The Rules of Summation

$$\sum_{i=1}^{n} x_i = x_1 + x_2 + \cdots + x_n$$

$$\sum_{i=1}^{n} a = na$$

$$\sum_{i=1}^{n} ax_i = a\sum_{i=1}^{n} x_i$$

$$\sum_{i=1}^{n} (x_i + y_i) = \sum_{i=1}^{n} x_i + \sum_{i=1}^{n} y_i$$

$$\sum_{i=1}^{n} (ax_i + by_i) = a\sum_{i=1}^{n} x_i + b\sum_{i=1}^{n} y_i$$

$$\sum_{i=1}^{n} (a + bx_i) = na + b\sum_{i=1}^{n} x_i$$

$$\bar{x} = \frac{\sum_{i=1}^{n} x_i}{n} = \frac{x_1 + x_2 + \cdots + x_n}{n}.$$

$$\sum_{i=1}^{n} (x_i - \bar{x}) = 0$$

$$\sum_{i=1}^{2}\sum_{j=1}^{3} f(x_i, y_j) = \sum_{i=1}^{2} [f(x_i, y_1) + f(x_i, y_2) + f(x_i, y_3)]$$

$$= f(x_1, y_1) + f(x_1, y_2) + f(x_1, y_3)$$
$$+ f(x_2, y_1) + f(x_2, y_2) + f(x_2, y_3)$$

Expected Values & Variances

$$E(X) = x_1 f(x_1) + x_2 f(x_2) + \cdots + x_n f(x_n)$$

$$= \sum_{i=1}^{n} x_i f(x_i) = \sum_{x} x f(x)$$

$$E[g(X)] = \sum_{x} g(x) f(x)$$

$$E[g_1(X) + g_1(X)] = \sum_{x} [g_1(x) + g_2(x)] f(x)$$

$$= \sum_{x} g_1(x) f(x) + \sum_{x} g_2(x) f(x)$$

$$= E[g_1(x)] + E[g_2(x)]$$

$$E(c) = c$$

$$E(cX) = cE(X)$$

$$E(a + cX) = a + cE(X)$$

$$var(X) = \sigma^2 = E[X - E(X)]^2 = E(X^2) - [E(X)]^2$$

$$var(a + cX) = E[(a + cX) - E(a + cX)]^2 = c^2 var(X)$$

Marginal and Conditional Distributions

$$f(x) = \sum_{y} f(x, y) \quad \text{for each value } X \text{ can take}$$

$$f(y) = \sum_{x} f(x, y) \quad \text{for each value } Y \text{ can take}$$

$$f(x|y) = P[X = x|Y = y] = \frac{f(x, y)}{f(y)}$$

If X and Y are independent random variables, then $f(x, y) = f(x) f(y)$ for each and every pair of values x and y. The converse is also true.

If X and Y are independent random variables, then the conditional probability density function of X given that

$$Y = y \text{ is } f(x|y) = \frac{f(x, y)}{f(y)} = \frac{f(x) f(y)}{f(y)} = f(x) \text{ for}$$

each and every pair of values x and y. The converse is also true.

Expectations, Vari

$$cov(X, Y) = E[(X - E[X])(Y - E[Y])]$$

$$= \sum_{x}\sum_{y} [x - E(X)][y - E(Y)] f(x, y)$$

$$\rho = \frac{cov(X, Y)}{\sqrt{var(X)var(Y)}}$$

$$E(c_1 X + c_2 Y) = c_1 E(X) + c_2 E(Y)$$

$$E(X + Y) = E(X) + E(Y)$$

$$var(aX + bY + cZ) = a^2 var(X) + b^2 var(Y) + c^2 var(Z) + 2ab\, cov(X, Y) + 2ac\, cov(X, Z) + 2bc\, cov(Y, Z)$$

If X, Y, and Z are independent, or uncorrelated, random variables, then the covariance terms are zero and:

$$var(aX + bY + cZ) = a^2 var(X) + b^2 var(Y) + c^2 var(Z)$$

Normal Probabilities

If $X \sim N(\mu, \sigma^2)$, then $Z = \dfrac{X - \mu}{\sigma} \sim N(0, 1)$

If $X \sim N(\mu, \sigma^2)$ and a is a constant, then

$$P(X \geq a) = P\left(Z \geq \frac{a - \mu}{\sigma}\right)$$

If $X \sim N(\mu, \sigma^2)$ and a and b are constants, then

$$P(a \leq X \leq b) = P\left(\frac{a - \mu}{\sigma} \leq Z \leq \frac{b - \mu}{\sigma}\right)$$

Assumptions of the Simple Linear Regression Model

SR1 The value of y, for each value of x, is $y = \beta_1 + \beta_2 x + e$

SR2 The average value of the random error e is $E(e) = 0$ since we assume that $E(y) = \beta_1 + \beta_2 x$

SR3 The variance of the random error e is $var(e) = \sigma^2 = var(y)$

SR4 The covariance between any pair of random errors, e_i and e_j is $cov(e_i, e_j) = cov(y_i, y_j) = 0$

SR5 The variable x is not random and must take at least two different values.

SR6 (optional) The values of e are normally distributed about their mean $e \sim N(0, \sigma^2)$

Least Squares Estimation

If b_1 and b_2 are the least squares estimates, then

$$\hat{y}_i = b_1 + b_2 x_i$$
$$\hat{e}_i = y_i - \hat{y}_i = y_i - b_1 - b_2 x_i$$

The Normal Equations

$$Nb_1 + \sum x_i b_2 = \sum y_i$$
$$\sum x_i b_1 + \sum x_i^2 b_2 = \sum x_i y_i$$

Least Squares Estimators

$$b_2 = \frac{\sum (x_i - \bar{x})(y_i - \bar{x})}{\sum (x_i - \bar{x})^2} \quad = b_2 = \beta_2 + \frac{\sum (x_i - \bar{x})e}{\sum (y_i - \bar{x})^2}$$

$$b_1 = \bar{y} - b_2 \bar{x}$$

x - no random, it has no distribution,
e is the only random variable

Principles of Econometrics

Third Edition

Principles of Econometrics

Third Edition

R. Carter Hill
Louisiana State University

William E. Griffiths
University of Melbourne

Guay C. Lim
University of Melbourne

John Wiley & Sons, Inc.

VP & Executive Publisher	Don Fowley
Associate Publisher	Judith Joseph
Editorial Assistant	Sarah Vernon
Associate Editor	Brian Kamins
Marketing Manager	Amy Scholz
Production Manager	Dorothy Sinclair
Senior Production Editor	Sandra Dumas
Senior Designer	Hope Miller
Media Editor	Allison Morris
Production Management Services	Thomson Digital
Bicentennial Logo Design	Richard J. Pacifico

This book was set in 10/12 Times Roman by Thomson Digital and printed and bound by RR Donnelley.

This book is printed on acid-free paper. ∞

To order books or for customer service please, call 1-800-CALL WILEY (225-5945).

ISBN 978-0471-72360-8

Printed in the United States of America

10 9 8 7 6 5 4

Carter Hill dedicates this work to his wife, Melissa Waters

Bill Griffiths dedicates this work to Jill, David, and Wendy Griffiths

Guay Lim dedicates this work to Tony Meagher

Brief Contents

Preface

Principles of Econometrics, 3rd edition, is an introductory book for undergraduate students in economics and finance, as well as first-year graduate students in economics, finance, accounting, agricultural economics, marketing, public policy, sociology, law, and political science. It is assumed that students have taken courses in the principles of economics and elementary statistics. Neither matrix algebra nor calculus is used, except for occasional references to the tools of calculus.

A brief explanation of the title is in order. This work is a revision of *Undergraduate Econometrics, 2nd edition*, by Hill, Griffiths, and Judge (Wiley, 2001). The former title was chosen to clearly differentiate the book from other more advanced books by the same authors. We have made the title change because the book is appropriate not only for undergraduates, but also for first-year graduate students in many fields, as well as MBA students. Furthermore, naming it *Principles of Econometrics* emphasizes our belief that econometrics should be a part of the economics curriculum, in the same way as the principles of microeconomics and the principles of macroeconomics. Those who have been studying and teaching econometrics as long as we have will remember that *Principles of Econometrics* was the title that Henri Theil used for his 1971 classic, which was also published by John Wiley & Sons. Our choice of the same title is not intended to signal that our book is similar in level and content. Theil's work was, and remains, a unique treatise on advanced graduate level econometrics. Our book is an introductory level econometrics text.

Book Objectives

Principles of Econometrics is designed to give students an understanding of why econometrics is necessary, and to provide them with a working knowledge of basic econometric tools so that

   (i) They can apply these tools to modeling, estimation, inference, and forecasting in the context of real world economic problems.
  (ii) They can evaluate critically the results and conclusions from others who use basic econometric tools.
 (iii) They have a foundation and understanding for further study of econometrics.
 (iv) They have an appreciation of the range of more advanced techniques that exist and that may be covered in later econometric courses.

The book is *not* an econometrics cookbook, nor is it in a theorem-proof format. It emphasizes motivation, understanding, and implementation. Motivation is achieved by introducing very simple economic models and asking economic questions that the student can answer. Understanding is aided by lucid description of techniques, clear interpretation, and appropriate applications. Learning is reinforced by doing, with clear worked examples in the text and exercises at the end of each chapter.

Overview of Contents

This third edition retains the spirit and structure of the second edition. The simple linear regression model is covered in Chapters 2–4. The multiple regression model is treated in Chapters 5–7. Chapters 8 and 9 introduce econometric problems that are unique to cross-sectional data (heteroskedasticity) and time-series data (dynamic models), respectively. Chapters 10 and 11 deal with random regressors, the failure of least squares when a regressor is endogenous, and instrumental variables estimation; first in the general case, and then in the simultaneous equations model. In Chapter 12, the analysis of time-series data is extended to discussions of nonstationarity and cointegration. Chapters 13 and 14 introduce econometric issues specific to macroeconomic models and the analysis of financial data, respectively. In Chapters 15 and 16, we introduce the microeconometric topics of panel data and models with qualitative and limited dependent variables. Guidelines for writing an empirical research paper and data sources are given in Chapter 17. Appendices A, B, and C review mathematical, probability, and statistical inference concepts that are used in the book.

Summary of Changes and New Material

This edition includes a great deal of new material, including new examples and exercises using real data, and some significant reorganizations. Important new features include

- Algebraic proofs and extensions are now presented in short chapter appendices.
- Learning objectives and keywords have been included at the beginning of each chapter.
- Additional emphasis is given to model interpretation, especially for nonlinear relationships involving logarithms. In particular the treatment of the log-linear model in Chapter 4 includes prediction, a generalized measure of goodness-of-fit, and prediction intervals.
- Polynomial regression, dummy variables, and interaction variables are combined in Chapter 7 on nonlinear relationships. More attention is given to the interpretation of dummy variables in log-linear models.
- In Chapter 8 feasible generalized least squares estimation of heteroskedastic error models and more general tests for heteroskedasticity are introduced.
- Dynamic economic relationships are considered in Chapter 9, where discussions of distributed lag models, lagged dependent variable models, and autocorrelation are combined and integrated.
- Problems created by correlation between the regression error term and explanatory variables are treated in Chapter 10. The importance of using strong and valid instruments is stressed, and a clear intuitive explanation of the regression-based Hausman test is provided.
- The complexities of using nonstationary time-series data in regression analysis are introduced in Chapter 12. Dickey–Fuller tests for alternative cases and cointegration are discussed and illustrated.
- Models useful in macroeconometrics, including the concepts of vector error correction models and vector autoregressive models, are investigated in Chapter 13.
- Financial econometrics is introduced to students in Chapter 14. The time-varying volatility of financial data and use of the ARCH model and its extensions are explained.

- In addition to probit and logit, Chapter 16 now contains additional material on multinomial choice and ordered choice models. Count data models are introduced and are linked to nonlinear regression analysis. The tobit model and sample selection issues are discussed.
- Math essentials, including exponents and logarithms, as well as the nature of linear and nonlinear relationships, are reviewed in Appendix A. Slopes and elasticities are provided for alternative functional forms.
- Statistical inference concepts of estimation, sampling properties, and hypothesis tests are reviewed in Appendix C in the context of estimating the mean of a population.
- Exercises are now divided into sections labeled "Problems," which can be done without a computer, and "Computer Exercises," which require the use of statistical software, although much can be done with spreadsheets such as Excel. Selected problems for which answers are provided in Appendix D are indicated by an asterisk, *. Exercises that are difficult, or that require the use of large data files, are marked with a diamond, ◆.

Computer Supplement Books

Two books are published by John Wiley & Sons as computer supplements to *Principles of Econometrics*.

- *Using EViews for the Principles of Econometrics,* by Griffiths, Hill, and Lim (ISBN 978-0471-78711-2). This supplementary book presents the EViews 6 (www.eviews.com) software commands required for the examples in *Principles of Econometrics* in a clear and concise way. It includes many illustrations that are student friendly. It is useful not only for students and instructors who will be using this software as part of their econometrics course, but also for those who wish to learn how to use EViews. This book includes the Student Version of EViews 6.
- *Using Stata for the Principles of Econometrics*, by Adkins and Hill [ISBN 978-0470-18546-9]. This supplementary book presents the Stata 10 (www .stata.com) software commands required for the examples in *Principles of Econometrics*. It is useful not only for students and instructors who will be using this software as part of their econometrics course, but also for those who wish to learn how to use Stata. Screen shots illustrate the use of Stata's drop-down menus. Stata commands are explained and the use of "do-files" illustrated. See http://stata.com/texts/s4poe for data files and more.

Electronic Computer Supplements

Extensive supplementary material is available to support both students and instructors at the Web site http://www.wiley.com/college/hill. In addition to published supplements explaining the use of EViews and Stata, two free electronic supplements are available to those using *Principles of Econometrics*. These are

- *Using Excel for Principles of Econometrics, 3rd Edition,* by Asli Ogunc and Carter Hill. This free supplement, readable using Adobe Acrobat, explains how to use

Excel to reproduce most of the examples in *Principles of Econometrics*. Detailed instructions and screen shots are provided explaining both the computations and clarifying the operations of Excel. Templates are developed for common tasks.

- *Using GRETL for Principles of Econometrics, 3rd Edition,* by Lee Adkins. This free supplement, readable using Adobe Acrobat, explains how to use the freely available statistical software GRETL (download from http://gretl.sourceforge .net). Professor Adkins explains in detail, and using screen shots, how to use GRETL to replicate the examples in *Principles of Econometrics*. See http:// www.learneconometrics.com/gretl.html for the GRETL manual, data files and more.

Data Files

Data files for the book are provided in a variety of formats at the book Web site http:// www.wiley.com/college/hill. These include

- ASCII format (*.dat). These are text files containing only data.
- Definition files (*.def). These are text files describing the data file contents, with a listing of variable names, variable definitions, and summary statistics.
- EViews (*.wf1) workfiles for each data file.
- Excel (*.xls) workbooks for each data file, including variable names in the first row.
- Stata (*.dta) data files.
- GRETL (*.gdt) data files.

Remark: In the text data files are referenced as *.dat; e.g. *food.dat*. Files in other formats will have the same name, but a different extension, such as *food.wf1*, *food.dta*, and so on. The corresponding data definition file will be *food.def*. These files are located at the book Web site http://www.wiley.com/college/hill.

The book Web site includes a complete list of the data files and where they are used in the book. Individual data files are available at http://www.principlesofeconometrics.com.

Additional Resources

The book Web site http://www.wiley.com/college/hill also includes

- Adobe Acrobat Reader.
- Links to other useful Web sites.
- A link to files containing SHAZAM instructions for the text examples produced by developers of the SHAZAM software package, http://shazam.econ.ubc.ca/.

Resources for Instructors

For instructors, also available at the Web site http://www.wiley.com/college/hill are

- Complete solutions, in both Microsoft Word and *.pdf formats, to *all* exercises in the text.
- PowerPoint slides and PowerPoint Viewer.

Acknowledgments

Several reviewers and colleagues have helped us improve our book. We thank Viera Chmelarova, Lee Adkins, Tom Fomby, Alicia Rambaldi, Chris O'Donnell, Robert Dixon, Andrew Clarke, Michael Coelli, Vance Martin, Chris Skeels, Jenny Williams, Wasana Karunanarathne, Simone Wong, Clarissa Messemer, Asli Ogune, Vera Tabakova, Randy Campbell, Eric Hillebrand, Dek Terrell, Melissa Waters, and many others, including our students, who made suggestions for improving the book over the years.

The following professors reviewed the text and made many valuable suggestions:

Nicholas Noble, Miami University of Ohio
Daniel Millimet, Southern Methodist University
Simon Power, Carleton University
William Latham, University of Delaware
Richard Fowels, University of Utah
Christopher Parmeter, Virginia Polytechnic University
Luca Flabbi, Georgetown University
Craig A. Depken, University of Texas at Arlington

Finally, authors Hill and Griffiths want to acknowledge the gifts given to them over the past 30 years by mentor, friend, and colleague George Judge. Neither this book nor any of the other books we have shared in the writing of, would have ever seen the light of day without his vision and inspiration.

R. Carter Hill
William E. Griffiths
Guay C. Lim

Contents

Chapter 3   Interval Estimation and Hypothesis Testing   48

Chapter 8   Heteroskedasticity   197

Chapter 9   Dynamic Models, Autocorrelation and Forecasting   226

Chapter 10   Random Regressors and Moment Based Estimation   268

Chapter 11   Simultaneous Equations Models   303

Chapter *1*

An Introduction to Econometrics

1.1 Why Study Econometrics?

The importance of econometrics extends far beyond the discipline of economics. Econometrics is a set of research tools also employed in the business disciplines of accounting, finance, marketing, and management. It is used by social scientists, specifically researchers in history, political science, and sociology. Econometrics plays an important role in such diverse fields as forestry and in agricultural economics. This breadth of interest in econometrics arises in part because economics is the foundation of business analysis. Thus research methods employed by economists, which include the field of econometrics, are useful to a broad spectrum of individuals.

Econometrics plays a special role in the training of economists. As a student of economics, you are learning to "think like an economist." You are learning economic concepts such as opportunity cost, scarcity, and comparative advantage. You are working with economic models of supply and demand, macroeconomic behavior, and international trade. Through this training you become a person who better understands the world in which we live; you become someone who understands how markets work, and the way in which government policies affect the marketplace.

If economics is your major or minor field of study, a wide range of opportunities is open to you upon graduation. If you wish to enter the business world, your employer will want to know the answer to the question, "What can you do for me?" Students taking a traditional economics curriculum answer, "I can think like an economist." While we may view such a response to be powerful, it is not very specific and may not be very satisfying to an employer who does not understand economics.

The problem is that a gap exists between what you have learned as an economics student and what economists actually do. Very few economists make their livings by studying economic theory alone, and those who do are usually employed by universities. Most economists, whether they work in the business world or for the government, or teach in universities, engage in economic analysis that is in part "empirical." By that, we mean that they use economic data to estimate economic relationships, test economic hypotheses, and predict economic outcomes.

Studying econometrics fills a gap between being "a student of economics" and being "a practicing economist." With the econometric skills you will learn from this book, including how to work with econometric software, you will be able to elaborate on your answer to the employer's question above by saying "I can predict the sales of your product." "I can estimate the effect on your sales if your competition lowers its price by $1 per unit." "I can test whether your new ad campaign is actually increasing your sales." These answers are music to an employer's ears, because they reflect your ability to think like an economist *and* to analyze economic data. Such pieces of information are keys to good business decisions. Being able to provide your employer with useful information will make you a valuable employee and increase your odds of getting a desirable job.

If you plan to continue your education by enrolling in graduate school, or law school, you will find that this introduction to econometrics is invaluable. If your goal is to earn a master's or Ph.D. degree in economics, finance, accounting, marketing, agricultural economics, sociology, political science, or forestry, you will encounter more econometrics in your future. The graduate courses tend to be quite technical and mathematical, and the forest often gets lost in studying the trees. By taking this introduction to econometrics you will gain an overview of what econometrics is about and develop some "intuition" about how things work, before entering a technically oriented course.

1.2 **What Is Econometrics About?**

At this point we need to describe the nature of econometrics. It all begins with a theory from your field of study, whether it is accounting, sociology, or economics, about how important variables are related to one another. In economics we express our ideas about relationships between economic variables using the mathematical concept of a function. For example, to express a relationship between income and consumption, we may write

$$CONSUMPTION = f(INCOME)$$

which says that the level of consumption is *some* function, $f(\cdot)$, of income.

The demand for an individual commodity, say the Honda Accord, might be expressed as

$$Q^d = f(P, P^s, P^c, INC)$$

which says that the quantity of Honda Accords demanded, Q^d, is a function $f(P, P^s, P^c, INC)$ of the price of Honda Accords P, the price of cars that are substitutes P^s, the price of items that are complements P^c, like gasoline, and the level of income INC.

The supply of an agricultural commodity such as beef might be written as

$$Q^s = f(P, P^c, P^f)$$

where Q^s is the quantity supplied, P is the price of beef, P^c is the price of competitive products in production (e.g., the price of hogs), and P^f is the price of factors or inputs (e.g., the price of corn) used in the production process.

Each of the above equations is a general economic model that describes how we visualize the way in which economic variables are interrelated. Economic models of this type *guide our economic analysis.*

For most economic decision or choice problems, it is not enough to know that certain economic variables are interrelated, or even the direction of the relationship. In addition, we must understand the magnitudes involved. That is, we must be able to say **how much** a change in one variable affects another.

Econometrics is about how we can use theory and data from economics, business, and the social sciences, along with tools from statistics, to answer "how much" type questions.

1.2.1 SOME EXAMPLES

As a case in point, consider the problem faced by a central bank. In the United States, this is the Federal Reserve System, with Ben Bernanke as Chairman of the Federal Reserve Board (FRB). When prices are observed to rise, suggesting an increase in the inflation rate, the FRB must make a decision about whether to dampen the rate of growth of the economy. It can do so by raising the interest rate it charges its member banks when they borrow money (the discount rate) or the rate on overnight loans between banks (the federal funds rate). Increasing these rates will then send a ripple effect through the economy causing increases in other interest rates, such as those faced by would-be investors, who may be firms seeking funds for capital expansion or individuals who wish to buy consumer durables like automobiles and refrigerators. This has the economic effect of increasing costs, and consumers would react by reducing the quantity of the durable goods demanded. Overall, aggregate demand falls and this is expected to slow the rate of inflation. These relationships are suggested by economic theory.

The real question facing Chairman Bernanke is *"How much should we increase the discount rate to slow inflation, and yet maintain a stable and growing economy?"* The answer will depend on the responsiveness of firms and individuals to increases in the interest rates and to the effects of reduced investment on Gross National Product. The key elasticities and multipliers are called **parameters**. The values of economic parameters are unknown and must be estimated using a sample of economic data when formulating economic policies.

Econometrics is about how to best estimate economic parameters given the data we have. "Good" econometrics is important, since errors in the estimates used by policy makers such as the FRB may lead to interest rate corrections that are too large or too small, which has consequences for all of us.

Every day decision makers face "how much" questions similar to those facing Chairman Bernanke. Some examples might include the following:

- A city council ponders the question of how much violent crime will be reduced if an additional million dollars is spent putting uniformed police on the street.

- U.S. Presidential candidate Clinton questions how many additional California voters will support her if she spends an additional million dollars in advertising in that state.

- The owner of a local Pizza Hut franchise must decide how much advertising space to purchase in the local newspaper, and thus must estimate the relationship between advertising and sales.

- Louisiana State University must estimate how much enrollment will fall if tuition is raised by $100 per semester, and thus whether its revenue from tuition will rise or fall.

- The CEO of Proctor & Gamble must estimate how much demand there will be in 10 years for the detergent Tide, and how much to invest in new plant and equipment.

- A real estate developer must predict by how much population and income will increase to the south of Baton Rouge, Louisiana, over the next few years, and if it will be profitable to begin construction of a new strip mall.

- You must decide how much of your savings will go into a stock fund and how much into the money market. This requires you to make predictions of the level of economic activity, the rate of inflation, and interest rates over your planning horizon.

- A public transportation council in Melbourne, Australia, must decide how an increase in fares for public transportation (trams, trains, and buses) will affect the number of travelers who switch to car or bike, and the effect of this switch on revenue going to public transportation.

To answer these questions of "how much," decision makers rely on information provided by empirical economic research. In such research, an economist uses economic theory and reasoning to construct relationships between the variables in question. Data on these variables are collected and econometric methods are used to estimate the key underlying parameters and to make predictions. The decision makers in the above examples obtain their "estimates" and "predictions" in different ways. The Federal Reserve Board has a large staff of economists to carry out econometric analyses. The CEO of Proctor & Gamble may hire econometric consultants to provide the firm with projections of sales. You may get advice about investing from a stockbroker, who in turn is provided with econometric projections made by economists working for the parent company. Whatever the source of your information about "how much" type questions, it is a good bet that there is an economist involved who is using econometric methods to analyze data that yield the answers.

In the next section, we show how to introduce parameters into an economic model and how to convert an economic model into an econometric model.

1.3 **The Econometric Model**

What is an econometric model, and where does it come from? We will give you a general overview, and we may use terms that are unfamiliar to you. Be assured that before you are too far into this book all the terminology will be clearly defined. In an econometric model we must first realize that economic relations are not exact. Economic theory does not claim to be able to predict the specific behavior of any individual or firm, but rather it describes the *average* or *systematic* behavior of *many* individuals or firms. When studying car sales we recognize that the *actual* number of Hondas sold is the sum of this systematic part and a random and unpredictable component e that we will call a **random error**. Thus an **econometric model** representing the sales of Honda Accords is

$$Q^d = f(P, P^s, P^c, INC) + e$$

The random error e accounts for the many factors that affect sales that we have omitted from this simple model, and it also reflects the intrinsic uncertainty in economic activity.

To complete the specification of the econometric model, we must also say something about the form of the algebraic relationship among our economic variables. For example, in your first economics courses quantity demanded was depicted as a *linear* function of price. We extend that assumption to the other variables as well, making the systematic part of the demand relation

$$f(P, P^s, P^c, INC) = \beta_1 + \beta_2 P + \beta_3 P^s + \beta_4 P^c + \beta_5 INC$$

The corresponding econometric model is

$$Q^d = \beta_1 + \beta_2 P + \beta_3 P^s + \beta_4 P^c + \beta_5 INC + e$$

The functional form represents a hypothesis about the relationship between the variables. In a particular problem our interest centers on trying to determine a form that is compatible with economic theory and the data.

In every econometric model, whether it is a demand equation, a supply equation, or a production function, there is a systematic portion and an unobservable random component. The systematic portion is the part we obtain from economic theory, and it includes an assumption about the functional form. The random component represents a "noise" component, which obscures our understanding of the relationship among variables, and which we represent using the random variable e.

1.4 How Do We Obtain Data?

Where does data come from? Economists and other social scientists work in a complex world in which data on variables are "observed" and rarely obtained from a controlled experiment. This makes the task of learning about economic parameters all the more difficult. Procedures for using such data to answer questions of economic importance are the subject matter of this book.

1.4.1 EXPERIMENTAL DATA

One way to acquire information about the unknown parameters of economic relationships is to conduct or observe the outcome of an experiment. In the physical sciences, and agriculture, it is easy to imagine controlled experiments. Scientists specify the values of key control variables and then observe the outcome. We might plant similar plots of land with a particular variety of wheat, and then vary the amounts of fertilizer and pesticide applied to each plot, observing at the end of the growing season the bushels of wheat produced on each plot. Repeating the experiment on N plots of land creates a sample of N observations. Such controlled experiments are extremely rare in business and the social sciences. The key aspect of experimental data is that the values of the explanatory variables can be fixed at specific values in repeated trials of the experiment.

One business example comes from marketing research. Suppose we are interested in the weekly sales of a particular item at a supermarket. As an item is sold it is passed over a scanning unit to record the price and the amount that will appear on your grocery bill. But, at the same time a data record is created, and at every point in time the price of the item and the prices of all its competitors are known, as well as current store displays and coupon usage. The prices and shopping environment are controlled by store management, and thus this "experiment" can be repeated a number of days or weeks using the same values of the "control" variables.

1.4.2 NONEXPERIMENTAL DATA

An example of nonexperimental data is survey data. The Public Policy Research Lab at Louisiana State University (http://www.survey.lsu.edu/) conducts telephone and mail surveys for clients. In a telephone survey numbers are selected randomly and called. Responses to questions are recorded and analyzed. In such an environment data on all variables are collected simultaneously and the values are neither fixed nor repeatable. These are nonexperimental data.

Data that are collected may be of several forms. As we analyze the data the form in which they are collected affects which methodological issues we may encounter. The data may be collected in a

- *time-series form*—data collected over discrete intervals of time—for example, the annual price of wheat in the United States from 1880 to 2007, or the daily price of General Electric stock from 1980 to 2007.
- *cross-section form*—data collected over sample units in a particular time period—for example, income by counties in California during 2006, or high school graduation rates by state in 2006.
- *panel data form*—data that follow individual microunits over time. Such data are increasingly available. For example, the U.S. Department of Education has several ongoing surveys, in which the same students are tracked over time, from the time they are in the 8th grade until their mid-twenties. These databases record not only student characteristics and performance, but also the socioeconomic characteristics of their families, their schools, and so on. Such data are rich sources of data for studies related to labor economics, economics of the household, health economics, and of course education.

These data may be collected at various levels of aggregation:

- *micro*—data collected on individual economic decision-making units such as individuals, households, or firms.
- *macro*—data resulting from a pooling or aggregating over individuals, households, or firms at the local, state, or national levels.

The data collected may also represent a flow or a stock:

- *flow*—outcome measures over a period of time, such as the consumption of gasoline during the last quarter of 2006.
- *stock*—outcome measured at a particular point in time, such as the quantity of crude oil held by Exxon in its U.S. storage tanks on April 1, 2006, or the asset value of the Wells Fargo Bank on July 1, 2007.

The data collected may be quantitative or qualitative:

- *quantitative*—outcomes such as prices or income that may be expressed as numbers or some transformation of them, such as real prices or per capita income.
- *qualitative*—outcomes that are of an "either–or" situation. For example, a consumer either did or did not make a purchase of a particular good, or a person either is or is not married.

In Chapter 17 we list sources of economic data that are available both in print, or electronic media, and on the Internet.

1.5 Statistical Inference

The phrase **statistical inference** will appear often in this book. By this we mean we want to "infer" or learn something about the real world by analyzing a sample of data. The ways in which statistical inference are carried out include

- Estimating economic parameters, such as elasticities, using econometric methods.

- Predicting economic outcomes, such as the enrollment in 2-year colleges in the United States for the next 10 years.

- Testing economic hypotheses, such as the question of whether newspaper advertising is better than store displays for increasing sales.

Econometrics includes all of these aspects of statistical inference, and as we proceed through this book you will learn how to properly estimate, predict, and test, given the characteristics of the data at hand.

1.6 A Research Format

Empirical economic research follows a pattern, and we will stress this orderly procedure throughout the book. The steps are as follows:

1. It all starts with a problem or question. The idea may come after lengthy study of all that has been written on a particular topic. You will find that "inspiration is 99% perspiration." That means, after you dig at a topic long enough, a new and interesting question will occur to you. Alternatively, you may be led by your natural curiosity to an interesting question. Professor Hal Varian ("How to Build an Economic Model in Your Spare Time," *The American Economist,* 41(2), Fall 1997, pp. 3–10) suggests you look for ideas outside academic journals—in newspapers, magazines, and so on. He relates a story about a research project that developed from his shopping for a new TV set.

2. Economic theory gives us a way of thinking about the problem: Which economic variables are involved and what is the possible direction of the relationship(s)? Every research project, given the initial question, begins by building an economic model and listing the questions (hypotheses) of interest. More questions will occur during the research project, but it is good to list those that motivate you at the beginning of the project.

3. The working economic model leads to an econometric model. We must choose a functional form and make some assumptions about the nature of the error term.

4. Sample data are obtained and a desirable method of statistical analysis is chosen, based on our initial assumptions and our understanding of how the data were collected.

5. Estimates of the unknown parameters are obtained with the help of a statistical software package, predictions are made, and hypothesis tests are performed.

6. Model diagnostics are performed to check the validity of assumptions we have made. For example, were all of the right-hand-side explanatory variables relevant? Was the correct functional form used?

7. The economic consequences and the implications of the empirical results are analyzed and evaluated. What economic resource allocation and distribution results are implied, and what are their policy-choice implications? What remaining questions might be answered with further study or new and better data?

This path is one we will follow in the following chapters. At the end of the work, a paper or report must be written, summarizing what you have found and the methods you used. Guidelines for writing economics papers are given in Chapter 17.

Chapter 2

The Simple Linear Regression Model

Learning Objectives

> **REMARK:** *Learning Objectives* and *Keywords* sections will appear at the beginning of each chapter. We urge you to think about, and possibly write out answers to the questions, and make sure you recognize and can define the keywords. If you are unsure about the questions or answers consult your instructor. When examples are requested in *Learning Objectives* sections, you should think of examples *not* in the book.

Based on the material in this chapter you should be able to

1. Explain the difference between an estimator and an estimate, and why the least squares estimators are random variables, and why least squares estimates are not.

2. Discuss the interpretation of the slope and intercept parameters of the simple regression model, and sketch the graph of an estimated equation.

3. Explain the theoretical decomposition of an observable variable y into its systematic and random components, and show this decomposition graphically.

4. Discuss and explain each of the assumptions of the simple linear regression model.

5. Explain how the least squares principle is used to fit a line through a scatter plot of data. Be able to define the least squares residual and the least squares fitted value of the dependent variable and show them on a graph.

6. Define the elasticity of y with respect to x and explain its computation in the simple linear regression model when y and x are not transformed in any way, and when y and x are transformed by taking the natural logarithm.

7. Explain the meaning of the statement "If regression model assumptions SR1–SR5 hold, then the least squares estimator b_2 is unbiased." In particular, what exactly does "unbiased" mean? Why is b_2 biased if an important variable has been omitted from the model.

8. Explain the meaning of the phrase "sampling variability."

9. Explain how the factors σ^2, $\sum(x_i - \bar{x})^2$, and N affect the precision with which we can estimate the unknown parameter β_2.

10. State and explain the Gauss–Markov theorem.

Keywords

assumptions	Gauss–Markov theorem	regression model
asymptotic	heteroskedastic	regression parameters
BLUE	homoskedastic	repeated sampling
biased estimator	independent variable	sampling precision
degrees of freedom	least squares estimates	sampling properties
dependent variable	least squares estimators	scatter diagram
deviation from the mean	least squares principle	simple linear regression function
form	least squares residuals	specification error
econometric model	linear estimator	unbiased estimator
economic model	prediction	
elasticity	random error term	

Economic theory suggests many relationships between economic variables. In microeconomics you considered demand and supply models in which the quantities demanded and supplied of a good depend on its price. You considered "production functions" and "total product curves" that explained the amount of a good produced as a function of the amount of an input, such as labor, that is used. In macroeconomics you specified "investment functions" to explain that the amount of aggregate investment in the economy depends on the interest rate and "consumption functions" that related aggregate consumption to the level of disposable income.

Each of these models involves a relationship between economic variables. In this chapter we consider how to use a sample of economic data to quantify such relationships. As economists we are interested in questions such as: If one variable (e.g., the price of a good) changes in a certain way, *by how much* will another variable (the quantity demanded or supplied) change? Also, given that we know the value of one variable, can we *forecast* or *predict* the corresponding value of another? We will answer these questions by using a **regression model**. Like all models the regression model is based on assumptions. In this chapter we hope to be very clear about these assumptions, as they are the conditions under which the analysis in subsequent chapters is appropriate.

2.1 An Economic Model

In order to develop the ideas of regression models we are going to use a simple, but important, economic example. Suppose that we are interested in studying the relationship between household income and expenditure on food. Consider the "experiment" of randomly selecting households from a particular population. The population might consist of households within a particular city, state, province, or country. For the present, suppose that we are interested only in households with an income of $1000 per week. In this experiment we randomly select a number of households from this population and interview them. We ask the question, "How much did you spend per person on food last week?" Weekly food expenditure, which we denote as *y*, is a *random variable* since the value is unknown to us until a household is selected and the question is asked and answered.

> **REMARK:** In Appendices B and C we distinguished random variables from their values by using uppercase (Y) letters for random variables and lowercase (y) letters for their values. We *will not* make this distinction any longer because it leads to complicated notation. We will use lowercase letters, like "y," to denote random variables as well as their values, and we will make the interpretation clear in the surrounding text.

The continuous random variable y has a probability density function (which we will abbreviate as *pdf*) that describes the probabilities of obtaining various food expenditure values. *If you are rusty or uncertain about probability concepts see Appendix B at the end of this book for a comprehensive review.* Clearly, the amount spent on food per person will vary from one household to another for a variety of reasons: some households will be devoted to gourmet food, some will contain teenagers, some will contain senior citizens, some will be vegetarian, and some will eat at restaurants more frequently. All of these factors and many others, including random, impulsive buying, will cause weekly expenditures on food to vary from one household to another, even if they all have the same income. The *pdf* $f(y)$ describes how expenditures are "distributed" over the population and might look like Figure 2.1.

The *pdf* in Figure 2.1a is actually a conditional probability density function since it is "conditional" upon household income. If x = weekly household income = \$1000, then the conditional *pdf* is $f(y|x = \$1000)$. The *conditional mean*, or *expected value*, of y is $E(y|x = \$1000) = \mu_{y|x}$ and is our population's mean weekly food expenditure per person.

> **REMARK:** The expected value of a random variable is called its "mean" value, which is really a contraction of *population mean*, the center of the probability distribution of the random variable. This is *not* the same as the *sample mean*, which is the arithmetic average of numerical values. Keep the distinction between these two usages of the term "mean" in mind.

The *conditional variance* of y is var($y|x = \$1000$) = σ^2, which measures the dispersion of household expenditures y about their mean $\mu_{y|x}$. The parameters $\mu_{y|x}$ and σ^2, if they were known, would give us some valuable information about the population we are considering. If we knew these parameters, and if we knew that the conditional distribution $f(y|x = \$1000)$ was *normal*, $N(\mu_{y|x}, \sigma^2)$, then we could calculate probabilities that y falls in specific intervals using properties of the normal distribution. That is, we could compute the proportion of the household population that spends between \$50 and \$75 per person on food, given \$1000 per week income.

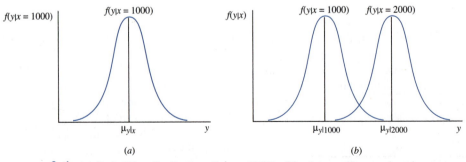

FIGURE **2.1** (*a*) Probability distribution $f(y|x = 1000)$ of food expenditure y given income $x = \$1000$. (*b*) Probability distributions of food expenditure y given incomes $x = \$1000$ and $x = \$2000$.

As economists we are usually more interested in studying relationships between variables, in this case the relationship between y = weekly food expenditure per person and x = weekly household income. Economic theory tells us that expenditure on economic goods depends on income. Consequently we call y the "dependent variable" and x the "independent" or "explanatory" variable. In econometrics, we recognize that real-world expenditures are random variables, and we want to use data to learn about the relationship.

An econometric analysis of the expenditure relationship can provide answers to some important questions, such as: If weekly income goes up by $100, *how much* will average weekly food expenditures rise? Or, could weekly food expenditures fall as income rises? How much would we predict the weekly per person expenditure on food to be for a household with an income of $2000 per week? The answers to such questions provide valuable information for decision makers.

> Using ... per person food spending information ... one can determine the similarities and disparities in the spending habits of households of differing sizes, races, incomes, geographic areas, and other socioeconomic and demographic features. This information is valuable for assessing existing market conditions, product distribution patterns, consumer buying habits, and consumer living conditions. Combined with demographic and income projections, this information may be used to anticipate consumption trends. The information may also be used to develop typical market baskets of food for special population groups, such as the elderly. These market baskets may, in turn, be used to develop price indices tailored to the consumption patterns of these population groups. [Blisard, Noel, Food Spending in American Households, 1997–1998, Electronic Report from the Economic Research Service, U.S. Department of Agriculture, Statistical Bulletin Number 972, June 2001]

From a business perspective, if we are managers of a supermarket chain (or restaurant, or health food store, etc.) we must consider long-range plans. If economic forecasters are predicting that local income will increase over the next few years, then we must decide whether to expand, and how much to expand, our facilities to serve our customers. Or, if we plan to open franchises in high-income and low-income neighborhoods, then forecasts of expenditures on food per person, along with neighborhood demographic information, give an indication of how large the stores in those areas should be.

In order to investigate the relationship between expenditure and income we must build an **economic model** and then a corresponding **econometric model** that forms the basis for a quantitative or *empirical* economic analysis. In our food expenditure example, economic theory suggests that average weekly per person household expenditure on food, represented mathematically by the conditional mean $E(y|x) = \mu_{y|x}$, depends on household income x. If we consider households with different levels of income, we expect the average expenditure on food to change. In Figure 2.1b we show the probability density functions of food expenditure for two different levels of weekly income, $1000 and $2000. Each conditional *pdf* $f(y|x)$ shows that expenditures will be distributed about a mean value $\mu_{y|x}$, but the mean expenditure by households with higher income is larger than the mean expenditure by lower income households.

In most economics textbooks "consumption" or "expenditure" functions relating consumption to income are depicted as *linear relationships,* and we will begin by assuming the same thing. The mathematical representation of our economic model of household food expenditure, depicted in Figure 2.2, is

$$E(y|x) = \mu_{y|x} = \beta_1 + \beta_2 x \tag{2.1}$$

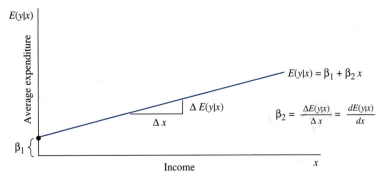

FIGURE 2.2 The economic model: a linear relationship between average per person food expenditure and income.

The conditional mean $E(y|x)$ in (2.1) is called a **simple regression function**. It is called *simple* regression not because it is easy, but because there is only one explanatory variable on the right-hand side of the equation. The unknown **regression parameters** β_1 and β_2 are the intercept and slope of the regression function, respectively. *If you need a review of the geometry, interpretation, and algebra of linear functions see Appendix A.3 at the end of the book.* In our food expenditure example the intercept β_1 represents the mean per person weekly household expenditure on food by a household with no weekly income, $x = \$0$. If income is measured in dollars, then the slope β_2 represents the change in $E(y|x)$ given a $1 change in weekly income; it could be called the marginal propensity to spend on food. Algebraically,

$$\beta_2 = \frac{\Delta E(y|x)}{\Delta x} = \frac{dE(y|x)}{dx} \tag{2.2}$$

where Δ denotes "change in" and $dE(y|x)/dx$ denotes the "derivative" of $E(y|x)$ with respect to x. We will not use derivatives to any great extent in this book, and if you are not familiar with the concept, you can think of "d" as a "stylized" version of Δ and go on.

The economic model (2.1) summarizes what theory tells us about the relationship between weekly household income (x) and expected household expenditure on food, $E(y|x)$. The parameters of the model, β_1 and β_2, are quantities that help characterize economic behavior in the population we are considering and are called **population parameters**. In order to use data we must now specify an *econometric model* that describes how the data on household income and expenditure are obtained, and that guides the econometric analysis.

2.2 An Econometric Model

The model $E(y|x) = \beta_1 + \beta_2 x$ describes economic behavior, but it is an abstraction from reality. If we take a random sample of households with weekly income $x = \$1000$, we know the actual expenditure values will be scattered around the mean value $E(y|x = 1000) = \mu_{y|x=1000} = \beta_1 + \beta_2(1000)$, as shown in Figure 2.1. If we were to sample household expenditures at other levels of income, we would expect the sample values to be scattered around their mean value $E(y|x) = \beta_1 + \beta_2 x$. In Figure 2.3 we arrange bell-shaped figures like Figure 2.1, depicting the *pdf*s of food expenditure $f(y|x)$, along the regression line for *each* level of income.

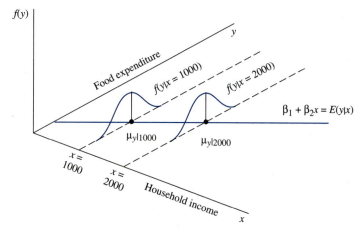

FIGURE 2.3   The probability density functions for y at two levels of income.

This figure shows that at each level of income the mean, or average, value of household expenditure is given by the regression function $E(y|x) = \beta_1 + \beta_2 x$. It also shows that we assume values of household expenditures on food will be distributed around the mean value $E(y|x) = \beta_1 + \beta_2 x$ at each level of income. This regression function is the foundation of an econometric model for household food expenditure.

In order to make the econometric model complete we have to make some assumptions.

> **REMARK:** You will hear a great deal about **assumptions** in this chapter and in the remainder of the book. Assumptions are the "if" part of an "if–then" type statement. If the assumptions we make are true, then certain things follow. And, as importantly, if the assumptions do not hold, then the conclusions we draw may not hold. Part of the challenge of econometric analysis is making realistic assumptions and then checking that they hold.

In Figure 2.1a we assumed that the *dispersion* of the values y about their mean is $\text{var}(y|x = \$1000) = \sigma^2$. We must make a similar assumption about the dispersion of values at each level of income. The basic assumption is that the dispersion of values y about their mean is the same for all levels of income x. That is, $\text{var}(y|x) = \sigma^2$ for all values of x. In Figure 2.1b the *pdfs* for two different incomes have different means, but they have identical variances. This assumption is also illustrated in Figure 2.3, as we have depicted the "spread" of each of the distributions, like Figure 2.1, to be the same.

The constant variance assumption $\text{var}(y|x) = \sigma^2$ implies that at each level of income x we are *equally* uncertain about how far values of y might fall from their mean value, $E(y|x) = \beta_1 + \beta_2 x$, and the uncertainty does not depend on income or anything else. Data satisfying this condition are said to be **homoskedastic**. If this assumption is violated, so that $\text{var}(y|x) \neq \sigma^2$ for all values of income x, the data are said to be **heteroskedastic**.

We have described the sample as *random*. This description means that when data are collected they are *statistically independent*. If y_i and y_j denote the per person food expenditures of two randomly selected households, then knowing the *value* of one of these (random) variables tells us nothing about the probability that the other will take a particular value or range of values.

Mathematicians spend their lives (we exaggerate slightly) trying to prove the same theorem with weaker and weaker sets of assumptions. This mindset spills over to econometricians to some degree. Consequently, econometric models often make an assumption that is weaker than statistical independence. If y_i and y_j are the expenditures of two randomly selected households, then we will assume that their *covariance* is zero, or $\text{cov}(y_i, y_j) = 0$. This is a weaker assumption than statistical independence (since independence implies zero covariance, but zero covariance does not imply independence); it implies only that there is no systematic *linear* association between y_i and y_j. Refer to Appendix B.4.3 for more discussion of this difference.

In order to carry out a regression analysis we must make two assumptions about the values of the variable x. The idea of regression analysis is to measure the effect of changes in one variable, x, on another, y. In order to do this x must take at least two values within the sample of data. If all the observations on x within the sample take the same value, say $x = \$1000$, then regression analysis fails. Secondly, we will assume that the x-values are given, and not random. All our results will be conditional on the given x-values. More will be said about this assumption soon.

Finally, it is sometimes assumed that the values of y are *normally* distributed. The usual justification for this assumption is that in nature the "bell-shaped" curve describes many phenomena, ranging from IQs to the length of corn stalks to the birth weights of Australian male children. It is reasonable, sometimes, to assume that an economic variable is normally distributed about its mean. We will say more about this assumption later, but for now we will make it an "optional" assumption, since we do not need to make it in many cases, and it is a very strong assumption when it is made.

These ideas, taken together, define our **econometric model**. They are a collection of assumptions that describe the data.

ASSUMPTIONS OF THE SIMPLE LINEAR REGRESSION MODEL-I

- The mean value of y, for each value of x, is given by the linear regression function

$$E(y|x) = \beta_1 + \beta_2 x$$

- For each value of x, the values of y are distributed about their mean value, following probability distributions that all have the same variance,

$$\text{var}(y|x) = \sigma^2$$

- The sample values of y are all uncorrelated and have zero covariance, implying that there is no linear association among them,

$$\text{cov}(y_i, y_j) = 0$$

This assumption can be made stronger by assuming that the values of y are all statistically independent.

- The variable x is not random and must take at least two different values.
- (*optional*) The values of y are normally distributed about their mean for each value of x,

$$y \sim N\big[(\beta_1 + \beta_2 x), \sigma^2\big]$$

2.2.1 INTRODUCING THE ERROR TERM

It is convenient to describe the assumptions of the simple linear regression model in terms of y, which in general is called the **dependent variable** in the regression model. However, for statistical purposes it is useful to characterize the assumptions another way.

The essence of regression analysis is that any observation on the dependent variable y can be decomposed into two parts: a systematic component and a random component. The systematic component of y is its mean, $E(y|x) = \beta_1 + \beta_2 x$, which itself is not random since it is a mathematical expectation. The random component of y is the difference between y and its conditional mean value $E(y|x)$. This is called a **random error term**, and it is defined as

$$e = y - E(y|x) = y - \beta_1 - \beta_2 x \qquad (2.3)$$

If we rearrange (2.3) we obtain the **simple linear regression model**

$$y = \beta_1 + \beta_2 x + e \qquad (2.4)$$

The dependent variable y is explained by a component that varies systematically with the **independent variable** x and by the random error term e.

Equation (2.3) shows that y and the error term e differ only by the term $E(y|x) = \beta_1 + \beta_2 x$, which is not random. Since y is random, so is the error term e. Given what we have already assumed about y, the properties of the random error e can be derived directly from (2.3). The expected value of the error term, given x, is

$$E(e|x) = E(y|x) - \beta_1 - \beta_2 x = 0$$

The mean value of the error term, given x, is zero.

Since y and e differ only by a constant (i.e., a factor that is not random), their variances must be identical and equal to σ^2. Thus the probability density functions for y and e are identical except for their location, as shown in Figure 2.4. Note that the center of the *pdf* for the error term, $f(e)$, is zero, which is its expected value, $E(e|x) = 0$.

We can now discuss a bit more the simplifying assumption that x is not random. The assumption that x is not random means that its value is known. In statistics such x-values are said to be "fixed in repeated samples." If we could perform controlled experiments, as described in Chapter 1, the same set of x-values could be used over and over, so that only the outcomes y are random. As an example, suppose that we are interested in how price affects the number of Big Macs sold weekly at the local McDonalds. The franchise owner can set the price (x) and then observe the number of Big Macs sold (y) during the week. The

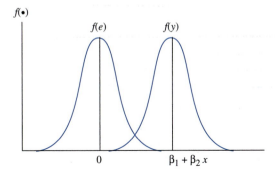

FIGURE **2.4**   Probability density functions for e and y.

following week the price could be changed, and again the data on sales collected. In this case $x =$ the price of a Big Mac is not random, but fixed.

The number of cases in which the x-values are fixed is small in the world of business and economics. When we survey households we obtain the data on variables like food expenditure per person and household income at the same time. Thus y and x are both random in this case; their values are unknown until they are actually observed. However, making the assumption that x is given, and not random, does not change the results we will discuss in the following chapters. The additional benefit from the assumption is notational simplicity. Since x is treated as a constant nonrandom term, we no longer need the conditioning notation "|". So, instead of $E(e|x) = 0$ you will see $E(e) = 0$. There are some important situations in which treating x as fixed is not acceptable, and these will be discussed in Chapter 10.

It is customary in econometrics to state the assumptions of the regression model in terms of the random error e. For future reference the assumptions are named SR1–SR6, "SR" denoting "simple regression." Remember, since we are treating x as fixed, and not random, henceforth we will *not* use the "conditioning" notation $y|x$.

ASSUMPTIONS OF THE SIMPLE LINEAR REGRESSION MODEL-II

SR1.   The value of y, for each value of x, is

[handwritten: when the mean value of E = φ the mean value for y for a given x is = β₁ + β₂x]

$$y = \beta_1 + \beta_2 x + e$$

SR2.   The expected value of the random error e is *[handwritten: - errors associated w/ different observations are independent]*

$$E(e) = 0$$

which is equivalent to assuming that

$$E(y) = \beta_1 + \beta_2 x$$

SR3.   The variance of the random error e is *[handwritten: - the spread of points around the regression line is similar for all x values]*

$$\text{var}(e) = \sigma^2 = \text{var}(y)$$

[handwritten: Homoskedastic - all have same variance.]

The random variables y and e have the same variance because they differ only by a constant.

SR4.   The covariance between any pair of random errors e_i and e_j is

$$\text{cov}(e_i, e_j) = \text{cov}(y_i, y_j) = 0$$

[handwritten: non auto - correlation - the error of 1 observation is not related to the error of another observation]

The stronger version of this assumption is that the random errors e are statistically independent, in which case the values of the dependent variable y are also statistically independent.

SR5.   The variable x is not random and must take at least two different values.

SR6.   (*optional*) The values of e are normally distributed about their mean

$$e \sim N(0, \sigma^2)$$

if the values of y are normally distributed, and vice versa.

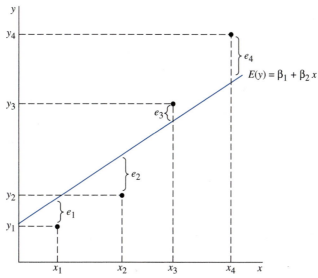

FIGURE 2.5   The relationship among y, e, and the true regression line.

The random error e and the dependent variable y are both random variables, and as we have shown the properties of one can be determined from the properties of the other. There is, however, one interesting difference between them, y is "observable" and e is "unobservable." If the regression parameters β_1 and β_2 were *known*, then for any value of y we could calculate $e = y - (\beta_1 + \beta_2 x)$. This is illustrated in Figure 2.5. Knowing the regression function $E(y) = \beta_1 + \beta_2 x$, we could separate y into its fixed and random parts. However, β_1 and β_2 *are never known*, and it is impossible to calculate e.

What comprises the error term e? The random error e represents all factors affecting y other than x. These factors cause individual observations y to differ from the mean value $E(y) = \beta_1 + \beta_2 x$. In the food expenditure example, what factors can result in a difference between household expenditure per person y and its mean, $E(y)$?

1. We have included income as the only explanatory variable in this model. Any *other* economic factors that affect expenditures on food are "collected" in the error term. Naturally, in any economic model, we want to include all the important and relevant explanatory variables in the model, so the error term e is a "storage bin" for unobservable and/or unimportant factors affecting household expenditures on food. As such, it adds noise that masks the relationship between x and y.

2. The error term e captures any approximation error that arises because the *linear* functional form we have assumed may be only an approximation to reality.

3. The error term captures any elements of random behavior that may be present in each individual. Knowing all the variables that influence a household's food expenditure might not be enough to perfectly predict expenditure. Unpredictable human behavior is also contained in e.

If we have omitted some important factor, or made any other serious **specification error**, then assumption SR2 $E(e) = 0$ will be violated, which will have serious consequences.

Table 2.1   **Food Expenditure and Income Data**

Observation (household)	Food expenditure ($)	Weekly income ($100)
i	y_i	x_i
1	115.22	3.69
2	135.98	4.39
	$\vdots$	
39	257.95	29.40
40	375.73	33.40
Summary statistics		
Sample mean	283.5735	19.6048
Median	264.4800	20.0300
Maximum	587.6600	33.4000
Minimum	109.7100	3.6900
Std. Dev.	112.7652	6.8478

2.3 Estimating the Regression Parameters

The economic and econometric models we developed in the previous section are the basis for using a sample of data to *estimate* the intercept and slope parameters, β_1 and β_2. For illustration we examine typical data on household food expenditure and weekly income from a random sample of 40 households. Representative observations and summary statistics are given in Table 2.1. We control for household size by considering only three-person households. The values of y are weekly food expenditures for a three-person household, in dollars. Instead of measuring income in dollars, we measure it in units of $100, because a $1 increase in income has a numerically small effect on food expenditure. Consequently, for the first household, the reported income is $369 per week with weekly food expenditure of $115.22. For the 40th household weekly income is $3340 and weekly food expenditure is $375.73. The complete data set of observations is in the file *food.dat*.

> **REMARK:** In the text, data files are referenced as *.dat; e.g., *food.dat*. Files in other formats will have the same name, but a different extension, such as *food.wf1*, *food.dta*, and so on. The corresponding data definition file will be *food.def*. These files are located at the book Web site (www.wiley.com/college/hill).

We assume that the expenditure data in Table 2.1 satisfy the assumptions SR1–SR5. That is, we assume that the expected value of household food expenditure is a linear function of income. This assumption about the expected value of y is equivalent to assuming that the random error has expected value zero, implying that we have not omitted any important factors. The variance of y, which is the same as the variance of the random error e, is assumed constant, implying that we are equally uncertain about the relationship between y and x for all observations. The values of y for different households are assumed

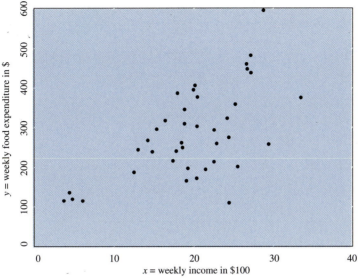

FIGURE **2.6** Data for the food expenditure example.

uncorrelated with each other, which follows if we obtained the data by random sampling. The values of x were actually obtained by random sampling, but we will make the analysis conditional on the x values in the sample, which allows us to treat them as nonrandom values that are fixed in repeated samples. At the end of the day, this simplification does not change the analysis.

Given this theoretical model for explaining the sample observations on household food expenditure, the problem now is how to use the sample information in Table 2.1, specific values of y_i and x_i, to estimate the unknown regression parameters β_1 and β_2. These parameters represent the unknown intercept and slope coefficients for the food expenditure–income relationship. If we represent the 40 data points as $(y_i, x_i), i = 1, \ldots, N = 40$, and plot them, we obtain the **scatter diagram** in Figure 2.6.

> **REMARK:** It will be our notational convention to use "i" subscripts for cross-sectional data observations, with the number of sample observations being N. For time-series data observations we use the subscript "t" and label the total number of observations as T. In purely algebraic or generic situations, we may use one or the other.

Our problem is to estimate the location of the mean expenditure line $E(y) = \beta_1 + \beta_2 x$. We would expect this line to be somewhere in the middle of all the data points since it represents mean, or average, behavior. To estimate β_1 and β_2 we could simply draw a freehand line through the middle of the data and then measure the slope and intercept with a ruler. The problem with this method is that different people would draw different lines, and the lack of a formal criterion makes it difficult to assess the accuracy of the method. Another method is to draw a line from the expenditure at the smallest income level, observation $i = 1$, to the expenditure at largest income level, $i = 40$. This approach does provide a formal rule. However, it may not be a very good rule because it ignores information on the exact position of the remaining 38 observations. It would be better if we could devise a rule that uses all the information from all the data points.

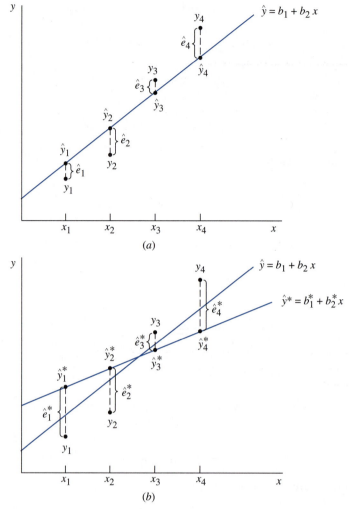

FIGURE 2.7 (*a*) The relationship among y, $\hat{e}$, and the fitted regression line. (*b*) The residuals from another fitted line.

2.3.1 THE LEAST SQUARES PRINCIPLE

To estimate β_1 and β_2 we want a rule, or formula, that tells us how to make use of the sample observations. Many rules are possible, but the one that we will use is based on the **least squares principle**. This principle asserts that to fit a line to the data values we should make the sum of the squares of the vertical distances from each point to the line as small as possible. The distances are squared to prevent large positive distances from being canceled by large negative distances. This rule is arbitrary, but very effective, and is simply one way to describe a line that runs through the middle of the data. The intercept and slope of this line, the line that best fits the data using the least squares principle, are b_1 and b_2, the least squares estimates of β_1 and β_2. The fitted line itself is then

$$\hat{y}_i = b_1 + b_2 x_i \tag{2.5}$$

The vertical distances from each point to the fitted line are the **least squares residuals**. They are given by

$$\hat{e}_i = y_i - \hat{y}_i = y_i - b_1 - b_2 x_i \tag{2.6}$$

These residuals are depicted in Figure 2.7a.

Now suppose we fit another line, *any other line*, to the data. Denote the new line as

$$\hat{y}_i^* = b_1^* + b_2^* x_i$$

where b_1^* and b_2^* are any other intercept and slope values. The residuals for this line, $\hat{e}_i^* = y_i - \hat{y}_i^*$, are shown in Figure 2.7b. The least squares estimates b_1 and b_2 have the property that the sum of their squared residuals is *less than* the sum of squared residuals for *any* other line. That is, if

$$SSE = \sum_{i=1}^{N} \hat{e}_i^2$$

is the sum of squared least squares residuals from (2.6) and

$$SSE^* = \sum_{i=1}^{N} \hat{e}_i^{*2} = \sum_{i=1}^{N} (y_i - \hat{y}_i^*)^2$$

is the sum of squared residuals based on any other estimates, then

$$SSE < SSE^*$$

no matter how the other line might be drawn through the data. The least squares principle says that the estimates b_1 and b_2 of β_1 and β_2 are the ones to use since the line using them as intercept and slope fits the data best.

The problem is to find b_1 and b_2 in a convenient way. Given the sample observations on y and x, we want to find values for the unknown parameters β_1 and β_2 that minimize the "sum of squares" function

$$S(\beta_1, \beta_2) = \sum_{i=1}^{N} (y_i - \beta_1 - \beta_2 x_i)^2$$

This is a straightforward calculus problem, the details of which are given in Appendix 2A, at the end of this chapter. The formulas for the least squares estimates of β_1 and β_2 that give the minimum of the sum of squared residuals are

---

THE LEAST SQUARES ESTIMATORS

$$b_2 = \frac{\sum(x_i - \bar{x})(y_i - \bar{y})}{\sum(x_i - \bar{x})^2} \tag{2.7}$$

$$b_1 = \bar{y} - b_2 \bar{x} \tag{2.8}$$

---

where $\bar{y} = \sum y_i / N$ and $\bar{x} = \sum x_i / N$ are the sample means of the observations on y and x.

The formula for b_2 reveals why we had to assume [SR5] that the values of x_i were not the same value for all observations. If $x_i = 5$, for example, for all observations, then b_2 is mathematically undefined and does not exist since the numerator and denominator of (2.7) are zero!

If we plug the sample values y_i and x_i into (2.7) and (2.8), then we obtain the least squares *estimates* of the intercept and slope parameters β_1 and β_2. It is interesting, however, and very important, that the formulas for b_1 and b_2 are perfectly general and can be used no matter what the sample values turn out to be. This should ring a bell. When the formulas for b_1 and b_2 are taken to be rules that are used whatever the sample data turn out to be, then b_1 and b_2 are random variables. When actual sample values are substituted into the formulas we obtain numbers that are the observed values of random variables. To distinguish these two cases we call the rules or general formulas for b_1 and b_2 the **least squares estimators**. We call the numbers obtained when the formulas are used with a particular sample **least squares estimates.**

- Least squares *estimators* are general formulas and are *random variables*.
- Least squares *estimates* are numbers that we obtain by applying the general formulas to the observed data.

The distinction between *estimators* and *estimates* is a fundamental concept that is essential to understand everything in the rest of this book.

2.3.2   ESTIMATES FOR THE FOOD EXPENDITURE FUNCTION

Using the least squares estimators (2.7) and (2.8), we can obtain the least squares estimates for the intercept and slope parameters β_1 and β_2 in the food expenditure example using the data in Table 2.1. From (2.7) we have

$$b_2 = \frac{\Sigma(x_i - \bar{x})(y_i - \bar{y})}{\Sigma(x_i - \bar{x})^2} = \frac{18671.2684}{1828.7876} = 10.2096$$

and from (2.8)

$$b_1 = \bar{y} - b_2\bar{x} = 283.5737 - (10.2096)(19.6048) = 83.4160$$

A convenient way to report the values for b_1 and b_2 is to write out the *estimated* or *fitted* regression line, with the estimates rounded appropriately:

$$\hat{y}_i = 83.42 + 10.21x_i$$

This line is graphed in Figure 2.8. The line's slope is 10.21 and its intercept, where it crosses the vertical axis, is 83.42. The least squares fitted line passes through the middle of the data in a very precise way, since one of the characteristics of the fitted line based on the least squares parameter estimates is that it passes through the point defined by the sample means, $(\bar{x}, \bar{y}) = (19.6048, 283.5735)$. This follows directly from rewriting (2.8) as $\bar{y} = b_1 + b_2\bar{x}$. Thus the "point of the means" is a useful reference value in regression analysis.

2.3.3   INTERPRETING THE ESTIMATES

Once obtained, the least squares estimates are interpreted in the context of the economic model under consideration. The value $b_2 = 10.21$ is an estimate of β_2. Recall that x, weekly household income, is measured in $100 units. The regression slope β_2 is the amount by which expected weekly expenditure on food per household increases when household weekly income increases by $100. Thus, we estimate that if weekly household income goes up by $100, expected weekly expenditure on food will increase by approximately $10.21. A supermarket executive with information on likely changes in the income and the number

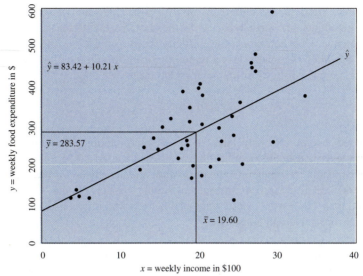

FIGURE **2.8**   The fitted regression.

of households in an area could estimate that it will sell $10.21 more per typical household per week for every $100 increase in income. This is a very valuable piece of information for long-run planning.

Strictly speaking, the intercept estimate $b_1 = 83.42$ is an estimate of the weekly food expenditure for a household with zero income. In most economic models we must be very careful when interpreting the estimated intercept. The problem is that we usually do not have any data points near $x = 0$, which is true for the food expenditure data shown in Figure 2.8. If we have no observations in the region where income is zero, then our estimated relationship may not be a good approximation to reality in that region. So, although our estimated model suggests that a household with zero income is expected to spend $83.42 per week on food, it might be risky to take this estimate literally. This is an issue that you should consider in each economic model that you estimate.

2.3.3a   Elasticities
Income elasticity is a useful way to characterize the responsiveness of consumer expenditure to changes in income. See Appendix A.3 for a discussion of elasticity calculations in a linear relationship. The elasticity of a variable y with respect to another variable x is

$$\varepsilon = \frac{\text{percentage change in } y}{\text{percentage change in } x} = \frac{\Delta y/y}{\Delta x/x} = \frac{\Delta y}{\Delta x} \cdot \frac{x}{y}$$

In the linear economic model given by (2.1) we have shown that

$$\beta_2 = \frac{\Delta E(y)}{\Delta x}$$

so the elasticity of mean expenditure with respect to income is

$$\varepsilon = \frac{\Delta E(y)/E(y)}{\Delta x/x} = \frac{\Delta E(y)}{\Delta x} \cdot \frac{x}{E(y)} = \beta_2 \cdot \frac{x}{E(y)} \tag{2.9}$$

To estimate this elasticity we replace β_2 by $b_2 = 10.21$. We must also replace "x" and "$E(y)$" by something, since in a linear model the elasticity is different on each point upon the regression line. Most commonly the elasticity is calculated at the "point of the means" $(\bar{x}, \bar{y}) = (19.60, 283.57)$ because it is a representative point on the regression line. If we calculate the income elasticity at the point of the means we obtain

$$\hat{\varepsilon} = b_2 \frac{\bar{x}}{\bar{y}} = 10.21 \times \frac{19.60}{283.57} = 0.71$$

This *estimated* income elasticity takes its usual interpretation. We estimate that a 1% increase in weekly household income will lead, on average, to a 0.71% increase in weekly household expenditure on food, when x and y take their sample mean values, $(\bar{x}, \bar{y}) = (19.60, 283.57)$. Since the estimated income elasticity is less than 1, we would classify food as a "necessity" rather than a "luxury," which is consistent with what we would expect for an average household.

2.3.3b   Prediction

The estimated equation can also be used for prediction or forecasting purposes. Suppose that we wanted to predict weekly food expenditure for a household with a weekly income of $2000. This prediction is carried out by substituting $x = 20$ into our estimated equation to obtain

$$\hat{y}_i = 83.42 + 10.21x_i = 83.42 + 10.21(20) = 287.61$$

We *predict* that a household with a weekly income of $2000 will spend $287.61 per week on food.

2.3.3c   Computer Output

Many different software packages can compute least squares estimates. Every software package's regression output looks different and uses different terminology to describe the output. Despite these differences, the various outputs provide the same basic information, which you should be able to locate and interpret. The matter is complicated somewhat by the fact that the packages also report various numbers whose meaning you may not know. For example, using the food expenditure data, the output from the software package EViews is shown in Figure 2.9.

In the EViews output the parameter estimates are in the "Coefficient" column, with names "C," for constant term (the estimate b_1), and *INCOME* (the estimate b_2). Software programs typically name the estimates with the name of the variable as assigned in the computer program (we named our variable *INCOME*) and an abbreviation for "constant." The estimates that we report in the text are rounded to two significant digits. The other numbers that you can recognize at this time are $SSE = \sum \hat{e}_i^2 = 304505.2$, which is called "Sum squared resid," and the sample mean of y, $\bar{y} = \sum y_i / N = 283.5735$, which is called "Mean dependent var."

We leave discussion of the rest of the output until later. By the end of this book, you will be able to interpret the remainder of the information.

2.3.4   OTHER ECONOMIC MODELS

We have used the household expenditure on food versus income relationship as an example to introduce the ideas of simple regression. The simple regression model can be applied to

[handwritten margin note: P-value — the smallest level of significance at which the null hypothesis is rejected.]

Dependent Variable: *FOOD_EXP*
Method: Least Squares
Sample: 1 40
Included observations: 40

	Coefficient	Std. Error	*t*-Statistic	Prob.
C	83.41600	43.41016	1.921578	0.0622
INCOME	10.20964	2.093264	4.877381	0.0000
R-squared	0.385002	Mean dependent var		283.5735
Adjusted R-squared	0.368818	S.D. dependent var		112.6752
S.E. of regression	89.51700	Akaike info criterion		11.87544
Sum squared resid	304505.2	Schwarz criterion		11.95988
Log likelihood	−235.5088	Hannan-Quinn criter		11.90597
F-statistic	23.78884	Durbin-Watson stat		1.893880
Prob(F-statistic)	0.000019			

FIGURE **2.9** EViews regression output.

estimate the parameters of many relationships in economics, business, and the social sciences. The applications of regression analysis are fascinating and useful. For example

- If the hourly wage rate of electricians rises by 5%, how much will new house prices increase?

- If the cigarette tax increases by $1, how much additional revenue will be generated in the state of Louisiana?

- If the central banking authority raises interest rates by one-half a percentage point, how much will consumer borrowing fall within 6 months? How much will it fall within 1 year? What will happen to the unemployment rate in the months following the increase?

- If we increase funding on preschool education programs in 2008, what will be the effect on high school graduation rates in 2020? What will be the effect on the crime rate by juveniles in 2012 and subsequent years?

The range of applications spans economics and finance, as well as most disciplines in the social and physical sciences. Any time you ask *how much* a change in one variable will affect another variable, regression analysis is a potential tool.

The simple linear regression model is much more flexible than it looks at first glance since the variables y and x can be transformations, involving logarithms, squares, cubes, or reciprocals, of the basic economic variables. Thus, the simple linear regression model can be used for nonlinear relationships between variables. The term *linear* in "linear regression" actually means that the parameters are not transformed in any way. In a linear regression model the parameters must not be raised to powers or transformed, so expressions like, $\ln(\beta_2)$, $\beta_1 \cdot \beta_2$, or $\beta_2^{\beta_1}$ are not permitted.

In Appendix A.4 we summarize a variety of nonlinear relationships between variables that can be estimated by using least squares estimation and the simple linear regression model. If y and x are transformed in some way, then the economic interpretations of the regression parameters change, and the calculation of elasticity changes as well. For example, a popular transformation in economics is the natural logarithm. Economic models like $\ln(y) = \beta_1 + \beta_2 \ln(x)$ are common. A nice feature of this model, if the assumptions of the regression model hold, is that the parameter β_2 *is* the elasticity of y with respect to x for all points on the regression line. Consequently the "log-log" model $\ln(y) = \beta_1 + \beta_2 \ln(x)$ is also called the *constant elasticity* model. See Table A.2 in Appendix A.4 for alternative algebraic functional forms, with the expressions for their slope and elasticity, and Figure A.2 for their geometric shapes. You will refer to Table A.2 and Figure A.2 often, so perhaps put a paper clip on the page for quick access.

2.4 Assessing the Least Squares Estimators

Using the food expenditure data we have estimated the parameters of the regression model $y_i = \beta_1 + \beta_2 x_i + e_i$ using the least squares formulas in (2.7) and (2.8). We obtained the least squares estimates $b_1 = 83.42$ and $b_2 = 10.21$. It is natural, but as we shall argue misguided, to ask the question "How good are these estimates?" This question is not answerable. We will never know the true values of the population parameters β_1 or β_2, consequently we cannot say how close $b_1 = 83.42$ and $b_2 = 10.21$ are to the true values. The least squares estimates are numbers that may or may not be close to the true parameter values, and we will never know.

Rather than asking about the quality of the estimates we will take a step back and examine the quality of the least squares estimation procedure. The motivation for this approach is this: If we were to collect another sample of data, by choosing another set of 40 households to survey, we would have obtained *different* estimates b_1 and b_2, even if we had carefully selected households with the same incomes as in the initial sample. This **sampling variation** is unavoidable. Different samples will yield different estimates because household food expenditures, $y_i, i = 1, \ldots, 40$, are random variables. Their values are not known until the sample is collected. Consequently, when viewed as an estimation procedure, b_1 and b_2 are also random variables, because their values depend on the random variable y. In this context we call b_1 and b_2 the *least squares estimators*.

We can investigate the properties of the estimators b_1 and b_2, which are called their **sampling properties**, and deal with the following important questions:

1. If the least squares estimators b_1 and b_2 are random variables, then what are their expected values, variances, covariances, and probability distributions?

2. The least squares principle is only *one* way of using the data to obtain estimates of β_1 and β_2. How do the least squares estimators compare with other procedures that might be used, and how can we compare alternative estimators? For example, is there another estimator that has a higher probability of producing an estimate that is close to β_2?

The answers to these questions will depend critically on whether the assumptions SR1–SR5 are satisfied. In later chapters we will discuss how to check if the assumptions we make hold in a specific application, and what we might do if one or more assumptions are shown not to hold.

> **REMARK:** We will summarize the properties of the least squares estimators in the next several sections. "Proofs" of important results appear in the appendices to this chapter. In many ways it is good to see these concepts in the context of a simpler problem before tackling them in the regression model. Appendix C covers the topics in this chapter, and the next, in the familiar and algebraically easier problem of estimating the mean of a population.

2.4.1   THE ESTIMATOR b_2

Formulas (2.7) and (2.8) are used to compute the least squares estimates b_1 and b_2. However, they are not well suited for examining theoretical properties of the estimators. In this section we rewrite the formula for b_2 to facilitate its analysis. In (2.7) b_2 is given by

$$b_2 = \frac{\sum(x_i - \bar{x})(y_i - \bar{y})}{\sum(x_i - \bar{x})^2}$$

This is called the *deviation from the mean* form of the estimator because the data have their sample means subtracted. Using assumption SR1 and a bit of algebra (Appendix 2C), we can write b_2 as a **linear estimator**,

$$b_2 = \sum_{i=1}^{N} w_i y_i \qquad (2.10)$$

where

$$w_i = \frac{x_i - \bar{x}}{\sum(x_i - \bar{x})^2} \qquad (2.11)$$

The term w_i depends only on x_i that are not random, so that w_i is not random either. Any estimator that is a weighted average of y_i's, as in (2.10), is called a linear estimator. This is an important classification that we will speak more of later. Then, with yet more algebra (Appendix 2D) we can express b_2 in a theoretically convenient way,

$$b_2 = \beta_2 + \sum w_i e_i \qquad (2.12)$$

where e_i is the random error in the linear regression model $y_i = \beta_1 + \beta_2 x_i + e_i$. This formula is not useful for computations, because it depends on β_2, which we do not know, and on e_i, which are unobservable. However, for understanding the sampling properties of the least squares estimator, (2.12) is very useful.

2.4.2   THE EXPECTED VALUES OF b_1 AND b_2

The estimator b_2 is a random variable since its value is unknown until a sample is collected. What we will show is that if our model assumptions hold, then $E(b_2) = \beta_2$; that is, the expected value of b_2 is equal to the true parameter β_2. When the expected value of *any* estimator of a parameter equals the true parameter value, then that estimator is **unbiased**. Since $E(b_2) = \beta_2$, the least squares estimator b_2 is an unbiased estimator of β_2. The intuitive meaning of unbiasedness comes from the repeated sampling interpretation of mathematical expectation. If many samples of size N are collected, and the formula for b_2 is used to estimate β_2 in each of those samples, then, if our assumptions are valid, the average value of the estimates b_2 obtained from all the samples will be β_2.

We will show that this result is true so that we can illustrate the part played by the assumptions of the linear regression model. In (2.12), what parts are random? The parameter β_2 is not random. It is a population parameter we are trying to estimate. If assumption SR5 holds, then x_i is not random. Then w_i is not random either, as it depends only on the values of x_i. The only random factors in (2.12) are the random error terms e_i.

We can find the expected value of b_2 using the fact that the expected value of a sum is the sum of the expected values:

$$
\begin{aligned}
E(b_2) &= E(\beta_2 + \Sigma w_i e_i) = E(\beta_2 + w_1 e_1 + w_2 e_2 + \cdots + w_N e_N) \\
&= E(\beta_2) + E(w_1 e_1) + E(w_2 e_2) + \cdots + E(w_N e_N) \\
&= E(\beta_2) + \Sigma E(w_i e_i) \\
&= \beta_2 + \Sigma w_i E(e_i) = \beta_2
\end{aligned}
\tag{2.13}
$$

The rules of expected values are fully discussed in Appendix B.4 at the end of the book. In the last line of (2.13) we use two assumptions. First, $E(w_i e_i) = w_i E(e_i)$ because w_i is not random, and constants can be factored out of expected values. Second, we have relied on the assumption that $E(e_i) = 0$. If $E(e_i) \neq 0$, then $E(b_2) \neq \beta_2$, in which case b_2 is a biased estimator of β_2. Recall that e_i contains, among other things, factors affecting y_i that are omitted from the economic model. If we have omitted anything that is important then we would expect that $E(e_i) \neq 0$ and $E(b_2) \neq \beta_2$. Thus, having an economic model that is correctly specified, in the sense that it includes all relevant explanatory variables, is a must in order for the least squares estimators to be unbiased.

The unbiasedness of the estimator b_2 is an important sampling property. When sampling repeatedly from a population the least squares estimator is "correct," on average, and this is one desirable property of an estimator. This statistical property by itself does not mean that b_2 is a good estimator of β_2, but it is part of the story. The unbiasedness property depends on having *many* samples of data from the same population. The fact that b_2 is unbiased does not imply *anything* about what might happen *in just one sample*. An individual estimate (a number) b_2 may be near to, or far from, β_2. Since β_2 is *never* known we will never know, given one sample, whether our estimate is "close" to β_2 or not. Thus the estimate $b_2 = 10.21$ may be close to β_2 or not.

The least squares estimator b_1 of β_1 is also an unbiased estimator, and $E(b_1) = \beta_1$ if the model assumptions hold.

2.4.3 REPEATED SAMPLING

To illustrate the concept of unbiased estimation in a slightly different way, we present in Table 2.2 least squares estimates of the food expenditure model from 10 random samples (*table2-2.dat*) of size $N = 40$ from the same population with the same incomes as the

Table 2.2   **Estimates from 10 Samples**

Sample	b_1	b_2
1	131.69	6.48
2	57.25	10.88
3	103.91	8.14
4	46.50	11.90
5	84.23	9.29
6	26.63	13.55
7	64.21	10.93
8	79.66	9.76
9	97.30	8.05
10	95.96	7.77

households given in Table 2.1. Note the variability of the least squares parameter estimates from sample to sample. This *sampling variation* is due to the fact that we obtained 40 *different* households in each sample, and their weekly food expenditure varies randomly.

The property of unbiasedness is about the *average* values of b_1 and b_2 if *many* samples of the same size are drawn from the same population. The average value of b_1 in these 10 samples is $\bar{b}_1 = 78.74$. The average value of b_2 is $\bar{b}_2 = 9.68$. If we took the averages of estimates from many samples, these averages would approach the true parameter values β_1 and β_2. Unbiasedness does not say that an estimate from any one sample is close to the true parameter value, and thus we cannot say that an *estimate* is unbiased. We can say that the least squares estimation procedure (or the least squares estimator) is unbiased.

2.4.4   THE VARIANCES AND COVARIANCE OF b_1 AND b_2

Table 2.2 shows that the least squares estimates of β_1 and β_2 vary from sample to sample. Understanding this variability is a key to assessing the reliability and sampling precision of an estimator. We now obtain the variances and covariance of the estimators b_1 and b_2. Before presenting the expressions for the variances and covariance, let us consider why they are important to know. The variance of the random variable b_2 is the average of the squared distances between the possible values of the random variable and its mean, which we now know is $E(b_2) = \beta_2$. The variance of b_2 is defined as

$$\mathrm{var}(b_2) = E[b_2 - E(b_2)]^2$$

It measures the spread of the probability distribution of b_2. In Figure 2.10 are graphs of two possible probability distributions of b_2, $f_1(b_2)$ and $f_2(b_2)$, that have the same mean value but different variances.

The probability density function $f_2(b_2)$ has a smaller variance than $f_1(b_2)$. Given a choice, we are interested in estimator precision and would prefer that b_2 have the pdf $f_2(b_2)$ rather than $f_1(b_2)$. With the distribution $f_2(b_2)$, the probability is more concentrated around the true parameter value β_2, giving, relative to $f_1(b_2)$, a higher probability of getting an estimate that is close to β_2. Remember, getting an estimate close to β_2 is our objective.

The variance of an estimator measures the *precision* of the estimator in the sense that it tells us how much the estimates can vary from sample to sample. Consequently, we often refer to the **sampling variance** or **sampling precision** of an estimator. The smaller the variance of an estimator is, the greater the sampling precision of that estimator. One estimator is more precise than another estimator if its sampling variance is less than that of the other estimator.

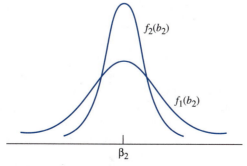

FIGURE 2.10   Two possible probability density functions for b_2.

We will now present and discuss the variances and covariance of b_1 and b_2. Appendix 2E contains the derivation of the variance of the least squares estimator b_2. If the regression model assumptions SR1–SR5 are correct (assumption SR6 is not required), then the variances and covariance of b_1 and b_2 are

$$\text{var}(b_1) = \sigma^2 \left[\frac{\sum x_i^2}{N\sum(x_i - \bar{x})^2} \right] \tag{2.14}$$

$$\text{var}(b_2) = \frac{\sigma^2}{\sum(x_i - \bar{x})^2} \tag{2.15}$$

$$\text{cov}(b_1, b_2) = \sigma^2 \left[\frac{-\bar{x}}{\sum(x_i - \bar{x})^2} \right] \tag{2.16}$$

At the beginning of this section we said that for unbiased estimators, smaller variances are better than larger variances. Let us consider the factors that affect the variances and covariance in (2.14)–(2.16).

1. The variance of the random error term, σ^2, appears in each of the expressions. It reflects the dispersion of the values y about their expected value $E(y)$. The greater the variance σ^2, the greater is that dispersion and the greater is the uncertainty about where the values of y fall relative to their mean $E(y)$. When σ^2 is larger, the information we have about β_1 and β_2 is less precise. In Figure 2.3 the variance is reflected in the spread of the probability distributions $f(y|x)$. The *larger* the variance term σ^2, the *greater is* the uncertainty in the statistical model, and the *larger* the variances and covariance of the least squares estimators.

2. The sum of squares of the values of x about their sample mean, $\sum(x_i - \bar{x})^2$, appears in each of the variances and in the covariance. This expression measures how *spread out* about their mean are the sample values of the independent or explanatory variable x. The more they are spread out, the larger the sum of squares. The less they are spread out, the smaller the sum of squares. You may recognize this sum of squares as the numerator of the sample variance of the x-values. See Appendix C.4. The *larger* the sum of squares, $\sum(x_i - \bar{x})^2$, the *smaller* the variances of the least squares estimators and the more *precisely* we can estimate the unknown parameters. The intuition behind this is demonstrated in Figure 2.11. In panel (b) is a data scatter in which the values of x are widely spread out along the x-axis. In panel (a) the data are "bunched." Which data scatter would you prefer given the task of fitting a line by hand? Pretty clearly, the data in panel (b) do a better job of determining where the least squares line must fall, because they are more spread out along the x-axis.

3. The larger the sample size N, the *smaller* the variances and covariance of the least squares estimators; it is better to have *more* sample data than *less*. The sample size N appears in each of the variances and covariance because each of the sums consists of N terms. Also, N appears explicitly in $\text{var}(b_1)$. The sum of squares term $\sum(x_i - \bar{x})^2$ gets larger as N increases because each of the terms in the sum is positive or zero (being zero if x happens to equal its sample mean value for an observation). Consequently, as N gets larger, both $\text{var}(b_2)$ and $\text{cov}(b_1, b_2)$ get smaller, since the sum of squares appears in their denominator. The sums in the numerator and denominator of $\text{var}(b_1)$ both get larger as N gets larger and offset one another, leaving

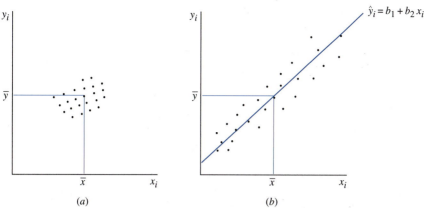

FIGURE 2.11 The influence of variation in the explanatory variable x on precision of estimation: (*a*) low x variation, low precision: (*b*) high x variation, high precision.

the N in the denominator as the dominant term, ensuring that var(b_1) also gets smaller as N gets larger.

4. The term $\sum x_i^2$ appears in var(b_1). The larger this term is, the larger the variance of the least squares estimator b_1. Why is this so? Recall that the intercept parameter β_1 is the expected value of y given that $x = 0$. The farther our data are from $x = 0$, the more difficult it is to interpret β_1, as in the food expenditure example, and the more difficult it is to accurately estimate β_1. The term $\sum x_i^2$ measures the distance of the data from the origin, $x = 0$. If the values of x are near zero then $\sum x_i^2$ will be small and this will reduce var(b_1). But if the values of x are large in magnitude, either positive or negative, the term $\sum x_i^2$ will be large and var(b_1) will be larger, other things being equal.

5. The sample mean of the x-values appears in cov(b_1, b_2). The absolute magnitude of the covariance *increases* with an increase in magnitude of the sample mean $\bar{x}$, and the covariance has a *sign* opposite to that of $\bar{x}$. The reasoning here can be seen from Figure 2.11. In panel (b) the least squares fitted line must pass through the point of the means. Given a fitted line through the data, imagine the effect of increasing the estimated slope b_2. Since the line must pass through the point of the means, the effect must be to lower the point where the line hits the vertical axis, implying a reduced intercept estimate b_1. Thus, when the sample mean is positive, as shown in Figure 2.11, there is a negative covariance between the least squares estimators of the slope and intercept.

2.5 The Gauss–Markov Theorem

What can we say about the least squares estimators b_1 and b_2 so far?

• The estimators are perfectly general. Formulas (2.7) and (2.8) can be used to estimate the unknown parameters β_1 and β_2 in the simple linear regression model no matter what the data turn out to be. Consequently, viewed in this way, the least squares estimators b_1 and b_2 are random variables.

• The least squares estimators are *linear* estimators, as defined in (2.10). Both b_1 and b_2 can be written as weighted averages of the y_i values.

- If assumptions SR1–SR5 hold then the least squares estimators are *unbiased*. This means that $E(b_1) = \beta_1$ and $E(b_2) = \beta_2$.

- We have expressions for the variances of b_1 and b_2 and their covariance. Furthermore, we have argued that for any unbiased estimator, having a smaller variance is better, as this implies we have a higher chance of obtaining an estimate close to the true parameter value.

Now we will state and discuss the famous Gauss–Markov theorem, which is proven in Appendix 2F.

> **GAUSS–MARKOV THEOREM:** Under the assumptions SR1–SR5 of the linear regression model, the estimators b_1 and b_2 have the smallest variance of all linear and unbiased estimators of β_1 and β_2. They are the **best linear unbiased estimators (BLUE)** of β_1 and β_2.

Let us clarify what the Gauss–Markov theorem does, and does not, say.

1. The estimators b_1 and b_2 are "best" when compared to similar estimators, those that are linear and unbiased. The theorem does *not* say that b_1 and b_2 are the best of all *possible* estimators.

2. The estimators b_1 and b_2 are best within their class because they have the minimum variance. When comparing two linear and unbiased estimators, we *always* want to use the one with the smaller variance, since that estimation rule gives us the higher probability of obtaining an estimate that is close to the true parameter value.

3. In order for the Gauss–Markov theorem to hold, assumptions SR1–SR5 must be true. If any of these assumptions are *not* true, then b_1 and b_2 are *not* the best linear unbiased estimators of β_1 and β_2.

4. The Gauss–Markov theorem does *not* depend on the assumption of normality (assumption SR6).

5. In the simple linear regression model, if we want to use a linear and unbiased estimator, then we have to do no more searching. The estimators b_1 and b_2 are the ones to use. This explains why we are studying these estimators (we would not have you study *bad* estimation rules, would we?) and why they are so widely used in research, not only in economics but in all social and physical sciences as well.

6. The Gauss–Markov theorem applies to the least squares estimators. It *does not* apply to the least squares *estimates* from a single sample.

2.6 The Probability Distributions of the Least Squares Estimators

The properties of the least squares estimators that we have developed so far do not depend in any way on the normality assumption SR6. If we also make this assumption that the random errors e_i are normally distributed with mean 0 and variance σ^2, then the probability distributions of the least squares estimators are also normal. This conclusion is obtained in two steps. First, based on assumption SR1, if e_i is normal then so is y_i. Second, the least squares estimators are linear estimators, of the form $b_2 = \Sigma w_i y_i$, and sums of normal random variables are normally distributed themselves. Consequently, *if* we make the normality assumption (assumption SR6 about the error term) then the least squares estimators are normally distributed.

$$b_1 \sim N\left(\beta_1, \frac{\sigma^2 \Sigma x_i^2}{N\Sigma(x_i - \bar{x})^2}\right) \qquad (2.17)$$

$$b_2 \sim N\left(\beta_2, \frac{\sigma^2}{\Sigma(x_i - \bar{x})^2}\right) \qquad (2.18)$$

As you will see in Chapter 3, the normality of the least squares estimators is of great importance in many aspects of statistical inference.

What if the errors are not normally distributed? Can we say anything about the probability distribution of the least squares estimators? The answer is, sometimes, yes.

> **A CENTRAL LIMIT THEOREM:** If assumptions SR1–SR5 hold, and if the sample size N is **sufficiently large**, then the least squares estimators have a distribution that approximates the normal distributions shown in (2.17) and (2.18).

The million dollar question is "How large is sufficiently large?" The answer is, there is no specific number. The reason for this vague and unsatisfying answer is that "how large" depends on many factors, such as what the distributions of the random errors look like (are they smooth? symmetric? skewed?) and what the x_i values are like. In the simple regression model some would say that $N = 30$ is sufficiently large. Others would say that $N = 50$ would be more a reasonable number. The bottom line is, however, that these are rules of thumb, and that the meaning of "sufficiently large" will change from problem to problem. Nevertheless, for better or worse, this *large sample*, or *asymptotic*, result is frequently invoked in regression analysis. This important result is an application of a central limit theorem, like the one discussed in Appendix C.3.4. If you are not familiar with this important theorem, you may want to review it now.

2.7 Estimating the Variance of the Error Term

The variance of the random error term, σ^2, is the one unknown parameter of the simple linear regression model that remains to be estimated. The variance of the random error e_i is

$$\text{var}(e_i) = \sigma^2 = E[e_i - E(e_i)]^2 = E(e_i^2)$$

if the assumption $E(e_i) = 0$ is correct. Since the "expectation" is an average value we might consider estimating σ^2 as the average of the squared errors,

$$\hat{\sigma}^2 = \frac{\Sigma e_i^2}{N}$$

This formula is unfortunately of no use since the random errors e_i are *unobservable*! However, while the random errors themselves are unknown we do have an analog to them, namely, the least squares residuals. Recall that the random errors are

$$e_i = y_i - \beta_1 - \beta_2 x_i$$

From (2.6) the least squares residuals are obtained by replacing the unknown parameters by their least squares estimates,

$$\hat{e}_i = y_i - \hat{y}_i = y_i - b_1 - b_2 x_i$$

It seems reasonable to replace the random errors e_i by their analogs, the least squares residuals, so that

$$\hat{\sigma}^2 = \frac{\Sigma \hat{e}_i^2}{N}$$

This estimator, though quite satisfactory in large samples, is a *biased* estimator of σ^2. There is a simple modification that produces an unbiased estimator, and that is

$$\hat{\sigma}^2 = \frac{\Sigma \hat{e}_i^2}{N-2} \tag{2.19}$$

The "2" that is subtracted in the denominator is the number of *regression parameters* (β_1, β_2) in the model, and this subtraction makes the estimator $\hat{\sigma}^2$ unbiased, so that $E(\hat{\sigma}^2) = \sigma^2$.

2.7.1 ESTIMATING THE VARIANCES AND COVARIANCE OF THE LEAST SQUARES ESTIMATORS

Having an unbiased estimator of the error variance means we can *estimate* the variances of the least squares estimators b_1 and b_2, and the covariance between them. Replace the unknown error variance σ^2 in (2.14)–(2.16) by $\hat{\sigma}^2$ to obtain

$$\widehat{\text{var}(b_1)} = \hat{\sigma}^2 \left[\frac{\Sigma x_i^2}{N \Sigma (x_i - \bar{x})^2} \right] \tag{2.20}$$

$$\widehat{\text{var}(b_2)} = \frac{\hat{\sigma}^2}{\Sigma (x_i - \bar{x})^2} \tag{2.21}$$

$$\widehat{\text{cov}(b_1, b_2)} = \hat{\sigma}^2 \left[\frac{-\bar{x}}{\Sigma (x_i - \bar{x})^2} \right] \tag{2.22}$$

The square roots of the estimated variances are the "standard errors" of b_1 and b_2. These quantities are used in hypothesis testing and confidence intervals. They are denoted as $\text{se}(b_1)$ and $\text{se}(b_2)$

$$\text{se}(b_1) = \sqrt{\widehat{\text{var}(b_1)}} \tag{2.23}$$

$$\text{se}(b_2) = \sqrt{\widehat{\text{var}(b_2)}} \tag{2.24}$$

Table 2.3 **Least Squares Residuals**

x	y	$\hat{y}$	$\hat{e} = y - \hat{y}$
3.69	115.22	121.09	−5.87
4.39	135.98	128.24	7.74
4.75	119.34	131.91	−12.57
6.03	114.96	144.98	−30.02
12.47	187.05	210.73	−23.68

2.7.2 CALCULATIONS FOR THE FOOD EXPENDITURE DATA

Let us make some calculations using the food expenditure data. The least squares estimates of the parameters in the food expenditure model are shown in Figure 2.9. First we will compute the least squares residuals from (2.6) and use them to calculate the estimate of the error variance in (2.19). In Table 2.3 are the least squares residuals for the first five households in Table 2.1.

Recall that we have estimated that for the food expenditure data the fitted least squares regression line is $\hat{y} = 83.42 + 10.21x$. For each observation we compute the least squares residual $\hat{e}_i = y_i - \hat{y}_i$. Using the residuals for all $N = 40$ observations we estimate the error variance to be

$$\hat{\sigma}^2 = \frac{\sum \hat{e}_i^2}{N - 2} = \frac{304505.2}{38} = 8013.29$$

The numerator, 304505.2, is the sum of squared least squares residuals, reported as "Sum squared resid" in Figure 2.9. The denominator is the number of sample observations, $N = 40$, minus the number of estimated regression parameters, 2; the quantity $N - 2 = 38$ is often called the "degrees of freedom" for reasons that will be explained in Chapter 3. In Figure 2.9, the value $\hat{\sigma}^2$ is not reported. Instead, EViews software reports $\hat{\sigma} = \sqrt{\hat{\sigma}^2} = \sqrt{8013.29} = 89.517$, labeled "S.E. of regression," which stands for "standard error of the regression."

It is typical for software not to report the estimated variances and covariance unless requested. However, all software packages automatically report the standard errors. For example, in the EViews output shown in Figure 2.9 the column labeled "Std. Error" contains $se(b_1) = 43.41$ and $se(b_2) = 2.09$. The entry called "S.D. dependent var" is the sample standard deviation of y, that is $\sqrt{\sum(y_i - \bar{y})^2/(N - 1)} = 112.6752$.

The full set of estimated variances and covariances for a regression is usually obtained by a simple computer command, or option, depending on the software being used. They are arrayed in a rectangular array, or matrix, with variances on the diagonal and covariances in the "off-diagonal" positions.

$$\begin{bmatrix} \widehat{\text{var}}(b_1) & \widehat{\text{cov}}(b_1, b_2) \\ \widehat{\text{cov}}(b_1, b_2) & \widehat{\text{var}}(b_2) \end{bmatrix}$$

For the food expenditure data the estimated covariance matrix of the least squares estimators is

	C	$INCOME$
C	1884.442	−85.90316
$INCOME$	−85.90316	4.381752

where C stands for the "constant term," which is the estimated intercept parameter in the regression, or b_1; similarly, the software reports the variable name *INCOME* for the column relating to the estimated slope b_2. Thus

$$\widehat{\text{var}}(b_1) = 1884.442, \quad \widehat{\text{var}}(b_2) = 4.381752, \quad \widehat{\text{cov}}(b_1, b_2) = -85.90316$$

The standard errors are

$$\text{se}(b_1) = \sqrt{\widehat{\text{var}}(b_1)} = \sqrt{1884.442} = 43.410$$

$$\text{se}(b_2) = \sqrt{\widehat{\text{var}}(b_2)} = \sqrt{4.381752} = 2.093$$

These values will be used extensively in Chapter 3.

2.8 Exercises

Answers to exercises marked "*" appear in Appendix D at the end of the book.

2.8.1 PROBLEMS

2.1 Consider the following five observations. You are to do all the parts of this exercise using only a calculator.

x	y	$x - \bar{x}$	$(x - \bar{x})^2$	$y - \bar{y}$	$(x - \bar{x})(y - \bar{y})$
3	5	2	4	3	6
2	2	1	1	0	0
1	3	0	0	1	12
−1	2	−2	4	0	0
0	−2	−1	1	−4	4
$\sum x_i =$	$\sum y_i =$	$\sum(x_i - \bar{x}) =$	$\sum(x_i - \bar{x})^2 =$	$\sum(y_i - \bar{y}) =$	$\sum(x_i - \bar{x})(y_i - \bar{y}) =$
5	10	0	10	0	10

(a) Complete the entries in the table. Put the sums in the last row. What are the sample means $\bar{x}$ and $\bar{y}$?

(b) Calculate b_1 and b_2 using (2.7) and (2.8) and state their interpretation.

(c) Compute $\sum_{i=1}^{5} x_i^2$, $\sum_{i=1}^{5} x_i y_i$. Using these numerical values show that

$$\sum(x_i - \bar{x})^2 = \sum x_i^2 - N\bar{x}^2 \quad \text{and} \quad \sum(x_i - \bar{x})(y_i - \bar{y}) = \sum x_i y_i - N\bar{x}\bar{y}$$

(d) Use the least squares estimates from part (b) to compute the fitted values of y, and complete the remainder of the table below. Put the sums in the last row.

x_i	y_i	$\hat{y}_i$	$\hat{e}_i$	$\hat{e}_i^2$	$x_i \hat{e}_i$
3	5				
2	2				
1	3				
−1	2				
0	−2				
$\sum x_i =$	$\sum y_i =$	$\sum \hat{y}_i =$	$\sum \hat{e}_i =$	$\sum \hat{e}_i^2 =$	$\sum x_i \hat{e}_i =$

(e) On graph paper, plot the data points and sketch the fitted regression line $\hat{y}_i = b_1 + b_2 x_i$.

(f) On the sketch in part (e), locate the point of the means $(\bar{x}, \bar{y})$. Does your fitted line pass through that point? If not, go back to the drawing board, literally.

(g) Show that for these numerical values $\bar{y} = b_1 + b_2\bar{x}$.

(h) Show that for these numerical values $\bar{\hat{y}} = \bar{y}$, where $\bar{\hat{y}} = \Sigma\hat{y}_i/N$.

(i) Compute $\hat{\sigma}^2$.

(j) Compute $\widehat{\text{var}(b_2)}$.

2.2   A household has weekly income \$1000. The mean weekly expenditure on food for households with this income is $E(y|x = \$1000) = \mu_{y|x=\$1000} = \$125$ and expenditures exhibit variance $\text{var}(y|x = \$1000) = \sigma^2_{y|x=\$1000} = 49$.

(a) Assuming that weekly food expenditures are normally distributed, find the probability that a household with this income spends between \$110 and \$140 on food in a week. Include a sketch with your solution.

(b) Find the probability in part (a) if the variance of weekly expenditures is $\text{var}(y|x = \$1000) = \sigma^2_{y|x=\$1000} = 81$.

2.3*   Graph the following observations of x and y on graph paper.

x	1	2	3	4	5	6
y	4	6	7	7	9	11

(a) Using a ruler, draw a line that fits through the data. Measure the slope and intercept of the line you have drawn.

(b) Use formulas (2.7) and (2.8) to compute, using only a hand calculator, the least squares estimates of the slope and the intercept. Plot this line on your graph.

(c) Obtain the sample means of $\bar{y} = \Sigma y_i/N$ and $\bar{x} = \Sigma x_i/N$. Obtain the predicted value of y for $x = \bar{x}$ and plot it on your graph. What do you observe about this predicted value?

(d) Using the least squares estimates from (b), compute the least squares residuals $\hat{e}_i$. Find their sum.

(e) Calculate $\Sigma x_i\hat{e}_i$.

2.4   We have defined the simple linear regression model to be $y = \beta_1 + \beta_2 x + e$. Suppose however that we knew, for a fact, that $\beta_1 = 0$.

(a) What does the linear regression model look like, algebraically, if $\beta_1 = 0$?

(b) What does the linear regression model look like, graphically, if $\beta_1 = 0$?

(c) If $\beta_1 = 0$ the least squares "sum of squares" function becomes $S(\beta_2) = \sum_{i=1}^{N}(y_i - \beta_2 x_i)^2$. Using the data,

x	1	2	3	4	5	6
y	4	6	7	7	9	11

plot the value of the sum of squares function for enough values of β_2 for you to locate the approximate minimum. What is the significance of the value of β_2 that minimizes $S(\beta_2)$? (*Hint*: Your computations will be simplified if you algebraically expand $S(\beta_2) = \sum_{i=1}^{N}(y_i - \beta_2 x_i)^2$ by squaring the term in parentheses and carrying the summation operator through.)

(d)◆Using calculus, show that the formula for the least squares estimate of β_2 in this model is $b_2 = \sum x_i y_i / \sum x_i^2$. Use this result to compute b_2 and compare this value to the value you obtained geometrically.

(e) Using the estimate obtained with the formula in (d), plot the fitted (estimated) regression function. On the graph locate the point $(\bar{x}, \bar{y})$. What do you observe?

(f) Using the estimates obtained with the formula in (d), obtain the least squares residuals, $\hat{e}_i = y_i - b_2 x_i$. Find their sum.

(g) Calculate $\sum x_i \hat{e}_i$.

2.5   A small business hires a consultant to predict the value of weekly sales of their product if their weekly advertising is increased to $600 per week. The consultant takes a record of how much the firm spent on advertising per week and the corresponding weekly sales over the past 6 months. The consultant writes "Over the past 6 months the average weekly expenditure on advertising has been $450 and average weekly sales have been $7500. Based on the results of a simple linear regression, I predict sales will be $8500 if $600 per week is spent on advertising."

(a) What is the estimated simple regression used by the consultant to make this prediction?

(b) Sketch a graph of the estimated regression line. Locate the average weekly values on the graph.

2.6*   A soda vendor at Louisiana State University football games observes that more sodas are sold the warmer the temperature at game time. Based on 32 home games covering 5 years, the vendor estimates the relationship between soda sales and temperature to be $\hat{y} = -240 + 6x$, where $y =$ the number of sodas she sells and $x =$ temperature in degrees Fahrenheit,

(a) Interpret the estimated slope and intercept. Do the estimates make sense? Why or why not?

(b) On a day when the temperature at game time is forecast to be $80°F$, predict how many sodas the vendor will sell.

(c) Below what temperature are the predicted sales zero?

(d) Sketch a graph of the estimated regression line.

2.7.   You have the results of a simple linear regression based on state-level data and the District of Columbia, a total of $N = 51$ observations.

(a) The estimated error variance $\hat{\sigma}^2 = 2.04672$. What is the sum of the squared least squares residuals?

(b) The estimated variance of b_2 is 0.00098. What is the standard error of b_2? What is the value of $\sum(x_i - \bar{x})^2$?

(c) Suppose the dependent variable $y_i =$ the state's mean income (in thousands of dollars) of males who are 18 years of age or older and x_i the percentage of males 18 years or older who are high school graduates. If $b_2 = 0.18$, interpret this result.

(d) Suppose $\bar{x} = 69.139$ and $\bar{y} = 15.187$, what is the estimate of the intercept parameter?

(e) Given the results in (b) and (d), what is $\sum x_i^2$?

(f) For the State of Arkansas the value of $y_i = 12.274$ and the value of $x_i = 58.3$. Compute the least squares residual for Arkansas. (*Hint*: Use the information in parts (c) and (d).).

2.8◆ Professor E.Z. Stuff has decided that the least squares estimator is too much trouble. Noting that two points determine a line, Dr. Stuff chooses two points from a sample of size N and draws a line between them, calling the slope of this line the EZ estimator of β_2 in the simple regression model. Algebraically, if the two points are (x_1, y_1) and (x_2, y_2), the EZ estimation rule is

$$b_{EZ} = \frac{y_2 - y_1}{x_2 - x_1}$$

Assuming that all the assumptions of the simple regression model hold:
(a) Show that b_{EZ} is a "linear" estimator.
(b) Show that b_{EZ} is an unbiased estimator.
(c) Find the variance of b_{EZ}.
(d) Find the probability distribution of b_{EZ}.
(e) Convince Professor Stuff that the EZ estimator is not as good as the least squares estimator. No proof is required here.

2.8.2 COMPUTER EXERCISES

2.9* An interesting and useful economic concept is the "learning curve." The idea is related to a phenomenon that occurs in assembly line production, such as in the automobile industry, or any time a task is performed repeatedly. Workers learn from experience and become more efficient in performing their task. This means it takes less time and labor costs to produce the final product. This idea forms the basis for an economic model relating cost per unit at time t ($UNITCOST_t$) to the *cumulative* production of a good up to, but not including, time t ($CUMPROD_t$). The relationship between the variables is often taken to be

$$UNITCOST_t = UNITCOST_1 \times CUMPROD_t^{\varepsilon}$$

where $UNITCOST_1$ equals the unit cost of production for the first unit produced, and ε equals the elasticity of unit costs with respect to cumulative production (which we expect to be negative). This nonlinear relationship between the variables is transformed to a linear one by taking logarithms of both sides:

$$\ln(UNITCOST_t) = \ln(UNITCOST_1) + \varepsilon\ln(CUMPROD_t)$$
$$= \beta_1 + \beta_2\ln(CUMPROD_t)$$

We have "renamed" $\ln(UNITCOST_1)$ and ε so that the model looks more familiar. Ernst Berndt is the author of an excellent book, more advanced than this one, entitled *The Practice of Econometrics: Classic and Contemporary* (Addison and Wesley, 1991). On page 85 of that book Berndt gives the example of learning in the production of a product called titanium dioxide, which is used as a thickener in paint. He provides data on production and unit costs from the DuPont Corporation for the years 1955–1970. The data are given in *learn.dat*.
(a) Use your computer software to plot a graph of $UNITCOST$ against $CUMPROD$, and $\ln(UNITCOST)$ against $\ln(CUMPROD)$.
(b) Obtain the least squares estimates b_1 and b_2 of β_1 and β_2 and give their economic interpretation. Do these numbers make sense? Make a sketch of the fitted regression line, by hand or using your software, in the plot from part (a).
(c) Find the estimated variances and covariance of the least squares estimators.
(d) Find $\hat{\sigma}^2$.

(e) Predict the unit cost of production when cumulative production is $CUMPROD_0 = 2000$.

2.10   The capital asset pricing model (CAPM) is an important model in the field of finance. It explains variations in the rate of return on a security as a function of the rate of return on a portfolio consisting of all publicly traded stocks, which is called the *market* portfolio. Generally the rate of return on any investment is measured relative to its opportunity cost, which is the return on a risk free asset. The resulting difference is called the *risk premium*, since it is the reward or punishment for making a risky investment. The CAPM says that the risk premium on security j is *proportional* to the risk premium on the market portfolio. That is

$$r_j - r_f = \beta_j(r_m - r_f)$$

where r_j and r_f are the returns to security j and the risk-free rate, respectively, r_m is the return on the market portfolio, and β_j is the jth security's "*beta*" value. A stock's *beta* is important to investors since it reveals the stock's volatility. It measures the sensitivity of security j's return to variation in the whole stock market. As such, values of *beta* less than 1 indicate that the stock is "defensive" since its variation is less than the market's. A *beta* greater than 1 indicates an "aggressive stock." Investors usually want an estimate of a stock's *beta* before purchasing it. The CAPM model shown above is the "economic model" in this case. The "econometric model" is obtained by including an intercept in the model (even though theory says it should be zero) and an error term,

$$r_j - r_f = \alpha_j + \beta_j(r_m - r_f) + e$$

(a) Explain why the econometric model above is a simple regression model like those discussed in this chapter.
(b) In the data file *capm2.dat* are data on the monthly returns of six firms (Microsoft, GE, GM, IBM, Disney, and Mobil-Exxon), the rate of return on the market portfolio (*MKT*), and the rate of return on the risk free asset (*RKFREE*). The 120 observations cover January 1995 to December 2004. Estimate the CAPM model for each firm, and comment on their estimated *beta* values. Which firm appears most aggressive? Which firm appears most defensive?
(c) Finance theory says that the intercept parameter α_j should be zero. Does this seem correct given your estimates? For the Microsoft stock, plot the fitted regression line along with the data scatter.
(d) Estimate the model for each firm under the assumption that $\alpha_j = 0$. Do the estimates of the *beta* values change much?

2.11   The file *br2.dat* contains data on 1080 houses sold in Baton Rouge, Louisiana during mid-2005. The data include sale price, the house size in square feet, its age, and whether it has a pool or fireplace or is on the waterfront. Also included is a variable named *style* included in the realtor's description. Variable descriptions are in the file *br2.def*.
(a) Plot house price against house size for all houses in the sample. Construct another plot for houses of traditional style.
(b) Estimate the regression model $PRICE = \beta_1 + \beta_2 SQFT + e$ for all the houses in the sample. Interpret the estimates. Draw a sketch of the fitted line.
(c) Estimate the regression model in (b) using only traditional style houses. Interpret the estimates. How do the estimates seem to compare to those in (b)?

(d) For each of the regressions in (b) and (c) compute the least squares residuals and plot them against *SQFT*. Do any of our assumptions appear violated?

2.12* The file *stockton2.dat* contains data on 880 houses sold in Stockton, CA, during mid-2005. Variable descriptions are in the file *stockton2.def*.
  (a) Plot house price against house size for all houses in the sample.
  (b) Estimate the regression model $PRICE = \beta_1 + \beta_2 SQFT + e$ for all the houses in the sample. Interpret the estimates. Draw a sketch of the fitted line.
  (c) Estimate the regression model in (b) using only houses that are vacant at the time of sale. Repeat the estimation for houses that were occupied (not vacant) at time of sale. Interpret the estimates. How do the estimates seem to compare to each other?
  (d) For each of the regressions in (c) compute the least squares residuals and plot them against *SQFT*. Do any of our assumptions appear violated?
  (e) Predict the price of a house with 2000 square feet of living area.

2.13 One would suspect that new home construction and sales depend on mortgage interest rates. If interest rates are high, fewer people will be able to afford to borrow the funds necessary to finance the purchase of a new home. Builders are aware of this fact, and thus when mortgage interest rates are high, they will be less inclined to build new homes. While this is intuitively reasonable, let us ask the question "If mortgage interest rates go up by 1%, how much does home construction fall?" Data on the 30-year fixed mortgage rate, housing starts (thousands), and houses sold (thousands) are contained in the file *house_starts.dat*. There are 184 monthly observations from January 1990 to April 2005.
  (a) Plot each of the series against time.
  (b) Plot housing starts (*STARTS*) against the 30-year fixed mortgage rate (*FIXED_RATE*).
  (c) Estimate the simple regression of *STARTS* on *FIXED_RATE*. Discuss the interpretation of the results as well as any comments you may have about how well the line fits the data. Plot the fitted regression line along with the data scatter from (b).
  (d) Plot houses sold (*SOLD*) against *FIXED_RATE*.
  (e) Estimate the simple regression of *SOLD* on *FIXED_RATE*. Discuss the interpretation of the results as well as any comments you may have about how well the line fits the data. Plot the fitted regression line along with the data scatter from (d).
  (f) If the 30-year fixed rate mortgage rate is 6%, predict the number of monthly housing starts.

2.14* Professor Ray C. Fair has for a number of years built and updated models that explain and predict the U.S. presidential elections. See his website at http://fairmodel. econ.yale.edu/vote2008/index2.htm, and see in particular his paper entitled "A Vote Equation for the 2004 Election." The basic premise of the model is that the incumbent party's share of the two-party (Democratic and Republican) popular vote (incumbent means the party in power at the time of the election) is affected by a number of factors relating to the economy and variables relating to the politics, such as how long the incumbent party has been in power and whether the President is running for reelection. Fair's data, 31 observations for the election years from 1880 to 2000, are in the file *fair.dat*. The dependent variable is *VOTE* = percentage share of the popular vote won by the incumbent party. Consider the explanatory variable

GROWTH = growth rate in real per capita GDP in the first three quarters of the election year (annual rate). One would think that if the economy is doing well, and growth is high, the party in power would have a better chance of winning the election.

(a) Plot a scatter diagram of *VOTE* against *GROWTH*. Does there appear to be positive association?

(b) Estimate the regression $VOTE = \beta_1 + \beta_2 GROWTH + e$ by least squares using all the data from 1880 to 2000. Report and discuss the estimation result. Sketch, by hand, the fitted line on the data scatter from (a).

(c) Economy wide inflation may spell doom for the incumbent party in an election. The variable *INFLATION* is the growth in prices over the first 15 quarters of an administration. Plot *VOTE* against *INFLATION*. Report and discuss the estimation results.

2.15 How much does education affect wage rates? The data file *cps_small.dat* contains 1000 observations on hourly wage rates, education, and other variables from the 1997 Current Population Survey (CPS).

(a) Obtain the summary statistics and histograms for the variables *WAGE* and *EDUC*. Discuss the data characteristics.

(b) Estimate the linear regression $WAGE = \beta_1 + \beta_2 EDUC + e$ and discuss the results.

(c) Calculate the least squares residuals and plot them against *EDUC*. Are any patterns evident? If assumptions SR1–SR5 hold, should any patterns be evident in the least squares residuals?

(d) Estimate separate regressions for males, females, blacks, and whites. Compare the results.

Appendix 2A Derivation of the Least Squares Estimates

Given the sample observations on y and x, we want to find values for the unknown parameters β_1 and β_2 that minimize the "sum of squares" function

$$S(\beta_1, \beta_2) = \sum_{i=1}^{N}(y_i - \beta_1 - \beta_2 x_i)^2 \tag{2A.1}$$

Since the points (y_i, x_i) have been observed, the sum of squares function S depends only on the unknown parameters β_1 and β_2. This function, which is a quadratic in terms of the unknown parameters β_1 and β_2, is a "bowl-shaped surface" like the one depicted in Figure 2A.1.

Our task is to find, out of all the possible values β_1 and β_2, the point (b_1, b_2) at which the sum of squares function S is a minimum. This minimization problem is a common one in calculus, and the minimizing point is at the "bottom of the bowl."

Those of you familiar with calculus and "partial differentiation" can verify that the partial derivatives of S with respect to β_1 and β_2 are

$$\frac{\partial S}{\partial \beta_1} = 2N\beta_1 - 2\sum y_i + 2(\sum x_i)\beta_2$$
$$\frac{\partial S}{\partial \beta_2} = 2(\sum x_i^2)\beta_2 - 2\sum x_i y_i + 2(\sum x_i)\beta_1 \tag{2A.2}$$

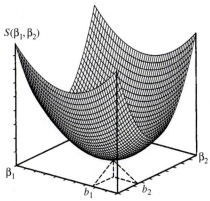

FIGURE **2A.1**   The sum of squares function and the minimizing values b_1 and b_2.

These derivatives are equations of the slope of the bowl-like surface in the directions of the axes. Intuitively, the "bottom of the bowl" occurs where the slope of the bowl, in the direction of each axis, $\partial S/\partial \beta_1$ and $\partial S/\partial \beta_2$, is zero.

Algebraically, to obtain the point (b_1, b_2) we set equations (2A.2) to zero and replace β_1 and β_2 by b_1 and b_2, respectively, to obtain

$$2[\Sigma y_i - Nb_1 - (\Sigma x_i)b_2] = 0$$

$$2[\Sigma x_i y_i - (\Sigma x_i)b_1 - (\Sigma x_i^2)b_2] = 0$$

Simplifying these gives equations usually known as the *normal equations,*

$$Nb_1 + (\Sigma x_i)b_2 = \Sigma y_i \tag{2A.3}$$

$$(\Sigma x_i)b_1 + (\Sigma x_i^2)b_2 = \Sigma x_i y_i \tag{2A.4}$$

These two equations have two unknowns b_1 and b_2. We can find the least squares estimates by solving these two linear equations for b_1 and b_2. To solve for b_2 multiply (2A.3) by Σx_i, multiply (2A.4) by N, then subtract the first equation from the second, and then isolate b_2 on the left-hand side.

$$b_2 = \frac{N\Sigma x_i y_i - \Sigma x_i \Sigma y_i}{N\Sigma x_i^2 - (\Sigma x_i)^2} \tag{2A.5}$$

This formula for b_2 is in terms of data sums, cross-products, and squares. The deviation from the mean form of the estimator is derived in Appendix 2B.

To solve for b_1, given b_2, divide both sides of (2A.3) by N and rearrange.

Appendix 2B Deviation from the Mean Form of b_2

The first step in the conversion of the formula for b_2 into (2.7) is to use some tricks involving summation signs. The first useful fact is that

$$\Sigma(x_i - \bar{x})^2 = \Sigma x_i^2 - 2\bar{x}\Sigma x_i + N\bar{x}^2 = \Sigma x_i^2 - 2\bar{x}\left(N\frac{1}{N}\Sigma x_i\right) + N\bar{x}^2$$
$$= \Sigma x_i^2 - 2N\bar{x}^2 + N\bar{x}^2 = \Sigma x_i^2 - N\bar{x}^2 \tag{2B.1}$$

Should you ever have to calculate $\sum(x_i - \bar{x})^2$, using the shortcut formula $\sum(x_i - \bar{x})^2 = \sum x_i^2 - N\bar{x}^2$ is much easier. Then

$$\sum(x_i - \bar{x})^2 = \sum x_i^2 - N\bar{x}^2 = \sum x_i^2 - \bar{x}\sum x_i = \sum x_i^2 - \frac{(\sum x_i)^2}{N} \qquad (2B.2)$$

To obtain this result we have used the fact that $\bar{x} = \sum x_i / N$, so $\sum x_i = N\bar{x}$.

The second useful fact is similar to the first, and it is

$$\sum(x_i - \bar{x})(y_i - \bar{y}) = \sum x_i y_i - N\bar{x}\bar{y} = \sum x_i y_i - \frac{\sum x_i \sum y_i}{N} \qquad (2B.3)$$

This result is proven in a similar manner.

If the numerator and denominator of b_2 in equation (2A.5) are divided by N, then using (2B.1)–(2B.3) we can rewrite b_2 in *deviation from the mean form* as

$$b_2 = \frac{\sum(x_i - \bar{x})(y_i - \bar{y})}{\sum(x_i - \bar{x})^2}$$

This formula for b_2 is one that you should remember, as we will use it time and time again in the next few chapters.

Appendix 2C b_2 Is a Linear Estimator

In order to derive (2.10) we make a further simplification using another property of sums. The sum of any variable about its average is zero, that is,

$$\sum(x_i - \bar{x}) = 0$$

Then, the formula for b_2 becomes

$$b_2 = \frac{\sum(x_i - \bar{x})(y_i - \bar{y})}{\sum(x_i - \bar{x})^2} = \frac{\sum(x_i - \bar{x})y_i - \bar{y}\sum(x_i - \bar{x})}{\sum(x_i - \bar{x})^2}$$

$$= \frac{\sum(x_i - \bar{x})y_i}{\sum(x_i - \bar{x})^2} = \sum\left[\frac{(x_i - \bar{x})}{\sum(x_i - \bar{x})^2}\right]y_i = \sum w_i y_i$$

where w_i is the constant given in (2.11).

Appendix 2D Derivation of Theoretical Expression for b_2

To obtain (2.12) replace y_i in (2.10) by $y_i = \beta_1 + \beta_2 x_i + e_i$ and simplify:

$$b_2 = \sum w_i y_i = \sum w_i(\beta_1 + \beta_2 x_i + e_i)$$

$$= \beta_1 \sum w_i + \beta_2 \sum w_i x_i + \sum w_i e_i$$

$$= \beta_2 + \sum w_i e_i$$

We used two more summation tricks to simplify this. First, $\sum w_i = 0$, this eliminates the term $\beta_1 \sum w_i$. Secondly, $\sum w_i x_i = 1$, so $\beta_2 \sum w_i x_i = \beta_2$, and (2.10) simplifies to (2.12).

The term $\Sigma w_i = 0$ because

$$\Sigma w_i = \Sigma \left[\frac{(x_i - \bar{x})}{\Sigma(x_i - \bar{x})^2} \right] = \frac{1}{\Sigma(x_i - \bar{x})^2} \Sigma(x_i - \bar{x}) = 0$$

where in the last step we used the fact that $\Sigma(x_i - \bar{x}) = 0$.

To show that $\Sigma w_i x_i = 1$ we again use $\Sigma(x_i - \bar{x}) = 0$. Another expression for $\Sigma(x_i - \bar{x})^2$ is

$$\begin{aligned} \Sigma(x_i - \bar{x})^2 &= \Sigma(x_i - \bar{x})(x_i - \bar{x}) \\ &= \Sigma(x_i - \bar{x})x_i - \bar{x}\Sigma(x_i - \bar{x}) \\ &= \Sigma(x_i - \bar{x})x_i \end{aligned}$$

Consequently

$$\Sigma w_i x_i = \frac{\Sigma(x_i - \bar{x})x_i}{\Sigma(x_i - \bar{x})^2} = \frac{\Sigma(x_i - \bar{x})x_i}{\Sigma(x_i - \bar{x})x_i} = 1$$

Appendix 2E Deriving the Variance of b_2

The starting point is (2.12), $b_2 = \beta_2 + \Sigma w_i e_i$. The least squares estimator is a random variable whose variance is defined to be

$$\text{var}(b_2) = E[b_2 - E(b_2)]^2$$

Substituting in (2.12) and using the unbiasedness of the least squares estimator, $E(b_2) = \beta_2$, we have

$$\begin{aligned} \text{var}(b_2) &= E(\beta_2 + \Sigma w_i e_i - \beta_2)^2 \\ &= E\left(\Sigma w_i e_i\right)^2 \\ &= E\left(\Sigma w_i^2 e_i^2 + 2\underset{i \neq j}{\Sigma\Sigma} w_i w_j e_i e_j\right) \quad \text{(square of bracketed term)} \\ &= \Sigma w_i^2 E(e_i^2) + 2\underset{i \neq j}{\Sigma\Sigma} w_i w_j E(e_i e_j) \quad \text{(because } w_i \text{ not random)} \\ &= \sigma^2 \Sigma w_i^2 \\ &= \frac{\sigma^2}{\Sigma(x_i - \bar{x})^2} \end{aligned}$$

The next to last line is obtained by using two assumptions: First,

$$\sigma^2 = \text{var}(e_i) = E[e_i - E(e_i)]^2 = E(e_i - 0)^2 = E(e_i^2)$$

Second, $\text{cov}(e_i, e_j) = E[(e_i - E(e_i))(e_j - E(e_j))] = E(e_i e_j) = 0$. Then, the very last step uses the fact that

$$\Sigma w_i^2 = \Sigma \left[\frac{(x_i - \bar{x})^2}{\left\{ \Sigma(x_i - \bar{x})^2 \right\}^2} \right] = \frac{\Sigma(x_i - \bar{x})^2}{\left\{ \Sigma(x_i - \bar{x})^2 \right\}^2} = \frac{1}{\Sigma(x_i - \bar{x})^2}$$

Alternatively, we can employ the rule for finding the variance of a sum. If X and Y are random variables, and a and b are constants, then

$$\text{var}(aX + bY) = a^2 \text{var}(X) + b^2 \text{var}(Y) + 2ab\,\text{cov}(X, Y)$$

Appendix B.4 reviews all the basic properties of random variables. In the second line below we use this rule extended to more than two random variables. Then,

$$\begin{aligned}
\text{var}(b_2) = \text{var}(\beta_2 + \Sigma w_i e_i) = \text{var}(\Sigma w_i e_i) \quad &\text{(since } \beta_2 \text{ is a constant)}\\
= \Sigma w_i^2 \text{var}(e_i) + \underset{i \neq j}{\Sigma\Sigma} w_i w_j \, \text{cov}(e_i, e_j) \quad &\text{(generalizing the variance rule)}\\
= \Sigma w_i^2 \text{var}(e_i) \quad &\text{(using cov}(e_i, e_j) = 0)\\
= \sigma^2 \Sigma w_i^2 \quad &\text{(using var}(e_i) = \sigma^2)\\
= \frac{\sigma^2}{\Sigma(x_i - \bar{x})^2} &
\end{aligned}$$

Carefully note that the derivation of the variance expression for b_2 depends on assumptions SR3 and SR4. If $\text{cov}(e_i, e_j) \neq 0$ then we cannot drop out all those terms in the double summation. If $\text{var}(e_i) \neq \sigma^2$ for all observations then σ^2 cannot be factored out of the summation. If either of these assumptions fails to hold then var(b_2) is *something else* and is not given by (2.15). The same is true for the variance of b_1 and the covariance.

Appendix 2F Proof of the Gauss–Markov Theorem

We will prove the Gauss–Markov theorem for the least squares estimator b_2 of β_2. Our goal is to show that in the class of linear and unbiased estimators the estimator b_2 has the smallest variance. Let $b_2^* = \Sigma k_i y_i$ (where k_i are constants) be any other linear estimator of β_2. To make comparison to the least squares estimator b_2 easier, suppose that $k_i = w_i + c_i$, where c_i is another constant and w_i is given in (2.11). While this is tricky, it is legal, since for any k_i that someone might choose we can find c_i. Into this new estimator substitute y_i and simplify, using the properties of w_i in Appendix 2D

$$\begin{aligned}
b_2^* = \Sigma k_i y_i = \Sigma(w_i + c_i) y_i &= \Sigma(w_i + c_i)(\beta_1 + \beta_2 x_i + e_i)\\
&= \Sigma(w_i + c_i)\beta_1 + \Sigma(w_i + c_i)\beta_2 x_i + \Sigma(w_i + c_i)e_i\\
&= \beta_1\Sigma w_i + \beta_1\Sigma c_i + \beta_2\Sigma w_i x_i + \beta_2\Sigma c_i x_i + \Sigma(w_i + c_i)e_i\\
&= \beta_1\Sigma c_i + \beta_2 + \beta_2\Sigma c_i x_i + \Sigma(w_i + c_i)e_i
\end{aligned} \tag{2F.1}$$

since $\Sigma w_i = 0$ and $\Sigma w_i x_i = 1$.

Take the mathematical expectation of the last line in (2F.1), using the properties of expectation and the assumption that $E(e_i) = 0$:

$$\begin{aligned}
E(b_2^*) &= \beta_1\Sigma c_i + \beta_2 + \beta_2\Sigma c_i x_i + \Sigma(w_i + c_i)E(e_i)\\
&= \beta_1\Sigma c_i + \beta_2 + \beta_2\Sigma c_i x_i
\end{aligned} \tag{2F.2}$$

In order for the linear estimator $b_2^* = \Sigma k_i y_i$ to be unbiased, it must be true that

$$\Sigma c_i = 0 \text{ and } \Sigma c_i x_i = 0 \tag{2F.3}$$

These conditions must hold in order for $b_2^* = \Sigma k_i y_i$ to be in the class of *linear* and *unbiased estimators*. So we will assume that conditions (2F.3) hold and use them to simplify expression (2F.1):

$$b_2^* = \Sigma k_i y_i = \beta_2 + \Sigma(w_i + c_i)e_i \tag{2F.4}$$

We can now find the variance of the linear unbiased estimator b_2^* following the steps in Appendix 2E and using the additional fact that

$$\Sigma c_i w_i = \Sigma \left[\frac{c_i(x_i - \bar{x})}{\Sigma(x_i - \bar{x})^2} \right] = \frac{1}{\Sigma(x_i - \bar{x})^2} \Sigma c_i x_i - \frac{\bar{x}}{\Sigma(x_i - \bar{x})^2} \Sigma c_i = 0$$

Use the properties of variance to obtain

$$\begin{aligned}
\text{var}(b_2^*) = \text{var}[\beta_2 + \Sigma(w_i + c_i)e_i] &= \Sigma(w_i + c_i)^2 \text{var}(e_i) \\
&= \sigma^2 \Sigma(w_i + c_i)^2 = \sigma^2 \Sigma w_i^2 + \sigma^2 \Sigma c_i^2 \\
&= \text{var}(b_2) + \sigma^2 \Sigma c_i^2 \\
&\geq \text{var}(b_2)
\end{aligned}$$

The last line follows since $\Sigma c_i^2 \geq 0$ and establishes that for the family of linear and unbiased estimators b_2^*, each of the alternative estimators has variance that is greater than or equal to that of the least squares estimator b_2. The *only* time that $\text{var}(b_2^*) = \text{var}(b_2)$ is when all the $c_i = 0$, in which case $b_2^* = b_2$. Thus there is no *other linear and unbiased estimator of* β_2 that is better than b_2, which proves the Gauss–Markov theorem.

Chapter 3

Interval Estimation and Hypothesis Testing

Learning Objectives

Based on the material in this chapter, you should be able to

1. Discuss how "repeated sampling theory" relates to interval estimation and hypothesis testing.

2. Explain why it is important for statistical inference that the least squares estimators b_1 and b_2 are normally distributed random variables.

3. Explain the "level of confidence" of an interval estimator, and exactly what it means in a repeated sampling context, and give an example.

4. Explain the difference between an interval estimator and an interval estimate. Explain how to interpret an interval estimate.

5. Explain the terms null hypothesis, alternative hypothesis, and rejection region, giving an example and a sketch of the rejection region.

6. Explain the logic of a statistical test, including why it is important that a test statistic have a known probability distribution if the null hypothesis is true.

7. Explain the term p-value and how to use a p-value to determine the outcome of a hypothesis test; provide a sketch showing a p-value.

8. Explain the difference between one-tail and two-tail tests. Explain, intuitively, how to choose the rejection region for a one-tail test.

9. Explain Type I error and illustrate it in a sketch. Define the level of significance of a test.

10. Explain the difference between economic and statistical significance.

11. Explain how to choose what goes in the null hypothesis, and what goes in the alternative hypothesis.

Keywords

alternative hypothesis	interval estimation	rejection region
confidence intervals	level of significance	test of significance
critical value	null hypothesis	test statistic
degrees of freedom	one-tail tests	two-tail tests
hypotheses	point estimates	Type I error
hypothesis testing	probability value	Type II error
inference	p-value	

In Chapter 2 we used the least squares estimators to develop **point estimates** for the parameters in the simple linear regression model. These estimates represent an **inference** about the regression function $E(y) = \beta_1 + \beta_2 x$ describing a relationship between economic variables. *Infer* means "to conclude by reasoning from something known or assumed." This dictionary definition describes statistical inference as well. We have assumed a relationship between economic variables and made various assumptions (SR1–SR5) about the regression model. Based on these assumptions, and given empirical estimates of regression parameters, we want to make inferences about the population from which the data were obtained.

In this chapter we introduce additional tools of statistical inference: **interval estimation** and **hypothesis testing**. Interval estimation is a procedure for creating ranges of values, sometimes called **confidence intervals**, in which the unknown parameters are likely to be located. Hypothesis tests are procedures for comparing conjectures that we might have about the regression parameters to the parameter estimates we have obtained from a sample of data. Hypothesis tests allow us to say that the data are compatible, or are not compatible, with a particular conjecture or hypothesis.

The procedures for hypothesis testing and interval estimation depend very heavily on assumption SR6 of the simple linear regression model and the resulting normality of the least squares estimators. If assumption SR6 does not hold, then the sample size must be sufficiently large so that the distributions of the least squares estimators are *approximately* normal. In this case the procedures we develop in this chapter can be used but are also approximate. In developing the procedures in this chapter we will be using the "Student's" t-distribution. You may want to refresh your memory about this distribution by reviewing Appendix B.5.3. Also, it is sometimes helpful to see the concepts we are about to discuss in a simpler setting. In Appendix C we examine statistical inference, interval estimation, and hypothesis testing in the context of estimating the mean of a normal population. You may want to review this material now, or read it along with this chapter as we proceed.

3.1 Interval Estimation

In Chapter 2 we estimated that household food expenditure would rise by $10.21 given a $100 increase in weekly income. The estimate $b_2 = 10.21$ is a *point* estimate of the unknown population parameter β_2 in the regression model. Interval estimation proposes a range of values in which the true parameter β_2 is likely to fall. Providing a range of values gives a sense of what the parameter value might be, and the precision with which we have estimated it. Such intervals are often called **confidence intervals**. We prefer to call them **interval estimates** because the term "confidence" is widely misunderstood and misused. As we will see, our confidence is in the procedure we use to obtain the intervals, not in the intervals themselves. This is consistent with how we assessed the properties of the least squares estimators in Chapter 2.

3.1.1   THE t-DISTRIBUTION

Let us assume that assumptions SR1–SR6 hold for the simple linear regression model. In this case we know that the least squares estimators b_1 and b_2 have normal distributions, as discussed in Section 2.6. For example, the normal distribution of b_2, the least squares estimator of β_2, is

$$b_2 \sim N\left(\beta_2, \frac{\sigma^2}{\sum(x_i - \bar{x})^2} \right)$$

A standardized normal random variable is obtained from b_2 by subtracting its mean and dividing by its standard deviation:

$$Z = \frac{b_2 - \beta_2}{\sqrt{\sigma^2/\Sigma(x_i - \bar{x})^2}} \sim N(0, 1) \tag{3.1}$$

The standardized random variable Z is normally distributed with mean 0 and variance 1. Using a table of normal probabilities (Table 1 at the end of the book) we know that

$$P(-1.96 \leq Z \leq 1.96) = 0.95$$

Substituting (3.1) into this expression we obtain

$$P\left(-1.96 \leq \frac{b_2 - \beta_2}{\sqrt{\sigma^2/\Sigma(x_i - \bar{x})^2}} \leq 1.96\right) = 0.95$$

Rearranging gives us

$$P\left(b_2 - 1.96\sqrt{\sigma^2/\Sigma(x_i - \bar{x})^2} \leq \beta_2 \leq b_2 + 1.96\sqrt{\sigma^2/\Sigma(x_i - \bar{x})^2}\right) = 0.95$$

This defines an interval that has probability 0.95 of containing the parameter β_2. The two endpoints $\left(b_2 \pm 1.96\sqrt{\sigma^2/\Sigma(x_i - \bar{x})^2}\right)$ provide an interval estimator. In repeated sampling 95% of the intervals constructed this way will contain the true value of the parameter β_2. This easy derivation of an interval estimator is based on both assumption SR6 *and* that we know the variance of the error term σ^2.

While we do not know the value of σ^2 we can estimate it. The least squares residuals are $\hat{e}_i = y_i - b_1 - b_2 x_i$ and our estimator of σ^2 is $\hat{\sigma}^2 = \Sigma\hat{e}_i^2/(N-2)$. Replacing σ^2 by $\hat{\sigma}^2$ in (3.1) creates a random variable we can work with, but this substitution changes the probability distribution from standard normal to a *t*-distribution with $N-2$ degrees of freedom,

$$t = \frac{b_2 - \beta_2}{\sqrt{\hat{\sigma}^2/\Sigma(x_i - \bar{x})^2}} = \frac{b_2 - \beta_2}{\sqrt{\widehat{\mathrm{var}(b_2)}}} = \frac{b_2 - \beta_2}{\mathrm{se}(b_2)} \sim t_{(N-2)} \tag{3.2}$$

The ratio $t = (b_2 - \beta_2)/\mathrm{se}(b_2)$ has a *t*-distribution with $N-2$ degrees of freedom, which we denote as $t \sim t_{(N-2)}$. A similar result holds for b_1, so in general we can say, if assumptions SR1–SR6 hold in the simple linear regression model, then

$$t = \frac{b_k - \beta_k}{\mathrm{se}(b_k)} \sim t_{(N-2)} \quad \text{for} \quad k = 1, 2 \tag{3.3}$$

This equation will be the basis for interval estimation and hypothesis testing in the simple linear regression model. The statistical argument of how we go from (3.1) to (3.2) is in Appendix 3A, at the end of this chapter.

When working with the *t*-distribution remember that it is a bell-shaped curve centered at zero. It looks like the standard normal distribution, except it is more spread out, with a larger variance and thicker tails. The shape of the *t*-distribution is controlled by a single parameter called the **degrees of freedom**, often abbreviated as *df*. We use the notation $t_{(m)}$ to specify a *t*-distribution with m degrees of freedom. In Table 2 at the end of the book (and inside the

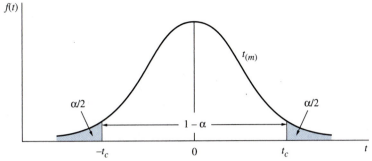

FIGURE 3.1   Critical values from a t-distribution.

front cover) are percentile values of the t-distribution for various degrees of freedom. For m degrees of freedom the 95th percentile of the t-distribution is denoted $t_{(0.95, m)}$. This value has the property that 0.95 of the probability falls to its left, so $P\left[t_{(m)} \leq t_{(0.95, m)}\right] = 0.95$. For example, if the degrees of freedom are $m = 20$, then, from Table 2, $t_{(0.95, 20)} = 1.725$. Should you encounter a problem requiring percentiles that we do not give, you can interpolate for an approximate answer, or use your computer software to obtain an exact value.

3.1.2   OBTAINING INTERVAL ESTIMATES

From Table 2 we can find a "critical value" t_c from a t-distribution such that $P(t \geq t_c) = P(t \leq - t_c) = \alpha/2$, where α is a probability often taken to be $\alpha = 0.01$ or $\alpha = 0.05$. The critical value t_c for degrees of freedom m is the percentile value $t_{(1-\alpha/2, m)}$. The values t_c and $-t_c$ are depicted in Figure 3.1.

Each shaded "tail" area contains $\alpha/2$ of the probability, so that $1 - \alpha$ of the probability is contained in the center portion. Consequently, we can make the probability statement

$$P(- t_c \leq t \leq t_c) = 1 - \alpha \tag{3.4}$$

For a 95% confidence interval the critical values define a central region of the t-distribution containing probability $1 - \alpha = 0.95$. This leaves probability $\alpha = 0.05$ divided equally between the two tails, so that $\alpha/2 = 0.025$. Then the critical value $t_c = t_{(1-0.025, m)} = t_{(0.975, m)}$. In the simple regression model the degrees of freedom are $m = N - 2$, so expression (3.4) becomes

$$P\left[- t_{(0.975, N-2)} \leq t \leq t_{(0.975, N-2)}\right] = 0.95$$

We find the percentile values $t_{(0.975, N-2)}$ in Table 2.

Now, let us see how we can put all these bits together to create a procedure for interval estimation. Substitute t from (3.3) into (3.4) to obtain

$$P\left[-t_c \leq \frac{b_k - \beta_k}{\mathrm{se}(b_k)} \leq t_c\right] = 1 - \alpha$$

Rearrange this expression to obtain

$$P[b_k - t_c \mathrm{se}(b_k) \leq \beta_k \leq b_k + t_c \mathrm{se}(b_k)] = 1 - \alpha \tag{3.5}$$

The interval endpoints $b_k - t_c \mathrm{se}(b_k)$ and $b_k + t_c \mathrm{se}(b_k)$ are random because they vary from sample to sample. These endpoints define an **interval estimator** of β_k. The probability statement in (3.5) says that the interval $b_k \pm t_c\text{se}(b_k)$ has probability $1-\alpha$ of containing the true but unknown parameter β_k.

When b_k and $\text{se}(b_k)$ in (3.5) are estimated values (numbers), based on a given sample of data, then $b_k \pm t_c\text{se}(b_k)$ is called a $100(1-\alpha)\%$ **interval estimate** of β_k. Equivalently it is called a $100(1-\alpha)\%$ **confidence interval**. Usually $\alpha = 0.01$ or $\alpha = 0.05$, so that we obtain a 99% confidence interval or a 95% confidence interval.

The interpretation of confidence intervals requires a great deal of care. The properties of the interval estimation procedure are based on the notion of repeated sampling. If we were to select *many* random samples of size N, compute the least squares estimate b_k and its standard error $\text{se}(b_k)$ for each sample, and then construct the interval estimate $b_k \pm t_c\text{se}(b_k)$ for each sample, then $100(1-\alpha)\%$ of all the intervals constructed would contain the true parameter β_k.

Any *one* interval estimate, based on one sample of data, may or may not contain the true parameter β_k, and because β_k is unknown, we will never know if it does or does not. When "confidence intervals" are discussed remember that our confidence is in the *procedure* used to construct the interval estimate; it is *not* in any one interval estimate calculated from a sample of data.

3.1.3 AN ILLUSTRATION

For the food expenditure data, $N = 40$ and the degrees of freedom are $N - 2 = 38$. For a 95% confidence interval $\alpha = 0.05$. The critical value $t_c = t_{(1-\alpha/2, N-2)} = t_{(0.975,38)} = 2.024$ is the 97.5 percentile from the t-distribution with 38 degrees of freedom. For β_2 the probability statement in (3.5) becomes

$$P[b_2 - 2.024\text{se}(b_2) \leq \beta_2 \leq b_2 + 2.024\text{se}(b_2)] = 0.95 \qquad (3.6)$$

To construct an interval estimate for β_2 we use the least squares estimate $b_2 = 10.21$ and its standard error

$$\text{se}(b_2) = \sqrt{\widehat{\text{var}}(b_2)} = \sqrt{4.38} = 2.09$$

Substituting these values into (3.6) we obtain a "95% confidence interval estimate" for β_2:

$$b_2 \pm t_c\text{se}(b_2) = 10.21 \pm 2.024(2.09) = [5.97, 14.45]$$

That is, we estimate "with 95% confidence" that from an additional $100 of weekly income households will spend between $5.97 and $14.45 on food.

Is β_2 actually in the interval $[5.97, 14.45]$? We do not know, and we will never know. What we *do* know is that when the procedure we used is applied to many random samples of data from the same population, then 95% of all the interval estimates constructed using this procedure will contain the true parameter. The interval estimation procedure "works" 95% of the time. What we can say about the interval estimate based on our one sample is that, given the reliability of the procedure, we would be "surprised" if β_2 is not in the interval $[5.97, 14.45]$.

What is the usefulness of an interval estimate of β_2? When reporting regression results we always give a point estimate, such as $b_2 = 10.21$. However, the point estimate alone gives no sense of its reliability. Thus, we might also report an interval estimate. Interval estimates incorporate both the point estimate and the standard error of the estimate, which is a measure of the variability of the least squares estimator. The interval estimate includes an allowance for the sample size as well, because for lower degrees of freedom the t-distribution critical value t_c is larger. If an interval estimate is wide (implying a large standard error), it suggests that there is not much information in the sample about β_2. If an interval estimate is narrow, it suggests that we have learned more about β_2.

What is "wide" and what is "narrow" depend on the problem at hand. For example, in our model $b_2 = 10.21$ is an estimate of how much weekly household food expenditure will rise given a $100 increase in weekly household income. A CEO of a supermarket chain can use this estimate to plan future store capacity requirements, given forecasts of income growth in an area. However, no decision will be based on this one number alone. The prudent CEO will carry out a sensitivity analysis by considering values of β_2 around 10.21. The question is "Which values?" One answer is provided by the interval estimate [5.97, 14.45]. While β_2 may or may not be in this interval, the CEO knows that the procedure used to obtain the interval estimate "works" 95% of the time. If varying β_2 within the interval has drastic consequences on company sales and profits, then the CEO may conclude that there is insufficient evidence upon which to make a decision and order a new and larger sample of data.

3.1.4 · THE REPEATED SAMPLING CONTEXT

In Section 2.4.3 we illustrated the sampling properties of the least squares estimators by showing what would happen if we collected 10 additional samples of size $N = 40$ from the same population that gave us the food expenditure data. The data are in the file *table2-2.dat*. In Table 3.1 we present the least squares estimates, the estimates of σ^2, and the coefficient standard errors from each sample. Note the sampling variation illustrated by these estimates. This variation is due to the simple fact that we obtained 40 *different* households in each sample. The 95% confidence interval estimates for the parameters β_1 and β_2 are given in Table 3.2 for the same samples.

Sampling variability causes the center of each of the interval estimates to change with the values of the least squares estimates, and it causes the widths of the intervals to change with the standard errors. If we ask the question "How many of these intervals contain the true parameters, and which ones are they?" we must answer that we do not know. But since 95% of all interval estimates constructed this way contain the true parameter values, we would expect perhaps 9 or 10 of these intervals to contain the true but unknown parameters.

Note the difference between point estimation and interval estimation. We have used the least squares estimators to obtain point estimates of unknown parameters. The estimated

Table 3.1   **Least Squares Estimates from 10 Random Samples**

Sample	b_1	$se(b_1)$	b_2	$se(b_2)$	$\hat{\sigma}^2$
1	131.69	40.58	6.48	1.96	7002.85
2	57.25	33.13	10.88	1.60	4668.63
3	103.91	37.22	8.14	1.79	5891.75
4	46.50	33.33	11.90	1.61	4722.58
5	84.23	41.15	9.29	1.98	7200.16
6	26.63	45.78	13.55	2.21	8911.43
7	64.21	32.03	10.93	1.54	4362.12
8	79.66	29.87	9.76	1.44	3793.83
9	97.30	29.14	8.05	1.41	3610.20
10	95.96	37.18	7.77	1.79	5878.71

Table 3.2 **Interval Estimates from 10 Random Samples**

Sample	$b_1 - t_c \text{se}(b_1)$	$b_1 + t_c \text{se}(b_1)$	$b_2 - t_c \text{se}(b_2)$	$b_2 + t_c \text{se}(b_2)$
1	49.54	213.85	2.52	10.44
2	−9.83	124.32	7.65	14.12
3	28.56	179.26	4.51	11.77
4	−20.96	113.97	8.65	15.15
5	0.93	167.53	5.27	13.30
6	−66.04	119.30	9.08	18.02
7	−0.63	129.05	7.81	14.06
8	19.19	140.13	6.85	12.68
9	38.32	156.29	5.21	10.89
10	20.69	171.23	4.14	11.40

variance $\widehat{\text{var}(b_k)}$, for $k = 1$ or 2, and its square root $\sqrt{\widehat{\text{var}(b_k)}} = \text{se}(b_k)$ provide information about the sampling variability of the least squares estimator from one sample to another. Interval estimators are a convenient way to report regression results because they combine point estimation with a measure of sampling variability to provide a range of values in which the unknown parameters might fall. When the sampling variability of the least squares estimator is relatively small, then the interval estimates will be relatively narrow, implying that the least squares estimates are "reliable." If the least squares estimators suffer from large sampling variability, then the interval estimates will be wide, implying that the least squares estimates are "unreliable."

3.2 Hypothesis Tests

Many business and economic decision problems require a judgment as to whether or not a parameter is a specific value. In the food expenditure example, it may make a good deal of difference for decision purposes whether β_2 is greater than 10, indicating that a $100 increase in income will increase expenditure on food by more than $10. Also, based on economic theory, we believe that β_2 should be positive. One check of our data and model is whether this theoretical proposition is supported by the data.

Hypothesis testing procedures compare a conjecture we have about a population to the information contained in a sample of data. Given an economic and statistical model, **hypotheses** are formed about economic behavior. These hypotheses are then represented as statements about model parameters. Hypothesis tests use the information about a parameter that is contained in a sample of data, its least squares point estimate, and its standard error, to draw a conclusion about the hypothesis.

In each and every hypothesis test five ingredients must be present:

> **COMPONENTS OF HYPOTHESIS TESTS**
>
> 1. A null hypothesis H_0
> 2. An alternative hypothesis H_1
> 3. A test statistic
> 4. A rejection region
> 5. A conclusion

3.2.1 THE NULL HYPOTHESIS

The null hypothesis, which is denoted by H_0 (*H-naught*), specifies a value for a regression parameter, which for generality we denote as β_k, for $k = 1$ or 2. The null hypothesis is stated as $H_0 : \beta_k = c$, where c is a constant, and is an important value in the context of a specific regression model. A null hypothesis is the belief we will maintain until we are convinced by the sample evidence that it is not true, in which case we *reject* the null hypothesis.

3.2.2 THE ALTERNATIVE HYPOTHESIS

Paired with every null hypothesis is a logical alternative hypothesis H_1 that we will accept if the null hypothesis is rejected. The alternative hypothesis is flexible and depends to some extent on economic theory. For the null hypothesis $H_0 : \beta_k = c$ the three possible alternative hypotheses are

- $H_1 : \beta_k > c$. Rejecting the null hypothesis that $\beta_k = c$ leads us to accept the conclusion that $\beta_k > c$. Inequality alternative hypotheses are widely used in economics because economic theory frequently provides information about the *signs* of relationships between variables. For example, in the food expenditure example we might well test the null hypothesis $H_0 : \beta_2 = 0$ against $H_1 : \beta_2 > 0$ because economic theory strongly suggests that necessities like food are normal goods, and that food expenditure will rise if income increases.

- $H_1 : \beta_k < c$. Rejecting the null hypothesis that $\beta_k = c$ in this case leads us to accept the conclusion that $\beta_k < c$.

- $H_1 : \beta_k \neq c$. Rejecting the null hypothesis that $\beta_k = c$ in this case leads us to accept the conclusion that β_k takes a value either larger or smaller than c.

3.2.3 THE TEST STATISTIC

The sample information about the null hypothesis is embodied in the sample value of a test statistic. Based on the value of a test statistic we decide either to reject the null hypothesis or not to reject it. A test statistic has a special characteristic: its probability distribution is completely *known* when the null hypothesis is true, and it has some *other* distribution if the null hypothesis is not true.

It all starts with the key result in (3.3), $t = (b_k - \beta_k)/\text{se}(b_k) \sim t_{(N-2)}$. **If** the null hypothesis $H_0 : \beta_k = c$ is *true*, **then** we can substitute c for β_k and it follows that

$$t = \frac{b_k - c}{\text{se}(b_k)} \sim t_{(N-2)} \tag{3.7}$$

If the null hypothesis is *not true*, then the *t*-statistic in (3.7) does *not* have a *t*-distribution with $N - 2$ degrees of freedom. This point is elaborated in Appendix 3B.

3.2.4 THE REJECTION REGION

The rejection region depends on the form of the alternative. It is the range of values of the test statistic that leads to *rejection* of the null hypothesis. It is possible to construct a rejection region only if we have

- a test statistic whose distribution is known when the null hypothesis is true
- an alternative hypothesis
- a level of significance

The rejection region consists of values that are *unlikely* and have low probability of occurring when the null hypothesis is true. The chain of logic is "If a value of the test statistic is obtained that falls in a region of low probability, then it is unlikely that the test statistic has the assumed distribution, and thus it is unlikely that the null hypothesis is true." If the alternative hypothesis is true, then values of the test statistic will tend to be unusually large or unusually small. The terms "large" and "small" are determined by choosing a probability α, called the **level of significance** of the test, which provides a meaning for "an *unlikely* event." The level of significance of the test α is usually chosen to be 0.01, 0.05 or 0.10.

If we reject the null hypothesis when it is true, then we commit what is called a **Type I error**. The level of significance of a test *is* the probability of committing a Type I error, so $P(\text{Type I error}) = \alpha$. Any time we reject a null hypothesis it is possible that we have made such an error—there is no avoiding it. The good news is that we can specify the amount of Type I error we will tolerate by setting the level of significance α. If such an error is costly, then we make α small. If we do not reject a null hypothesis that is false, then we have committed a **Type II error**. In a real-world situation we cannot control or calculate the probability of this type of error because it depends on the unknown true parameter β_k. For more about Type I and Type II errors see Appendix C.6.9.

3.2.5 A CONCLUSION

When you have completed testing a hypothesis you should state your conclusion. Do you reject the null hypothesis, or do you not reject the null hypothesis? As we will argue below you should avoid saying that you "accept" the null hypothesis, which can be very misleading. Also, we urge you to make it standard practice to say what the conclusion means in the economic context of the problem you are working on and the economic significance of the finding. Statistical procedures are not ends in themselves. They are carried out for a reason and have meaning, which you should be able to explain.

3.3 Rejection Regions for Specific Alternatives

In this section we hope to be very clear about the nature of the rejection rules for each of the three possible alternatives to the null hypothesis $H_0 : \beta_k = c$. As noted in the previous section, to have a rejection region for a null hypothesis we need a test statistic, which we have; it is given in (3.7). Second, we need a specific alternative, $\beta_k > c$, $\beta_k < c$, or $\beta_k \neq c$. Third, we need to specify the level of significance of the test. The level of significance of a test, α, is the probability that we reject the null hypothesis when it is actually true, which is called a Type I error.

3.3.1 ONE-TAIL TESTS WITH ALTERNATIVE "GREATER THAN" ($>$)

When testing the null hypothesis $H_0 : \beta_k = c$, if the *alternative* hypothesis $H_1 : \beta_k > c$ is true, then the value of the t-statistic (3.7) tends to become larger than usual for the t-distribution. We will reject the null hypothesis if the test statistic is larger than the critical value for the level of significance α. The critical value that leaves probability α in the right

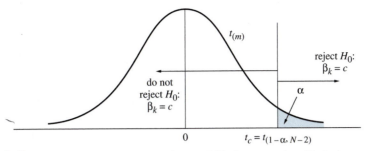

FIGURE *3.2*   Rejection region for a one-tail test of $H_0 : \beta_k = c$ against $H_1 : \beta_k > c$.

tail is the $(1-\alpha)$-percentile $t_{(1-\alpha, N-2)}$, as shown in Figure 3.2. For example, if $\alpha = 0.05$ and $N - 2 = 30$, then from Table 2 the critical value is the 95th percentile value $t_{(0.95, 30)} = 1.697$.

The rejection rule is

> When testing the null hypothesis $H_0 : \beta_k = c$ against the alternative hypothesis $H_1 : \beta_k > c$, reject the null hypothesis and accept the alternative hypothesis if $t \geq t_{(1-\alpha, N-2)}$.

The test is called a "one-tail" test because unlikely values of the t-statistic fall only in one tail of the probability distribution. If the null hypothesis is true, then the test statistic (3.7) has a t-distribution, and its value would tend to fall in the center of the distribution, to the left of the critical value, where most of the probability is contained. The level of significance α is chosen so that if the null hypothesis is true, then the probability that the t-statistic value falls in the extreme right tail of the distribution is small; an event that is unlikely to occur by chance. If we obtain a test statistic value in the rejection region, we take it as evidence *against* the null hypothesis, leading us to conclude that the null hypothesis is unlikely to be true. Evidence against the null hypothesis is evidence in support of the alternative hypothesis. Thus if we reject the null hypothesis then we conclude that the alternative is true.

If the null hypothesis $H_0 : \beta_k = c$ is *true*, then the test statistic (3.7) has a t-distribution and its values fall in the nonrejection region with probability $1 - \alpha$. If $t < t_{(1-\alpha, N-2)}$, then there is no statistically significant evidence against the null hypothesis, and we do not reject it.

3.3.2   ONE-TAIL TESTS WITH ALTERNATIVE "LESS THAN" ($<$)

If the alternative hypothesis $H_1 : \beta_k < c$ is true, then the value of the t-statistic (3.7) tends to become smaller than usual for the t-distribution. We reject the null hypothesis if the test statistic is smaller than the critical value for the level of significance α. The critical value that leaves probability α in the left tail is the α-percentile $t_{(\alpha, N-2)}$, as shown in Figure 3.3.

When using Table 2 to locate critical values, recall that the t-distribution is symmetric about zero, so that the α-percentile $t_{(\alpha, N-2)}$ is the negative of the $(1-\alpha)$-percentile $t_{(1-\alpha, N-2)}$. For example, if $\alpha = 0.05$ and $N - 2 = 20$, then from Table 2 the 95th percentile of the t-distribution is $t_{(0.95, 20)} = 1.725$ and the 5th percentile value is $t_{(0.05, 20)} = -1.725$.

The rejection rule is:

> When testing the null hypothesis $H_0 : \beta_k = c$ against the alternative hypothesis $H_1 : \beta_k < c$, reject the null hypothesis and accept the alternative hypothesis if $t \leq t_{(\alpha, N-2)}$.

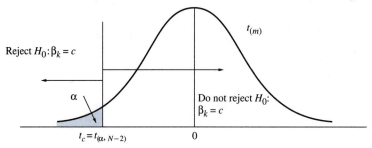

FIGURE 3.3   The rejection region for a one-tail test of $H_0 : \beta_k = c$ against $H_1 : \beta_k < c$.

The nonrejection region consists of t-statistic values greater than $t_{(\alpha, N-2)}$. When the null hypothesis is true, the probability of obtaining such a t-value is $1 - \alpha$, which is chosen to be large. Thus if $t > t_{(\alpha, N-2)}$ then do not reject $H_0 : \beta_k = c$.

Remembering where the rejection region is located may be facilitated by the following trick:

> **MEMORY TRICK:** The rejection region for a one-tail test is in the direction of the arrow in the alternative. If the alternative is ">", then reject in the right tail. If the alternative is "<", reject in the left tail.

3.3.3   TWO-TAIL TESTS WITH ALTERNATIVE "NOT EQUAL TO" ($\neq$)

When testing the null hypothesis $H_0 : \beta_k = c$, if the alternative hypothesis $H_1 : \beta_k \neq c$ is true, then the value of the t-statistic (3.7) tends to become either larger *or* smaller than usual for the t-distribution. To have a test with level of significance α we define the critical values so that the probability of the t-statistic falling in either tail is $\alpha/2$. The left-tail critical value is the percentile $t_{(\alpha/2, N-2)}$ and the right-tail critical value is the percentile $t_{(1-\alpha/2, N-2)}$. We reject the null hypothesis that $H_0 : \beta_k = c$ in favor of the alternative that $H_1 : \beta_k \neq c$ if the test statistic $t \leq t_{(\alpha/2, N-2)}$ or $t \geq t_{(1-\alpha/2, N-2)}$, as shown in Figure 3.4. For example, if $\alpha = 0.05$ and $N - 2 = 30$, then $\alpha/2 = 0.025$ and the left-tail critical value is the 2.5-percentile value $t_{(0.025,30)} = -2.042$; the right-tail critical value is the 97.5-percentile $t_{(0.975,30)} = 2.042$. The right-tail critical value is found in Table 2, and the left-tail critical value is found using the symmetry of the t-distribution.

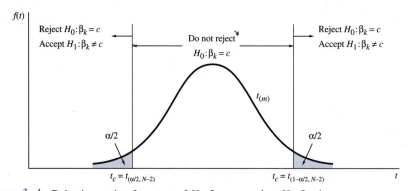

FIGURE 3.4   Rejection region for a test of $H_0 : \beta_k = c$ against $H_1 : \beta_k \neq c$.

Since the rejection region is composed of portions of the t-distribution in the left and right tails, this test is called a **two-tail test**. When the null hypothesis is true, the probability of obtaining a value of the test statistic that falls in *either* tail area is "small." The sum of the tail probabilities is α. Sample values of the test statistic that are in the tail areas are incompatible with the null hypothesis and are evidence against the null hypothesis being true. On the other hand, if the null hypothesis $H_0 : \beta_k = c$ is true, then the probability of obtaining a value of the test statistic t in the central nonrejection region is high. Sample values of the test statistic in the central nonrejection area are compatible with the null hypothesis and are not taken as evidence against the null hypothesis being true. Thus the rejection rule is

> When testing the null hypothesis $H_0 : \beta_k = c$ against the alternative hypothesis $H_1 : \beta_k \neq c$, reject the null hypothesis and accept the alternative hypothesis if $t \leq t_{(\alpha/2, N-2)}$ **or** if $t \geq t_{(1-\alpha/2, N-2)}$.

We do not reject the null hypothesis if $t_{(\alpha/2, N-2)} < t < t_{(1-\alpha/2, N-2)}$.

3.4 Examples of Hypothesis Tests

We illustrate the mechanics of hypothesis testing using the food expenditure model. We give examples of right-tail, left-tail, and two-tail tests. In each case we will follow a prescribed set of steps, closely following the list of required components for all hypothesis tests listed at the beginning of Section 3.2. A standard procedure for all hypothesis testing problems and situations is

> **STEP-BY-STEP PROCEDURE FOR TESTING HYPOTHESES**
> 1. Determine the null and alternative hypotheses.
> 2. Specify the test statistic and its distribution if the null hypothesis is true.
> 3. Select α and determine the rejection region.
> 4. Calculate the sample value of the test statistic.
> 5. State your conclusion.

3.4.1 RIGHT-TAIL TESTS

3.4.1a One-Tail Test of Signficance
Usually our first concern is whether there is a relationship between the variables, as we have specified in our model. If $\beta_2 = 0$ then there is no linear relationship between food expenditure and income. Economic theory suggests that food is a normal good, and that as income increases food expenditure will also increase, and thus that $\beta_2 > 0$. The least squares estimate of β_2 is $b_2 = 10.21$, which is certainly greater than zero. However, simply observing that the estimate has the right sign does not constitute scientific proof. We want to determine if there is convincing, or *significant*, statistical evidence that would lead us to conclude that $\beta_2 > 0$. When testing the null hypothesis that a parameter is zero, we are asking if the estimate b_2 is significantly different from zero, and the test is called a **test of significance**.

A statistical test procedure cannot prove the truth of a null hypothesis. When we fail to reject a null hypothesis, all the hypothesis test can establish is that the information in a sample of data is *compatible* with the null hypothesis. Conversely, a statistical test can lead us to *reject* the null hypothesis, with only a small probability α of rejecting the null hypothesis when it is actually true. Thus rejecting a null hypothesis is a stronger conclusion than failing to reject it. For this reason the null hypothesis is usually stated in such a way that if our theory is correct, then we will reject the null hypothesis. In our example, economic theory implies that there should be a positive relationship between income and food expenditure. We would like to establish that there is statistical evidence to support this theory using a hypothesis test. With this goal we set up the null hypothesis that there is *no* relation between the variables, $H_0 : \beta_2 = 0$. In the alternative hypothesis we put the conjecture that we would like to establish, $H_1 : \beta_2 > 0$. If we then reject the null hypothesis we can make a direct statement, concluding that β_2 is positive, with only a small (α) probability that we are in error.

The steps of this hypothesis test are as follows:

1. The null hypothesis is $H_0 : \beta_2 = 0$. The alternative hypothesis is $H_1 : \beta_2 > 0$.

2. The test statistic is (3.7). In this case $c = 0$, so $t = b_2/\text{se}(b_2) \sim t_{(N-2)}$ if the null hypothesis is true.

3. Let us select $\alpha = 0.05$. The critical value for the right-tail rejection region is the 95th percentile of the t-distribution with $N - 2 = 38$ degrees of freedom, $t_{(0.95,38)} = 1.686$. Thus we will reject the null hypothesis if the calculated value of $t \geq 1.686$. If $t < 1.686$, we will not reject the null hypothesis.

4. Using the food expenditure data, we found that $b_2 = 10.21$ with standard error $\text{se}(b_2) = 2.09$. The value of the test statistic is

$$t = \frac{b_2}{\text{se}(b_2)} = \frac{10.21}{2.09} = 4.88$$

5. Since $t = 4.88 > 1.686$, we reject the null hypothesis that $\beta_2 = 0$ and accept the alternative that $\beta_2 > 0$. That is, we reject the hypothesis that there is no relationship between income and food expenditure, and conclude that there is a *statistically significant* positive relationship between household income and food expenditure.

The last part of the conclusion is important. When you report your results to an audience, you will want to describe the outcome of the test in the context of the problem you are investigating, not just in terms of Greek letters and symbols.

What if we had not been able to reject the null hypothesis in this example? Would we have concluded that economic theory is wrong and that there is no relationship between income and food expenditure? No. Remember that failing to reject a null hypothesis **does not** mean that the null hypothesis is true.

3.4.1b   One-Tail Test of an Economic Hypothesis

Suppose that the economic profitability of a new supermarket depends on households spending at least \$5.50 out of each additional \$100 weekly income on food and that construction will not proceed unless there is strong evidence to this effect. In this case the conjecture we want to establish, the one that will go in the alternative hypothesis, is that $\beta_2 > 5.5$. If $\beta_2 \leq 5.5$, then the supermarket will be unprofitable and the owners would not want to build it. The least squares estimate of β_2 is $b_2 = 10.21$, which is greater than 5.5. What we want to determine is if there is convincing statistical evidence that would lead us to conclude, based on the available data, that $\beta_2 > 5.5$. This judgment is based not only on the estimate b_2, but also on its precision as measured by $\text{se}(b_2)$.

What will the null hypothesis be? We have been stating null hypotheses as equalities, such as $\beta_2 = 5.5$. This null hypothesis is too limited because it is theoretically possible that $\beta_2 < 5.5$. It turns out that the hypothesis testing procedure for testing the null hypothesis that $H_0 : \beta_2 \leq 5.5$ against the alternative hypothesis $H_1 : \beta_2 > 5.5$ is *exactly the same* as testing $H_0 : \beta_2 = 5.5$ against the alternative hypothesis $H_1 : \beta_2 > 5.5$. The test statistic and rejection region are exactly the same. For a right-tail test you can form the null hypothesis in either of these ways depending upon the problem at hand.

The steps of this hypothesis test are as follows:

1. The null hypothesis is $H_0 : \beta_2 \leq 5.5$. The alternative hypothesis is $H_1 : \beta_2 > 5.5$.

2. The test statistic $t = (b_2 - 5.5)/\text{se}(b_2) \sim t_{(N-2)}$ if the null hypothesis is true.

3. Let us select $\alpha = .01$. The critical value for the right-tail rejection region is the 99th percentile of the t-distribution with $N - 2 = 38$ degrees of freedom, $t_{(0.99,38)} = 2.429$. We will reject the null hypothesis if the calculated value of $t \geq 2.429$. If $t < 2.429$ we will not reject the null hypothesis.

4. Using the food expenditure data, $b_2 = 10.21$ with standard error $\text{se}(b_2) = 2.09$. The value of the test statistic is

$$t = \frac{b_2 - 5.5}{\text{se}(b_2)} = \frac{10.21 - 5.5}{2.09} = 2.25$$

5. Since $t = 2.25 < 2.429$ we do not reject the null hypothesis that $\beta_2 \leq 5.5$. We are *not* able to conclude that the new supermarket will be profitable and will not begin construction.

In this example we have posed a situation where the choice of the level of significance α becomes of great importance. A construction project worth millions of dollars depends on having *convincing* evidence that households will spend at least \$5.50 out of each additional \$100 income on food. While the "usual" choice is $\alpha = 0.05$, we have chosen a conservative value of $\alpha = 0.01$ because we seek a test that has a low chance of rejecting the null hypothesis when it is actually true. Recall that the level of significance of a test defines what we mean by an unlikely value of the test statistic. In this example, if the null hypothesis is true, then building the supermarket will be unprofitable. We want the probability of building an unprofitable market to be very small, and therefore we want the probability of rejecting the null hypothesis when it is true to be very small. In each real-world situation, the choice of α must be made on an assessment of *risk* and the *consequences* of making an incorrect decision.

A CEO unwilling to make a decision based on the above evidence may well order a new and larger sample of data to be analyzed. Recall that as the sample size increases, the least squares estimator becomes more precise (as measured by estimator variance) and consequently hypothesis tests become more powerful tools for statistical inference.

3.4.2 LEFT-TAIL TESTS

For completeness we will illustrate a test with the rejection region in the left tail. Consider the null hypothesis that $\beta_2 \geq 15$ and the alternative hypothesis $\beta_2 < 15$. Recall our memory trick for determining the location of the rejection region for a t-test. The rejection region is in the direction of the arrow "$<$" in the alternative hypothesis. That tells us that the rejection region is in the left tail of the t-distribution. The steps of this hypothesis test are as follows:

1. The null hypothesis is $H_0 : \beta_2 \geq 15$. The alternative hypothesis is $H_1 : \beta_2 < 15$.

2. The test statistic $t = (b_2 - 15)/\text{se}(b_2) \sim t_{(N-2)}$ if the null hypothesis is true.

3. Let us select $\alpha = 0.05$. The critical value for the left-tail rejection region is the 5th percentile of the t-distribution with $N - 2 = 38$ degrees of freedom, $t_{(0.05,38)} = -1.686$. We will reject the null hypothesis if the calculated value of $t \leq -1.686$. If $t > -1.686$ we will not reject the null hypothesis. A left-tail rejection region is illustrated in Figure 3.3.

4. Using the food expenditure data, $b_2 = 10.21$ with standard error $\text{se}(b_2) = 2.09$. The value of the test statistic is

$$t = \frac{b_2 - 15}{\text{se}(b_2)} = \frac{10.21 - 15}{2.09} = -2.29$$

5. Since $t = -2.29 < -1.686$ we reject the null hypothesis that $\beta_2 \geq 15$ and accept the alternative that $\beta_2 < 15$. We conclude that households spend less than \$15 from each additional \$100 income on food.

3.4.3 Two-Tail Tests

3.4.3a Two-Tail Test of an Economic Hypothesis

A consultant voices the opinion that based on other similar neighborhoods the households near the proposed market will spend an additional \$7.50 per additional \$100 income. In terms of our economic model we can state this conjecture as the null hypothesis $\beta_2 = 7.5$. If we want to test whether this is true or not, then the alternative is that $\beta_2 \neq 7.5$. This alternative makes no claim about whether β_2 is greater than 7.5 or less than 7.5, simply that it is not 7.5. In such cases we use a two-tail test, as follows:

1. The null hypothesis is $H_0 : \beta_2 = 7.5$. The alternative hypothesis is $H_1 : \beta_2 \neq 7.5$.

2. The test statistic $t = (b_2 - 7.5)/\text{se}(b_2) \sim t_{(N-2)}$ if the null hypothesis is true.

3. Let us select $\alpha = 0.05$. The critical values for this two-tail test are the 2.5-percentile $t_{(0.025,38)} = -2.024$ and the 97.5-percentile $t_{(0.975,38)} = 2.024$. Thus we will reject the null hypothesis if the calculated value of $t \geq 2.024$ **or** if $t \leq -2.024$. If $-2.024 < t < 2.024$ we will not reject the null hypothesis.

4. For the food expenditure data $b_2 = 10.21$ with standard error $\text{se}(b_2) = 2.09$. The value of the test statistic is

$$t = \frac{b_2 - 7.5}{\text{se}(b_2)} = \frac{10.21 - 7.5}{2.09} = 1.29$$

5. Since $-2.204 < t = 1.29 < 2.204$ we do not reject the null hypothesis that $\beta_2 = 7.5$. The sample data are consistent with the conjecture households will spend an additional \$7.50 per additional \$100 income on food.

We must avoid reading into this conclusion more than it means. We **do not** conclude from this test that $\beta_2 = 7.5$, only that the data are not incompatible with this parameter value. The data are also compatible with the null hypotheses $H_0 : \beta_2 = 8.5$ ($t = 0.82$), $H_0 : \beta_2 = 6.5$ ($t = 1.77$), and $H_0 : \beta_2 = 12.5$ ($t = -1.09$). A hypothesis test **cannot** be used to prove that a null hypothesis is true.

There is a trick relating two-tail tests and confidence intervals that is sometimes useful. Let c be a value within a $100(1 - \alpha)\%$ confidence interval, so that if $t_c = t_{(1-\alpha/2, N-2)}$, then

$$b_k - t_c \text{se}(b_k) \leq c \leq b_k + t_c \text{se}(b_k)$$

If we test the null hypothesis $H_0 : \beta_k = c$ against $H_1 : \beta_k \neq c$, when c is inside the confidence interval, then we will *not* reject the null hypothesis at the level of significance α. If c is outside the confidence interval, then the two-tail test will reject the null hypothesis. We do not advocate using confidence intervals to test hypotheses, they serve a different purpose, but if you are given a confidence interval this trick is handy.

3.4.3b Two–Tail Test of Significance

While we are confident that a relationship exists between food expenditure and income, models are often proposed that are more speculative, and the purpose of hypothesis testing is to ascertain whether a relationship between variables exists or not. In this case the null hypothesis is $\beta_2 = 0$; that is, no linear relationship exists between x and y. The alternative is $\beta_2 \neq 0$, which would mean that a relationship exists, but that there may be either a positive or negative association between the variables. This is the most common form of a **test of significance**. The test steps are as follows:

1. The null hypothesis is $H_0 : \beta_2 = 0$. The alternative hypothesis is $H_1 : \beta_2 \neq 0$.

2. The test statistic $t = b_2/\text{se}(b_2) \sim t_{(N-2)}$ *if the null hypothesis is true.*

3. Let us select $\alpha = 0.05$. The critical values for this two-tail test are the 2.5-percentile $t_{(0.025,38)} = -2.024$ and the 97.5-percentile $t_{(0.975,38)} = 2.024$. We will reject the null hypothesis if the calculated value of $t \geq 2.024$ *or* if $t \leq -2.024$. If $-2.024 < t < 2.024$ we will not reject the null hypothesis.

4. Using the food expenditure data, $b_2 = 10.21$ with standard error $\text{se}(b_2) = 2.09$. The value of the test statistic is $t = b_2/\text{se}(b_2) = 10.21/2.09 = 4.88$.

5. Since $t = 4.88 > 2.024$ we reject the null hypothesis that $\beta_2 = 0$ and conclude that there is a statistically significant relationship between income and food expenditure.

Two points should be made about this result. First, the value of the t-statistic we computed in this two-tail test is the same as the value computed in the one-tail test of significance in Section 3.4.1a. The difference between the two tests is the rejection region and the critical values. Second, the two-tail test of significance is something that should be done each time a regression model is estimated, and consequently computer software automatically calculates the t-values for null hypotheses that the regression parameters are zero. Refer back to Figure 2.9. Consider the portion that reports the estimates:

Variable	Coefficient	Std. Error	t-Statistic	Prob.
C	83.41600	43.41016	1.921578	0.0622
INCOME	10.20964	2.093264	4.877381	0.0000

Note that there is a column labeled t-Statistic. This is the t-statistic value for the null hypothesis that the corresponding parameter is zero. It is calculated as $t = b_k/\text{se}(b_k)$. Dividing the least squares estimates (Coefficient) by their standard errors (Std. Error) gives the t-statistic values (t-Statistic) for testing the hypothesis that the parameter is zero. The t-statistic value for the variable *INCOME* is 4.877381, which is relevant for testing the null hypothesis $H_0 : \beta_2 = 0$. We have rounded this value to 4.88 in our discussions.

The t-value for testing the hypothesis that the intercept is zero equals 1.92. The $\alpha = 0.05$ critical values for these two-tail tests are $t_{(0.025,38)} = -2.024$ and $t_{(0.975,38)} = 2.024$ whether we are testing a hypothesis about the slope or intercept, so we fail to reject the null hypothesis that $H_0 : \beta_1 = 0$ given the alternative $H_1 : \beta_1 \neq 0$.

The final column, labeled "Prob." is the subject of the next section.

REMARK: "Statistically significant" does not necessarily imply "economically significant." For example, suppose the CEO of a supermarket chain plans a certain course of action *if* $\beta_2 \neq 0$. Furthermore, suppose a large sample is collected from which we obtain the estimate $b_2 = 0.0001$ with $se(b_2) = 0.00001$, yielding the t-statistic $t = 10.0$. We would reject the null hypothesis that $\beta_2 = 0$ and accept the alternative that $\beta_2 \neq 0$. Here $b_2 = 0.0001$ is statistically different from zero. However, 0.0001 may not be "economically" different from 0, and the CEO may decide not to proceed with the plans. The message here is that one must think carefully about the importance of a statistical analysis before reporting or using the results.

3.5 The p-Value

When reporting the outcome of statistical hypothesis tests, it has become standard practice to report the **p-value** (an abbreviation for **probability value**) of the test. If we have the p-value of a test, p, we can determine the outcome of the test by comparing the p-value to the chosen level of significance, α, *without* looking up or calculating the critical values. The rule is

---

p-VALUE RULE: Reject the null hypothesis when the p-value is less than, or equal to, the level of significance α. That is, if $p \leq \alpha$ then reject H_0. If $p > \alpha$ then do not reject H_0.

If you have chosen the level of significance to be $\alpha = 0.01$, 0.05, 0.10, or any other value, you can compare it to the p-value of a test and then reject, or not reject, without checking the critical value. In written works reporting the p-value of a test allows the reader to apply his or her own judgment about the appropriate level of significance.

How the p-value is computed depends on the alternative. If t is the calculated value of the t-statistic, then

- if $H_1 : \beta_k > c$, $p =$ probability to the right of t
- if $H_1 : \beta_k < c$, $p =$ probability to the left of t
- if $H_1 : \beta_k \neq c$, $p = $ *sum* of probabilities to the right of $|t|$ *and* to the left of $-|t|$

MEMORY TRICK: The direction of the alternative indicates the tail(s) of the distribution in which the p-value falls.

3.5.1 p-Value for a Right-Tail Test

In Section 3.4.1b we tested the null hypothesis $H_0 : \beta_2 \leq 5.5$ against the one-sided alternative $H_1 : \beta_2 > 5.5$. The calculated value of the t-statistic was

$$t = \frac{b_2 - 5.5}{se(b_2)} = \frac{10.21 - 5.5}{2.09} = 2.25$$

In this case, since the alternative is "greater than" ($>$), the p-value of this test is the probability that a t-random variable with $N - 2 = 38$ degrees of freedom is greater than 2.25, or $p = P\left[t_{(38)} \geq 2.25\right] = 0.0152$.

   This probability value cannot be found in the usual t-table of critical values, but it is easily found using the computer. Statistical software packages, and spreadsheets such as Excel, have simple commands to evaluate the *cumulative distribution function* (*cdf*) (see Appendix B.2) for a variety of probability distributions. If $F_X(x)$ is the *cdf* for a random variable X, then for any value $x = c$ the cumulative probability is $P[X \leq c] = F_X(c)$. Given such a function for the t-distribution, we compute the desired p-value

$$p = P\left[t_{(38)} \geq 2.25\right] = 1 - P\left[t_{(38)} \leq 2.25\right] = 1 - 0.9848 = 0.0152$$

Following the p-value rule we conclude that at $\alpha = 0.01$ we do not reject the null hypothesis. If we had chosen $\alpha = 0.05$ we would reject the null hypothesis in favor of the alternative.

   The logic of the p-value rule is shown in Figure 3.5. The probability of obtaining a t-value greater than 2.25 is 0.0152, $p = P\left[t_{(38)} \geq 2.25\right] = 0.0152$. The 99th percentile $t_{(0.99,38)}$, which is the critical value for a right-tail test with level of significance of $\alpha = 0.01$, must fall to the right of 2.25. This means that $t = 2.25$ does not fall in the rejection region if $\alpha = 0.01$ and we will not reject the null hypothesis at this level of significance. This is consistent with the p-value rule: When the p-value (0.0152) is greater than the chosen level of significance (0.01) we do not reject the null hypothesis.

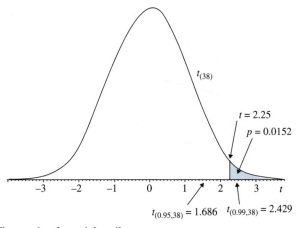

FIGURE **3.5**   The p-value for a right-tail test.

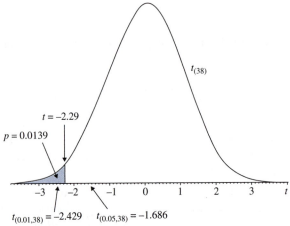

FIGURE *3.6* The p-value for a left-tail test.

On the other hand, the 95th percentile $t_{(0.95,38)}$, which is the critical value for a right-tail test with $\alpha = 0.05$, must be to the left of 2.25. This means that $t = 2.25$ falls in the rejection region and we reject the null hypothesis at the level of significance $\alpha = 0.05$. This is consistent with the *p-value rule*: When the p-value (0.0152) is less than or equal to the chosen level of significance (0.05) we will reject the null hypothesis.

3.5.2 *p*-VALUE FOR A LEFT-TAIL TEST

In Section 3.4.2 we carried out a test with the rejection region in the left tail of the t-distribution. The null hypothesis was $H_0 : \beta_2 \geq 15$ and the alternative hypothesis was $H_1 : \beta_2 < 15$. The calculated value of the t-statistic was $t = -2.29$. To compute the p-value for this left-tail test we calculate the probability of obtaining a t-statistic to the left of -2.29. Using your computer software you will find this value to be $P\left[t_{(38)} \leq -2.29\right] = 0.0139$. Following the p-value rule we conclude that at $\alpha = 0.01$ we do not reject the null hypothesis. If we choose $\alpha = 0.05$ we will reject the null hypothesis in favor of the alternative. See Figure 3.6 to see this graphically. Locate the 1st and 5th percentiles. These will be the critical values for left-tail tests with $\alpha = 0.01$ and $\alpha = 0.05$ levels of significance. When the p-value (0.0139) is greater than the level of significance ($\alpha = 0.01$) then the t-value -2.29 is not in the test rejection region. When the p-value (0.0139) is less than or equal to the level of significance ($\alpha = 0.05$) then the t-value -2.29 is in the test rejection region.

3.5.3 *p*-VALUE FOR A TWO-TAIL TEST

For a two-tail test, the rejection region is in the two tails of the t-distribution, and the p-value is similarly calculated in the two tails of the distribution. In Section 3.4.3a we tested the null hypothesis that $\beta_2 = 7.5$ against the alternative hypothesis $\beta_2 \neq 7.5$. The calculated value of the t-statistic was $t = 1.29$. For this two-tail test the p-value is the combined probability to the right of 1.29 and to the left of -1.29:

$$p = P\left[t_{(38)} \geq 1.29\right] + P\left[t_{(38)} \leq -1.29\right] = 0.2033$$

This calculation is depicted in Figure 3.7. Once the p-value is obtained its use is unchanged. If we choose $\alpha = 0.05$, $\alpha = 0.10$, or even $\alpha = 0.20$ we will fail to reject the null hypothesis because $p > \alpha$.

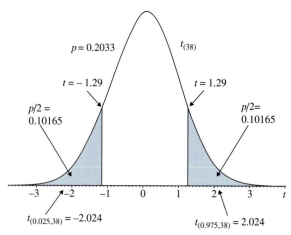

FIGURE **3.7** The p-value for a two-tail test of significance.

At the beginning of this section we stated the following rule for computing p-values for two-tail tests: if $H_1 : \beta_k \neq c$, $p = sum$ of probabilities to the right of $|t|$ *and* to the left of $-|t|$. The reason for the use of absolute values in this rule is that it will apply equally well if the value of the t-statistic turns out to be positive or negative.

3.5.4 p-VALUE FOR A TWO-TAIL TEST OF SIGNIFICANCE

All statistical software computes the p-value for the two-tail test of significance for each coefficient when a regression analysis is performed. In Section 3.4.3b we discussed testing the null hypothesis $H_0 : \beta_2 = 0$ against the alternative hypothesis $H_1 : \beta_2 \neq 0$. For the calculated value of the t-statistic $t = 4.88$ the p-value is

$$p = P\left[t_{(38)} \geq 4.88\right] + P\left[t_{(38)} \leq -4.88\right] = 0.0000$$

Your software will automatically compute and report this p-value for a two-tail test of significance. Refer back to Figure 2.9 and consider just the portion reporting the estimates:

Variable	Coefficient	Std. Error	t-Statistic	Prob.
C	83.41600	43.41016	1.921578	0.0622
INCOME	10.20964	2.093264	4.877381	0.0000

Next to each t-statistic value is the two-tail p-value, which is labeled "Prob" by the EViews software. Other software packages will use similar names. When inspecting computer output we can immediately decide if an estimate is statistically significant (statistically different from zero using a two-tail test) by comparing the p-value to whatever level of significance we care to use. The estimated intercept has p-value 0.0622 so it is not statistically different from zero at the level of significance $\alpha = 0.05$, but it is statistically significant if $\alpha = 0.10$.

The estimated coefficient for income has a p-value that is zero to four places. Thus $p \le \alpha = 0.01$ or even $\alpha = 0.0001$, and thus we reject the null hypothesis that income has no effect on food expenditure at these levels of significance. The p-value for this two-tail test of significance is not actually zero. If more places are used then $p = 0.00001946$. Regression software usually does not print out more than four places because in practice levels of significance less than $\alpha = 0.001$ are rare.

3.6 Exercises

Answers to exercises marked * appear in Appendix D at the end of the book.

3.6.1 PROBLEMS

3.1 Using the regression output for the food expenditure model shown in Figure 2.9:

(a) Construct a 95% interval estimate for β_1 and interpret.

(b) Test the null hypothesis that β_1 is zero, against the alternative that it is not, at the 5% level of significance without using the reported p-value. What is your conclusion?

(c) Draw a sketch showing the p-value 0.0622 shown in Figure 2.9, the critical value from the t-distribution used in (b) and how the p-value could have been used to answer (b).

(d) Test the null hypothesis that β_1 is zero, against the alternative that it is positive, at the 5% level of significance. Draw a sketch of the rejection region and compute the p-value. What is your conclusion?

(e) Explain the differences and similarities between the "level of significance" and the "level of confidence."

(f) The results in (d) show that we are 95% confident that β_1 is positive. True or false? If false, explain.

3.2 The general manager of an engineering firm wants to know if a technical artist's experience influences the quality of their work. A random sample of 24 artists is selected and their years of work experience and quality rating (as assessed by their supervisors) recorded. Work experience (*EXPER*) is measured in years and quality rating (*RATING*) takes a value of 1 through 7, with 7 = excellent and 1 = poor. The simple regression model $RATING = \beta_1 + \beta_2 EXPER + e$ is proposed. The least squares estimates of the model, and the standard errors of the estimates, are

$$\widehat{RATING} = 3.204 + 0.076\,EXPER$$
$$(\text{se}) \qquad (0.709) \quad (0.044)$$

(a) Sketch the estimated regression function. Interpret the coefficient of *EXPER*.

(b) Construct a 95% confidence interval for β_2, the slope of the relationship between quality rating and experience. In what are you 95% confident?

(c) Test the null hypothesis that β_2 is zero against the alternative that it is not using a two-tail test and the $\alpha = 0.05$ level of significance. What do you conclude?

(d) Test the null hypothesis that β_2 is zero against the one-tail alternative that it is positive at the $\alpha = 0.05$ level of significance. What do you conclude?

(e) For the test in part (c), the *p*-value is 0.0982. If we choose the probability of a Type I error to be $\alpha = 0.05$, do we reject the null hypothesis or not, just based on an inspection of the *p*-value? Show, in a diagram, how this *p*-value is computed.

3.3* In an estimated simple regression model, based on 24 observations, the estimated slope parameter is 0.310 and the estimated standard error is 0.082.
  (a) Test the hypothesis that the slope is zero, against the alternative that it is not, at the 1% level of significance.
  (b) Test the hypothesis that the slope is zero, against the alternative that it is positive at the 1% level of significance.
  (c) Test the hypothesis that the slope is zero against the alternative that it is negative at the 5% level of significance. Draw a sketch showing the rejection region.
  (d) Test the hypothesis that the estimated slope is 0.5, against the alternative that it is not, at the 5% level of significance.
  (e) Obtain a 99% interval estimate of the slope.

3.4 Consider a simple regression in which the dependent variable *MIM* = mean income of males who are 18 years of age or older, in thousands of dollars. The explanatory variable *PMHS* = percent of males 18 or older who are high school graduates. The data consist of 51 observations on the 50 states plus the District of Columbia. Thus *MIM* and *PMHS* are "state averages." The estimated regression, along with standard errors and *t*-statistics, is

$$\widehat{MIM} = \quad (a) \quad + \quad 0.180PMHS$$
$$\text{(se)} \quad (2.174) \quad (b)$$
$$\text{(t)} \quad (1.257) \quad (5.754)$$

  (a) What is the estimated equation intercept? Show your calculation. Sketch the estimated regression function.
  (b) What is the standard error of the estimated slope? Show your calculation.
  (c) What is the *p*-value for the two-tail test of the hypothesis that the equation intercept is zero? Draw a sketch to illustrate.
  (d) State the economic interpretation of the estimated slope. Is the sign of the coefficient what you would expect from economic theory?
  (e) Construct a 99% confidence interval estimate of the slope of this relationship.
  (f) Test the hypothesis that the slope of the relationship is 0.2, against the alternative that it is not. State in words the meaning of the null hypothesis in the context of this problem.

3.6.2 COMPUTER EXERCISES

3.5 A life insurance company wishes to examine the relationship between the amount of life insurance held by a family and family income. From a random sample of 20 households, the company collected the data in the file *insur.dat*. The data are in units of thousands of dollars.
  (a) Estimate the linear regression with dependent variable *INSURANCE* and independent variable *INCOME*. Write down the fitted model and draw a sketch of the fitted function. Identify the estimated slope and intercept on the sketch. Locate the point of the means on the plot.

(b) Discuss the relationship you estimated in (a). In particular
   (i) What is your estimate of the resulting change in the amount of life insurance when income increases by $1000?
   (ii) What is the standard error of the estimate in (i) and how do you use this standard error for interval estimation and hypothesis testing?
(c) One member of the management board claims that, for every $1000 increase in income, the amount of life insurance held will go up by $5000. Choose an alternative hypothesis and explain your choice. Does your estimated relationship support this claim? Use a 5% significance level.
(d) Test the hypothesis that as income increases the amount of life insurance increases by the same amount. That is, test the hypothesis that the slope of the relationship is 1.
(e) Write a short report (200–250 words) summarizing your findings about the relationship between income and the amount of life insurance held.

3.6* Consider the learning curve example introduced in Exercise 2.9.
   (a) Construct a 95% interval estimate for β_2 and interpret.
   (b) Test at the 5% level of significance whether there is no learning against the alternative that there is learning. Formulate the null and alternative hypotheses and discuss your reasoning. Explain your conclusion.

3.7 Consider the capital asset pricing model (CAPM) in Exercise 2.10.
   (a) Test at the 5% level of significance the hypothesis that each stock's "*beta*" value is 1 against the alternative that it is not equal to 1. What is the economic interpretation of a *beta* equal to 1?
   (b) Test at the 5% level of significance the null hypothesis that Mobil-Exxon's "*beta*" value is greater than or equal to 1 against the alternative that it is less than 1. What is the economic interpretation of a *beta* less than 1?
   (c) Test at the 5% level of significance the null hypothesis that Microsoft's "*beta*" value is less than or equal to 1 against the alternative that it is greater than 1. What is the economic interpretation of a *beta* more than 1?
   (d) Construct a 95% interval estimate of Microsoft's "*beta*." Assume that you are a stockbroker. Explain this result to an investor who has come to you for advice.
   (e) Test (at a 5% significance level) the hypothesis that the intercept term in the CAPM model for each stock is zero, against the alternative that it is not. What do you conclude?

3.8 Consider the housing starts data (*house_starts.dat*) introduced in Exercise 2.13.
   (a) Estimate the simple regression of housing starts (*STARTS*) on the 30-year fixed rate (*FIXED_RATE*). Using a 5% significance level, test the null hypothesis that there is no linear relationship between these variables against the alternative that there is an inverse relationship.
   (b) It is conjectured that if the 30-year fixed interest rate increases by 1% then house starts will fall by 150,000. Test this hypothesis at the 5% level of significance using a two-tail test.
   (c) Construct a 95% interval estimate of the slope from the regression estimated in part (a). State the meaning of this interval estimate. In part (b) you tested that the slope of the relationship was $\beta_2 = -150$. Is the value -150 inside the 95% interval estimate? How does this finding relate to the hypothesis test in (b)?

3.9* Reconsider the presidential voting data (*fair.dat*) introduced in Exercise 2.14.
  (a) Using the regression model $VOTE = \beta_1 + \beta_2 GROWTH + e$, test (at a 5% significance level) the null hypothesis that economic growth has no effect on the percentage vote earned by the incumbent party. Select an alternative hypothesis and a rejection region. Explain your choice.
  (b) Using the regression model in part (a), construct a 95% interval estimate for β_2, and interpret.
  (c) Using the regression model $VOTE = \beta_1 + \beta_2 INFLATION + e$, test the null hypothesis that inflation has no effect on the percentage vote earned by the incumbent party. Select an alternative hypothesis, a rejection region, and a significance level. Explain your choice.
  (d) Using the regression model in part (c), construct a 95% interval estimate for β_2, and interpret.

3.10 The file *br.dat* contains data on 1080 houses sold in Baton Rouge, Louisiana during mid-2005.
  (a) Estimate the regression model $PRICE = \beta_1 + \beta_2 SQFT + e$ for (i) all the houses in the sample, (ii) town houses, and (iii) French style homes. Construct a 95% interval estimate for β_2 in each case and discuss the differences.
  (b) Test the hypothesis that an additional square foot of living area increases house price by $80 for each of the cases in part (a). Use a two-tail test using the $\alpha = 0.05$ level of significance.

3.11* The file *stockton2.dat* contains data on 880 houses sold in Stockton, CA during mid-2005. This data was considered in Exercise 2.12.
  (a) Estimate the regression model $PRICE = \beta_1 + \beta_2 SQFT + e$ for all the houses in the sample. Test the hypothesis that an additional square foot of living area increases house price by $80. Use a two-tail test using the $\alpha = 0.05$ level of significance.
  (b) Repeat part (a) using houses that were vacant at the time of sale.
  (c) Repeat part (a) using houses that were occupied (not vacant) at time of sale.
  (d) Using the houses that were occupied at the time of sale, test the null hypothesis that the value of an additional square foot of living area is less than or equal to $80, against the alternative that the value of an additional square foot is worth more than $80.
  (e) Using the houses that were vacant at the time of sale, test the null hypothesis that the value of an additional square foot of living area is more than or equal to $80, against the alternative that the value of an additional square foot is worth less than $80.
  (f) Construct a 95% interval estimate for β_2 using (i) the full sample, (ii) houses vacant at the time of sale, and (iii) occupied at the time of sale.

3.12 How much does experience affect wage rates? The data file *cps_small.dat* contains 1000 observations on hourly wage rates, experience, and other variables from the 1997 Current Population Survey (CPS).
  (a) Estimate the linear regression $WAGE = \beta_1 + \beta_2 EXPER + e$ and discuss the results. Using your software plot a scatter diagram with $WAGE$ on the vertical axis and $EXPER$ on the horizontal axis. Sketch in by hand, or using your software, the fitted regression line.
  (b) Test the statistical significance of the estimated slope of the relationship at the 5% level. Use a one-tail test.

(c) Repeat part (a) for the subsamples consisting of (i) females, (ii) males, (iii) blacks, and (iv) white males. What differences, if any, do you notice?

(d) For each of the estimated regression models in (a) and (c), calculate the least squares residuals and plot them against *EXPER*. Are any patterns evident?

3.13◆ Repeat Exercise 3.12 using the data file *cps.dat*, which contains 4733 observations. This exercise may not work with "student" versions of software.

Appendix 3A Derivation of the *t*-Distribution

Interval estimation and hypothesis testing procedures in this chapter involve the *t*-distribution. Here we develop the key result.

The first result that is needed is the normal distribution of the least squares estimator. Consider, for example, the normal distribution of b_2 the least squares estimator of β_2, which we denote as

$$b_2 \sim N\left(\beta_2, \frac{\sigma^2}{\Sigma(x_i - \bar{x})^2}\right)$$

A standardized normal random variable is obtained from b_2 by subtracting its mean and dividing by its standard deviation:

$$Z = \frac{b_2 - \beta_2}{\sqrt{\text{var}(b_2)}} \sim N(0, 1) \qquad (3A.1)$$

That is, the standardized random variable Z is normally distributed with mean 0 and variance 1.

The second piece of the puzzle involves a chi-square random variable. If assumption SR6 holds, then the random error term e_i has a normal distribution, $e_i \sim N(0, \sigma^2)$. Again, we can standardize the random variable by dividing by its standard deviation so that $e_i/\sigma \sim N(0, 1)$. The square of a standard normal random variable is a chi-square random variable (see Appendix B.5.2) with one degree of freedom, so $(e_i/\sigma)^2 \sim \chi^2_{(1)}$. If all the random errors are independent then

$$\Sigma\left(\frac{e_i}{\sigma}\right)^2 = \left(\frac{e_1}{\sigma}\right)^2 + \left(\frac{e_2}{\sigma}\right)^2 + \cdots + \left(\frac{e_N}{\sigma}\right)^2 \sim \chi^2_{(N)} \qquad (3A.2)$$

Since the true random errors are unobservable we replace them by their sample counterparts, the least squares residuals $\hat{e}_i = y_i - b_1 - b_2 x_i$ to obtain

$$V = \frac{\Sigma \hat{e}_i^2}{\sigma^2} = \frac{(N-2)\hat{\sigma}^2}{\sigma^2} \qquad (3A.3)$$

The random variable V in (3A.3) does not have a $\chi^2_{(N)}$ distribution because the least squares residuals are *not* independent random variables. All N residuals $\hat{e}_i = y_i - b_1 - b_2 x_i$ depend on the least squares estimators b_1 and b_2. It can be shown that only $N - 2$ of the least squares residuals are independent in the simple linear regression model. Consequently, the random variable in (3A.3) has a chi-square distribution with $N - 2$ degrees of freedom. That is, when multiplied by the constant $(N-2)/\sigma^2$, the random variable $\hat{\sigma}^2$ has a *chi-square distribution with $N-2$ degrees of freedom,*

$$V = \frac{(N-2)\hat{\sigma}^2}{\sigma^2} \sim \chi^2_{(N-2)} \tag{3A.4}$$

We have *not* established the fact that the chi-square random variable V is statistically independent of the least squares estimators b_1 and b_2, but it is. The proof is beyond the scope of this book. Consequently, V and the standard normal random variable Z in (3A.1) are independent.

From the two random variables V and Z we can form a t-random variable. A t-random variable is formed by dividing a standard normal random variable, $Z \sim N(0,1)$, by the square root of an *independent* chi-square random variable, $V \sim \chi^2_{(m)}$, that has been divided by its degrees of freedom, m. That is,

$$t = \frac{Z}{\sqrt{V/m}} \sim t_{(m)}$$

The t-distribution's shape is completely determined by the degrees of freedom parameter, m, and the distribution is symbolized by $t_{(m)}$. See Appendix B.5.3. Using Z and V from (3A.1) and (3A.4), respectively, we have

$$t = \frac{Z}{\sqrt{V/(N-2)}}$$

$$= \frac{(b_2 - \beta_2) \Big/ \sqrt{\sigma^2/\Sigma(x_i - \bar{x})^2}}{\sqrt{\dfrac{(N-2)\hat{\sigma}^2/\sigma^2}{N-2}}} \tag{3A.5}$$

$$= \frac{b_2 - \beta_2}{\sqrt{\dfrac{\hat{\sigma}^2}{\Sigma(x_i - \bar{x})^2}}} = \frac{b_2 - \beta_2}{\sqrt{\widehat{\operatorname{var}(b_2)}}} = \frac{b_2 - \beta_2}{\operatorname{se}(b_2)} \sim t_{(N-2)}$$

The last line is the key result that we state in (3.2), with its generalization in (3.3).

Appendix 3B Distribution of the t-Statistic Under H_1

To examine the distribution of the t-statistic in (3.7) when the null hypothesis is not true, suppose that the true $\beta_2 = 1$. Following the steps in (3A.5) in Appendix 3A we would find that

$$t = \frac{b_2 - 1}{\operatorname{se}(b_2)} \sim t_{(N-2)}$$

If $\beta_2 = 1$ and $c \neq 1$ then the test statistic in (3.7) does not have a t-distribution since, in its formation, the numerator of (3A.5) is *not* standard normal. It is not standard normal because the incorrect value $\beta_2 = c$ is subtracted from b_2.

If $\beta_2 = 1$ and we *incorrectly* hypothesize that $\beta_2 = c$, then the numerator in (3A.5) that is used in forming (3.7) has the distribution

$$\frac{b_2 - c}{\sqrt{\text{var}(b_2)}} \sim N\left(\frac{1 - c}{\sqrt{\text{var}(b_2)}}, 1\right) \tag{3B.1}$$

where

$$\text{var}(b_2) = \frac{\sigma^2}{\Sigma(x_i - \bar{x})^2}$$

Since its mean is not zero, the distribution of the variable in (3B.1) is not standard normal, as required in the formation of a *t*-random variable.

Chapter *4*

Prediction, Goodness-of-Fit, and Modeling Issues

Learning Objectives

Based on the material in this chapter, you should be able to

1. Explain how to use the simple linear regression model to predict the value of y for a given value of x.

2. Explain, intuitively and technically, why predictions for x values further from $\bar{x}$ are less reliable.

3. Explain the meaning of *SST*, *SSR*, and *SSE*, and how they are related to R^2.

4. Define and explain the meaning of the coefficient of determination.

5. Explain the relationship between correlation analysis and R^2.

6. Report the results of a fitted regression equation in such a way that confidence intervals and hypothesis tests for the unknown coefficients can be constructed quickly and easily.

7. Describe how estimated coefficients and other quantities from a regression equation will change when the variables are scaled. Why would you want to scale the variables?

8. Appreciate the wide range of nonlinear functions that can be estimated using a model that is linear in the parameters.

9. Write down the equations for the log-log, log-linear, and linear-log functional forms.

10. Explain the difference between the slope of a functional form and the elasticity from a functional form.

11. Explain how you would go about choosing a functional form and deciding that a functional form is adequate?

12. Explain how to test whether the equation "errors" are normally distributed?

13. Explain how to compute a prediction, a prediction interval, and a goodness-of-fit measure in a log-linear model.

Keywords

coefficient of determination	Jarque–Bera test	log-normal distribution
correlation	kurtosis	prediction
data scale	least squares predictor	prediction interval
forecast error	linear model	R^2
forecast standard error	linear relationship	residual
functional form	linear-log model	skewness
goodness-of-fit	log-linear model	
growth model	log-log model	

In Chapter 3 we focused on making statistical inferences, constructing confidence intervals, and testing hypotheses about regression parameters. Another purpose of the regression model, and the one we focus on first in this chapter, is **prediction**. A prediction is a forecast of an unknown value of the dependent variable y given a particular value of x. A **prediction interval**, much like a confidence interval, is a range of values in which the unknown value of y is likely to be located. Examining the **correlation** between sample values of y and their predicted values provides a **goodness-of-fit** measure called R^2 that describes how well our model fits the data. For each observation in the sample the difference between the predicted value of y and the actual value is a **residual**. Diagnostic measures constructed from the residuals allow us to check the adequacy of the **functional form** used in the regression analysis and give us some indication of the validity of the regression assumptions. We will examine each of these ideas and concepts in turn.

4.1 Least Squares Prediction

In Section 2.3.3b we briefly introduced the idea that the least squares estimates of the linear regression model provide a way to predict the value of y for any value of x. The ability to predict is important to business economists and financial analysts who attempt to forecast the sales and revenues of specific firms; it is important to government policy makers who attempt to predict the rates of growth in national income, inflation, investment, saving, social insurance program expenditures, and tax revenues; and it is important to local businesses to have predictions of growth in neighborhood populations and income so that they may expand, or contract, their provision of services. Accurate predictions provide a basis for better decision making in every type of planning context. In this section we explore the use of linear regression as a tool for prediction.

Given the simple linear regression model and assumptions SR1–SR6, let x_0 be a value of the explanatory variable. We want to predict the corresponding value of y, which we call y_0. In order to use regression analysis as a basis for prediction, we must assume that y_0 and x_0 are related to one another by the same regression model that describes our sample of data, so that, in particular, SR1 holds for these observations

$$y_0 = \beta_1 + \beta_2 x_0 + e_0 \tag{4.1}$$

where e_0 is a random error. We assume that $E(y_0) = \beta_1 + \beta_2 x_0$ and $E(e_0) = 0$. We also assume that e_0 has the same variance as the regression errors, $\text{var}(e_0) = \sigma^2$, and e_0 is

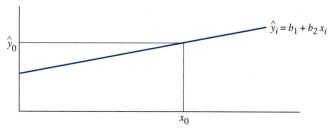

FIGURE **4.1** A point prediction.

uncorrelated with the random errors that are part of the sample data, so that $\mathrm{cov}(e_0, e_i) = 0$
$i = 1, 2, \ldots, N$. The **least squares predictor** of y_0 comes from the fitted regression line

$$\hat{y}_0 = b_1 + b_2 x_0 \tag{4.2}$$

That is, the predicted value $\hat{y}_0$ is given by the point on the least squares fitted line where
$x = x_0$, as shown in Figure 4.1. How good is this prediction procedure? The least squares
estimators b_1 and b_2 are random variables—their values vary from one sample to another. It
follows that the least squares predictor $\hat{y}_0 = b_1 + b_2 x_0$ must also be random. To evaluate
how well this predictor performs we define the **forecast error**, which is analogous to the
least squares residual,

$$f = y_0 - \hat{y}_0 = (\beta_1 + \beta_2 x_0 + e_0) - (b_1 + b_2 x_0) \tag{4.3}$$

We would like the forecast error to be small, implying that our forecast is close to the value
we are predicting. Taking the expected value of f we find

$$\begin{aligned}
E(f) &= \beta_1 + \beta_2 x_0 + E(e_0) - [E(b_1) + E(b_2)x_0] \\
&= \beta_1 + \beta_2 x_0 + 0 - [\beta_1 + \beta_2 x_0] \\
&= 0
\end{aligned}$$

which means, on average, the forecast error is zero, and $\hat{y}_0$ is an **unbiased predictor** of y_0.
However, unbiasedness does not necessarily imply that a particular forecast will be close to
the actual value. The probability of a small forecast error also depends on the variance of the
forecast error. While we will not prove it, $\hat{y}_0$ is the **best linear unbiased predictor (BLUP)**
of y_0 if assumptions SR1–SR5 hold. This result is reasonable given that the least squares
estimators b_1 and b_2 are best linear unbiased estimators.

Using (4.3) and what we know about the variances and covariance of the least squares
estimators, we can show (see Appendix 4A at the end of this chapter) that the variance of the
forecast error is

$$\mathrm{var}(f) = \sigma^2 \left[1 + \frac{1}{N} + \frac{(x_0 - \bar{x})^2}{\Sigma(x_i - \bar{x})^2} \right] \tag{4.4}$$

Notice that some of the elements of this expression appear in the formulas for the variances
of the least squares estimators and affect the precision of prediction in the same way that they
affect the precision of estimation. We would prefer that the variance of the forecast error be
small, which would increase the probability that the prediction $\hat{y}_0$ is close to the value y_0 we
are trying to predict. Note that the variance of the forecast error is smaller when

i.   the overall uncertainty in the model is smaller, as measured by the variance of the random errors σ^2;

ii. the sample size N is larger;

iii. the variation in the explanatory variable is larger; and

iv. the value of $(x_0 - \bar{x})^2$ is small.

The new addition is the term $(x_0 - \bar{x})^2$, which measures how far x_0 is from the center of the x-values. The more distant x_0 is from the center of the sample data the larger the forecast variance will become. Intuitively, this means that we are able to do a better job predicting in the region where we have more sample information, and we will have less accurate predictions when we try to predict outside the limits of our data.

In practice we replace σ^2 in (4.4) by its estimator $\hat{\sigma}^2$ to obtain

$$\widehat{\mathrm{var}(f)} = \hat{\sigma}^2 \left[1 + \frac{1}{N} + \frac{(x_0 - \bar{x})^2}{\Sigma(x_i - \bar{x})^2} \right]$$

The square root of this estimated variance is the **standard error of the forecast**

$$\mathrm{se}(f) = \sqrt{\widehat{\mathrm{var}(f)}} \tag{4.5}$$

Defining the critical value t_c to be the $100(1 - \alpha/2)$-percentile from the t-distribution, we can obtain a $100(1-\alpha)\%$ **prediction interval** as

$$\hat{y}_0 \pm t_c \mathrm{se}(f) \tag{4.6}$$

See Appendix 4A for some details related to the development of this result.

Following our discussion of $\mathrm{var}(f)$ in (4.4), the farther x_0 is from the sample mean $\bar{x}$, the larger the variance of the prediction error and the less reliable the prediction is likely to be. In other words, our predictions for values of x_0 close to the sample mean $\bar{x}$ are more reliable than our predictions for values of x_0 far from the sample mean $\bar{x}$. This fact shows up in the size of our prediction intervals. The relationship between point and interval predictions for different values of x_0 is illustrated in Figure 4.2. A point prediction is given by the fitted least squares line $\hat{y}_0 = b_1 + b_2 x_0$. The prediction interval takes the form of two bands around the fitted least squares line. Because the forecast variance increases the farther x_0 is from the

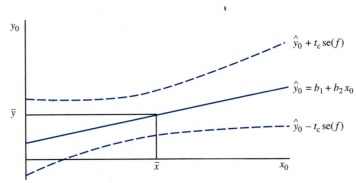

FIGURE 4.2   Point and interval prediction.

sample mean of $\bar{x}$, the confidence bands are their narrowest when $x_0 = \bar{x}$, and increase in width as $|x_0 - \bar{x}|$ increases.

4.1.1 PREDICTION IN THE FOOD EXPENDITURE MODEL

In Section 2.3.3b we predicted that a household with $x_0 = \$2000$ weekly income would spend $287.61 on food using the calculation

$$\hat{y}_0 = b_1 + b_2 x_0 = 83.4160 + 10.2096(20) = 287.6089$$

Now we are able to attach a "confidence interval" to this prediction. The estimated variance of the forecast error is

$$\widehat{\text{var}(f)} = \hat{\sigma}^2 \left[1 + \frac{1}{N} + \frac{(x_0 - \bar{x})^2}{\Sigma(x_i - \bar{x})^2} \right]$$

$$= \hat{\sigma}^2 + \frac{\hat{\sigma}^2}{N} + (x_0 - \bar{x})^2 \frac{\hat{\sigma}^2}{\Sigma(x_i - \bar{x})^2}$$

$$= \hat{\sigma}^2 + \frac{\hat{\sigma}^2}{N} + (x_0 - \bar{x})^2 \widehat{\text{var}(b_2)}$$

In the last line we have recognized the estimated variance of b_2 from (2.21). In Section 2.7.2 we obtained the values $\hat{\sigma}^2 = 8013.2941$ and $\widehat{\text{var}(b_2)} = 4.3818$. For the food expenditure data $N = 40$ and the sample mean of the explanatory variable is $\bar{x} = 19.6048$. Using these values we obtain the standard error of the forecast $\text{se}(f) = \sqrt{\widehat{\text{var}(f)}} = \sqrt{8214.31} = 90.6328$. If we select $1 - \alpha = 0.95$, then $t_c = t_{(0.975, 38)} = 2.0244$ and the 95% prediction interval for y_0 is

$$\hat{y}_0 \pm t_c \text{se}(f) = 287.6069 \pm 2.0244(90.6328) = [104.1323, \ 471.0854]$$

Our prediction interval suggests that a household with $2000 weekly income will spend somewhere between $104.13 and $471.09 on food. Such a wide interval means that our point prediction $287.61 is not very reliable. We have obtained this wide prediction interval for the value of $x_0 = 20$ that is close to the sample mean $\bar{x} = 19.60$. For values of x that are more extreme the prediction interval would be even wider. The unreliable predictions may be slightly improved if we collect a larger sample of data, which will improve the precision with which we estimate the model parameters. However, in this example the magnitude of the estimated error variance $\hat{\sigma}^2$ is very close to the estimated variance of the forecast error $\widehat{\text{var}(f)}$, suggesting that the primary uncertainty in the forecast comes from large uncertainty in the model. This should not be a surprise, since we are predicting household behavior, which is a complicated phenomenon, on the basis of a single household characteristic, income. While income is a key factor in explaining food expenditure, we can imagine many other household demographic characteristics that may play a role. To more accurately predict food expenditure we may need to include these additional factors into the regression model. Extending the simple regression model to include other factors will begin in Chapter 5.

4.2 **Measuring Goodness-of-Fit**

Two major reasons for analyzing the model

$$y_i = \beta_1 + \beta_2 x_i + e_i \tag{4.7}$$

are to explain how the dependent variable (y_i) changes as the independent variable (x_i) changes, and to predict y_0 given an x_0. These two objectives come under the broad headings of estimation and prediction. Closely allied with the prediction problem discussed in the previous section is the desire to use x_i to explain as much of the variation in the dependent variable y_i as possible. In the regression model (4.7) we call x_i the "explanatory" variable because we hope that its variation will "explain" the variation in y_i.

To develop a measure of the variation in y_i that is explained by the model, we begin by separating y_i into its explainable and unexplainable components. We have assumed that

$$y_i = E(y_i) + e_i \tag{4.8}$$

where $E(y_i) = \beta_1 + \beta_2 x_i$ is the explainable, "systematic" component of y_i, and e_i is the random, unsystematic and unexplainable component of y_i. While both of these parts are unobservable to us, we can estimate the unknown parameters β_1 and β_2 and, analogous to (4.8), decompose the value of y_i into

$$y_i = \hat{y}_i + \hat{e}_i \tag{4.9}$$

where $\hat{y}_i = b_1 + b_2 x_i$ and $\hat{e}_i = y_i - \hat{y}_i$.

In Figure 4.3 the "point of the means" $(\bar{x}, \bar{y})$ is shown, with the least squares fitted line passing through it. This is a characteristic of the least squares fitted line whenever the regression model includes an intercept term. Subtract the sample mean $\bar{y}$ from both sides of the equation to obtain

$$y_i - \bar{y} = (\hat{y}_i - \bar{y}) + \hat{e}_i \tag{4.10}$$

As shown in Figure 4.3 the difference between y_i and its mean value $\bar{y}$ consists of a part that is "explained" by the regression model $\hat{y}_i - \bar{y}$ and a part that is unexplained $\hat{e}_i$.

The breakdown in (4.10) leads to a decomposition of the total sample variability in y into explained and unexplained parts. Recall from your statistics courses (see Appendix C.4) that

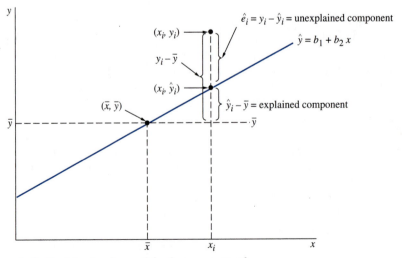

FIGURE **4.3**   Explained and unexplained components of y_i.

if we have a sample of observations $y_1, y_2, \ldots, y_N$, two descriptive measures are the sample mean $\bar{y}$ and the sample variance

$$\hat{\sigma}_y^2 = \frac{\Sigma(y_i - \bar{y})^2}{N - 1}$$

The numerator of this quantity, the sum of squared differences between the sample values y_i and the sample mean $\bar{y}$, is a measure of the total variation in the sample values. If we square and sum both sides of (4.10), and using the fact that the cross-product term $\Sigma(\hat{y}_i - \bar{y})\hat{e}_i = 0$ (see Appendix 4B), we obtain

$$\Sigma(y_i - \bar{y})^2 = \Sigma(\hat{y}_i - \bar{y})^2 + \Sigma\hat{e}_i^2 \tag{4.11}$$

Equation (4.11) gives us a decomposition of the "total sample variation" in y into explained and unexplained components. Specifically, these "sums of squares" are

1. $\Sigma(y_i - \bar{y})^2$ = total sum of squares = SST: a measure of *total variation* in y about the sample mean.
2. $\Sigma(\hat{y}_i - \bar{y})^2$ = sum of squares due to the regression = SSR: that part of total variation in y, about the sample mean, that is explained by, or due to, the regression. Also known as the "explained sum of squares."
3. $\Sigma\hat{e}_i^2$ = sum of squares due to error = SSE: that part of total variation in y about its mean that is not explained by the regression. Also known as the unexplained sum of squares, the residual sum of squares, or the sum of squared errors.

Using these abbreviations (4.11) becomes

$$SST = SSR + SSE$$

This decomposition of the total variation in y into a part that is explained by the regression model and a part that is unexplained allows us to define a measure, called the **coefficient of determination**, or R^2, that is the proportion of variation in y explained by x within the regression model.

$$R^2 = \frac{SSR}{SST} = 1 - \frac{SSE}{SST} \tag{4.12}$$

The closer R^2 is to 1, the closer the sample values y_i are to the fitted regression equation $\hat{y}_i = b_1 + b_2 x_i$. If $R^2 = 1$, then all the sample data fall exactly on the fitted least squares line, so $SSE = 0$, and the model fits the data "perfectly." If the sample data for y and x are uncorrelated and show no linear association, then the least squares fitted line is "horizontal," and identical to $\bar{y}$, so that $SSR = 0$ and $R^2 = 0$. When $0 < R^2 < 1$, it is interpreted as "the proportion of the variation in y about its mean that is explained by the regression model."

4.2.1 CORRELATION ANALYSIS

In Appendix B.4.3 we discuss the **covariance** and **correlation** between two random variables x and y. The correlation coefficient ρ_{xy} between x and y is defined in (B.20) as

$$\rho_{xy} = \frac{\text{cov}(x, y)}{\sqrt{\text{var}(x)}\sqrt{\text{var}(y)}} = \frac{\sigma_{xy}}{\sigma_x \sigma_y} \tag{4.13}$$

We did not discuss *estimating* the correlation coefficient. We will do so now to develop a useful relationship between the sample correlation coefficient and R^2.

Given a sample of data pairs $(x_i, y_i), i = 1, \ldots, N$, the sample correlation coefficient is obtained by replacing the covariance and standard deviations in (4.13) by their sample analogs:

$$r_{xy} = \frac{\hat{\sigma}_{xy}}{\hat{\sigma}_x \hat{\sigma}_y} \tag{4.14}$$

where

$$\hat{\sigma}_{xy} = \Sigma(x_i - \bar{x})(y_i - \bar{y})/(N-1)$$

$$\hat{\sigma}_x = \sqrt{\Sigma(x_i - \bar{x})^2/(N-1)} \tag{4.15}$$

$$\hat{\sigma}_y = \sqrt{\Sigma(y_i - \bar{y})^2/(N-1)}$$

The sample correlation coefficient r_{xy} has a value between -1 and 1, and it measures the strength of the linear association between observed values of x and y.

4.2.2 CORRELATION ANALYSIS AND R^2

There are two interesting relationships between R^2 and r_{xy} in the simple linear regression model.

1. The first is that $r_{xy}^2 = R^2$. That is, the square of the sample correlation coefficient between the sample data values x_i and y_i is algebraically equal to R^2 in a simple regression model. Intuitively this relationship makes sense: r_{xy}^2 falls between 0 and 1 and measures the strength of the linear association between x and y. This interpretation is not far from that of R^2: the proportion of variation in y about its mean explained by x in the linear regression model.

2. The second, and more important, relation is that R^2 can also be computed as the square of the sample correlation coefficient between y_i and $\hat{y}_i = b_1 + b_2 x_i$. That is, $R^2 = r_{y\hat{y}}^2$. As such it measures the linear association, or goodness-of-fit, between the sample data and their predicted values. Consequently R^2 is sometimes called a measure of "goodness-of-fit." This result is valid not only in simple regression models but also in multiple regression models that we introduce in Chapter 5. Furthermore, as you will see in Section 4.4, the concept of obtaining a goodness-of-fit measure by predicting y as well as possible and finding the squared correlation coefficient between this prediction and the sample values of y can be extended to situations in which the usual R^2 does not strictly apply.

4.2.3 THE FOOD EXPENDITURE EXAMPLE

Look at the food expenditure example in Section 2.3.2, and in particular the data scatter and fitted regression line in Figure 2.8, and the computer output Figure 2.9. Go ahead. I will wait until you get back. The question we would like to answer is "How well does our model fit the data?" To compute the R^2 we can use the sums of squares

$$SST = \Sigma(y_i - \bar{y})^2 = 495132.160$$
$$SSE = \Sigma(y_i - \hat{y}_i)^2 = \Sigma\hat{e}_i^2 = 304505.176$$

Then

$$R^2 = 1 - \frac{SSE}{SST} = 1 - \frac{304505.176}{495132.160} = 0.385$$

We conclude that 38.5% of the variation in food expenditure (about its sample mean) is explained by our regression model, which uses only income as an explanatory variable. Is this a good R^2? We would argue that such a question is not useful. While finding and reporting R^2 provides information about the relative magnitudes of the different sources of variation, debates about whether a particular R^2 is "large enough" are not particularly constructive. Microeconomic household behavior is very difficult to explain fully. With cross-sectional data R^2-values from 0.10 to 0.40 are very common even with much larger regression models. Macroeconomic analyses using time-series data, which often trend together smoothly over time, routinely report R^2-values of 0.90 and higher. You should *not* evaluate the quality of the model based only on how well it predicts the sample data used to construct the estimates. To evaluate the model it is as important to consider factors such as the signs and magnitudes of the estimates, their statistical and economic significance, the precision of their estimation, and the ability of the fitted model to predict values of the dependent variable that were not in the estimation sample. Other model diagnostic issues will be discussed in the next section.

Correlation analysis leads to the same conclusions and numbers, but it is worthwhile to consider this approach in more detail. The sample correlation between the y and x sample values is

$$r_{xy} = \frac{\hat{\sigma}_{xy}}{\hat{\sigma}_x \hat{\sigma}_y} = \frac{478.75}{(6.848)(112.675)} = 0.62$$

The correlation is positive, indicating a positive association between food expenditure and income. The sample correlation measures the strength of the linear association, with a maximum value of 1. The value $r_{xy} = 0.62$ indicates a non-negligible but less than perfect fit. As expected $r_{xy}^2 = 0.62^2 = 0.385 = R^2$.

In Figure 4.4 we plot the sample values of y_i and their corresponding fitted values $\hat{y}_i$. You can confirm that the correlation between these values is $r_{\hat{y}y} = 0.62$.

4.2.4 REPORTING THE RESULTS

In any paper where you write the results of a simple regression, with only one explanatory variable, these results can be presented quite simply. The key ingredients are the coefficient estimates, the standard errors (or t-values), an indication of statistical significance, and R^2. Also, when communicating regression results avoid using symbols like x and y. Use abbreviations for the variables that are readily interpreted, defining the variables precisely in a separate section of the report. For the food expenditure example, we might have the variable definitions:

$FOOD\_EXP$ = weekly food expenditure by a household of size 3, in dollars

$INCOME$ = weekly household income, in \$100 units

Then the estimated equation results are

$$FOOD\_EXP = 83.42 + 10.21\, INCOME \qquad R^2 = 0.385$$
$$(\text{se}) \qquad (43.41)^* \quad (2.09)^{***}$$

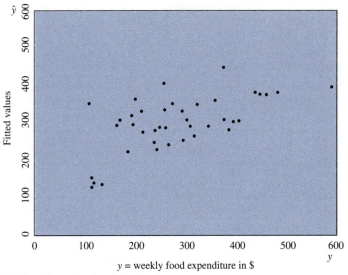

FIGURE *4.4* Plot of predicted y, $\hat{y}$, against y.

Report the standard errors below the estimated coefficients. The reason for showing the standard errors is that an approximate 95% interval estimate (if the degrees of freedom $N-2$ are greater than 30) is $b_k \pm 2 \times se$. The reader may then divide the estimate by the standard error to obtain the value of the t-statistic if desired. Furthermore, testing other hypotheses is facilitated by having the standard error present. To test the null hypothesis $H_0 : \beta_2 = 8.0$, we can quickly construct the t-statistic $t = [(10.21 - 8)/2.09)]$ and proceed with the steps of the test procedure.

Asterisks are often used to show the reader the statistically significant (that is, significantly different from zero using a two-tail test) coefficients, with explanations in a table footnote:

    * indicates significant at the 10% level

    ** indicates significant at the 5% level

  *** indicates significant at the 1% level

The asterisks are assigned by checking the p-values from the computer output, as in Figure 2.9.

4.3 Modeling Issues

4.3.1 THE EFFECTS OF SCALING THE DATA

Data we obtain are not always in a convenient form for presentation in a table or use in a regression analysis. When the *scale* of the data is not convenient, it can be altered without changing any of the real underlying relationships between variables. For example, the real personal consumption in the United States, as of the 1st quarter of 2006, was $8023.6 *billion* annually. That is, written out, $8,023,600,000,000, or 8 trillion 23 billion 600 million dollars. While we *could* use the long form of the number in a table or in a regression analysis, there is no advantage to doing so. By choosing the units of measurement to be "billions of dollars," we have taken a long number and made it comprehensible. What are the effects of scaling the variables in a regression model?

Consider the food expenditure model. In Table 2.1 we report weekly expenditures in *dollars* but we report income in $100 units, so a weekly income of $2000 is reported as $x = 20$. Why did we scale the data in this way? If we had estimated the regression using income in dollars, the results would have been

$$FOOD\_EXP = 83.42 + 0.1021\,INCOME(\$) \quad R^2 = 0.385$$
$$(\text{se}) \qquad (43.41)^* (0.0209)^{***}$$

There are two changes. First, the estimated coefficient of income is now 0.1021. The interpretation is "If weekly household income increases by $1 then we estimate that weekly food expenditure will increase by about 10 cents." There is nothing mathematically wrong with this, but it leads to a discussion of changes that are so small as to seem irrelevant. An increase in income of $100 leads to an estimated increase in food expenditure of $10.21, as before, but these magnitudes are more easily discussed.

The other change that occurs in the regression results when income is in dollars is that the standard error becomes smaller, by a factor of 100. Since the estimated coefficient is smaller by a factor of 100 also, this leaves the t-statistic and all other results unchanged.

Such a change in the units of measurement is called *scaling the data*. The choice of the scale is made by the researcher to make interpretation meaningful and convenient. The choice of the scale does not affect the measurement of the underlying relationship, but it does affect the interpretation of the coefficient estimates and some summary measures. Let us list the possibilities:

1. **Changing the scale of x:** In the linear regression model $y = \beta_1 + \beta_2 x + e$, suppose we change the units of measurement of the explanatory variable x by dividing it by a constant c. In order to keep intact the equality of the left- and right-hand sides, the coefficient of x must be multiplied by c. That is, $y = \beta_1 + \beta_2 x + e = \beta_1 + (c\beta_2)(x/c) + e = \beta_1 + \beta_2^* x^* + e$, where $\beta_2^* = c\beta_2$ and $x^* = x/c$. For example, if x is measured in dollars, and $c = 100$, then x^* is measured in hundreds of dollars. Then β_2^* measures the expected change in y given a $100 increase in x, and β_2^* is 100 times larger than β_2. When the scale of x is altered the only other change occurs in the standard error of the regression coefficient, but it changes by the same multiplicative factor as the coefficient, so that their ratio, the t-statistic, is unaffected. All other regression statistics are unchanged.

2. **Changing the scale of y:** If we change the units of measurement of y, but not x, then all the coefficients must change in order for the equation to remain valid. That is, $y/c = (\beta_1/c) + (\beta_2/c)x + (e/c)$ or $y^* = \beta_1^* + \beta_2^* x + e^*$. In this rescaled model β_2^* measures the change we expect in y^* given a 1-unit change in x. Because the error term is scaled in this process the least squares residuals will also be scaled. This will affect the standard errors of the regression coefficients, but it will not affect t-statistics or R^2.

3. If the scale of y and the scale of x are changed by the same factor, then there will be no change in the reported regression results for b_2, but the estimated intercept and residuals will change; t-statistics and R^2 are unaffected. The interpretation of the parameters is made relative to the new units of measurement.

4.3.2 CHOOSING A FUNCTIONAL FORM

In our ongoing example, we have assumed that the mean household food expenditure is a linear function of household income. That is, we assumed the underlying economic relationship to be $E(y) = \beta_1 + \beta_2 x$, which implies that there is a linear, straight-line relationship between $E(y)$ and x. Why did we do that? While the world is not "linear," a straight line is a good approximation to many nonlinear or curved relationships over narrow ranges. Also, in your principles of economics classes you may have begun with straight lines for supply, demand and consumption functions, and we wanted to ease you into the more "artistic" aspects of econometrics.

The starting point in all econometric analyses is economic theory. What does economics really say about the relation between food expenditure and income, holding all else constant? We expect there to be a positive relationship between these variables because food is a normal good. But nothing says the relationship must be a straight line. In fact, we do *not* expect that as household income rises that food expenditures will continue to rise indefinitely at the same constant rate. Instead, as income rises we expect food expenditures to rise, but we expect such expenditures to increase at a decreasing rate. This is a phrase that is used many times in economics classes. What it means graphically is that there is not a straight-line relationship between the two variables, and that it might look something like Figure 4.5.

The simple linear regression model is much more flexible than it appears at first glance. By *transforming* the variables y and x we can represent many curved, nonlinear relationships and still use the linear regression model. If you have not done so, read Appendix A.2.4 and Appendix A.4. Mark Table A.2 and Figure A.3 with paper clips so that you can find them easily.

Choosing an algebraic form for the relationship means choosing *transformations* of the original variables. This is not an easy process and it requires good analytic geometry skills and some experience. It may *not* come to you easily. The variable transformations that we begin with are

1. Power: if x is a variable then x^p means raising the variable to the power p; examples are quadratic (x^2) and cubic (x^3) transformations.

2. The natural logarithm: if x is a variable then its natural logarithm is $\ln(x)$.

3. The reciprocal: if x is a variable then its reciprocal is $1/x$.

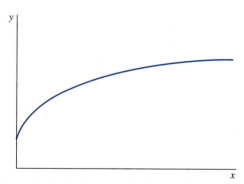

FIGURE *4.5* A nonlinear relationship between food expenditure and income.

Using just these three algebraic transformations there are amazing varieties of "shapes" that we can represent, as shown in Figure A.3.

A difficulty introduced when transforming variables is that regression result interpretations change. For each different functional form, shown in Table A.2, the expressions for both the slope and elasticity change from the linear relationship case. This is so because the variables are related nonlinearly. What this means for the practicing economist is that great attention must be given to result interpretation whenever variables are transformed. Because you may be less familiar with logarithmic transformations, let us summarize the interpretation in three possible configurations. You should read Appendix A.4.4–A.4.6 for a complete discussion of the algebra.

1. In the **log-log model** both the dependent and independent variables are transformed by the "natural" logarithm. The model is $\ln(y) = \beta_1 + \beta_2 \ln(x)$. In order to use this model both y and x must be greater than zero, because the logarithm is defined only for positive numbers. The parameter β_2 is the elasticity of y with respect to x. Referring to Figure A.3, you can see why economists use the constant elasticity, log-log model specification so frequently. In panel (c), if $\beta_2 > 1$ the relation could depict a supply curve, or if $0 < \beta_2 < 1$ a production relation. In panel (d), if $\beta_2 < 0$ it could represent a demand curve. In each case interpretation is convenient because the elasticity is constant.

2. In the **log-linear model** $\ln(y) = \beta_1 + \beta_2 x$ only the dependent variable is transformed by the logarithm. The dependent variable must be greater than zero to use this form. A convenient interpretation for the log-linear model is developed in Appendix A.4.5. A one-unit increase in x leads to (approximately) a $100 \times \beta_2\%$ change in y. The log-linear form is common; we will treat it fully in Section 4.4. For now, note its possible shapes in Figure A.3e. If $\beta_2 > 0$ the function increases at an increasing rate; its slope is larger for larger values of y. If $\beta_2 < 0$, the function decreases, but at a decreasing rate.

3. In the **linear-log model** $y = \beta_1 + \beta_2 \ln(x)$ the variable x is transformed by the natural logarithm. See Figure A.3f. The slope of this function is $\Delta y/\Delta x = \beta_2/x$ and it changes at every point. We can interpret β_2 by rewriting the slope expression as

$$\frac{\Delta y}{100(\Delta x/x)} = \frac{\beta_2}{100}$$

The term $100(\Delta x/x)$ is the *percentage change in x*. Thus in the linear-log model we can say that a 1% increase in x leads to a $\beta_2/100$ *unit* change in y. For example, suppose that we are considering a production relationship where y is output, and x is an input, such as labor. In this case the slope of the function is the "marginal product" of labor, which we expect to be positive but diminishing, as implied by the linear-log model. Let y be daily manufacturing output and x the number of hours of labor input per day. If the estimated relationship is

$\widehat{OUTPUT} = 100 + 700 \ln(LABOR)$, then we estimate that a 1% increase in labor input leads to a 7-*unit* increase in y, or a 10% increase in labor will increase daily output by 70 units.

4.3.3   THE FOOD EXPENDITURE MODEL

Suppose that, in the food expenditure model, we wish to choose a functional form that is consistent with Figure 4.5. From the array of shapes in Figure A.3 two possible choices that are similar in some aspects to Figure 4.5 are the reciprocal model and the linear-log model.

These two functional forms are different ways of modeling the data and lead to estimates of the unknown parameters that have different economic interpretations.

The reciprocal model in this case is

$$FOOD\_EXP = \beta_1 + \beta_2 \frac{1}{INCOME} + e$$

For the food expenditure model we might assume that $\beta_1 > 0$ and $\beta_2 < 0$. If this is the case, then as income increases, household consumption of food increases at a decreasing rate and reaches an upper bound β_1. This model is *linear in the parameters* but it is *nonlinear in the variables*. Even so, if the error term e satisfies our usual assumptions, then the unknown parameters can be estimated by least squares, and inferences can be made in the usual way.

Another property of the reciprocal model, ignoring the error term, is that when $INCOME < -\beta_2/\beta_1$, the model predicts expenditure on food to be negative. This property is unrealistic; it implies that this functional form is inappropriate for small values of income.

When choosing a functional form, one practical guideline is to consider how the dependent variable changes with the independent variable. In the reciprocal model the slope of the food expenditure relationship is $-\beta_2/INCOME^2$. If the parameter $\beta_2 < 0$, then there is a positive relationship between food expenditure and income, and, as income increases, this "marginal propensity to spend on food" diminishes, as economic theory predicts. Indeed, in the reciprocal model, as x becomes very large the slope approaches zero, which says that as income increases the household expenditure on food stops increasing after some point.

An alternative to the reciprocal model is the linear-log model

$$FOOD\_EXP = \beta_1 + \beta_2 \ln(INCOME) + e$$

For $\beta_2 > 0$ this function is increasing, but at a decreasing rate. As $INCOME$ increases the slope $\beta_2/INCOME$ decreases. As noted above, in this context the slope is the marginal propensity to spend on food from additional income. Similarly, the elasticity, $\beta_2/FOOD\_EXP$, becomes smaller for larger levels of food expenditure. These results are consistent with the idea that at high incomes, and large food expenditures, the effect of an increase in income on food expenditure is small.

REMARK: Given this array of models, that involve different transformations of the dependent and independent variables, and some of which have similar shapes, what are some guidelines for choosing a functional form?

1. Choose a shape that is consistent with what economic theory tells us about the relationship.
2. Choose a shape that is sufficiently flexible to "fit" the data.
3. Choose a shape so that assumptions SR1–SR6 are satisfied, ensuring that the least squares estimators have the desirable properties described in Chapters 2 and 3.

While these objectives are easily stated, the reality of model building is much more difficult. You must recognize that we **never** know the "true" functional relationship between economic variables and the functional form that we select, no matter how elegant, is only an approximation. Our job is to choose a functional form that satisfactorily meets the three objectives stated above.

4.3.4   ARE THE REGRESSION ERRORS NORMALLY DISTRIBUTED?

Recall that hypothesis tests and interval estimates for the coefficients rely on the assumption that the errors, and hence the dependent variable y, are normally distributed. While our tests and confidence intervals are valid in large samples whether the data are normally distributed or not, it is nevertheless desirable to have a model in which the regression errors are normally distributed, so that we do not have to rely on large sample approximations. If the errors are not normally distributed we might be able to improve our model by considering an alternative functional form or transforming the dependent variable. As noted in the last "Remark," when choosing a functional form, one of the criteria we might examine is whether a model specification satisfies regression assumptions, and in particular whether it leads to errors that are normally distributed (SR6). How do we check out the assumption of normally distributed errors?

We cannot observe the true random errors, so we must base our analysis of their normality on the least squares residuals, $\hat{e}_i = y_i - \hat{y}_i$. Most computer software will create a histogram of the residuals for this purpose and may also give statistics that can be used to formally test a null hypothesis that the residuals (and thus the true errors) come from a normal distribution. The relevant EViews output for the food expenditure example, using the linear relationship with no transformation of the variables, appears in Figure 4.6. What does this histogram tell us? First, notice that it is centered at zero. This is not surprising because the mean of the least squares residuals is always zero if the model contains an intercept, as shown in Appendix 4B. Second, it seems symmetrical, but there are some large gaps, and it does not really appear bell-shaped. However, just checking the shape of the histogram is not a statistical "test."

There are many tests for normality. The **Jarque–Bera test** for normality is based on two measures, skewness and kurtosis. In the present context, **skewness** refers to how symmetric the residuals are around zero. Perfectly symmetric residuals will have a skewness of zero. The skewness value for the food expenditure residuals is -0.097. **Kurtosis** refers to the "peakedness" of the distribution. For a normal distribution the kurtosis value is 3. For more on skewness and kurtosis see Appendices B.4.2 and C.4.2. From Figure 4.6, we see that the food expenditure residuals have a kurtosis of 2.99. The skewness and kurtosis values are close to the values for the normal distribution. So, the question we have to ask is

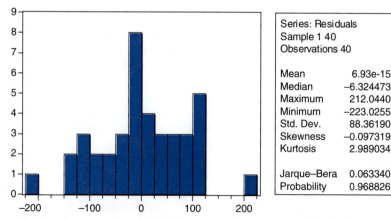

FIGURE **4.6** EViews output: residuals histogram and summary statistics for food expenditure example.

whether 2.99 is sufficiently different from 3, and -0.097 sufficiently different from zero, to conclude the residuals are not normally distributed. The Jarque–Bera statistic is given by

$$JB = \frac{N}{6}\left(S^2 + \frac{(K-3)^2}{4}\right)$$

where N is the sample size, S is skewness, and K is kurtosis. Thus, large values of the skewness, and/or values of kurtosis quite different from 3, will lead to a large value of the Jarque–Bera statistic. When the residuals are normally distributed, the Jarque–Bera statistic has a chi-squared distribution with two degrees of freedom. We reject the hypothesis of normally distributed errors if a calculated value of the statistic exceeds a critical value selected from the chi-squared distribution with 2 degrees of freedom. The 5% critical value from a χ^2-distribution with two degrees of freedom is 5.99, and the 1% critical value is 9.21.

Applying these ideas to the food expenditure example, we have

$$JB = \frac{40}{6}\left(-0.097^2 + \frac{(2.99-3)^2}{4}\right) = 0.063$$

Because $0.063 < 5.99$ there is insufficient evidence from the residuals to conclude that the normal distribution assumption is unreasonable at the 5% level of significance. The same conclusion could have been reached by examining the p-value. The p-value appears in the EViews output described as "Probability." Thus, we also fail to reject the null hypothesis on the grounds that $0.9688 > 0.05$.

4.3.5 ANOTHER EMPIRICAL EXAMPLE

How does one choose the best transformation for y and x, and hence the best functional form for describing the relationship between y and x. Unfortunately there are no hard and fast rules that will work for all situations. The best we can do is give examples and describe all the issues that are worth considering. So far, we have focused on theoretical issues, with questions like: Does a selected function possess the theoretical properties considered desirable in the economic relationship being examined? We also mentioned that we should choose a function such that the properties of the simple regression model hold. More will be said on these points as we move through the text. In this section we turn to some empirical issues related to the choice of functional form.

Figure 4.7 describes a plot of average wheat yield (in tonnes per hectare—a hectare is about 2.5 acres, and a tonne is a metric ton that is 1000 kg or 2205 lb—we are speaking Australian here!) for the Greenough Shire in Western Australia, against time. The observations are for the period 1950–1997, and time is measured using the values 1, 2, ... , 48. These data can be found in the file *wa-wheat.dat*. Notice in Figure 4.7 that wheat yield fluctuates quite a bit, but, overall, it tends to increase over time, and the increase is at an increasing rate, particularly toward the end of the time period. An increase in yield is expected because of technological improvements, such as the development of varieties of wheat that are higher yielding and more resistant to pests and diseases. Suppose that we are interested in measuring the effect of technological improvement on yield. Direct data on changes in technology are not available, but we can examine how wheat yield has changed over time as a consequence of changing technology. The equation of interest relates *YIELD* to *TIME*, where *TIME* = 1, ... , 48. One problem with the linear equation

$$YIELD_t = \beta_1 + \beta_2 TIME_t + e_t$$

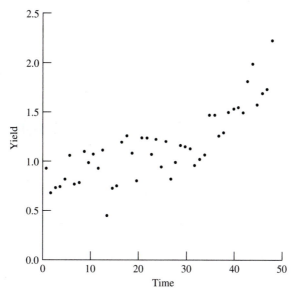

FIGURE **4.7**   Scatter plot of wheat yield over time.

is that it implies that yield increases at the same constant rate β_2, when, from Figure 4.7, we expect this rate to be increasing. The least squares fitted line (standard errors in parentheses) is

$$\widehat{YIELD}_t = 0.638 + 0.0210 \ TIME_t \qquad R^2 = 0.649$$
$$(\text{se}) \quad \cdot \quad (0.064) \ (0.0022)$$

The fitted values from this regression $\left(\widehat{YIELD}_t\right)$, along with the actual values for *YIELD*, are displayed in the upper part of Figure 4.8. The lower part of the graph displays the residuals, centered around zero. The values on the *x*-axis represent the years 1950–1997. Notice that there is a concentration of positive residuals at each end of the sample and a concentration of

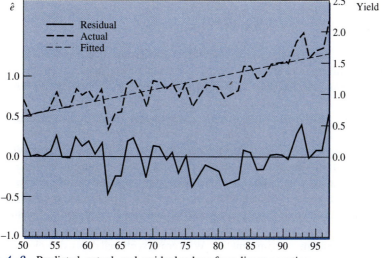

FIGURE **4.8**   Predicted, actual, and residual values from linear equation.

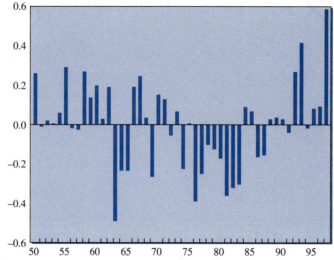

FIGURE **4.9**   Bar chart of residuals from linear equation.

negative residuals in the middle. The bar chart in Figure 4.9 makes these concentrations even more apparent. They are caused by the inability of a straight line to capture the fact that yield is increasing at an increasing rate. What alternative can we try? Two possibilities are x^2 and x^3. It turns out that x^3 provides the better fit, and so we consider instead the functional form

$$YIELD_t = \beta_1 + \beta_2 TIME_t^3 + e_t$$

The slope of the expected yield function is $3\beta_2 TIME^2$. So, providing the estimate of β_2 turns out to be positive, the function will be increasing. Furthermore, the slope is increasing as well. Thus the function itself is "increasing at an increasing rate." Before estimating the cubic equation note that the values of $TIME^3$ can get very large. This variable is a good candidate for scaling. If we define $TIMECUBE_t = TIME_t^3/1,000,000$ the estimated equation is

$$\widehat{YIELD_t} = 0.874 + 9.68\,TIMECUBE_t \qquad R^2 = 0.751$$
$$(\text{se}) \quad\;\; (0.036)\;\; (0.082)$$

The fitted, actual, and residual values from this equation appear in Figure 4.10. Notice how the predicted (fitted) values are now increasing at an increasing rate. Also, the predominance of positive residuals at the ends and negative residuals in the middle no longer exists. Furthermore, the R^2-value has increased from 0.649 to 0.751, indicating that the equation with $TIMECUBE$ fits the data better than the one with just $TIME$. Both these equations have the same dependent variable and the same number of explanatory variables (only 1). In these circumstances the R^2 can be used legitimately to compare goodness of fit. What lessons have we learned from this example? First, a plot of the original dependent variable series y against the explanatory variable x is a useful starting point for deciding on a functional form in a simple regression model. Secondly, examining a plot of the residuals is a useful device for uncovering inadequacies in any chosen functional form. Runs of positive and/or negative residuals can suggest an alternative. In this example, with time-series data, plotting the residuals against time was informative. With cross-sectional data using plots of residuals against both independent and dependent variables is recommended. Ideally we will see no

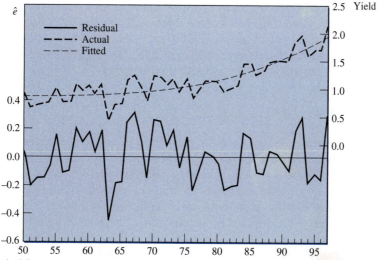

FIGURE **4.10** Fitted, actual, and residual values from equation with cubic term.

patterns, and the residual histogram and Jarque–Bera test will not rule out the assumption of normality. As we travel through the book, you will discover that patterns in the residuals can also mean many other specification inadequacies, such as omitted variables, heteroskedasticity, and autocorrelation. Thus, as you become more knowledgeable and experienced, you should be careful to consider other options. For example, wheat yield in Western Australia is heavily influenced by rainfall. Inclusion of a rainfall variable might be an option worth considering. Also, it makes sense to include *TIME* and *TIME*^{2} in addition to *TIME*-cubed. A further possibility is the constant growth rate model that we consider in the next section.

4.4 **Log-Linear Models**

Econometric models that employ natural logarithms are very common. In this section we discuss this topic further and give some examples. You should review Appendix A.2.4 where basic properties of logarithms are introduced, and Appendices A.4.4–A.4.6 and Section 4.3 where regression models involving logarithmic transformations of variables are discussed. Logarithmic transformations are often used for variables that are monetary values, such as wages, salaries, income, prices, sales, and expenditures, and in general for variables that measure the "size" of something. These variables have the characteristic that they are positive and often have distributions that are positively skewed, with a long tail to the right. Figure B.2 in Appendix B is representative of the income distribution in the United States. In fact the probability density function $f(x)$ shown is called the "log-normal," because $\ln(x)$ has a normal distribution. Because the transformation $\ln(x)$ has the effect of making larger values of x less extreme, $\ln(x)$ will often be closer to a normal distribution for variables of this kind. The log-normal distribution is discussed in Appendix 4C.

The basic interpretation of β_2 in the log-linear model $\ln(y) = \beta_1 + \beta_2 x$ is discussed in Appendix A.4, with the slope and elasticity given in Table A.2. The slope for this functional form is $\beta_2 y$. Since $y > 0$, the slope is increasing as y increases if $\beta_2 > 0$, so that the relationship between y and x is said to be "increasing at an increasing rate." To make a discussion relevant in a specific context the slope can be evaluated at the sample mean $\bar{y}$, or another interesting value. The elasticity of y with respect to x is $\beta_2 x$, and for specificity we might compute this value at the mean of the x-values, $\bar{x}$, or some other value.

An easier interpretation can be obtained by using the properties of logarithms. See equation (A.13) and the discussion surrounding it. In the log-linear model, a one-unit increase in x leads, approximately, to a $100\beta_2\%$ change in y.

4.4.1 A GROWTH MODEL

Earlier in this chapter, in Section 4.3.5, we considered an empirical example in which the production of wheat was tracked over time, with improvements in technology leading to wheat production increasing at an increasing rate. Another way to represent such a relationship is using a log-linear model. To see how, suppose that due to advances in technology the yield of wheat produced (tonnes per hectare) is growing at approximately a constant rate per year. Specifically, suppose that the yield in year t is $YIELD_t = (1+g)YIELD_{t-1}$, with g being the fixed growth rate in 1 year. By substituting repeatedly we obtain $YIELD_t = YIELD_0(1+g)^t$. Here $YIELD_0$ is the yield in year "0," the year before the sample begins, so it is probably unknown. Taking logarithms we obtain

$$\ln(YIELD_t) = \ln(YIELD_0) + [\ln(1+g)] \times t$$
$$= \beta_1 + \beta_2 t$$

This is simply a log-linear model with dependent variable $\ln(YIELD_t)$ and explanatory variable t, or time. We expect growth to be positive, so that $\beta_2 > 0$, in which case the plot of $YIELD$ against time looks like the upward sloping curve in Appendix A, Figure A.3, which closely resembles the scatter diagram in Figure 4.7.

Estimating the log-linear model for yield we obtain

$$\widehat{\ln(YIELD_t)} = -0.3434 + 0.0178t$$
$$\text{(se)} \quad\quad (0.0584) \quad (0.0021)$$

The estimated coefficient $b_2 = \widehat{\ln(1+g)} = 0.0178$. Using the property that $\ln(1+x) \cong x$ if x is small [see Appendix A, equation (A.11) and the discussion following it], we estimate that the growth rate in wheat yield is approximately $\hat{g} = 0.0178$, or about 1.78% per year, over the period of the data.

4.4.2 A WAGE EQUATION

The relationship between wages and education is a key relationship in labor economics (and no doubt in your mind). Suppose that the rate of return to an extra year of education is a constant r. That is, in the first year after an additional year of education your wage rate rises from an initial value $WAGE_0$ to $WAGE_1 = (1+r)WAGE_0$. For an extra 2 years of education this becomes $WAGE_2 = (1+r)^2 WAGE_0$, and so on. Taking logarithms we have a relationship between $\ln(WAGE)$ and years of education ($EDUC$)

$$\ln(WAGE) = \ln(WAGE_0) + [\ln(1+r)] \times EDUC$$
$$= \beta_1 + \beta_2 EDUC$$

An additional year of education leads to an approximate $100\beta_2\%$ increase in wages.

Data on hourly wages, years of education and other variables are in the file *cps_small.dat*. These data consist of 1000 observations from the 1997 Current Population Survey (CPS). The CPS is a monthly survey of about 50,000 households conducted in the United States by the Bureau of the Census for the Bureau of Labor Statistics. The survey has been conducted for more than 50 years. Using this data the estimated log-linear model is

$$\widehat{\ln(WAGE)} = 0.7884 + 0.1038 \times EDUC$$
$$\text{(se)} \qquad (0.0849) \ (0.0063)$$

We estimate that an additional year of education increases the wage rate by approximately 10.4%. A 95% interval estimate for the value of an additional year of education is 9.1% to 11.6%.

4.4.3 PREDICTION IN THE LOG-LINEAR MODEL

You may have noticed that when reporting regression results in this section we did not include an R^2-value. In a log-linear regression the R^2-value automatically reported by statistical software is the percent of the variation in $\ln(y)$ explained by the model. However, our objective is to explain the variations in y, not $\ln(y)$. Furthermore, the fitted regression line predicts $\widehat{\ln(y)} = b_1 + b_2 x$, whereas we want to predict y. The problems of obtaining a useful measure of goodness-of-fit and prediction are connected, as we discussed in Section 4.2.2.

How shall we obtain the predicted value of y? A first inclination might be to take the antilog of $\widehat{\ln(y)} = b_1 + b_2 x$. For the natural logarithm the antilog is the exponential function, so that a natural choice for prediction is

$$\hat{y}_n = \exp(\widehat{\ln(y)}) = \exp(b_1 + b_2 x)$$

In the log-linear model this is not necessarily the best we can do. Using properties of the log-normal distribution it can be shown (see Appendix 4C) that an alternative predictor is

$$\hat{y}_c = \widehat{E(y)} = \exp(b_1 + b_2 x + \hat{\sigma}^2/2) = \hat{y}_n e^{\hat{\sigma}^2/2}$$

If the sample size is large, the "corrected" predictor $\hat{y}_c$ is, on average, closer to the actual value of y and should be used. In small samples (less than 30) the "natural" predictor may actually be a better choice. The reason for this incongruous result is that the estimated value of the error variance $\hat{\sigma}^2$ adds a certain amount of "noise" when using $\hat{y}_c$, leading it to have increased variability relative to $\hat{y}_n$ that can outweigh the benefit of the correction in small samples.

The effect of the correction can be illustrated using the wage equation. What would we predict the wage to be for a worker with 12 years of education? The predicted value of $\ln(WAGE)$ is

$$\widehat{\ln(WAGE)} = 0.7884 + 0.1038 \times EDUC = 0.7884 + 0.1038 \times 12 = 2.0335$$

Then the value of the natural predictor is $\hat{y}_n = \exp(\widehat{\ln(y)}) = \exp(2.0335) = 7.6408$. The value of the corrected predictor, using $\hat{\sigma}^2 = 0.2402$ from the regression output, is

$$\hat{y}_c = \widehat{E(y)} = \hat{y}_n e^{\hat{\sigma}^2/2} = 7.6408 \times 1.1276 = 8.6161$$

We predict that the wage for a worker with 12 years of education will be $7.64 per hour if we use the natural predictor, and $8.62 if we use the corrected predictor. In this case the sample is large ($N = 1000$) so we would use the corrected predictor. Among the 1000 workers there are 379 with 12 years of education. Their average wage is $8.30, so the corrected predictor is consistent with the sample of data.

How does the correction affect our prediction? Recall that $\hat{\sigma}^2$ must be greater than zero and $e^0 = 1$. Therefore the effect of the correction is always to increase the value of the prediction because $e^{\hat{\sigma}^2/2}$ is always greater than 1. The natural predictor tends to systematically under-predict the value of y in a log-linear model, and the correction offsets the downward bias in large samples.

4.4.4   A GENERALIZED R^2 MEASURE

It is a general rule that the squared simple correlation between y and its fitted value $\hat{y}$, where $\hat{y}$ is the "best" prediction one can obtain, is a valid measure of goodness-of-fit that we can use as an R^2 in many contexts. As we have seen, what we may consider the "best" predictor can change depending upon the model under consideration. That is, a general goodness-of-fit measure, or general R^2 is

$$R_g^2 = [\text{corr}(y, \hat{y})]^2 = r_{y\hat{y}}^2$$

In the wage equation $R_g^2 = [\text{corr}(y, \hat{y}_c)]^2 = 0.4739^2 = 0.2246$, as compared to the reported $R^2 = 0.2146$ from the regression of $\ln(WAGE)$ on $EDUC$. (In this case since the corrected and natural predictors differ only by a constant factor, the correlation is the same for both.) These R^2-values are small, but we repeat our earlier message: R^2-values tend to be small with microeconomic, cross-sectional data, because the variations in individual behavior are difficult to fully explain.

4.4.5   PREDICTION INTERVALS IN THE LOG-LINEAR MODEL

We have a corrected predictor $\hat{y}_c$ for y in the log-linear model. It is the "point" predictor, or point forecast, that is relevant if we seek the single number that is our best prediction of y. If we prefer a prediction or forecast interval for y, then we must rely on the natural predictor $\hat{y}_n$.[1] Specifically we follow the procedure outlined in Section 4.1, and then take antilogs. That is, compute $\widehat{\ln(y)} = b_1 + b_2 x$ and then $\widehat{\ln(y)} \pm t_c \text{se}(f)$, where the critical value t_c is the $100(1-\alpha/2)$-percentile from the t-distribution and $\text{se}(f)$ is given in (4.5). Then a $100(1-\alpha)\%$ prediction interval for y is

$$\left[\exp\left(\widehat{\ln(y)} - t_c \text{se}(f) \right), \exp\left(\widehat{\ln(y)} + t_c \text{se}(f) \right) \right]$$

For the wage data, a 95% prediction interval for the wage of a worker with 12 years of education is

$$[\exp(2.0335 - 1.96 \times 0.4905), \exp(2.0335 + 1.96 \times 0.4905)] = [2.9184, 20.0046]$$

---

[1] See Appendix 4A. The corrected predictor includes the estimated error variance, making the t-distribution no longer relevant in (4A.1).

The interval prediction is $2.92–$20.00, which is so wide that it is basically useless. What does this tell us? Nothing we did not already know. Our model is not an accurate predictor of individual behavior in this case. In later chapters we will see if we can improve this model by adding additional explanatory variables, such as experience, that should be relevant.

4.5 Exercises

Answer to exercises marked * appear in Appendix D at the end of the book.

4.5.1 PROBLEMS

4.1* (a) Suppose that a simple regression has quantities $\sum(y_i - \bar{y})^2 = 631.63$ and $\sum \hat{e}_i^2 = 182.85$, find R^2.
 (b) Suppose that a simple regression has quantities $N = 20$, $\sum y_i^2 = 5930.94$, $\bar{y} = 16.035$, and $SSR = 666.72$, find R^2.
 (c) Suppose that a simple regression has quantities $R^2 = 0.7911$, $SST = 552.36$, and $N = 20$, find $\hat{\sigma}^2$.

4.2* Consider the following estimated regression equation (standard errors in parentheses):

$$\hat{y} = 5.83 + 0.869x \quad R^2 = 0.756$$
$$(se) \ (1.23) \ (0.117)$$

 Rewrite the estimated equation that would result if
 (a) All values of x were divided by 10 before estimation.
 (b) All values of y were divided by 10 before estimation.
 (c) All values of y and x were divided by 10 before estimation.

4.3 Using the data in Exercise 2.1 and only a calculator (show your work) compute
 (a) the predicted value of y for $x_0 = 5$.
 (b) the $se(f)$ corresponding to part (a).
 (c) a 95% prediction interval for y given $x_0 = 5$.
 (d) a 99% prediction interval for y given $x_0 = 5$.
 (e) a 95% prediction interval for y given $x = \bar{x}$. Compare the width of this interval to the one computed in part (c).

4.4 Given the simple linear model $y = \beta_1 + \beta_2 x + e$, and the least squares estimators, we can estimate $E(y)$ for any value of $x = x_0$ as $\widehat{E(y_0)} = b_1 + b_2 x_0$.
 (a) Describe the difference between predicting y_0 and estimating $E(y_0)$.
 (b) Find the expected value and variance of $\widehat{E(y_0)} = b_1 + b_2 x_0$.
 (c) When discussing the unbiasedness of the least squares predictor we showed that $E(f) = E(y_0 - \hat{y}_0) = 0$, where f is the forecast error. Why did we define unbiasedness in this strange way? What is wrong with saying, as we have in other unbiasedness demonstrations, that $E(\hat{y}_0) = y_0$?

4.5 Suppose you are estimating a simple linear regression model.
 (a) If you multiply all the x values by 10, but not the y values, what happens to the parameter values β_1 and β_2? What happens to the least squares estimates b_1 and b_2? What happens to the variance of the error term?
 (b) Suppose you are estimating a simple linear regression model. If you multiply all the y values by 10, but not the x values, what happens to the parameter values β_1

and β_2? What happens to the least squares estimates b_1 and b_2? What happens to the variance of the error term?

4.6   The fitted least squares line is $\hat{y}_i = b_1 + b_2 x_i$.

(a) Algebraically, show that the fitted line passes through the point of the means, $(\bar{x}, \bar{y})$.

(b) Algebraically show that the average value of $\hat{y}_i$ equals the sample average of y. That is, show that $\bar{\hat{y}} = \bar{y}$, where $\bar{\hat{y}} = \Sigma \hat{y}_i / N$.

4.7   In a simple linear regression model suppose we know that the intercept parameter is zero, so the model is $y_i = \beta_2 x_i + e_i$. The least squares estimator of β_2 is developed in Exercise 2.4.

(a) What is the least squares predictor of y in this case?

(b) When an intercept is not present in a model, R^2 is often defined to be $R_u^2 = 1 - SSE / \Sigma y_i^2$, where SSE is the usual sum of squared residuals. Compute R_u^2 for the data in Exercise 2.4.

(c) Compare the value of R_u^2 in part (b) to the generalized $R^2 = r_{y\hat{y}}^2$, where $\hat{y}$ is the predictor based on the restricted model in part (a).

(d) Compute $SST = \Sigma (y_i - \bar{y})^2$ and $SSR = \Sigma (\hat{y}_i - \bar{y})^2$, where $\hat{y}$ is the predictor based on the restricted model in part (a). Does the sum of squares decomposition $SST = SSR + SSE$ hold in this case?

4.5.2   COMPUTER EXERCISES

4.8   The first three columns in the file *wa-wheat.dat* contain observations on wheat yield in the Western Australian shires Northampton, Chapman Valley, and Mullewa, respectively. There are 48 annual observations for the years 1950–1997. For the Chapman Valley shire, consider the three equations

$$y_t = \beta_0 + \beta_1 t + e_t$$
$$y_t = \alpha_0 + \alpha_1 \ln(t) + e_t$$
$$y_t = \gamma_0 + \gamma_1 t^2 + e_t$$

(a) Estimate each of the three equations.

(b) Taking into consideration (i) plots of the fitted equations, (ii) plots of the residuals, (iii) error normality tests, and (iv) values for R^2, which equation do you think is preferable? Explain.

4.9*   For each of the three functions in Exercise 4.8

(a) Find the predicted value for yield when $t = 49$.

(b) Find estimates of the slopes dy_t / dt at the point $t = 49$.

(c) Find estimates of the elasticities $(dy_t / dt)(t / y_t)$ at the point $t = 49$.

(d) Comment on the estimates you obtained in parts (b) and (c). What is their importance?

4.10   The file *london.dat* is a cross section of 1519 households drawn from the 1980–1982 British Family Expenditure Surveys. Data have been selected to include only households with one or two children living in Greater London. Self-employed and retired households have been excluded. Variable definitions are in the file *london.def*. The budget share of a commodity, say food, is defined as

$$WFOOD = \frac{\text{expenditure on food}}{\text{total expenditure}}$$

A functional form that has been popular for estimating expenditure functions for commodities is

$$WFOOD = \beta_1 + \beta_2 \ln(TOTEXP) + e$$

(a) Estimate this function for households with one child and households with two children. Report and comment on the results. (You may find it more convenient to use the files *lon1.dat* and *lon2.dat* that contain the data for the one and two children households, with 594 and 925 observations, respectively.)

(b) It can be shown that the expenditure elasticity for food is given by

$$\varepsilon = \frac{\beta_1 + \beta_2[\ln(TOTEXP) + 1]}{\beta_1 + \beta_2\ln(TOTEXP)}$$

Find estimates of this elasticity for one and two children households, evaluated at average total expenditure in each case. Do these estimates suggest food is a luxury or a necessity? (*Hint*: Are the elasticities greater than 1 or less than 1?)

(c) Analyze the residuals from each estimated function. Does the functional form seem appropriate? Is it reasonable to assume the errors are normally distributed?

4.11* Reconsider the presidential voting data (*fair.dat*) introduced in Exercises 2.14 and 3.9.

(a) Using all the data from 1880 to 2000, estimate the regression model $VOTE = \beta_1 + \beta_2 GROWTH + e$. Based on these estimates, what is the predicted value of *VOTE* in 2000? What is the least squares residual for the 2000 election observation?

(b) Estimate the regression in (a) using only data up to 1996 (observations 1–30). Predict the value of *VOTE* in 2000 using the actual value of *GROWTH* for 2000, which was 1.603%. What is the prediction error in this forecast? Is it larger or smaller than the error computed in part (b).

(c) Using the regression results from (b), construct a 95% interval estimate for the 2000 value of *VOTE* using the actual value of $GROWTH = 1.603\%$.

(d) Using the estimation results in (b), what value of *GROWTH* would have led to a prediction that the nonincumbent party (Democrats) would have won 50.1% of the vote?

4.12 Consider the housing starts data (*house_starts.dat*) introduced in Exercises 2.13 and 3.8. The data extend to April 2005.

(a) The fixed interest rates for May and June 2005 were 6.00% and 5.82%, respectively. Predict the number of housing starts in May and June 2005.

(b) The actual number of housing starts in May and June 2005 were 2041 and 2065 (thousands), respectively. (*Source*: Economagic.com.) How large were your prediction errors?

(c) Construct 95% prediction intervals for the number of housing starts in May and June 2005, based on the sample data. Did your intervals contain the true values?

4.13* The file *stockton2.dat* contains data on 880 houses sold in Stockton, CA, during mid-2005. Variable descriptions are in the file *stockton2.def*. These data were considered in Exercises 2.12 and 3.11.

(a) Estimate the log-linear model $\ln(PRICE) = \beta_1 + \beta_2 SQFT + e$. Interpret the estimated model parameters. Calculate the slope and elasticity at the sample means, if necessary.

(b) Estimate the log-log model $\ln(PRICE) = \beta_1 + \beta_2 \ln(SQFT) + e$. Interpret the estimated parameters. Calculate the slope and elasticity at the sample means, if necessary.

(c) Compare the R^2-value from the linear model $PRICE = \beta_1 + \beta_2 SQFT + e$ to the "generalized" R^2 measure for the models in (b) and (c).

(d) Construct histograms of the least squares residuals from each of the models in (a), (b), and (c) and obtain the Jarque–Bera statistics. Based on your observations, do you consider the distributions of the residuals to be compatible with an assumption of normality?

(e) For each of the models (a)–(c) plot the least squares residuals against $SQFT$. Do you observe any patterns?

(f) For each model in (a)–(c), predict the value of a house with 2700 square feet.

(g) For each model in (a)–(c), construct a 95% prediction interval for the value of a house with 2700 square feet.

(h) Based on your work in this problem, discuss the choice of functional form. Which functional form would you use? Explain.

4.14   How much does education affect wage rates? This question will explore the issue further. The data file *cps_small.dat* contains 1000 observations on hourly wage rates, education, and other variables from the 1997 Current Population Survey (CPS).

(a) Construct histograms of the *WAGE* variable and its logarithm, $\ln(WAGE)$. Which appears more normally distributed?

(b) Estimate the linear regression $WAGE = \beta_1 + \beta_2 EDUC + e$ and log-linear regression $\ln(WAGE) = \beta_1 + \beta_2 EDUC + e$. What is the estimated return to education in each model? That is, for an additional year of education, what percentage increase in wages can the average worker expect?

(c) Construct histograms of the residuals from the linear and log-linear models in (b), and the Jarque–Bera test for normality. Does one set of residuals appear more compatible with normality than the other?

(d) Compare the R^2 of the linear model to the "generalized" R^2 for the log-linear model. Which model fits the data better?

(e) Plot the least squares residuals from each model against *EDUC*. Do you observe any patterns?

(f) Using each model, predict the wage of a worker with 16 years of education. Compare these predictions to the actual average wage of all workers in the sample with 16 years of education.

(g) Based on the results in parts (a)–(f), which functional form would you use? Explain.

4.15   Does the return to education differ by race and gender? For this exercise use the file *cps.dat*. (This is a large file with 4733 observations. If your software is a student version, you can use the smaller file *cps_small.dat*.) In this exercise you will extract subsamples of observations consisting of (i) all males, (ii) all females, (iii) all whites, (iv) all blacks, (v) white males, (vi) white females, (vii) black males, and (viii) black females.

(a) For each sample partition, obtain the summary statistics of *WAGE*.

(b) A variable's *coefficient of variation* is 100 times the ratio of its sample standard deviation to its sample mean. For a variable y it is

$$CV = 100 \times \frac{\hat{\sigma}_y}{\bar{y}}$$

It is a measure of variation that takes into account the size of the variable. What is the coefficient of variation for *WAGE* within each sample partition?

(c) For each sample partition estimate the log-linear model

$$\ln(WAGE) = \beta_1 + \beta_2 EDUC + e$$

What is the approximate percentage return to another year of education for each group?

(d) Does the model fit the data equally well for each sample partition?

(e) For each sample partition, test the null hypothesis that the rate of return to education is 10% against the alternative that it is not, using a two-tail test at the 5% level of significance.

4.16 The November 2000 U.S. Presidential Election was won by George Bush over Al Gore. In Florida, especially Palm Beach county, voting irregularities were claimed. In the file *florida.dat* are county voting data for candidates Bush, Gore, and two minor candidates, Pat Buchanan and Ralph Nader.

(a) Estimate a simple regression using as a dependent variable the votes for Buchanan and as the explanatory variable the votes for Bush. Use the data on the 66 counties excluding Palm Beach. Interpret the model R^2. How well does the model explain the Buchanan vote?

(b) Predict the Buchanan vote for Palm Beach county and construct a 99.9% prediction interval. Is the actual vote for Buchanan within the prediction interval?

(c) Plot a scatter diagram of the actual Buchanan vote (vertical axis) against the predicted Buchanan vote (horizontal axis) using data on all 67 observations.

(d) Repeat parts (a)–(c) based on a regression using as dependent variable the votes for Buchanan and as explanatory variable the votes for Gore.

(e) To control for total county population, create variables that are the shares of votes by county. That is, Buchanan's share of the vote is Buchanan's county vote divided by the total number of votes cast in the county. Estimate the simple regression of Buchanan's share on Bush's share using data on the 66 counties excluding Palm Beach. Construct a 99.9% prediction interval for Buchanan's share of the vote in Palm Beach county. Multiply the endpoints of the prediction interval by the total votes cast in Palm Beach county to determine a prediction interval for Buchanan's vote. Where does Buchanan's actual vote in Palm Beach county fall relative to this interval?

Appendix 4A Development of a Prediction Interval

The forecast error is $f = y_0 - \hat{y}_0 = (\beta_1 + \beta_2 x_0 + e_0) - (b_1 + b_2 x_0)$. To obtain its variance let us first obtain the variance of $\hat{y}_0 = b_1 + b_2 x_0$. The variances and covariance of the least squares estimators are given in Section 2.4.4. Using them, we obtain

$$\text{var}(\hat{y}_0) = \text{var}(b_1 + b_2 x_0) = \text{var}(b_1) + x_0^2 \text{var}(b_2) + 2x_0 \text{cov}(b_1, b_2)$$

$$= \frac{\sigma^2 \sum x_i^2}{N \sum (x_i - \bar{x})^2} + x_0^2 \frac{\sigma^2}{\sum (x_i - \bar{x})^2} + 2x_0 \sigma^2 \frac{-\bar{x}}{\sum (x_i - \bar{x})^2}$$

Now we use a trick. Add the term $\sigma^2 N\bar{x}^2 / N\Sigma(x_i - \bar{x})^2$ after the first term (inside braces below) and subtract the same term at the end. Then combine the terms in brackets, as shown below:

$$
\begin{aligned}
\text{var}(\hat{y}_0) &= \left[\frac{\sigma^2 \Sigma x_i^2}{N\Sigma(x_i - \bar{x})^2} - \left\{ \frac{\sigma^2 N\bar{x}^2}{N\Sigma(x_i - \bar{x})^2} \right\} \right] \\
&\quad + \left[\frac{\sigma^2 x_0^2}{\Sigma(x_i - \bar{x})^2} + \frac{\sigma^2 (-2x_0\bar{x})}{\Sigma(x_i - \bar{x})^2} + \left\{ \frac{\sigma^2 N\bar{x}^2}{N\Sigma(x_i - \bar{x})^2} \right\} \right] \\
&= \sigma^2 \left[\frac{\Sigma x_i^2 - N\bar{x}^2}{N\Sigma(x_i - \bar{x})^2} + \frac{x_0^2 - 2x_0\bar{x} + \bar{x}^2}{\Sigma(x_i - \bar{x})^2} \right] \\
&= \sigma^2 \left[\frac{\Sigma(x_i - \bar{x})^2}{N\Sigma(x_i - \bar{x})^2} + \frac{(x_0 - \bar{x})^2}{\Sigma(x_i - \bar{x})^2} \right] \\
&= \sigma^2 \left[\frac{1}{N} + \frac{(x_0 - \bar{x})^2}{\Sigma(x_i - \bar{x})^2} \right]
\end{aligned}
$$

Taking into account that x_0 and the unknown parameters β_1 and β_2 are not random, you should be able to show that $\text{var}(f) = \text{var}(\hat{y}_0) + \text{var}(e_0) = \text{var}(\hat{y}_0) + \sigma^2$. A little factoring gives the result in (4.4).

We can construct a standard normal random variable as

$$
\frac{f}{\sqrt{\text{var}(f)}} \sim N(0, 1)
$$

If the forecast error variance in (4.4) is estimated by replacing σ^2 by its estimator $\hat{\sigma}^2$,

$$
\widehat{\text{var}(f)} = \hat{\sigma}^2 \left[1 + \frac{1}{N} + \frac{(x_0 - \bar{x})^2}{\Sigma(x_i - \bar{x})^2} \right]
$$

then

$$
\frac{f}{\sqrt{\widehat{\text{var}(f)}}} = \frac{y_0 - \hat{y}_0}{\text{se}(f)} \sim t_{(N-2)} \tag{4A.1}
$$

where the square root of the estimated variance is the standard error of the forecast given in (4.5)

Using these results we can construct an interval prediction procedure for y_0 just as we constructed confidence intervals for the parameters β_k. If t_c is a critical value from the $t_{(N-2)}$-distribution such that $P(t \ge t_c) = \alpha/2$, then

$$
P(-t_c \le t \le t_c) = 1 - \alpha \tag{4A.2}
$$

Substitute the t-random variable from (4A.1) into (4A.2) to obtain

$$
P\left[-t_c \le \frac{y_0 - \hat{y}_0}{\text{se}(f)} \le t_c \right] = 1 - \alpha
$$

Simplify this expression to obtain

$$P[\hat{y}_0 - t_c \text{se}(f) \leq y_0 \leq \hat{y}_0 + t_c \text{se}(f)] = 1 - \alpha$$

A $100(1-\alpha)\%$ confidence interval, or prediction interval, for y_0 is given by (4.6).

Appendix 4B The Sum of Squares Decomposition

To obtain the sum of squares decomposition in (4.11), we square both sides of (4.10)

$$(y_i - \bar{y})^2 = [(\hat{y}_i - \bar{y}) + \hat{e}_i]^2 = (\hat{y}_i - \bar{y})^2 + \hat{e}_i^2 + 2(\hat{y}_i - \bar{y})\hat{e}_i$$

Then sum

$$\Sigma(y_i - \bar{y})^2 = \Sigma(\hat{y}_i - \bar{y})^2 + \Sigma\hat{e}_i^2 + 2\Sigma(\hat{y}_i - \bar{y})\hat{e}_i$$

Expanding the last term we obtain

$$\Sigma(\hat{y}_i - \bar{y})\hat{e}_i = \Sigma\hat{y}_i\hat{e}_i - \bar{y}\Sigma\hat{e}_i = \Sigma(b_1 + b_2x_i)\hat{e}_i - \bar{y}\Sigma\hat{e}_i$$
$$= b_1\Sigma\hat{e}_i + b_2\Sigma x_i\hat{e}_i - \bar{y}\Sigma\hat{e}_i$$

Consider first the term $\Sigma\hat{e}_i$

$$\Sigma\hat{e}_i = \Sigma(y_i - b_1 - b_2x_i) = \Sigma y_i - Nb_1 - b_2\Sigma x_i = 0$$

This last expression is zero because of the first normal equation, (2A.3). The first normal equation is valid *only if the model contains an intercept*. The sum of the least squares residuals is always zero *if* the model contains an intercept. It follows then that the *sample mean* of the least squares residuals is also zero (since it is the sum of the residuals divided by the sample size) if the model contains an intercept. That is, $\bar{\hat{e}} = \Sigma\hat{e}_i/N = 0$.

The next term $\Sigma x_i\hat{e}_i = 0$ because

$$\Sigma x_i\hat{e}_i = \Sigma x_i(y_i - b_1 - b_2x_i) = \Sigma x_iy_i - b_1\Sigma x_i - b_2\Sigma x_i^2 = 0$$

This result follows from the second normal equation, (2A.4). This result always holds for the least squares estimator and does not depend on the model having an intercept. See Appendix 2A for discussion of the normal equations. Substituting $\Sigma\hat{e}_i = 0$ and $\Sigma x_i\hat{e}_i = 0$ back into the original equation, we obtain $\Sigma(\hat{y}_i - \bar{y})\hat{e}_i = 0$.

Thus if the model contains an intercept it is guaranteed that $SST = SSR + SSE$. If, however, the model does not contain an intercept, then $\Sigma\hat{e}_i \neq 0$ and $SST \neq SSR + SSE$.

Appendix 4C The Log-Normal Distribution

Suppose that the variable y has a normal distribution, with mean μ and variance σ^2. By now you are familiar with this bell-shaped distribution. If we consider $w = e^y$, then $y = \ln(w) \sim N(\mu, \sigma^2)$ and w is said to have a **log-normal** distribution. The question then is, what are the mean and variance of w? Recall that the "expected value of a sum is the sum of the expected values." But, unfortunately, the exponential function is nonlinear, and the expected value of nonlinear function of y is *not* just the same function of $E(y)$. That is, if $g(y)$ is some function of y, then in general $E[g(y)] \neq g[E(y)]$. So the expectation $E(w) = E(e^y) \neq e^{E(y)}$. Happily the expected value and variance of w have been worked out and are

$$E(w) = e^{\mu + \sigma^2/2}$$

and

$$\text{var}(w) = e^{2\mu + \sigma^2}\left(e^{\sigma^2} - 1\right)$$

These results relate to the log-linear regression model in several ways. First, given the log-linear model $\ln(y) = \beta_1 + \beta_2 x + e$, if we assume that $e \sim N(0, \sigma^2)$, then

$$E(y_i) = E\left(e^{\beta_1 + \beta_2 x_i + e_i}\right) = E\left(e^{\beta_1 + \beta_2 x_i} e^{e_i}\right) = e^{\beta_1 + \beta_2 x_i} E(e^{e_i}) = e^{\beta_1 + \beta_2 x_i} e^{\sigma^2/2} = e^{\beta_1 + \beta_2 x_i + \sigma^2/2}$$

Consequently, if we want to predict $E(y)$ we should use

$$\widehat{E(y_i)} = e^{b_1 + b_2 x_i + \hat{\sigma}^2/2}$$

where b_1, b_2, and $\hat{\sigma}^2$ are from the log-linear regression.

The second implication comes from the growth and wage equations discussed in Section 4.4. For example, in the wage equation we estimated $\beta_2 = \ln(1 + r)$. Solving for r we obtain $r = e^{\beta_2} - 1$. If assumption SR6 holds, then the least squares estimator is normally distributed $b_2 \sim N\left(\beta_2, \text{var}(b_2) = \sigma^2/\sum(x_i - \bar{x})^2\right)$. Then

$$E[e^{b_2}] = e^{\beta_2 + \text{var}(b_2)/2}$$

Therefore, an estimator of the rate of return r is

$$\hat{r} = e^{b_2 + \widehat{\text{var}(b_2)}/2} - 1$$

where $\widehat{\text{var}(b_2)} = \hat{\sigma}^2/\sum(x_i - \bar{x})^2$.

Chapter 5

The Multiple Regression Model

Learning Objectives

Based on the material in this chapter, you should be able to

1. Recognize a multiple regression model and be able to interpret the coefficients in that model.

2. Understand and explain the meanings of the assumptions for the multiple regression model.

3. Use your computer to find least squares estimates of the coefficients in a multiple regression model. Interpret those estimates.

4. Explain the meaning of the Gauss–Markov theorem.

5. Use your computer to obtain variance and covariance estimates, and standard errors, for the estimated coefficients in a multiple regression model.

6. Explain the circumstances under which coefficient variances (and standard errors) are likely to be relatively high, and relatively low.

7. Find interval estimates for single coefficients. Interpret the interval estimates.

8. Test hypotheses about single coefficients in a multiple regression model. In particular
   (a) What is the difference between a one-tail and a two-tail test?
   (b) How do you compute the p-value for a one-tail test, and for a two-tail test?
   (c) What is meant by "testing the significance of a coefficient"?
   (d) What is the meaning of the t-values and p-values that appear in your computer output?

9. Compute and explain the meaning of R^2 in a multiple regression model.

Keywords

BLU estimator	interval estimate	regression coefficients
covariance matrix of	least squares estimates	standard errors
least squares estimator	least squares estimation	sum of squared errors
critical value	least squares estimators	sum of squares of regression
error variance estimate	multiple regression model	testing significance
error variance estimator	one-tail test	total sum of squares
goodness-of-fit	p-value	two-tail test

The model in Chapters 2–4 is called a simple regression model because the dependent variable y is related to only *one* explanatory variable x. While this model is useful for a range of situations, in most economic models there are two or more explanatory variables that influence the dependent variable y. For example, in a demand equation the quantity demanded of a commodity depends on the price of that commodity, the prices of substitute and complementary goods, and income. Output in a production function will be a function of more than one input. Aggregate money demand will be a function of aggregate income and the interest rate. Investment will depend on the interest rate and changes in income.

When we turn an economic model with more than one explanatory variable into its corresponding econometric model, we refer to it as a **multiple regression model**. Most of the results we developed for the simple regression model in Chapters 2–4 can be extended naturally to this general case. There are slight changes in the interpretation of the β parameters, the degrees of freedom for the t-distribution will change, and we will need to modify the assumption concerning the characteristics of the explanatory (x) variables. These and other consequences of extending the simple regression model to a multiple regression model are described in this chapter.

As an example for introducing and analyzing the multiple regression model, we consider a model used to explain sales revenue for a fast-food hamburger chain with outlets in small U.S. cities.

5.1 Introduction

5.1.1   THE ECONOMIC MODEL

We will set up an economic model for a hamburger chain that we call Big Andy's Burger Barn.[1] Important decisions made by the management of Big Andy's are its pricing policy for different products and how much to spend on advertising. To assess the effect of different price structures and different levels of advertising expenditure, Big Andy's Burger Barn sets different prices and spends varying amounts on advertising in different cities. Of particular interest to management is how sales revenue changes as the level of advertising expenditure changes. Does an increase in advertising expenditure lead to an increase in sales? If so, is the increase in sales sufficient to justify the increased advertising expenditure? Management is also interested in pricing strategy. Will reducing prices lead to an increase or decrease in sales revenue? If a reduction in price leads only to a small increase in the quantity sold, sales revenue will fall (demand is price inelastic); a price reduction that leads to a large increase in quantity sold will produce an increase in revenue (demand is price elastic). This economic information is essential for effective management.

The first step is to set up an economic model in which sales revenue depends on one or more explanatory variables. We initially hypothesize that sales revenue is linearly related to price and advertising expenditure. The economic model is

$$S = \beta_1 + \beta_2 P + \beta_3 A \tag{5.1}$$

where S represents monthly sales revenue in a given city, P represents price in that city, and A is monthly advertising expenditure in that city. Both S and A are measured in terms of thousands of dollars. Because sales in bigger cities will tend to be greater than sales in smaller cities, we focus on smaller cities with comparable populations.

---

[1] The data we use reflect a real fast-food franchise whose identity we disguise under the name Big Andy's.

Since a hamburger outlet sells a number of products: burgers, fries, and shakes, and each product has its own price, it is not immediately clear what price should be used in equation (5.1). What we need is some kind of average price for all products and information on how this average price changes from city to city. For this purpose management has constructed a single price index P, measured in dollars and cents, that describes overall prices in each city.

The remaining symbols in (5.1) are the unknown parameters β_1, β_2, and β_3 that describe the dependence of sales (S) on price (P) and advertising (A). Mathematically, the intercept parameter β_1 is the value of the dependent variable when each of the independent, explanatory variables takes the value zero. However, in many cases this parameter has no clear economic interpretation. In this particular case it is not realistic to have a situation where $P = A = 0$. Except in very special circumstances, we always include an intercept in the model, even if it has no direct economic interpretation. Omitting it can lead to a model that fits the data poorly and does not predict well.

The other parameters in the model measure the change in the value of the dependent variable given a unit change in an explanatory variable, *all other variables held constant*. For example, in (5.1)

> β_2 = the change in monthly sales S ($1000) when the price index P is increased by one unit ($1) and advertising expenditure A is held constant
>
> $$= \frac{\Delta S}{\Delta P_{(A \text{ held constant})}} = \frac{\partial S}{\partial P}$$

The symbol "∂" stands for "partial differentiation." Those of you familiar with calculus may have seen this operation. It means that, as the definition states, we calculate the change in one variable, S, when the variable P changes, all other factors, A, held constant. We will occasionally use this symbol, but you will not be asked to evaluate such derivatives.

The sign of β_2 could be positive or negative. If an increase in price leads to an increase in sales revenue, then $\beta_2 > 0$, and the demand for the chain's products is price inelastic. Conversely, a price elastic demand exists if an increase in price leads to a decline in revenue, in which case $\beta_2 < 0$. Thus, knowledge of the *sign* of β_2 provides information on the price elasticity of demand. The *magnitude* of β_2 measures the amount of change in revenue for a given price change.

The parameter β_3 describes the response of sales revenue to a change in the level of advertising expenditure. That is,

> β_3 = the change in monthly sales S ($1000) when advertising expenditure A is increased by one unit ($1000) and the price index P is held constant
>
> $$= \frac{\Delta S}{\Delta A_{(P \text{ held constant})}} = \frac{\partial S}{\partial A}$$

We expect the sign of β_3 to be positive. That is, we expect that an increase in advertising expenditure, unless the ad is offensive, will lead to an increase in sales revenue. Whether or not the increase in revenue is sufficient to justify the added advertising expenditure, and the added cost of producing more hamburgers, is another question. With $\beta_3 < 1$, an increase of $1000 in advertising expenditure will yield an increase in revenue that is less than $1000. For $\beta_3 > 1$, it will be greater. Thus, in terms of the chain's advertising policy, knowledge of β_3 is very important.

The next step along the road to learning about β_1, β_2, and β_3, is to convert the economic model into an econometric model.

5.1.2   THE ECONOMETRIC MODEL

The economic model (5.1) describes the expected or average behavior of many individual franchises that make up the complete chain run by Big Andy's Burger Barn. As such we should write it as $E(S) = \beta_1 + \beta_2 P + \beta_3 A$, where $E(S)$ is the "expected value" of sales revenue. Data for sales revenue, price, and advertising for different cities will not follow an exact linear relationship. Equation (5.1) describes, not a line as in Chapters 2–4, but a *plane*. As illustrated in Figure 5.1, the plane intersects the vertical axis at β_1. The parameters β_2 and β_3 measure the slope of the plane in the directions of the "price axis" and the "advertising axis," respectively. Representative observations for sales revenue, price, and advertising for some cities are displayed in Table 5.1. The complete set of observations can be found in the file *andy.dat* and is represented by the dots in Figure 5.1. These data do not fall exactly on a plane, but instead resemble a "cloud."

To allow for a difference between observable sales revenue and the expected value of sales revenue, we add a *random error term*, $e = S - E(S)$. This random error represents all factors, other than price and advertising revenue, which cause sales revenue to differ from its expected value. These factors might include the weather, the behavior of competitors, a new Surgeon General's report on the deadly effects of fat intake, and so on, as well as differences in burger-buying behavior across cities. Denoting the observation for city i by the subscript i, we have

$$S_i = E(S_i) + e_i = \beta_1 + \beta_2 P_i + \beta_3 A_i + e_i \tag{5.2}$$

The economic model in (5.1) describes the average, systematic relationship between the variables S, P, and A. The expected value $E(S)$ is the nonrandom, systematic component, to which we add the random error e to determine S. Thus S is a random variable. We do not know what the value of sales revenue will be until we observe it.

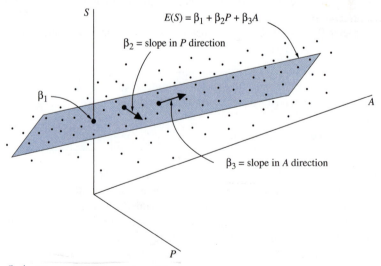

FIGURE 5.1   The multiple regression plane.

T a b l e 5 . 1   **Observations on Monthly Sales, Price, and Advertising in Big Andy's Burger Barn**

City	Sales (S) $1000 units	Price (P) $1 units	Advertising (A) $1000 units
1	73.2	5.69	1.3
2	71.8	6.49	2.9
3	62.4	5.63	0.8
4	67.4	6.22	0.7
5	89.3	5.02	1.5
.	.	.	.
.	.	.	.
.	.	.	.
73	75.4	5.71	0.7
74	81.3	5.45	2.0
75	75.0	6.05	2.2
	Summary statistics		
Sample mean	77.37	5.69	1.84
Median	76.50	5.69	1.80
Maximum	91.20	6.49	3.10
Minimum	62.40	4.83	0.50
Std. Dev.	6.4885	0.5184	0.8317

The introduction of the error term and assumptions about its probability distribution turn the economic model into the **econometric model** in (5.2). The econometric model provides a more realistic description of the relationship between the variables as well as a framework for developing and assessing estimators of the unknown parameters.

5.1.2a   The General Model

It is useful to digress for a moment and summarize how the concepts developed so far relate to the general case. In a general multiple regression model, a dependent variable y is related to a number of **explanatory variables** $x_2, x_3, \ldots, x_K$ through a linear equation that can be written as

$$y_i = \beta_1 + \beta_2 x_{i2} + \beta_3 x_{i3} + \cdots + \beta_K x_{iK} + e_i \tag{5.3}$$

The coefficients $\beta_2, \beta_3, \ldots, \beta_K$ are unknown coefficients corresponding to the explanatory variables $x_2, x_3, \ldots, x_K$. A single parameter, call it β_k, measures the effect of a change in the variable x_k upon the expected value of y, all other variables held constant. In terms of partial derivatives,

$$\beta_k = \frac{\Delta E(y)}{\Delta x_k}\bigg|_{\text{other } x\text{'s held constant}} = \frac{\partial E(y)}{\partial x_k}$$

The parameter β_1 is the intercept term. We can think of it as being attached to a variable x_1 that is always equal to 1. That is, $x_{i1} = 1$. We use K to denote the number of unknown parameters in (5.3).

The equation for sales revenue can be viewed as a special case of (5.3) where $K = 3$, $y_i = S_i$, $x_{i1} = 1$, $x_{i2} = P_i$, and $x_{i3} = A_i$. Thus we rewrite (5.2) as

$$y_i = \beta_1 + \beta_2 x_{i2} + \beta_3 x_{i3} + e_i \tag{5.4}$$

In this chapter we will introduce point and interval estimation in terms of this model with $K = 3$. The results generally will hold for models with more explanatory variables ($K > 3$).

5.1.2b   The Assumptions of the Model

To make the econometric model in (5.4) complete, assumptions about the probability distribution of the random errors e_i need to be made. The assumptions that we introduce for e_i are similar to those introduced for the simple regression model in Chapter 2. They are

1. $E(e_i) = 0$. Each random error has a probability distribution with zero mean. Some errors will be positive, some will be negative; over a large number of observations, they will average out to zero.

2. $\text{var}(e_i) = \sigma^2$. Each random error has a probability distribution with variance σ^2. The variance σ^2 is an unknown parameter and it measures the uncertainty in the statistical model. It is the same for each observation, so that for no observations will the model uncertainty be more, or less, nor is it directly related to any economic variable. Errors with this property are said to be **homoskedastic**.

3. $\text{cov}(e_i, e_j) = 0$. The covariance between the two random errors corresponding to any two different observations is zero. The size of an error for one observation has no bearing on the likely size of an error for another observation. Thus, any pair of errors is uncorrelated.

4. We will sometimes further assume that the random errors e_i have normal probability distributions. That is, $e_i \sim N(0, \sigma^2)$.

Because each observation on the dependent variable y_i depends on the random error term e_i, each y_i is also a random variable. The statistical properties of y_i follow from those of e_i. These properties are

1. $E(y_i) = \beta_1 + \beta_2 x_{i2} + \beta_3 x_{i3}$. The expected (average) value of y_i depends on the values of the explanatory variables and the unknown parameters. It is equivalent to $E(e_i) = 0$. This assumption says that the average value of y_i changes for each observation and is given by the **regression function** $E(y_i) = \beta_1 + \beta_2 x_{i2} + \beta_3 x_{i3}$.

2. $\text{var}(y_i) = \text{var}(e_i) = \sigma^2$. The variance of the probability distribution of y_i does not change with each observation. Some observations on y_i are not more likely to be further from the regression function than others.

3. $\text{cov}(y_i, y_j) = \text{cov}(e_i, e_j) = 0$. Any two observations on the dependent variable are uncorrelated. For example, if one observation is above $E(y_i)$, a subsequent observation is not more or less likely to be above $E(y_i)$.

4. We sometimes will assume that the values of y_i are normally distributed about their mean. That is, $y_i \sim N[(\beta_1 + \beta_2 x_{i2} + \beta_3 x_{i3}), \sigma^2]$, which is equivalent to assuming that $e_i \sim N(0, \sigma^2)$.

In addition to the above assumptions about the error term (and hence about the dependent variable), we make two assumptions about the explanatory variables. The first is that the explanatory variables are not random variables. Thus we are assuming that the values of the explanatory variables are known to us prior to observing the values of the dependent variable. This assumption is realistic for our hamburger chain where a decision about prices and advertising is made for each city and values for these variables are set accordingly. For cases in which this assumption is untenable, our analysis will be conditional upon the values of the explanatory variables in our sample, or further assumptions must be made. This issue is taken up further in Chapter 10.

The second assumption is that any one of the explanatory variables is not an exact linear function of the others. This assumption is equivalent to assuming that no variable is redundant. As we will see, if this assumption is violated, a condition called **exact collinearity**, the least squares procedure fails.

To summarize, we construct a list of the assumptions for the general multiple regression model in (5.3), much as we have done in the earlier chapters, to which we can refer as needed:

ASSUMPTIONS OF THE MULTIPLE REGRESSION MODEL

MR1. $y_i = \beta_1 + \beta_2 x_{i2} + \cdots + \beta_K x_{iK} + e_i, \ i = 1, \ldots, N$

MR2. $E(y_i) = \beta_1 + \beta_2 x_{i2} + \cdots + \beta_K x_{iK} \Leftrightarrow E(e_i) = 0$

MR3. $\text{var}(y_i) = \text{var}(e_i) = \sigma^2$

MR4. $\text{cov}(y_i, y_j) = \text{cov}(e_i, e_j) = 0$

MR5. The values of each x_{ik} are not random and are not exact linear functions of the other explanatory variables

MR6. $y_i \sim N[(\beta_1 + \beta_2 x_{i2} + \cdots + \beta_K x_{iK}), \sigma^2] \Leftrightarrow e_i \sim N(0, \sigma^2)$

5.2 Estimating the Parameters of the Multiple Regression Model

In this section we consider the problem of using the least squares principle to estimate the unknown parameters of the multiple regression model. We will discuss estimation in the context of the model in (5.4), which we repeat here for convenience.

$$y_i = \beta_1 + \beta_2 x_{i2} + \beta_3 x_{i3} + e_i \tag{5.4}$$

This model is simpler than the full model and yet all the results we present carry over to the general case with only minor modifications.

5.2.1 LEAST SQUARES ESTIMATION PROCEDURE

To find an estimator for estimating the unknown parameters we follow the least squares procedure that was first introduced in Chapter 2 for the simple regression model. With the least squares principle we minimize the sum of squared differences between the observed values of y_i and its expected value $E(y_i) = \beta_1 + x_{i2}\beta_2 + x_{i3}\beta_3$. Mathematically we minimize the sum of squares function $S(\beta_1, \beta_2, \beta_3)$, which is a function of the unknown parameters, given the data

$$S(\beta_1, \beta_2, \beta_3) = \sum_{i=1}^{N} [y_i - E(y_i)]^2$$

$$= \sum_{i=1}^{N} (y_i - \beta_1 - \beta_2 x_{i2} - \beta_3 x_{i3})^2 \tag{5.5}$$

Given the sample observations y_i, minimizing the sum of squares function is a straightforward exercise in calculus. Details of this exercise are given in Appendix 5A at the end of this chapter. The solutions give us formulas for the least squares estimators for the β coefficients in a multiple regression model with two explanatory variables. They are extensions of those given in equations (2.7) and (2.8) for the simple regression model with one explanatory variable. There are three reasons for relegating these formulas to Appendix 5A instead of inflicting them on you here. First, they are complicated formulas that we do not expect you to memorize. Second, we never use these formulas explicitly; computer software uses the formulas to calculate least squares estimates. Third, we frequently have models with more than two explanatory variables in which case the formulas become even more complicated. If you proceed with more advanced study in econometrics, you will discover that there is one relatively simple matrix algebra expression for the least squares estimator that can be used for all models, irrespective of the number of explanatory variables.

Although we always get the computer to do the work for us, it is important to understand the least squares principle and the difference between least squares estimators and least squares estimates. Looked at as a general way to use sample data, formulas for b_1, b_2, and b_3, obtained by minimizing (5.5), are estimation procedures, which are called the **least squares estimators** of the unknown parameters. In general, since their values are not known until the data are observed and the estimates calculated, the least squares estimators are random variables. Computer software applies the formulas to a specific sample of data producing **least squares estimates**, which are numeric values. To avoid too much notation, we use b_1, b_2, and b_3 to denote both the estimators and the estimates.

5.2.2   LEAST SQUARES ESTIMATES USING HAMBURGER CHAIN DATA

Table 5.2 contains the least squares results for the sales equation for Big Andy's Burger Barn. For the moment, we are concerned only with the least squares estimates, which are

$$b_1 = 118.91 \quad b_2 = -7.908 \quad b_3 = 1.863$$

The various other entries on the output will be discussed as we move through the remainder of this chapter.

To interpret the coefficient estimates, note that the regression function that we are estimating is

$$E(y_i) = \beta_1 + \beta_2 x_{i2} + \beta_3 x_{i3}$$

and the fitted regression line is

$$\hat{y}_i = b_1 + b_2 x_{i2} + b_3 x_{i3}$$
$$= 118.91 - 7.908 x_{i2} + 1.863 x_{i3}$$

Table 5.2   **Least Squares Estimates for Sales Equation for Big Andy's Burger Barn**

Variable	Coefficient	Std. Error	t-Statistic	Prob.
C	118.9136	6.3516	18.7217	0.0000
P	−7.9079	1.0960	−7.2152	0.0000
A	1.8626	0.6832	2.7263	0.0080
$R^2 = 0.4483$	$SSE = 1718.943$	$\hat{\sigma} = 4.8861$	$\hat{\sigma}_y = 6.48854.$	

In terms of the original economic variables,

$$\hat{S}_i = 118.91 - 7.908 P_i + 1.863 A_i \qquad (5.6)$$

If you were writing a paper you might use variable names that are more informative, such as

$$\widehat{SALES} = 118.91 - 7.908\,PRICE + 1.863\,ADVERT$$

Based on these results, what can we say?

1. The negative coefficient on P_i suggests that demand is price elastic; we estimate that, with advertising held constant, an increase in price of \$1 will lead to a fall in monthly revenue of \$7908. Or, expressed differently, a reduction in price of \$1 will lead to an increase in revenue of \$7908. If such is the case, a strategy of price reduction through the offering of specials would be successful in increasing sales revenue. We do need to consider carefully the magnitude of the price change, however. A \$1 change in price is a relatively large change. The sample mean of price is 5.69 and its standard deviation is 0.52. A 10 cent change is more realistic, in which case we estimate the revenue change to be \$791.

2. The coefficient on advertising is positive; we estimate that, with price held constant, an increase in advertising expenditure of \$1000 will lead to an increase in sales revenue of \$1863. We can use this information, along with the costs of producing the additional hamburgers, to determine whether an increase in advertising expenditures will increase profit.

3. The estimated intercept implies that if both price and advertising expenditure were zero the sales revenue would be \$118,914. Clearly, this outcome is not possible; a zero price implies zero sales revenue. In this model, as in many others, it is important to recognize that the model is an approximation to reality in the region for which we have data. Including an intercept improves this approximation even when it is not directly interpretable.

In addition to providing information about how sales change when price or advertising change, the estimated equation can be used for prediction. Suppose Big Andy is interested in predicting sales revenue for a price of \$5.50 and an advertising expenditure of \$1200. Including extra decimal places to get an accurate hand calculation, this prediction is

$$
\begin{aligned}
\hat{S} &= 118.91 - 7.908 PRICE + 1.863 ADVERT \\
&= 118.914 - 7.9079 \times 5.5 + 1.8626 \times 1.2 \\
&= 77.656
\end{aligned}
$$

The predicted value of sales revenue for $P = 5.5$ and $A = 1.2$ is \$77,656.

> **REMARK:** A word of caution is in order about interpreting regression results. The negative sign attached to price implies that reducing the price will increase sales revenue. If taken literally, why should we not keep reducing the price to zero? Obviously that would not keep increasing total revenue. This makes the following important point: Estimated regression models describe the relationship between the economic variables for values *similar* to those found in the sample data. Extrapolating the results to extreme values is generally not a good idea. Predicting the value of the dependent variable for values of the explanatory variables far from the sample values invites disaster. Refer to Figure 4.2 and the surrounding discussion.

5.2.3   ESTIMATION OF THE ERROR VARIANCE σ^2

There is one remaining parameter to estimate, the variance of the error term. For this parameter we follow the same steps that were outlined in Section 2.7. We know that

$$\sigma^2 = \text{var}(e_i) = E\left(e_i^2\right)$$

Thus, we can think of σ^2 as the expectation or population mean of the squared errors e_i^2. A natural estimator of this population mean is the sample mean $\hat{\sigma}^2 = \Sigma e_i^2/N$. However, the squared errors e_i^2 are unobservable and so we develop an estimator for σ^2 that is based on the squares of the least squares residuals. For the model in (5.4) these residuals are

$$\hat{e}_i = y_i - \hat{y}_i = y_i - (b_1 + b_2 x_{i2} + b_3 x_{i3})$$

An estimator for σ^2 that uses the information from $\hat{e}_i^2$ and has good statistical properties is

$$\hat{\sigma}^2 = \frac{\sum_{i=1}^{N}\hat{e}_i^2}{N-K} \tag{5.7}$$

where K is the number of β parameters being estimated in the multiple regression model. We can think of $\hat{\sigma}^2$ as an average of $\hat{e}_i^2$ with the denominator in the averaging process being $N-K$ instead of N. It can be shown that replacing e_i^2 by $\hat{e}_i^2$ requires the use of $N-K$ instead of N for $\hat{\sigma}^2$ to be unbiased. Note that in Chapter 2, equation (2.19), where there was one explanatory variable and two coefficients, we had $K=2$.

To appreciate further why $\hat{e}_i$ provide information about σ^2, recall that σ^2 measures the variation in e_i or, equivalently, the variation in y_i around the mean function $\beta_1 + \beta_2 x_{i2} + \beta_3 x_{i3}$. Since $\hat{e}_i$ are estimates of e_i, big values of $\hat{e}_i$ suggest σ^2 is large while small $\hat{e}_i$ suggest σ^2 is small. When we refer to "big" values of $\hat{e}_i$, we mean big positive ones or big negative ones. Using the squares of the residuals $\hat{e}_i^2$ means that positive values do not cancel with negative ones; thus, $\hat{e}_i^2$ provide information about the parameter σ^2.

In the hamburger chain example we have $K=3$. The estimate for our sample of data in Table 5.1 is

$$\hat{\sigma}^2 = \frac{\sum_{i=1}^{75}\hat{e}_i^2}{N-K} = \frac{1718.943}{75-3} = 23.874$$

Go back and have a look at Table 5.2. There are two quantities in this table that relate to the above calculation. The first is the sum of squared errors

$$SSE = \sum_{i=1}^{N}\hat{e}_i^2 = 1718.943$$

The second is the square root of $\hat{\sigma}^2$, given by

$$\hat{\sigma} = \sqrt{23.874} = 4.8861$$

Both these quantities typically appear in the output from your computer software. Different software refer to it in different ways. Sometimes $\hat{\sigma}$ is referred to as the *standard error of the regression*. Sometimes it is called the *root mse* (short for mean squared error).

A major reason for estimating the error variance is to enable us to get an estimate of the unknown variances and covariances for the least squares estimators. We now consider those variances and covariances in the context of the overall properties of the least squares estimator.

5.3 Sampling Properties of the Least Squares Estimator

In a general context, the least squares estimators (b_1, b_2, b_3) are random variables; they take on different values in different samples and their values are unknown until a sample is collected and their values computed. The sampling properties of a least squares estimator tell us how the estimates vary from sample to sample. They provide a basis for assessing the reliability of the estimates. In Chapter 2 we found that the least squares estimator was unbiased and that there is no other linear unbiased estimator that has a smaller variance, if the model assumptions are correct. This result remains true for the *general* multiple regression model that we are considering in this chapter.

> **THE GAUSS–MARKOV THEOREM:** For the multiple regression model, if assumptions MR1–MR5 listed at the beginning of the chapter hold, then the least squares estimators are the best linear unbiased estimators (BLUE) of the parameters.

If we are able to assume that the errors are *normally distributed*, then y will also be a normally distributed random variable. The least squares estimators will also have normal probability distributions, since they are linear functions of y. If the errors are not normally distributed, then the least squares estimators are approximately normally distributed in large samples. What constitutes large is tricky. It depends on a number of factors specific to each application. Frequently, $N - K = 50$ will be large enough. These facts are of great importance for the construction of interval estimates and the testing of hypotheses about the parameters of the regression model.

5.3.1   THE VARIANCES AND COVARIANCES OF THE LEAST SQUARES ESTIMATORS

The variances and covariances of the least squares estimators give us information about the reliability of the estimators b_1, b_2, and b_3. Since the least squares estimators are unbiased, the smaller their variances the higher is the probability that they will produce estimates "near" the true parameter values. For $K = 3$ we can express the variances and covariances in an algebraic form that provides useful insights into the behavior of the least squares estimator. For example, we can show that

$$\text{var}(b_2) = \frac{\sigma^2}{(1 - r_{23}^2)\Sigma_{i=1}^{N}(x_{i2} - \bar{x}_2)^2} \tag{5.8}$$

where r_{23} is the sample correlation coefficient between the values of x_2 and x_3; see equation (B.20) in Appendix B.4.3 and Section 4.2.1. Its formula is given by

$$r_{23} = \frac{\Sigma(x_{i2} - \bar{x}_2)(x_{i3} - \bar{x}_3)}{\sqrt{\Sigma(x_{i2} - \bar{x}_2)^2 \Sigma(x_{i3} - \bar{x}_3)^2}} \tag{5.9}$$

For the other variances and covariances there are formulas of a similar nature. It is important to understand the factors affecting the variance of b_2:

1. Larger error variances σ^2 lead to larger variances of the least squares estimators. This is to be expected since σ^2 measures the overall uncertainty in the model specification. If σ^2 is large, then data values may be widely spread about the regression function

$E(y_i) = \beta_1 + \beta_2 x_{i2} + \beta_3 x_{i3}$ and there is less information in the data about the parameter values. If σ^2 is small then data values are compactly spread about the regression function $E(y_i) = \beta_1 + \beta_2 x_{i2} + \beta_3 x_{i3}$ and there is more information about what the parameter values might be.

2. Larger sample sizes N imply smaller variances of the least squares estimators. A larger value of N means a larger value of the summation $\sum(x_{i2} - \bar{x}_2)^2$. Since this term appears in the denominator of (5.8), when it is large, $var(b_2)$ is small. This outcome is also an intuitive one; more observations yield more precise parameter estimation.

3. More variation in an explanatory variable around its mean, measured in this case by $\sum(x_{i2} - \bar{x}_2)^2$, leads to a smaller variance of the least squares estimator. To estimate β_2 precisely, we prefer a large amount of variation in x_{i2}. The intuition here is that, if the variation or change in x_2 is small, it is difficult to measure the effect of that change. This difficulty will be reflected in a large variance for b_2.

4. A larger correlation between x_2 and x_3 leads to a larger variance of b_2. Note that $1 - r_{23}^2$ appears in the denominator of (5.8). A value of $|r_{23}|$ close to 1 means $1 - r_{23}^2$ will be small, which in turn means $var(b_2)$ will be large. The reason for this fact is that variation in x_{i2} about its mean adds most to the precision of estimation when it is not connected to variation in the other explanatory variables. When the variation in one explanatory variable is connected to variation in another explanatory variable, it is difficult to disentangle their separate effects. In Chapter 6 we discuss "collinearity," which is the situation when the explanatory variables are correlated with one another. Collinearity leads to increased variances of the least squares estimators.

Although our discussion has been in terms of a model where $K = 3$, these factors affect the variances of the least squares estimators in the same way in larger models.

It is customary to arrange the estimated variances and covariances of the least squares estimators in a square array, which is called a matrix. This matrix has variances on its diagonal and covariances in the off-diagonal positions. It is called a **variance–covariance matrix** or, more simply, a **covariance matrix**. When $K = 3$, the arrangement of the variances and covariances in the covariance matrix is

$$\text{cov}(b_1, b_2, b_3) = \begin{bmatrix} var(b_1) & \text{cov}(b_1, b_2) & \text{cov}(b_1, b_3) \\ \text{cov}(b_1, b_2) & var(b_2) & \text{cov}(b_2, b_3) \\ \text{cov}(b_1, b_3) & \text{cov}(b_2, b_3) & var(b_3) \end{bmatrix}$$

Using the estimate $\hat{\sigma}^2 = 23.874$ and our computer software package, the estimated variances and covariances for b_1, b_2, and b_3 in the Big Andy's Burger Barn example are

$$\overline{\text{cov}(b_1, b_2, b_3)} = \begin{bmatrix} 40.343 & -6.795 & -0.7484 \\ -6.795 & 1.201 & -0.0197 \\ -0.7484 & -0.0197 & 0.4668 \end{bmatrix} \tag{5.10}$$

Thus, we have

$$\overline{var(b_1)} = 40.343 \quad \overline{\text{cov}(b_1, b_2)} = -6.795$$

$$\overline{var(b_2)} = 1.201 \quad \overline{\text{cov}(b_1, b_3)} = -0.7484$$

$$\overline{var(b_3)} = 0.4668 \quad \overline{\text{cov}(b_2, b_3)} = -0.0197$$

Table 5.3   **Covariance Matrix for Coefficient Estimates**

	C	P	A
C	40.3433	−6.7951	−0.7484
P	−6.7951	1.2012	−0.0197
A	−0.7484	−0.0197	0.4668

Table 5.3 shows how this information is typically reported in the output from computer software.

Of particular relevance are the standard errors of b_1, b_2, and b_3; they are given by the square roots of the corresponding estimated variances. That is,

$$se(b_1) = \sqrt{\widehat{\text{var}(b_1)}} = \sqrt{40.3433} = 6.3516$$

$$se(b_2) = \sqrt{\widehat{\text{var}(b_2)}} = \sqrt{1.2012} = 1.0960$$

$$se(b_3) = \sqrt{\widehat{\text{var}(b_3)}} = \sqrt{0.4668} = 0.6832$$

Again, it is time to go back and look at Table 5.2. Notice that these values appear in the standard error column.

These standard errors can be used to say something about the range of the least squares estimates if we were to obtain more samples of 75 burger barns from different cities. For example, the standard error of b_2 is approximately $se(b_2) = 1.1$. We know that the least squares estimator is unbiased, so its mean value is $E(b_2) = \beta_2$. If b_2 is normally distributed, then based on statistical theory we expect 95% of the estimates b_2, obtained by applying the least squares estimator to other samples, to be within approximately two standard deviations of the mean β_2. Given our sample, $2 \times se(b_2) = 2.2$, so we estimate that 95% of the b_2 values would lie within the interval $\beta_2 \pm 2.2$. It is in this sense that the estimated variance of β_2, or its corresponding standard error, tells us something about the reliability of the least squares estimates. If the difference between b_2 and β_2 can be large, b_2 is not reliable; if the difference between b_2 and β_2 is likely to be small, then b_2 is reliable. Whether a particular difference is "large" or "small" will depend on the context of the problem and the use to which the estimates are to be put. This issue is considered again in later sections when we use the estimated variances and covariances to test hypotheses about the parameters and to construct interval estimates.

5.3.2 THE PROPERTIES OF THE LEAST SQUARES ESTIMATORS ASSUMING NORMALLY DISTRIBUTED ERRORS

We have asserted that, under the multiple regression model assumptions MR1–MR5, listed at the end of Section 5.1, the least squares estimator b_k is the best linear unbiased estimator of the parameter β_k in the model

$$y_i = \beta_1 + \beta_2 x_{i2} + \beta_3 x_{i3} + \cdots + \beta_K x_{iK} + e_i$$

If we add assumption MR6 that the random errors e_i have normal probability distributions, then the dependent variable y_i is normally distributed,

$$y_i \sim N[(\beta_1 + \beta_2 x_{i2} + \cdots + \beta_K x_{iK}), \sigma^2] \Leftrightarrow e_i \sim N(0, \sigma^2)$$

Since the least squares estimators are linear functions of dependent variables it follows that the least squares estimators are also normally distributed,

$$b_k \sim N[\beta_k, \text{var}(b_k)]$$

That is, each b_k has a normal distribution with mean β_k and variance $\text{var}(b_k)$. By subtracting its mean and dividing by the square root of its variance, we can transform the normal random variable b_k into the *standard normal variable Z*,

$$Z = \frac{b_k - \beta_k}{\sqrt{\text{var}(b_k)}} \sim N(0, 1), \quad \text{for } k = 1, 2, \ldots, K \tag{5.11}$$

that has mean zero and a variance of 1. The variance of b_k depends on the unknown variance of the error term, σ^2, as illustrated in (5.8) for the $K = 3$ case. When we replace σ^2 by its estimator $\hat{\sigma}^2$, from (5.7), we obtain the estimated $\text{var}(b_k)$ which we denote as $\widehat{\text{var}(b_k)}$. Replacing $\text{var}(b_k)$ by $\widehat{\text{var}(b_k)}$ in (5.11) changes the $N(0,1)$ random variable to a t-random variable. That is,

$$t = \frac{b_k - \beta_k}{\sqrt{\widehat{\text{var}(b_k)}}} = \frac{b_k - \beta_k}{\text{se}(b_k)} \sim t_{(N-K)} \tag{5.12}$$

One difference between this result and that in Chapter 3, see equation (3.2), is the degrees of freedom of the t-random variable. In Chapter 3, where there were two coefficients to be estimated, the number of degrees of freedom was $N - 2$. In this chapter there are K unknown coefficients in the general model and *the number of degrees of freedom for t-statistics is $N - K$*.

We now examine how the result in (5.12) can be used for interval estimation and hypothesis testing. The procedures are identical to those described in Chapter 3, only the degrees of freedom change.

5.4 Interval Estimation

Suppose we are interested in finding a 95% interval estimate for β_2, the response of sales revenue to a change in price at Big Andy's Burger Barn. Following the procedures described in Section 3.1, and noting that we have $N - K = 75 - 3 = 72$ degrees of freedom, the first step is to find a value from the $t_{(72)}$-distribution, call it t_c, such that

$$P(-t_c < t_{(72)} < t_c) = 0.95 \tag{5.13}$$

Using the notation introduced in Section 3.1, $t_c = t_{(0.975, N-K)}$ is the 97.5-percentile of the $t_{(N-K)}$-distribution (the area or probability to the left of t_c is 0.975), and $-t_c = t_{(0.025, N-K)}$ is the 2.5-percentile of the $t_{(N-K)}$-distribution (the area or probability to the left of $-t_c$ is 0.025). Consulting the t-table inside the front cover of the book, we discover there is no entry for 72 degrees of freedom, but, from the entries for 70 and 80 degrees of freedom, it is clear that, correct to two decimal places, $t_c = 1.99$. If greater accuracy is required, your computer software can be used to find $t_c = 1.993$. Using this value, and the result in (5.12) for the second coefficient ($k = 2$), we can rewrite (5.13) as

$$P\left(-1.993 \leq \frac{b_2 - \beta_2}{\text{se}(b_2)} \leq 1.993\right) = 0.95 \tag{5.14}$$

Rearranging (5.14) we obtain

$$P[b_2 - 1.993 \times \mathrm{se}(b_2) \leq \beta_2 \leq b_2 + 1.993 \times \mathrm{se}(b_2)] = 0.95$$

The interval endpoints

$$[b_2 - 1.993 \times \mathrm{se}(b_2), \ b_2 + 1.993 \times \mathrm{se}(b_2)] \tag{5.15}$$

define a 95% interval estimator of β_2. If this interval estimator is used in many samples from the population, then 95% of them will contain the true parameter β_2. We can establish this fact before any data are collected, based on the model assumptions alone. Before the data are collected we have confidence in the **interval estimation procedure (estimator)** because of its performance when used repeatedly.

A 95% interval estimate for β_2 based on our particular sample is obtained from (5.15) by replacing b_2 and $\mathrm{se}(b_2)$ by their values $b_2 = -7.908$ and $\mathrm{se}(b_2) = 1.096$. Thus, our 95% interval estimate for β_2 is given by

$$(-10.092, -5.724)$$

This interval estimate suggests that decreasing price by $1 will lead to an increase in revenue somewhere between $5724 and $10,092. Or, in terms of a price change whose magnitude is more realistic, a 10 cent price reduction will lead to a revenue increase between $572 and $1009. Based on this information, and the cost of making and selling more burgers, Big Andy can decide whether to proceed with a price reduction.

Following a similar procedure for β_3, the response of sales revenue to advertising, we find a 95% interval estimate is given by[2]

$$(1.8626 - 1.993 \times 0.6832, \ 1.8626 + 1.993 \times 0.6832) = (0.501, 3.224)$$

We estimate that an increase in advertising expenditure of $1000 leads to an increase in sales revenue of between $501 and $3224. This interval is a relatively wide one; it implies that extra advertising expenditure could be unprofitable (the revenue increase is less than $1000), or it may lead to a revenue increase more than three times the cost of the advertising. Another way of describing this situation is to say that the point estimate $b_3 = 1.8626$ is not very reliable, as its standard error (which measures sampling variability) is relatively large.

In general, if an interval estimate is uninformative because it is too wide, there is nothing immediate that can be done. A wide interval for the parameter β_3 arises because the estimated sampling variability of the least squares estimator b_3 is large. In the computation of an interval estimate, a large sampling variability is reflected by a large standard error. A narrower interval can only be obtained by reducing the variance of the estimator. Based on the variance expression in (5.8), one solution is to obtain more and better data, exhibiting more independent variation. Big Andy could collect data from other cities and set a wider range of price and advertising combinations. It might be expensive to do so, however, and so he would need to assess whether the extra information is worth the extra cost. This solution is generally not open to economists, who rarely use controlled experiments to obtain data. Alternatively we might introduce some kind of nonsample information on the coefficients. The question of how to use both sample and nonsample information in the estimation process is taken up in Chapter 6.

---

[2] For this calculation we used more digits so that it would match the more accurate computer output. You may see us do this occasionally.

We cannot say, in general, what constitutes an interval that is too wide, or too uninformative. It depends on the context of the problem being investigated and how the information is to be used.

To give a general expression for an interval estimate we need to recognize that the critical value t_c will depend on the degree of confidence specified for the interval estimate and the number of degrees of freedom. We denote the degree of confidence by $1 - \alpha$; in the case of a 95% interval estimate $\alpha = 0.05$ and $1 - \alpha = 0.95$. The number of degrees of freedom is $N - K$; in Big Andy's Burger Barn example this value was $75 - 3 = 72$. The value t_c is the percentile value $t_{(1-\alpha/2,N-K)}$, which has the property that $P\left[t_{(N-K)} \leq t_{(1-\alpha/2,N-K)}\right] = 1 - \alpha/2$. In the case of a 95% confidence interval, $1 - \alpha/2 = 0.975$; we use this value because we require 0.025 in each tail of the distribution. Thus, we write the general expression for a $100(1 - \alpha)\%$ confidence interval as

$$\left[b_k - t_{(1-\alpha/2,N-K)} \times \text{se}(b_k), \quad b_k + t_{(1-\alpha/2,N-K)} \times \text{se}(b_k)\right]$$

5.5 Hypothesis Testing for a Single Coefficient

As well as being useful for interval estimation, the t-distribution result in equation (5.12) provides the foundation for testing hypotheses about individual coefficients. As you discovered in Chapter 3, hypotheses of the form $H_0 : \beta_2 = c$ versus $H_1 : \beta_2 \neq c$, where c is a specified constant, are called two-tail tests. Hypotheses with inequalities such as $H_0 : \beta_2 \leq c$ versus $H_1 : \beta_2 > c$ are called one-tail tests. In this section we consider examples of each type of hypothesis. For a two-tail test, we consider testing the significance of an individual coefficient; for one-tail tests some hypotheses of economic interest are considered. We will follow the step-by-step procedure for testing hypotheses that was introduced in Section 3.4. To refresh your memory, here again are the steps:

STEP-BY-STEP PROCEDURE FOR TESTING HYPOTHESES

1. Determine the null and alternative hypotheses.
2. Specify the test statistic and its distribution if the null hypothesis is true.
3. Select α and determine the rejection region.
4. Calculate the sample value of the test statistic and, if desired, the p-value.
5. State your conclusion.

At the time these steps were introduced in Chapter 3 you had not discovered p-values. Knowing about p-values (see Section 3.5) means that steps 3–5 can be framed in terms of the test statistic and its value and/or the p-value. We will use both.

5.5.1   TESTING THE SIGNIFICANCE OF A SINGLE COEFFICIENT

When we set up a multiple regression model, we do so because we believe the explanatory variables influence the dependent variable y. If we are to confirm this belief, we need to examine whether or not it is supported by the data. That is, we need to ask whether the data provide any evidence to suggest that y is related to each of the explanatory variables. If a given explanatory variable, say x_k, has no bearing on y, then $\beta_k = 0$. Testing this null hypothesis is sometimes called a test of significance for the explanatory variable x_k. Thus, to find whether the data contain any evidence suggesting y is related to x_k, we test the null hypothesis

$$H_0 : \beta_k = 0$$

against the alternative hypothesis

$$H_1 : \beta_k \neq 0$$

To carry out the test we use the test statistic (5.12), which, if the null hypothesis is true, is

$$t = \frac{b_k}{se(b_k)} \sim t_{(N-K)}$$

For the alternative hypothesis "not equal to" we use a two-tail test, introduced in Section 3.3.3, and reject H_0 if the computed t-value is greater than or equal to t_c (the critical value from the right side of the distribution) or less than or equal to $-t_c$ (the critical value from the left side of the distribution). For a test with level of significance α, $t_c = t_{(1-\alpha/2, N-K)}$ and $-t_c = t_{(\alpha/2, N-K)}$. Alternatively, if we state the acceptance–rejection rule in terms of the p-value, we reject H_0 if $p \leq \alpha$ and do not reject H_0 if $p > \alpha$.

In the Big Andy's Burger Barn example we test, following our standard testing format, whether sales revenue is related to price:

1. The null and alternative hypotheses are $H_0 : \beta_2 = 0$ and $H_1 : \beta_2 \neq 0$.
2. The test statistic, if the null hypothesis is true, is $t = b_2 / se(b_2) \sim t_{(N-K)}$.
3. Using a 5% significance level ($\alpha = 0.05$), and noting that there are 72 degrees of freedom, the critical values that lead to a probability of 0.025 in each tail of the distribution are $t_{(0.975,72)} = 1.993$ and $t_{(0.025,72)} = -1.993$. Thus we reject the null hypothesis if the calculated value of t from step 2 is such that $t \geq 1.993$ or $t \leq -1.993$. If $-1.993 < t < 1.993$, we do not reject H_0. Stating the acceptance–rejection rule in terms of the p-value, we reject H_0 if $p \leq 0.05$ and do not reject H_0 if $p > 0.05$.
4. The computed value of the t-statistic is

$$t = \frac{-7.908}{1.096} = -7.215$$

From your computer software the p-value in this case can be found as

$$P(t_{(72)} > 7.215) + P(t_{(72)} < -7.215) = 2 \times (2.2 \times 10^{-10}) = 0.000$$

Correct to three decimal places the result is p-value $= 0.000$.

5. Since $-7.215 < -1.993$, we reject $H_0 : \beta_2 = 0$ and conclude that there is evidence from the data to suggest sales revenue depends on price. Using the p-value to perform the test, we reject H_0 because $0.000 < 0.05$.

For testing whether sales revenue is related to advertising expenditure, we have

1. $H_0 : \beta_3 = 0$ and $H_1 : \beta_3 \neq 0$.
2. The test statistic, if the null hypothesis is true, is $t = b_3 / se(b_3) \sim t_{(N-K)}$.

3. Using a 5% significance level, we reject the null hypothesis if $t \geq 1.993$ or $t \leq -1.993$. In terms of the p-value, we reject H_0 if $p \leq 0.05$. Otherwise, we do not reject H_0.

4. The value of test statistic is

$$t = \frac{1.8626}{0.6832} = 2.726$$

The p-value is given by

$$P(t_{(72)} > 2.726) + P(t_{(72)} < -2.726) = 2 \times 0.004 = 0.008$$

5. Because $2.726 > 1.993$, we reject H_0; the data support the conjecture that revenue is related to advertising expenditure. The same test outcome can be obtained using the p-value. In this case we reject H_0 because $0.008 < 0.05$.

Note that the t-values -7.215 and 2.726 and their corresponding p-values 0.000 and 0.008 were reported in Table 5.2 at the same time as we reported the original least squares estimates and their standard errors. Hypothesis tests of this kind are carried out routinely by computer software, and their outcomes can be read immediately from the computer output that will be similar to Table 5.2.

Significance of a coefficient estimate is desirable. It confirms an initial prior belief that a particular explanatory variable is a relevant variable to include in the model. However, as mentioned in Section 3.4.3, statistical significance should not be confused with economic importance. If the estimated response of sales revenue to advertising had been $b_3 = 0.01$ with a standard error of $se(b_3) = 0.005$, then we would have concluded b_3 is significantly different from zero; but, since the estimate implies increasing advertising by $1000 increases revenue by only $10, we would not conclude advertising is important. We should also be cautious about concluding that statistical significance implies precise estimation. The advertising coefficient $b_3 = 1.8626$ was found to be significantly different from zero, but we also concluded the corresponding 95% interval estimate $(0.501, 3.224)$ was too wide to be very informative. In other words, we were not able to get a precise estimate of β_3.

5.5.2 ONE-TAIL HYPOTHESIS TESTING FOR A SINGLE COEFFICIENT

In Section 5.1 we noted that two important considerations for the management of Big Andy's Burger Barn were whether demand was price elastic or inelastic and whether the additional sales revenue from additional advertising expenditure would cover the costs of the advertising. We now are in a position to state these questions as testable hypotheses and to ask whether the hypotheses are compatible with the data.

5.5.2a Testing for Elastic Demand

With respect to demand elasticity, we wish to know if

- $\beta_2 \geq 0$: a decrease in price leads to a decrease in sales revenue (demand is price inelastic), or

- $\beta_2 < 0$: a decrease in price leads to an increase in sales revenue (demand is price elastic).

If we are not prepared to accept that demand is elastic unless there is strong evidence from the data to support this claim, it is appropriate to take the assumption of an inelastic demand as our null hypothesis. Following our standard testing format, we first state the null and alternative hypotheses:

1. $H_0 : \beta_2 \geq 0$ (demand is unit elastic or inelastic).
   $H_1 : \beta_2 < 0$ (demand is elastic).

2. To create a test statistic we act as if the null hypothesis is the equality $\beta_2 = 0$. Doing so is valid because if we reject H_0 for $\beta_2 = 0$, we also reject it for any $\beta_2 > 0$. Then, assuming $H_0 : \beta_2 = 0$ is true, from (5.12) the test statistic is $t = b_2 / \text{se}(b_2) \sim t_{(N-K)}$.

3. The rejection region consists of values from the t-distribution that are unlikely to occur if the null hypothesis is true. If we define "unlikely" in terms of a 5% significance level, then unlikely values of t are those less than the critical value $t_{(0.05,72)} = -1.666$. Thus, we reject H_0 if $t \leq -1.666$ or if the p-value < 0.05.

4. The value of the test statistic is

$$t = \frac{b_2}{\text{se}(b_2)} = \frac{-7.908}{1.096} = -7.215$$

   The corresponding p-value is $P(t_{(72)} < -7.215) = 0.000$.

5. Since $-7.215 < -1.666$, we reject $H_0 : \beta_2 \geq 0$ and conclude that $H_1 : \beta_2 < 0$ (demand is elastic) is more compatible with the data. The sample evidence supports the proposition that a reduction in price will bring about an increase in sales revenue. Since $0.000 < 0.05$, the same conclusion is reached using the p-value.

Note the similarities and the differences between this test and the two-tail test of significance performed in Section 5.5.1. The calculated t-values are the same, but the critical t-values are different. Not only are the values themselves different, with a two-tail test there are two critical values, one from each side of the distribution. With a one-tail test there is only one critical value, from one side of the distribution. Also, the p-value from the one-tail test is usually half that of the two-tail test, although this fact is harder to appreciate from this example because both p-values are essentially zero.

5.5.2b Testing Advertising Effectiveness

The other hypothesis of interest is whether an increase in advertising expenditure will bring an increase in sales revenue that is sufficient to cover the increased cost of advertising. Since such an increase will be achieved if $\beta_3 > 1$, we set up the hypotheses:

1. $H_0 : \beta_3 \leq 1$ and $H_1 : \beta_3 > 1$.

2. Treating the null hypothesis as the equality $H_0 : \beta_3 = 1$, the test statistic that has the t-distribution when H_0 is true is, from (5.12),

$$t = \frac{b_3 - 1}{\text{se}(b_3)} \sim t_{(N-K)}$$

3. Choosing $\alpha = 0.05$ as our level of significance, the relevant critical value is $t_{(0.95,72)} = 1.666$. We reject H_0 if $t \geq 1.666$ or if the p-value ≤ 0.05.

4. The value of the test statistic is

$$t = \frac{b_3 - \beta_3}{se(b_3)} = \frac{1.8626 - 1}{0.6832} = 1.263$$

The p-value of the test is $P(t_{(72)} > 1.263) = 0.105$.

5. Since $1.263 < 1.666$, we do not reject H_0. There is insufficient evidence in our sample to conclude that advertising will be cost effective. Using the p-value to perform the test, we again conclude that H_0 cannot be rejected because $0.105 > 0.05$. Another way of thinking about the test outcome is as follows: Because the estimate $b_2 = 1.8626$ is greater than 1, this estimate by itself suggests advertising will be effective. However, when we take into account the precision of estimation, measured by the standard error, we find that $b_2 = 1.8626$ is not significantly greater than 1. In the context of our hypothesis testing framework, we cannot conclude with a sufficient degree of certainty that $\beta_3 > 1$.

5.6 Measuring Goodness-of-Fit

For the simple regression model studied in Chapter 4, we introduced R^2 as a measure of the proportion of variation in the dependent variable that is explained by variation in the explanatory variable. In the multiple regression model the same measure is relevant, and the same formulas are valid, but now we talk of the proportion of variation in the dependent variable explained by *all* the explanatory variables included in the linear model. The coefficient of determination is

$$R^2 = \frac{SSR}{SST} = \frac{\sum_{i=1}^{N}(\hat{y}_i - \bar{y})^2}{\sum_{i=1}^{N}(y_i - \bar{y})^2}$$
$$= 1 - \frac{SSE}{SST} = 1 - \frac{\sum_{i=1}^{N}\hat{e}_i^2}{\sum_{i=1}^{N}(y_i - \bar{y})^2} \tag{5.16}$$

where SSR is the variation in y "explained" by the model (sum of squares of regression), SST is the total variation in y about its mean (sum of squares total), and SSE is the sum of squared least squares residuals (errors) and is the portion of the variation in y that is not explained by the model.

The notation $\hat{y}_i$ refers to the predicted value of y for each of the sample values of the explanatory variables. That is,

$$\hat{y}_i = b_1 + b_2 x_{i2} + b_3 x_{i3} + \cdots + b_K x_{iK}$$

The sample mean $\bar{y}$ is both the mean of y_i and the mean of $\hat{y}_i$, providing the model includes an intercept (β_1 in this case).

The value for SSE will be reported by almost all computer software, but sometimes SST is not reported. Recall, however, that the sample standard deviation for y, which is readily computed by most software, is given by

$$\hat{\sigma}_y = \sqrt{\frac{1}{N-1}\sum_{i=1}^{N}(y_i - \bar{y})^2} = \sqrt{\frac{SST}{N-1}}$$

and so

$$SST = (N - 1)\hat{\sigma}_y^2$$

For Big Andy's Burger Barn we find that $SST = 74 \times 6.48854^2 = 3115.485$ and $SSE = 1718.943$. Using these sums of squares, we have

$$R^2 = 1 - \frac{\sum_{i=1}^{N} \hat{e}_i^2}{\sum_{i=1}^{N} (y_i - \bar{y})^2} = 1 - \frac{1718.943}{3115.485} = 0.448$$

The interpretation of R^2 is that 44.8% of the variation in sales revenue is explained by the variation in price and by the variation in the level of advertising expenditure. It means that, *in our sample*, 55.2% of the variation in revenue is left unexplained and is due to variation in the error term or to variation in other variables that implicitly form part of the error term.

As mentioned in Section 4.2.2, the coefficient of determination is also viewed as a measure of the predictive ability of the model over the sample period or as a measure of how well the estimated regression fits the data. The value of R^2 is equal to the squared sample correlation coefficient between $\hat{y}_i$ and y_i. Since the sample correlation measures the linear association between two variables, if R^2 is high, it means that there is a close association between the values of y_i and the values predicted by the model, $\hat{y}_i$. In this case the model is said to "fit" the data well. If R^2 is low, there is not a close association between the values of y_i and the values predicted by the model, $\hat{y}_i$, and the model does not fit the data well.

One difficulty with R^2 using as a goodness-of-fit measure is that it can be made large by adding more and more variables, even if the variables added have no economic justification. Algebraically it is a fact that as variables are added the sum of squared errors SSE goes down and thus R^2 goes up. If the model contains $N - 1$ variables, then $R^2 = 1$. The manipulation of a model just to obtain a high R^2 is not wise.

An alternative measure of goodness-of-fit called the adjusted R^2, and often symbolized as $\bar{R}^2$, is usually reported by regression programs; it is computed as

$$\bar{R}^2 = 1 - \frac{SSE/(N - K)}{SST/(N - 1)}$$

For the data from Big Andy's Burger Barn the value of this descriptive measure is $\bar{R}^2 = 0.433$. This measure does not always go up when a variable is added, because of the degrees of freedom term $N - K$ in the numerator. As the number of variables K increases, SSE goes down, and so does $N - K$. The effect on $\bar{R}^2$ depends on the amount by which SSE falls. While solving one problem, this corrected measure of goodness of fit unfortunately introduces another one. It loses its interpretation; $\bar{R}^2$ is no longer the percent of variation explained. This modified $\bar{R}^2$ is sometimes used and misused as a device for selecting the appropriate set of explanatory variables. This practice should be avoided. We prefer to concentrate on the unadjusted R^2 and think of it as a descriptive device for telling us about the "fit" of the model; it describes the proportion of variation in the dependent variable explained by the explanatory variables and the predictive ability of the model over the sample period.

One final note is in order. The intercept parameter β_1 is the y-intercept of the regression "plane," as shown in Figure 5.1. If, for theoretical reasons, you are *certain* that the regression plane passes through the origin, then $\beta_1 = 0$ and can be omitted from the model. While this is not a common practice, it does occur, and regression software includes an option that removes the intercept from the model. If the model does not contain an intercept parameter, then the measure R^2 given in (5.16) is no longer appropriate. The reason it is no longer appropriate is that, without an intercept term in the model,

$$\sum_{i=1}^{N}(y_i - \bar{y})^2 \neq \sum_{i=1}^{N}(\hat{y}_i - \bar{y})^2 + \sum_{i=1}^{N}\hat{e}_i^2$$

or $SST \neq SSR + SSE$. To understand why, go back and check the proof in Appendix 4B of Chapter 4. In the sum of squares decomposition the cross-product term $\sum_{i=1}^{N}(\hat{y}_i - \bar{y})\hat{e}_i$ no longer disappears. Under these circumstances it does not make sense to talk of the proportion of total variation that is explained by the regression. Thus, when your model does not contain a constant, it is better not to report R^2, even if your computer displays one.

5.6.1 REPORTING THE REGRESSION RESULTS

The discussion and calculation of R^2 completes our description of all the entries in Table 5.2. We are now in a position to report the results along the lines described in Section 4.2.4. When writing a report or paper, the information from estimating a multiple regression equation is summarized by writing down (i) the estimated equation using informative variable names, (ii) standard errors of coefficients below the estimated coefficients (or the t-values for testing zero null hypothesis), and (iii) the R^2-value.

For Big Andy's Burger Barn we have

$$\widehat{SALES} = 118.9 - 7.908PRICE + 1.8626ADVERT \quad R^2 = 0.448$$
$$\text{(se)} \quad (6.4) \quad (1.096) \quad \quad (0.6832) \tag{5.17}$$

From this summary we can read off the estimated effects of changes in the explanatory variables on the dependent variable and we can predict values of the dependent variable for given values of the explanatory variables. For the construction of an interval estimate we need the least squares estimate, its standard error, and a critical value from the t-distribution. For a 95% interval estimate and at least moderate degrees of freedom the critical t-value is approximately 2. Thus, from the information in (5.17), an approximate 95% interval estimate can be obtained by mentally calculating the points two standard errors either side of the least squares estimate.

Similarly, the t-value used to test a null hypothesis of the form $H_0: \beta_k = 0$ is given by the ratio of the least squares estimate to its standard error that appears underneath. It too can be calculated mentally by inspection of (5.17). If the ratio of an estimate to its standard error is absolutely greater than 2 (approximately), you know that a null hypothesis of the form $H_0: \beta_k = 0$ would be rejected at the $\alpha = 0.05$ level of significance. Furthermore, as discussed in Section 3.4.3, from an interval estimate we can tell whether any hypothesis of the form $H_0: \beta_k = c$ would be rejected or not in a two-tail test. If c is within the interval, H_0 is not rejected, otherwise H_0 is rejected. Remembering these quick "inspection techniques" will help you make "on the spot" assessments of reported results.

Table 5.4   **Data for Exercise 5.1**

y_i	x_{i1}	x_{i2}	x_{i3}
1	1	0	1
2	1	1	-2
3	1	2	1
-1	1	-2	0
0	1	1	-1
-1	1	-2	-1
2	1	0	1
1	1	-1	1
2	1	1	0

5.7 Exercises

Answers to exercises marked * appear in Appendix D at the end of book.

5.7.1 PROBLEMS

5.1*   Consider the multiple regression model

$$y_i = x_{i1}\beta_1 + x_{i2}\beta_2 + x_{i3}\beta_3 + e_i$$

with the nine observations on y_i, x_{i1}, x_{i2} and x_{i3} given in Table 5.4.

Use a hand calculator to answer the following questions:
(a) Calculate the observations in terms of deviations from their means. That is, find

$$x_{i2}^* = x_{i2} - \bar{x}_2, \qquad x_{i3}^* = x_{i3} - \bar{x}_3, \qquad y_i^* = y_i - \bar{y}$$

(b) Calculate $\sum y_i^* x_{i2}^*$, $\sum x_{i2}^{*2}$, $\sum y_i^* x_{i3}^*$, $\sum x_{i2}^* x_{i3}^*$, and $\sum x_{i3}^{*2}$.
(c) Use the expressions in Appendix 5A to find least squares estimates b_1, b_2, and b_3.
(d) Find the least squares residuals $\hat{e}_1, \hat{e}_2, \ldots, \hat{e}_9$.
(e) Find the variance estimate $\hat{\sigma}^2$.
(f) Use equation (5.9) to find the sample correlation between x_2 and x_3.
(g) Find the standard error for b_2.
(h) Find SSE, SST, SSR, and R^2.

5.2*   Use your answers to Exercise 5.1 to
(a) Compute a 95% interval estimate for β_2.
(b) Test the hypothesis $H_0 : \beta_2 = 1$ against the alternative that $H_1 : \beta_2 \neq 1$.

5.3   Consider the following model that relates the proportion of a household's budget spent on alcohol WALC to total expenditure TOTEXP, age of the household head AGE, and the number of children in the household NK.

$$WALC = \beta_1 + \beta_2 \ln(TOTEXP) + \beta_3 AGE + \beta_4 NK + e$$

The data in the file *london.dat* were used to estimate this model. See Exercise 4.10 for more details about the data. Note that only households with one or two children are being considered. Thus, NK takes only the values 1 or 2. Output from estimating this equation appears in Table 5.5.

Table 5.5 Output for Exercise 5.3

Dependent Variable: *WALC*
Included observations: 1519

Variable	Coefficient	Std. Error	t-Statistic	Prob.
C	0.0091	0.0191		0.6347
ln(*TOTEXP*)	0.0276		6.6086	0.0000
AGE		0.0002	−6.9624	0.0000
NK	−0.0133	0.0033	−4.0750	0.0000

R-squared			Mean dependent var	0.0606
S.E. of regression			S.D. dependent var	0.0633
Sum squared resid	5.752896 (SSE)			

$\Sigma \hat{e}_i^2$

(a) Fill in the following blank spaces that appear in this table.
  (i) The t-statistic for b_1.
  (ii) The standard error for b_2.
  (iii) The estimate b_3.
  (iv) R^2.
  (v) $\hat{\sigma}$.
(b) Interpret each of the estimates b_2, b_3, and b_4.
(c) Compute a 95% interval estimate for β_3. What does this interval tell you?
(d) Test the hypothesis that the budget proportion for alcohol does not depend on the number of children in the household. Can you suggest a reason for the test outcome?

5.4* The data set used in Exercise 5.3 is used again. This time it is used to estimate how the proportion of the household budget spent on transportation *WTRANS* depends on the log of total expenditure ln(*TOTEXP*), *AGE*, and number of children *NK*. The output is reported in Table 5.6.
(a) Write out the estimated equation in the standard reporting format with standard errors below the coefficient estimates.
(b) Interpret the estimates b_2, b_3, and b_4. Do you think the results make sense from an economic or logical point of view?
(c) Are there any variables that you might exclude from the equation? Why?
(d) What proportion of variation in the budget proportion allocated to transport is explained by this equation.

Table 5.6 Output for Exercise 5.4

Dependent Variable: *WTRANS*
Included observations: 1519

Variable	Coefficient	Std. Error	t-Statistic	Prob.
C	−0.0315	0.0322	−0.9776	0.3284
ln(*TOTEXP*)	0.0414	0.0071	5.8561	0.0000
AGE	−0.0001	0.0004	−0.1650	0.8690
NK	−0.0130	0.0055	−2.3542	0.0187

R-squared	0.0247		Mean dependent var	0.1323
			S.D. dependent var	0.1053

Table 5.7 **Output for Exercise 5.5**

Dependent Variable: *VALUE*
Included observations: 506

Variable	Coefficient	Std. Error	t-Statistic	Prob.
C	28.4067	5.3659	5.2939	0.0000
CRIME	−0.1834	0.0365	−5.0275	0.0000
NITOX	−22.8109	4.1607	−5.4824	0.0000
ROOMS	6.3715	0.3924	16.2378	0.0000
AGE	−0.0478	0.0141	−3.3861	0.0008
DIST	−1.3353	0.2001	−6.6714	0.0000
ACCESS	0.2723	0.0723	3.7673	0.0002
TAX	−0.0126	0.0038	−3.3399	0.0009
PTRATIO	−1.1768	0.1394	−8.4409	0.0000

(e) Predict the proportion of a budget that will be spent on transportation, for both one- and two-children households, when total expenditure and age are set at their sample means, which are 98.7 and 36, respectively.

5.5 This question is concerned with the value of houses in towns surrounding Boston. It uses the data of Harrison, D. and D.L. Rubinfeld (1978), "Hedonic Prices and the Demand for Clean Air," *Journal of Environmental Economics and Management*, 5, 81–102. The output appears in Table 5.7. The variables are defined as follows:

VALUE = median value of owner-occupied homes in thousands of dollars,
CRIME = per capita crime rate,
NITOX = nitric oxide concentration (parts per million),
ROOMS = average number of rooms per dwelling,
AGE = proportion of owner-occupied units built prior to 1940,
DIST = weighted distances to five Boston employment centers,
ACCESS = index of accessibility to radial highways,
TAX = full-value property-tax rate per $10,000, and
PTRATIO = pupil–teacher ratio by town.

(a) Report briefly on how each of the variables influences the value of a home.
(b) Find 95% interval estimates for the coefficients of *CRIME* and *ACCESS*.
(c) Test the hypothesis that increasing the number of rooms by one, increases the value of a house by $7000.
(d) Test as an alternative hypothesis H_1 that reducing the pupil–teacher ratio by 10 will increase the value of a house by more than $10,000.

5.7.2 COMPUTER EXERCISES

5.6 Use a computer to verify your answers to Exercise 5.1, parts (c), (e), (f), (g), and (h).

5.7 (a) The file *lond_small.dat* contains a subset of 500 observations from the bigger file *london.dat*. Use the data in the file *lond_small.dat* to estimate budget share equations of the form

$$W = \beta_1 + \beta_2 \ln(TOTEXP) + \beta_3 AGE + \beta_4 NK + e$$

for all budget shares (food, fuel, clothing, alcohol, transportation, and other) in the data set. Report and discuss your results. In your discussion comment on how total expenditure, age, and number of children influence the various budget proportions. Also comment on the significance of your coefficient estimates.

(b) Commodities are regarded as luxuries if $\beta_2 > 0$ and necessities if $\beta_2 < 0$. For each commodity group test $H_0 : \beta_2 \leq 0$ against $H_1 : \beta_2 > 0$ and comment on the outcomes.

5.8   The file *cocaine.dat* contains 56 observations on variables related to sales of cocaine powder in northeastern California over the period 1984–1991. The data are a subset of those used in the study Caulkins, J.P. and R. Padman (1993), "Quantity Discounts and Quality Premia for Illicit Drugs," *Journal of the American Statistical Association*, 88, 748–757. The variables are

$PRICE$ = price per gram in dollars for a cocaine sale,
$QUANT$ = number of grams of cocaine in a given sale,
$QUAL$ = quality of the cocaine expressed as percentage purity, and
$TREND$ = a time variable with 1984 = 1 up to 1991 = 8.

Consider the regression model

$$PRICE = \beta_1 + \beta_2 QUANT + \beta_3 QUAL + \beta_4 TREND + e$$

(a) What signs would you expect on the coefficients β_2, β_3, and β_4?

(b) Use your computer software to estimate the equation. Report the results and interpret the coefficient estimates. Have the signs turned out as you expected?

(c) What proportion of variation in cocaine price is explained jointly by variation in quantity, quality, and time?

(d) It is claimed that the greater the number of sales, the higher the risk of getting caught. Thus, sellers are willing to accept a lower price if they can make sales in larger quantities. Set up H_0 and H_1 that would be appropriate to test this hypothesis. Carry out the hypothesis test.

(e) Test the hypothesis that the quality of cocaine has no influence on price against the alternative that a premium is paid for better quality cocaine.

(f) What is the average annual change in the cocaine price? Can you suggest why price might be changing in this direction?

5.9* Data on per capita consumption of beef, the price of beef, the price of lamb, the price of pork, and per capita disposable income for Australia, for the period 1949–1965, are given in the file *meat.dat*. All prices and income have been deflated with 1953 as the base year. Consider the log-log demand curve

$$\ln(QB_t) = \beta_1 + \beta_2 \ln(PB_t) + \beta_3 \ln(PL_t) + \beta_4 \ln(PP_t) + \beta_5 \ln(IN_t) + e_t$$

Because the data are observations over time, we use a t subscript instead of an i subscript. The variables are defined as

QB_t is per capita consumption of beef in year t (pounds),
PB_t is the price of beef in year t (pence per pound),
PL_t is the price of lamb in year t (pence per pound),
PP_t is the price of pork in year t (pence per pound), and
IN_t is per capita disposable income in year t (Australian currency pounds).

(a) What signs do you expect on each of the coefficients?

(b) Estimate β_2, β_3, and β_4 using least squares. Interpret the results. Do they seem reasonable?

(c) Compute and interpret the estimated covariance matrix for the least squares estimator and the standard errors.

(d) Compute 95% interval estimates for each of the parameters.

5.10 The file *br.dat* contains data on 1080 houses sold in Baton Rouge, Louisiana, during mid-2005.

(a) Estimate the regression model $PRICE = \beta_1 + \beta_2 SQFT + \beta_3 AGE + e$ for (i) all the houses in the sample, (ii) town houses, and (iii) French style homes. Construct a 95% interval estimate for β_3 in each case and discuss the differences.

(b) For each of the cases in part (a), test the hypothesis that having an older house reduces the price by $1000 per year for each year of its age. Use a two-tail test with an $\alpha = 0.05$ level of significance.

5.11* Reconsider the presidential voting data (*fair.dat*) introduced in Exercise 2.14.

(a) Estimate the regression model

$$VOTE = \beta_1 + \beta_2 GROWTH + \beta_3 INFLATION + e$$

Report the results in standard format. Are the estimates for β_2 and β_3 significantly different from zero at a 10% significance level. Did you use one-tail tests or two-tail tests? Why?

(b) Predict the percentage vote for the incumbent party when the inflation rate is 4% and the growth rate is −4%.

(c) Suppose that the inflation rate is 4% and the growth rate is −4%. Also assume that $\beta_1 = b_1$ and $\beta_3 = b_3$. For what values of β_2 will the incumbent party get the majority of the vote. Using this range of values as the null hypothesis, test the hypothesis that the incumbent party will get the majority of the vote against the alternative that it will not.

5.12 Each morning between 6:30 AM and 8:00 AM Bill leaves the Melbourne suburb of Carnegie to drive to work at the University of Melbourne. The time it takes Bill to drive to work (*TIME*) depends on the departure time (*DEPART*), the number of red lights that he encounters (*REDS*), and the number of trains that he has to wait for at the Murrumbeena level crossing (*TRAINS*). Observations on these variables for the 231 working days in 2006 appear in the file *commute.dat*. *TIME* is measured in minutes. *DEPART* is the number of minutes after 6:30 AM that Bill departs.

(a) Estimate the equation

$$TIME = \beta_1 + \beta_2 DEPART + \beta_3 REDS + \beta_4 TRAINS + e$$

Report the results and interpret each of the coefficient estimates, including the intercept β_1.

(b) Find 95% interval estimates for each of the coefficients. Have you obtained precise estimates of each of the coefficients?

(c) Using a 5% significance level, test the hypothesis that each red light delays Bill by 2 minutes or more against the alternative that the delay is less than 2 minutes.

(d) Using a 10% significance level, test the hypothesis that each train delays Bill by 3 minutes.

(e) Using a 5% significance level, test the null hypothesis that leaving at 7:30 AM instead of 7:00 AM will make the trip at least 10 minutes longer (other things equal).

(f) Using a 5% significance level test the hypothesis that the minimum time it takes Bill is less than or equal to 20 minutes against the alternative that it is more than 20 minutes. What assumptions about the true values of β_2, β_3, and β_4 did you have to make to perform this test?

5.13* The file *rice.dat* contains 352 observations on 44 rice farmers in the Tarlac region of the Philippines for the 8 years 1990 to 1997. Variables in the data set are tonnes of freshly threshed rice (*PROD*), hectares planted (*AREA*), person-days of hired and family labor (*LABOR*), and kilograms of fertilizer (*FERT*). Treating the data set as one sample with $N = 352$, proceed with the following questions:
(a) Estimate the production function

$$\ln(PROD) = \beta_1 + \beta_2\ln(AREA) + \beta_3\ln(LABOR) + \beta_4\ln(FERT) + e$$

Report the results, interpret the estimates, and comment on the statistical significance of the estimates.
(b) Using a 1% level of significance, test the hypothesis that the elasticity of production with respect to land is equal to 0.5.
(c) Find a 95% interval estimate for the elasticity of production with respect to fertilizer. Has this elasticity been precisely measured?
(d) Using a 5% level of significance, test the hypothesis that the elasticity of production with respect to labor is less than or equal to 0.3 against the alternative that it is greater than 0.3. What happens if you reverse the null and alternative hypotheses?

5.14◆ Reconsider the production function for rice estimated in Exercise 5.13.
(a) Predict rice production from 1 hectare of land, 50 person-days of labor, and 100 kg of fertilizer.
(b) Your economic principles suggest that a farmer should continue to apply fertilizer as long as the marginal product of fertilizer $\partial PROD/\partial FERT$ is greater than the price of fertilizer divided by the price of output. Suppose that this price ratio is 0.004. For $FERT = 100$ and the predicted value for $PROD$ found in part (a), show that the farmer should continue to apply fertilizer as long as $\beta_4 > 0.1242$.
(c) Using $H_1 : \beta_4 > 0.1242$ as the alternative hypothesis, test whether the farmer should apply more fertilizer. Use a 5% significance level. Why did we choose $\beta_4 > 0.1242$ as the alternative rather than the null hypothesis?
(d) Find a 95% interval estimate for rice production from 1 hectare of land, 50 person-days of labor and 1 kg of fertilizer.

5.15 Consider the following aggregate production function for the U.S. manufacturing sector

$$Y_t = \alpha K_t^{\beta_2} L_t^{\beta_3} E_t^{\beta_4} M_t^{\beta_5} \exp\{e_t\}$$

where $e_t \sim N(0, \sigma^2)$, Y_t is gross output in time t, K_t is capital, L_t is labor, E_t is energy, and M_t denotes other intermediate materials. The data underlying these variables are given in index form in the file *manuf.dat*.
(a) Show that taking logarithms of the production function puts it in a form suitable for least squares estimation.

(b) Estimate the unknown parameters of the production function and find the corresponding standard errors.

(c) Discuss the economic and statistical implications of these results.

Appendix 5A Derivation of Least Squares Estimators

In Appendix 2A we derived expressions for the least squares estimators b_1 and b_2 in the simple regression model. In this appendix we proceed with a similar exercise for the multiple regression model; we describe how to obtain expressions for b_1, b_2, and b_3 in a model with two explanatory variables. Given sample observations on y, x_2, and x_3, the problem is to find values for β_1, β_2, and β_3 that minimize

$$S(\beta_1, \beta_2, \beta_3) = \sum_{i=1}^{N} (y_i - \beta_1 - \beta_2 x_{i2} - \beta_3 x_{i3})^2$$

The first step is to partially differentiate S with respect to β_1, β_2, and β_3 and to set the first-order partial derivatives to zero. This yields

$$\frac{\partial S}{\partial \beta_1} = 2N\beta_1 + 2\beta_2 \Sigma x_{i2} + 2\beta_3 \Sigma x_{i3} - 2\Sigma y_i$$

$$\frac{\partial S}{\partial \beta_2} = 2\beta_1 \Sigma x_{i2} + 2\beta_2 \Sigma x_{i2}^2 + 2\beta_3 \Sigma x_{i2} x_{i3} - 2\Sigma x_{i2} y_i$$

$$\frac{\partial S}{\partial \beta_3} = 2\beta_1 \Sigma x_{i3} + 2\beta_2 \Sigma x_{i2} x_{i3} + 2\beta_3 \Sigma x_{i3}^2 - 2\Sigma x_{i3} y_i$$

Setting these partial derivatives equal to zero, dividing by 2, and rearranging yields

$$\begin{aligned} Nb_1 + \Sigma x_{i2} b_2 + \Sigma x_{i3} b_3 &= \Sigma y_i \\ \Sigma x_{i2} b_1 + \Sigma x_{i2}^2 b_2 + \Sigma x_{i2} x_{i3} b_3 &= \Sigma x_{i2} y_i \\ \Sigma x_{i3} b_1 + \Sigma x_{i2} x_{i3} b_2 + \Sigma x_{i3}^2 b_3 &= \Sigma x_{i3} y_i \end{aligned} \qquad (5A.1)$$

The least squares estimators for b_1, b_2, and b_3 are given by the solution of this set of three *simultaneous equations*, known as the **normal equations**. To write expressions for this solution it is convenient to express the variables as deviations from their means. That is, let

$$y_i^* = y_i - \bar{y}, \quad x_{i2}^* = x_{i2} - \bar{x}_2, \quad x_{i3}^* = x_{i3} - \bar{x}_3$$

Then the least squares estimates b_1, b_2, and b_3 are

$$b_1 = \bar{y} - b_2 \bar{x}_2 - b_3 \bar{x}_3$$

$$b_2 = \frac{(\Sigma y_i^* x_{i2}^*)(\Sigma x_{i3}^{*2}) - (\Sigma y_i^* x_{i3}^*)(\Sigma x_{i2}^* x_{i3}^*)}{(\Sigma x_{i2}^{*2})(\Sigma x_{i3}^{*2}) - (\Sigma x_{i2}^* x_{i3}^*)^2}$$

$$b_3 = \frac{(\Sigma y_i^* x_{i3}^*)(\Sigma x_{i2}^{*2}) - (\Sigma y_i^* x_{i2}^*)(\Sigma x_{i3}^* x_{i2}^*)}{(\Sigma x_{i2}^{*2})(\Sigma x_{i3}^{*2}) - (\Sigma x_{i2}^* x_{i3}^*)^2}$$

For models with more than three parameters the solutions become quite messy without using matrix algebra; we will not show them. Computer software used for multiple regression computations solves normal equations like those in (5A.1) to obtain the least squares estimates.

Chapter 6

Further Inference in the Multiple Regression Model

Learning Objectives

Based on the material in this chapter, you should be able to

1. Explain the concepts of restricted and unrestricted sums of squared errors and how they are used to test hypotheses.

2. Use the F-test to test single null hypotheses or joint null hypotheses.

3. Use your computer to perform an F-test.

4. Test the overall significance of a regression model, and identify the components of this test from your computer output.

5. Explain how to test a single null hypothesis involving two or more coefficients when (a) H_1 is a "not equal to" hypothesis and (b) H_1 is a "greater than" or "less than" hypothesis.

6. From output of your computer software, locate (a) the sum of squared errors, (b) the F-value for the overall significance of a regression model, (c) the estimated covariance matrix for the least squares estimates, and (d) the correlation matrix for the explanatory variables.

7. Obtain restricted least squares estimates that include nonsample information in the estimation procedure.

8. Explain the properties of the restricted least squares estimator. In particular, how does its bias and variance compare with those of the unrestricted least squares estimator?

9. Explain the issues that need to be considered when choosing a regression model.

10. Explain what is meant by (a) an omitted variable and (b) an irrelevant variable. Explain the consequences of omitted and irrelevant variables for the properties of the least squares estimator.

11. Explain what is meant by collinearity and the consequences for least squares estimation.

12. Explain how the RESET test can pick up model misspecification.

Keywords

auxiliary regressions	omitted variable bias	restricted *SSE*
collinearity	overall significance	single and joint null hypotheses
F-test	RESET	testing many parameters
irrelevant variable	restricted least	unrestricted model
nonsample information	squares	unrestricted *SSE*
omitted variable	restricted model	

Economists develop and evaluate theories about economic behavior. Hypothesis testing procedures are used to test these theories. In Chapter 5 we developed *t*-tests for null hypotheses consisting of a single restriction on one parameter β_k from the multiple regression model. This analysis can be extended in two ways. We may encounter a null hypothesis consisting of a single restriction that involves more than one parameter, or we may be concerned with testing a null hypothesis with two or more restrictions on two or more parameters. The tools for these tests are considered in this chapter. An important new development is the *F*-test used to test a null hypothesis with two or more restrictions on the parameters.

The theories that economists develop sometimes provide **nonsample** information that can be used along with the information in a sample of data to estimate the parameters of a regression model. A procedure that combines these two types of information is called **restricted least squares**. It can be a useful technique when the data are not information-rich, a condition called collinearity, and the theoretical information is good. The restricted least squares procedure also plays a useful practical role when testing hypotheses. In addition to these topics we discuss model specification for the multiple regression model, prediction, and the construction of prediction intervals. Model specification involves choosing a functional form and choosing a set of explanatory variables. In this chapter we focus on issues related to variable choice. What happens if we omit a relevant variable? What happens if we include an irrelevant one? We also discuss the problems that arise if our data are not sufficiently rich because the variables are collinear or lack adequate variation.

The assumptions MR1–MR6 listed in Section 5.1 are adopted throughout this chapter. In particular, we assume the errors are normally distributed. This assumption is needed for the *t*- and *F*-test statistics to have their required distributions in samples of all sizes. If the errors are not normal, then the results presented in this chapter are still valid in the sense that they hold approximately if the sample size is large.

6.1 The *F*-Test

In Chapter 5 we learned how to use *t*-tests to test hypotheses about single parameters in a multiple regression model. There are, however, many instances where tests involving more than one parameter are appropriate. For example, we might want to test whether a group of explanatory variables should be included in a particular model. Should variables on socioeconomic background, along with variables describing education and experience, be used to explain a person's wage? Does the quantity demanded of a product depend on the prices of substitute goods or only on its own price? Other questions that lead to hypothesis tests involving more than one parameter, but do not involve testing the relevance of a group of variables, are: Does a production function exhibit constant returns to scale? If all prices and income go up by the same proportion, will quantity demanded for a commodity remain unchanged?

We distinguish between a **single null hypothesis** that is a null hypothesis with a single restriction on one or more parameters and a **joint null hypothesis** that contains two or more restrictions on two or more parameters. What we discover in this chapter is that a two-tail test for a single null hypothesis can be conducted via a t-test or an F-test. The two tests are equivalent. A one-tail test for a single null hypothesis must be tested via a t-test. The F-test must be used to test a joint null hypothesis.

The F-test for a joint null hypothesis is based on a comparison of the sum of squared errors from the original, unrestricted multiple regression model with the sum of squared errors from a regression model in which the null hypothesis is assumed to be true. To illustrate what is meant by an unrestricted multiple regression model and a model that is restricted by the null hypothesis, consider the Big Andy's Burger Barn example where sales (S) are a function of a price index of all products sold (P) and expenditure on advertising (A)

$$S_i = \beta_1 + \beta_2 P_i + \beta_3 A_i + e_i \qquad -unrestricted \qquad (6.1)$$

Suppose that we wish to test the hypothesis that changes in price have no effect on sales revenue against the alternative that changes in price do have an effect. The null and alternative hypotheses are $H_0: \beta_2 = 0$ and $H_1: \beta_2 \neq 0$. The restricted model, which assumes the null hypothesis is true, is

$$S_i = \beta_1 + \beta_3 A_i + e_i \qquad -restricted \qquad (6.2)$$

Setting $\beta_2 = 0$ in the **unrestricted model** in (6.1) means that the price variable P_i does not appear in the **restricted model** in (6.2).

When estimating a model where a null hypothesis is assumed to be true, we place conditions, or constraints, on the values that the parameters can take. Instead of finding least squares estimates that minimize the sum of squared errors, we find estimates that minimize the sum of squared errors *subject to parameter constraints*. The imposition of the parameter constraints means the sum of squared errors will increase; a constrained minimum is larger than an unconstrained minimum. Thus, the sum of squared errors from (6.2) will be larger than that from (6.1). The idea of the F-test is that if these sums of squared errors are substantially different, then the assumption that the null hypothesis is true has significantly reduced the ability of the model to fit the data, and thus the data do not support the null hypothesis. Conversely, if the null hypothesis is true, we expect that the data are compatible with the conditions placed on the parameters. Thus, we expect little change in the sum of squared errors when the null hypothesis is true.

The sum of squared errors in a model that assumes a null hypothesis is true is called the **restricted sum of squared errors** or SSE_R; the subscript R indicates that the parameters have been restricted or constrained. To make a clear distinction between the restricted sum of squared errors and the sum of squared errors from the original, unrestricted model, the sum of squared errors from the original model is called the **unrestricted sum of squared errors** or SSE_U. It is *always* true that $SSE_R - SSE_U \geq 0$. The null hypothesis can be a single null hypothesis or a joint null hypothesis. Let J be the number of restrictions in the null hypothesis. For example, for testing the null hypothesis that led to the restricted model in (6.2), $J = 1$. The general F-statistic is given by

$$F = \frac{(SSE_R - SSE_U)/J}{SSE_U/(N - K)} \qquad (6.3)$$

If the null hypothesis is true, then the statistic F has what is called an F-distribution with J numerator degrees of freedom and $N - K$ denominator degrees of freedom. Some details about this distribution are given in Appendix B.5.4, with its typical shape illustrated in Figure B.8; the reason why the expression in (6.3) has an F-distribution is given in an appendix to this chapter, Appendix 6A. *If the null hypothesis is not true*, then the difference between SSE_R and SSE_U becomes large, implying that the constraints placed on the model by the null hypothesis have a large effect on the ability of the model to fit the data. A large value for $SSE_R - SSE_U$ means the value of F tends to be *large*. Thus, we *reject* the null hypothesis if the value of the F-test statistic becomes too large. What is too large is decided by comparing the value of F to a critical value F_c, which leaves a probability α in the upper tail of the F-distribution with J and $N - K$ degrees of freedom. Tables of critical values for $\alpha = 0.01$ and $\alpha = 0.05$ are provided in Tables 4 and 5 at the end of the book. The rejection region where $F > F_c$ is illustrated in Figure B.8.

Using the hypothesis testing steps introduced in Chapter 3, the F-test procedure for testing whether price should be excluded from the sales equation is as follows:

1. Specify the null and alternative hypotheses: $H_0: \beta_2 = 0$ and $H_1: \beta_2 \neq 0$.
2. Specify the test statistic and its distribution if the null hypothesis is true: Having one restriction in H_0 means $J = 1$. Also, recall that $N = 75$, so the distribution of the F-test statistic when H_0 is true is

$$F = \frac{(SSE_R - SSE_U)/1}{SSE_U/(75 - 3)} \sim F_{(1,72)}$$

3. Set α and determine the rejection region: Using $\alpha = 0.05$, the critical value from the $F_{(1,72)}$-distribution is $F_c = F_{(0.95,1,72)} = 3.97$. Thus, H_0 is rejected if $F \geq 3.97$. Alternatively, H_0 is rejected if p-value ≤ 0.05.
4. Calculate the sample value of the test statistic and, if desired, the p-value: For the unrestricted and restricted models in equations (6.1) and (6.2), respectively, we find

$$SSE_U = 1718.943, \quad SSE_R = 2961.827$$

Imposing the null hypothesis $H_0: \beta_2 = 0$ on the model has increased the sum of squared errors from 1718.943 to 2961.827. The value of the F-test statistic is

$$F = \frac{(SSE_R - SSE_U)/J}{SSE_U/(N - K)} = \frac{(2961.827 - 1718.943)/1}{1718.943/(75 - 3)} = 52.06$$

The p-value for the test is $p = P\left[F_{(1,72)} \geq 52.06\right] = 0.0000$, correct to four decimal places.

5. State your conclusion: Since $F = 52.06 \geq F_c$, we reject the null hypothesis and conclude that price does have a significant effect on sales revenue. Alternatively, we reject H_0 because $p = 0.0000 \leq 0.05$.

You might ask where the value $F_c = F_{(0.95,1,72)} = 3.97$ came from. The F critical values in Tables 4 and 5 at the end of the book are reported for only a limited number of degrees of freedom. However, exact critical values like the one for this problem can be obtained for any number of degrees of freedom using your statistical software.

6.1.1   THE RELATIONSHIP BETWEEN t- AND F-TESTS

Do you remember that we used a t-test to test $H_0 : \beta_2 = 0$ against $H_1 : \beta_2 \neq 0$ in Chapter 5? Why are we now using an F-test? What is the relationship between the t- and F-tests? When testing a single "equality" null hypothesis (a single restriction) against a "not equal to" alternative hypothesis, either a t-test or an F-test can be used and the test outcomes will be identical. The reason for this correspondence is an exact relationship between the t- and F-distributions. The square of a t-random variable with m degrees of freedom is an F-random variable with one degree of freedom in the numerator and m degrees of freedom in the denominator. It has distribution $F_{(1, m)}$. When using a t-test for $H_0 : \beta_2 = 0$ against $H_1 : \beta_2 \neq 0$, we found that $t = -7.215$ and $t_c = 1.993$. The F-value that we calculated is $F = 52.06 = t^2 = (-7.215)^2$ and the corresponding critical value is $F_c = 3.97 = t_c^2 = (1.993)^2$. Because of this exact relationship, the p-values for the two tests are identical, meaning that we will always reach the same conclusion whichever approach we take.

There is no equivalence when using a one-tail t-test since the F-test is not appropriate when the alternative is an inequality such as ">" or "<". The equivalence between t-tests and F-tests also does not carry over when a null hypothesis consists of more than a single restriction. Under these circumstances, where $J \geq 2$, the t-test cannot be used, but an F-test is available. Examples of F-tests where $J \geq 2$ are given in the next two sections of this chapter.

We can summarize the elements of an F-test as follows:

1. The null hypothesis H_0 consists of one or more equality restrictions. The number of restrictions is denoted by J. When $J = 1$, the null hypothesis is called a single null hypothesis. When $J \geq 2$, it is called a joint null hypothesis. The null hypothesis may not include any "greater than or equal to" or "less than or equal to" hypotheses.

2. The alternative hypothesis states that one or more of the equalities in the null hypothesis is not true. The alternative hypothesis may not include any "greater than" or "less than" options.

3. The test statistic is the F-statistic in (6.3).

4. If the null hypothesis is true, F has the F-distribution with J numerator degrees of freedom and $N - K$ denominator degrees of freedom. The null hypothesis is *rejected* if $F > F_c$, where $F_c = F_{(1-\alpha, J, N-K)}$ is the critical value that leaves α percent of the probability in the upper tail of the F-distribution.

5. When testing a single equality null hypothesis it is perfectly correct to use either the t- or F-test procedure. They are equivalent. In practice, it is customary to test single restrictions using a t-test. The F-test is usually reserved for joint hypotheses.

6.2 Testing the Significance of the Model

An important application of the F-test is for what is called testing the overall significance of a model. In Section 5.5.1, we tested whether the dependent variable y is related to a particular explanatory variable x_k using a t-test. In this section we extend this idea to a joint test of the relevance of *all* the included explanatory variables. Consider again the general multiple regression model with $K - 1$ explanatory variables and K unknown coefficients

$$y_i = \beta_1 + x_{i2}\beta_2 + x_{i3}\beta_3 + \cdots + x_{iK}\beta_K + e_i \tag{6.4}$$

To examine whether we have a viable explanatory model, we set up the following null and alternative hypotheses

$$H_0 : \beta_2 = 0, \beta_3 = 0, \ldots, \beta_K = 0$$

$$H_1 : At\ least\ one\ \text{of the } \beta_k \text{ is nonzero for } k = 2, 3, \ldots, K$$

(6.5)

The null hypothesis is a joint one because it has $K - 1$ components. It states as a conjecture that each and every one of the parameters β_k, other than the intercept parameter β_1, is zero. If this null hypothesis is true, none of the explanatory variables influence y, and thus our model is of little or no value. If the alternative hypothesis H_1 is true, then at least one of the parameters is not zero, and thus one or more of the explanatory variables should be included in the model. The alternative hypothesis does not indicate, however, which variables those might be. Since we are testing whether or not we have a viable explanatory model, the test for (6.5) is sometimes referred to as a **test of the overall significance of the regression model**. Given the t-distribution can only be used to test a single null hypothesis, we use the F-test for testing the joint null hypothesis in (6.5). The unrestricted model is that given in equation (6.4). The restricted model, obtained assuming the null hypothesis is true, is

$$y_i = \beta_1 + e_i \tag{6.6}$$

The least squares estimator of β_1 in this restricted model is $b_1^* = \sum_{i=1}^{N} y_i / N = \bar{y}$, which is the sample mean of the observations on the dependent variable. The *restricted* sum of squared errors from the hypothesis (6.5) is

$$SSE_R = \sum_{i=1}^{N} (y_i - b_1^*)^2 = \sum_{i=1}^{N} (y_i - \bar{y})^2 = SST$$

In this one case, in which we are testing the null hypothesis that all the model parameters are zero *except the intercept*, the restricted sum of squared errors is the total sum of squares (SST) from the original unconstrained model. The unrestricted sum of squared errors is, as before, the sum of squared errors from the unconstrained model. That is, $SSE_U = SSE$. The number of restrictions is $J = K - 1$. Thus, to test the overall significance of a model, the F-test statistic can be modified and written as

$$F = \frac{(SST - SSE)/(K - 1)}{SSE/(N - K)} \tag{6.7}$$

The calculated value of this test statistic is compared to a critical value from the $F_{(K-1, N-K)}$-distribution. It is used to test the overall significance of a regression model. The outcome of the test is of fundamental importance when carrying out a regression analysis, and it is usually automatically reported by computer software as the "F-value".

To illustrate, we test the overall significance of the regression used to explain Big Andy's sales revenue. We want to test whether the coefficients of price and of advertising expenditure are both zero, against the alternative that at least one of these coefficients is not zero. Recalling that the model is $S_i = \beta_1 + \beta_2 P_i + \beta_3 A_i + e_i$, the hypothesis testing steps are as follows:

1. We want to test

$$H_0 : \beta_2 = 0, \quad \beta_3 = 0$$

against the alternative

$$H_1 : \beta_2 \neq 0 \text{ or } \beta_3 \neq 0, \text{ or both are nonzero}$$

2. If H_0 is true $F = \dfrac{(SST - SSE)/(3-1)}{SSE/(75-3)} \sim F_{(2,72)}$.

3. Using a 5% significance level, we find the critical value for the F-statistic with $(2,72)$ degrees of freedom is $F_c = 3.12$. Thus, we reject H_0 if $F \geq 3.12$.

4. From Section 5.6, we have $SST = 3115.485$ and $SSE = 1718.943$, which give an F-value of

$$F = \frac{(SST - SSE)/(K-1)}{SSE/(N-K)} = \frac{(3115.485 - 1718.943)/2}{1718.943/(75-3)} = 29.25$$

Also, p-value $= P[F \geq 29.25] = 0.0000$, correct to four decimal places.

5. Since $29.25 > 3.12$, we reject H_0 and conclude that the estimated relationship is a significant one. A similar conclusion is reached using the p-value. We conclude that price or advertising expenditure or both have an influence on sales. Note that this conclusion is consistent with conclusions reached using separate t-tests for testing the significance of price and the significance of advertising expenditure in Section 5.1.1.

Go back and check the output from your computer software. Can you find the F-value 29.25 and the corresponding p-value of 0.0000 that form part of the routine output?

6.3 An Extended Model

So far in Chapters 5 and 6 we have hypothesized that Big Andy's sales revenue is explained by product price and advertising expenditures,

$$S = \beta_1 + \beta_2 P + \beta_3 A + e \tag{6.8}$$

One aspect of this model that is worth questioning is whether the *linear* relationship between revenue, price, and advertising expenditure is a good approximation to reality. Having a linear model implies that increasing advertising expenditure will continue to increase sales revenue at the same rate irrespective of the existing levels of sales revenue and advertising expenditure. That is, the coefficient β_3, which measures the response of $E(S)$ to a change in A, is constant; it does not depend on the level of A. In reality, as the level of advertising expenditure increases, we would expect diminishing returns to set in. An extra \$100 spent on advertising is likely to have a bigger marginal impact on sales when the level of advertising is, say, \$600, than when it is \$1600.

To illustrate what is meant by diminishing returns consider the relationship between sales and advertising (assuming a fixed price) graphed in Figure 6.1. The figure shows the effect on sales of an increase of \$200 in advertising expenditure when the original level of advertising is (a) \$600 and (b) \$1600. Note that the units in the graph are thousands of dollars and so these points appear as 0.6 and 1.6. At the smaller level of advertising, sales increase from \$72,400 to \$74,000, whereas at the higher level of advertising the increase is a much smaller one, from \$78,500 to \$79,000. The linear model in (6.8) with the constant slope β_3 will not capture these kinds of diminishing returns. What is required is a model where the slope changes as the level of A increases. One such model with this characteristic is obtained by including the squared value of advertising A^2 as another explanatory variable, making the new model

$$S = \beta_1 + \beta_2 P + \beta_3 A + \beta_4 A^2 + e \tag{6.9}$$

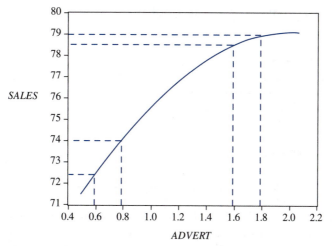

FIGURE **6.1**   A model where sales exhibits diminishing returns to advertising expenditure.

Adding the term $\beta_4 A^2$ to our original specification yields a model in which the response of expected revenue to a change in advertising expenditure depends on the level of advertising. Specifically, using a little calculus, it can be shown that the response of $E(S)$ to a change in A is

$$\frac{\Delta E(S)}{\Delta A}_{\,(P\,\text{held constant})} = \frac{\partial E(S)}{\partial A} = \beta_3 + 2\beta_4 A \tag{6.10}$$

To find the expected signs for β_3 and β_4, note that we expect the response of sales revenue to a change in advertising to be positive when $A = 0$. That is, we expect $\beta_3 > 0$. Also, to achieve diminishing returns the response must decline as A increases. That is, we expect $\beta_4 < 0$.

Having proposed an extended model that might be more realistic, our next step is to estimate it. For estimation purposes the squared value of advertising is "just another variable." That is, we can write (6.9) as

$$y_i = \beta_1 + \beta_2 x_{i2} + \beta_3 x_{i3} + \beta_4 x_{i4} + e_i$$

where

$$y_i = S_i, \quad x_{i2} = P_i, \quad x_{i3} = A_i, \quad x_{i4} = A_i^2$$

The least squares estimates, using the data in the file *andy.dat*, are

$$\hat{S}_i = 109.72 - 7.640 P_i + 12.151 A_i - 2.768 A_i^2$$
$$\text{(se)} \quad (6.80) \quad (1.046) \quad (3.556) \quad (0.941) \tag{6.11}$$

What can we say about the addition of A^2 to the equation? Its coefficient has the expected negative sign and is significantly different from zero at a 5% significance level. Moreover, the coefficient of A has retained its positive sign and continues to be significant. Allowing for diminishing returns to advertising expenditure has improved our model both statistically and in terms of meeting our expectations about how sales will respond to changes in advertising.

6.4 Testing Some Economic Hypotheses

As well as being more realistic, the extended model of the previous section provides a vehicle for testing some interesting economic hypotheses, illustrating the use of *t*- and *F*-tests in economic analysis. The first hypothesis relates to the significance of advertising.

6.4.1 THE SIGNIFICANCE OF ADVERTISING

In the context of our extended model,

$$S_i = \beta_1 + \beta_2 P_i + \beta_3 A_i + \beta_4 A_i^2 + e_i \qquad (6.12)$$

how do we test whether advertising has an effect upon sales revenue? If either β_3 or β_4 is not zero, then advertising has an effect on revenue. Based on two separate one-tail *t*-tests we can conclude, in turn, that β_3 is not zero and β_4 is not zero, and in both cases they are of the correct sign. But the question we are now asking involves testing both β_3 and β_4 at the *same time*. A joint test is appropriate. The joint test uses the *F*-statistic in (6.3) to test $H_0: \beta_3 = 0, \beta_4 = 0$. We will compare the unrestricted model in (6.12) to the restricted model, which assumes the null hypothesis is true. The restricted model is

$$S_i = \beta_1 + \beta_2 P_i + e_i \qquad (6.13)$$

The steps for carrying out the test are as follows:

1. The joint null hypothesis is $H_0: \beta_3 = 0, \beta_4 = 0$. The alternative hypothesis is $H_1: \beta_3 \neq 0$ or $\beta_4 \neq 0$ or both are nonzero.

2. The test statistic and its distribution if the null hypothesis is true are

$$F = \frac{(SSE_R - SSE_U)/2}{SSE_U/(75 - 4)} \sim F_{(2,71)}$$

3. Selecting a 5% significance level, we find that the critical value is $F_c = F_{(0.95,2,71)} = 3.126$, giving a rejection region of $F \geq 3.126$.

4. The sum of squared errors from (6.12) is $SSE_U = 1532.084$; the sum of squared errors from (6.13) is $SSE_R = 1896.391$, leading to a value for the test statistic of $F = 8.44$. The corresponding *p*-value is $P\left[F_{(2,71)} > 8.44\right] = 0.0005$.

5. Since $F = 8.44 > F_c = 3.126$, we reject the null hypothesis that both $\beta_3 = 0$ and $\beta_4 = 0$ and conclude that at least one of them is not zero. Advertising does have a significant effect upon sales revenue. The same conclusion is reached by noting that *p*-value $= 0.0005 < 0.05$.

6.4.2 THE OPTIMAL LEVEL OF ADVERTISING

Economic theory tells us that we should undertake all those actions for which the marginal benefit is greater than the marginal cost. This optimizing principle applies to Big Andy's Burger Barn as it attempts to choose the optimal level of advertising expenditure.

From (6.10) the marginal benefit from another unit of advertising is the increase in expected sales revenue:

$$\frac{\Delta E(S)}{\Delta A}_{(P \text{ held constant})} = \beta_3 + 2\beta_4 A$$

The marginal cost of another unit of advertising is the cost of the advertising plus the cost of preparing the additional products sold due to effective advertising. If we ignore the latter costs, advertising expenditures should be increased to the point where the marginal benefit from \$1 of advertising falls to \$1, or where

$$\beta_3 + 2\beta_4 A_o = 1$$

with A_o denoting the optimal level of advertising. Using the least squares estimates for β_3 and β_4 in (6.11) we can estimate A_o from

$$12.1512 + 2\times(-2.76796)\hat{A}_o = 1$$

Solving, we obtain $\hat{A}_o = 2.014$, implying the optimal monthly advertising expenditure is \$2014.

Big Andy has been spending \$1900 per month on advertising. He wants to know whether this amount could be optimal. Does the information from the estimated equation provide sufficient evidence to reject a hypothesis that \$1900 per month is optimal? The null and alternative hypotheses for this test are

$$H_0: \beta_3 + 2\times\beta_4\times1.9 = 1, \quad H_1: \beta_3 + 2\times\beta_4\times1.9 \neq 1$$

After carrying out the multiplication, these hypotheses can be written as

$$H_0: \beta_3 + 3.8\beta_4 = 1, \quad H_1: \beta_3 + 3.8\beta_4 \neq 1$$

This hypothesis can be tested using either a t-test or an F-test. The t-test statistic

$$t = \frac{(b_3 + 3.8b_4) - 1}{se(b_3 + 3.8b_4)}$$

has a $t_{(71)}$-distribution if the null hypothesis is true. The tricky part of this test is calculating the denominator of the t-statistic. Using the property of variance given in (B.21) of Appendix B.4.3,

$$\widehat{\text{var}(b_3 + 3.8b_4)} = \widehat{\text{var}(b_3)} + 3.8^2 \times \widehat{\text{var}(b_4)} + 2\times3.8\times\widehat{\text{cov}(b_3, b_4)}$$

$$= 12.6463 + 3.8^2\times0.884774 - 2\times3.8\times3.288746$$

$$= 0.427967$$

The estimated variances and covariance are provided by your statistical software. The calculated value of the t-statistic is

$$t = \frac{1.6330 - 1}{\sqrt{0.427967}} = \frac{0.633}{0.65419} = 0.9676$$

The critical value for this two-tailed test comes from the $t_{(71)}$-distribution. At the $\alpha = 0.05$ level of significance $t_c = 1.994$. Thus, because $-1.994 < 0.9676 < 1.994$, we cannot reject the null hypothesis that the optimal level of advertising is \$1900 per month. There is insufficient evidence to suggest Andy should change his advertising strategy.

Alternatively, using an F-test, the test statistic is

$$F = \frac{(SSE_R - SSE_U)/J}{SSE_U/(N - K)}$$

where $J = 1$, $N = 75$, and $K = 4$. The sum of squared errors from the full unrestricted model in (6.12) is $SSE_U = 1532.084$. Some algebra is required to obtain the restricted model that is needed to obtain a value for SSE_R. When H_0 is true, $\beta_3 = 1 - 3.8\beta_4$ and the restricted model becomes

$$S_i = \beta_1 + \beta_2 P_i + (1 - 3.8\beta_4)A_i + \beta_4 A_i^2 + e_i$$

Collecting terms and rearranging this equation to put it in a form convenient for estimation yields

$$(S_i - A_i) = \beta_1 + \beta_2 P_i + \beta_4 (A_i^2 - 3.8A_i) + e_i$$

Estimating this model by least squares with dependent variable $y_i = S_i - A_i$ and explanatory variables $x_{i2} = P_i$ and $x_{i3} = A_i^2 - 3.8A_i$ yields the restricted sum of squared errors $SSE_R = 1552.286$. The calculated value of the F-statistic is

$$F = \frac{(1552.286 - 1532.084)/1}{1532.084/71} = 0.9362$$

The value $F = 0.9362$ is equal to $t^2 = (0.9676)^2$, obeying the relationship between t- and F-random variables that we mentioned previously. The critical value F_c comes from the $F_{(1,71)}$-distribution. For $\alpha = 0.05$ the critical value is $F_c = 3.976 = t_c^2 = (1.994)^2$.

Given that $F = 0.9362 < F_c = 3.976$, using the F-test yields the same result as using the t-test. If the test is done on the basis of its p-value, we find

$$p\text{-value} = P[F_{(1,71)} > 0.9362] = P[t_{(71)} > 0.9676] + P[t_{(71)} < -0.9676] = 0.3365$$

The result $0.3365 > 0.05$ leads us to conclude that Andy's advertising strategy is compatible with the data.

You may have noticed that our description of this test has deviated slightly from the step-by-step hypothesis testing format introduced in Chapter 3 and used so far in the book. The same ingredients were there but their arrangement varied. From now on we will be less formal about following these steps. By being less formal we can expose you to the type of discussion you will find in research reports. Please remember, however, that the steps were introduced for a purpose: To teach you good habits. Following the steps ensures you include a description of all the relevant components of the test and that you think about the steps in the correct order. It is not correct, for example, to decide on the hypotheses or the rejection region after you observe the value of the statistic.

6.4.2a A One-Tail Test with More than One Parameter

Suppose that, instead of wanting to test whether the data supports the conjecture that $A = 1.9$ is optimal, Big Andy wants to test whether the optimal value of A is greater than 1.9. If he has been spending $1900 per month on advertising, and he does not want to increase this amount unless there is convincing evidence that the optimal amount is greater than $1900, he will set up the hypotheses

$$H_0: \beta_3 + 3.8\beta_4 \le 1, \quad H_1: \beta_3 + 3.8\beta_4 > 1$$

In this case we obtain the same calculated t-value of $t = 0.9676$, but the rejection region for a 5% significance level is different. For the two-tail test the $\alpha = 0.05$ rejection region was: Reject H_0 if $t \ge 1.994$ or $t \le -1.994$. In this case, for the one-tail test, it is: Reject H_0 if $t \ge 1.667$. Because $0.9676 < 1.667$, we do not reject H_0. There is not enough evidence in the data to suggest the optimal level of advertising expenditure is greater than $1900.

Because the F-distribution is not well suited for performing one-tail tests of this type, we restrict ourselves to the t-distribution when considering alternative hypotheses that have inequality signs like "<" or ">".

6.4.3 USING COMPUTER SOFTWARE

While it is possible and instructive to compute an F-value by using the restricted and unrestricted sums of squares, it is often more convenient to use the power of modern statistical software. Most statistical software packages have commands that will automatically compute t- and F-values and their corresponding p-values when provided with a null hypothesis. You should check your software. Can you work out how to get it to test null hypotheses like those we constructed? These tests belong to a class of tests called "Wald tests." Your software might refer to them in this way. Can you reproduce the answers we got for Big Andy's tests?

We conclude this section with a joint test of two of Big Andy's conjectures. In addition to proposing that the optimal level of monthly advertising expenditure is $1900, Big Andy is planning staffing and purchasing of inputs on the assumption that a price of $P = \$6$ and advertising expenditure of $A = 1.9$ will, on average, yield sales revenue of $80,000. That is, in the context of our model

$$
\begin{aligned}
E(S) &= \beta_1 + \beta_2 P + \beta_3 A + \beta_4 A^2 \\
&= \beta_1 + 6\beta_2 + 1.9\,\beta_3 + 1.9^2\,\beta_4 \\
&= 80
\end{aligned}
$$

Is this conjecture about sales, and the conjecture about optimal advertising, compatible with the evidence contained in the sample of data? We formulate the joint null hypothesis

$$H_0: \beta_3 + 3.8\beta_4 = 1 \quad and \quad \beta_1 + 6\beta_2 + 1.9\beta_3 + 3.61\beta_4 = 80$$

The alternative is that at least one of these restrictions is not true. Because there are $J = 2$ restrictions to test jointly, we use an F-test. Constructing the restricted model requires substituting both of these restrictions into our extended model, which is left as an exercise. Using instead computer output obtained by supplying the two hypotheses directly to the software, we obtain a computed value for the F-statistic of 5.74 and a corresponding p-value of 0.0049. At a 5% significance level, the joint null hypothesis is rejected. As an exercise, use the least squares estimates to predict sales revenue for $P = 6$ and $A = 1.9$. Has Andy been too optimistic or too pessimistic about the level of sales?

6.5 The Use of Nonsample Information

In many estimation problems we have information over and above the information contained in the sample observations. This nonsample information may come from many places, such as economic principles or experience. When it is available it seems intuitive that we should find a way to use it. If the nonsample information is correct, and if we combine it with the sample information, the precision with which we can estimate the parameters is improved.

To illustrate how we might go about combining sample and nonsample information, consider a model designed to explain the demand for beer. From the theory of consumer choice in microeconomics, we know that the demand for a good will depend on the price of that good, on the prices of other goods, particularly substitutes and complements, and on income. In the case of beer, it is reasonable to relate the quantity demanded (Q) to the price of beer (PB), the price of liquor (PL), the price of all other remaining goods and services (PR), and income (I). To estimate this demand relationship we need a further assumption about the functional form. Using "ln" to denote the natural logarithm, we assume, for this case, that the log-log functional form is appropriate

$$\ln(Q) = \beta_1 + \beta_2 \ln(PB) + \beta_3 \ln(PL) + \beta_4 \ln(PR) + \beta_5 \ln(I) \qquad (6.14)$$

This model is a convenient one because it precludes infeasible negative prices, quantities, and income, and because the coefficients β_2, β_3, β_4, and β_5 are elasticities. See Appendix A.4.4.

A relevant piece of nonsample information can be derived by noting that, if all prices and income go up by the same proportion, we would expect there to be no change in quantity demanded. For example, a doubling of all prices and income should not change the quantity of beer consumed. This assumption is that economic agents do not suffer from "money illusion." Let us impose this assumption on our demand model and see what happens. Having all prices and income change by the same proportion is equivalent to multiplying each price and income by a constant. Denoting this constant by λ, and multiplying each of the variables in (6.14) by λ, yields

$$\begin{aligned} \ln(Q) &= \beta_1 + \beta_2\ln(\lambda PB) + \beta_3\ln(\lambda PL) + \beta_4\ln(\lambda PR) + \beta_5\ln(\lambda I) \\ &= \beta_1 + \beta_2\ln(PB) + \beta_3\ln(PL) + \beta_4\ln(PR) + \beta_5\ln(I) \\ &\quad + (\beta_2 + \beta_3 + \beta_4 + \beta_5)\ln(\lambda) \end{aligned} \qquad (6.15)$$

Comparing (6.14) with (6.15) shows that multiplying each price and income by λ will give a change in $\ln(Q)$ equal to $(\beta_2 + \beta_3 + \beta_4 + \beta_5) \ln(\lambda)$. Thus, for there to be no change in $\ln(Q)$ when all prices and income go up by the same proportion, it must be true that

$$\beta_2 + \beta_3 + \beta_4 + \beta_5 = 0 \qquad (6.16)$$

Thus, we can say something about how quantity demanded should not change when prices and income change by the same proportion, and this information can be written in terms of a specific restriction on the parameters of the demand model. We call such a restriction **nonsample information**. If we believe that this nonsample information makes sense, and hence that the parameter restriction in (6.16) holds, then it seems desirable to be able to obtain estimates that obey this restriction.

To obtain estimates that obey (6.16), we begin with the multiple regression model

$$\ln(Q_t) = \beta_1 + \beta_2 \ln(PB_t) + \beta_3 \ln(PL_t) + \beta_4 \ln(PR_t) + \beta_5 \ln(I_t) + e_t \qquad (6.17)$$

Table 6.1 Summary Statistics for Data Used to Estimate Beer Demand

	Q	PB	PL	PR	I
Sample mean	56.11	3.08	8.37	1.25	32,602
Median	54.90	3.11	8.39	1.18	32,457
Maximum	81.70	4.07	9.52	1.73	41,593
Minimum	44.30	1.78	6.95	0.67	25,088
Std. Dev.	7.8574	0.6422	0.7696	0.2983	4,542

and a sample of data consisting of 30 years of annual data on beer consumption collected from a randomly selected household. These data are stored in the file *beer.dat*. Because the data are time-series rather than cross-sectional data, a subscript t (instead of i) has been used to denote the tth observation. Summary statistics for the data appear in Table 6.1.

To introduce the nonsample information, we solve the parameter restriction $\beta_2 + \beta_3 + \beta_4 + \beta_5 = 0$ for one of the β_k's. Which one is not important mathematically, but for reasons explained below we solve for β_4

$$\beta_4 = -\beta_2 - \beta_3 - \beta_5$$

Substituting this expression into the original model in (6.17) gives

$$\ln(Q_t) = \beta_1 + \beta_2 \ln(PB_t) + \beta_3 \ln(PL_t) + (-\beta_2 - \beta_3 - \beta_5)\ln(PR_t) + \beta_5 \ln(I_t) + e_t$$

$$= \beta_1 + \beta_2\left[\ln(PB_t) - \ln(PR_t)\right] + \beta_3\left[\ln(PL_t) - \ln(PR_t)\right]$$
$$+ \beta_5\left[\ln(I_t) - \ln(PR_t)\right] + e_t$$

$$= \beta_1 + \beta_2 \ln\left(\frac{PB_t}{PR_t}\right) + \beta_3 \ln\left(\frac{PL_t}{PR_t}\right) + \beta_5 \ln\left(\frac{I_t}{PR_t}\right) + e_t \qquad (6.18)$$

We have used the parameter restriction to eliminate the parameter β_4 and in so doing, and using the properties of logarithms, we have constructed the new variables $\ln(PB_t/PR_t)$, $\ln(PL_t/PR_t)$, and $\ln(I_t/PR_t)$. The last line in (6.18) is our restricted model. To get least squares estimates that satisfy the parameter restriction, called **restricted least squares estimates**, we apply the least squares estimation procedure directly to the restricted model in (6.18). The estimated equation is

$$\widehat{\ln(Q_t)} = -4.798 - 1.2994 \ln\left(\frac{PB_t}{PR_t}\right) + 0.1868 \ln\left(\frac{PL_t}{PR_t}\right) + 0.9458 \ln\left(\frac{I_t}{PR_t}\right) \qquad (6.19)$$
$$(\text{se}) \qquad\qquad (0.166) \qquad\qquad (0.284) \qquad\qquad (0.427)$$

Let the restricted least squares estimates in (6.19) be denoted by $b_1^*, b_2^*, b_3^*,$ and b_5^*. To obtain an estimate for β_4 we use the restriction

$$b_4^* = -b_2^* - b_3^* - b_5^* = -(-1.2994) - 0.1868 - 0.9458 = 0.1668$$

By using the restriction *within* the model we have ensured that the estimates obey the constraint, so that $b_2^* + b_3^* + b_4^* + b_5^* = 0$. While it is always possible to obtain restricted estimates by substituting the constraints into the model, it may become messy if there are a number of restrictions or if the restrictions involve several parameters. Some software packages have commands that automatically compute the restricted least squares estimates when provided with the constraints. You should check out the commands available in your software.

What are the properties of this restricted least squares estimation procedure? First, the restricted least squares *estimator* is biased, $E(b_k^*) \neq \beta_k$, *unless* the constraints we impose are *exactly* true. This result makes an important point about econometrics. A good *economist* will obtain more reliable parameter estimates than a poor one, because a good economist will introduce better nonsample information. This is true at the time of model specification and later, when constraints might be applied to the model. Nonsample information is not restricted to constraints on the parameters; it is also used for model specification. *Good economic theory* is a very important ingredient in empirical research.

The second property of the restricted least squares estimator is that its variance is smaller than the variance of the least squares estimator, *whether the constraints imposed are true or not*. By combining nonsample information with the sample information we reduce the variation in the estimation procedure caused by random sampling. This reduction in variance obtained by imposing restrictions on the parameters is not at odds with the Gauss–Markov theorem. The Gauss–Markov result that the least squares estimator is the best linear unbiased estimator applies to linear and unbiased estimators that use data alone, and no constraints on the parameters. Including additional information with the data gives the added reward of a reduced variance. If the additional nonsample information is correct, we are unambiguously better off; the restricted least squares estimator is unbiased and has lower variance. If the additional nonsample information is incorrect, the reduced variance comes at the cost of biasedness. This bias can be a big price to pay if it leads to estimates substantially different from their corresponding true parameter values. Evidence on whether or not a restriction is true can be obtained by testing the restriction along the lines of the previous section. In the case of this particular demand example, the test is left as an exercise.

6.6 Model Specification

In what has been covered so far, we have generally taken the role of the model as given. Questions have been of the following type: Given a particular regression model, what is the best way to estimate its parameters? Given a particular model, how do we test hypotheses about the parameters of that model? How do we construct interval estimates for the parameters of a model? What are the properties of estimators in a given model? Given that all these questions require knowledge of the model, it is natural to ask where the model comes from. In any econometric investigation, choice of the model is one of the first steps. In this section we focus on the following questions: What are the important considerations when choosing a model? What are the consequences of choosing the wrong model? Are there ways of assessing whether a model is adequate?

Three essential features of model choice are (1) choice of functional form, (2) choice of explanatory variables (regressors) to be included in the model, and (3) whether the multiple regression model assumptions MR1–MR6, listed in Chapter 5, hold. Later chapters on heteroskedasticity, autocorrelation, and random regressors deal with violations of the assumptions. For choice of functional form and regressors, economic principles and logical reasoning play a prominent and vital role. We need to ask: What variables are likely to influence the dependent variable y? How is y likely to respond when these variables change? At a constant rate? At a decreasing rate? Is it reasonable to assume constant elasticities over the whole range of the data? The answers to these questions have a bearing on regressor choice and choice of a suitable functional form. Alternative functional forms were considered in Appendix A and Sections 2.3.4, 4.3, and 4.4; further issues in relation to functional form are addressed in Chapter 7. We turn now to consider the consequences of choosing the wrong set of regressors and some questions about regressor choice.

6.6.1 OMITTED VARIABLES

It is possible that a chosen model may have important variables omitted. Our economic principles may have overlooked a variable, or lack of data may lead us to drop a variable even when it is prescribed by economic theory. To introduce the **omitted-variable problem**, we consider a sample of married couples where both husbands and wives work. This sample was used by labor economist Tom Mroz in a classic paper on female labor force participation. The variables from this sample that we use in our illustration are stored in the file *edu_inc.dat*. The dependent variable is annual family income *FAMINC* defined as the combined income of husband and wife. We are interested in the impact of level of education, both the husband's education and the wife's education, on family income. Summary statistics for the data appear in Table 6.2 with *HEDU* and *WEDU* denoting years of education for the husband and wife, respectively. We define the other variables as they are introduced. The estimated relationship is

$$\widehat{FAMINC}_i = -5534 + 3132\,HEDU_i + 4523\,WEDU_i$$

$$\text{(se)} \qquad (11230) \quad (803) \qquad\qquad (1066) \qquad\qquad\qquad (6.20)$$

$$(p\text{-value}) \qquad (0.622) \quad (0.000) \qquad\quad (0.000)$$

We estimate that an additional year of education for the husband will increase annual income by \$3132, and an additional year of education for the wife will increase income by \$4523.

What happens if we now incorrectly omit wife's education from the equation? Then, the estimated equation becomes

$$\widehat{FAMINC}_i = -26191 + 5155\,HEDU_i$$

$$\text{(se)} \qquad\qquad (8541) \quad (658) \qquad\qquad\qquad\qquad (6.21)$$

$$(p\text{-value}) \qquad\quad (0.002) \quad (0.000)$$

Table 6.2   **Summary Statistics for Data Used for Family Income Example**

	FAMINC	HEDU	WEDU	KL6	X_5	X_6
Sample mean	91213	12.61	12.65	0.14	12.57	25.13
Median	83013	12	12	0	12.60	24.91
Maximum	344146	17	17	2	20.82	37.68
Minimum	9072	4	5	0	2.26	9.37
Std. Dev.	44147	3.035	2.285	0.392	3.427	5.052
Correlation matrix						
FAMINC	1.000					
HEDU	0.355	1.000				
WEDU	0.362	0.594	1.000			
KL6	−0.072	0.105	0.129	1.000		
X_5	0.290	0.836	0.518	0.149	1.000	
X_6	0.351	0.821	0.799	0.160	0.900	1.000

Relative to (6.20), omitting *WEDU* leads us to overstate the effect of an extra year of education for the husband by about $2000. This change in the magnitude of a coefficient is typical of the effect of incorrectly omitting a relevant variable. Omission of a relevant variable (defined as one whose coefficient is nonzero) leads to an estimator that is biased. Naturally enough, this bias is known as **omitted-variable bias**. To give a general expression for this bias for the case where one explanatory variable is omitted from a model with two explanatory variables, we write the underlying model for (6.20) as

$$y_i = \beta_1 + \beta_2 x_{i2} + \beta_3 x_{i3} + e_i \tag{6.22}$$

where $y_i = FAMINC_i$, $x_{i2} = HEDU_i$, and $x_{i3} = WEDU_i$. Omitting x_3 from the equation is equivalent to imposing the restriction $\beta_3 = 0$. It can be viewed as an example of imposing an incorrect constraint on the parameters. As discussed in the previous section, the implications of an incorrect constraint are biased coefficient estimates, but a reduced variance. Let b_2^* be the least squares estimator for β_2 when x_3 is omitted from the equation. In an appendix to this chapter, Appendix 6B, we show that

$$\text{bias}(b_2^*) = E(b_2^*) - \beta_2 = \beta_3 \frac{\widehat{\text{cov}}(x_2, x_3)}{\widehat{\text{var}}(x_2)} \tag{6.23}$$

Knowing the sign of β_3 and the sign of the covariance between x_2 and x_3 tells us the direction of the bias. Also, while omitting a variable from the regression usually biases the least squares estimator, if the sample covariance (or sample correlation) between x_2 and the omitted variable x_3 is zero, then the least squares estimator in the misspecified model is still unbiased.

Analyzing (6.23) in the context of our example, first note that $\beta_3 > 0$ because husband's education has a positive effect on family income. Also, from Table 6.2, $\widehat{\text{cov}}(x_2, x_3) > 0$ because husband's and wife's levels of education are positively correlated. Thus, the bias exhibited in (6.21) is positive. There are, of course, other variables that could be included in (6.20) as explanators of family income. In the following equation we include *KL6*, the number of children less than 6 years old. The larger the number of young children, the fewer the number of hours likely to be worked and hence a lower family income would be expected.

$$\widehat{FAMINC}_i = -7755 + 3211\,HEDU_i + 4777\,WEDU_i - 14311\,KL6_i$$

(se)	(11163)	(797)	(1061)	(5004)	(6.24)
(*p*-value)	(0.488)	(0.000)	(0.000)	(0.004)	

We estimate that a child under 6 reduces family income by $14,311. Notice that, compared to (6.20), the coefficient estimates for *HEDU* and *WEDU* have not changed a great deal. This outcome occurs because *KL6* is not highly correlated with the education variables. From a general modeling perspective, it means that useful results can still be obtained when a relevant variable is omitted if that variable is uncorrelated with the included variables, and our interest is on the coefficients of the included variables. Such instances can arise, for example, if data are not available for the relevant omitted variable.

6.6.2   IRRELEVANT VARIABLES

The consequences of omitting relevant variables may lead you to think that a good strategy is to include as many variables as possible in your model. However, doing so will not only complicate your model unnecessarily, it may also inflate the variances of your estimates because of the presence of **irrelevant variables**. To see the effect of irrelevant variables, we add two artificially generated variables X_5 and X_6 to (6.24). These variables were constructed so that they are correlated with *HEDU* and *WEDU*, but are not expected to influence family income. The resulting estimated equation is

$$\widehat{FAMINC}_i = -7759 + 3340\,HEDU_i + 5869\,WEDU_i - 14200\,KL6_i + 889X_{i5} - 1067X_{i6}$$

(se)	(11195)	(1250)	(2278)	(5044)	(2242)	(1982)
(p-value)	(0.500)	(0.008)	(0.010)	(0.005)	(0.692)	(0.591)

What can we observe from these estimates? First, as expected, the coefficients of X_5 and X_6 have p-values greater than 0.05. They do indeed appear to be irrelevant variables. Also, the standard errors of the coefficients estimated for all other variables have increased, with p-values increasing correspondingly. The inclusion of irrelevant variables has reduced the precision of the estimated coefficients for other variables in the equation. This result follows because, by the Gauss–Markov theorem, the least squares estimator of the correct model is the minimum variance linear unbiased estimator.

6.6.3   CHOOSING THE MODEL

The possibilities of omitted-variable bias or inflated variances from irrelevant variables mean that it is important to specify an appropriate set of explanatory variables. Unfortunately, doing so is often not an easy task. There is no one set of mechanical rules that can be applied to come up with the best model. What is needed is an intelligent application of both theoretical knowledge and the outcomes of various statistical tests. Better choices come with experience. What is important is to recognize ways of assessing whether a model is reasonable or not. Some points worth keeping in mind are as follows:

1. Choose variables and a functional form on the basis of your theoretical and general understanding of the relationship.
2. If an estimated equation has coefficients with unexpected signs, or unrealistic magnitudes, they could be caused by a misspecification such as the omission of an important variable.
3. One method for assessing whether a variable or a group of variables should be included in an equation is to perform significance tests. That is, t-tests for hypotheses such as $H_0: \beta_3 = 0$ or F-tests for hypotheses such as $H_0: \beta_3 = \beta_4 = 0$. Failure to reject hypotheses such as these can be an indication that the variable(s) are irrelevant. However, it is important to remember that failure to reject a null hypothesis can also occur if the data are not sufficiently rich to disprove the hypothesis. More will be said about poor data in the next section. For the moment we note that, when a variable has an insignificant coefficient, it can either be (a) discarded as an irrelevant variable or (b) retained because the theoretical reason for its inclusion is a strong one.
4. The adequacy of a model can be tested using a general specification test known as RESET. We conclude this section with a description of this test.

6.6.3a   The RESET Test

Testing for model misspecification is a way of asking is our model adequate, or can we improve on it? It could be misspecified if we have omitted important variables, included irrelevant ones, chosen a wrong functional form, or have a model that violates the assumptions of the multiple regression model. The RESET test (Regression Specification Error Test) is designed to detect omitted variables and incorrect functional form. It proceeds as follows.

Suppose that we have specified and estimated the regression model

$$y_i = \beta_1 + \beta_2 x_{i2} + \beta_3 x_{i3} + e_i$$

Let (b_1, b_2, b_3) be the least squares estimates and let

$$\hat{y}_i = b_1 + b_2 x_{i2} + b_3 x_{i3} \tag{6.25}$$

be the predicted values of y_i. Consider the following two artificial models

$$y_i = \beta_1 + \beta_2 x_{i2} + \beta_3 x_{i3} + \gamma_1 \hat{y}_i^2 + e_i \tag{6.26}$$

$$y_i = \beta_1 + \beta_2 x_{i2} + \beta_3 x_{i3} + \gamma_1 \hat{y}_i^2 + \gamma_2 \hat{y}_i^3 + e_i \tag{6.27}$$

In (6.26) a test for misspecification is a test of $H_0: \gamma_1 = 0$ against the alternative $H_1: \gamma_1 \neq 0$. In (6.27), testing $H_0: \gamma_1 = \gamma_2 = 0$ against $H_1: \gamma_1 \neq 0$ and/or $\gamma_2 \neq 0$ is a test for misspecification. In the first case a t- or an F-test can be used. An F-test is required for the second equation. Rejection of H_0 implies the original model is inadequate and can be improved. A failure to reject H_0 says the test has not been able to detect any misspecification.

To understand the idea behind the test, note that $\hat{y}_i^2$ and $\hat{y}_i^3$ will be polynomial functions of x_{i2} and x_{i3}. If you square and cube both sides of (6.25), you will get terms like x_{i2}^2, x_{i3}^3, $x_{i2} x_{i3}$, $x_{i2} x_{i3}^2$, and so on. Since polynomials can approximate many different kinds of functional forms, if the original functional form is not correct the polynomial approximation that includes $\hat{y}_i^2$ and $\hat{y}_i^3$ may significantly improve the fit of the model. If it does, this fact will be detected through nonzero values of γ_1 and γ_2. Furthermore, if we have omitted variables, and these variables are correlated with x_{i2} and x_{i3}, then they are also likely to be correlated with terms like x_{i2}^2 and x_{i3}^2, and so some of their effect may be picked up by including the terms $\hat{y}_i^2$ and/or $\hat{y}_i^3$. Overall, the general philosophy of the test is: If we can significantly improve the model by artificially including powers of the predictions of the model, then the original model must have been inadequate.

Applying the two RESET tests in (6.26) and (6.27) to the family income equation in (6.24) yields the following results

$$H_0: \gamma_1 = 0 \qquad F = 5.984 \quad p\text{-value} = 0.015$$

$$H_0: \gamma_1 = \gamma_2 = 0 \quad F = 3.123 \quad p\text{-value} = 0.045$$

In both cases the null hypothesis of no misspecification is rejected at a 5% significance level. So, although this equation was a useful one for illustrating the effect of omitted-variable bias, it could be improved upon as a model for explaining family income. Perhaps age and experience could be included in the model, along with whether the household is in a city or the country. Perhaps the linear functional form is inappropriate.

Although the RESET test is often useful for picking up poorly specified models, it needs to be kept in mind that it will not always discriminate between alternative models. For example, if two different functional forms are being considered for a particular relationship, it is possible for RESET to reject neither of them.

6.7 Poor Data, Collinearity, and Insignificance

Most economic data that are used for estimating economic relationships are nonexperi-mental. Indeed, in most cases they are simply "collected" for administrative or other purposes. They are not the result of a planned experiment in which an experimental design is specified for the explanatory variables. In controlled experiments the right-hand-side variables in the model can be assigned values in such a way that their individual effects can be identified and estimated with precision. When data are the result of an uncontrolled experiment many of the economic variables may move together in systematic ways. Such variables are said to be **collinear**, and the problem is labeled **collinearity**. In this case there is no guarantee that the data will be "rich in information," nor that it will be possible to isolate the economic relationship or parameters of interest.

As an example, consider the problem faced by the marketing executives at Big Andy's Burger Barn when they are trying to estimate the increase in sales revenue attributable to advertising that appears in newspapers *and* the increase in sales revenue attributable to coupon advertising. Suppose it has been common practice to coordinate these two advertising devices, so that at the same time advertising appears in the newspapers there are flyers distributed containing coupons for price reductions on hamburgers. If variables measuring the expenditures on these two forms of advertising appear on the right-hand side of a sales revenue equation like (5.2), then the data on these variables will show a systematic, positive relationship; intuitively, it will be difficult for such data to reveal the separate effects of the two types of ads. Although it is clear that total advertising expenditure increases sales revenue, because the two types of advertising expenditure move together, it may be difficult to sort out their separate effects on sales revenue.

As a second example, consider a production relationship explaining output over time as a function of the amounts of various quantities of inputs employed. There are certain factors of production (inputs), such as labor and capital, that are used in *relatively fixed proportions*. As production increases, the changing amounts of two or more such inputs reflect equi-proportionate increases. Proportional relationships between variables are the very sort of systematic relationships that epitomize "collinearity." Any effort to measure the individual or separate effects (marginal products) of various mixes of inputs from such data will be difficult.

It is not just relationships between variables in a sample of data that make it difficult to isolate the separate effects of individual explanatory variables. If the values of an explanatory variable do not vary or change much within a sample of data, then it is clearly difficult to use that data to estimate a coefficient that describes the effect of change in that variable. It is hard to estimate the effect of change if there has been no change.

6.7.1 THE CONSEQUENCES OF COLLINEARITY

The consequences of collinearity and/or lack of variation depend on whether we are examin-ing an extreme case where estimation breaks down or a bad but not extreme case where estimation can still proceed but our estimates lack precision. In Section 5.3.1, we considered the model

$$y_i = \beta_1 + \beta_2 x_{i2} + \beta_3 x_{i3} + e_i$$

and wrote the variance of the least squares estimator for β_2 as

$$\text{var}(b_2) = \frac{\sigma^2}{\left(1 - r_{23}^2\right)\sum_{i=1}^{N}(x_{i2} - \bar{x}_2)^2} \tag{6.28}$$

where r_{23} is the correlation between x_2 and x_3. Exact or extreme collinearity exists when x_2 and x_3 are perfectly correlated, in which case $r_{23} = 1$ and var(b_2) goes to infinity. Similarly, if x_2 exhibits no variation $\sum(x_{i2} - \bar{x}_2)^2$ equals zero and var(b_2) again goes to infinity. In this case x_2 is collinear with the constant term. In general, w*henever there are one or more* **exact** *linear relationships among the explanatory variables, then the condition of exact collinearity exists. In this case the least squares estimator is not defined.* We *cannot* obtain estimates of β_k's using the least squares principle. One of our least squares assumptions MR5, which says the values of x_{ik} are not exact linear functions of the other explanatory variables, is violated.

The more usual case is where correlations between explanatory variables might be high, but not exactly one, variation in explanatory variables may be low but not zero, or linear dependencies between more than two explanatory variables could be high but not exact. These circumstances do *not* constitute a violation of least squares assumptions. By the Gauss–Markov theorem, the least squares estimator is still the best linear unbiased estimator. There may be a problem, however, if the best we can do is not very good because of the poor characteristics of our data. From (6.28) we can see that when r_{23} is close to 1 or $\sum(x_{i2} - \bar{x}_2)^2$ is close to zero, the variance of b_2 will be large. A large variance means a large standard error, which means the estimate may not be significantly different from zero and an interval estimate will be wide. The sample data have provided relatively imprecise information about the unknown parameters. The effects of this imprecise information can be summarized as follows.

1. When estimator standard errors are large, it is likely that the usual t-tests will lead to the conclusion that parameter estimates are not significantly different from zero. This outcome occurs despite possibly high R^2- or F-values indicating significant explanatory power of the model as a whole. The problem is that collinear variables do not provide enough information to estimate their separate effects, even though economic theory may indicate their importance in the relationship.

2. Estimators may be very sensitive to the addition or deletion of a few observations, or the deletion of an apparently insignificant variable.

3. Despite the difficulties in isolating the effects of individual variables from such a sample, accurate forecasts may still be possible if the nature of the collinear relationship remains the same within the out-of-sample observations. For example, in an aggregate production function where the inputs labor and capital are nearly collinear, accurate forecasts of output may be possible for a particular ratio of inputs but not for various mixes of inputs.

6.7.2 AN EXAMPLE

The file *cars.dat* contains observations on the following variables for 392 cars:

    MPG = miles per gallon
    CYL = number of cylinders
    ENG = engine displacement in cubic inches
    WGT = vehicle weight in pounds

Suppose we are interested in estimating the effect of *CYL, ENG*, and *WGT* on *MPG*. All the explanatory variables are related to the power and size of the car. Although there are exceptions, overall we would expect the values for *CYL, ENG,* and *WGT* to be large for large cars and small for small cars. They are variables that are likely to be highly correlated and whose separate effect on *MPG* may be difficult to estimate. A regression of *MPG* on *CYL* yields

$$\widehat{MPG}_i \;=\; 42.9 \;-\; 3.558\,CYL_i$$

$$(\text{se}) \qquad (0.83) \quad (0.146)$$

$$(p\text{-value}) \qquad (0.000) \quad (0.000)$$

We estimate that an additional cylinder reduces the gasoline consumption by 3.6 miles per gallon, and the significance of its coefficient suggests it is an important variable. Now, observe what happens when *ENG* and *WGT* are included. The estimated model becomes

$$\widehat{MPG}_i \;=\; 44.4 \;-\; 0.268\,CYL_i \;-\; 0.0127 ENG_i \;-\; 0.00571\,WGT_i$$

$$(\text{se}) \qquad (1.5) \quad (0.413) \qquad\quad (0.0083) \qquad\quad (0.00071)$$

$$(p\text{-value}) \quad (0.000) \quad (0.517) \qquad\quad (0.125) \qquad\quad\quad (0.000)$$

The estimated coefficient on *CYL* has changed dramatically, and although we know that number of cylinders and engine size are important variables, when considered separately, their coefficients are not significantly different from zero at a 5% significance level. The null hypotheses $H_0:\beta_2 = 0$ and $H_0:\beta_3 = 0$ are not rejected by separate t-tests, where β_2 is the coefficient of *CYL* and β_3 is the coefficient of *ENG*. What is happening is that the high correlation between *CYL* and *ENG* ($r = 0.95$) is making it difficult to accurately estimate the effects of each variable. When we test the null hypothesis $H_0:\beta_2 = \beta_3 = 0$ against the alternative $H_1:\beta_2 \neq 0$ and/or $\beta_3 \neq 0$, we obtain an F-value of 4.30 with corresponding p-value of 0.014. The null hypothesis is firmly rejected. The data are telling us that together *CYL* and *ENG* influence *MPG*, but it is difficult to sort out the influence of each. If one coefficient is free to take any value, the data are not good enough to prove the other coefficient must be nonzero. Should you drop one of the insignificant variables, say *CYL*? Doing so will reduce the variances of the remaining estimates, but, given *CYL* is an important variable that is highly correlated with *ENG* and *WGT*, it is also likely to introduce omitted-variable bias.

6.7.3 IDENTIFYING AND MITIGATING COLLINEARITY

Because nonexact collinearity is not a violation of least squares assumptions, it does not make sense to go looking for a problem if there is no evidence that one exists. If you have estimated an equation where the coefficients are precisely estimated and significant, they have the expected signs and magnitudes, and they are not sensitive to adding or deleting a few observations, or an insignificant variable, then there is no reason to try and identify or mitigate collinearity. If there are highly correlated variables, they are not causing you a problem. However, if you have a poorly estimated equation, which does not live up to expectations, it is useful to establish why the estimates are poor.

One simple way to detect collinear relationships is to use sample correlation coefficients between pairs of explanatory variables. These sample correlations are descriptive measures of linear association. However, in some cases where collinear relationships involve more than two of the explanatory variables, the collinearity may not be detected by examining pairwise correlations. In such instances, a second simple and effective procedure for identifying the presence of collinearity is to estimate the so-called auxiliary regressions. In these least squares regressions, the left-hand-side variable is one of the *explanatory* variables and the right-hand-side variables are all the remaining explanatory variables. For example, a general auxiliary regression for x_2 is

$$x_{i2} = a_1 x_{i1} + a_3 x_{i3} + \cdots + a_K x_{iK} + error$$

If R^2 from this artificial model is high, above 0.80 say, the implication is that a large portion of the variation in x_2 is explained by variation in the other explanatory variables. In Section 5.3.1 we made the point that it is variation in a variable that is *not* associated with any other explanatory variable that is valuable for improving the precision of the least squares estimator b_2. If R^2 from the auxiliary regression is not high, then the variation in x_2 is not explained by the other explanatory variables, and the estimator b_2's precision is not affected by this problem.

The collinearity problem is that the data do not contain enough "information" about the individual effects of explanatory variables to permit us to estimate all the parameters of the statistical model precisely. Consequently, one solution is to obtain more information and include it in the analysis. One form the new information can take is more, and better, sample data. Unfortunately, in economics, this is not always possible. Cross-sectional data are expensive to obtain, and, with time-series data, one must wait for the data to appear. Alternatively, if new data are obtained via the same nonexperimental process as the original sample of data, then the new observations may suffer the same collinear relationships and provide little in the way of new, independent information. Under these circumstances the new data will help little to improve the precision of the least squares estimates.

A second way of adding new information is to introduce, as we did in Section 6.5, *nonsample* information in the form of restrictions on the parameters. This nonsample information may then be combined with the sample information to provide restricted least squares estimates. The good news is that using nonsample information in the form of linear constraints on the parameter values reduces estimator sampling variability. The bad news is that the resulting restricted estimator is *biased* unless the restrictions are *exactly* true. Thus, it is important to use good nonsample information, so that the reduced sampling variability is not bought at a price of large estimator biases.

6.8 Prediction

The prediction problem for a linear model with one explanatory variable was covered in depth in Section 4.1. The results in this section extend naturally to the more general model that has more than one explanatory variable.

To describe the extensions, consider a model with an intercept term and two explanatory variables x_2 and x_3. That is

$$y_i = \beta_1 + x_{i2}\beta_2 + x_{i3}\beta_3 + e_i \tag{6.29}$$

where the e_i are uncorrelated random variables with mean 0 and variance σ^2. Given a set of values for the explanatory variables, say $(1, x_{02}, x_{03})$, the prediction problem is to predict the value of the dependent variable y_0, which is given by

$$y_0 = \beta_1 + x_{02}\beta_2 + x_{03}\beta_3 + e_0$$

If the data are time-series data, $(1, x_{02}, x_{03})$ will be future values for the explanatory variables; for cross-section data they represent values for an individual or some other economic unit that was not sampled. We are assuming that the parameter values determining y_0 are the same as those in the model (6.29) describing how the original sample of data was generated. Also, we assume the random error e_0 to be uncorrelated with each of the sample errors e_i and to have the same mean 0 and variance σ^2. Under these assumptions, the best linear unbiased predictor of y_0 is given by

$$\hat{y}_0 = b_1 + x_{02}b_2 + x_{03}b_3$$

where b_k's are the least squares estimators. This predictor is unbiased in the sense that the average value of the forecast error is zero. That is, if $f = (y_0 - \hat{y}_0)$ is the forecast error, then $E(f) = 0$. The predictor is best in the sense that the variance of the forecast error for all other linear and unbiased predictors of y_0 is not less than $\text{var}(y_0 - \hat{y}_0)$.

The variance of forecast error $\text{var}(y_0 - \hat{y}_0)$ contains two components. One component occurs because b_1, b_2, and b_3 are estimates of the true parameters, and the other component is a consequence of the unknown random error e_0. The expression for $\text{var}(y_0 - \hat{y}_0)$ is given by

$$\begin{aligned}
\text{var}(f) &= \text{var}[(\beta_1 + \beta_2 x_{02} + \beta_3 x_{03} + e_0) - (b_1 + b_2 x_{02} + b_3 x_{03})] \\
&= \text{var}(e_0 - b_1 - b_2 x_{02} - b_3 x_{03}) \\
&= \text{var}(e_0) + \text{var}(b_1) + x_{02}^2 \text{var}(b_2) + x_{03}^2 \text{var}(b_3) \\
&\quad + 2x_{02}\, \text{cov}(b_1, b_2) + 2x_{03}\, \text{cov}(b_1, b_3) + 2x_{02}x_{03}\, \text{cov}(b_2, b_3)
\end{aligned}$$

To obtain $\text{var}(f)$ we recognized that the unknown parameters and the values of the explanatory variables are constants, and that e_0 is uncorrelated with the sample data, and thus is uncorrelated with the least squares estimators (b_1, b_2, b_3). The remaining variances and covariances of the least squares estimators are obtained using the rule for calculating the variance of a weighted sum in Appendix B.4.3.

Each of the terms in the expression for $\text{var}(f)$ involves σ^2. To obtain the estimated variance of the forecast error $\widehat{\text{var}(f)}$, we replace σ^2 with its estimator $\hat{\sigma}^2$. The standard error of the forecast is given by $\text{se}(f) = \sqrt{\widehat{\text{var}(f)}}$. If the random errors e_i and e_0 are normally distributed, or if the sample is large, then

$$\frac{f}{\text{se}(f)} = \frac{y_0 - \hat{y}_0}{\sqrt{\widehat{\text{var}(y_0 - \hat{y}_0)}}} \sim t_{(N-K)}$$

Following the steps we have used many times, a $100(1-\alpha)\%$ interval predictor for y_0 is $\hat{y}_0 \pm t_c \text{se}(f)$, where t_c is a critical value from the $t_{(N-K)}$-distribution.

Thus, the methods for prediction in the model with $K = 3$ are straightforward extensions of the results from the simple linear regression model. For $K > 3$, the methods extend in a similar way.

6.9 Exercises

Answers to exercises marked * appear in Appendix D at the end of the book.

6.9.1 PROBLEMS

6.1 When using $N = 40$ observations to estimate the model

$$y_i = \beta_1 + \beta_2 x_i + \beta_3 z_i + e_i$$

you obtain $SSE = 979.830$ and $\hat{\sigma}_y = 13.45222$. Find
(a) R^2.
(b) The value of the F-statistic for testing $H_0 : \beta_2 = \beta_3 = 0$. Do you reject or fail to reject H_0?

6.2   Consider again the model in Exercise 6.1. After augmenting this model with the squares and cubes of predictions $\hat{y}_i^2$ and $\hat{y}_i^3$, we obtain $SSE = 696.5357$. Use RESET to test for misspecification.

6.3*   Consider the model

$$y_i = \beta_1 + x_{i2}\beta_2 + x_{i3}\beta_3 + e_i$$

and suppose that application of least squares to 20 observations on these variables yields the following results $\left(\text{cov}[b]\right.$ denotes the estimated covariance matrix$)$:

$$\begin{bmatrix} b_1 \\ b_2 \\ b_3 \end{bmatrix} = \begin{bmatrix} 0.96587 \\ 0.69914 \\ 1.7769 \end{bmatrix}, \quad \widehat{\text{cov}[b]} = \begin{bmatrix} 0.21812 & 0.019195 & -0.050301 \\ 0.019195 & 0.048526 & -0.031223 \\ -0.050301 & -0.031223 & 0.037120 \end{bmatrix}$$

$$\hat{\sigma}^2 = 2.5193 \qquad R^2 = 0.9466$$

(a) Find the total variation, unexplained variation, and explained variation for this model.
(b) Find 95% interval estimates for β_2 and β_3.
(c) Use a t-test to test the hypothesis $H_0 : \beta_2 \geq 1$ against the alternative $H_1 : \beta_2 < 1$.
(d) Use your answers in part (a) to test the joint hypothesis $H_0 : \beta_2 = 0, \beta_3 = 0$.
(e) Test the hypothesis $H_0 : 2\beta_2 = \beta_3$.

6.4   Suppose that, from a sample of 63 observations, the least squares estimates and the corresponding estimated covariance matrix are given by

$$\begin{bmatrix} b_1 \\ b_2 \\ b_3 \end{bmatrix} = \begin{bmatrix} 2 \\ 3 \\ -1 \end{bmatrix}, \quad \widehat{\text{cov}[b]} = \begin{bmatrix} 3 & -2 & 1 \\ -2 & 4 & 0 \\ 1 & 0 & 3 \end{bmatrix}$$

Test each of the following hypotheses and state the conclusion:

(a) $\beta_2 = 0$.
(b) $\beta_1 + 2\beta_2 = 5$.
(c) $\beta_1 - \beta_2 + \beta_3 = 4$.

6.5   The RESET test suggests augmenting an existing model with the squares of the predictions $\hat{y}_i^2$, or their squares and cubes $(\hat{y}_i^2, \hat{y}_i^3)$. What would happen if you augmented the model with the predictions themselves $\hat{y}_i$?

6.6   Table 6.3 contains output for the two models

$$y_i = \beta_1 + \beta_2 x_i + \beta_3 w_i + e_i$$
$$y_i = \beta_1 + \beta_2 x_i + e_i$$

obtained using $N = 35$ observations. RESET tests applied to the second model yield F-values of 17.98 (for $\hat{y}_i^2$) and 8.72 (for $\hat{y}_i^2$ and $\hat{y}_i^3$). The correlation between x and w is $r_{xw} = 0.975$. Discuss the following questions:

(a) Should w_i be included in the model?
(b) What can you say about omitted-variable bias?
(c) What can you say about the existence of collinearity and its possible effect?

Table 6.3 **Output for Exercise 6.6**

Variable	Coefficient	Std. Error	t-value	Coefficient	Std. Error	t-value
C	3.6356	2.763	1.316	-5.8382	2.000	-2.919
X	-0.99845	1.235	-0.8085	4.1072	0.3383	12.14
W	0.49785	0.1174	4.240			

Table 6.4 Least Squares Output for Exercise 6.7

Dependent Variable: ln(VC)
Included observations: 268

Variable	Coefficient	Std. Error	t-value	p-value
C	7.528901	0.582172	12.93244	0.0000
ln(Y)	0.679157	0.053399	12.71856	0.0000
ln(K)	0.350305	0.052879	6.624638	0.0000
ln(PL)	0.275366	0.043807	6.285921	0.0000
ln(PF)	0.321864	0.036098	8.916433	0.0000
ln(PM)	−0.068318	0.100338	−0.680879	0.4966
ln(STAGE)	−0.194390	0.028577	−6.802349	0.0000

R-squared	0.989528	Mean dependent var	6.243818
Adjusted R-squared	0.989287	S.D. dependent var	1.135334
S.E. of regression	0.117512	F-statistic	4110.310
Sum squared resid	3.604139	Prob(F-statistic)	0.000000

6.7* In the paper Baltagi, B.H., J.M. Griffen, and S.R. Vadali (1998), "Excess Capacity: A Permanent Characteristic of U.S. Airlines," *Journal of Applied Econometrics*, 13, 645–657, the authors consider estimation of airline cost functions. Tables 6.4–6.6 contain output obtained using their data to estimate a function of the form

$$\ln(VC) = \beta_1 + \beta_2 \ln(Y) + \beta_3 \ln(K) + \beta_4 \ln(PL) + \beta_5 \ln(PF) + \beta_6 \ln(PM)$$
$$+ \beta_7 \ln(STAGE) + e$$

where VC = variable cost; Y = output; K = capital stock; PL = price of labor; PF = price of fuel; PM = price of materials; and $STAGE$ = average flight length.
(a) Interpret the coefficients of $\ln(Y)$, $\ln(K)$, and $\ln(PF)$.
(b) Do the estimated coefficients have the anticipated signs?
(c) Which coefficients are not significantly different from zero?
(d) Does the RESET test suggest the model is misspecified?
(e) Constant returns to scale exist if $\beta_2 + \beta_3 = 1$. Test this hypothesis.
(f) If all input prices increase by the same proportion, variable cost will increase by the same proportion if $\beta_4 + \beta_5 + \beta_6 = 1$. Test this hypothesis.
(g) The tests in parts (e) and (f) could also be carried out using t-statistics. Explain how you would use the information in Tables 6.4 and 6.5 to compute these t-statistics.

Table 6.5 Covariance Matrix for Least Squares Estimates: Exercise 6.7

	C	ln(Y)	ln(K)	ln(PL)	ln(PF)	ln(PM)	ln(STAGE)
C	0.338924	0.007059	−0.005419	0.011217	0.017152	−0.056298	−0.004939
ln(Y)	0.007059	0.002851	−0.002753	−9.89E(05	0.000179	−0.000364	−0.001097
ln(K)	−0.005419	−0.002753	0.002796	2.83E-05	−0.000110	0.000294	0.000887
ln(PL)	0.011217	−9.89E-05	2.83E-05	0.001919	−8.60E-05	−0.002159	3.64E-05
ln(PF)	0.017152	0.000179	−0.000110	−8.60E-05	0.001303	−0.002929	−0.000102
ln(PM)	−0.056298	−0.000364	0.000294	−0.002159	−0.002929	0.010068	0.000104
ln(STAGE)	−0.004939	−0.001097	0.000887	3.64E-05	−0.000102	0.000104	0.000817

Table 6.6   **Test Results for Exercise 6.7**

Ramsey RESET Test:			
F-statistic (1 term)	3.380323	*p*-value	0.067120
F-statistic (2 terms)	1.860108	*p*-value	0.157729
Wald Test:			
Null Hypothesis:	$\beta_2 + \beta_3 = 1$		
F-statistic	6.104834	*p*-value	0.014121
Wald Test:			
Null Hypothesis:	$\beta_4 + \beta_5 + \beta_6 = 1$		
F-statistic	75.43246	*p*-value	0.000000

6.8   In Section 6.4.3 we tested the joint null hypothesis

$$H_0 : \beta_3 + 3.8\,\beta_4 = 1 \quad \text{and} \quad \beta_1 + 6\,\beta_2 + 1.9\,\beta_3 + 3.61\,\beta_4 = 80$$

in the model
$$S_i = \beta_1 + \beta_2 P_i + \beta_3 A_i + \beta_4 A_i^2 + e_i$$

By substituting the restrictions into the model and rearranging variables, show how the model can be written in a form where least squares estimation will yield restricted least squares estimates.

6.9.2   COMPUTER EXERCISES

6.9   In Exercise 5.15 we expressed the model

$$Y_t = \alpha K_t^{\beta_2} L_t^{\beta_3} E_t^{\beta_4} M_t^{\beta_5} \exp\{e_t\}$$

in terms of logarithms and estimated it using data in the file *manuf.dat*. Use the data and results from Exercise 5.15 to test the following hypotheses:
(a) $H_0 : \beta_2 = 0$ against $H_1 : \beta_2 \neq 0$.
(b) $H_0 : \beta_2 = 0, \beta_3 = 0$ against $H_1 : \beta_2 \neq 0$ and/or $\beta_3 \neq 0$.
(c) $H_0 : \beta_2 = 0, \beta_4 = 0$ against $H_1 : \beta_2 \neq 0$ and/or $\beta_4 \neq 0$.
(d) $H_0 : \beta_2 = 0, \beta_3 = 0, \ \beta_4 = 0$ against $H_1 : \beta_2 \neq 0$ and/or $\beta_3 \neq 0$ and/or $\beta_4 \neq 0$.
(e) $H_0 : \beta_2 + \beta_3 + \beta_4 + \beta_5 = 1$ against $H_1 : \beta_2 + \beta_3 + \beta_4 + \beta_5 \neq 1$.
(f) Analyze the impact of collinearity on this model.

6.10* Use the sample data for beer consumption in the file *beer.dat* to
(a) Estimate the coefficients of the demand relation (6.14) using only sample information. Compare and contrast these results to the restricted coefficient results given in (6.19).
(b) Does collinearity appear to be a problem?
(c) Test the validity of the restriction that implies demand will not change if prices and income go up in the same proportion.
(d) Use model (6.19) to construct a 95% prediction interval for Q when $PB = 3.00, PL = 10, PR = 2.00$, and $I = 50,000$. (*Hint*: Construct the interval for $\ln(Q)$ and then take antilogs.)
(e) Repeat part (d) using the unconstrained model from part (a). Comment.

6.11   Consider production functions of the form $Q = f(L, K)$, where Q is the output measure and L and K are labor and capital inputs, respectively. A popular functional form is the Cobb–Douglas equation

$$\ln(Q) = \beta_1 + \beta_2 \ln(L) + \beta_3 \ln(K) + e$$

(a) Use the data in the file *cobb.dat* to estimate the Cobb–Douglas production function. Is there evidence of collinearity?

(b) Re-estimate the model with the restriction of constant returns to scale, that is, $\beta_2 + \beta_3 = 1$, and comment on the results.

6.12* Using data in the file *beer.dat*, perform RESET tests on the two alternative models

$$\ln(Q_t) = \beta_1 + \beta_2 \ln(PB_t) + \beta_3 \ln(PL_t) + \beta_4 \ln(PR_t) + \beta_5 \ln(I_t) + e_t$$

$$Q_t = \beta_1 + \beta_2 PB_t + \beta_3 PL_t + \beta_4 PR_t + \beta_5 I_t + e_t$$

Which model seems to better reflect the demand for beer?

6.13   The file *toodyay.dat* contains 48 annual observations on a number of variables related to wheat yield in the Toodyay Shire of Western Australia, for the period 1950–1997. Those variables are

Y = wheat yield in tonnes per hectare,
 t = trend term to allow for technological change,
RG = rainfall at germination (May–June),
RD = rainfall at development stage (July–August), and
RF = rainfall at flowering (September–October).

The unit of measurement for rainfall is centimeters. A model that allows for the yield response to rainfall to be different for the three different periods is

$$Y_t = \beta_1 + \beta_2 t + \beta_3 RG_t + \beta_4 RD_t + \beta_5 RF_t + e_t$$

(a) Estimate this model. Report the results and comment on the signs and significance of the estimated coefficients.

(b) Test the hypothesis that the response of yield to rainfall is the same irrespective of whether the rain falls during germination, development, or flowering.

(c) Estimate the model under the restriction that the three responses to rainfall are the same. Comment on the results.

6.14   Following on from the example in Section 6.6.1, the file *hwage.dat* contains another subset of the data used by labor economist Tom Mroz. The variables with which we are concerned are

HW = husband's wage in 2006 dollars,
HE = husband's education attainment in years,
HA = husband's age, and
CIT = a variable equal to 1 if living in a large city, otherwise 0.

(a) Estimate the model

$$HW = \beta_1 + \beta_2 HE + \beta_3 HA + e$$

What effect do changes in the level of education and age have on wages?

(b) Does a RESET test suggest the model in part (a) is adequate?

(c) Add the variables HE^2 and HA^2 to the original equation and reestimate it. Describe the effect that education and age have on wages in this newly estimated model.

(d) Does a RESET test suggest the model in part (c) is adequate?

(e) Reestimate the model in part (c) with the variable *CIT* included. What can you say about the level of wages in large cities relative to outside those cities?

(f) Do you think *CIT* should be included in the equation?

(g) For both the model estimated in part (c) and the model estimated in part (e) evaluate the following four derivatives:

(i) $\dfrac{\partial HW}{\partial HE}$ for $HE = 6$ and $HE = 15$

(ii) $\dfrac{\partial HW}{\partial HA}$ for $HA = 35$ and $HA = 50$

Does the omission of *CIT* lead to omitted-variable bias? Can you suggest why?

6.15 In Exercise 5.10 you used data in the file *br.dat* to estimate the regression model $PRICE = \beta_1 + \beta_2 SQFT + \beta_3 AGE + e$ for (i) all the houses in the sample, (ii) town houses, and (iii) French style homes.

(a) For each of these categories test that, on average, the price of a 40-year-old house of size 3600 square feet is more than double that of a 5-year-old house with 1800 square feet. Set up this conjecture as the alternative hypothesis and use a 5% significance level.

(b) Using all the houses in the sample, and a 5% significance level, test the hypothesis that, on average, the following houses are all equally priced: (i) a new house of 2000 square feet, (ii) a 20-year-old house of 2200 square feet, and (iii) a 40-year-old house of 2400 square feet. (Carry out the test in terms of the expected price $E(PRICE)$.)

(c) Does a RESET test suggest this model is a reasonable one? If not, can you make suggestions for improving it?

6.16* Reconsider the presidential voting data (*fair.dat*) introduced in Exercise 2.14 and used again in Exercise 5.11 to estimate the regression model

$$VOTE = \beta_1 + \beta_2 GROWTH + \beta_3 INFLATION + e$$

In order to get reelected, President Willie B. Great believes it is worth sacrificing some inflation as long as more growth is achieved.

(a) Test the hypothesis that a 1% increase in both *GROWTH* and *INFLATION* will leave *VOTE* unchanged against the alternative that *VOTE* will increase.

(b) Test the hypothesis that Willie will not get reelected against the alternative that he will get reelected when the growth rate is 4% and the inflation rate is 5%. (Carry out the test in terms of the expected vote $E(VOTE)$ and use a 5% significance level.)

6.17 Reconsider the commuting time model estimated in Exercise 5.12 using the data file *commute.dat*

$$TIME = \beta_1 + \beta_2 DEPART + \beta_3 REDS + \beta_4 TRAINS + e$$

(a) Using a 5% significance level, test the hypothesis that the delay from a train is equal to three times the delay from a red light.

(b) Using a 5% significance level, test the null hypothesis that the delay from a train is at least three times greater than the delay from a red light against the alternative that it is less than three times greater.

(c) Worried that he may miss an important meeting if there are three trains, Bill leaves for work at 7:10 AM instead of 7:15 AM. Using a 5% significance level, test the null hypothesis that leaving 5 minutes earlier is enough time to allow for three trains against the alternative that it is not enough time.

(d) Suppose that Bill encounters no red lights and no trains. Using a 5% significance level, test the hypothesis that leaving Carnegie at 7:15 AM is early enough to get him to the University before 8:00 AM against the alternative it is not. (Carry out the test in terms of the expected time *E(TIME)*.)

(e) Suppose that Bill leaves Carnegie at 7:00 AM and encounters six red lights and one train. Find a 95% interval estimate for the time he arrives at the University.

6.18* Reconsider the production function for rice estimated in Exercise 5.13 using data in the file *rice.dat*

$$\ln(PROD) = \beta_1 + \beta_2 \ln(AREA) + \beta_3 \ln(LABOR) + \beta_4 \ln(FERT) + e$$

(a) Using a 5% level of significance, test the hypothesis that the elasticity of production with respect to land is equal to the elasticity of production with respect to labor.

(b) Using a 10% level of significance, test the hypothesis that the production function exhibits constant returns to scale. That is, $H_0 : \beta_2 + \beta_3 + \beta_4 = 1$.

(c) Using a 5% level of significance, jointly test the two hypotheses in parts (a) and (b). That is, $H_0 : \beta_2 = \beta_3$ and $\beta_2 + \beta_3 + \beta_4 = 1$.

(d) Using a 5% level of significance, test the hypothesis that the mean of log output equals 1.5 when $AREA = 2$, $LABOR = 100$, and $FERT = 175$. State the null and alternative hypotheses in terms of β_1, β_2, β_3, and β_4.

6.19* Reestimate the model in Exercise 6.18 with (i) *FERT* omitted, (ii) *LABOR* omitted, and (iii) *AREA* omitted. In each case discuss the effect of omitting a variable on the estimates of the remaining two elasticities. Also, in each case check to see if the RESET test has picked up the omitted variable.

Appendix 6A Chi-Square and *F*-tests: More Details

This appendix has two objectives. The first is to explain why the statistic

$$F = \frac{(SSE_R - SSE_U)/J}{SSE_U/(N-K)} \tag{6A.1}$$

has an $F_{(J, N-K)}$-distribution when a specified null hypothesis is true. The other is to introduce a χ^2 (chi-square) statistic that is also used for testing null hypotheses containing single or joint hypotheses about the coefficients in a regression relationship. You may already have noticed and wondered about computer output that gives a χ^2-value and corresponding *p*-value in addition to the *F*-value and its *p*-value.

The starting point is the result that, when the null hypothesis being tested is true,

$$V_1 = \frac{(SSE_R - SSE_U)}{\sigma^2} \sim \chi^2_{(J)} \tag{6A.2}$$

In words, V_1 has a χ^2-distribution with J degrees of freedom. If σ^2 was known, V_1 could be used to test the null hypothesis. There are two ways of overcoming the problem of an unknown σ^2. One leads to the F-statistic in (6A.1); the other yields the χ^2-statistic you may have been wondering about. Considering the second one first, one way to obtain a workable test statistic is to replace σ^2 in (6A.2) with its estimate $\hat{\sigma}^2$ from the unrestricted model. If sample size is sufficiently large, it will be approximately true that

$$\hat{V}_1 = \frac{(SSE_R - SSE_U)}{\hat{\sigma}^2} \sim \chi^2_{(J)} \tag{6A.3}$$

This statistic can be used to test hypotheses about the unknown regression coefficients. At a 5% significance level we reject H_0 if $\hat{V}_1$ is greater than the critical value $\chi^2_{(0.95, J)}$, or if the p-value $P[\chi^2_{(J)} > \hat{V}_1]$ is less than 0.05.

To describe the second way of eliminating the unknown σ^2 we introduce the result

$$V_2 = \frac{(N - K)\hat{\sigma}^2}{\sigma^2} \sim \chi^2_{(N-K)} \tag{6A.4}$$

This result is the multiple regression extension of the simple regression result given in equation (3A.4) of the appendix to Chapter 3. We are now in a position to use the result that the ratio of two independent χ^2 random variables, each divided by their respective degrees of freedom, is an F random variable. That is, from (B.35) in Appendix B at the end of the book,

$$F = \frac{V_1/m_1}{V_2/m_2} \sim F(m_1, m_2)$$

In the context of our problem

$$F = \frac{\dfrac{(SSE_R - SSE_U)}{\sigma^2} \Big/ J}{\dfrac{(N - K)\hat{\sigma}^2}{\sigma^2} \Big/ (N - K)} \tag{6A.5}$$

$$= \frac{(SSE_R - SSE_U)/J}{\hat{\sigma}^2} \sim F_{(J, N-K)}$$

The two σ^2's in V_1 and V_2 cancel. Also, although we have not done so, it is possible to prove that V_1 and V_2 are independent.

Noting that $\hat{\sigma}^2 = SSE_U/(N - K)$, we can see that (6A.5) and (6A.1) are identical. The F-statistic in (6A.5) is the one we have used throughout this chapter for testing hypotheses.

What is the relationship between $\hat{V}_1$ and F given in (6A.3) and (6A.5), respectively? A moment's thought reveals that

$$F = \frac{\hat{V}_1}{J}$$

The F-value is equal to the χ^2-value divided by the number of restrictions in the null hypothesis. We can confirm this relationship by reexamining some examples.

When testing $H_0: \beta_3 = \beta_4 = 0$ in the equation

$$S_i = \beta_1 + \beta_2 P_i + \beta_3 A_i + \beta_4 A_i^2 + e_i$$

we obtain

$$F = 8.44 \quad p\text{-value} = 0.0005$$

$$\chi^2 = 16.88 \quad p\text{-value} = 0.0002$$

Because there are two restrictions ($J = 2$), the F-value is half the χ^2-value. The p-values are different because the tests are different.

For testing $H_0: \beta_3 + 3.8\,\beta_4 = 1$ (see Section 6.4.2), we obtain

$$F = 0.936 \quad p\text{-value} = 0.3365$$
$$\chi^2 = 0.936 \quad p\text{-value} = 0.3333$$

The F- and χ^2-values are equal because $J = 1$, but again the p-values are different.

Appendix 6B   Omitted–Variable Bias: A Proof

Consider the model

$$y_i = \beta_1 + \beta_2 x_{i2} + \beta_3 x_{i3} + e_i$$

Suppose that we incorrectly omit x_3 from the model and estimate instead

$$y_i = \beta_1 + \beta_2 x_{i2} + v_i$$

where $v_i = \beta_3 x_{i3} + e_i$. Then, the estimator used for β_2 is

$$b_2^* = \frac{\sum (x_{i2} - \bar{x}_2)(y_i - \bar{y})}{\sum (x_{i2} - \bar{x}_2)^2} = \beta_2 + \sum w_i v_i \qquad (6B.1)$$

where

$$w_i = \frac{(x_{i2} - \bar{x}_2)}{\sum (x_{i2} - \bar{x}_2)^2}$$

The second equality in (6B.1) follows from Appendix 2D in Chapter 2. Substituting for v_i in (6B.1) yields

$$b_2^* = \beta_2 + \beta_3 \sum w_i x_{i3} + \sum w_i e_i$$

Hence, the mean of b_2^* is

$$
\begin{aligned}
E(b_2^*) &= \beta_2 + \beta_3 \sum w_i x_{i3} \\
&= \beta_2 + \beta_3 \frac{\sum (x_{i2} - \bar{x}_2) x_{i3}}{\sum (x_{i2} - \bar{x}_2)^2} \\
&= \beta_2 + \beta_3 \frac{\sum (x_{i2} - \bar{x}_2)(x_{i3} - \bar{x}_3)}{\sum (x_{i2} - \bar{x}_2)^2} \\
&= \beta_2 + \beta_3 \frac{\widehat{\mathrm{cov}(x_2, x_3)}}{\widehat{\mathrm{var}(x_2)}} \neq \beta_2
\end{aligned}
$$

Thus, the restricted estimator is biased. Knowing the sign of β_3 and the sign of the covariance between x_2 and x_3 tells us the direction of the bias. Also, while omitting a variable from the regression usually biases the least squares estimator, if the sample covariance (or the simple correlation) between x_2 and the omitted variable x_3 is zero, then the least squares estimator in the misspecified model is still unbiased. Way back in Section 2.2, we suggested that omitting an important factor will lead to violation of the assumption SR2 $E(e) = 0$ and that such a violation can have serious consequences. We can now be more precise about that statement. Omitting an important variable that is correlated with variables included in the equation yields an error that we have called v_i in the above discussion. This error will have a nonzero mean and the consequences are biased estimates for the coefficients of the remaining variables in the model.

Chapter 7

Nonlinear Relationships

Learning Objectives

Based on the material in this chapter you should be able to explain

1. The difference between qualitative and quantitative economic variables.
2. How to include a 0–1 dummy variable on the right-hand side of a regression, how this affects model interpretation, and give an example.
3. How to interpret the coefficient on a dummy variable in a log-linear equation.
4. How to include a slope dummy variable in a regression, how this affects model interpretation, and give an example.
5. How to include a product of two dummy variables in a regression, how this affects model interpretation, and give an example.
6. How to model qualitative factors with more than two categories (like region of the country), how to interpret the resulting model, and give an example.
7. The consequences of ignoring a structural change in parameters during part of the sample.
8. How to test the equivalence of two regression equations using dummy variables.
9. How to interpret the coefficient of an interaction between two continuous variables.

Keywords

annual dummy variables	dummy variable trap	nonlinear relationship
binary variable	exact collinearity	polynomial
Chow test	hedonic model	reference group
collinearity	interaction variable	regional dummy variable
dichotomous variable	intercept dummy variable	seasonal dummy variables
dummy variable	log-linear models	slope dummy variable

In this chapter we consider methods for adding more flexibility to the regression model. The tools we introduce allow us to deal with the fact that most economic relationships are not linear. By that, we mean that relationships between economic variables cannot always be represented by straight lines. The essence of a linear relationship is that its slope is constant and does not depend on the values of the variables. If the slope of the relationship changes for any reason, then the relationship is said to be **nonlinear**. This problem was introduced in Sections 4.3 and 4.4, where we examined the choice of model functional form and discovered that by creatively using logarithms, reciprocals, squares, and cubes of variables we could accommodate relationships with many different shapes. See Appendix A, Sections A.3 and A.4, for further discussion of linearity versus nonlinearity.

We will consider several procedures for extending the multiple regression model to situations in which the slope of the relationship changes in one way or another. First, we consider usefulness of **polynomials** to capture curvilinear relationships. Second, we explain the use of **dummy variables, which** are explanatory variables that take only two values, usually 0 and 1. These simple variables are very powerful tools for capturing qualitative characteristics of individuals, such as gender, race, and geographic region of residence. In general, we use dummy variables to describe any event that has only two possible outcomes. Finally, we make use of **interaction variables**. These are variables formed by multiplying two or more explanatory variables together. When using either polynomial terms, dummy variables, or interaction variables, some changes in model interpretation are required, and we will discuss each of these cases.

7.1 Polynomials

Polynomials are a rich class of functions that can parsimoniously describe relationships that are curved, with one or more peaks and valleys. Consider the following examples.

7.1.1 COST AND PRODUCT CURVES

In microeconomics you studied "cost" curves and "product" curves that describe a firm. Total cost and total product curves are mirror images of each other, taking the standard "cubic" shapes shown in Figure 7.1. Average and marginal cost curves, and their mirror images, average and marginal product curves, take quadratic shapes, usually represented as shown in Figure 7.2. The slopes of these relationships are not constant and cannot be represented by regression models that are "linear in the variables." However, these shapes are easily represented by polynomials. For example, if we consider the average cost relationship, in Figure 7.2a, a suitable regression model is

$$AC = \beta_1 + \beta_2 Q + \beta_3 Q^2 + e \tag{7.1}$$

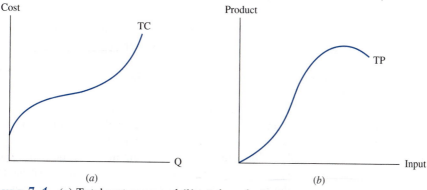

FIGURE 7.1 (a) Total cost curve and (b) total product curve.

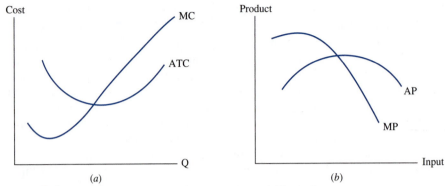

FIGURE 7.2   Average and marginal (*a*) cost curves and (*b*) product curves.

This quadratic function can take the "U" shape we associate with average cost functions. For the total cost curve in Figure 7.1a a cubic polynomial is in order,

$$TC = \alpha_1 + \alpha_2 Q + \alpha_3 Q^2 + \alpha_4 Q^3 + e \tag{7.2}$$

These functional forms, which represent nonlinear shapes, can still be estimated using the least squares methods we have studied. The variables Q^2 and Q^3 are explanatory variables that are treated no differently from any others.

An interesting aspect of models of nonlinear relationships is the interpretation of the parameters—they are no longer slopes. Indeed, the slope of the average cost curve (7.1) is

$$\frac{dE(AC)}{dQ} = \beta_2 + 2\beta_3 Q \tag{7.3}$$

That is, the slope of the average cost curve changes for every value of Q and depends on the parameters β_2 and β_3. For this U-shaped curve we expect $\beta_2 < 0$ and $\beta_3 > 0$.

The slope of the total cost curve (7.2), which is the marginal cost, is

$$\frac{dE(TC)}{dQ} = \alpha_2 + 2\alpha_3 Q + 3\alpha_4 Q^2 \tag{7.4}$$

The slope is a quadratic function of Q, involving the parameters α_2, α_3, and α_4. For a U-shaped marginal cost curve we expect the parameter signs to be $\alpha_2 > 0$, $\alpha_3 < 0$, and $\alpha_4 > 0$.

Another example of a polynomial nonlinear relationship is the quadratic nonlinear relationship between sales and advertising expenditure introduced in Section 6.3. It was similar to (7.1) with a slope that depended on advertising expenditure.

Using polynomial terms is an easy and flexible way to capture nonlinear relationships between variables. As we have shown care must be taken when interpreting the parameters of models containing polynomial terms. Their inclusion does not complicate least squares estimation, with one exception. It is sometimes true that having a variable and its square or cube in the same model causes **collinearity** problems. See Section 6.7.

Table 7.1   **Wage Equation with Quadratic Experience**

Variable	Coefficient	Std. Error	t-Statistic	Prob.
C	−9.8177	1.0550	−9.3062	0.0000
EDUC	1.2101	0.0702	17.2282	0.0000
EXPER	0.3409	0.0514	6.6292	0.0000
$EXPER^2$	−0.0051	0.0012	−4.2515	0.0000

$R^2 = 0.2709$ $SSE = 28420.08$

7.1.2 A WAGE EQUATION

In Section 4.4.2 we introduced a wage equation, and we expressed ln(wages) as a function of education. Now we add another important determinant of wages to the model, namely the worker's years of experience. What we expect is that young, inexperienced workers will have relatively low wages; with additional experience their wages will rise, but the wages will begin to decline after middle age, as the worker nears retirement.[1] To capture this life-cycle pattern of wages we introduce experience and experience squared to explain the level of wages

$$WAGE = \beta_1 + \beta_2 EDUC + \beta_3 EXPER + \beta_4 EXPER^2 + e \qquad (7.5)$$

To obtain the inverted-U shape, we expect $\beta_3 > 0$ and $\beta_4 < 0$. The marginal effect of experience on wage, holding education and other factors constant, is

$$\frac{\partial E(WAGE)}{\partial EXPER} = \beta_3 + 2\beta_4 EXPER \qquad (7.6)$$

The peak of the wage–experience curve occurs where $EXPER = -\beta_3/2\beta_4$. This is the point at which the slope in (7.6) is zero.

To illustrate we use data on 1000 workers from the 1997 Current Population Survey contained in the file *cps_small.dat*. The estimation results are in Table 7.1. The estimated coefficients on education, experience, and experience squared have the anticipated signs and are statistically significant.

For these 1997 data, the dependent variable is earnings per hour ($). Thus we estimate that each additional year of education leads to an increase in hourly earnings of $1.21. Using (7.6), the estimate of the marginal effect of experience at the sample median experience of 18 years is

$$\left.\frac{\widehat{\partial E(WAGE)}}{\partial EXPER}\right|_{EXPER=18} = 0.3409 + 2(-0.0051)18 = 0.1576$$

---

[1] This important economic relationship, still widely studied by labor economists, was discussed by economist Jacob Mincer (1958) "Investment in Human Capital and Personal Income Distribution," *Journal of Political Economy*, 66(4), 281-302. Wages are often expressed in logarithmic form, as we do in Section 7.5, and with this addition the relation in equation (7.5) is called the "Mincer equation." Both the theory and empirical issues are neatly summarized in Ernst Berndt (1991) *The Practice of Econometrics: Classic and Contemporary*, Reading, MA: Addison-Wesley, Chapter 5.

We estimate for a worker with 18 years of experience, that an additional year of experience increases hourly wage by 15.76 cents. The turning point in the relationship, after which wages are expected to diminish with additional experience, is estimated to occur at $EXPER = -\beta_3/2\beta_4 = -0.3409/2(-0.0051) = 33.47$ years.

7.2 Dummy Variables

Dummy variables allow us to construct models in which some or all regression model parameters, including the intercept, change for some observations in the sample. To make matters specific, let us consider an example from real estate economics. Buyers and sellers of homes, tax assessors, real estate appraisers, and mortgage bankers are interested in predicting the current market value of a house. A common way to predict the value of a house is to use a **hedonic model**, in which the price of the house is explained as a function of its characteristics, such as its size, location, number of bedrooms, age, and so on. The idea is to break down a good into its component pieces, and then estimate the value of each characteristic.[2]

For the present, let us assume that the size of the house, measured in square feet, $SQFT$, is the only relevant variable in determining house price, $PRICE$. Specify the regression model as

$$PRICE = \beta_1 + \beta_2 SQFT + e \qquad (7.7)$$

In this model β_2 is the value of an additional square foot of living area, and β_1 is the value of the land alone.

In real estate the three most important words are "location, location, and location." How can we take into account the effect of a property being in a desirable neighborhood, such as one near a university, or near a golf course? Thought of this way, location is a "qualitative" characteristic of a house.

Dummy variables are used to account for qualitative factors in econometric models. They are often called **binary** or **dichotomous** variables as they take just two values, usually 1 or 0, to indicate the presence or absence of a characteristic. This choice of values is arbitrary but very convenient as we will see. Generally we define a dummy variable D as

$$D = \begin{cases} 1 & \text{if characteristic is present} \\ 0 & \text{if characteristic is not present} \end{cases} \qquad (7.8)$$

Thus, for the house price model, we can define a dummy variable, to account for a desirable neighborhood, as

$$D = \begin{cases} 1 & \text{if property is in the desirable neighborhood} \\ 0 & \text{if property is not in the desirable neighborhood} \end{cases}$$

---

[2] Such models have been used for many types of goods, including personal computers, automobiles and wine. This famous idea was introduced by Sherwin Rosen (1978) "Hedonic Prices and Implicit Markets," *Journal of Political Economy*, 82, 357-369. The ideas are summarized and applied to asparagus and personal computers in Ernst Berndt (1991) *The Practice of Econometrics: Classic and Contemporary*, Reading, MA: Addison-Wesley, Chapter 4.

Dummy variables can be used to capture changes in the model intercept, or slopes, or both. We consider these possibilities in turn.

7.2.1 INTERCEPT DUMMY VARIABLES

The most common use of dummy variables is to modify the regression model intercept parameter. Adding the dummy variable D to the regression model, along with a new parameter δ, we obtain

$$PRICE = \beta_1 + \delta D + \beta_2 SQFT + e \qquad (7.9)$$

The effect of the inclusion of a dummy variable D into the regression model is best seen by examining the regression function, $E(PRICE)$, in the two locations. If the model in (7.9) is correctly specified, then $E(e) = 0$ and

$$E(PRICE) = \begin{cases} (\beta_1 + \delta) + \beta_2 SQFT & \text{when } D = 1 \\ \beta_1 + \beta_2 SQFT & \text{when } D = 0 \end{cases} \qquad (7.10)$$

In the desirable neighborhood $D = 1$, and the intercept of the regression function is $(\beta_1 + \delta)$. In other areas the regression function intercept is simply β_1. This difference is depicted in Figure 7.3, assuming that $\delta > 0$.

Adding the dummy variable D to the regression model causes a parallel shift in the relationship by the amount δ. In the context of the house price model the interpretation of the parameter δ is that it is a "location premium," the difference in house price due to being located in the desirable neighborhood. A dummy variable like D that is incorporated into a regression model to capture a shift in the intercept as the result of some qualitative factor is called an **intercept dummy variable**. In the house price example we expect the price to be higher in a desirable location, and thus we anticipate that δ will be positive.

The least squares estimator's properties are not affected by the fact that one of the explanatory variables consists only of zeros and ones—D is treated as any other explanatory variable. We can construct an interval estimate for δ, or we can test the significance of its least squares estimate. Such a test is a statistical test of whether the neighborhood effect on house price is "statistically significant." If $\delta = 0$, then there is no location premium for the neighborhood in question.

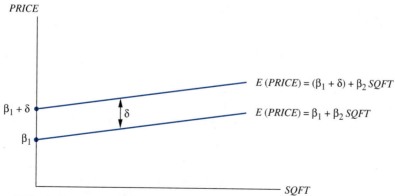

FIGURE **7.3** An intercept dummy variable.

7.2.1a   Choosing the Reference Group

The convenience of the values $D = 0$ and $D = 1$ is seen in (7.10). The value $D = 0$ defines the **reference group**, or **base group**, of houses that are not in the desirable neighborhood. The expected price of these houses is simply $E(PRICE) = \beta_1 + \beta_2 SQFT$. Using (7.9) we are comparing the house prices in the desirable neighborhood to those in the base group.

A researcher can choose whichever neighborhood is most convenient for expository purposes, to be the reference group. For example, we can define the dummy variable LD to denote the less desirable neighborhood

$$LD = \begin{cases} 1 & \text{if property is not in the desirable neighborhood} \\ 0 & \text{if property is in the desirable neighborhood} \end{cases}$$

This dummy variable is defined just the opposite from D, and $LD = 1 - D$. If we include LD in the model specification

$$PRICE = \beta_1 + \lambda LD + \beta_2 SQFT + e$$

then we make the reference group, $LD = 0$, the houses in the desirable neighborhood.

You may be tempted to include both D and LD in the regression model to capture the effect of each neighborhood on house prices. That is, you might consider the model

$$PRICE = \beta_1 + \delta D + \lambda LD + \beta_2 SQFT + e$$

In this model the variables D and LD are such that $D + LD = 1$. Since the intercept variable $x_1 = 1$, we have created a model with **exact collinearity**, and as explained in Section 6.7, the least squares estimator is not defined in such cases. This error is sometimes described as falling into the **dummy variable trap**. By including only one of the dummy variables, either D or LD, the omitted variable defines the reference group, and we avoid the problem.[3]

7.2.2   SLOPE DUMMY VARIABLES

Instead of assuming that the effect of location on house price causes a change in the intercept of the hedonic regression equation (7.7), let us assume that the change is in the slope of the relationship. We can allow for a change in a slope by including in the model an additional explanatory variable that is equal to the product of a dummy variable and a continuous variable. In our model the slope of the relationship is the value of an additional square foot of living area. If we assume this is one value for homes in the desirable neighborhood, and another value for homes in other neighborhoods, we can specify

$$PRICE = \beta_1 + \beta_2 SQFT + \gamma(SQFT \times D) + e \qquad (7.11)$$

The new variable $(SQFT \times D)$ is the product of house size and the dummy variable, and is called an **interaction variable**, as it captures the interaction effect of location and size on house price. Alternatively, it is called a **slope dummy variable**, because it allows for a

---

[3] Another way to avoid the dummy variable trap is to omit the intercept from the model. This choice is less desirable than omitting one dummy variable, since omitting the intercept alters several of the key numerical properties of the least squares estimator. See Appendix 4B and Section 5.6. Omitting the intercept causes the basic definition of model R^2 to fail, which is inconvenient.

change in the slope of the relationship. The slope dummy variable takes a value equal to size for houses in the desirable neighborhood, when $D = 1$, and it is zero for homes in other neighborhoods. Despite its unusual nature, a slope dummy variable is treated just like any other explanatory variable in a regression model. Examining the regression function for the two different locations best illustrates the effect of the inclusion of the slope dummy variable into the economic model,

$$E(PRICE) = \beta_1 + \beta_2 SQFT + \gamma(SQFT \times D) = \begin{cases} \beta_1 + (\beta_2 + \gamma)SQFT & \text{when } D = 1 \\ \beta_1 + \beta_2 SQFT & \text{when } D = 0 \end{cases}$$

In the desirable neighborhood, the price per square foot of a home is $(\beta_2 + \gamma)$; it is β_2 in other locations. We would anticipate $\gamma > 0$ if price per square foot is higher in the more desirable neighborhood. This situation is depicted in Figure 7.4a.

Another way to see the effect of including a slope dummy variable is to use calculus. The partial derivative of expected house price with respect to size (measured in square feet), which gives the slope of the relation, is

$$\frac{\partial E(PRICE)}{\partial SQFT} = \begin{cases} \beta_2 + \gamma & \text{when } D = 1 \\ \beta_2 & \text{when } D = 0 \end{cases}$$

If the assumptions of the regression model hold for (7.11), then the least squares estimators have their usual good properties, as discussed in Section 5.3. A test of the hypothesis that the

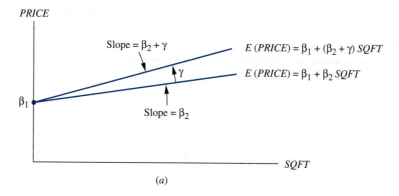

(a)

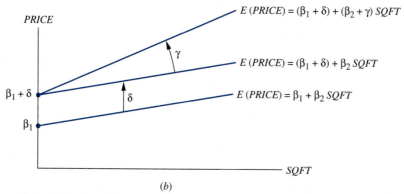

(b)

FIGURE **7.4** (a) A slope dummy variable. (b) A slope and intercept dummy variable.

Table 7.2   **Representative Real Estate Data Values**

PRICE	SQFT	AGE	UTOWN	POOL	FPLACE
205.452	23.46	6	0	0	1
185.328	20.03	5	0	0	1
248.422	27.77	6	0	0	0
287.339	23.67	28	1	1	0
255.325	21.30	0	1	1	1
301.037	29.87	6	1	0	1

value of a square foot of living area is the same in the two locations is carried out by testing the null hypothesis $H_0 : \gamma = 0$ against the alternative $H_1 : \gamma \neq 0$. In this case, we might test $H_0 : \gamma = 0$ against $H_1 : \gamma > 0$, since we expect the effect to be positive.

If we assume that house location affects *both* the intercept and the slope, then both effects can be incorporated into a single model. The resulting regression model is

$$PRICE = \beta_1 + \delta D + \beta_2 SQFT + \gamma(SQFT \times D) + e \qquad (7.12)$$

In this case the regression functions for the house prices in the two locations are

$$E(PRICE) = \begin{cases} (\beta_1 + \delta) + (\beta_2 + \gamma)SQFT & \text{when } D = 1 \\ \beta_1 + \beta_2 SQFT & \text{when } D = 0 \end{cases}$$

In Figure 7.4b we depict the house price relations assuming that $\delta > 0$ and $\gamma > 0$.

7.2.3   AN EXAMPLE: THE UNIVERSITY EFFECT ON HOUSE PRICES

A real estate economist collects information on 1000 house price sales from two similar neighborhoods, one called "University Town" bordering a large state university, and one that is a neighborhood about 3 miles from the university. A few of the observations are shown in Table 7.2. The complete data file is *utown.dat*.

House prices are given in $1000; size (*SQFT*) is the number of hundreds of square feet of living area. For example, the first house sold for $205,452 and has 2346 square feet of living area. Also recorded are the house *AGE* (in years), location (*UTOWN* = 1 for homes near the university, 0 otherwise), whether the house has a pool (*POOL* = 1 if a pool is present, 0 otherwise) and whether the house has a fireplace (*FPLACE* = 1 if a fireplace is present, 0 otherwise).

The economist specifies the regression equation as

$$\begin{aligned} PRICE = \beta_1 &+ \delta_1 UTOWN + \beta_2 SQFT + \gamma(SQFT \times UTOWN) \\ &+ \beta_3 AGE + \delta_2 POOL + \delta_3 FPLACE + e \end{aligned} \qquad (7.13)$$

We anticipate that all the coefficients in this model will be positive except β_3, which is an estimate of the effect of age, or depreciation, on house price. Note that *POOL* and *FPLACE* are intercept dummy variables. By introducing these variables we are asking if, and by how much, these features change house price. Because these variables stand alone, and are not interacted with *SQFT,* we are assuming that they do not affect the price per square foot. The estimated regression results are shown in Table 7.3. The goodness-of-fit statistic is

Table 7.3   **House Price Equation Estimates**

Variable	Coefficient	Std. Error	t-Statistic	Prob.
C	24.5000	6.1917	3.9569	0.0001
UTOWN	27.4530	8.4226	3.2594	0.0012
SQFT	7.6122	0.2452	31.0478	0.0000
SQFT×UTOWN	1.2994	0.3320	3.9133	0.0001
AGE	−0.1901	0.0512	−3.7123	0.0002
POOL	4.3772	1.1967	3.6577	0.0003
FPLACE	1.6492	0.9720	1.6968	0.0901

$R^2 = 0.8706$ $SSE = 230184.4$

$R^2 = 0.8706$ indicating that the model fits the data well. The slope dummy variable is $SQFT \times UTOWN$. Based on one-tail t-tests of significance, at the $\alpha = 0.05$ level we reject zero null hypotheses for each of the parameters and accept the alternatives that they are positive, except for the coefficient on AGE, which we accept to be negative. In particular, based on these t-tests, we conclude that houses near the university have a significantly higher base price and their price per square foot is significantly higher than the comparison neighborhood.

The estimated regression function for the houses near the university is

$$\widehat{PRICE} = (24.5 + 27.453) + (7.6122 + 1.2994)SQFT - 0.1901AGE$$
$$+ 4.3772POOL + 1.6492FPLACE$$

$$= 51.953 + 8.9116SQFT - 0.1901AGE + 4.3772POOL + 1.6492FPLACE$$

For houses in other areas, the estimated regression function is

$$\widehat{PRICE} = 24.5 + 7.6122SQFT - 0.1901AGE + 4.3772POOL + 1.6492FPLACE$$

Based on these regression results, we estimate

- the location premium for lots near the university is $27,453
- the price per square foot is $89.12 for houses near the university and $76.12 for houses in other areas
- that houses depreciate $190.10 per year
- that a pool increases the value of a home by $4377.20
- that a fireplace increases the value of a home by $1649.20

7.3 Applying Dummy Variables

Dummy variables can be used to ask, and answer, a rich variety of questions. In this section we consider some common applications.

7.3.1 INTERACTIONS BETWEEN QUALITATIVE FACTORS

We have seen how dummy variables can be used to represent qualitative factors in a regression model. Intercept dummy variables for qualitative factors are *additive*. That is, the effect of each qualitative factor is added to the regression intercept, and the effect of any dummy variable is independent of any other qualitative factor. Sometimes, however, we might question whether qualitative factors' effects are independent.

For example, suppose we are estimating a wage equation, in which an individual's wages are explained as a function of their experience, skill, and other factors related to productivity. It is customary to include dummy variables for race and gender in such equations. If we have modeled productivity attributes well, and if wage determination is not discriminatory, then the coefficients of the race and gender dummy variables should not be significant. Including just race and gender dummies, however, will not capture interactions between these qualitative factors. Is there a differential in wages for black women? Separate dummy variables for being "black" and "female" will not capture this extra interaction effect. To allow for such a possibility consider the following specification, where for simplicity we use only education (*EDUC*) as a productivity measure,

$$WAGE = \beta_1 + \beta_2 EDUC + \delta_1 BLACK$$
$$+ \delta_2 FEMALE + \gamma(BLACK \times FEMALE) + e \qquad (7.14)$$

where *BLACK* and *FEMALE* are dummy variables, and thus so is their interaction. These are intercept dummy variables because they are not interacted with any continuous explanatory variable. They have the effect of causing a parallel shift in the regression, as in Figure 7.3. When multiple dummy variables are present, and especially when there are interactions between dummies, it is important for proper interpretation to write out the regression function, *E(WAGE)*, for each dummy variable combination.

$$E(WAGE) = \begin{cases} \beta_1 + \beta_2 EDUC & WHITE-MALE \\ (\beta_1 + \delta_1) + \beta_2 EDUC & BLACK-MALE \\ (\beta_1 + \delta_2) + \beta_2 EDUC & WHITE-FEMALE \\ (\beta_1 + \delta_1 + \delta_2 + \gamma) + \beta_2 EDUC & BLACK-FEMALE \end{cases}$$

In this specification white males are the reference group, because this is the group defined when all dummy variables take the value zero, in this case $BLACK = 0$ and $FEMALE = 0$. The parameter δ_1 measures the effect of being black, relative to the reference group; the parameter δ_2 measures the effect of being female, and the parameter γ measures the effect of being black and female.

Using the CPS data (*cps_small.dat*) we obtain the results in Table 7.4. Holding the effect of education constant, we estimate that black males earn $1.83 per hour less than white males, white females earn $2.55 less than white males, and black females earn $3.80 less than white males. The coefficients of *EDUC, BLACK,* and *FEMALE* are all significantly different from zero using individual *t*-tests. The interaction effect between *BLACK* and

Table 7.4 **Wage Equation with Race and Gender**

Variable	Coefficient	Std. Error	t-Statistic	Prob.
C	−3.2303	0.9675	−3.3388	0.0009
EDUC	1.1168	0.0697	16.0200	0.0000
BLACK	−1.8312	0.8957	−2.0444	0.0412
FEMALE	−2.5521	0.3597	−7.0953	0.0000
BLACK×FEMALE	0.5879	1.2170	0.4831	0.6291

$R^2 = 0.2482$ $\qquad SSE = 29307.71$

FEMALE is not estimated very precisely using this sample of 1000 observations, and it is not statistically significant.[4]

Suppose we are asked to test the joint significance of all the qualitative factors. How do we test the hypothesis that neither race nor gender affects wages? We do it by testing the joint null hypothesis $H_0 : \delta_1 = 0$, $\delta_2 = 0$, $\gamma = 0$ against the alternative that at least one of the indicated parameters is not zero. If the null hypothesis is true, race and gender fall out of the regression, and thus they have no effect on wages.

To test this hypothesis we use the F-test procedure that is described in Section 6.1. The test statistic for a joint hypothesis is

$$F = \frac{(SSE_R - SSE_U)/J}{SSE_U/(N-K)}$$

where SSE_R is the sum of squared least squares residuals from the "restricted" model in which the null hypothesis is assumed to be true, SSE_U is the sum of squared residuals from the original, "unrestricted," model, J is the number of joint hypotheses, and $N - K$ is the number of degrees of freedom in the unrestricted model. If the null hypothesis is true, then the test statistic F has an F-distribution with J numerator degrees of freedom and $N - K$ denominator degrees of freedom, $F_{(J, N-K)}$. We reject the null hypothesis if $F \geq F_c$, where F_c is the critical value, illustrated in Figure B.8 of Appendix B, for the level of significance α. To test the $J = 3$ joint null hypotheses $H_0 : \delta_1 = 0$, $\delta_2 = 0$, $\gamma = 0$, we obtain the unrestricted sum of squared errors $SSE_U = 29308$ from the model reported in Table 7.4. The restricted sum of squares is obtained by estimating the model that assumes the null hypothesis is true, leading to the fitted model

$$\widehat{WAGE} = -4.9122 + 1.1385EDUC$$
$$\text{(se)} \quad (0.9668) \quad (0.0716)$$

which has $SSE_R = 31093$. The degrees of freedom $N - K = 1000 - 5 = 995$ come from the unrestricted model. The value of the F-statistic is

$$F = \frac{(SSE_R - SSE_U)/J}{SSE_U/(N-K)} = \frac{(31093 - 29308)/3}{29308/995} = 20.20$$

The 1% critical value (i.e., the 99th percentile value) is $F_{(0.99,3,995)} = 3.80$. Thus we conclude that race and/or gender affect the wage equation.

7.3.2 QUALITATIVE FACTORS WITH SEVERAL CATEGORIES

Many qualitative factors have more than two categories. An example is the variable region of the country in our wage equation. The CPS data record worker residence within one of the four regions: Northeast, Midwest, South, and West. Again, using just the simple wage

---

[4] Estimating this model using the larger data set *cps.dat*, which contains 4733 observations, yields a coefficient estimate of 1.2685 with a *t*-value of 2.37. Recall from Sections 2.4.4 and 5.3.1 that larger sample sizes lead to smaller standard errors and thus more precise estimation. Labor economists tend to use large data sets so that complex effects and interactions can be estimated precisely. We use the smaller data set as a text example so that results can be replicated with student versions of software.

specification for illustration, we can incorporate dummy variables into the wage equation as

$$WAGE = \beta_1 + \beta_2 EDUC + \delta_1 SOUTH + \delta_2 MIDWEST + \delta_3 WEST + e \qquad (7.15)$$

Notice that we have not included the dummy variables for all regions. Doing so would have created a model in which exact collinearity exists. Since the regional categories are exhaustive, the sum of the region dummy variables is $NORTHEAST + SOUTH + MIDWEST + WEST = 1$. Thus the "intercept variable" $x_1 = 1$ is an exact linear combination of the region dummies. Recall, from Section 6.7, that the least squares estimator is not defined in such cases. Failure to omit one dummy variable will lead to your computer software returning a message saying that least squares estimation fails. This error is the **dummy variable trap** that we mentioned in Section 7.2.1a.

The usual solution to this problem is to omit one dummy variable, which defines a **reference group**, as we shall see by examining the regression function,

$$E(WAGE) = \begin{cases} (\beta_1 + \delta_3) + \beta_2 EDUC & WEST \\ (\beta_1 + \delta_2) + \beta_2 EDUC & MIDWEST \\ (\beta_1 + \delta_1) + \beta_2 EDUC & SOUTH \\ \beta_1 + \beta_2 EDUC & NORTHEAST \end{cases}$$

The omitted dummy variable, $NORTHEAST$, identifies the reference group for the equation, to which workers in other regions are compared. It is the group that remains when the regional dummy variables $WEST$, $MIDWEST$, and $SOUTH$ are set to zero. Mathematically it does not matter which dummy variable is omitted and the choice can be made that is most convenient for interpretation. The intercept parameter β_1 represents the base wage for a worker with no education who lives in the northeast. The parameter δ_1 measures the expected wage differential between southern workers relative to those in the northeast; δ_2 measures the expected wage differential between midwestern workers and those in the northeast.

Using the CPS data *cps_small.dat*, let us take the specification in Table 7.4 and add the regional dummies $SOUTH$, $MIDWEST$, and $WEST$. The results are in Table 7.5. Based on those results we can say that workers in the south earn significantly less per hour than workers in the northeast, holding constant the factors education, experience, race, and gender. We estimate that workers in the south earn $1.24 less per hour than workers in the northeast.

Table 7.5 **Wage Equation with Regional Dummy Variables**

Variable	Coefficient	Std. Error	t-Statistic	Prob.
C	−2.4557	1.0510	−2.3365	0.0197
EDUC	1.1025	0.0700	15.7526	0.0000
BLACK	−1.6077	0.9034	−1.7795	0.0755
FEMALE	−2.5009	0.3600	−6.9475	0.0000
BLACK×FEMALE	0.6465	1.2152	0.5320	0.5949
SOUTH	−1.2443	0.4794	−2.5953	0.0096
MIDWEST	−0.4996	0.5056	−0.9880	0.3234
WEST	−0.5462	0.5154	−1.0597	0.2895

$R^2 = 0.2535$ $\qquad$ $SSE = 29101.3$

How would we test the hypothesis that there are no regional differences? This would be a joint test of the null hypothesis that the coefficients of the regional dummies are all zero. In the context of the CPS data, $SSE_U = 29101$ for the wage equation in Table 7.5. Under the null hypothesis the model in Table 7.5 reduces to that in Table 7.4 where $SSE_R = 29308$. This yields an F-statistic value of 2.3452. The $\alpha = 0.05$ critical value (95th percentile) is $F_{(0.95,3,992)} = 2.6138$ and for $\alpha = 0.10$ (90th percentile) it is $F_{(0.90,3,992)} = 2.0893$. At the 10% level of significance we reject the null hypothesis and conclude that that there are significant regional differences. We cannot make this statement at the 5% level.[5]

7.3.3 TESTING THE EQUIVALENCE OF TWO REGRESSIONS

In the Section 7.2.2 we introduced both an intercept and slope dummy variable into the hedonic equation for house price. The result was given in equation (7.12)

$$PRICE = \beta_1 + \delta D + \beta_2 SQFT + \gamma(SQFT \times D) + e$$

The regression functions for the house prices in the two locations are

$$E(PRICE) = \begin{cases} \alpha_1 + \alpha_2 SQFT & D = 1 \\ \beta_1 + \beta_2 SQFT & D = 0 \end{cases}$$

where $\alpha_1 = \beta_1 + \delta$ and $\alpha_2 = \beta_2 + \gamma$. Figure 7.4b shows that by introducing both intercept and slope dummy variables we have essentially assumed that the regressions in the two neighborhoods are completely different. We could obtain the estimates for (7.12) by estimating separate regressions for each of the neighborhoods. In this section we generalize this idea, which leads to the **Chow test**, named after econometrician Gregory Chow. The Chow test is an F-test for the equivalence of two regressions.

By including an intercept dummy variable and an interaction variable for *each* additional variable in an equation we allow all coefficients to differ based on a qualitative factor. Consider again the wage equation in (7.14)

$$WAGE = \beta_1 + \beta_2 EDUC + \delta_1 BLACK + \delta_2 FEMALE + \gamma(BLACK \times FEMALE) + e$$

We might ask "Are there differences between the wage regressions for the south and for the rest of the country?" If there are no differences, then the data from the south and other regions can be pooled into one sample, with no allowance made for differing slope or intercept. How can we test this? We can carry out the test by creating an intercept and slope dummy for *every* variable in the model, and then jointly testing the significance of the dummy variable coefficients using an F-test. That is, we specify the model

$$\begin{aligned} WAGE = {} & \beta_1 + \beta_2 EDUC + \delta_1 BLACK + \delta_2 FEMALE + \gamma(BLACK \times FEMALE) \\ & + \theta_1 SOUTH + \theta_2(EDUC \times SOUTH) + \theta_3(BLACK \times SOUTH) \\ & + \theta_4(FEMALE \times SOUTH) + \theta_5(BLACK \times FEMALE \times SOUTH) + e \end{aligned} \quad (7.16)$$

In (7.16) we have twice the number of parameters and variables than in (7.14). We have added five new variables, the $SOUTH$ intercept dummy variable and interactions between $SOUTH$ and the other four variables, and corresponding parameters. Estimating (7.16) is

---

[5] Using the larger CPS data file *cps.dat*, $F = 8.7909$, which is significant at the 1% level.

Table 7.6 **Comparison of Fully Interacted to Separate Models**

Variable	(1) Full sample Coefficient	Std. Error	(2) Non-south Coefficient	Std. Error	(3) South Coefficient	Std. Error
C	−3.5775	1.1513	−3.5775	1.2106	−2.2752	1.5550
EDUC	1.1658	0.0824	1.1658	0.0866	0.9741	0.1143
BLACK	−0.4312	1.3482	−0.4312	1.4176	−2.1756	1.0804
FEMALE	−2.7540	0.4257	−2.7540	0.4476	−1.8421	0.5896
BLACK×FEMALE	0.0673	1.9063	0.0673	2.0044	0.6101	1.4329
SOUTH	1.3023	2.1147				
EDUC×SOUTH	−0.1917	0.1542				
BLACK×SOUTH	−1.7444	1.8267				
FEMALE×SOUTH	0.9119	0.7960				
BLACK×FEMALE×SOUTH	0.5428	2.5112				
SSE	29012.7		22031.3		6981.4	
N	1000		685		315	

equivalent to estimating (7.14) twice—once for the southern workers and again for workers in the rest of the country. To see this examine the regression functions

$$
E(WAGE) = \begin{cases} \beta_1 + \beta_2 EDUC + \delta_1 BLACK + \delta_2 FEMALE \\ \quad + \gamma(BLACK \times FEMALE) \hspace{3cm} SOUTH = 0 \\ (\beta_1 + \theta_1) + (\beta_2 + \theta_2)EDUC + (\delta_1 + \theta_3)BLACK \\ \quad + (\delta_2 + \theta_4)FEMALE + (\gamma + \theta_5)(BLACK \times FEMALE) \hspace{1cm} SOUTH = 1 \end{cases}
$$

Note that each variable has a separate coefficient for southern and non-southern workers.

In column (1) of Table 7.6 we report the estimates and standard errors for the fully interacted model (7.16), using the full sample. The base model (7.14) is estimated once for workers outside the south [column (2)] and again for southern workers [column (3)]. Note that the coefficient estimates on the non-south data in (2) are identical to those using the full sample in (1). The standard errors differ because the estimates of the error variance, σ^2, differ. The coefficient estimates using only southern workers are obtained from the full model by adding the dummy variable interaction coefficients θ_i to the corresponding non-south coefficients. For example, the coefficient estimate for *BLACK* in column (3) is obtained as $(\hat{\delta}_1 + \hat{\theta}_3) = -0.4312 - 1.7444 = -2.1756$. Similarly the coefficient on *FEMALE* in (3) is $(\hat{\delta}_2 + \hat{\theta}_4) = -2.7540 + 0.9119 = -1.8421$. Furthermore, note that the sum of squared residuals for the full model in column (1) is the sum of the *SSE* from the two separate regressions

$$
SSE_{full} = SSE_{non\text{-}south} + SSE_{south} = 22031.3 + 6981.4 = 29012.7
$$

Using this dummy variable approach we can test for a southern regional difference. We estimate (7.16) and test the joint null hypothesis

$$
H_0 : \theta_1 = \theta_2 = \theta_3 = \theta_4 = \theta_5 = 0
$$

against the alternative that at least one $\theta_i \neq 0$. This is the Chow test. If we reject this null hypothesis we conclude that there is some difference in the wage equation in the southern region relative to the rest of the country. The test can also be thought of as comparing the estimates in the non-south and south in columns (2) and (3) in Table 7.6.

The test ingredients are the unrestricted $SSE_U = 29012.7$ from the full model in Table 7.6 (or the sum of the *SSE*s from the two separate regressions), and the restricted $SSE_R = 29307.7$ from Table 7.4. The test statistic for the $J = 5$ hypotheses is

$$F = \frac{(SSE_R - SSE_U)/J}{SSE_U/(N-K)} = \frac{(29307.7 - 29012.7)/5}{29012.7/990} = 2.0132$$

The denominator degrees of freedom come from the unrestricted model, $N - K = 1000 - 10$. The 10% critical value is $F_c = 1.85$, and thus we reject the hypothesis that the wage equation is the same in the southern region and the remainder of the country at the 10% level of significance.[6] The *p*-value of this test is $p = 0.0744$.[7]

> **REMARK:** The usual *F*-test of a joint hypothesis relies on the assumptions MR1–MR6 of the linear regression model. Of particular relevance for testing the equivalence of two regressions is assumption MR3 that the variance of the error term, $\text{var}(e_i) = \sigma^2$, is the same *for all* observations. If we are considering possibly different slopes and intercepts for parts of the data, it might also be true that the error variances are different in the two parts of the data. In such a case the usual *F*-test is not valid. Testing for equal variances is covered in Section 8.4.2, and the question of pooling in this case is covered in Section 8.3.3. For now, be aware that we are assuming constant error variances in the calculations above.

7.3.4 CONTROLLING FOR TIME

The earlier examples we have given apply to cross-sectional data. Dummy variables are also used in regressions using time-series data, as the following examples illustrate.

7.3.4a Seasonal Dummies

Summer means outdoor cooking on barbeque grills. What effect might this have on the sales of charcoal briquettes, a popular fuel for grilling? To investigate let us define a model with dependent variable y_t = the number of 20 pound bags of Royal Oak charcoal sold in week *t* at a supermarket. Explanatory variables would include the price of Royal Oak, the price of competitive brands (Kingsford and the store brand), the prices of complementary goods (charcoal lighter fluid, pork ribs and sausages), and advertising (newspaper ads and coupons). While these standard demand factors are all relevant, we may also find strong seasonal effects. All other things being equal, more charcoal is sold in the warm summer months than in other seasons. Thus we may want to include either monthly dummies (for example $AUG = 1$ if month is August, $AUG = 0$ otherwise) or seasonal dummies (in North America, $SUMMER = 1$ if month = June, July, or August; $SUMMER = 0$ otherwise) into the regression. In addition to these seasonal effects, holidays are special occasions for cookouts. In the United States these are Memorial Day (last Monday in May), Independence Day (July 4), and Labor Day (first Monday in September). Additional sales can be expected in the

---

[6] Using the larger data file *cps.dat* $F = 3.975$, which is significant at the 1% level.

[7] The joint test is significant at the 10% level despite the fact none of the individual coefficients on the south interaction variables are significant at even the 20% level, reminding us that joint and individual tests are fundamentally different.

week before these holidays, meaning that dummy variables for each should be included into the regression.

7.3.4b   Annual Dummies

In the same spirit as seasonal dummies, annual dummy variables are used to capture year effects not otherwise measured in a model. The real estate model discussed earlier in this chapter provides an example. Real estate data are available continuously, every month, every year. Suppose we have data on house prices for a certain community covering a 10-year period. In addition to house characteristics, such as those employed in (7.13), the overall price level is affected by demand factors in the local economy, such as population change, interest rates, unemployment rate, and income growth. Economists creating "cost-of-living" or "house price" indexes for cities must include a component for housing that takes the pure price effect into account. Understanding the price index is important for tax assessors, who must reassess the market value of homes in order to compute the annual property tax. It is also important to mortgage bankers and other home lenders, who must reevaluate the value of their portfolio of loans with changing local conditions, and to homeowners trying to sell their houses as well as potential buyers, as they attempt to agree upon a selling price.

The simplest method for capturing these price effects is to include annual dummies (for example, $D99 = 1$ if year $= 1999$; $D99 = 0$ otherwise) into the hedonic regression model. An example can be found in Exercise 7.4.

7.3.4c   Regime Effects

An economic regime is a set of structural economic conditions that exist for a certain period. The idea is that economic relations may behave one way during one regime, but they may behave differently during another. Economic regimes may be associated with political regimes (conservatives in power, liberals in power), unusual economic conditions (oil embargo, recession, hyperinflation), or changes in the legal environment (tax law changes). An investment tax credit[8] was enacted in 1962 in an effort to stimulate additional investment. The law was suspended in 1966, reinstated in 1970, and eliminated in the Tax Reform Act of 1986. Thus we might create a dummy variable

$$ITC = \begin{cases} 1 & 1962 - 1965, \ 1970 - 1986 \\ 0 & otherwise \end{cases}$$

A macroeconomic investment equation might be

$$INV_t = \beta_1 + \delta ITC_t + \beta_2 GNP_t + \beta_3 GNP_{t-1} + e_t$$

If the tax credit was successful then $\delta > 0$.

7.4 Interactions Between Continuous Variables

When the product of two continuous variables is included in a regression model the effect is to alter the relationship between each of them and the dependent variable. We will consider a

---

[8] Intriligator, Bodkin and Hsiao, *Econometric Models, Techniques and Applications*, 2nd edition, Upper Saddle River, NJ: Prentice-Hall, 1996, p. 53.

Table 7.7 **Pizza Expenditure Data**

PIZZA	INCOME	AGE
109	15000	25
0	30000	45
0	12000	20
108	20000	28
220	15000	25

life-cycle model to illustrate this idea. Suppose we are economists for Gutbusters Pizza and wish to study the effect of income and age on an individual's expenditure on pizza. For that purpose we take a random sample of 40 individuals, age 18 and older, and record their annual expenditure on pizza (*PIZZA*), their income (*INCOME*), and age (*AGE*). The first five observations are shown in Table 7.7. The full data set is contained in the file *pizza.dat*.

As an initial model let us consider

$$PIZZA = \beta_1 + \beta_2 AGE + \beta_3 INCOME + e \qquad (7.17)$$

The implications of this specification are as follows:

1. $\partial E(PIZZA)/\partial AGE = \beta_2$: For a *given level of income,* the expected expenditure on pizza changes by the amount β_2 with an additional year of age. What would you expect here? Based on our casual observation of college students, who appear to consume massive quantities of pizza, we expect the sign of β_2 to be negative. With the effects of income removed, we expect that as a person ages their pizza expenditure will fall.

2. $\partial E(PIZZA)/\partial INCOME = \beta_3$: For individuals of a *given age,* an increase in income of \$1 increases expected expenditures on pizza by β_3. Since pizza is probably a normal good, we expect the sign of β_3 to be positive. The parameter β_3 might be called the marginal propensity to spend on pizza.

Estimates of (7.17), with *t*-statistics in parentheses, are

$$\widehat{PIZZA} = 342.88 - 7.58AGE + 0.0024INCOME$$
$$(t) \qquad\qquad (-3.27) \qquad (3.95)$$

The signs of the estimated parameters are as we anticipated. Both *AGE* and *INCOME* have significant coefficients, based on their *t*-statistics.

These are the implications of the model in (7.17). However, is it reasonable to expect that, *regardless* of the age of the individual, an increase in income by \$1 should lead to an increase in pizza expenditure by β_3 dollars? Probably not. It would seem more reasonable to assume that as a person grows older, their marginal propensity to spend on pizza declines. That is, as a person ages, less of each extra dollar is expected to be spent on pizza. This is a case in which the effect of income depends on the age of the individual. That is, the effect of one variable is modified by another. One way of accounting for such interactions is to include an interaction variable that is the product of the two variables involved. Since *AGE* and *INCOME* are the variables that interact we will add the variable (*AGE×INCOME*) to the regression model. The result is

$$PIZZA = \beta_1 + \beta_2 AGE + \beta_3 INCOME + \beta_4(AGE \times INCOME) + e \qquad (7.18)$$

Just as in the cases when we interacted a continuous variable with a dummy variable, and when we interacted a continuous variable with itself, when the product of two continuous variables is included in a model the interpretation of the parameters requires care. The effects of *INCOME* and *AGE* are as follows:

1. $\partial E(PIZZA)/\partial AGE = \beta_2 + \beta_4 INCOME$: The effect of *AGE* now depends on income. As a person ages their pizza expenditure is expected to fall, and, because β_4 is expected to be negative, the greater the income the greater will be the fall attributable to a change in age.

2. $\partial E(PIZZA)/\partial INCOME = \beta_3 + \beta_4 AGE$: The effect of a change in income on expected pizza expenditure, which is the marginal propensity to spend on pizza, now depends on *AGE*. If our logic concerning the effect of aging is correct then β_4 should be negative. Then, as *AGE* increases, the value of the partial derivative declines.

The estimated model (7.18) including the product ($AGE \times INCOME$) is

$$\widehat{PIZZA} = 161.47 - 2.98AGE + 0.009INCOME - 0.00016(AGE \times INCOME)$$
$$(t) \qquad\qquad (-0.89) \qquad (2.47) \qquad\qquad (-1.85)$$

The estimated coefficient of the interaction term is negative and significant at the $\alpha = 0.05$ level using a one-tail test. The signs of other coefficients remain the same, but *AGE*, by itself, no longer appears to be a significant explanatory factor. This suggests that *AGE* affects pizza expenditure through its interaction with income, that is, on the marginal propensity to spend on pizza.

Using these estimates let us estimate the marginal effect of age upon pizza expenditure for two individuals; one with \$25,000 income and the other with \$90,000 income.

$$\frac{\widehat{\partial E(PIZZA)}}{\partial AGE} = b_2 + b_4\ INCOME$$
$$= -2.98 - 0.00016\ INCOME$$
$$= \begin{cases} -6.98 & \text{for } INCOME = \$25,000 \\ -17.40 & \text{for } INCOME = \$90,000 \end{cases}$$

That is, we expect that an individual with \$25,000 income will reduce pizza expenditures by \$6.98 per year, while the individual with \$90,000 income will reduce pizza expenditures by \$17.40 per year, all other factors held constant.

7.5 Log-Linear Models

In Section 4.4 and Appendix 4C we examined the log-linear model in some detail. You might have noticed that the example in Section 4.4.2 was of a wage equation with dependent variable ln(*WAGE*), but then in (7.5) we changed the example to have wage *level* as the dependent variable. The reason for the change was to simplify exposition of models with polynomial terms, dummy variables and interaction terms. In this section we explore the interpretation of dummy variables and interaction terms in log-linear models. Some additional detail is provided in Appendix 7A.

7.5.1 DUMMY VARIABLES

Let us consider the log-linear model

$$\ln(WAGE) = \beta_1 + \beta_2 EDUC + \delta FEMALE \qquad (7.19)$$

What is the interpretation of the parameter δ? *FEMALE* is an intercept dummy variable, creating a parallel shift of the log-linear relationship when *FEMALE* = 1. That is

$$\ln(WAGE) = \begin{cases} \beta_1 + \beta_2 EDUC & MALES \\ (\beta_1 + \delta) + \beta_2 EDUC & FEMALES \end{cases}$$

But what about the fact that the dependent variable is $\ln(WAGE)$? Does that have an effect? The answer is yes and there are two solutions.

7.5.1a A Rough Calculation
First, take the difference between $\ln(WAGE)$ of females and males

$$\ln(WAGE)_{FEMALES} - \ln(WAGE)_{MALES} = \Delta \ln(WAGE) = \delta$$

Recall from Appendix A.4.5, equation (A.12), that 100 times the log difference is approximately the percentage difference, so that $100\Delta \ln(WAGE) \cong \%\Delta WAGE = 100\delta\%$. Using the data file *cps_small.dat*, the estimated log-linear model (7.19) is

$$\overline{\ln(WAGE)} = 0.9290 + 0.1026 EDUC - 0.2526 FEMALE$$
$$\text{(se)} \qquad (0.0837) \quad (0.0061) \qquad (0.0300)$$

Thus we estimate that there is a 25.26% differential between male and female wages. This is quick and simple, but as shown in Table A.2 there is close to a 10% approximation error with this large a difference.

7.5.1b An Exact Calculation
We can overcome the approximation error by doing a little algebra. The wage difference is

$$\ln(WAGE)_{FEMALES} - \ln(WAGE)_{MALES} = \ln\left(\frac{WAGE_{FEMALES}}{WAGE_{MALES}}\right) = \delta$$

using the property of logarithms that $\ln(x) - \ln(y) = \ln(x/y)$. These are natural logarithms, and the anti-log is the exponential function,

$$\frac{WAGE_{FEMALES}}{WAGE_{MALES}} = e^{\delta}$$

Subtract 1 from each side (in a tricky way) to obtain

$$\frac{WAGE_{FEMALES}}{WAGE_{MALES}} - \frac{WAGE_{MALES}}{WAGE_{MALES}} = \frac{WAGE_{FEMALES} - WAGE_{MALES}}{WAGE_{MALES}} = e^{\delta} - 1$$

The percentage difference between wages of females and males is $100(e^{\delta} - 1)\%$. From this, we estimate the wage differential between males and females to be

$$100(e^{\hat{\delta}} - 1)\% = 100(e^{-0.2526} - 1)\% = -22.32\%$$

The approximate standard error for this estimate is 2.33%, which is a calculation that may be provided by your software, making this exact calculation more than one standard error different from the approximate value of -25.26%.

7.5.2 INTERACTION AND QUADRATIC TERMS

In the simple log-linear model $\ln(y) = \beta_1 + \beta_2 x$, we give an interpretation to β_2 by saying that given a 1-unit change in x the approximate percentage change in y is $100\beta_2\%$. See Appendix A, (A.13) and the surrounding discussion. How do we extend this result to higher order models? Consider the wage equation

$$\ln(WAGE) = \beta_1 + \beta_2 EDUC + \beta_3 EXPER + \gamma(EDUC \times EXPER) \qquad (7.20)$$

What is the effect of another year of experience, holding education constant? Roughly,

$$\left. \frac{\Delta \ln(WAGE)}{\Delta EXPER} \right|_{EDUC\ fixed} = \beta_3 + \gamma EDUC$$

In Appendix A, equation (A.12), we show that 100 times the log difference is approximately the percentage difference. Using this result, the approximate percentage change in wage given a 1-year increase in experience is $100(\beta_3 + \gamma EDUC)\%$. Using the data file *cps_small.dat* we estimate (7.20) to obtain

$$\widehat{\ln(WAGE)} = 0.1528 + 0.1341 EDUC + 0.0249 EXPER - 0.000962(EDUC \times EXPER)$$
$$(se) \quad (0.1722) \ (0.0127) \qquad (0.0071) \qquad (0.00054)$$

For a person with 16 years of education, we estimate that an additional year of experience leads to an increase in wages of approximately $100(0.0249 - 0.000962 \times 16)\% = 0.9518\%$, with standard error 0.216.

What if there is a quadratic term on the right-hand side, as in

$$\ln(WAGE) = \beta_1 + \beta_2 EDUC + \beta_3 EXPER + \beta_4 EXPER^2 + \gamma(EDUC \times EXPER)$$

Then, using a little calculus, we find that a 1-year increase in experience leads to an approximate percentage wage change of

$$\%\Delta WAGE \cong 100(\beta_3 + 2\beta_4 EXPER + \gamma EDUC)\%$$

7.6 Exercises

Answers to exercises marked * appear in Appendix D at the end of the book.

7.6.1 PROBLEMS

7.1 An Economics department at a large state university keeps track of its majors' starting salaries. Does taking econometrics effect starting salary? Let $SAL =$ salary in dollars, *GPA* = grade point average on a 4.0 scale, *METRICS* = 1 if student took econometrics, and *METRICS* = 0 otherwise. Using the data file *metrics.dat*, which contains information on 50 recent graduates, we obtain the estimated regression

$$\widehat{SAL} = 24200 + 1643GPA + 5033METRICS \quad R^2 = 0.74$$
$$\text{(se)} \quad (1078) \quad (352) \quad \quad (456)$$

(a) Interpret the estimated equation.
(b) How would you modify the equation to see if women had lower starting salaries than men? (Hint: Define a dummy variable *FEMALE* = 1, if female; 0 otherwise.)
(c) How would you modify the equation to see if the value of econometrics was the same for men and women?

7.2* In September 1998, a local TV station contacted an econometrician to analyze some data for them. They were going to do a Halloween story on the legend of full moons affecting behavior in strange ways. They collected data from a local hospital on emergency room cases for the period from January 1, 1998 until mid-August. There were 229 observations. During this time there were eight full moons and seven new moons (a related myth concerns new moons) and three holidays (New Year's Day, Memorial Day, and Easter). If there is a full-moon effect, then hospital administrators will adjust numbers of emergency room doctors and nurses, and local police may change the number of officers on duty.

Using the data in the file *fullmoon.dat* we obtain the regression results in the following table: *T* is a time trend ($T = 1,2,3,\ldots,229$) and the rest are dummy variables. *HOLIDAY* = 1 if the day is a holiday; 0 otherwise. *FRIDAY* = 1 if the day is a Friday; 0 otherwise. *SATURDAY* = 1 if the day is a Saturday; 0 otherwise. *FULLMOON* = 1 if there is a full moon; 0 otherwise. *NEWMOON* = 1 if there is a new moon; 0 otherwise.

Emergency Room Cases Regression—Model 1

Variable	Coefficient	Std. Error	t-Statistic	Prob.
C	93.6958	1.5592	60.0938	0.0000
T	0.0338	0.0111	3.0580	0.0025
HOLIDAY	13.8629	6.4452	2.1509	0.0326
FRIDAY	6.9098	2.1113	3.2727	0.0012
SATURDAY	10.5894	2.1184	4.9987	0.0000
FULLMOON	2.4545	3.9809	0.6166	0.5382
NEWMOON	6.4059	4.2569	1.5048	0.1338

$R^2 = 0.1736$ $SSE = 27108.82$

(a) Interpret these regression results. When should emergency rooms expect more calls?
(b) The model was reestimated omitting the variables *FULLMOON* and *NEW-MOON*, as shown below. Comment on any changes you observe.
(c) Test the joint significance of *FULLMOON* and *NEWMOON*. State the null and alternative hypotheses and indicate the test statistic you use. What do you conclude?

Emergency Room Cases Regression—Model 2

Variable	Coefficient	Std. Error	t-Statistic	Prob.
C	94.0215	1.5458	60.8219	0.0000
T	0.0338	0.0111	3.0568	0.0025
HOLIDAY	13.6168	6.4511	2.1108	0.0359
FRIDAY	6.8491	2.1137	3.2404	0.0014
SATURDAY	10.3421	2.1153	4.8891	0.0000

$R^2 = 0.1640$ $SSE = 27424.19$

7.3   Henry Saffer and Frank Chaloupka ("The Demand for Illicit Drugs," *Economic Inquiry*, 37(3), 1999, 401–411) estimate demand equations for alcohol, marijuana, cocaine, and heroin using a sample of size $N = 44,889$. The estimated equation for alcohol use after omitting a few control variables is

Demand for Illicit Drugs

Variable	Coefficient	|t-statistic|
C	4.099	17.98
ALCOHOL PRICE	−0.045	5.93
INCOME	0.000057	17.45
GENDER	1.637	29.23
MARITAL STATUS	−0.807	12.13
AGE 12–20	−1.531	17.97
AGE 21–30	0.035	0.51
BLACK	−0.580	8.84
HISPANIC	−0.564	6.03

The variable definitions (sample means in parentheses) are as follows:

The dependent variable is the number of days alcohol was used in the past 31 days (3.49)

ALCOHOL PRICE—price of a liter of pure alcohol in 1983 dollars (24.78)
INCOME—total personal income in 1983 dollars (12,425)
GENDER—a binary variable = 1 if male (0.479)
MARITAL STATUS—a binary variable = 1 if married (0.569)
AGE 12–20—a binary variable = 1 if individual is 12–20 years of age (0.155)
AGE 21–30—a binary variable = 1 if individual is 21–30 years of age (0.197)
BLACK—a binary variable = 1 if individual is black (0.116)
HISPANIC—a binary variable = 1 if individual is Hispanic (0.078)

(a) Interpret the coefficient of alcohol price.
(b) Compute the price elasticity at the means of the variables.
(c) Compute the price elasticity at the means of alcohol price and income, for a married black male, age 21–30.
(d) Interpret the coefficient of income. If we measured income in $1000 units, what would the estimated coefficient be?
(e) Interpret the coefficients of the dummy variables, and their significance.

7.4 In the file *stockton.dat* we have data from January 1991 to December 1996 on house prices, square footage, and other characteristics of 4682 houses that were sold in Stockton, CA. One of the key problems regarding housing prices in a region concerns construction of "house price indexes," as discussed in Section 7.3.4b. To illustrate, we estimate a regression model for house price, including as explanatory variables the size of the house (*SQFT*), the age of the house (*AGE*), and annual dummy variables, omitting the dummy variable for the year 1991.

$$PRICE = \beta_1 + \beta_2 SQFT + \beta_3 AGE + \delta_1 D92 + \delta_2 D93 + \delta_3 D94 + \delta_4 D95 + \delta_5 D96 + e$$

The results are as follows:

Stockton House Price Index Model

Variable	Coefficient	Std. Error	t-Statistic	Prob.
C	21456.2000	1839.0400	11.6671	0.0000
SQFT	72.7878	1.0001	72.7773	0.0000
AGE	−179.4623	17.0112	−10.5496	0.0000
D92	−4392.8460	1270.9300	−3.4564	0.0006
D93	−10435.4700	1231.8000	−8.4717	0.0000
D94	−13173.5100	1211.4770	−10.8739	0.0000
D95	−19040.8300	1232.8080	−15.4451	0.0000
D96	−23663.5100	1194.9280	−19.8033	0.0000

(a) Discuss the estimated coefficients on *SQFT* and *AGE*, including their interpretation, signs, and statistical significance.
(b) Discuss the estimated coefficients on the dummy variables.
(c) What would have happened if we had included a dummy variable for 1991?

7.5* An agricultural economist carries out an experiment to study the production relationship between the dependent variable *YIELD* = peanut yield (pounds per acre) and the production inputs

NITRO = amount of nitrogen applied (hundreds of pounds per acre)
PHOS = amount of phosphorus fertilizer (hundreds of pounds per acre)

A total $N = 27$ observations were obtained using different test fields. The estimated quadratic model, with an interaction term, is

$$\widehat{YIELD} = 1.385 + 8.011 NITRO + 4.800 PHOS - 1.944 NITRO^2$$
$$\quad (1.264) \ (0.941) \qquad (0.941) \qquad (0.220)$$

$$\quad - 0.778 PHOS^2 - 0.567 NITRO \times PHOS$$
$$\quad (0.220) \qquad (0.155)$$

(a) Find and comment on the estimated functions describing the marginal response of yield to nitrogen, when *PHOS* = 1, *PHOS* = 2, and *PHOS* = 3.
(b) Find and comment on the estimated functions describing the marginal response of yield to phosphorus, when *NITRO* = 1, *NITRO* = 2, and *NITRO* = 3.

(c) Test the hypothesis that the marginal response of yield to nitrogen is zero, when
   (i) *PHOS* = 1 and *NITRO* = 1
   (ii) *PHOS* = 1 and *NITRO* = 2
   (iii) *PHOS* = 1 and *NITRO* = 3
   Note: The following information may be useful:

$$\overline{\text{var}(b_2 + 2b_4 + b_6)} = 0.233$$

$$\overline{\text{var}(b_2 + 4b_4 + b_6)} = 0.040$$

$$\overline{\text{var}(b_2 + 6b_4 + b_6)} = 0.233$$

(d)◆ (This part requires the use of calculus.) For the function estimated, what levels of nitrogen and phosphorus give maximum yield? Are these levels the optimal fertilizer applications for the peanut producer?

7.6.2   COMPUTER EXERCISES

7.6 In (7.13) we specified a hedonic model for house price. The dependent variable was the price of the house, in dollars. Real estate economists have found that for many data sets a more appropriate model has the dependent variable ln(*PRICE*).
   (a) Using the data in the file *utown.dat,* estimate the model (7.13) using ln(*PRICE*) as the dependent variable.
   (b) Discuss the estimated coefficients on *SQFT* and *AGE*. Refer to Section 4.4 for help with interpreting the coefficients in this log-linear functional form.
   (c) Compute the percentage change in price due to the presence of a pool. Use both the rough approximation in Section 7.5.1a and the exact calculation in Section 7.5.1b.
   (d) Compute the percentage change in price due to the presence of a fireplace. Use both the rough approximation in Section 7.5.1a and the exact calculation in Section 7.5.1b.
   (e) Compute the percentage change in price of a 2500 square foot home near the university relative to the same house in another location using the methodology in Section 7.5.1b.

7.7 Data on the weekly sales of a major brand of canned tuna by a supermarket chain in a large midwestern U.S. city during a mid-1990's calendar year are contained in the file *tuna.dat*. There are 52 observations on the variables

SAL1 = unit sales of brand no. 1 canned tuna
APR1 = price per can of brand no. 1 canned tuna
APR2, APR3 = price per can of brands nos. 2 and 3 of canned tuna
DISP = a dummy variable that takes the value 1 if there is a store display for brand no. 1 during the week but no newspaper ad; 0 otherwise
DISPAD = a dummy variable that takes the value 1 if there is a store display *and* a newspaper ad during the week; 0 otherwise

(a) Estimate, by least squares, the log-linear model

$$\ln(SAL1) = \beta_1 + \beta_2 APR1 + \beta_3 APR2 + \beta_4 APR3 + \beta_5 DISP + \beta_6 DISPAD + e$$

(b) Discuss and interpret the estimates of β_2, β_3, and β_4.

(c) Are the signs and *relative* magnitudes of the estimates of β_5 and β_6 consistent with economic logic? Interpret these estimates using the approaches in Sections 7.5.1a and 7.5.1b.

(d) Test, at the $\alpha = 0.05$ level of significance, each of the following hypotheses:

    (i) $H_0 : \beta_5 = 0$, $H_1 : \beta_5 \neq 0$

    (ii) $H_0 : \beta_6 = 0$, $H_1 : \beta_6 \neq 0$

    (iii) $H_0 : \beta_5 = 0, \beta_6 = 0$; $H_1 : \beta_5 \text{ or } \beta_6 \neq 0$

    (iv) $H_0 : \beta_6 \leq \beta_5$, $H_1 : \beta_6 > \beta_5$

(e) Discuss the relevance of the hypothesis tests in (d) for the supermarket chain's executives.

7.8   F.G. Mixon and R.W. Ressler (2000) in "A Note on Elasticity and Price Dispersions in the Music Recording Industry" (*Review of Industrial Organization, 17*, 465–470) investigate the pricing of compact disks. They note that it is common for new releases to be priced lower than older CDs. Their explanation of this pricing scheme is differences in the price elasticity of demand. The number of substitutes for old CDs is less than for new. For example, new music can be heard on VH1, MTV, in movie and TV-program soundtracks, on radio, and live. That old favorite you had on vinyl record or tape, and now want on CD, has much more limited competition. To empirically test this they obtain data on 118 CDs. The data are in the file *music.dat*. The variables are

$PRICE$ = retail price of the CD (US $)
AGE = age of the recording (1999—copyright date)
OLD = a dummy variable = 1 if the recording is not a new release
NET = a dummy variable = 1 for Internet prices (Tower Records and Amazon web sites).

(a) Estimate the model $PRICE = \beta_1 + \beta_2 AGE + \delta NET + e$. Interpret the estimated model.

(b) Estimate the model $PRICE = \beta_1 + \beta_2 OLD + \delta NET + e$. Interpret the estimated model.

7.9* In Section 7.4 the effect of income on pizza expenditure was permitted to vary by the age of the individual.

(a) Use the data in the file *pizza.dat* to estimate the regression model in which pizza expenditure depends *only* on income. Before estimating this model, and *for the remainder of this exercise,* use income measured in $1000s. (It might be simplest to create a new variable $INC = INCOME/1000$.)

(b) Estimate the model in (7.17). Comment on the signs and significance of the parameter estimates and on the effect of scaling the income variable.

(c) Estimate the model in (7.18). Comment on the signs and significance of the parameter estimates. Is there a significant interaction effect between age and income? What is the effect of scaling income?

(d) In (7.18) test the hypothesis that age does not affect pizza expenditure. That is, test the joint null hypothesis $H_0 : \beta_2 = 0, \beta_4 = 0$. What do you conclude?

(e) Construct point estimates and 95% interval estimates of the marginal propensity to spend on pizza for individuals of age 20, 30, 40, and 50. Comment on these estimates.

(f) Modify (7.18) to permit a "life-cycle" effect in which the marginal effect of income on pizza expenditure increases with age, up to a point, and then falls. Do so by adding the term $(AGE^2 \times INC)$ to the model. What sign do you anticipate on this term? Estimate the model and test the significance of the coefficient for this variable.

(g) Check the model used in part (f) for collinearity (See Section 6.7.3). Add the term $(AGE^3 \times INC)$ to the model in (f) and check the resulting model for collinearity.

7.10 The file *pizza.dat* includes additional information about the 40 individuals used in the pizza expenditure example in Section 7.4. The dummy variable $FEMALE = 1$ for females; 0 otherwise. The variables *HS, COLLEGE,* and *GRAD* are dummy variables indicating level of educational attainment. $HS = 1$ for individuals whose highest degree is a high school diploma. $COLLEGE = 1$ for individuals whose highest degree is a college diploma. $GRAD = 1$ if individuals have a graduate degree. If *HS, COLLEGE,* and *GRAD* are all 0, the individual did not complete high school.

(a) Begin with the model in (7.17). Include gender (*FEMALE*) as an explanatory variable and estimate the resulting model. What is the effect of including this dummy variable? Is gender a relevant explanatory variable?

(b) Begin with the model in (7.17). Include the dummy variables *HS, COLLE-GE,* and *GRAD* as explanatory variables and estimate the resulting model. What is the effect of including these dummy variables? Is level of educational attainment a significant explanatory variable?

(c) Consider (7.17). Test the hypothesis that separate regression equations for males and females are identical, against the alternative that they are not. Use the 5% level of significance and discuss the consequences of your findings.

7.11 Use the data in *pizza.dat* to do the following:

(a) Estimate the model (7.18) and compare your results to those in Section 7.4.

(b) Calculate the marginal effect $\partial E(PIZZA)/\partial INCOME$ for an individual of average age and income and test the statistical significance of the estimate.

(c) Calculate a 95% interval estimate for the marginal effect in (b).

(d) Calculate the marginal effect $\partial E(PIZZA)/\partial AGE$ for an individual of average age and income and test the statistical significance of the estimate.

(e) Calculate a 95% interval estimate for the marginal effect in (d).

(f) (This part requires the completion of Exercise 7.10.) Write a report (250 + words) to the president of Gutbusters summarizing your findings from Exercises 7.10 and 7.11.

7.12* Lion Forest has been a very successful golf professional. However, at age 45 his game is not quite what it used to be. He started the pro-tour when he was only 20 and he has been looking back examining how his scores have changed as he got older. In the file *golf.dat*, the first column contains his final score (Actual score – par) for 150 tournaments. The second column contains his age (in units of 10 years). There are scores for six major tournaments in each year for the last 25 years. Denoting his score by *SCORE* and his age by *AGE*, estimate the following model and obtain the within-sample predictions.

$$SCORE = \beta_1 + \beta_2 AGE + \beta_3 AGE^2 + \beta_4 AGE^3 + e$$

(a) Test the null hypothesis that a quadratic function is adequate against the cubic function as an alternative. What are the characteristics of the cubic equation that might make it appropriate?

(b) Use the within-sample predictions to answer the following questions:
  (i) At what age was Lion at the peak of his career?
  (ii) When was Lion's game improving at an increasing rate?

(iii) When was Lion's game improving at a decreasing rate?
(iv) At what age did Lion start to play worse than he had played when he was 20 years old?
(v) When could he no longer score less than par (on average)?
(c) When he is aged 70, will he be able to break 100? Assume par is 72.

7.13   Use the data in the file *cps2.dat* to estimate the following wage equation:

$$\ln(WAGE) = \beta_1 + \beta_2 EDUC + \beta_3 EXPER + \beta_4 FEMALE + \beta_5 BLACK + \beta_6 MARRIED$$
$$+ \beta_7 UNION + \beta_8 SOUTH + \beta_9 FULLTIME + \beta_{10} METRO + e$$

(a) Discuss the results of the estimation. Interpret *each* coefficient, and comment on its sign and significance. Are things as you would expect?
(b)♦ (large data set) Use the data *cps.dat* to reestimate the equation. What changes do you observe?

7.14♦ (large data set) Use the data file *cps.dat* for the following.
(a) Reestimate the model reported in Table 7.1. What changes do you observe? Estimate the marginal effect of experience on wage and compare the result to that based on Table 7.1.
(b) Estimate the model given in (7.14). Compare the results to those in Table 7.4. Test the hypothesis that the interaction between *BLACK* and *FEMALE* is significant.
(c) Estimate the model reported in Table 7.5. Discuss the results and compare them to those reported in Table 7.5. Test the hypothesis that there is no regional effect.
(d) Estimate the model in (7.16) and test the hypothesis that there is no difference between the wage equations for southern and non-southern workers.
(e) Estimate the log-linear model in (7.19). Estimate the percentage difference in wages between males and females.

7.15* Professor Ray C. Fair's voting model was introduced in Exercise 2.14. He builds models that explain and predict the U.S. presidential elections. See his website at http://fairmodel.econ.yale.edu/vote2008/index2.htm, and see in particular his paper entitled "A Vote Equation for the 2004 Election." The basic premise of the model is that the incumbent party's share of the two-party (Democratic and Republican) popular vote (incumbent means the party in power at the time of the election) is affected by a number of factors relating to the economy, and variables relating to the politics, such as how long the incumbent party has been in power, and whether the President is running for reelection. Fair's data, 31 observations for the election years from 1880 to 2000, are in the file *fair.dat*. The dependent variable is *VOTE* = percentage share of the popular vote won by the incumbent party.

The explanatory variables include

PARTY = 1 if there is a Democratic incumbent at the time of the election and −1 if there is a Republican incumbent.
PERSON = 1 if the incumbent is running for election and 0 otherwise.
DURATION = 0 if the incumbent party has been in power for one term, 1 if the incumbent party has been in power for two consecutive terms, 1.25 if the incumbent party has been in power for three consecutive terms, 1.50 for four consecutive terms, and so on.

WAR = 1 for the elections of 1920, 1944, and 1948 and 0 otherwise.

GROWTH = growth rate of real per capita GDP in the first three quarters of the election year (annual rate).

INFLATION = absolute value of the growth rate of the GDP deflator in the first 15 quarters of the administration (annual rate) except for 1920, 1944, and 1948, where the values are zero.

GOODNEWS = number of quarters in the first 15 quarters of the administration in which the growth rate of real per capita GDP is greater than 3.2% at an annual rate except for 1920, 1944, and 1948, where the values are zero.

(a) Consider the regression model

$$VOTE = \beta_1 + \beta_2 GROWTH + \beta_3 INFLATION + \beta_4 GOODNEWS$$
$$+ \beta_5 PERSON + \beta_6 DURATION + \beta_7 PARTY + \beta_8 WAR + e$$

Discuss the anticipated effects of the dummy variables *PERSON* and *WAR*.

(b) The binary variable *PARTY* is somewhat different from the dummy variables we have considered. Write out the regression function $E(VOTE)$ for the two values of *PARTY*. Discuss the effects of this specification.

(c) Use the data for the period 1916-2000 to estimate the proposed model. Discuss the estimation results. Are the signs as expected? Are the estimates statistically significant? How well does the model fit the data?

(d) Predict the outcome of the 2004 election using $PARTY = -1$, $DURATION = 0$, $WAR = 0$, and $PERSON = 1$. For the other variables specify $GOODNEWS = 1$, $GROWTH = 2.0$, and $INFLATION = 1.7$.

(e) Construct a 95% prediction interval for the outcome of the 2004 election.

(f) Using data values of your choice (you must explain them), predict the outcome of the 2008 election.

7.16 The data file *br2.dat* contains data on 1080 house sales in Baton Rouge, Louisiana, during July and August 2005. The variables are *PRICE* ($), *SQFT* (total square feet), *BEDROOMS* (number), *BATHS* (number), *AGE* (years), *OWNER* (=1 if occupied by owner; 0 if vacant or rented), *POOL* (=1 if present), *TRADITIONAL* (=1 if traditional style; 0 if other style), *FIREPLACE* (=1 if present), and *WATERFRONT* (=1 if on waterfront).

(a) Compute the data summary statistics and comment. In particular construct a histogram of *PRICE*. What do you observe?

(b) Estimate a regression model explaining $\ln(PRICE/1000)$ as a function of the remaining variables. Divide the variable *SQFT* by 100 prior to estimation. Comment on how well the model fits the data. Discuss the signs and statistical significance of the estimated coefficients. Are the signs what you expect? Give an exact interpretation of the coefficient of *WATERFRONT*.

(c) Create a variable that is the product of *WATERFRONT* and *TRADITIONAL*. Add this variable to the model and reestimate. What is the effect of adding this variable? Interpret the coefficient of this interaction variable, and discuss its sign and statistical significance.

(d) It is arguable that the traditional style homes may have a different regression function from the diverse set of nontraditional styles. Carry out a Chow test of the equivalence of the regression models for traditional versus nontraditional styles. What do you conclude?

(e) Using the equation estimated in part (d), predict the value of a traditional style house with 2500 square feet of area, that is 20 years old, which is owner occupied at the time of sale, with a fireplace, 3 bedrooms and 2 baths, but no pool and not on the waterfront.

7.17* Recent data on 880 house sales from Stockton, California, are contained in the data file *stockton2.dat*. The variables are *PRICE* ($), *SQFT* (total square feet of living area), *BEDS* (number bedrooms), *BATHS* (number), *AGE* (years), *STORIES* (number), and a dummy variable *VACANT* that equals one if the house was vacant at the time of sale.
  (a) Examine the histogram of the variable *PRICE*. What do you observe? Create the variable ln(*PRICE*) and examine its histogram. Comment on the difference.
  (b) Estimate a regression of ln(*PRICE*/1000) on the remaining variables. Divide *SQFT* by 100 prior to estimation. Discuss the estimation results. Comment on the signs and significance of all variables except *VACANT*.
  (c) How does vacancy at the time of sale affect house price?
  (d) Omitting *VACANT*, estimate the regression model separately for those houses that are vacant at the time of sale and those that are occupied at the time of sale (not vacant). Compare the estimation results.
  (e) Carry out a Chow test of the equivalence of the regression models in (d).

Appendix 7A Details of Log-Linear Model Interpretation

You may have noticed that in Section 7.5 while discussing the interpretation of the log-linear model we omitted the error term, and we did not discuss the regression function $E(WAGE)$. To do so we make use of the properties of the log-normal distribution in Appendix 4C. There we noted that for the log-linear model $\ln(y) = \beta_1 + \beta_2 x + e$, if the error term $e \sim N(0, \sigma^2)$ then the expected value of y is

$$E(y) = \exp(\beta_1 + \beta_2 x + \sigma^2/2) = \exp(\beta_1 + \beta_2 x) \times \exp(\sigma^2/2)$$

Starting from this equation we can explore the interpretation of dummy variables and interaction terms.

Let D be a dummy variable. Adding this to our log-linear model we have $\ln(y) = \beta_1 + \beta_2 x + \delta D + e$ and

$$E(y) = \exp(\beta_1 + \beta_2 x + \delta D) \times \exp(\sigma^2/2)$$

If we let $E(y_1)$ and $E(y_0)$ denote the cases when $D = 1$ and $D = 0$, respectively, then we can compute their percentage difference as

$$\%\Delta E(y) = 100 \left[\frac{E(y_1) - E(y_0)}{E(y_0)} \right] \%$$

$$= 100 \left[\frac{\exp(\beta_1 + \beta_2 x + \delta) \times \exp(\sigma^2/2) - \exp(\beta_1 + \beta_2 x) \times \exp(\sigma^2/2)}{\exp(\beta_1 + \beta_2 x) \times \exp(\sigma^2/2)} \right] \%$$

$$= 100 \left[\frac{\exp(\beta_1 + \beta_2 x)\exp(\delta) - \exp(\beta_1 + \beta_2 x)}{\exp(\beta_1 + \beta_2 x)} \right] \% = 100[\exp(\delta) - 1]\%$$

The interpretation of dummy variables in log-linear models carries over to the regression function. The percentage difference in the *expected* value of y is $100[\exp(\delta) - 1]\%$.

Instead of a dummy variable, let us introduce another variable z and its interaction with x, $\ln(y) = \beta_1 + \beta_2 x + \beta_3 z + \gamma(xz) + e$. Then

$$E(y) = \exp(\beta_1 + \beta_2 x + \beta_3 z + \gamma(xz)) \times \exp(\sigma^2/2)$$

The derivative of this expression, with respect to z, holding x constant, is

$$\frac{\partial E(y)}{\partial z} = \exp(\beta_1 + \beta_2 x + \beta_3 z + \gamma(xz)) \times \exp(\sigma^2/2) \times (\beta_3 + \gamma x))$$

Dividing both sides by $E(y)$ and multiplying by 100 gives

$$100\left[\frac{\partial E(y)/E(y)}{\partial z}\right] = 100(\beta_3 + \gamma x)\%$$

Interpreting "∂" as "Δ", then the left-hand-side numerator is the percentage change in the expected value of y resulting from a 1-unit change in z. The interpretations we developed in Section 7.5 hold in general; the only refinement is that here we have calculated the percentage change in the *expected* value of y.

Chapter *8*

Heteroskedasticity

Learning Objectives

Based on the material in this chapter you should be able to

1. Explain the meaning of heteroskedasticity and give examples of data sets likely to exhibit heteroskedasticity.

2. Describe and compare the properties of the least squares and generalized least squares estimators when heteroskedasticity exists.

3. Compute heteroskedasticity-consistent standard errors for least squares.

4. Compute generalized least squares estimates for heteroskedastic models where (a) the variance is known except for the proportionality constant σ^2, (b) the variance is a function of explanatory variables and unknown parameters, and (c) the sample is partitioned into two subsamples with different variances.

5. Describe how to transform a model to eliminate heteroskedasticity.

6. Explain how and why plots of least squares residuals can reveal heteroskedasticity.

7. Specify a variance function and use it to test for heteroskedasticity with (a) a Breusch–Pagan test, and (b) a White test.

8. Test for heteroskedasticity using a Goldfeldt–Quandt test applied to (a) two subsamples with potentially different variances and (b) a model where the variance is hypothesized to depend on an explanatory variable.

Keywords

Breusch–Pagan test	heteroskedasticity-consistent	residual plot
generalized least squares	standard errors	transformed model
Goldfeld–Quandt test	homoskedasticity	variance function
heteroskedastic partition	Lagrange multiplier test	weighted least squares
heteroskedasticity	mean function	White test

8.1 The Nature of Heteroskedasticity

In Chapter 2 the relationship between average or mean household expenditure on food $E(y)$ and household income x was described by the linear function

$$E(y) = \beta_1 + \beta_2 x \qquad (8.1)$$

The unknown parameters β_1 and β_2 convey information about this expenditure function. The response parameter β_2 describes how mean household food expenditure changes when household income increases by one unit. The intercept parameter β_1 measures expenditure on food for a zero income level. Knowledge of these parameters aids planning by institutions such as government agencies or food retail chains. To estimate β_1 and β_2 we considered a sample of $N = 40$ households indexed by $i = 1, 2, \ldots, 40$, with the pair (y_i, x_i) denoting expenditure on food and income for the ith household.

To recognize that not all households with a particular income will have the same food expenditure, and in line with our general specification of the regression model, we let e_i be the difference between expenditure on food by the ith household y_i and mean expenditure on food for all households with income x_i. That is,

$$e_i = y_i - E(y_i) = y_i - \beta_1 - \beta_2 x_i \tag{8.2}$$

Thus, the model used to describe expenditure on food for the ith household is written as

$$y_i = \beta_1 + \beta_2 x_i + e_i \tag{8.3}$$

We can view $E(y_i) = \beta_1 + \beta_2 x_i$ as that part of food expenditure explained by income x_i and e_i as that part of food expenditure explained by other factors.

We begin this chapter by asking whether the mean function $E(y) = \beta_1 + \beta_2 x$ is better at explaining expenditure on food for low-income households than it is for high-income households. If you were to guess food expenditure for a low-income household and food expenditure for a high-income household, which guess do you think would be easier? Low-income households do not have the option of extravagant food tastes. Comparatively, they have few choices and are almost forced to spend a particular portion of their income on food. High-income households on the other hand could have simple food tastes or extravagant food tastes. They might dine on caviar or spaghetti, while their low-income counterparts have to take the spaghetti. Thus, income is relatively less important as an explanatory variable for food expenditure of high-income households. It is harder to guess their food expenditure.

Another way of describing what we have just said is to say the probability of getting large positive or negative values for e_i is higher for high incomes than it is for low incomes. Factors other than income can have a larger impact on food expenditure when household income is high. How can we model this phenomenon? A random variable, in this case e_i, has a higher probability of taking on large values if its variance is high. Thus, we can capture the effect we are describing by having $var(e_i)$ depend directly on income x_i. An equivalent statement is to say $var(y_i)$ increases as x_i increases. Food expenditure y_i can deviate further from its mean $E(y_i) = \beta_1 + \beta_2 x_i$ when x_i is large. In such a case, when the variances for all observations are not the same, we say that **heteroskedasticity** exists. Alternatively, we say the random variable y_i and the random error e_i are **heteroskedastic**. Conversely, if all observations come from probability density functions with the same variance, we say that **homoskedasticity** exists, and y_i and e_i are **homoskedastic**.

The heteroskedastic assumption is illustrated in Figure 8.1. At x_1, the probability density function $f(y_1|x_1)$ is such that y_1 will be close to $E(y_1)$ with high probability. When we move to x_2, the probability density function $f(y_2|x_2)$ is more spread out; we are less certain about where y_2 might fall, and larger values are possible. When homoskedasticity exists, the probability density function for the errors does not change as x changes, as we illustrated in Figure 2.3.

Note that the existence of heteroskedasticity is a violation of one of our least squares assumptions that were listed in Section 5.1. When we previously considered the model in

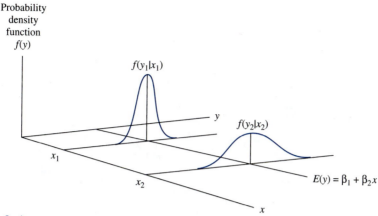

FIGURE **8.1**   Heteroskedastic errors.

(8.3), we assumed that the e_i were uncorrelated random error terms with mean zero and constant variance σ^2. That is,

$$E(e_i) = 0 \quad \text{var}(e_i) = \sigma^2 \quad \text{cov}(e_i, e_j) = 0$$

The assumption we are questioning now is the constant variance assumption MR3 that states $\text{var}(y_i) = \text{var}(e_i) = \sigma^2$. Our discussion suggests that it should be replaced with an assumption of the form

$$\text{var}(y_i) = \text{var}(e_i) = h(x_i) \tag{8.4}$$

where $h(x_i)$ is a function of x_i that increases as x_i increases.

This chapter is concerned with the consequences of a variance assumption like (8.4). What are the consequences for the properties of least squares estimators? Is there a better estimation technique? How do we detect the existence of heteroskedasticity?

We can further illustrate the nature of heteroskedasticity, and at the same time demonstrate an informal way of detecting heteroskedasticity, by reexamining least squares estimation of the mean function $E(y_i) = \beta_1 + \beta_2 x_i$ and the corresponding least squares residuals. The least squares estimated equation from the observations in the file *food.dat* is

$$\hat{y}_i = 83.42 + 10.21\, x_i$$

A graph of this estimated function, along with all the observed expenditure-income points (y_i, x_i), appears in Figure 8.2. Notice that, as income (x_i) grows, the prevalence of data points that deviate further from the estimated mean function increases. There are more points scattered further away from the line as x_i gets larger. Another way of describing this feature is to say that there is a tendency for the least squares residuals, defined by

$$\hat{e}_i = y_i - 83.42 - 10.21 x_i$$

to increase in absolute value as income grows.

Since the observable least squares residuals $(\hat{e}_i)$ are estimates of the unobservable errors (e_i), given by $e_i = y_i - \beta_1 - \beta_2 x_i$, Figure 8.2 also suggests that the unobservable errors tend

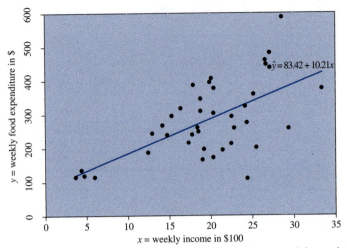

FIGURE **8.2**   Least squares estimated expenditure function and observed data points.

to increase in absolute value as income increases. That is, the variation of food expenditure y_i around mean food expenditure $E(y_i)$ increases as income x_i increases. This observation is consistent with the hypothesis that we posed earlier, namely, that the mean food expenditure function is better at explaining food expenditure for low-income (spaghetti-eating) households than it is for high-income households who might be spaghetti eaters or caviar eaters. We can capture the increasing variation of y_i around its mean by the heteroskedasticity assumption given in (8.4).

Heteroskedasticity is often encountered when using **cross-sectional data**. The term cross-sectional data refers to having data on a number of economic units such as firms or households, *at a given point in time*. The household data on income and food expenditure fall into this category. Other possible examples include data on costs, outputs, and inputs for a number of firms, and data on quantities purchased and prices for some commodity, or commodities, in a number of retail establishments. Cross-sectional data invariably involve observations on economic units of varying sizes. For example, data on households will involve households with varying numbers of household members and different levels of household income. With data on a number of firms, we might measure the size of the firm by the quantity of output it produces. Frequently, the larger the firm, or the larger the household, the more difficult it is to explain the variation in some outcome variable y_i by the variation in a set of explanatory variables. Larger firms and households are likely to be more diverse and flexible with respect to the way in which values for y_i are determined. What this means for the linear regression model is that, as the size of the economic unit becomes larger, there is more uncertainty associated with the outcomes y_i. This greater uncertainty is modeled by specifying an error variance that is larger, the larger the size of the economic unit.

Heteroskedasticity is not a property that is necessarily restricted to cross-sectional data. With time-series data, where we have data *over time* on *one* economic unit, such as a firm, a household, or even a whole economy, it is possible that the error variance will change. This would be true if there was an external shock or change in circumstances that created more or less uncertainty about y.

The plotting of least squares residuals is an informal way of detecting heteroskedasticity. More formal tests are considered later in the chapter. First, however, we examine the consequences of heteroskedasticity for least squares estimation.

8.2 Using the Least Squares Estimator

Since the existence of heteroskedasticity means that the least squares assumption $\text{var}(e_i) = \sigma^2$ is violated, we need to ask what consequences this violation has for our least squares estimator and what we can do about it. There are two implications:

Consequences for violation [handwritten margin note]

1. The least squares estimator is still a linear and unbiased estimator, but it is no longer best. There is another estimator with a smaller variance.

2. The standard errors usually computed for the least squares estimator are incorrect. Confidence intervals and hypothesis tests that use these standard errors may be misleading.

We consider the second implication first. What happens to the standard errors? For the simple linear regression model without heteroskedasticity

$$y_i = \beta_1 + \beta_2 x_i + e_i \quad \text{var}(e_i) = \sigma^2 \tag{8.5}$$

we showed in Chapter 2 that the variance of the least squares estimator for b_2 is

$$\text{var}(b_2) = \frac{\sigma^2}{\sum_{i=1}^{N}(x_i - \bar{x})^2} \tag{8.6}$$

Now suppose the error variances for each observation are different, and that we recognize this difference by putting a subscript i on σ^2, so that we have

$$y_i = \beta_1 + \beta_2 x_i + e_i \quad \text{var}(e_i) = \sigma_i^2 \tag{8.7}$$

It is shown in Appendix 8A at the end of this chapter that the variance of the least squares estimator for β_2 under the heteroskedastic specification in (8.7) is

$$\text{var}(b_2) = \sum_{i=1}^{N} w_i^2 \sigma_i^2 = \frac{\sum_{i=1}^{N}\left[(x_i - \bar{x})^2 \sigma_i^2\right]}{\left[\sum_{i=1}^{N}(x_i - \bar{x})^2\right]^2} \tag{8.8}$$

where $w_i = (x_i - \bar{x})/\sum(x_i - \bar{x})^2$. Consequently, if we proceed to use the least squares estimator and its usual standard errors when $\text{var}(e_i) = \sigma_i^2$, we will be using an estimate of (8.6) to compute the standard error of b_2 when we should be using an estimate of (8.8).

This problem can be overcome by using an estimator for the variance of b_2 given in (8.8). Such an estimator was suggested by econometrician Hal White. The resulting standard errors (the standard error for b_2 and the standard errors for the least squares estimator of other coefficients in the multiple regression model) have become known as White's **heteroskedasticity-consistent standard errors**, or **heteroskedasticity robust**, or simply **robust, standard errors**. The term "robust" is used because they are valid in large samples for both heteroskedastic and homoskedastic errors.

To obtain the White standard error for b_2 corresponding to (8.8), we obtain the least squares residuals $\hat{e}_i = y_i - b_1 - b_2 x_i$ and replace σ_i^2 in (8.8) with the squares of the least squares residuals. The White variance estimator is given by

$$\widehat{\text{var}(b_2)} = \sum_{i=1}^{N} w_i^2 \hat{e}_i^2 = \frac{\sum_{i=1}^{N}\left[(x_i - \bar{x})^2 \hat{e}_i^2\right]}{\left[\sum_{i=1}^{N}(x_i - \bar{x})^2\right]^2} \tag{8.9}$$

and the White standard error is given by the square root of this quantity. In multiple regression models the formulas are more complex, but the principle is the same. Replacing σ_i^2 with the squared residuals $\hat{e}_i^2$ leads to a variance estimator with good properties in large samples because large variances tend to lead to large values of the squared residuals.

Most regression packages include an option for calculating standard errors using White's estimator. If we do so for the food expenditure example, we obtain

$$\hat{y}_i = 83.42 + 10.21x_i$$
$$\quad (27.46) \quad (1.81) \quad \text{(White se)}$$
$$\quad (43.41) \quad (2.09) \quad \text{(incorrect se)}$$

In this case, ignoring heteroskedasticity and using incorrect standard errors, based on the usual formula in (8.6), tends to understate the precision of estimation; we tend to get confidence intervals that are wider than they should be. Specifically, following the result in (3.6) in Chapter 3, we can construct two corresponding 95% confidence intervals for β_2.

$$\text{White}: \quad b_2 \pm t_c \text{se}(b_2) = 10.21 \pm 2.024 \times 1.81 = [6.55, \ 13.87]$$
$$\text{Incorrect}: \quad b_2 \pm t_c \text{se}(b_2) = 10.21 \pm 2.024 \times 2.09 = [5.97, \ 14.45]$$

If we ignore heteroskedasticity, we estimate that β_2 lies between 5.97 and 14.45. When we recognize the existence of heteroskedasticity, our information is more precise, and we estimate that β_2 lies between 6.55 and 13.87.

White's estimator for the standard errors helps us avoid computing incorrect interval estimates or incorrect values for test statistics in the presence of heteroskedasticity. However, it does not address the first implication of heteroskedasticity that we mentioned at the beginning of this section, that the least squares estimator is no longer best. In the next section we describe an alternative estimator that has a smaller variance than the least squares estimator.

8.3 The Generalized Least Squares Estimator

Consider again the food expenditure example and the heteroskedasticity assumption employed in the last section, namely

$$y_i = \beta_1 + \beta_2 x_i + e_i$$
$$E(e_i) = 0, \quad \text{var}(e_i) = \sigma_i^2, \quad \text{cov}(e_i, e_j) = 0 \tag{8.10}$$

Although it is possible to obtain the White heteroskedasticity-consistent variance estimates by simply assuming the error variances σ_i^2 can be different for each observation, to develop an estimator that is better than the least squares estimator we need to make a further assumption about how the variances σ_i^2 change with each observation. This further assumption becomes necessary because the best linear unbiased estimator in the presence of heteroskedasticity, an estimator known as the **generalized least squares** estimator, depends on the unknown σ_i^2. It is not practical to estimate N unknown variances $\sigma_1^2, \sigma_2^2, \ldots, \sigma_N^2$ with only N observations without making a restrictive assumption about how the σ_i^2 change. Thus, to make the generalized least squares estimator operational, some structure is imposed on σ_i^2. Three alternative structures are considered in the next three subsections. Details of the generalized least squares estimator and the issues involved will become clear as we work our way through these sections.

8.3.1 TRANSFORMING THE MODEL

Our earlier inspection of the least squares residuals for the food expenditure example suggested that the error variance increases as income increases. One possible assumption for the variance σ_i^2 that has this characteristic is

$$\text{var}(e_i) = \sigma_i^2 = \sigma^2 x_i \tag{8.11}$$

That is, we assume that the variance of the ith error term σ_i^2 is given by a positive unknown constant parameter σ^2 multiplied by the positive income variable x_i, so that $\text{var}(e_i)$ is proportional to income. As explained earlier, in economic terms this assumption implies that, for low levels of income (x_i), food expenditure (y_i) will be clustered closer to the mean function $E(y_i) = \beta_1 + \beta_2 x_i$. Expenditure on food for low-income households will be largely explained by the level of income. At high levels of income, food expenditures can deviate more from the mean function. This means that there are likely to be many other factors, such as specific tastes and preferences, that reside in the error term, and that lead to a greater variation in food expenditure for high-income households.

The least squares estimator is not the best linear unbiased estimator when the errors are heteroskedastic. What is the best linear unbiased estimator under these circumstances? We approach this problem by *changing or transforming the model into one with homoskedastic errors*. Leaving the basic structure of the model intact, it is possible to turn the heteroskedastic error model into a homoskedastic error model. Once this transformation has been carried out, application of least squares to the transformed model gives a best linear unbiased estimator.

To demonstrate these facts, we begin by dividing both sides of the original model in (8.10) by $\sqrt{x_i}$

$$\frac{y_i}{\sqrt{x_i}} = \beta_1 \left(\frac{1}{\sqrt{x_i}} \right) + \beta_2 \left(\frac{x_i}{\sqrt{x_i}} \right) + \frac{e_i}{\sqrt{x_i}} \tag{8.12}$$

Now, define the following *transformed variables*

$$y_i^* = \frac{y_i}{\sqrt{x_i}}, \quad x_{i1}^* = \frac{1}{\sqrt{x_i}}, \quad x_{i2}^* = \frac{x_i}{\sqrt{x_i}} = \sqrt{x_i}, \quad e_i^* = \frac{e_i}{\sqrt{x_i}} \tag{8.13}$$

so that (8.12) can be rewritten as

$$y_i^* = \beta_1 x_{i1}^* + \beta_2 x_{i2}^* + e_i^* \tag{8.14}$$

The beauty of this transformed model is that the new transformed error term e_i^* is homoskedastic. The proof of this result is:

$$\text{var}(e_i^*) = \text{var}\left(\frac{e_i}{\sqrt{x_i}} \right) = \frac{1}{x_i} \text{var}(e_i) = \frac{1}{x_i} \sigma^2 x_i = \sigma^2 \tag{8.15}$$

Also, the transformed error term will retain the properties of zero mean, $E(e_i^*) = 0$, and zero correlation between different observations, $\text{cov}(e_i^*, e_j^*) = 0$ for $i \neq j$. As a consequence, we can apply least squares to the transformed variables, y_i^*, x_{i1}^*, and x_{i2}^* to obtain the best linear unbiased estimator for β_1 and β_2. Note that the transformed variables y_i^*, x_{i1}^*, and x_{i2}^* are all observable; it is a straightforward matter to compute "the observations" on these variables. An important difference, however, is that the model no longer contains a constant term. The old x_{i1} is implicitly equal to 1 for all observations. The new transformed variable $x_{i1}^* = 1/\sqrt{x_i}$ is no longer constant. You will have to be careful to exclude a constant if your software automatically inserts one, but you can still proceed. The transformed model is linear in the unknown parameters β_1 and β_2. These are the original parameters that we are interested in estimating. They have not been affected by the transformation. In short, the transformed model is a linear model to which we can apply least squares estimation. The transformed model satisfies the conditions of the Gauss–Markov theorem, and the least squares estimators defined in terms of the transformed variables are BLUE.

To summarize, to obtain the best linear unbiased estimator for a model with heteroskedasticity of the type specified in equation (8.11)

1. Calculate the transformed variables given in (8.13).

2. Use least squares to estimate the transformed model given in (8.14).

The estimator obtained in this way is called a generalized least squares estimator.

One way of viewing the generalized least squares estimator is as a **weighted least squares** estimator. Recall that the least squares estimator yields values of β_1 and β_2 that minimize the sum of squared errors. In this case, we are minimizing the sum of squared transformed errors that is given by

$$\sum_{i=1}^{N} e_i^{*2} = \sum_{i=1}^{N} \frac{e_i^2}{x_i} = \sum_{i=1}^{N} (x_i^{-1/2} e_i)^2$$

The errors are *weighted* by $x_i^{-1/2}$, the reciprocal of $\sqrt{x_i}$. When $\sqrt{x_i}$ is small, the data contain more information about the regression function and the observations are weighted heavily. When $\sqrt{x_i}$ is large, the data contain less information and the observations are weighted lightly. In this way we take advantage of the heteroskedasticity to improve parameter estimation.

Most software has a weighted least squares or generalized least squares option. If your software falls into this category, you do not have to worry about transforming the variables before estimation, nor do you have to worry about omitting the constant. The computer will do both the transforming and the estimating. If you do the transforming yourself, that is, you create y_i^*, x_{i1}^*, and x_{i2}^* and apply least squares, be careful not to include a constant in the regression. As noted before, there is no constant because $x_{i1}^* \neq 1$.

Applying the generalized (weighted) least squares procedure to our household expenditure data yields the following estimates:

$$\hat{y}_i = 78.68 + 10.45 x_i$$
$$\text{(se)} \quad (23.79) \quad (1.39) \tag{8.16}$$

That is, we estimate the intercept term as $\hat{\beta}_1 = 78.68$ and the slope coefficient that shows the response of food expenditure to a change in income as $\hat{\beta}_2 = 10.45$. These estimates are somewhat different from the least squares estimates $b_1 = 83.42$ and $b_2 = 10.21$ that did not allow for the existence of heteroskedasticity. It is important to recognize that the interpretations for β_1 and β_2 are the same in the transformed model in (8.14) as they are in the untransformed model in (8.10). *Transformation of the variables should be regarded as a device for converting a heteroskedastic error model into a homoskedastic error model, not as something that changes the meaning of the coefficients.*

The standard errors in (8.16), namely $\text{se}(\hat{\beta}_1) = 23.79$ and $\text{se}(\hat{\beta}_2) = 1.39$, are both lower than their least squares counterparts that were calculated from White's estimator, namely $\text{se}(b_1) = 27.46$ and $\text{se}(b_2) = 1.81$. Since generalized least squares is a better estimation procedure than least squares, we do expect the generalized least squares standard errors to be lower. This statement needs to be qualified in two ways, however. First, remember that standard errors are square roots of *estimated* variances; in a single sample the relative magnitudes of variances may not always be reflected by their corresponding variance estimates. Thus, lower standard errors do not always mean better estimation. Second, the reduction in variance has come at the cost of making an additional assumption, namely, that the variances have the structure given in (8.11).

The smaller standard errors have the advantage of producing narrower more informative confidence intervals. For example, using the generalized least squares results, a 95% confidence interval for β_2 is given by

$$\hat{\beta}_2 \pm t_c \text{se}(\hat{\beta}_2) = 10.451 \pm 2.024 \times 1.386 = [7.65, 13.26]$$

The least squares confidence interval computed using White's standard errors was [6.55, 13.87].

8.3.2 ESTIMATING THE VARIANCE FUNCTION

In the previous section we assumed that heteroskedasticity could be described by the variance function $\text{var}(e_i) = \sigma^2 x_i$. There are other alternatives, however. For example, both $\text{var}(e_i) = \sigma^2 x_i^2$ and $\text{var}(e_i) = \sigma^2 x_i^{1/2}$ have the property that the error variance increases as x_i increases. Why not choose one of these functions? A more general specification that includes all these specifications as special cases is

$$\text{var}(e_i) = \sigma_i^2 = \sigma^2 x_i^{\gamma} \tag{8.17}$$

where γ is an unknown parameter.

How do we proceed with estimation with an assumption like (8.17)? Our earlier discussion suggests that we should transform our model by dividing the ith observation on each variable by $x_i^{\gamma/2}$. Doing so will lead to a transformed error term with constant variance σ^2. Do you understand why? Go back to (8.15) and redo the little proof in this equation with γ included.

Because γ is unknown, we must estimate it before we can proceed with the transformation. To do so it is convenient to consider a framework more general than (8.17). To motivate this framework we take logs of (8.17) to yield

$$\ln(\sigma_i^2) = \ln(\sigma^2) + \gamma \ln(x_i)$$

Then, taking the exponential of both sides,

$$\sigma_i^2 = \exp\left[\ln(\sigma^2) + \gamma \ln(x_i)\right] = \exp(\alpha_1 + \alpha_2 z_i) \tag{8.18}$$

where $\alpha_1 = \ln(\sigma^2), \alpha_2 = \gamma$, and $z_i = \ln(x_i)$. Writing the variance function in this form is convenient because it shows how the variance can be related to any explanatory variable z_i that may or may not be one of the variables in the mean function $E(y_i) = \beta_1 + \beta_2 x_i$. Also, if we believe the variance is likely to depend on more than one explanatory variable, say z_{i2}, $z_{i3}, \ldots, z_{iS}$, (8.18) can be extended to the function

$$\sigma_i^2 = \exp(\alpha_1 + \alpha_2 z_{i2} + \cdots + \alpha_S z_{iS}) \qquad (8.19)$$

The exponential function is convenient because it ensures that we will get positive values for the variances σ_i^2 for all possible values of the parameters $\alpha_1, \alpha_2, \ldots, \alpha_S$.

Returning to (8.18), we rewrite it as

$$\ln(\sigma_i^2) = \alpha_1 + \alpha_2 z_i \qquad (8.20)$$

and now address the question of how to estimate α_1 and α_2. Recall how we get the least squares estimator for the mean function $E(y_i) = \beta_1 + \beta_2 x_i$. We expressed the observations y_i as

$$y_i = E(y_i) + e_i = \beta_1 + \beta_2 x_i + e_i$$

and then applied least squares. We can follow a similar strategy for estimating the variance function using the squares of the least squares residuals $\hat{e}_i^2$ as our observations. That is, we write

$$\ln(\hat{e}_i^2) = \ln(\sigma_i^2) + v_i = \alpha_1 + \alpha_2 z_i + v_i \qquad (8.21)$$

and apply least squares. Regressing $\ln(\hat{e}_i^2)$ on a constant and z_i yields least squares estimates for α_1 and α_2.

Whether or not this procedure is a legitimate one depends on the properties of the new error term v_i that we introduced in (8.21). Does it have a zero mean? Is it uncorrelated and homoskedastic? The answer to these questions is no; $E(v_i) \neq 0$ and the v_i are both correlated and heteroskedastic. However, it can be shown that the least squares estimator for α_2 (and any other slope parameters that might be present) is unbiased in large samples. The least squares estimator for the intercept α_1 is asymptotically biased downward by the amount 1.2704, and thus the obvious "fix" is to use the intercept estimator $\hat{\hat{\alpha}}_1 = \hat{\alpha}_1 + 1.2704$. Interestingly, this correction has no effect on the generalized least squares estimates of the β coefficients because α_1 cancels out during the calculations.[1]

In the food expenditure example, with z_i defined as $z_i = \ln(x_i)$, the least squares estimate of (8.21) is

$$\ln(\hat{\sigma}_i^2) = 0.9378 + 2.329 z_i$$

Notice that the estimate $\hat{\alpha}_2 = \hat{\gamma} = 2.329$ is more than twice the value of $\gamma = 1$ that was an implicit assumption of the variance specification used in Section 8.3.1. It suggests the earlier assumption could be too restrictive.

The next step is to transform the observations in such a way that the transformed model has a constant error variance. As suggested earlier, we could do so by dividing both sides of the equation $y_i = \beta_1 + \beta_2 x_i + e_i$ by $x_i^{\hat{\gamma}/2}$. However, in line with the more general specification in (8.19), we can obtain variance estimates from

$$\hat{\sigma}_i^2 = \exp(\hat{\alpha}_1 + \hat{\alpha}_1 z_i)$$

---

[1] Further discussion of this advanced point can be found in *Introduction to the Theory and Practice of Econometrics, 2nd Edition* (Wiley, 1988) by Judge, Hill, Griffiths, Lütkepohl and Lee, pp. 365–369.

and then divide both sides of the equation by $\hat{\sigma}_i$. Both strategies ultimately lead to the same generalized least squares estimates for β_1 and β_2. Why does the second one work? Dividing (8.10) by σ_i yields

$$\left(\frac{y_i}{\sigma_i}\right) = \beta_1 \left(\frac{1}{\sigma_i}\right) + \beta_2 \left(\frac{x_i}{\sigma_i}\right) + \left(\frac{e_i}{\sigma_i}\right)$$

The variance of the transformed error is constant (homoskedastic) because

$$\text{var}\left(\frac{e_i}{\sigma_i}\right) = \left(\frac{1}{\sigma_i^2}\right) \text{var}(e_i) = \left(\frac{1}{\sigma_i^2}\right) \sigma_i^2 = 1 \tag{8.22}$$

Thus, to obtain a generalized least squares estimator for β_1 and β_2, using the estimates $\hat{\sigma}_i^2$ in place of the unknown σ_i^2, we define the transformed variables

$$y_i^* = \left(\frac{y_i}{\hat{\sigma}_i}\right) \quad x_{i1}^* = \left(\frac{1}{\hat{\sigma}_i}\right) \quad x_{i2}^* = \left(\frac{x_i}{\hat{\sigma}_i}\right) \tag{8.23}$$

and apply least squares to the equation

$$y_i^* = \beta_1 x_{i1}^* + \beta_2 x_{i2}^* + e_i^* \tag{8.24}$$

To summarize these steps for the general case, suppose we are estimating the model

$$y_i = \beta_1 + \beta_2 x_{i2} + \cdots + \beta_K x_{iK} + e_i \tag{8.25}$$

where

$$\text{var}(e_i) = \sigma_i^2 = \exp(\alpha_1 + \alpha_2 z_{i2} + \cdots + \alpha_S z_{iS}) \tag{8.26}$$

The steps for obtaining a generalized least squares estimator for $\beta_1, \beta_2, \ldots, \beta_K$ are

1. Estimate (8.25) by least squares and compute the squares of the least squares residuals $\hat{e}_i^2$.
2. Estimate $\alpha_1, \alpha_2, \ldots, \alpha_S$ by applying least squares to the equation $\ln(\hat{e}_i^2) = \alpha_1 + \alpha_2 z_{i2} + \cdots + \alpha_S z_{iS} + v_i$.
3. Compute variance estimates $\hat{\sigma}_i^2 = \exp(\hat{\alpha}_1 + \hat{\alpha}_2 z_{i2} + \cdots + \hat{\alpha}_S z_{iS})$.
4. Compute the transformed observations defined by (8.23), including $x_{i3}^*, \ldots, x_{iK}^*$ if $K > 2$.
5. Apply least squares to (8.24), or to an extended version of (8.24), if $K > 2$.

Steps 4 and 5 can be replaced by weighted least squares with weights defined by $\hat{\sigma}_i^{-1}$ if your software automatically computes weighted least squares estimates. If you are very fortunate, you will have software that performs all five steps with one click of your mouse.

Following these steps to obtain generalized least squares estimates for the food expenditure example yields

$$\begin{aligned} \hat{y}_i &= 76.05 + 10.63x \\ (\text{se}) \quad &\quad (9.71) \quad (0.97) \end{aligned} \tag{8.27}$$

Compared to the generalized least squares results for the variance specification $\sigma_i^2 = \sigma^2 x_i$, the estimates for β_1 and β_2 have not changed a great deal, but there has been a considerable drop in the standard errors that, under the previous specification, were $se(\hat{\beta}_1) = 23.79$ and $se(\hat{\beta}_2) = 1.39$.

As mentioned earlier, because standard errors are themselves estimates, we cannot conclude with certainty that allowing for a more general variance specification has improved the precision with which we have estimated β_1 and β_2. However, in this particular case it is distinctly possible that our improved results are attributable to better modeling and better estimation.

8.3.3 A Heteroskedastic Partition

To introduce a third form of heteroskedasticity and the generalized least squares estimator corresponding to it, we return to a data set that was used in Chapter 7 to estimate wage equations and to illustrate the use of dummy variables. In that chapter several equations were estimated using variables such as level of education, race, gender, and region of residence to explain differences in the mean level of wages. Although the equations were simplifications designed to aid the interpretation of dummy variables, the explanatory variables that were used are typical of those included in labor market applications. In this section our illustrative example is another simplified wage equation where earnings per hour (*WAGE*) depends on years of education (*EDUC*), years of experience (*EXPER*), and a dummy variable *METRO* that is equal to 1 for workers who live in a metropolitan area and 0 for workers who live outside a metropolitan area. Using data in the file *cps2.dat* the least squares estimated equation for this model is

$$\widehat{WAGE} = -9.914 + 1.234EDUC + 0.133EXPER + 1.524METRO \tag{8.28}$$
$$\text{(se)} \quad (1.08) \quad (0.070) \quad\quad (0.015) \quad\quad\quad (0.431)$$

The results suggest education and experience have a positive effect on the level of wages and that, given a particular level of education and experience, the average metropolitan wage is $1.52 per hour higher than the average wage in a rural area.

The question we now ask is: How does the variance of wages in a metropolitan area compare with the variance of wages in a rural area? Are the variances likely to be the same or different? One might suspect that the greater range of different types of jobs in a metropolitan area will lead to city wages having a higher variance. To introduce a framework for investigating this question, we partition our sample into two parts, one for the metropolitan observations (for which we use the subscript "*M*") and the other for the rural observations (for which we use the subscript "*R*")

$$WAGE_{Mi} = \beta_{M1} + \beta_2 EDUC_{Mi} + \beta_3 EXPER_{Mi} + e_{Mi} \quad i = 1, 2, \dots, N_M \tag{8.29a}$$

$$WAGE_{Ri} = \beta_{R1} + \beta_2 EDUC_{Ri} + \beta_3 EXPER_{Ri} + e_{Ri} \quad i = 1, 2, \dots, N_R \tag{8.29b}$$

Implicit in the above specification is the assumption that the coefficients for *EDUC* and *EXPER* (β_2 and β_3) are the same in both metropolitan and rural areas, but the intercepts differ. This assumption is in line with the estimated equation in (8.28) where the estimate for β_{R1} is $b_{R1} = -9.914$ and the estimate for β_{M1} is

$$b_{M1} = -9.914 + 1.524 = -8.39$$

The new assumption in (8.29) is that the variances of the two error terms e_{Mi} and e_{Ri} are not equal. For the least squares estimates in (8.28) to be best linear unbiased, we require $\mathrm{var}(e_{Mi}) = \mathrm{var}(e_{Ri}) = \sigma^2$; the error variance is constant for all observations. We now assume that the error variances in the metropolitan and rural regions are different. That is,

$$\mathrm{var}(e_{Mi}) = \sigma_M^2, \quad \mathrm{var}(e_{Ri}) = \sigma_R^2 \tag{8.30}$$

Having two subsets of observations, each with a different variance, partitions the sample into what we have called a **heteroskedastic partition**.

In the file *cps2.dat* there are $N_M = 808$ metropolitan observations and $N_R = 192$ rural observations. Using these observations and least squares to estimate (8.29a) and (8.29b) separately yields variance estimates

$$\hat{\sigma}_M^2 = 31.824, \quad \hat{\sigma}_R^2 = 15.243$$

The estimated error variance for the metropolitan wage equation is approximately double that for the rural wage equation. Whether this difference could be attributable to sampling error, or is sufficiently large to conclude that $\sigma_M^2 \neq \sigma_R^2$, is something to decide using a hypothesis test. We defer such a test until the next section and, for the moment, assume that $\sigma_M^2 \neq \sigma_R^2$.

One set of estimates that recognizes that the error variances are different are the separate least squares estimates of (8.29a) and (8.29b) that turn out to be

$$b_{M1} = -9.052, \quad b_{M2} = 1.282, \quad b_{M3} = 0.1346$$
$$b_{R1} = -6.166, \quad b_{R2} = 0.956, \quad b_{R3} = 0.1260$$

However, a problem with these estimates is that we have two estimates for β_2 and two estimates for β_3, when in (8.29) we are assuming the effect of education and experience on wages is the same for both metropolitan and rural areas. Given this assumption is correct, better estimates (ones with lower variances) can be obtained by combining both subsets of data and applying a generalized least squares estimator to the complete set of data, with recognition given to the existence of heteroskedasticity.

The strategy for obtaining generalized least squares estimates is the same as it was in the previous section. The variables are transformed by dividing each observation by the standard deviation of the corresponding error term. In our example of a heteroskedastic partition, that means that all metropolitan observations are divided by σ_M and all rural observations are divided by σ_R. Equations (8.29a) and (8.29b) become

$$\left(\frac{WAGE_{Mi}}{\sigma_M}\right) = \beta_{M1}\left(\frac{1}{\sigma_M}\right) + \beta_2\left(\frac{EDUC_{Mi}}{\sigma_M}\right) + \beta_3\left(\frac{EXPER_{Mi}}{\sigma_M}\right) + \left(\frac{e_{Mi}}{\sigma_M}\right)$$

$$i = 1, 2, \ldots, N_M \tag{8.31a}$$

$$\left(\frac{WAGE_{Ri}}{\sigma_R}\right) = \beta_{R1}\left(\frac{1}{\sigma_R}\right) + \beta_2\left(\frac{EDUC_{Ri}}{\sigma_R}\right) + \beta_3\left(\frac{EXPER_{Ri}}{\sigma_R}\right) + \left(\frac{e_{Ri}}{\sigma_R}\right)$$

$$i = 1, 2, \ldots, N_R \tag{8.31b}$$

The variances of the transformed error terms (e_{Mi}/σ_M) and (e_{Ri}/σ_R) are the same. They are both equal to 1. Is this fact obvious to you? No? Go back and check out (8.15) and (8.22).

When you are comfortable, it will be clear to you that the combined set of error terms is homoskedastic. Thus, application of least squares to the complete set of transformed observations yields best linear unbiased estimators.

There are two complications, however. The first is that σ_M and σ_R are unknown. We solve this problem by transforming the observations with their estimates $\hat{\sigma}_M$ and $\hat{\sigma}_R$. Doing so yields a generalized least squares estimator that has good properties in large samples. The second complication relates to the fact that the metropolitan and rural intercepts are different. This complication will not necessarily be present in all models with a heteroskedastic partition, but it arises in this case because both the mean and variance of wage depend on the dummy variable *METRO*.

The different intercepts are accommodated by including *METRO* as we did in the original equation (8.28), but this time it is transformed in the same way as the other variables. Collecting all these facts together, we can combine equations (8.31a) and (8.31b) and summarize the method for obtaining generalized least squares estimates in the following way.

1. Obtain estimates $\hat{\sigma}_M$ and $\hat{\sigma}_R$ by applying least squares separately to the metropolitan and rural observations.

2. Let $\hat{\sigma}_i = \begin{cases} \hat{\sigma}_M & \text{when } METRO_i = 1 \\ \hat{\sigma}_R & \text{when } METRO_i = 0 \end{cases}$

3. Apply least squares to the transformed model

$$\left(\frac{WAGE_i}{\hat{\sigma}_i}\right) = \beta_{R1}\left(\frac{1}{\hat{\sigma}_i}\right) + \beta_2\left(\frac{EDUC_i}{\hat{\sigma}_i}\right) + \beta_3\left(\frac{EXPER_i}{\hat{\sigma}_i}\right)$$
$$+ \delta\left(\frac{METRO_i}{\hat{\sigma}_i}\right) + \left(\frac{e_i}{\hat{\sigma}_i}\right)$$

(8.32)

where $\beta_{M1} = \beta_{R1} + \delta$.

Following these steps using the data in the file *cps2.dat* yields the estimated equation

$$\widehat{WAGE} = -9.398 + 1.196EDUC + 0.132EXPER + 1.539METRO$$
$$(se) \quad (1.02) \quad (0.069) \quad \quad (0.015) \quad \quad (0.346)$$

(8.33)

These coefficient estimates are similar in magnitude to those in (8.28), an outcome that is not surprising given that both least squares and generalized least squares are unbiased in the presence of heteroskedasticity. We would hope, however, that the greater precision of the generalized least squares estimator is reflected in smaller standard errors. The standard errors in (8.28) are not a good basis for comparison because they are incorrect under heteroskedasticity. However, we compare those in (8.33) with those obtained by applying least squares separately to the metropolitan and rural observations. For *EDUC* they are $se(b_{M2}) = 0.080$ and se $(b_{R2}) = 0.133$, and for *EXPER* they are se $(b_{M3}) = 0.018$ and se $(b_{R3}) = 0.025$. Using the larger combined set of observations has led to a reduction in the standard errors.

> **REMARK:** The generalized least squares estimators described in the last three subsections require an assumption about the form of the heteroskedasticity. Using least squares with White standard errors avoids the need to make an assumption about the form of heteroskedasticity, but does not realize the potential efficiency gains from generalized least squares.

8.4 Detecting Heteroskedasticity

In our discussion of the food expenditure equation, we used the nature of the economic problem and data to argue why heteroskedasticity of a particular form might be present. However, in this and in other equations that use other types of data, there will be uncertainty about whether a heteroskedastic assumption is warranted. It is natural to ask: How do I know if heteroskedasticity is likely to be a problem for my model and my set of data? Is there a way of detecting heteroskedasticity so that I know whether to use generalized least squares techniques? We consider three ways of investigating these questions. The first is the informal use of residual plots. The other two are more formal classes of statistical tests.

8.4.1 RESIDUAL PLOTS

One way of investigating the existence of heteroskedasticity is to estimate your model using least squares and to plot the least squares residuals. If the errors are homoskedastic, there should be no patterns of any sort in the residuals. If the errors are heteroskedastic, they may tend to exhibit greater variation in some systematic way. For example, for the household expenditure data, we suspect that the variance increases as incomes increases. Earlier in this chapter (Section 8.1) we plotted the estimated least squares function and the residuals and reported them in Figure 8.2. We discovered that the absolute values of the residuals do indeed tend to increase as income increases. This method of investigating heteroskedasticity can be followed for any simple regression.

When we have more than one explanatory variable, the estimated least squares function is not so easily depicted on a diagram. However, what we can do is plot the least squares residuals against each explanatory variable, or against $\hat{y}_i$, to see if those residuals vary in a systematic way relative to the specified variable.

8.4.2 THE GOLDFELD–QUANDT TEST

Our second test for heteroskedasticity is designed for two subsamples with possibly different variances. In Section 8.3.3, under the title "A Heteroskedastic Partition," we considered metropolitan and rural subsamples for estimating a wage equation. Suspecting that the error variances could be different for these two groups, we estimated their variances as $\hat{\sigma}_M^2 = 31.824$ and $\hat{\sigma}_R^2 = 15.243$. We now ask: Are these values sufficiently different to conclude that $\sigma_M^2 \neq \sigma_R^2$?

The background for this test appears in Appendix C.7.3. The only difference is that the degrees of freedom change because we are considering the error variances from two subsamples of a regression equation rather than the variances from two independent samples of data. In the context of the example we are considering, it can be shown that

$$F = \frac{\hat{\sigma}_M^2/\sigma_M^2}{\hat{\sigma}_R^2/\sigma_R^2} \sim F_{(N_M - K_M, N_R - K_R)} \tag{8.34}$$

where $N_M - K_M$ and $N_R - K_R$ are the degrees of freedom for the two subsample regressions. Usually, $K_M = K_R$. In words, (8.34) says: The F statistic that has a numerator equal to the ratio of one variance estimate to its true population value, and a denominator equal to the ratio of the other variance estimate to its population value, has an F distribution with $(N_M - K_M, N_R - K_R)$ degrees of freedom. Suppose we want to test

$$H_0 : \sigma_M^2 = \sigma_R^2 \quad \text{against} \quad H_1 : \sigma_M^2 \neq \sigma_R^2 \qquad (8.35)$$

Then, when H_0 is true, (8.34) reduces to $F = \hat{\sigma}_M^2 / \hat{\sigma}_R^2$, and its value for the wage equation is

$$F = \frac{\hat{\sigma}_M^2}{\hat{\sigma}_R^2} = \frac{31.824}{15.243} = 2.09$$

Given that (8.35) is a two-tail test, and recalling that $N_M = 808$, $N_R = 192$, and $K_M = K_R = 3$, the relevant lower and upper critical values for a 5% significance level are $F_{Lc} = F_{(0.025,805,189)} = 0.81$ and $F_{Uc} = F_{(0.975,805,189)} = 1.26$. We reject H_0 if $F < F_{Lc}$ or $F > F_{Uc}$. Since $2.09 > 1.26$, in this case we reject H_0 and conclude the wage variances for the rural and metropolitan regions are not equal.

When following the above procedure, it does not matter whether you put the larger variance estimate in the numerator or the denominator of the F-statistic. However, if you always put the larger estimate in the numerator, then you reject H_0 at a 5% level of significance if $F > F_{Uc} = F_{(0.975,N_M-K_M,N_R-K_R)}$. For a one-tail test the critical value changes. For $H_1 : \sigma_M^2 > \sigma_R^2$, we reject H_0 at a 5% level of significance if $F > F_c = F_{(0.95,805,189)} = 1.22$. Since we originally hypothesized that greater job variety in the metropolitan area might lead to a greater variance, one could argue that a one-tail test is appropriate.

Although the Goldfeld–Quandt test is specifically designed for instances where the sample divides naturally into two subsamples, it can also be used where, under H_1, the variance is a function of a single explanatory variable, say z_i. To perform the test under these circumstances, we order the observations according to z_i so that, if heteroskedasticity exists, the first half of the sample will correspond to observations with lower variances and the last half of the sample will correspond to observations with higher variances. Then, we split the sample into approximately two equal halves, carry out two separate least squares regressions that yield variance estimates, say $\hat{\sigma}_1^2$ and $\hat{\sigma}_2^2$, and proceed with the test as described previously.

Following these steps for the food expenditure example, with the observations ordered according to income x_i, and the sample split into two equal subsamples of 20 observations each, yields $\hat{\sigma}_1^2 = 3574.8$ and $\hat{\sigma}_2^2 = 12921.9$, from which we obtain

$$F = \frac{\hat{\sigma}_2^2}{\hat{\sigma}_1^2} = \frac{12921.9}{3574.8} = 3.61$$

Believing that the variances could increase, but not decrease with income, we use a one-tail test with 5% critical value $F_{(0.95,18,18)} = 2.22$. Since $3.61 > 2.22$, a null hypothesis of homoskedasticity is rejected in favor of the alternative that the variance increases with income.

8.4.3 TESTING THE VARIANCE FUNCTION

In this section we consider a test for heteroskedasticity based on the variance function. The form of the variance function used for testing is slightly different from that used for estimation in Section 8.3, but the idea is the same. As before, it is important to distinguish between the mean function $E(y_i)$ and the variance function $\text{var}(y_i)$. The mean function appears in the regression model

$$y_i = E(y_i) + e_i = \beta_1 + \beta_2 x_{i2} + \cdots + \beta_K x_{iK} + e_i \tag{8.36}$$

The variance function is relevant when heteroskedasticity is a possibility and we hypothesize that the variance depends on a set of explanatory variables $z_{i2}, z_{i3}, \ldots, z_{iS}$. A general form for the variance function is

$$\text{var}(y_i) = \sigma_i^2 = E(e_i^2) = h(\alpha_1 + \alpha_2 z_{i2} + \cdots + \alpha_S z_{iS}) \tag{8.37}$$

This is a *general* form because we have not been specific about the function $h(\cdot)$. One of the desirable features of the test that we develop is that it is valid for all reasonable functions $h(\cdot)$. Examples are the function specified in Section 8.3.2, namely

$$h(\alpha_1 + \alpha_2 z_{i2} + \cdots + \alpha_S z_{iS}) = \exp(\alpha_1 + \alpha_2 z_{i2} + \cdots + \alpha_S z_{iS})$$

and its special case that appears in (8.18)

$$h(\alpha_1 + \alpha_2 z_i) = \exp\left[\ln(\sigma^2) + \gamma \ln(x_i)\right]$$

Another example is the linear function

$$h(\alpha_1 + \alpha_2 z_{i2} + \cdots + \alpha_S z_{iS}) = \alpha_1 + \alpha_2 z_{i2} + \cdots + \alpha_S z_{iS} \tag{8.38}$$

Notice what happens to the function $h(\cdot)$ when $\alpha_2 = \alpha_3 = \cdots = \alpha_S = 0$. It collapses to

$$h(\alpha_1 + \alpha_2 z_{i2} + \cdots + \alpha_S z_{iS}) = h(\alpha_1)$$

The term $h(\alpha_1)$ is a constant; it does not depend on any explanatory variables. In other words, when $\alpha_2 = \alpha_3 = \cdots = \alpha_S = 0$, heteroskedasticity is not present; the variance is constant. In terms of notation that you are familiar with, we can write $\sigma^2 = h(\alpha_1)$. Consequently, the null and alternative hypotheses for a test for heteroskedasticity based on the variance function are

$$\begin{aligned} H_0 &: \quad \alpha_2 = \alpha_3 = \cdots = \alpha_S = 0 \\ H_1 &: \quad \text{not all the } \alpha_s \text{ in } H_0 \text{ are zero} \end{aligned} \tag{8.39}$$

The null and alternative hypotheses are the first components of a test. The next component is a test statistic. To obtain a test statistic we consider the linear variance function in (8.38) that we substitute into (8.37) to obtain

$$\text{var}(y_i) = \sigma_i^2 = E(e_i^2) = \alpha_1 + \alpha_2 z_{i2} + \cdots + \alpha_S z_{iS} \tag{8.40}$$

Let $v_i = e_i^2 - E(e_i^2)$ be the difference between a squared error and its mean. Then, from (8.40), we can write

$$e_i^2 = E(e_i^2) + v_i = \alpha_1 + \alpha_2 z_{i2} + \cdots + \alpha_S z_{iS} + v_i \tag{8.41}$$

Notice that the addition of v_i to the variance function serves a similar purpose to addition of e_i to the mean function in (8.36). There is an important difference, however. In (8.36) the dependent variable y_i is observable. If we try to estimate (8.41), we find that the "dependent variable" e_i^2 is not observable. We overcome this problem by replacing e_i^2 with the squares of the least squares residuals $\hat{e}_i^2$, obtained from estimating (8.36). Thus, we write an operational version of (8.41) as

$$\hat{e}_i^2 = \alpha_1 + \alpha_2 z_{i2} + \cdots + \alpha_S z_{iS} + v_i \qquad (8.42)$$

Strictly speaking, replacing e_i^2 by $\hat{e}_i^2$ also changes the definition of v_i, but we will retain the same notation to avoid unnecessary complication.

The variance function test for heteroskedasticity uses quantities obtained from least squares estimation of (8.42). We are interested in discovering whether the variables z_{i2}, $z_{i3}, \ldots, z_{iS}$ help explain the variation in $\hat{e}_i^2$. Since the R^2 goodness-of-fit statistic from (8.42) measures the proportion of variation in $\hat{e}_i^2$ explained by the z's, it is a natural candidate for a test statistic. It can be shown that, when H_0 is true, the sample size multiplied by R^2 has a chi-square (χ^2) distribution with $S - 1$ degrees of freedom. That is,

$$\chi^2 = N \times R^2 \sim \chi^2_{(S-1)} \qquad (8.43)$$

It is likely that, so far, your exposure to the χ^2-distribution has been limited. It was introduced in Appendix B.5.2, it was used for testing for normality in Section 4.3.4, and its relationship with the F-test was explored in an appendix to Chapter 6, Appendix 6A. It is a distribution that is used for testing many different kinds of hypotheses. Like an F random variable, a χ^2 random variable takes only positive values. Because a large R^2 value provides evidence against the null hypothesis (it suggests the z variables explain changes in the variance), the rejection region for the statistic in (8.43) is in the right tail of the distribution. Thus, for a 5% significance level, we reject H_0 and conclude that heteroskedasticity exists when $\chi^2 > \chi^2_{(0.95, S-1)}$.

There are several important features of this test:

1. It is a large sample test. The result in (8.43) holds approximately in large samples.

2. You will often see the test referred to as a **Lagrange multiplier test** or a **Breusch–Pagan test** for heteroskedasticity. Breusch and Pagan used the Lagrange multiplier principle (see Appendix C.8.4) to derive an earlier version of the test that was later modified by other researchers to the form in (8.43). The test values for these and other slightly different versions of the test, one of which is an F-test, are automatically calculated by a number of software packages. The one provided by your software may or may not be exactly the same as the $N \times R^2$ version in (8.43). The relationships between the different versions of the test are described in Appendix 8B. As you proceed through the book and study more econometrics, you will find that many Lagrange multiplier tests can be written in the form $N \times R^2$ where R^2 comes from a convenient auxiliary regression related to the hypothesis being tested.

3. We motivated the test in terms of an alternative hypothesis with the very general variance function $\sigma_i^2 = h(\alpha_1 + \alpha_2 z_{i2} + \cdots + \alpha_S z_{iS})$, yet we proceeded to carry out the test using the linear function $\hat{e}_i^2 = \alpha_1 + \alpha_2 z_{i2} + \cdots + \alpha_S z_{iS} + v_i$. One of the amazing features of the Breusch–Pagan test is that the value of the statistic computed from the linear function is valid for testing an alternative hypothesis of heteroskedasticity where the variance function can be of any form given by (8.37).

8.4.3a The White Test

One problem with the variance function test described so far is that it presupposes that we have knowledge of what variables will appear in the variance function if the alternative hypothesis of heteroskedasticity is true. In other words, it assumes we are able to specify z_2, $z_3,\ldots,z_S$. In reality we may wish to test for heteroskedasticity without precise knowledge of the relevant variables. With this point in mind, econometrician Hal White suggested defining the z's as equal to the x's, the squares of the x's, and possibly their cross products. Frequently, the variables that affect the variance are the same as those in the mean function. Also, by using a quadratic function we can approximate a number of other possible variance functions. Suppose the mean function has two explanatory variables

$$E(y_i) = \beta_1 + \beta_2 x_{i2} + \beta_3 x_{i3}$$

The White test without cross-product terms (interactions) specifies

$$z_2 = x_2 \quad z_3 = x_3 \quad z_4 = x_2^2 \quad z_5 = x_3^2$$

Including interactions adds one further variable, $z_6 = x_2 x_3$. If the mean function contains quadratic terms (e.g., $x_3 = x_2^2$), then some of the z's are redundant and are deleted.

The White test is performed as an F-test (see Appendix 8B for details) or using the $\chi^2 = N \times R^2$ test defined in (8.43). Its test values are routinely calculated by many econometric software packages and can often be found by the simple click of a mouse.

8.4.3b Testing the Food Expenditure Example

To test for heteroskedasticity in the food expenditure example where the variance is potentially a function of income, we test $H_0 : \alpha_2 = 0$ against the alternative $H_1 : \alpha_2 \neq 0$ in the variance function $\sigma_i^2 = h(\alpha_1 + \alpha_2 x_i)$. We begin by estimating the function $\hat{e}_i^2 = \alpha_1 + \alpha_2 x_i + v_i$ by least squares, from which we obtain

$$SST = 4,610,749,441 \quad SSE = 3,759,556,169$$
$$R^2 = 1 - \frac{SSE}{SST} = 0.1846$$

and

$$\chi^2 = N \times R^2 = 40 \times 0.1846 = 7.38$$

Since there is only one parameter in the null hypothesis, the χ^2-test has one degree of freedom. The 5% critical value is 3.84. Because 7.38 is greater than 3.84, we reject H_0 and conclude that the variance depends on income.

For the White version of the test we estimate the equation $\hat{e}_i^2 = \alpha_1 + \alpha_2 x_i + \alpha_3 x_i^2 + v_i$ and test $H_0 : \alpha_2 = \alpha_3 = 0$ against $H_1 : \alpha_2 \neq 0$ or $\alpha_3 \neq 0$. In this case, including both the test and p-values, we have

$$\chi^2 = N \times R^2 = 40 \times 0.18888 = 7.555 \qquad p\text{-value} = 0.023$$

The 5% critical value is $\chi^2_{(0.95,2)} = 5.99$. Again, we conclude that heteroskedasticity exists with the variance dependent on income.

8.5 Exercises

8.5.1 PROBLEMS

8.1   Show that the variance of the least squares estimator given in (8.8) simplifies to that given in (8.6) when $\sigma_i^2 = \sigma^2$. That is

$$\frac{\sum_{i=1}^{N}\left[(x_i - \bar{x})^2\sigma_i^2\right]}{\left[\sum_{i=1}^{N}(x_i - \bar{x})^2\right]^2} = \frac{\sigma^2}{\sum_{i=1}^{N}(x_i - \bar{x})^2}$$

8.2   Consider the model $y_i = \beta_1 + \beta_2 x_i + e_i$ with heteroskedastic variance $\text{var}(e_i) = \sigma_i^2$ and its transformed homoskedastic version $y_i^* = \beta_1\sigma_i^{-1} + \beta_2 x_i^* + e_i^*$ where $y_i^* = \sigma_i^{-1}y_i$, $x_i^* = \sigma_i^{-1}x_i$, and $e_i^* = \sigma_i^{-1}e_i$. The normal equations whose solution yields the generalized least squares estimators $\hat{\beta}_1$ and $\hat{\beta}_2$ are

$$\left(\sum\sigma_i^{-2}\right)\hat{\beta}_1 + \left(\sum\sigma_i^{-1}x_i^*\right)\hat{\beta}_2 = \sum\sigma_i^{-1}y_i^*$$
$$\left(\sum\sigma_i^{-1}x_i^*\right)\hat{\beta}_1 + \left(\sum x_i^{*2}\right)\hat{\beta}_2 = \sum x_i^*y_i^*$$

(a) Show that $\hat{\beta}_1$ and $\hat{\beta}_2$ can be written as

$$\hat{\beta}_2 = \frac{\dfrac{\sum\sigma_i^{-2}y_ix_i}{\sum\sigma_i^{-2}} - \left(\dfrac{\sum\sigma_i^{-2}y_i}{\sum\sigma_i^{-2}}\right)\left(\dfrac{\sum\sigma_i^{-2}x_i}{\sum\sigma_i^{-2}}\right)}{\dfrac{\sum\sigma_i^{-2}x_i^2}{\sum\sigma_i^{-2}} - \left(\dfrac{\sum\sigma_i^{-2}x_i}{\sum\sigma_i^{-2}}\right)^2} \qquad \hat{\beta}_1 = \frac{\sum\sigma_i^{-2}y_i}{\sum\sigma_i^{-2}} - \left(\frac{\sum\sigma_i^{-2}x_i}{\sum\sigma_i^{-2}}\right)\hat{\beta}_2$$

(b) Show that $\hat{\beta}_1$ and $\hat{\beta}_2$ are equal to the least squares estimators b_1 and b_2 when $\sigma_i^2 = \sigma^2$ for all i. That is, the error variances are constant.

(c) Does a comparison of the formulas for $\hat{\beta}_1$ and $\hat{\beta}_2$ with those for b_1 and b_2 suggest an interpretation for $\hat{\beta}_1$ and $\hat{\beta}_2$?

8.3   Consider the simple regression model

$$y_i = \beta_1 + \beta_2 x_i + e_i$$

where the e_i are independent errors with $E(e_i) = 0$ and $\text{var}(e_i) = \sigma^2 x_i^2$. Suppose that you have the following five observations

$$y = (4, 3, 1, 0, 2) \quad x = (1, 2, 1, 3, 4)$$

Use a hand calculator to find generalized least squares estimates of β_1 and β_2.

8.4   A sample of 200 Chicago households was taken to investigate how far American households tend to travel when they take vacation. Measuring distance in miles per year, the following model was estimated

$$MILES = \beta_1 + \beta_2 INCOME + \beta_3 AGE + \beta_4 KIDS + e$$

The variables are self-explanatory except perhaps for AGE that is the average age of the adult members of the household. The data are in the file *vacation.dat*.

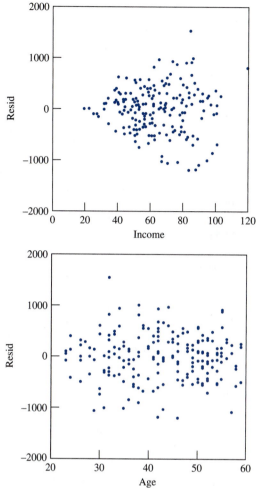

FIGURE **8.3** Residual plots for Exercise 8.4: vacation data.

(a) The equation was estimated by least squares and the residuals are plotted against age and income in Figure 8.3. What do these graphs suggest to you?

(b) Ordering the observations according to descending values of *INCOME*, and applying least squares to the first 100 observations, and again to the second 100 observations, yields the sums of squared errors

$$SSE_1 = 2.9471 \times 10^7 \quad SSE_2 = 1.0479 \times 10^7$$

Use the Goldfeld–Quandt test to test for heteroskedastic errors. Include specification of the null and alternative hypotheses.

(c) Table 8.1 contains three sets of estimates, those from least squares, those from least squares with White's standard errors, and those from generalized least squares under the assumption $\sigma_i^2 = \sigma^2 \times INCOME^2$.

  (i) How do vacation miles traveled depend on income, age, and the number of kids in the household?

  (ii) How do White's standard errors compare with the least squares standard errors? Do they change your assessment of the precision of estimation?

Table 8.1   **Output for Exercise 8.4**

Variable	Coefficient	Std. Error	t-Value	p-Value
Least squares estimates				
C	−391.55	169.78	−2.31	0.022
INCOME	14.20	1.80	7.89	0.000
AGE	15.74	3.76	4.19	0.000
KIDS	−81.83	27.13	−3.02	0.003
Least squares estimates with White standard errors				
C	−391.55	142.65	−2.74	0.007
INCOME	14.20	1.94	7.32	0.000
AGE	15.74	3.97	3.97	0.000
KIDS	−81.83	29.15	−2.81	0.006
Generalized least squares estimates				
C	−425.00	121.44	−3.50	0.001
INCOME	13.95	1.48	9.42	0.000
AGE	16.72	3.02	5.53	0.000
KIDS	−76.81	21.85	−3.52	0.001

      (iii) Is there evidence to suggest the generalized least squares estimates are better estimates?

8.5 In Exercise 5.5 an equation used for the valuation of homes in towns surrounding Boston was estimated. Reestimating that equation with White's standard errors yields the output in Table 8.2.

    (a) For the coefficients of *CRIME, ROOMS, AGE,* and *TAX,* compare 95% confidence intervals obtained using the standard errors from Exercise 5.5 with those from Table 8.2.

Table 8.2   **Estimated Mean Function for Exercise 8.5**

Dependent Variable: *VALUE*
Observations: 506
Heteroskedasticity-Consistent Standard Errors

Variable	Coefficient	Std. Error	t-Value	p-Value
C	28.407	7.380	3.849	0.000
CRIME	−0.183	0.035	−5.283	0.000
NITOX	−22.811	4.360	−5.232	0.000
ROOMS	6.372	0.665	9.574	0.000
AGE	−0.048	0.011	−4.433	0.000
DIST	−1.335	0.190	−7.019	0.000
ACCESS	0.272	0.075	3.644	0.000
TAX	−0.013	0.003	−4.430	0.000
PTRATIO	−1.177	0.124	−9.522	0.000

$R^2 = 0.657$ $SSE = 14,652.22$ $SST = 42,716.29$

Table 8.3   **Estimated Variance Function for Exercise 8.6**

Dependent Variable: *EHAT_SQ*
Included observations: 506

Variable	Coefficient	Std. Error	t-Value	p-Value
C	1007.037	204.522	4.92	0.000
ROOMS	−305.311	63.088	−4.84	0.000
ROOMS^2	23.822	4.844	4.92	0.000
CRIME	2.285	1.242	1.84	0.067
CRIME^2	−0.039	0.019	−2.04	0.042
DIST	−4.419	2.466	−1.79	0.074

$R^2 = 0.08467$ $SSE = 5,038,458$ $SST = 5,504,525$

    (b) Do you think heteroskedasticity is likely to be a problem?

    (c) What misleading inferences are likely if the incorrect standard errors are used?

8.6 Continuing with the example in Exercise 8.5, Table 8.3 contains output for the following least squares regression

$$\hat{e}_i^2 = \alpha_1 + \alpha_2 ROOMS_i + \alpha_3 ROOMS_i^2 + \alpha_4 CRIME_i + \alpha_5 CRIME_i^2 + \alpha_6 DIST_i + v_i$$

where $\hat{e}_i$ are the least squares residuals from the mean function estimated in Exercise 8.5.

    (a) Discuss how each of the variables *ROOMS*, *CRIME*, and *DIST* influences the variance of house values.

    (b) Test for heteroskedasticity.

8.7* Consider the model

$$y_i = \beta_1 + \beta_2 x_i + e_i \quad E(e_i) = 0 \quad var(e_i) = \sigma_i^2 = \exp(\alpha z_i)$$

You have the following eight observations on y_i, x_i, and z_i.

y	1.1	−0.5	18.9	−0.9	6.4	1.8	4.5	−0.2
x	−0.5	−3	3.2	−1.8	3.4	−3.5	2.4	−0.2
z	3.3	0.3	7.0	4.7	1.9	6.8	2.3	6.4

Use a hand calculator to:

    (a) Find least squares estimates of β_1 and β_2.

    (b) Find the least squares residuals.

    (c) Estimate α.

    (d) Find variance estimates $\hat{\sigma}_i^2$.

    (e) Find generalized least squares estimates of β_1 and β_2. (*Hint*: Use the results in Exercise 8.2)

8.5.2 COMPUTER EXERCISES

8.8 The file *stockton96.dat* contains 940 observations on home sales in Stockton, CA in 1996. They are a subset of the data in the file *stockton.dat* used for Exercise 7.4.

(a) Use least squares to estimate a linear equation that relates house price *PRICE* to the size of the house in square feet *SQFT* and the age of the house in years *AGE*. Comment on the estimates.

(b) Suppose that you own two houses. One has 1400 square feet; the other has 1800 square feet. Both are 20 years old. What price do you estimate you will get for each house.

(c) Use the White test (with cross-product term included) to test for heteroskedasticity.

(d) Estimate α_1 and α_2 in the variance function $\sigma_i^2 = \exp(\alpha_1 + \alpha_2 SQFT)$.

(e) Using the variance assumption from part (d), find generalized least squares estimates for the parameters of the equation estimated by least squares in part (a). Comment on the results.

(f) Use the results from part (e) to estimate the prices you will get for your two houses.

8.9 (a) Using the estimates obtained in part (a) of Exercise 8.8 as the parameter values, and assuming normally distributed errors, find the probability that (i) your 1400 square feet house sells for more than \$115,000 and (ii) your 1800 square feet house sells for less than \$110,000.

(b) After making the correction $\hat{\alpha}_1 = \hat{\alpha}_1 + 1.2704$, use the estimates obtained in parts (d) and (e) of Exercise 8.8 as the parameter values, and assuming normally distributed errors, find the probability that (i) your 1400 square feet house sells for more than \$115,000 and (ii) your 1800 square feet house sells for less than \$110,000.

(c) Comment on and compare the answers you obtained in parts (a) and (b).

8.10* (a) The purpose of this exercise is to test whether the variance specification $\sigma_i^2 = \sigma^2 x_i$ introduced in Section 8.3.1 has been adequate to eliminate heteroskedasticity in the food expenditure example in the text. Compute the squares of the residuals from the transformed model used to obtain the estimates in (8.16). Regress the squares of the residuals on x_i and test for heteroskedasticity.

(b) We now ask whether the variance specification $\sigma_i^2 = \sigma^2 x_i^\gamma$ introduced in Section 8.3.2 eliminates heteroskedasticity. Compute the squares of the residuals from the transformed model used to obtain the estimates in (8.27). Regress the squares of the residuals on x_i and test for heteroskedasticity.

8.11 Reconsider the household expenditure model that appears in the text, and the data for which are in the file *food.dat*. That is, we have the model

$$y_i = \beta_1 + \beta_2 x_i + e_i$$

where y_i is food expenditure for the ith household and x_i is income. Find generalized least squares estimates for β_1 and β_2 under the assumptions

(a) $\text{var}(e_i) = \sigma^2 \sqrt{x_i}$

(b) $\text{var}(e_i) = \sigma^2 x_i^2$

(c) $\text{var}(e_i) = \sigma^2 \ln(x_i)$

Comment on the sensitivity of the estimates and their standard errors to the heteroskedastic specification. For each case, use the White $N \times R^2$ statistic and the residuals from the transformed model to test to see whether heteroskedasticity has been eliminated.

8.12   In the file *pubexp.dat* there are data on public expenditure on education (*EE*), gross domestic product (*GDP*), and population (*P*) for 34 countries in the year 1980. It is hypothesized that per capita expenditure on education is linearly related to per capita *GDP*. That is,

$$y_i = \beta_1 + \beta_2 x_i + e_i$$

where

$$y_i = \left(\frac{EE_i}{P_i}\right) \quad \text{and} \quad x_i = \left(\frac{GDP_i}{P_i}\right)$$

It is suspected that e_i may be heteroskedastic with a variance related to x_i.
(a) Why might the suspicion about heteroskedasticity be reasonable?
(b) Estimate the equation using least squares, plot the least squares function and the residuals. Is there any evidence of heteroskedasticity?
(c) Test for the existence of heteroskedasticity using a White test.
(d) Use White's formula for least squares variance estimates to find some alternative standard errors for the least squares estimates obtained in part (b). Use these standard errors and those obtained in part (b) to construct two alternative 95% confidence intervals for β_2. What can you say about the confidence interval that ignores the heteroskedasticity?
(e) Reestimate the equation under the assumption that $\text{var}(e_i) = \sigma^2 x_i$. Report the results. Construct a 95% confidence interval for β_2. Comment on its width relative to that of the confidence intervals found in part (d).

8.13* Consider the following cost function where C denotes cost and Q denotes output. Assume that $\text{var}(e_{1t}) = \sigma^2 Q_{1t}$. We use a subscript t because the observations are time-series data. They are stored in the file *cloth.dat*.

$$C_{1t} = \beta_1 + \beta_2 Q_{1t} + \beta_3 Q_{1t}^2 + \beta_4 Q_{1t}^3 + e_{1t}$$

(a) Find generalized least squares estimates of $\beta_1, \beta_2, \beta_3,$ and β_4.
(b) Test the hypothesis $\beta_1 = \beta_4 = 0$.
(c) What can you say about the nature of the average cost function if the hypothesis in (b) is true?
(d) Under what assumption about the error term would it be more appropriate to estimate the average cost function than the total cost function?

8.14* In the file *cloth.dat* there are 28 time-series observations on total cost (C) and output (Q) for two clothing manufacturing firms. It is hypothesized that both firms' cost functions are cubic and can be written as:

$$\text{firm 1: } C_{1t} = \beta_1 + \beta_2 Q_{1t} + \beta_3 Q_{1t}^2 + \beta_4 Q_{1t}^3 + e_{1t}$$
$$\text{firm 2: } C_{2t} = \delta_1 + \delta_2 Q_{2t} + \delta_3 Q_{2t}^2 + \delta_4 Q_{2t}^3 + e_{2t}$$

where $E(e_{1t}) = E(e_{2t}) = 0$, $\text{var}(e_{1t}) = \sigma_1^2$, and $\text{var}(e_{2t}) = \sigma_2^2$. Also, e_{1t} and e_{2t} are independent of each other and over time.
(a) Estimate each function using least squares. Report and comment on the results. Do the estimated coefficients have the expected signs?

(b) Using a 10% significance level, test the hypothesis that $H_0 : \sigma_1^2 = \sigma_2^2$ against the alternative that $H_1 : \sigma_1^2 \neq \sigma_2^2$.

(c) Estimate both equations jointly assuming that $\beta_1 = \delta_1$, $\beta_2 = \delta_2$, $\beta_3 = \delta_3$, and $\beta_4 = \delta_4$. Report and comment on the results.

(d) Test the hypothesis

$$H_0 : \beta_1 = \delta_1, \; \beta_2 = \delta_2, \; \beta_3 = \delta_3 \text{ and } \beta_4 = \delta_4$$

Comment on the test outcome.

8.15* (a) Reconsider the wage equation that was estimated in Section 8.3.3. Instead of estimating the variances from two separate subsamples, one for metropolitan and the other for rural, estimate the two variances using the model

$$\sigma_i^2 = \exp(\alpha_1 + \alpha_2 METRO_i)$$

and one single combined sample. Are your variance estimates different from those obtained using two separate sub-samples? Why?

(b) Find a new set of generalized least squares estimates for the mean function and compare them with those in (8.33).

(c) Find White standard errors for the least squares estimates of the mean function. How do they compare with the generalized least squares standard errors obtained in part (b)?

8.16 Consider the following model used to explain gasoline consumption per car in Germany and Austria for the period 1960–1978:

$$\ln(GAS) = \beta_1 + \beta_2 \ln(INC) + \beta_3 \ln(PRICE) + \beta_4 \ln(CARS) + e$$

where INC is per capita real income, $PRICE$ is the real gasoline price, and $CARS$ is the per capita stock of cars. Data on these variables appear in the file *gasga.dat*.

(a) Using separate least squares estimations, estimate the error variance for Germany σ_G^2, and the error variance for Austria σ_A^2.

(b) Test the hypothesis $H_0 : \sigma_G^2 = \sigma_A^2$ against the alternative $H_1 : \sigma_G^2 \neq \sigma_A^2$ at a 5% significance level.

(c) Find generalized least squares estimates of the coefficients β_1, β_2, β_3, β_4.

(d) Use the results in (c) to test the null hypothesis that demand is price inelastic ($\beta_3 \geq -1$) against the alternative that demand is elastic $\beta_3 < -1$.

Appendix 8A Properties of the Least Squares Estimator

We are concerned with the properties of the least squares estimator for β_2 in the model

$$y_i = \beta_1 + \beta_2 x_i + e_i$$

where

$$E(e_i) = 0 \quad \text{var}(e_i) = \sigma_i^2 \quad \text{cov}(e_i, e_j) = 0 \quad (i \neq j)$$

Note that we are assuming the existence of heteroskedasticity. In Appendix 2D of Chapter 2, we wrote the least squares estimator for β_2 as

$$b_2 = \beta_2 + \Sigma w_i e_i \tag{8A.1}$$

where

$$w_i = \frac{x_i - \bar{x}}{\Sigma(x_i - \bar{x})^2}$$

This expression is a useful one for exploring the properties of least squares estimation under heteroskedasticity. The first property that we establish is that of unbiasedness. This property was derived under homoskedasticity in equation (2.13). The same proof holds under heteroskedasticity because the only error term assumption that was used is $E(e_i) = 0$. We summarize the results here for completeness:

$$E(b_2) = E(\beta_2) + E(\Sigma w_i e_i)$$
$$= \beta_2 + \Sigma w_i E(e_i) = \beta_2$$

The next result is that the least squares estimator is no longer best. That is, although it is still unbiased, it is no longer *the best* linear unbiased estimator. We showed this result in Section 8.3 by considering alternative variance specifications, and deriving alternative estimators that were best under these specifications.

The final consequence of using least squares under heteroskedasticity is that the usual formulas for the least squares standard errors are incorrect. To prove this result we write, from (8A.1),

$$\text{var}(b_2) = \text{var}(\Sigma w_i e_i)$$
$$= \Sigma w_i^2 \text{var}(e_i) + \underset{i \neq j}{\Sigma\Sigma} w_i w_j \text{cov}(e_i, e_j)$$
$$= \Sigma w_i^2 \sigma_i^2 \tag{8A.2}$$
$$= \frac{\Sigma\left[(x_i - \bar{x})^2 \sigma_i^2\right]}{\left[\Sigma(x_i - \bar{x})^2\right]^2}$$

If the variances are all the same ($\sigma_i^2 = \sigma^2$), then the next to last line becomes $\sigma^2 \Sigma w_i^2$. This simplification is not possible under heteroskedasticity, and so the result in (8A.2) is different to that derived in Appendix 2E. Specifically, it follows from (8A.2) that

$$\text{var}(b_2) \neq \frac{\sigma^2}{\Sigma(x_i - \bar{x})^2} \tag{8A.3}$$

Thus, if we use the least squares estimation procedure and ignore heteroskedasticity when it is present, we will be using an estimate of (8A.3) to obtain the standard error for b_2 when in fact we should be using an estimate of (8A.2). Using incorrect standard errors means that interval estimates and hypothesis tests will no longer be valid. Note that standard computer software for least squares regression will compute the estimated variance for b_2 based on (8A.3), unless told specifically to compute White standard errors.

Appendix 8B Variance Function Tests for Heteroskedasticity

More insights into variance function tests can be developed by relating them to the F-test introduced in equation (6.7) for testing the significance of a mean function. To put that test in the context of a variance function consider equation (8.42)

$$\hat{e}_i^2 = \alpha_1 + \alpha_2 z_{i2} + \cdots + \alpha_S z_{iS} + v_i \tag{8B.1}$$

and assume our objective is to test $H_0 : \alpha_2 = \alpha_3 = \cdots = \alpha_S = 0$ against the alternative that at least one α_s, for $s = 2, \ldots, S$, is nonzero. In Section 8.4.3 we considered a more general variance function than that in (8B.1), but we also pointed out that using the linear function in (8B.1) is valid for testing more general alternative hypotheses.

Adapting the F-value reported in equation (6.7) to test the overall significance of (8B.1), we have

$$F = \frac{(SST - SSE)/(S-1)}{SSE/(N-S)} \tag{8B.2}$$

where

$$SST = \sum_{i=1}^{N} \left[\hat{e}_i^2 - \overline{\hat{e}^2} \right]^2 \quad \text{and} \quad SSE = \sum_{i=1}^{N} \hat{v}_i^2$$

are the total sum of squares and sum of squared errors from estimating (8B.1). Note that $\overline{\hat{e}^2}$ is the mean of the dependent variable in (8B.1), or, equivalently, the average of the squares of the least squares residuals from the mean function. At a 5% significance level, a valid test is to reject H_0 if the F-value is greater than a critical value given by $F_{(0.95, S-1, N-S)}$.

Two further tests, the original Breusch–Pagan test and the $N \times R^2$ version of it can be obtained by modifying (8B.2). Please be patient as we work through these modifications. We begin by rewriting (8B.2) as

$$\chi^2 = (S-1) \times F = \frac{SST - SSE}{SSE/(N-S)} \sim \chi^2_{(S-1)} \tag{8B.3}$$

The chi-square statistic $\chi^2 = (S-1) \times F$ has an approximate $\chi^2_{(S-1)}$-distribution in large samples. That is, multiplying an F-statistic by its numerator degrees of freedom gives another statistic that follows a chi-square distribution. The degrees of freedom of the chi-square distribution are $S - 1$, the same as that for the numerator of the F-distribution. The background for this result is given in Appendix 6A.

Next, note that

$$\widehat{\text{var}(e_i^2)} = \widehat{\text{var}(v_i)} = \frac{SSE}{N-S} \tag{8B.4}$$

That is, the variance of the dependent variable is the same as the variance of the error, which can be estimated from the sum of squared errors in (8B.1). Substituting (8B.4) into (8B.3) yields

$$\chi^2 = \frac{SST - SSE}{\widehat{\text{var}(e_i^2)}} \tag{8B.5}$$

This test statistic represents the basic form of the Breusch–Pagan statistic. Its two different versions occur because of the alternative estimators used to replace $\widehat{\text{var}(e_i^2)}$.

If it is assumed that e_i is normally distributed, it can be shown that $\text{var}(e_i^2) = 2\sigma_e^4$, and the statistic for the first version of the Breusch–Pagan test is

$$\chi^2 = \frac{SST - SSE}{2\hat{\sigma}_e^4} \tag{8B.6}$$

Note that $\sigma_e^4 = (\sigma_e^2)^2$ is the square of the error variance from the mean function; unlike SST and SSE, its estimate comes from estimating (8.36). The result $\text{var}(e_i^2) = 2\sigma_e^4$ might be unexpected. Here is a little proof so that you know where it comes from. When $e_i \sim N(0, \sigma_e^2)$, then $(e_i/\sigma_e) \sim N(0, 1)$, and $(e_i^2/\sigma_e^2) \sim \chi_{(1)}^2$. The variance of a $\chi_{(1)}^2$ random variable is 2. Thus,

$$\text{var}\left(\frac{e_i^2}{\sigma_e^2}\right) = 2 \Rightarrow \frac{1}{\sigma_e^4}\text{var}(e_i^2) = 2 \Rightarrow \text{var}(e_i^2) = 2\sigma_e^4$$

Using (8B.6), we reject a null hypothesis of homoskedasticity when the χ^2-value is greater than a critical value from the $\chi_{(S-1)}^2$ distribution.

For the second version of (8B.5) the assumption of normally distributed errors is not necessary. Because this assumption is not used, it is often called the robust version of the Breusch–Pagan test. The sample variance of the squared least squares residuals, the $\hat{e}_i^2$, is used as an estimator for $\text{var}(e_i^2)$. Specifically, we set

$$\widehat{\text{var}(e_i^2)} = \frac{1}{N}\sum_{i=1}^{N}\left[\hat{e}_i^2 - \overline{\hat{e}^2}\right]^2 = \frac{SST}{N} \tag{8B.7}$$

This quantity is an estimator for $\text{var}(e_i^2)$ under the assumption H_0 is true. It can also be written as the total sum of squares from estimating the variance function divided by the sample size. Substituting (8B.7) into (8B.5) yields

$$\chi^2 = \frac{SST - SSE}{SST/N}$$
$$= N \times \left(1 - \frac{SSE}{SST}\right) \tag{8B.8}$$
$$= N \times R^2$$

where R^2 is the R^2 goodness-of-fit statistic from estimating the variance function. At a 5% significance level, a null hypothesis of homoskedasticity is rejected when $\chi^2 = N \times R^2$ exceeds the critical value $\chi_{(0.95, S-1)}^2$.

Software often reports the outcome of the White test described in Section 8.4.3a as an F-value or a χ^2-value. The F-value is from the statistic in (8B.4), with the z's chosen as the x's and their squares and possibly cross products. The χ^2-value is from the statistic in (8B.8), with the z's chosen as the x's and their squares and possibly cross products.

Chapter *9*

Dynamic Models, Autocorrelation, and Forecasting

Learning Objectives

Based on the material in this chapter, you should be able to

1. Explain why lags are important in models that use time-series data and the ways in which lags can be included in dynamic econometric models.
2. Describe the properties of an AR(1) error.
3. Compute nonlinear least squares estimates for a model with an AR(1) error.
4. Use a correlogram of residuals to test for autocorrelation.
5. Use a Lagrange multiplier test to test for autocorrelation.
6. Estimate an autoregressive model and use it to obtain forecasts.
7. Specify, estimate, and interpret the estimates from a finite distributed lag model.
8. Compute and explain delay and interim multipliers and the total multiplier.
9. Specify and estimate autoregressive distributed lag models.
10. Find distributed lag weights from an estimated ARDL model.

Keywords

autocorrelation	dynamic models	lag length
autoregressive distributed lag models	finite distributed lag	lagged dependent variable
	forecast error	*LM* test
autoregressive error	forecasting	nonlinear least squares
autoregressive model	HAC standard errors	sample autocorrelation function
correlogram	impact multiplier	standard error of forecast error
delay multiplier	infinite distributed lag	total multiplier
distributed lag weight	interim multiplier	$T \times R^2$ form of *LM* test

9.1 Introduction

When modeling relationships between variables, the nature of the data that have been collected has an important bearing on the appropriate choice of an econometric model. In particular, it is important to distinguish between cross-section data (data on a number of economic units at a particular point in time) and time-series data (data collected over time on one particular economic unit). Examples of economic units from which we often obtain observations are individuals, households, firms, geographical regions, and countries. Because cross-section data are often generated by way of a random sample, cross-section observations on a particular variable are typically uncorrelated. The level of income observed in the Smith's household, for example, does not impact on, or is not affected by, the level of income in the Jones' household. There is no particular ordering of the observations that is more natural or better than another.

With time-series data on the other hand, there is a natural ordering; the observations are ordered according to time. Moreover, with time-series data it is likely that the observations will be correlated over time. The level of income observed in the Smith's household in one year is likely to be related to the level of income in the Smith's household in the year before. In addition, relationships between variables can become dynamic. A change in the level of an explanatory variable may have behavioral implications beyond the time period in which it occurred. The consequences of economic decisions that result in changes in economic variables can last a long time. When the income tax rate is increased, consumers have less disposable income, reducing their expenditures on goods and services, which reduces profits of suppliers, which reduces the demand for productive inputs, which reduces the profits of the input suppliers, and so on. The effect of the tax increase ripples through the economy. These effects do not occur instantaneously but are spread, or *distributed*, over future time periods. As shown in Figure 9.1, economic actions or decisions taken at one point in time t have effects on the economy at time t, but also at times $t + 1$, $t + 2$, and so on.

Given that the effects of changes in variables are not all instantaneous, we need to ask how to model the dynamic nature of relationships. We begin by recognizing three different ways of doing so. One way is to specify that a dependent variable y_t is a function of current and past values of an explanatory variable. That is,

$$y_t = f(x_t, x_{t-1}, x_{t-2}, \ldots) \tag{9.1}$$

We are saying, for example, that the current rate of unemployment depends not just on the current interest rate, but also on the rates in previous time periods. Turning this interpretation around slightly, it means that a change in the interest rate now will have an impact on unemployment now and in future periods; it takes time for the effect of an interest rate change to work its way through the economy.

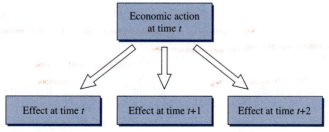

FIGURE *9.1* The distributed lag effect.

A second way of capturing the dynamic characteristics of time-series data is to specify a model with a lagged dependent variable as one of the explanatory variables. For example,

$$y_t = f(y_{t-1}, x_t) \tag{9.2}$$

In this case we are saying that the unemployment rate in one period will depend (among other things) on what it was in the previous period. Assuming a positive relationship, periods of high unemployment will tend to follow periods of high unemployment and periods of low unemployment will tend to follow periods of low unemployment.

A third way of modeling the continuing impact of change over several periods is via the error term. For example, we can write

$$y_t = f(x_t) + e_t \qquad e_t = f(e_{t-1}) \tag{9.3}$$

where the function $e_t = f(e_{t-1})$ is used to denote the dependence of the error on its value in the previous period. Because (9.3) implies $e_{t+1} = f(e_t)$, the dynamic nature of this relationship is such that the impact of any unpredictable shock that feeds into the error term will be felt not just in period t, but also in future periods. The current error e_t affects not just the current value of the dependent variable y_t, but also its future values $y_{t+1}, y_{t+2}, \ldots$. As an example, suppose that a terrorist act creates fear of an oil shortage, which then drives up the price of oil. The terrorist act is an unpredictable shock that forms part of the error term e_t. It is likely to affect the price of oil in the future as well as during the current period.

In this chapter we consider these three ways in which dynamics can enter a regression relationship—lagged values of the explanatory variable, lagged values of the dependent variable, and lagged values of the error term. What we discover is that these three ways are not as distinct as one might at first think. Including a lagged dependent variable can capture similar effects to those obtained by including a lagged error, or a long history of past values of an explanatory variable. Thus, we not only consider the three kinds of dynamic relationships, but also explore the relationships between them.

Related to the idea of modeling dynamic relationships between time-series variables is the important concept of forecasting. We are not only interested in tracing the impact of a change in an explanatory variable or an error shock through time. Forecasting future values of economic time series, such as the inflation rate, unemployment, or the exchange rate, is something that attracts the attention of business, governments, and the general public. Describing how dynamic models can be used for forecasting is another objective of this chapter.

An assumption that we maintain throughout the chapter is that the variables in our equations are stationary. This assumption will take on more meaning in Chapter 12 when it is relaxed. For the moment we simply illustrate the nature of stationary and nonstationary variables with some graphs. Figure 9.2 contains graphs of the observations on three different variables, plotted against the observation number. Because the observations are ordered according to time, the graphs show how the value of each variable changes over time. Plots of this kind are routinely considered when examining time-series variables. The variable y_1 that appears in Figure 9.2a is considered stationary because it tends to fluctuate around a constant mean without wandering or trending. On the other hand, y_2 and y_3 that appear in Figure 9.2b and 9.2c possess characteristics of nonstationary variables. In Figure 9.2b y_2 tends to wander or is "slow turning," while y_3 in Figure 9.2c is trending. These concepts will be defined more precisely in Chapter 12. At the present time the important thing to remember is that this chapter is concerned with modeling and estimating dynamic relationships between stationary variables whose time series have similar characteristics to those of y_1. That is, they neither "wander" nor "trend."

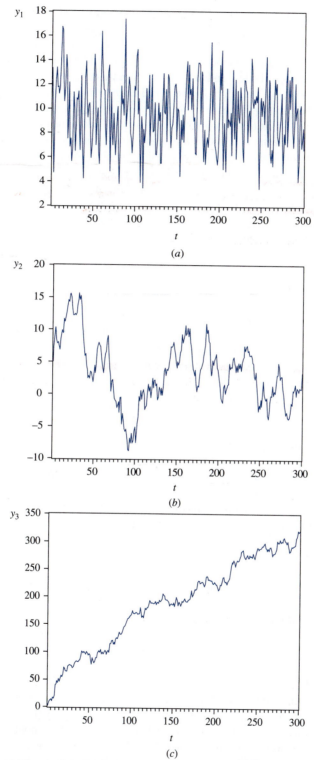

FIGURE **9.2** (a) Time series of a stationary variable; (b) time series of a nonstationary variable that is "slow turning" or "wandering"; (c) time series of a nonstationary variable that "trends".

9.2 Lags in the Error Term: Autocorrelation

The first dynamic model that we consider is one with a lag in the error term. This model is a convenient one to introduce first because it leads naturally into other models that involve lags in the dependent variable y and lags in one or more explanatory variables, say x. We introduce a direct way of modeling impacts of the error term that last beyond the current period. We ask the question: Is there a way of including lags in the error term to recognize that any unexpected shock felt through the error term will take time to work its way through the economy or the industry described by the equation? Given that a shock does take several periods to work through the system, if we consider an error term in any one period, it will contain not only the effect of a current shock, but also the carryover from previous shocks. This carryover will be related to, or **correlated with**, the earlier shocks. When circumstances such as these lead to error terms that are correlated, we say that **autocorrelation** exists. To make these concepts more concrete, we introduce them in the context of an area response model for sugarcane.

9.2.1   AREA RESPONSE MODEL FOR SUGARCANE

One way of modeling supply response for an agricultural crop is to specify a model in which area planted (acres) depends on price. When the price of the crop's output is high, farmers plant more of that crop than when its price is low. Letting A denote area planted, and P denote output price, and assuming a log-log (constant elasticity) functional form, an area response model of this type can be written as

$$\ln(A) = \beta_1 + \beta_2 \ln(P)$$

We use this model to explain the area of sugarcane planted in a region of the Southeast Asian country of Bangladesh. Information on the area elasticity β_2 is useful for government planning. It is important to know whether existing sugar processing mills are likely to be able to handle predicted output, whether there is likely to be excess milling capacity, and whether a pricing policy linking production, processing, and consumption is desirable.

Data comprising 34 annual observations on area and price are given in the file *bangla.dat*. To convert our economic model into an econometric one, we use the subscript t to describe area and price in year t, and add a random error term e_t to give

$$\ln(A_t) = \beta_1 + \beta_2 \ln(P_t) + e_t \tag{9.4}$$

In line with our earlier notation, we can write this equation as

$$y_t = \beta_1 + \beta_2 x_t + e_t \tag{9.5}$$

where $y_t = \ln(A_t)$ and $x_t = \ln(P_t)$.

Suppose now that we wish to investigate how to include lags in the error term where e_t depends on one or more of its past values $e_{t-1}, e_{t-2}, \ldots$. It is likely that farmers' decisions about the area of sugarcane planted will depend on their perceptions about future prices, and about government policies on prices and the establishment of processing mills. Since variables for these perceptions are not explicitly included in the model, their effect on area planted will be felt through the error term e_t. Also, if perceptions change slowly over time, or at least not in a completely random manner, the current perceptions that form part of e_t will be related to perceptions held in the previous period that form part of the lagged error e_{t-1}. A model that captures these effects is

$$e_t = \rho e_{t-1} + v_t \qquad (9.6)$$

where ρ (rho) is a parameter that describes the dependence of e_t on e_{t-1} and v_t is a new random error term. The rationale for (9.6) is a simple one. The random component e_t in time period t is composed of two parts: (i) ρe_{t-1} is a carryover from the random error in the previous period, due to the inertia in economic systems, with the magnitude of the parameter ρ determining the extent of the carryover, and (ii) v_t is a "new" shock to the level of the economic variable. In our example, the "carryover" might be farmers' perceptions of government policies on pricing and the establishment of mills. A new shock could be the announcement of a new policy or information on sugarcane shortages or excesses. This model asserts that shocks to an economic variable do not work themselves out in one period. The parameter ρ in (9.6) determines how quickly the effect of a shock dissipates. The larger the magnitude of ρ the greater the carryover from one period to another and the more slowly the shock dissipates.

Given a particular set of assumptions about v_t, the model in (9.6) is known as a first-order autoregressive model or, more simply, an AR(1) model. It is called "first-order" because there is a one-period lag on the right side of the equation. The existence of AR(1) errors has implications for estimation of the unknown parameters in our regression equation, β_1 and β_2. Before turning to those implications, we need to investigate the properties of AR(1) errors.

9.2.2 FIRST-ORDER AUTOREGRESSIVE ERRORS

We begin by summarizing the model and stating the new assumptions about the AR(1) error. We are considering the regression model

$$y_t = \beta_1 + \beta_2 x_t + e_t \qquad (9.7)$$

Only one explanatory variable is included to keep the discussion relatively simple and to use the framework of the sugarcane example. Extension to more than one explanatory variable is straightforward. The error e_t is assumed to follow a first-order autoregressive AR(1) model (sometimes called an AR(1) process)

$$e_t = \rho e_{t-1} + v_t \qquad (9.8)$$

The random errors v_t are assumed to have the properties assumed about e_t in Chapters 2 through 7. That is, the v_t are uncorrelated random variables with mean zero and a constant variance σ_v^2 (see assumptions MR2, MR3, and MR4 stated in Section 5.1):

$$E(v_t) = 0, \quad \text{var}(v_t) = \sigma_v^2, \quad \text{cov}(v_t, v_s) = 0 \quad \text{for } t \neq s \qquad (9.9)$$

We also assume that ρ is less than 1 in absolute value. That is,

$$-1 < \rho < 1 \qquad (9.10)$$

This assumption implies that the e_t are stationary and have properties that do not change from period to period.

What are the implications of the AR(1) error model defined by (9.8), (9.9), and (9.10) for the properties (mean, variance, and correlations) of the errors e_t? This question is an important one because, as we saw in Chapters 2, 5 and 8, the properties of the least squares estimator for β_1 and β_2 depend on the properties of the e_t. We need to assess whether the least squares estimator is still the best, linear unbiased estimator. It can be shown that the mean of e_t is

$$E(e_t) = 0 \tag{9.11}$$

That is, when the equation errors follow an AR(1) model, they continue to have a zero mean. For the variance of the e_t, it can be shown that

$$\text{var}(e_t) = \sigma_e^2 = \frac{\sigma_v^2}{1 - \rho^2} \tag{9.12}$$

This equation describes the relationship between the variance σ_e^2 of the original equation error e_t and the variance σ_v^2 of the uncorrelated homoskedastic error v_t. Because σ_v^2 does not change over time, the error e_t is also homoskedastic. Where the properties of the e_t differ from those assumed in Chapters 2 through 7, is in the covariance between the errors corresponding to different observations. Since we are using time-series data, when we say "the covariance between errors corresponding to different observations," we are referring to the covariance between errors for different time periods. This covariance will be nonzero because of the existence of a lagged relationship between the errors from different time periods. Specifically, it can be shown that the covariance between any two errors that are k periods apart is

$$\text{cov}(e_t, e_{t-k}) = \sigma_e^2 \rho^k \quad k > 0 \tag{9.13}$$

In Chapters 2 through 7, we assumed this covariance was zero. So, we will need to examine the implications of (9.13) for estimation. However, before doing so, it is useful to get a better understanding of (9.13) and what it means for the sugarcane example. Note that the symbol k is used to represent the time between errors. The expression in (9.13) says that the covariance between two errors that are k periods apart depends on the variance σ_e^2, and on the parameter ρ raised to the power k.

To describe the *correlation* implied by the covariance in (9.13), we use the correlation formula (B.20) from Appendix B.4.3. Writing this formula in terms of our quantities of interest yields

$$\text{corr}(e_t, e_{t-k}) = \frac{\text{cov}(e_t, e_{t-k})}{\sqrt{\text{var}(e_t)\text{var}(e_{t-k})}} = \frac{\text{cov}(e_t, e_{t-k})}{\text{var}(e_t)} = \frac{\sigma_e^2 \rho^k}{\sigma_e^2} = \rho^k \tag{9.14}$$

An interpretation or definition of the unknown parameter ρ can be obtained by setting $k = 1$. Specifically,

$$\text{corr}(e_t, e_{t-1}) = \rho \tag{9.15}$$

Thus, ρ represents the correlation between two errors that are one period apart; it is sometimes called the autocorrelation coefficient. Also, when the errors in different time periods are correlated, we say that **autocorrelation** exists. There are a variety of dynamic error models that lead to the existence of autocorrelation. The AR(1) error model that leads to (9.14) is one of those models. However, because the AR(1) error model has, historically, been the most commonly used one, the more general term "autocorrelation" is sometimes used to describe a regression model with AR(1) errors.

From (9.14), we can also consider the sequence of correlations between errors as they become further apart in time. Considering one period apart, two periods apart, three periods apart, and so on, we obtain the sequence

$$\rho, \rho^2, \rho^3, \ldots$$

Since $-1 < \rho < 1$, the values in this sequence are declining. The greatest correlation between errors is for those that are one period apart; as the errors become further apart, the correlation between them becomes smaller and smaller, and eventually negligible. This characteristic of an AR(1) error model is one that seems reasonable for many economic phenomena.

Let us investigate the errors in the sugarcane model to see if they might exhibit autocorrelation. Because the e_t are not observable, we cannot investigate directly whether they are correlated. However, we can use (9.7) to find least squares estimates b_1 and b_2 and then compute the least squares residuals $\hat{e}_t = y_t - b_1 - b_2 x_t$. Because the $\hat{e}_t$ will have characteristics similar to those of the errors e_t, autocorrelation can be investigated by examining the characteristics of the $\hat{e}_t$. Application of least squares to the area response model in (9.4) yields the following estimated equation

$$\hat{y}_t = 3.893 + 0.776x_t$$
$$\text{(se)} \quad (0.061) \quad (0.277)$$
(9.16)

The results indicate that both coefficients are significantly different from zero, and suggest that the elasticity of area response to price is approximately 0.8. The residuals from this equation appear in Table 9.1 and are plotted against time in Figure 9.3.

From both the table and the figure we can see that there is a tendency for negative residuals to follow negative residuals and for positive residuals to follow positive residuals. For example, there is a run of positive residuals from observation 2 to observation 5, followed by a long run of negative residuals from observation 6 to observation 11. Can you see some more of these "runs"? This kind of behavior is consistent with an assumption of positive correlation between successive residuals. With uncorrelated errors, we would not

Table 9.1 **Least Squares Residuals for the Sugarcane Example**

Time	$\hat{e}_t$	Time	$\hat{e}_t$	Time	$\hat{e}_t$	Time	$\hat{e}_t$
1	−0.303	10	−0.254	19	−0.036	27	−0.651
2	0.254	11	−0.145	20	0.361	28	−0.218
3	0.182	12	0.091	21	−0.138	29	0.137
4	0.503	13	0.304	22	0.017	30	0.121
5	0.275	14	0.656	23	0.336	31	−0.040
6	−0.115	15	0.134	24	−0.175	32	−0.048
7	−0.437	16	−0.059	25	−0.517	33	0.183
8	−0.423	17	0.435	26	−0.137	34	0.184
9	−0.367	18	−0.106				

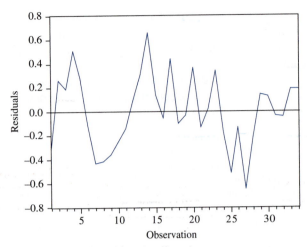

FIGURE **9.3** Least squares residuals plotted against time.

expect to see any particular pattern. If the errors are negatively autocorrelated, we would expect the residuals to show a tendency to oscillate in sign.

The magnitude of the correlation between residuals that are one period apart is given by the sample correlation between $\hat{e}_t$ and $\hat{e}_{t-1}$. Recall from Section 4.2 that the sample correlation between two variables x_t and y_t is given by

$$r_{xy} = \frac{\widehat{\operatorname{cov}(x_t, y_t)}}{\sqrt{\widehat{\operatorname{var}(x_t)}\,\widehat{\operatorname{var}(y_t)}}} = \frac{\sum_{t=1}^{T}(x_t - \bar{x})(y_t - \bar{y})}{\sqrt{\sum_{t=1}^{T}(x_t - \bar{x})^2 \sum_{t=1}^{T}(y_t - \bar{y})^2}} \tag{9.17}$$

To obtain an expression for the correlation between $\hat{e}_t$ and $\hat{e}_{t-1}$, we can replace x_t by $\hat{e}_t$ and y_t by $\hat{e}_{t-1}$. Before doing so, it is convenient to note two simplifications that can be used. In (9.17), $\bar{x}$ and $\bar{y}$ are estimates of the population means $E(x)$ and $E(y)$. We are assuming that all errors have zero means. That is, $E(e_t) = E(e_{t-1}) = 0$. Thus, when replacing x_t by e_t and y_t by e_{t-1}, we can replace $\bar{x}$ and $\bar{y}$ by zero. The second simplification comes from the assumption that the variance of e_t is constant over time, and hence $\operatorname{var}(e_t) = \operatorname{var}(e_{t-1})$. This result means that only one term is required in the denominator. The sample correlation between $\hat{e}_t$ and $\hat{e}_{t-1}$ is then given by

$$r_1 = \frac{\widehat{\operatorname{cov}(e_t, e_{t-1})}}{\widehat{\operatorname{var}(e_t)}} = \frac{\sum_{t=2}^{T}\hat{e}_t \hat{e}_{t-1}}{\sum_{t=2}^{T}\hat{e}_{t-1}^2} \tag{9.18}$$

We have used the subscript "1" on r because we are considering errors that are one period apart. The summations start from $t = 2$ to accommodate the lagged residual $\hat{e}_{t-1}$.

In some books and some software you will find slight variations of (9.18) that give slightly different numerical values. For example, sometimes the denominator is written as $\sum_{t=1}^{T}\hat{e}_t^2$ to include all observations.

Applying (9.18) to the residuals from the sugarcane response equation yields a correlation of $r_1 = 0.404$, suggesting the residuals are moderately correlated; although a formal hypothesis test is needed to assess whether this value is sufficiently large to be significantly different from zero. We consider such tests later in this chapter. Our next task is to suggest how to estimate a model with autocorrelated errors.

9.3 Estimating an AR(1) Error Model

Given that an AR(1) error model is being used to capture autocorrelation in the errors and to model the dynamic effects of the error term, we need to ask how to estimate such a model. Three procedures are considered—least squares estimation, nonlinear least squares estimation, and least squares estimation of a more general model.

9.3.1 LEAST SQUARES ESTIMATION

When the errors follow an AR(1) model $e_t = \rho e_{t-1} + v_t$, the least squares assumption MR4, $\text{cov}(e_t, e_s) = 0$ for $t \neq s$, is violated. Suppose we proceed with least squares estimation anyway, without recognizing the AR(1) error. What are the consequences? They are essentially the same as ignoring heteroskedasticity should it exist.

1. The least squares estimator is still a linear unbiased estimator, but it is no longer best. It is possible to find an alternative estimator with a lower variance. Having a lower variance means there is a higher probability of obtaining a coefficient estimate close to its true value. It also means hypothesis tests have greater power and a lower probability of a Type II error.

2. The formulas for the standard errors usually computed for the least squares estimator are no longer correct, and hence confidence intervals and hypothesis tests that use these standard errors may be misleading.

Although the usual least squares standard errors are not the correct ones, it is possible to compute correct standard errors for the least squares estimator when the errors are autocorrelated. These standard errors are known as HAC (heteroskedasticity and autocorrelation consistent) standard errors, or Newey-West standard errors, and are analogous to the heteroskedasticity consistent standard errors introduced in Chapter 8. They have the advantage of being consistent for autocorrelated errors that are not necessarily AR(1) and do not require specification of the dynamic error model that is needed to get an estimator with a lower variance.

To illustrate how confidence intervals can be misleading, it is instructive to compute correct and incorrect standard errors for the least squares estimator of the sugarcane example. The two sets of standard errors, along with the estimated equation are

$$\hat{y}_t = 3.893 + 0.776 x_t$$
$$(0.061) \ (0.277) \quad \text{incorrect se's}$$
$$(0.062) \ (0.378) \quad \text{correct se's}$$

Note that the correct standard errors are larger than the incorrect ones. If we ignored the autocorrelation, we would tend to overstate the reliability of the least squares estimates. The confidence intervals would be narrower than they should be. For example, using $t_c = 2.037$, we find the following 95% confidence intervals for β_2:

$$(0.211, 1.340) \quad \text{(incorrect)}$$
$$(0.006, 1.546) \quad \text{(correct)}$$

If we are unaware of the autocorrelation, we estimate that the elasticity of area response lies between 0.211 and 1.340. In reality, the reliability of least squares estimation is such that the interval estimate should be from 0.006 to 1.546. Although autocorrelation can lead to either overstatement or understatement of the reliability of the least squares estimates, overstatement of reliability, as illustrated in this example, is the more common occurrence.

9.3.2 NONLINEAR LEAST SQUARES ESTIMATION

While it is possible to compute correct standard errors for the least squares estimator when the errors follow an AR(1) error model, it is preferable to employ a better estimation procedure that gives us narrower, more informative confidence intervals than the correct ones from least squares.

To develop such an estimator, we return to the model in (9.7)

$$y_t = \beta_1 + \beta_2 x_t + e_t \tag{9.19}$$

and the AR(1) error representation

$$e_t = \rho e_{t-1} + v_t \tag{9.20}$$

Substituting (9.20) into (9.19) yields

$$y_t = \beta_1 + \beta_2 x_t + \rho e_{t-1} + v_t \tag{9.21}$$

Now note that (9.19) holds for every single observation. In particular, in terms of the previous period we can write

$$e_{t-1} = y_{t-1} - \beta_1 - \beta_2 x_{t-1} \tag{9.22}$$

Multiplying (9.22) by ρ yields

$$\rho e_{t-1} = \rho y_{t-1} - \rho \beta_1 - \rho \beta_2 x_{t-1} \tag{9.23}$$

Substituting (9.23) into (9.21) yields

$$y_t = \beta_1(1 - \rho) + \beta_2 x_t + \rho y_{t-1} - \rho \beta_2 x_{t-1} + v_t \tag{9.24}$$

What have we done? We have transformed the original model in (9.19) with the autocorrelated error term e_t into a new model given by (9.24) that has an error term v_t that is uncorrelated over time. The advantage of doing so is that we can now proceed to find estimates for (β_1, β_2, ρ) that minimize the sum of squares of uncorrelated errors $S_v = \sum_{t=2}^{T} v_t^2$. Minimizing the sum of squares of the correlated errors $S_e = \sum_{t=1}^{T} e_t^2$ yields the least squares estimator that is not the best, and whose standard errors are not correct. However, minimizing the sum of squares of uncorrelated errors S_v yields an estimator that is best and whose standard errors are correct (in large samples). Note that this result is in line with earlier practice in the book. The least squares estimator used in Chapters 2 through 7 minimizes a sum of squares of uncorrelated errors.

There are, however, two important distinctive features about the transformed model in (9.24). To appreciate the first, note that the coefficient of x_{t-1} is equal to $-\rho \beta_2$ that is the negative product of ρ (the coefficient of y_{t-1}) and β_2 (the coefficient of x_t). This fact means that, although (9.24) is a linear function of the variables x_t, y_{t-1}, and x_{t-1}, it is not a linear function of the parameters (β_1, β_2, ρ). The usual linear least squares formulas cannot be obtained by using calculus to find the values of (β_1, β_2, ρ) that minimize S_v. Nevertheless, modern computer software can be used to find the estimates numerically. Numerical methods use a systematic procedure for trying a sequence of alternative parameter values until those that minimize the sum of squares function are found. Because these estimates are not computed from a linear formula, but they still minimize a sum of squares function, they are called **nonlinear least squares estimates**. Estimates obtained in this way have the usual desirable properties in large samples and are computed routinely by econometric software.

The second distinguishing feature about the model in (9.24) is that it contains the lagged dependent variable y_{t-1}, as well as x_t and x_{t-1}, the current and lagged values of the explanatory variable. For this reason the summation $S_v = \sum_{t=2}^{T} v_t^2$ begins at $t = 2$.

Returning to the sugarcane example and applying nonlinear least squares to estimate β_1, β_2, and ρ yields the following estimated equation

$$\widehat{\ln(A_t)} = 3.899 + 0.888 \ln (P_t) \quad e_t = 0.422 e_{t-1} + v_t$$
$$\text{(se)} \quad (0.092) \ (0.259) \quad\quad\quad (0.166) \quad\quad\quad\quad (9.25)$$

These estimates are similar to the least squares estimates ($b_1 = 3.893$, $b_2 = 0.776$), but suggest a slightly higher area response elasticity. The estimate $\hat{\rho} = 0.422$ is also similar but not exactly the same as the estimate $r_1 = 0.404$ obtained from the correlation between least squares residuals that are one period apart. The standard error $\text{se}(\hat{\beta}_2) = 0.259$ is smaller than the corresponding correct least squares standard error $[\text{se}(b_2) = 0.378]$, suggesting a more reliable estimate, but the standard error for $\hat{\beta}_1$ is unexpectedly larger, something that we do not expect since we have used an estimation procedure with a lower variance. It has to be kept in mind, however, that standard errors are themselves estimates of true underlying standard deviations. Also, a sample size larger than $T = 34$ might be necessary to realize the potential lower variance benefits from the better estimator.

9.3.2a   Generalized Least Squares Estimation

In Chapter 8 we discovered that the problem of heteroskedasticity could be overcome by using an estimation procedure known as generalized least squares, and that a convenient way to obtain generalized least squares estimates is to first transform the model, so that it has a new uncorrelated homoskedastic error term, and then apply least squares to the transformed model. This same kind of approach can be pursued when autocorrelation exists. Indeed, it can be shown that nonlinear least squares estimation of (9.24) is equivalent to using an iterative generalized least squares estimator called the Cochrane–Orcutt procedure. Details are provided in Appendix 9A.

9.3.3   ESTIMATING A MORE GENERAL MODEL

The results for the sugarcane example presented in (9.25) came from estimating the AR(1) error model written as the transformed model

$$y_t = \beta_1(1 - \rho) + \beta_2 x_t - \rho\beta_2 x_{t-1} + \rho y_{t-1} + v_t \quad\quad\quad (9.26)$$

Suppose, now, that we consider the model

$$y_t = \delta + \delta_0 x_t + \delta_1 x_{t-1} + \theta_1 y_{t-1} + v_t \tag{9.27}$$

How do (9.26) and (9.27) differ? What characteristics do they have in common? The first thing to notice is that they contain the same variables; in both cases y_t depends on x_t, x_{t-1}, and y_{t-1}. There is a difference in the number of parameters, however. In (9.26) there are three unknown parameters, β_1, β_2, and ρ. In (9.27) there are four unknown parameters, δ, δ_0, δ_1, and θ_1. Also, the notation in (9.27) is new; we have used the symbols δ (delta) and θ (theta). The intercept is denoted by δ, the coefficients of x and its lag are denoted by subscripted δs, and the coefficient of the lagged dependent variable y_{t-1} is given by a subscripted θ. This new notation will prove to be convenient in Section 9.7 where we discuss a general class of **autoregressive distributed lag** (ARDL) models. Equation (9.27) is a member of this class.

To establish the relationship between (9.26) and (9.27), note that (9.27) is the same as (9.26) if we set

$$\delta = \beta_1(1 - \rho) \quad \delta_0 = \beta_2 \quad \delta_1 = -\rho\beta_2 \quad \theta_1 = \rho$$

Then, it can be seen that (9.26) is a restricted version of (9.27) with the restriction $\delta_1 = -\theta_1\delta_0$. If this restriction is imposed on (9.27), the number of parameters reduces from four to three and (9.27) is equivalent to the AR(1) error model.

These observations raise a number of questions. Instead of estimating the AR(1) error model, would it be better to estimate the more general model in (9.27)? What technique should be used for estimating (9.27)? Is it possible to estimate (9.27) and then test the validity of the AR(1) error model by testing a null hypothesis $H_0: \delta_1 = -\theta_1\delta_0$?

Considering estimation first, we note that (9.27) can be estimated by least squares providing the v_t satisfy the usual assumptions required for least squares estimation, namely, they have zero mean, constant variance, and are uncorrelated. The presence of the lagged dependent variable y_{t-1} means that a large sample is required for the desirable properties of the least squares estimator to hold, but the least squares procedure is still valid. We can no longer make this statement if the v_t are correlated, however. Such correlation will lead to the least squares estimator being biased, even in large samples.

In the introduction to this chapter we observed that dynamic characteristics of time-series relationships can occur through lags in the dependent variable, lags in the explanatory variables, or lags in the error term. We went on to examine how a lag in the error term can be modeled through an AR(1) process, and showed such a model is equivalent to (9.26), which in turn is a special case of (9.27). Notice that (9.26) and (9.27) do not have lagged error terms, but they do have a lagged dependent variable and a lagged explanatory variable. Thus, the dynamic features of a model implied by an AR(1) error can be captured by using instead a model with a lagged y and a lagged x. This observation raises issues about a general modeling strategy for dynamic economic relationships. Instead of explicitly modeling lags through an autocorrelated error, we can capture the same dynamic effects by simply adding lagged variables y_{t-1} and x_{t-1} to the original linear equation.

Is it possible to test $H_0: \delta_1 = -\theta_1\delta_0$ and hence decide whether the AR(1) model is a reasonable restricted version of (9.27), or whether the more general model in (9.27) would be preferable? The answer is "yes"; the test is similar to, but more complicated, than those considered in Chapter 6. Complications occur because the hypothesis involves an equation that is nonlinear in the parameters, but, nevertheless, it can be performed using modern software.

Applying the least squares estimator to (9.27) using the data for the sugarcane example yields

$$\hat{y}_t = 2.366 + 0.777x_t - 0.611x_{t-1} + 0.404y_{t-1}$$
$$(\text{se}) \quad (0.656) \ (0.280) \quad (0.297) \qquad (0.167)$$

(9.28)

Because the lagged variables y_{t-1} and x_{t-1} appear on the right side of the equation, 33 rather than 34 observations are used for estimation. The estimate $\hat{\beta}_2 = 0.777$ is similar to the least squares estimate from the original equation relating log of area to log of price, while the estimate $\hat{\rho} = 0.404$ is the same as the correlation obtained using least squares residuals. The intercept estimate is lower than the values obtained in our earlier estimations. All estimated coefficients are significantly different from zero at a 0.05 level of significance. Using a chi-square (Wald) test to test the hypothesis $H_0 : \delta_1 = -\theta_1 \delta_0$ yields a value of $\chi^2_{(1)} = 1.115$ with a corresponding p-value $= 0.29$. Thus, we do not reject the restriction implied by the AR(1) error model. Modeling the dynamics of area response of sugarcane via an AR(1) error model appears to be a reasonable strategy.

9.4 Testing for Autocorrelation

We have discovered that the existence of autocorrelation has an important bearing on the modeling of dynamic relationships and the choice of estimation technique. The existence of AR(1) errors means we should transform our model into one with lagged dependent and lagged explanatory variables and estimate it with nonlinear or linear least squares depending on whether or not we impose the coefficient restriction implied by the AR(1) error model. It is important, therefore, to be able to test for the existence of correlated errors.

We consider two testing procedures in this section and a third in Appendix 9B. The main two procedures are (1) examination of a device known as a **residual correlogram**, and (2) a **Lagrange multiplier test**, so called because it is based on a testing principle with that name. See Appendix C.8.4c for some general information about Lagrange multiplier tests.

The third testing procedure, considered in Appendix 9B, is the **Durbin–Watson** test. You will almost certainly see a value for a Durbin–Watson statistic d routinely reported on your computer output. Because $d \approx 2(1 - r_1)$, values of d near 2 suggest no autocorrelation and smaller values (less than about 1.4) suggest positive autocorrelation. Although it is a long-standing traditional test, the Durbin–Watson is less convenient than the correlogram or the Lagrange multiplier test. These latter two tests are easier to implement and, because their assumptions are less restrictive, they are applicable to a wider variety of situations.

9.4.1 RESIDUAL CORRELOGRAM

Our objective is to test whether the errors e_t in the regression model $y_t = \beta_1 + \beta_2 x_t + e_t$ are correlated. In the AR(1) error model $e_t = \rho e_{t-1} + v_t$, we assume that the v_t are uncorrelated random errors with zero mean and constant variance. That is, $v_t \sim (0, \sigma_v^2)$ and $E(v_t v_s) = 0$ for $t \neq s$. It follows that the e_t will be uncorrelated when $\rho = 0$, because then $e_t = v_t$. Thus, in the context of the AR(1) error model, the null and alternative hypotheses for a test for autocorrelation are

$$H_0 : \rho = 0 \quad H_1 : \rho \neq 0$$

When looking at the sugarcane example in Section 9.2.2, we computed the correlation between the least squares residuals $\hat{e}_t$ and those residuals lagged by one period $\hat{e}_{t-1}$ and found it to be $r_1 = 0.404$. We recognized that this value is an estimate of the autocorrelation coefficient ρ. Thus, one way to test for autocorrelation is to examine whether $r_1 = 0.404$ is significantly different from zero.

To obtain a test statistic for testing H_0 against the alternative H_1, we use a relatively simple result that holds in large samples when H_0 is true, namely

$$Z = \sqrt{T}r_1 \sim N(0,1) \tag{9.29}$$

The product of the square root of the sample size and the correlation r_1 has an approximate standard normal distribution. Consequently, at a 5% significance level, we reject $H_0 : \rho = 0$ when $\sqrt{T}r_1 \geq 1.96$ or $\sqrt{T}r_1 \leq -1.96$.

In the sugarcane example where $T = 34$ and $r_1 = 0.404$, we have

$$Z = \sqrt{34} \times 0.404 = 2.36 \geq 1.96 \tag{9.30}$$

Hence, we reject the null hypothesis of no autocorrelation and conclude the errors are correlated.

Most econometric software automatically performs the test in (9.30) in a slightly different and more general form. To describe this form, note that rejecting H_0 when $\sqrt{T}r_1 \geq 1.96$ or $\sqrt{T}r_1 \leq -1.96$ is equivalent to rejecting H_0 when

$$r_1 \geq \frac{1.96}{\sqrt{T}} \quad \text{or} \quad r_1 \leq -\frac{1.96}{\sqrt{T}}$$

We can view $1.96/\sqrt{T}$ and $-1.96/\sqrt{T}$ as bounds on r_1 outside of which r_1 is significantly different from zero. This result can be generalized to all lags. Suppose r_k is the correlation between $\hat{e}_t$ and $\hat{e}_{t-k}$; in other words, it is the correlation between residuals that are k periods apart. Then, r_k is significantly different from zero at a 5% significance level if

$$r_k \geq \frac{1.96}{\sqrt{T}} \quad \text{or} \quad r_k \leq -\frac{1.96}{\sqrt{T}} \tag{9.31}$$

The sequence of correlations r_k, $k = 1, 2, \ldots$, is called the **sample autocorrelation function** or the **correlogram** of the residuals. It shows the correlation between residuals that are one period apart, two periods apart, three periods apart, and so on. These correlations are estimates of the population correlation function given by $\rho_1, \rho_2, \rho_3, \ldots$, where

$$\rho_k = \frac{\text{cov}(e_t, e_{t-k})}{\text{var}(e_t)} = \frac{E(e_t e_{t-k})}{E(e_t^2)} \tag{9.32}$$

To provide an easy way of checking the inequalities in (9.31), most econometric software provides a graph of the correlogram with the bounds $\pm 1.96/\sqrt{T}$ superimposed on that graph so that the econometrician can see at a glance which correlations are significant. In the sugar example the correlations up to six lags are

$$r_1 = 0.404 \quad r_2 = 0.122 \quad r_3 = 0.084 \quad r_4 = -0.353 \quad r_5 = -0.420 \quad r_6 = -0.161$$

and the bounds are $\pm 1.96/\sqrt{T} = \pm 0.336$. These results appear in the correlogram in Figure 9.4.

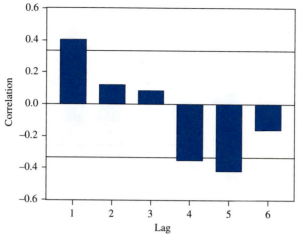

FIGURE **9.4**   Correlogram for least squares residuals from sugar cane example.

The bars in Figure 9.4 represent the correlations and the horizontal lines at ± 0.336 are the significance bounds. They suggest the correlations r_1, r_4, and r_5 are significantly different from zero. The significant negative correlations at lags 4 and 5 are not captured by an AR(1) error model. In Section 9.2.2 we found that, for the AR(1) model, $\rho_k = \rho^k$. The correlation between errors k periods apart is equal to the correlation between errors one period apart, raised to the power of k. The correlations r_4 and r_5 do not conform to this expectation, and they are hard to explain in terms of sugarcane area response. It might be a spurious correlation or it might suggest some other kind of model misspecification.

Your software will not produce a correlogram that is exactly the same as Figure 9.4. It might have the correlations on the x-axis and the lags on the y-axis. It could use spikes instead of bars to denote the correlations, it might provide a host of additional information, and its significance bounds might be slightly different than ours. So, be prepared! Learn to isolate and focus on the information corresponding to that in Figure 9.4 and do not be disturbed if the output is slightly but not substantially different. If the significance bounds are slightly different, it is because they use a refinement of the large sample approximation $\sqrt{T}r_k \sim N(0,1)$.

Figure 9.4 illustrates the correlogram for the residuals $\hat{e}_t$ from least squares estimation of the model

$$y_t = \beta_1 + \beta_2 x_t + e_t$$

Following detection of a significant correlation at lag 1, a reasonable strategy is to assume an AR(1) error model $e_t = \rho e_{t-1} + v_t$ and then estimate the derived model (9.24)

$$y_t = \beta_1(1-\rho) + \beta_2 x_t + \rho y_{t-1} - \rho\beta_2 x_{t-1} + v_t$$

If the assumption that the errors v_t are uncorrelated is a reasonable one, we would expect the residuals from estimating this model, the $\hat{v}_t$'s, to be uncorrelated. This fact can be checked using the correlogram for the $\hat{v}_t$'s that appears in Figure 9.5. From this figure we note that the correlation at lag 1 has been eliminated, although the large correlations at lags 4 and 5 remain.

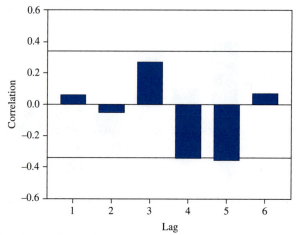

FIGURE *9.5*   Correlogram for nonlinear least squares residuals from sugarcane example.

9.4.2   A LAGRANGE MULTIPLIER TEST

A second test that we consider for testing for autocorrelation is derived from a general set of hypothesis testing principles that produce Lagrange multiplier (*LM*) tests. In more advanced courses you will learn the origin of the term Lagrange multiplier. The general principle is described in Appendix C.8.4c. To introduce this test, return to equation (9.21) that was written as

$$y_t = \beta_1 + \beta_2 x_t + \rho e_{t-1} + v_t \tag{9.33}$$

If e_{t-1} was observable, an obvious way to test the null hypothesis $H_0 : \rho = 0$ is to regress y_t on x_t and e_{t-1} and to use a t- or F-test to test the significance of the coefficient of e_{t-1}. Because e_{t-1} is not observable, we replace it by the lagged least squares residuals $\hat{e}_{t-1}$, and then perform the test in the usual way.

Proceeding in this way for the sugarcane example yields

$$t = 2.439 \quad F = 5.949 \quad p\text{-value} = 0.021$$

The p-value is less than 0.05 and thus the *LM* test rejects the null hypothesis of no autocorrelation at a 5% significance level.

As we discovered in Chapter 8, *LM* tests are such that they can frequently be written as the simple expression $T \times R^2$, where T is the number of sample observations and R^2 is the goodness-of-fit statistic from an auxiliary regression. To derive the relevant auxiliary regression for the autocorrelation *LM* test, we begin by writing the test equation from (9.33) as

$$y_t = \beta_1 + \beta_2 x_t + \rho \, \hat{e}_{t-1} + \hat{v}_t \tag{9.34}$$

Noting that $y_t = b_1 + b_2 x_t + \hat{e}_t$, we can rewrite (9.34) as

$$b_1 + b_2 x_t + \hat{e}_t = \beta_1 + \beta_2 x_t + \rho \, \hat{e}_{t-1} + \hat{v}_t$$

Rearranging this equation yields

$$\hat{e}_t = (\beta_1 - b_1) + (\beta_2 - b_2)x_t + \rho\,\hat{e}_{t-1} + \hat{v}_t$$
$$= \gamma_1 + \gamma_2 x_t + \rho\,\hat{e}_{t-1} + \hat{v}_t \qquad (9.35)$$

where $\gamma_1 = \beta_1 - b_1$ and $\gamma_2 = \beta_2 - b_2$. When testing for autocorrelation by testing the significance of the coefficient of $\hat{e}_{t-1}$, one can estimate (9.34) or (9.35). Both yield the same test result—the same coefficient estimate for $\hat{e}_{t-1}$ and the same t-value. The estimates for the intercept and the coefficient of x_t will be different, however, because in (9.35) we are estimating $(\beta_1 - b_1)$ and $(\beta_2 - b_2)$ instead of β_1 and β_2. The auxiliary regression from which the $T \times R^2$ version of the LM test is obtained is (9.35). Because $(\beta_1 - b_1)$ and $(\beta_2 - b_2)$ are centered around zero, if (9.35) is a regression with significant explanatory power, that power will come from $\hat{e}_{t-1}$.

If $H_0 : \rho = 0$ is true, then $LM = T \times R^2$ has an approximate $\chi^2_{(1)}$-distribution where T and R^2 are the sample size and goodness-of-fit statistic, respectively, from least squares estimation of (9.35). For the sugarcane example

$$LM = T \times R^2 = 34 \times 0.16101 = 5.474$$

The 5% critical value from a $\chi^2_{(1)}$-distribution is 3.84, leading us to reject the null hypothesis of autocorrelation. Alternatively, we can reject H_0 by examining the p-value for $LM = 5.474$, which is 0.019.

Further variations and generalizations of the LM test are available. You should note the following:

1. When estimating the regressions in (9.34) or (9.35), using the first observation $(t = 1)$ requires knowledge of $\hat{e}_0$. Two ways of overcoming this lack of knowledge are often employed. One is to set $\hat{e}_0 = 0$. The other is to omit the first observation. In our calculations we set $\hat{e}_0 = 0$. The results change very little if the first observation is omitted instead.

2. We have been concerned with testing for autocorrelation involving only one lagged error e_{t-1}. To test for more complicated autocorrelation structures, involving higher order lags such as e_{t-2}, e_{t-3}, and so on, the LM test can be used by including the additional lagged errors in (9.34) or (9.35). An F-test can be used to test the relevance of their inclusion, or, a χ^2-test can be used for the $T \times R^2$ version of the test. The degrees of freedom for the χ^2-test and the numerator degrees of freedom for the F-test is the number of lagged residuals that are included.

9.4.3 RECAPPING AND LOOKING FORWARD

In the introduction to this chapter we indicated that we would consider three ways of introducing lags into a regression equation—through the error term, through lagged values of the dependent variable, and through lagged values of the explanatory variables. Our focus so far has been on a particular model for a lagged error term, the first-order autoregressive model. However, it is important that you appreciate that some of the things that we have covered have wider applicability. The simple regression model with AR(1) error was expressed as a model with a lagged explanatory variable and a lagged dependent variable. In Section 9.7 we study a class of models known as autoregressive distributed lag (ARDL) models. These are models containing both lagged explanatory variables and lagged dependent variables. Thus, the AR(1) error model can be viewed as a special case ARDL model. In general, ARDL models can capture very flexible dynamic relationships.

The AR(1) error model was not only a convenient model for leading into a discussion of more general ARDL models, it was a convenient one for introducing tests for autocorrelation in the errors. What needs to be emphasized is that the correlogram and the Lagrange multiplier test, designed for picking up correlated errors, are valid testing procedures in more general models. Before we formally introduce ARDL models in Section 9.7, we discuss AR models (that contain lagged values of the dependent variable) in Section 9.5 and finite distributed lag models (that contain lagged values of the explanatory variable) in Section 9.6. In all these types of models (AR, DL, and ARDL), it is important to test for autocorrelation in the errors. The correlogram and the Lagrange multiplier test are appropriate procedures for doing so.

Finally, as you read through the next three sections keep in mind the two general reasons for estimating dynamic relationships: (1) To forecast future values of a dependent variable and (2) to trace out the time path of the effect of a change in an explanatory variable on a dependent variable. The AR model discussed in Section 9.5 is useful for forecasting and so the discussion in that section concentrates on the important ingredients of forecasting—how to forecast, and find forecast standard errors and forecast intervals. The finite distributed lag model discussed in Section 9.6 is useful for estimating the impact of a change in an explanatory variable; here we are concerned with delay and interim multipliers. The more general ARDL model is used for forecasting and estimating multiplier effects.

9.5 An Introduction to Forecasting: Autoregressive Models

The forecasting of values of economic variables is a major activity for many institutions including firms, banks, governments, and individuals. Accurate forecasts are important for decision making on government economic policy, investment strategies, the supply of goods to retailers, and a multitude of other things that affect our everyday lives. Because of its importance, you will find that there are whole books and courses that are devoted to the various aspects of forecasting—methods and models for forecasting, ways of evaluating forecasts and their reliability, and practical examples. In this section we give a brief introduction to forecasting using one class of models known as autoregressive (AR) models.

In the earlier sections of this chapter we were concerned with an AR(1) error model $e_t = \rho e_{t-1} + v_t$ and its implications for estimating β_1 and β_2 in the regression model $y_t = \beta_1 + \beta_2 x_t + e_t$. However, the AR class of models has wider applicability than its use for modeling dynamic error terms. It is also used for modeling observed values of a time series y_t. In this context, an autoregressive model of order p, denoted as AR(p), is given by

$$y_t = \delta + \theta_1 y_{t-1} + \theta_2 y_{t-2} + \cdots + \theta_p y_{t-p} + v_t \tag{9.36}$$

In this model the current value of a variable y_t depends on its values in the last p periods and a random error that is assumed to have a zero mean, a constant variance and be uncorrelated over time. The order of the model p is equal to the largest lag of y on the right side of the equation. Notice that there are no explanatory variables in (9.36). The value of y_t depends only on a history of its past values and no x's. Thus, when (9.36) is used for forecasting, we are using the current and past values of a variable to forecast its future value. The model relies on correlations between values of the variable over time to help produce a forecast.

Suppose that it is May 2006, and that you are interested in forecasting the U.S. inflation rate for each of the next 3 months. To find past data on the inflation rate you collect 270 monthly observations on the consumer price index (*CPI*) from December 1983 to May 2006. Then, you compute values of the inflation rate y_t as follows

$$y_t = [\ln(CPI_t) - \ln(CPI_{t-1})] \times 100 \approx \left(\frac{CPI_t - CPI_{t-1}}{CPI_{t-1}}\right) \times 100$$

Recall from Appendix A.4.5 that the rate of change in a variable can be approximated by a change in the logarithm of that variable. Also, it is conventional to express rates of change in terms of percentages; to do so we multiply the change in logarithms by 100. Defining y_t as the change in the log of the *CPI* means the number of observations on y_t is one less, namely 269. The data are stored in the file *inflation.dat*.

To use an AR model to forecast the inflation rate, the next step is to estimate the model in (9.36). What technique should be used to estimate this model? How do we decide on the number of lags p? Providing the errors v_t are uncorrelated, then, following the line of discussion in Section 9.3.3, equation (9.36) can be estimated using least squares. Having lagged values of the dependent variable as our explanatory variable does not present any problem. Also, the requirement that v_t be uncorrelated provides one way of selecting a suitable p. Recall from Section 9.3.3 that including lagged values of the dependent variable can eliminate autocorrelation in the errors. Thus, one way to proceed is to include enough lagged y's to eliminate autocorrelation. There are also other issues, however. A simple model with fewer lags is preferred to a complicated one with many lags. Thus, one may not want to be concerned about eliminating autocorrelations at long lags. In addition, estimates of the coefficients can be checked to see if they are significantly different from zero.

The estimated AR model for the inflation rate, with $p = 3$, is given by

$$\widehat{INFLN}_t = 0.1883 + 0.3733\,INFLN_{t-1} - 0.2179\,INFLN_{t-2} + 0.1013\,INFLN_{t-3} \tag{9.37}$$
$$\text{(se)} \quad (0.0253)\ (0.0615) \qquad\qquad (0.0645) \qquad\qquad (0.0613)$$

Having three lags means that the equation is estimated for $t = 4, 5, \ldots, 269$; the number of observations used in estimation is reduced by three from 269 to 266. To ensure you understand how observations are "lost," try substituting $t = 1$ into (9.37). You will discover that observations are needed for $INFLN_0$, $INFLN_{-1}$, and $INFLN_{-2}$. These presample observations are not available. For all observations to be available for estimation, we begin from $t = p + 1$. Most software automatically makes this adjustment.

In (9.37) the estimated coefficients at lags 1 and 2 are significant at a 1% significance level; that for lag 3 is significant at a 10% significance level. The residual correlogram for autocorrelations up to lag 24 appears in Figure 9.6. Most of the estimated autocorrelations are not significantly different from zero, with those for the early lags being negligible. There are significant but not large autocorrelations at lags 6, 11, 13, and 14. It was decided that including distant lags to eliminate these relatively small correlations would unnecessarily complicate the model.

To see how the estimated AR(3) model in (9.37) can be used to forecast the inflation rate for 3 months into the future, we begin by rewriting the more general model in (9.36) for the case where $p = 3$

$$y_t = \delta + \theta_1 y_{t-1} + \theta_2 y_{t-2} + \theta_3 y_{t-3} + v_t \tag{9.38}$$

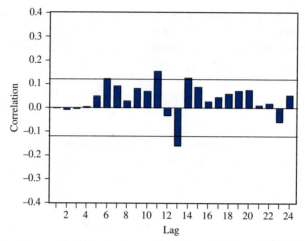

FIGURE 9.6 Correlogram for least squares residuals from AR(3) model for inflation.

Now suppose we have observed the last sample observation y_T and we wish to forecast y_{T+1}, y_{T+2}, and y_{T+3}. Using (9.38), we can obtain the equation that generates y_{T+1} by changing the time subscripts appropriately. This equation is

$$y_{T+1} = \delta + \theta_1 y_T + \theta_2 y_{T-1} + \theta_3 y_{T-2} + v_{T+1}$$

and the forecast of this value given by the estimated equation is

$$\begin{aligned}
\hat{y}_{T+1} &= \hat{\delta} + \hat{\theta}_1 y_T + \hat{\theta}_2 y_{T-1} + \hat{\theta}_3 y_{T-2} \\
&= 0.1883 + 0.3733 \times 0.4468 - 0.2179 \times 0.5988 + 0.1013 \times 0.3510 \\
&= 0.2602
\end{aligned}$$

Moving to the forecast for two months ahead, we have

$$\begin{aligned}
\hat{y}_{T+2} &= \hat{\delta} + \hat{\theta}_1 \hat{y}_{T+1} + \hat{\theta}_2 y_T + \hat{\theta}_3 y_{T-1} \\
&= 0.1883 + 0.3733 \times 0.2602 - 0.2179 \times 0.4468 + 0.1013 \times 0.5988 \qquad (9.39) \\
&= 0.2487
\end{aligned}$$

There is an important difference in the way the forecasts $\hat{y}_{T+1}$ and $\hat{y}_{T+2}$ are obtained. It is possible to calculate $\hat{y}_{T+1}$ using only past observations on y. However, because $\hat{y}_{T+2}$ depends on y_{T+1}, which is unobserved at time T, on the right side of the equation for $\hat{y}_{T+2}$, we replace y_{T+1} by its forecast $\hat{y}_{T+1}$. For forecasting y_{T+3}, the forecasts for both y_{T+2} and y_{T+1} are needed on the right side of the equation, and for forecasts further into the future, all values for the lagged y's are forecasts obtained for earlier periods. The forecasts obtained for 3 months into the future are given in Table 9.2.

Also appearing in Table 9.2 are standard errors for the forecast errors and 95% forecast intervals. How are they obtained? The forecast error at time $T + 1$ is

$$u_1 = y_{T+1} - \hat{y}_{T+1} = (\delta - \hat{\delta}) + (\theta_1 - \hat{\theta}_1)y_T + (\theta_2 - \hat{\theta}_2)y_{T-1} + (\theta_3 - \hat{\theta}_3)y_{T-2} + v_{T+1}$$

The difference between the forecast $\hat{y}_{T+1}$ and the corresponding realized value y_{T+1} can be attributed to the difference between the actual coefficients and the estimated coefficients and

Table 9.2 **Forecasts and Forecast Intervals for Inflation Rate**

Month	Forecast $\hat{y}_{T+j}$	Standard error of forecast error ($\hat{\sigma}_j$)	Forecast interval $(\hat{y}_{T+j} - 1.969\,\hat{\sigma}_j, \hat{y}_{T+j} + 1.969\,\hat{\sigma}_j)$
Jun 06 ($j = 1$)	0.2602	0.1972	(−0.1282, 0.6485)
Jul 06 ($j = 2$)	0.2487	0.2105	(−0.1658, 0.6633)
Aug 06 ($j = 3$)	0.2697	0.2111	(−0.1460, 0.6854)

the unpredictable random error v_{T+1}. A similar situation arose in Sections 4.1 and 6.8 when we were forecasting using the regression model. What we are going to do differently now is to ignore the error from estimating the coefficients. Usually the variance of the random error is large relative to the variances of the estimated coefficients and so, when examining forecast errors from AR models, and computing their standard errors, it is common to ignore the error from estimating the coefficients. Doing so means we can write the forecast error for 1 month ahead as

$$u_1 = v_{T+1} \tag{9.40}$$

For 2 months ahead the forecast error gets more complicated because we have to allow for not only v_{T+2}, but also for the error that occurs from using $\hat{y}_{T+1}$ instead of y_{T+1} on the right side of (9.39). Thus, the forecast error for two periods ahead is

$$u_2 = \theta_1(y_{T+1} - \hat{y}_{T+1}) + v_{T+2} = \theta_1 u_1 + v_{T+2} = \theta_1 v_{T+1} + v_{T+2} \tag{9.41}$$

For three periods ahead the error can be shown to be

$$u_3 = \theta_1 u_2 + \theta_2 u_1 + v_{T+3} = (\theta_1^2 + \theta_2)v_{T+1} + \theta_1 v_{T+2} + v_{T+3} \tag{9.42}$$

Because the v_t's are uncorrelated, expressing the forecast errors in terms of them is convenient for deriving expressions for the forecast error variances. From (9.40), (9.41), and (9.42), we have

$$\sigma_1^2 = \text{var}(u_1) = \sigma_v^2$$
$$\sigma_2^2 = \text{var}(u_2) = \sigma_v^2(1 + \theta_1^2)$$
$$\sigma_3^2 = \text{var}(u_3) = \sigma_v^2[(\theta_1^2 + \theta_2)^2 + \theta_1^2 + 1]$$

Then, along the lines of confidence intervals that were constructed for parameters in earlier chapters, in large samples a 95% confidence interval for a forecast of y_{T+j} is given by

$$(\hat{y}_{T+j} - t_c\hat{\sigma}_j, \quad \hat{y}_{T+j} + t_c\hat{\sigma}_j) \tag{9.43}$$

The standard errors in Table 9.2 are σ_1, σ_2, and σ_3, evaluated at the coefficient estimates $(\hat{\delta}, \hat{\theta}_1, \hat{\theta}_2, \hat{\theta}_3)$ and the error standard deviation estimate $\hat{\sigma}_v = 0.1972$. The forecast intervals are computed from (9.43) with $t_c = t_{(0.975, 262)} = 1.969$. The wide intervals that include negative as well as positive values suggest that the forecasts are not very reliable. Notice how the forecast standard errors and the widths of the intervals increase as we forecast further into the future, reflecting the additional uncertainty from doing so.

The AR model is just one of a large number of forecasting models where the history of a variable can be used to forecast its future values. In Appendix 9D we examine another popular model, the exponential smoothing model.

9.6 Finite Distributed Lags

In the previous section we used the framework of an autoregressive model to investigate how the past history of the inflation rate can be used to forecast future inflation rates. Now, we turn to a different question. What impact do wage changes have on the inflation rate? On the supply side we expect wage increases to increase the costs of production and to drive up prices. On the demand side wage increases mean greater disposable income, and a greater demand for goods and services, that also pushes up prices. Irrespective of the line of reasoning, the relationship between wage changes and inflation is unlikely to be a totally instantaneous one; it takes time for wage changes to impact on inflation. One way of modeling the impact of wage changes on inflation is through a finite distributed lag model.

To introduce the concept of a finite distributed lag, let y_t be the inflation rate and let x_t be the rate of change in the wage rate in period t. If we assume a linear relationship between the inflation rate and the rate of change in wages, and also that wage changes up to q months into the past have an influence on the current rate of inflation, then the econometric model for this relationship can be written as

$$y_t = \alpha + \beta_0 x_t + \beta_1 x_{t-1} + \beta_2 x_{t-2} + \cdots + \beta_q x_{t-q} + v_t, \quad t = q+1, \ldots, T \quad (9.44)$$

where we assume that $E(v_t) = 0$, $\text{var}(v_t) = \sigma^2$, and $\text{cov}(v_t, v_s) = 0$. If we have T observations on the pairs (y_t, x_t), then only $T - q$ *complete* observations are available for estimation since q observations are "lost" in the creation of $x_{t-1}, x_{t-2}, \ldots, x_{t-q}$, an issue we also encountered for the AR model of the previous section.

Equation (9.44) is called a **distributed lag model** because the effect of changes in x_t is distributed over time. It is called a **finite** distributed lag model because it is assumed that after a finite number of periods q, changes in x no longer have an impact on y. The parameter α is the intercept and β_s is called a **distributed-lag weight** or an *s*-**period delay multiplier**. It measures the effect of past changes in the growth of wages Δx_{t-s} on expected current inflation, when the growth of wages is held constant in other periods. That is,

$$\frac{\partial E(y_t)}{\partial x_{t-s}} = \beta_s$$

To appreciate further the interpretation of the lag weights β_s suppose that x and y have been constant for at least the last q periods and that x_t is increased by 1 unit (1% in our example), and then returned to its original level. Then, ignoring the error term, the immediate effect will be an increase in y_t by β_0 units. One period later y_{t+1} will increase by β_1 units, then y_{t+2} will increase by β_2 units, and so on, up to period $t + q$ when y_{t+q} will increase by β_q units. In period $t + q + 1$ the value of y will return to its original level. Thus, β_s is the *s*-period delayed effect of a change in x. If the rate of growth of wages increases by 1% in period t and then returns to its original level, there will be a β_s% increase in the inflation rate in period $t + s$. Setting $s = 0$ yields what is called the **impact multiplier** β_0.

It is also relevant to ask what happens if x_t is increased by 1 unit and then maintained at its new level in subsequent periods $(t + 1), (t + 2), \ldots$. In this case the immediate impact will again be β_0; the total effect in period $t + 1$ will be $\beta_0 + \beta_1$, in period $t + 2$, it will be $\beta_0 + \beta_1 + \beta_2$, and so on. We add together the effects from the changes in all proceeding periods. These quantities are called **interim multipliers**. For example, the two-period interim multiplier is $(\beta_0 + \beta_1 + \beta_2)$. The **total multiplier** is the final effect on y of the sustained increase after q or more periods have elapsed; it is given by $\sum_{s=0}^{q} \beta_s$.

Table 9.3 **Least Squares Estimates for Finite Distributed Lag Model**

Variable	Coefficient	Std. Error	t-value	p-value
Constant	0.1219	0.0487	2.505	0.013
x_t	0.1561	0.0885	1.764	0.079
x_{t-1}	0.1075	0.0851	1.264	0.207
x_{t-2}	0.0495	0.0853	0.580	0.562
x_{t-3}	0.1990	0.0879	2.264	0.024

For estimation of the lag weight coefficients, we can use least squares. Providing the errors v_t are uncorrelated and homoskedastic, least squares estimation of (9.44) yields best linear unbiased estimates of α and the β_s. The data used for estimation are in the file *inflation.dat*. Construction of the data series for the inflation rate was discussed in the previous section. In a similar way, we denote the percentage rate of change in wages as

$$x_t = [\ln(WAGE_t) - \ln(WAGE_{t-1})] \times 100 \approx \left(\frac{WAGE_t - WAGE_{t-1}}{WAGE_{t-1}} \right) \times 100$$

where $WAGE_t$ is the average hourly earnings (\$/hour) in private industries. The data we use are for the U.S. economy from January 1984 to May 2006.

Allowing for a 3-month lag for our inflation example, we set $q = 3$ and compute the least squares estimates reported in Table 9.3. We find that a 1% increase in wage growth leads to an immediate increase in the inflation rate of 0.16%, a 1-month lagged increase of 0.11%, a 2-month lagged increase of 0.05%, and a 3-month lagged increase of 0.20%. The biggest impacts are felt immediately and after a 3 month lag. The lag weights for lags 1 and 2 are not significantly different from zero at a 10% level of significance. The lag-weights or *delay multipliers* are reported again in Table 9.4 alongside the corresponding interim multipliers. The interim multipliers suggest that a sustained increase of 1% in the growth of wages will, after 3 months, lead to an increase of 0.51% in the inflation rate.

Finite distributed lag models can also be used for forecasting. Values of x are used in the estimated equation to forecast future values of y. Because future values of x will generally be unknown, it may be necessary to independently predict these values before proceeding to forecast y, with a consequent increase in the forecast standard error. Also, if the x variable is a policy variable like the interest rate or the level of taxation, a distributed lag model can be used to forecast the effects of different policies.

Table 9.4 **Multipliers for Inflation Example**

Lag	Multipliers	
	Delay	Interim
0	0.1561	0.1561
1	0.1075	0.2636
2	0.0495	0.3131
3	0.1990	0.5121

9.7 Autoregressive Distributed Lag Models

It is useful at this point to stop and think about what we have covered and what we have not covered, and to ask where improvements are needed. We have seen how the dynamic aspects of modeling time-series data can lead to (i) a model with a lagged error term (the AR(1) error model), (ii) a forecasting model with lagged values of y_t (the AR(p) model), and (iii) a model with lagged values of an explanatory variable x_t (a finite distributed lag model that shows how a change in x_t has multiplier effects over a number of time periods). What we have not covered explicitly is a model that contains both lagged values of x_t and lagged values of y_t, although we did see how the AR(1) error model could be conveniently transformed into a model that includes y_{t-1} and x_{t-1}.

An autoregressive distributed lag (ARDL) model is one that contains both lagged x_t's and lagged y_t's. In its general form, with p lags of y and q lags of x, an ARDL(p, q) model can be written as

$$y_t = \delta + \delta_0 x_t + \delta_1 x_{t-1} + \cdots + \delta_q x_{t-q} + \theta_1 y_{t-1} + \cdots + \theta_p y_{t-p} + v_t \qquad (9.45)$$

As we will discover, the ARDL model overcomes two potential problems with the finite distributed lag model. In the finite distributed lag model it is necessary to choose a value for q, the point in the past beyond which it is assumed changes in x no longer have an impact on y. In the inflation example we chose $q = 3$, but it is possible that wage rate changes have an impact on inflation beyond 3 months. At first glance it is not clear how the model in (9.45) overcomes that problem. It still contains a finite number (q) of lagged x_t's. However, it can be shown that an ARDL model can be transformed into one with lagged x_t's going back to the infinite past

$$y_t = \alpha + \beta_0 x_t + \beta_1 x_{t-1} + \beta_2 x_{t-2} + \beta_3 x_{t-3} + \cdots + e_t$$
$$= \alpha + \sum_{s=0}^{\infty} \beta_s x_{t-s} + e_t \qquad (9.46)$$

Because it does not have a finite cutoff point, this model is called an **infinite distributed lag model**. Like before, the parameter β_s is the distributed lag weight or the s-period delay multiplier showing the effect of a change in x_t on y_{t+s}. The total or long run multiplier showing the long-run effect of a sustained change in x_t is $\sum_{s=0}^{\infty} \beta_s$. We expect the effect of a change to gradually die out in which case the values of β_s for large s will be small and decreasing, a property that is necessary for the infinite sum $\sum_{s=0}^{\infty} \beta_s$ to be finite. Estimates for the lag weights β_s can be found from estimates of the δ_j's and θ_k's in (9.45). The precise relationship between them depends on the values for p and q.

A second potential problem with a finite distributed lag model that can be corrected by using an ARDL model is that of autocorrelated errors. The inclusion of lagged values of the dependent variable can serve to eliminate such correlation.

To make these ideas concrete, we return to the inflation example. The correlogram for the residuals from the finite distributed lag model (whose estimates appear in Table 9.3) is given in Figure 9.7. The relatively large autocorrelation at lag 1 is significantly different from zero at a 5% significance level, and there are several correlations at longer lags that are marginally significant. These results suggest that the assumption of uncorrelated errors v_t in the finite distributed lag model is not a reasonable one.

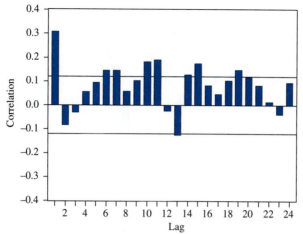

FIGURE **9.7**   Correlogram for least squares residuals from finite distributed lag model.

As an alternative, consider the following least squares estimated ARDL(2,3) model

$$\widehat{INFLN}_t = 0.0989 + 0.1149\,PCWAGE_t + 0.0377\,PCWAGE_{t-1} + 0.0593\,PCWAGE_{t-2}$$

(se)   (0.0468) (0.0834)   (0.0812)   (0.0812)

$$+\,0.2361\,PCWAGE_{t-3} + 0.3536\,INFLN_{t-1} - 0.1976\,INFLN_{t-2}$$

(0.0829)   (0.0604)   (0.0604)   (9.47)

where $x_t = PCWAGE_t$ is the percentage change in wages. The setting $p = 2$ implies there are two lags of the dependent variable $INFLN$ while the setting $q = 3$ means that the current value and three lagged values of $PCWAGE$ appear on the right side of the equation. How were these values for p and q chosen? In general there is no one unambiguous way of choosing p and q. Two things to consider are whether the estimated coefficients are significant and whether the resulting residuals are uncorrelated. In (9.47) the coefficient estimates for $PCWAGE_{t-3}$, $INFLN_{t-1}$, and $INFLN_{t-2}$ are significant at a 5% significance level, but those for $PCWAGE_t$, $PCWAGE_{t-1}$, and $PCWAGE_{t-2}$ are not. We have nevertheless retained the current and early lags of $PCWAGE$, given its clear importance at lag 3. The correlogram for the residuals appears in Figure 9.8. With the exception of a few marginally significant correlations at long lags (correlations that are relatively small despite being significant), the correlogram does not suggest the residuals are autocorrelated.

The next question to address is the implications of the estimated model in (9.47) for the distributed lag weights that describe how the impact of a change in the wage rate on the rate of inflation is distributed over time. Writing (9.47) in terms of its coefficients, we have

$$y_t = \delta + \delta_0 x_t + \delta_1 x_{t-1} + \delta_2 x_{t-2} + \delta_3 x_{t-3} + \theta_1 y_{t-1} + \theta_2 y_{t-2} + v_t$$

Then, using the results in equation (9C.6) of Appendix 9C.2, and the estimates from (9.47), the first five lag weights for the infinite distributed lag representation in (9.46) are

$$\hat{\beta}_0 = \hat{\delta}_0 = 0.1149$$
$$\hat{\beta}_1 = \hat{\theta}_1\hat{\beta}_0 + \hat{\delta}_1 = 0.3536 \times 0.1149 + 0.0377 = 0.0784$$
$$\hat{\beta}_2 = \hat{\theta}_1\hat{\beta}_1 + \hat{\theta}_2\hat{\beta}_0 + \hat{\delta}_2 = 0.0643$$
$$\hat{\beta}_3 = \hat{\theta}_1\hat{\beta}_2 + \hat{\theta}_2\hat{\beta}_1 + \hat{\delta}_3 = 0.2434$$
$$\hat{\beta}_4 = \hat{\theta}_1\hat{\beta}_3 + \hat{\theta}_2\hat{\beta}_2 = 0.0734$$

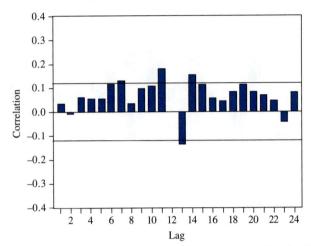

FIGURE **9.8**   Correlogram for least squares residuals from autoregressive distributed lag model.

The weights decrease at first, increase at lag 3, and then decline, suggesting that a change in the growth of wages has its largest effect on the inflation rate after a 3-month lag. A graph of the first 12 weights appears in Figure 9.9. There is a small negative effect at lags 5, 6, and 7, after which the weights are close to zero indicating that there is little effect on inflation after 7 months. The sum of the lag weights giving the total impact of a 1% change in the growth of wages on inflation is 0.53%.

Our focus in this section has been on the use of autoregressive distributed lag models for modeling the lagged effect of a change in one variable on another. These models can also be used for forecasting along the lines described for pure autoregressive models in Section 9.5.

With respect to a general modeling strategy, because ARDL models are more general than AR models, finite distributed lag models, and AR error models, any dynamic modeling exercise should not focus on one of the more restrictive classes of models without giving due consideration to an ARDL model. There are other important issues to be considered, however. These will become apparent in Chapter 12.

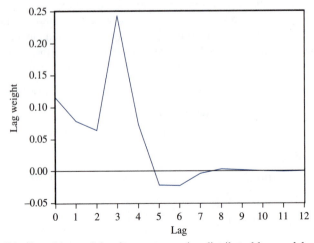

FIGURE **9.9**   Distributed lag weights for autoregressive distributed lag model.

9.8 Exercises

9.8.1 PROBLEMS

9.1   Consider the AR(1) error model

$$e_t = \rho e_{t-1} + v_t$$

where $E(v_t) = 0$, $\text{var}(v_t) = \sigma_v^2$, and $E(v_t v_s) = 0$ for $t \neq s$. Given that $\text{var}(e_t) = \text{var}(e_{t-1}) = \sigma_e^2$, prove that

$$\sigma_e^2 = \frac{\sigma_v^2}{1 - \rho^2}$$

Also, show that

$$E(e_t e_{t-1}) = \sigma_e^2 \rho \quad \text{and} \quad E(e_t e_{t-2}) = \sigma_e^2 \rho^2$$

9.2*   The following least squares residuals come from a sample of size $T = 10$:

t	1	2	3	4	5	6	7	8	9	10
$\hat{e}_t$	0.28	−0.31	−0.09	0.03	−0.37	−0.17	−0.39	−0.03	0.03	1.02

(a) Use a hand calculator to compute the sample autocorrelations

$$r_1 = \frac{\sum_{t=2}^{T} \hat{e}_t \hat{e}_{t-1}}{\sum_{t=2}^{T} \hat{e}_{t-1}^2} \qquad r_2 = \frac{\sum_{t=3}^{T} \hat{e}_t \hat{e}_{t-2}}{\sum_{t=3}^{T} \hat{e}_{t-2}^2}$$

(b) Test whether (i) r_1 is significantly different from zero and (ii) r_2 is significantly different from zero.

9.3   Consider the model

$$DISP = \beta_1 + \beta_2 DUR + e$$

where *DISP* represents factory shipments of disposers and *DUR* is durable goods expenditures. Using 26 annual observations from the Department of Commerce's Survey of Current Business, the following least squares regression was estimated

$$\widehat{DISP}_t = -388 + 24.8 DUR_t$$
$$\text{(se)} \qquad (112) \quad (1.2) \tag{9.48}$$

Let $\hat{e}_t$ denote the residuals from this equation. Consider the following estimated equation

$$\hat{e}_t = 16.6 - 0.194 DUR_t + 0.428\,\hat{e}_{t-1} \quad R^2 = 0.165$$
$$\text{(se)} \qquad\quad (0.911) \qquad\quad (0.201) \tag{9.49}$$

(a) Use the results from (9.49) to conduct two separate tests for first-order auto-regressive errors.

(b) The model with AR(1) errors was estimated as

$$\widehat{DISP}_t = -343 + 24.4DUR_t \quad e_t = 0.419e_{t-1} + v_t$$
$$\text{(se)} \quad \quad (200) \quad (2.6) \quad \quad \quad (0.201)$$

What effect does ignoring autocorrelation have on inferences about the relationship between disposer shipments and durable goods expenditure?

9.4   Consider the model

$$e_t = \rho e_{t-1} + v_t$$

(a) Suppose $\rho = 0.9$ and $\sigma_v^2 = 1$. What is
   (i) the correlation between e_t and e_{t-1},
   (ii) the correlation between e_t and e_{t-4},
   (iii) the variance σ_e^2?
(b) Repeat part (a) with $\rho = 0.4$ and $\sigma_v^2 = 1$. Comment on the difference between your answers for parts (a) and (b).

9.5*   Consider the model

$$y_t = \beta_1 + \beta_2 x_t + e_t \quad \quad e_t = \rho e_{t-1} + v_t$$

with the usual assumptions about v_t.
(a) Suppose (unrealistically) that you can observe e_t, $t = 1, 2, \ldots, T$. What formula would you use to forecast
   (i) e_{T+1}
   (ii) e_{T+2}
   Hint: Review Section 9.5.
(b) Suppose the above model is applied to the sugarcane example in this chapter. Use equation (9.25) to find

$$\tilde{e}_T = \ln(A_T) - \hat{\beta}_1 - \hat{\beta}_2 \ln(P_T)$$

Note that T refers to the last sample observation.
(c) Using $\tilde{e}_T$ from part (b), the estimate for ρ in (9.25), and the formulas you gave in part (a), find forecasts for e_{T+1} and e_{T+2}.
(d) Assuming $P_{T+1} = 1$ and $P_{T+2} = 1.2$, find forecasts for $\ln(A_{T+1})$ and $\ln(A_{T+2})$.
(e) In light of the discussion in Section 4.4.3, and given $\hat{\sigma}_v = 0.2854$, suggest two alternative forecasts for A_{T+1} and A_{T+2}.

9.6   Consider the infinite lag representation

$$y_t = \alpha + \sum_{s=0}^{\infty} \beta_s x_{t-s} + e_t$$

for the ARDL model

$$y_t = \delta + \delta_3 x_{t-3} + \theta_1 y_{t-1} + \theta_2 y_{t-2} + \theta_3 y_{t-3} + v_t$$

Show that

$$\beta_0 = \beta_1 = \beta_2 = 0$$
$$\beta_3 = \delta_3$$
$$\beta_4 = \theta_1\beta_3$$
$$\beta_5 = \theta_1\beta_4 + \theta_2\beta_3$$
$$\beta_s = \theta_1\beta_{s-1} + \theta_2\beta_{s-2} + \theta_3\beta_{s-3} \quad \text{for } s \geq 6$$

9.7   Using monthly observations on changes in the U.S. index of industrial production (*DIP*) for the period January 1985 to December 2005, the following autoregressive model was estimated

$$\widehat{DIP}_t = 0.109 + 0.033DIP_{t-1} + 0.236DIP_{t-2} + 0.200DIP_{t-3} \quad \hat{\sigma}_v = 0.4293$$

(a) Use this estimated equation to forecast *DIP* for January, February, and March 2006. (Values for October, November and December, 2005, are $DIP_{T-2} = 1.221$, $DIP_{T-1} = 1.006$ and $DIP_T = 1.041$, respectively.)
(b) Find 95% confidence intervals for your forecasts.

9.8*   Using the estimates in equation (9.28), find the first six lag weights of the infinite lag representation

$$y_t = \alpha + \sum_{s=0}^{\infty} \beta_s x_{t-s} + e_t$$

that shows the effect of lagged prices on area sown to sugarcane. Comment on this lag distribution.

9.8.2   COMPUTER EXERCISES

9.9*   To investigate the relationship between job vacancies (*JV*) and the unemployment rate (*U*), a researcher sets up the model

$$\ln(JV_t) = \beta_1 + \beta_2 \ln(U_t) + e_t$$

and assumes that the e_t are independent $N(0, \sigma_e^2)$ random variables.
(a) Use the data in the file *vacan.dat* to find least squares estimates for β_1 and β_2. Construct a 95% confidence interval for β_2.
(b) Use an *LM* test to test for AR(1) errors. In light of this result, what can you say about the original assumptions for the error e_t; what can you say about the confidence interval for β_2 found in (a)?
(c) Reestimate the model assuming the errors follow an AR(1) error model. Find a new 95% confidence interval for β_2 and comment on the results, particularly in relation to your answers for part (a). Does the correlogram for the residuals from this model show any evidence of autocorrelation?

9.10   As an alternative to the model in Exercise 9.9, consider the relationship

$$\ln(JV_t) = \delta + \delta_0 \ln(U_t) + \delta_1 \ln(U_{t-1}) + \theta_1 \ln(JV_{t-1}) + v_t$$

(a) Estimate this relationship and test the hypothesis $H_0 : \delta_1 = -\theta_1\delta_0$. Comment on the result.
(b) Forecast $\ln(JV)$ for two periods beyond the sample observations. Assume $U_{T+1} = U_{T+2} = 5$.

9.11◆ Data for a monopolist's total revenue (TR), total cost (TC) and output (Q), for 48 consecutive months, appear in the file *monop.dat*. Suppose that the monopolist's economic models for total revenue and total cost are given, respectively, by

$$TR = \beta_1 Q + \beta_2 Q^2$$
$$TC = \alpha_1 + \alpha_2 Q + \alpha_3 Q^2$$

(a) Show that marginal cost and marginal revenue are given by

$$MC = \alpha_2 + 2\alpha_3 Q \qquad MR = \beta_1 + 2\beta_2 Q$$

(b) Show that the profit maximizing quantity that equates marginal revenue and marginal cost is

$$Q^* = \frac{\alpha_2 - \beta_1}{2(\beta_2 - \alpha_3)}$$

(c) Use the least squares estimator to estimate the total revenue and total cost functions. Under what assumptions are these estimates appropriate? What do the least squares estimates suggest is the profit maximizing level of output?

(d) After rounding the optimizing output to an integer, use that output to predict total revenue, total cost, and profit for the next 3 months. (Continue to assume the least squares statistical assumptions are appropriate.)

(e) Separately test the errors for each of the functions to see if these errors might be autocorrelated.

(f) Where autocorrelation has been suggested by the tests in part (e), reestimate the equations assuming AR(1) errors.

(g) What is the profit maximizing level of output suggested by the results in part (f)?

(h) Given the output level found in part (g), and the autocorrelation assumption, predict total revenue, total cost, and hence profit for the next 3 months. Compare the predictions with those from part (d).

9.12 In the sugarcane example in Sections 9.1–9.4 it was assumed that farmers' decisions about area sown depend on current price. Suppose, instead, that expectations about future price depend not just on current price but also on prices over the last 4 years. That is

$$\ln(A_t) = \alpha + \beta_0 \ln(P_t) + \beta_1 \ln(P_{t-1}) + \beta_2 \ln(P_{t-2})$$
$$+ \beta_3 \ln(P_{t-3}) + \beta_4 \ln(P_{t-4}) + e_t$$

(a) Use the observations in the file *bangla.dat* to estimate this model. What are the estimated delay and interim multipliers? Comment on the results.

(b) You will have discovered that the lag weights obtained in part (a) are not sensible. One way to try and overcome this problem is to insist that the weights lie on a straight line

$$\beta_i = \alpha_0 + \alpha_1 i \quad i = 0, 1, 2, 3, 4$$

If $\alpha_0 > 0$ and $\alpha_1 < 0$, these weights will decline implying farmers place a larger weight on more recent prices when forming their expectations. Substitute

$\beta_i = \alpha_0 + \alpha_1 i$ into the original equation and hence show that this equation can be written as

$$\ln(A_t) = \alpha + \alpha_0 z_{t0} + \alpha_1 z_{t1} + e_t$$

where

$$z_{t0} = \ln(P_t) + \ln(P_{t-1}) + \ln(P_{t-2}) + \ln(P_{t-3}) + \ln(P_{t-4})$$
$$z_{t1} = \ln(P_{t-1}) + 2\ln(P_{t-2}) + 3\ln(P_{t-3}) + 4\ln(P_{t-4})$$

(c) Create the variables z_{t0} and z_{t1} and find least squares estimates of α_0 and α_1.
(d) Use the estimates for α_0 and α_1 to find estimates for $\beta_i = \alpha_0 + \alpha_1 i$ and comment on them. Has the original problem been cured? Do the weights now satisfy a priori expectations?
(e) How do the delay and interim multipliers compare with those obtained earlier?

9.13   The file *housing.dat* contains monthly observations on new privately owned housing starts (in thousands) and the 30-year mortgage rate from January 1985 to December 2005. Let these variables be denoted by $HOUSE_t$ and IR_t, respectively. Define y_t and x_t as the monthly changes in *HOUSE* and *IR*. That is

$$y_t = HOUSE_t - HOUSE_{t-1} \quad x_t = IR_t - IR_{t-1}$$

We are interested in the dynamic relationship between y_t and x_t.
(a) Estimate the model

$$y_t = \delta + \delta_0 x_t + \delta_1 x_{t-1} + \theta_1 y_{t-1} + v_t$$

   (i) Comment on the results. Are the signs of the coefficients in line with your expectations? Do tests of significance on the estimated coefficients suggest the model is a reasonable one?
   (ii) Test the hypothesis $H_0 : \delta_1 = -\theta_1 \delta_0$ against the alternative $H_1 : \delta_1 \neq -\theta_1 \delta_0$. What does the result of this test tell you?
   (iii) Does the residual correlogram suggest that v_t are correlated?
(b) Estimate the model

$$y_t = \delta + \delta_3 x_{t-3} + \theta_1 y_{t-1} + \theta_2 y_{t-2} + \theta_3 y_{t-3} + v_t$$

   (i) Comment on the results.
   (ii) Use the result in Exercise 9.6 to find estimates of the lag weights up to lag 12 for the infinite lag representation

$$y_t = \alpha + \sum_{s=0}^{\infty} \beta_s x_{t-s} + e_t$$

   Comment on the results.
   (iii) Does the residual correlogram suggest that v_t are correlated?
   (iv) Forecast y_t for January, February, and March 2006.
   (v) Forecast housing starts for January, February, and March 2006.

9.14 Consider the learning curve data and model given in Exercise 2.9 and the file *learn.dat*. The model is

$$\ln(UNITCOST_t) = \beta_1 + \beta_2 \ln(CUMPROD_t) + e_t$$

(a) Use an *LM* test to test whether the errors in this model are correlated.
(b) Estimate an ARDL model relating *UNITCOST* to *CUMPROD*. How many lags did you use for *UNITCOST*? For *CUMPROD*? Why?
(c) Find estimates of the first five lag weights of the infinite lag representation. Comment on these estimates.
(d) Suppose that cumulative production in year 1971 is 3800. Do you expect cost per unit in 1971 to be more or less than it was in 1970?

9.15 In the file *mining.dat* are seasonally adjusted quarterly observations on indices of mining production (*PRO*), and electric power use for mining (*POW*), in the United States. Consider the model

$$\ln(POW_t) = \beta_1 + \beta_2 t + \beta_3 t^2 + \beta_4 \ln(PRO_t) + e_t$$

where *t* is a time trend.
(a) Estimate the model using least squares. Comment on the signs of the estimated coefficients and what they imply. Does autocorrelation appear to be a problem?
(b) Estimate an ARDL model that also includes *t* and t^2. How many lags of *POW* and *PRO* did you include? Why?
(c) Suppose that you wish to test the null hypothesis that the coefficient of $\ln(PRO_t)$ equals 1. Compare the *p*-value of this test performed on the model in part (a) with that from part (b). Comment.
(d) What is the total multiplier estimated from the model in part (b)?

9.16 Reconsider Exercise 9.15.
(a) Re-estimate the models in Exercise 9.15(a) and (b) assuming that

$$\beta_1 = \alpha_1 + \delta_1 D_t$$

where D_t is dummy variable that takes the value 1 for the period 1985:1 to 1999:3 and is zero otherwise.
(b) For both models in part (a) test the hypothesis $H_0 : \delta_1 = 0$. Does the test outcome depend on which model is estimated? What can you conclude about the effects of model misspecification on tests for structural change?

9.17* The file *robbery.dat* contains monthly data on the number of armed robberies (*ROB*) in Boston from January 1966 to October 1975.
(a) Estimate the model

$$ROB_t = \beta_1 + \beta_2 t + \theta ROB_{t-1} + e_t$$

Does the residual correlogram from this model suggest that the errors are correlated?
(b) Find 95% confidence intervals for the number of armed robberies in November and December 1975.

9.18 The file *consumption.dat* contains quarterly observations on U.S. per capita real disposable personal income (*INC*), real personal consumption (*CONS*), and real personal consumption of durables (*DUR*) for the period 1952Q1 to 2006Q1.

(a) Construct the rate of change variables

$$x_t = [\ln(INC_t) - \ln(INC_{t-1})] \times 100$$
$$y_t = [\ln(CONS_t) - \ln(CONS_{t-1})] \times 100$$
$$z_t = [\ln(DUR_t) - \ln(DUR_{t-1})] \times 100$$

(b) Estimate ARDL models for
   (i) y_t on x_t,
   (ii) z_t on x_t.
   Explain your choice of lags.
(c) In each case find estimates for
   (i) the lag weights for eight quarters,
   (ii) the total multiplier.
   Comment on these results.

Appendix 9A Generalized Least Squares Estimation

We are considering the simple regression model with AR(1) errors

$$y_t = \beta_1 + \beta_2 x_t + e_t \qquad e_t = \rho e_{t-1} + v_t$$

Our objective is to obtain the generalized least squares estimator for β_1 and β_2 by transforming the model so that it has a new uncorrelated homoskedastic error term, enabling us to apply least squares to the transformed model. To specify the transformed model we begin with (9.24), which is

$$y_t = \beta_1 + \beta_2 x_t + \rho y_{t-1} - \rho\beta_1 - \rho\beta_2 x_{t-1} + v_t \qquad (9A.1)$$

and then rearrange it to give

$$y_t - \rho y_{t-1} = \beta_1(1 - \rho) + \beta_2(x_t - \rho x_{t-1}) + v_t \qquad (9A.2)$$

After defining the following transformed variables

$$y_t^* = y_t - \rho y_{t-1}, \quad x_{t2}^* = x_t - \rho x_{t-1}, \quad x_{t1}^* = 1 - \rho$$

we can rewrite (9A.2) as

$$y_t^* = x_{t1}^* \beta_1 + x_{t2}^* \beta_2 + v_t \qquad (9A.3)$$

We have formed a new model with transformed variables y_t^*, x_{t1}^*, and x_{t2}^* and, *importantly*, with an error term that is *not* the correlated e_t, but the uncorrelated v_t that we assumed to be distributed $(0, \sigma_v^2)$. We would expect application of least squares to (9A.3) to yield the best linear unbiased estimator for β_1 and β_2.

There are two additional problems that we need to solve, however:

1. Because lagged values of y_t and x_t had to be formed, only $(T - 1)$ new observations were created by the transformation. We have values $(y_t^*, x_{t1}^*, x_{t2}^*)$ for $t = 2, 3, \ldots, T$. But, we have no $(y_1^*, x_{11}^*, x_{12}^*)$.

2. The value of the autoregressive parameter ρ is not known. Since y_t^*, x_{t1}^*, and x_{t2}^* depend on ρ, we cannot compute these transformed observations without estimating ρ.

Considering the second problem first, we can use the sample correlation r_1 defined in (9.15) as an estimator for ρ. Alternatively, (9A.1) can be rewritten as

$$y_t - \beta_1 - \beta_2 x_t = \rho(y_{t-1} - \beta_1 - \beta_2 x_{t-1}) + v_t \tag{9A.4}$$

which is the same as $e_t = \rho e_{t-1} + v_t$. After replacing β_1 and β_2 with the least squares estimates b_1 and b_1, least squares can be applied to (9A.4) to estimate ρ.

Equations (9A.3) and (9A.4) can be estimated iteratively. That is, we use $\hat{\rho}$ from (9A.4) to estimate β_1 and β_2 from (9A.3). Then, we use these new estimates for β_1 and β_2 in (9A.4) to reestimate ρ, which we then use again in (9A.3) to reestimate β_1 and β_2, and so on. This iterative procedure is known as the Cochrane–Orcutt estimator. On convergence, it is identical to the nonlinear least squares estimator described in Section 9.3.2.

What about the problem of having $(T - 1)$ instead of T transformed observations? One way to solve this problem is to ignore it and to proceed with estimation on the basis of the $(T - 1)$ observations. That is the strategy adopted by the estimators we have considered so far. If T is large, it is a reasonable strategy. However, if we wish to improve efficiency by including a transformation of the first observation, we need to create a transformed error that has the same variance as the errors $(v_2, v_3, \ldots, v_T)$.

The first observation in the regression model is

$$y_1 = \beta_1 + x_1 \beta_2 + e_1$$

with error variance $\text{var}(e_1) = \sigma_e^2 = \sigma_v^2/(1 - \rho^2)$. The transformation that yields an error variance of σ_v^2 is multiplication by $\sqrt{1 - \rho^2}$. The result is

$$\sqrt{1 - \rho^2} y_1 = \sqrt{1 - \rho^2} \beta_1 + \sqrt{1 - \rho^2} x_1 \beta_2 + \sqrt{1 - \rho^2} e_1$$

or

$$y_1^* = x_{11}^* \beta_1 + x_{12}^* \beta_2 + e_1^* \tag{9A.5}$$

where

$$\begin{aligned} y_1^* = \sqrt{1 - \rho^2} y_1 \quad x_{11}^* = \sqrt{1 - \rho^2} \\ x_{12}^* = \sqrt{1 - \rho^2} x_1 \quad e_1^* = \sqrt{1 - \rho^2} e_1 \end{aligned} \tag{9A.6}$$

To confirm that the variance of e_1^* is the same as that of the errors $(v_2, v_3, \ldots, v_T)$, note that

$$\text{var}(e_1^*) = (1 - \rho^2)\, \text{var}(e_1) = (1 - \rho^2)\frac{\sigma_v^2}{1 - \rho^2} = \sigma_v^2$$

We also require that e_1^* be uncorrelated with $(v_2, v_3, \ldots, v_T)$. This result will hold because each of the v_t does not depend on any past values for e_t. The transformed first observation in (9A.5) can be used with the remaining transformed observations in (9A.3) to obtain generalized least squares estimates that utilize all T observations. This procedure is sometimes known as the Prais–Winsten estimator.

Appendix 9B The Durbin-Watson Test

In Section 9.4 two testing procedures for testing for autocorrelation, the sample correlogram and a Lagrange multiplier test, were considered. These are two large sample tests; their test statistics have their specified distributions in large samples. An alternative test, one that is exact in the sense that its distribution does not rely on a large sample approximation, is the Durbin–Watson test. It was developed in 1950 and, for a long time, was the standard test for $H_0 : \rho = 0$ in the AR(1) error model $e_t = \rho e_{t-1} + v_t$. It is used less frequently today because of the need to examine upper and lower bounds, as we describe below, and because its distribution no longer holds when the equation contains a lagged dependent variable.

It is assumed that the v_t are independent random errors with distribution $N(0, \sigma_v^2)$, and that the alternative hypothesis is one of positive autocorrelation. That is

$$H_0 : \rho = 0 \quad H_1 : \rho > 0$$

The statistic used to test H_0 against H_1 is

$$d = \frac{\sum_{t=2}^{T} (\hat{e}_t - \hat{e}_{t-1})^2}{\sum_{t=1}^{T} \hat{e}_t^2} \tag{9B.1}$$

where the $\hat{e}_t$ are the least squares residuals $\hat{e}_t = y_t - b_1 - b_2 x_t$. To see why d is a reasonable statistic for testing for autocorrelation, we expand (9B.1) as

$$d = \frac{\sum_{t=2}^{T} \hat{e}_t^2 + \sum_{t=2}^{T} \hat{e}_{t-1}^2 - 2\sum_{t=2}^{T} \hat{e}_t \hat{e}_{t-1}}{\sum_{t=1}^{T} \hat{e}_t^2}$$

$$= \frac{\sum_{t=2}^{T} \hat{e}_t^2}{\sum_{t=1}^{T} \hat{e}_t^2} + \frac{\sum_{t=2}^{T} \hat{e}_{t-1}^2}{\sum_{t=1}^{T} \hat{e}_t^2} - \frac{2\sum_{t=2}^{T} \hat{e}_t \hat{e}_{t-1}}{\sum_{t=1}^{T} \hat{e}_t^2} \tag{9B.2}$$

$$\approx 1 + 1 - 2r_1$$

The last line in (9B.2) holds only approximately. The first two terms differ from one through the exclusion of $\hat{e}_1^2$ and $\hat{e}_T^2$ from the first and second numerator summations, respectively. The last term differs from $2r_1$ through the inclusion of $\hat{e}_T^2$ in the denominator summation. Thus, we have

$$d \approx 2(1 - r_1) \tag{9B.3}$$

If the estimated value of ρ is $r_1 = 0$, then the Durbin–Watson statistic $d \approx 2$, which is taken as an indication that the model errors are not autocorrelated. If the estimate of ρ happened to be $r_1 = 1$ then $d \approx 0$, and thus a low value for the Durbin–Watson statistic implies that the model errors are correlated, and $\rho > 0$.

The question we need to answer is: How close to zero does the value of the test statistic have to be before we conclude that the errors are correlated? In other words, what is a critical value d_c such that we reject H_0 when

$$d \leq d_c$$

Determination of a critical value and a rejection region for the test requires knowledge of the probability distribution of the test statistic under the assumption that the null hypothesis, $H_0: \rho = 0$, is true. For a 5% significance level, knowledge of the probability distribution $f(d)$ under H_0 allows us to find d_c such that $P(d \leq d_c) = 0.05$. Then, as illustrated in Figure 9A.1, we reject H_0 if $d \leq d_c$ and fail to reject H_0 if $d > d_c$. Alternatively, we can state the test procedure in terms of the p-value of the test. For this one-tail test, the p-value is given by the area under $f(d)$ to the left of the calculated value of d. Thus, if the p-value is less than or equal to 0.05, it follows that $d \leq d_c$ and H_0 is rejected. If the p-value is greater than 0.05, then $d > d_c$, and H_0 is accepted.

In any event, whether the test result is found by comparing d with d_c, or by computing the p-value, the probability distribution $f(d)$ is required. A difficulty associated with $f(d)$, and one that we have not previously encountered when using other test statistics, is that this probability distribution depends on the values of the explanatory variables. Different sets of explanatory variables lead to different distributions for d. Because $f(d)$ depends on the values of the explanatory variables, the critical value d_c for any given problem will also depend on the values of the explanatory variables. This property means that it is impossible to tabulate critical values that can be used for every possible problem. With other test statistics, such as t, F, and χ^2, the tabulated critical values are relevant for all models.

There are two ways to overcome this problem. The first way is to use software that computes the p-value for the explanatory variables in the model under consideration. Instead of comparing the calculated d value with some tabulated values of d_c, we get our computer to calculate the p-value of the test. If this p-value is less than the specified significance level, $H_0: \rho = 0$ is rejected and we conclude that autocorrelation does exist.

In the sugarcane area response model, the calculated value for the Durbin–Watson statistic is $d = 1.169$. Is this value sufficiently close to zero (or sufficiently less than 2), to reject H_0, and conclude that autocorrelation exists? Using suitable software,[1] we find that

$$p\text{-value} = P(d \leq 1.169) = 0.0044$$

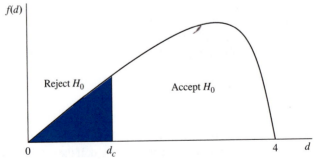

FIGURE **9A.1**   Testing for positive autocorrelation.

---

[1]The software packages SHAZAM and SAS, for example, will compute the exact Durbin–Watson p-value.

This value is much less than a conventional 0.05 significance level; we conclude, therefore, that the equation's error is positively autocorrelated.

9B.1 THE DURBIN–WATSON BOUNDS TEST

In the absence of software that computes a p-value, a test known as the bounds test can be used to partially overcome the problem of not having general critical values. Durbin and Watson considered two other statistics d_L and d_U whose probability distributions do not depend on the explanatory variables and which have the property that

$$d_L < d < d_U$$

That is, irrespective of the explanatory variables in the model under consideration, d will be bounded by an upper bound d_U and a lower bound d_L. The relationship between the probability distributions $f(d_L), f(d),$ and $f(d_U)$ is depicted in Figure 9A.2. Let d_{Lc} be the 5% critical value from the probability distribution for d_L. That is, d_{Lc} is such that $P(d_L < d_{Lc}) = 0.05$. Similarly, let d_{Uc} be such that $P(d_U < d_{Uc}) = 0.05$. Since the probability distributions $f(d_L)$ and $f(d_U)$ do not depend on the explanatory variables, it is possible to tabulate the critical values d_{Lc} and d_{Uc}. These values do depend on T and K, but it is possible to tabulate the alternative values for different T and K.

Thus, in Figure 9A.2 we have three critical values. The values d_{Lc} and d_{Uc} can be readily tabulated. The value d_c, the one in which we are really interested for testing purposes, cannot be found without a specialized computer program. However, it is clear from the figure that if the calculated value d is such that $d < d_{Lc}$, then it must follow that $d < d_c$, and H_0 is rejected. Also, if $d > d_{Uc}$, then it follows that $d > d_c$, and H_0 is accepted. If it turns out that $d_{Lc} < d < d_{Uc}$, then, because we do not know the location of d_c, we cannot be sure whether to accept or reject. These considerations led Durbin and Watson to suggest the following decision rules, which are known collectively as the Durbin–Watson *bounds test*.

If $d < d_{Lc}$, reject $H_0 : \rho = 0$ and accept $H_1 : \rho > 0$;

if $d > d_{Uc}$, do not reject $H_0 : \rho = 0$;

if $d_{Lc} < d < d_{Uc}$, the test is inconclusive.

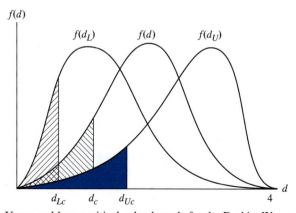

FIGURE **9A.2** Upper and lower critical value bounds for the Durbin–Watson test.

The presence of a range of values where no conclusion can be reached is an obvious disadvantage of the test. For this reason it is preferable to have software that can calculate the required p-value if such software is available.

The critical bounds for the sugarcane example for $T = 34$ are

$$d_{Lc} = 1.393 \quad d_{Uc} = 1.514$$

These bounds can be found in the previous edition of this book.[2] Since $d = 1.169 < d_{Lc}$, we conclude that $d < d_c$, and hence we reject H_0; there is evidence to suggest that autocorrelation exists.

Appendix 9C Deriving ARDL Lag Weights

In this appendix we are concerned with showing how the distributed lag weights β_0, β_1, β_2, ... in the infinite distributed lag representation

$$y_t = \alpha + \beta_0 x_t + \beta_1 x_{t-1} + \beta_2 x_{t-2} + \beta_3 x_{t-3} + \cdots + e_t = \alpha + \sum_{s=0}^{\infty} \beta_s x_{t-s} + e_t$$

can be derived from the coefficients in the ARDL representation

$$y_t = \delta + \delta_0 x_t + \delta_1 x_{t-1} + \cdots + \delta_q x_{t-q} + \theta_1 y_{t-1} + \cdots + \theta_p y_{t-p} + v_t$$

To do so, we will examine two special cases.

Appendix 9C.1 THE GEOMETRIC LAG

The simplest ARDL model is that where $p = 1$ and $q = 0$, leading to the ARDL(1,0) model

$$y_t = \delta + \delta_0 x_t + \theta_1 y_{t-1} + v_t \tag{9C.1}$$

To derive its lag weights we will ignore the error term. The error term in the infinite lag representation will be different from v_t, and for that reason we have called it e_t in earlier equations, but it does not affect the lag weights. Then, noting that the equation for y_{t-1} is given by

$$y_{t-1} = \delta + \delta_0 x_{t-1} + \theta_1 y_{t-2} \tag{9C.2}$$

and substituting (9C.2) into (9C.1), yields

$$y_t = \delta + \delta_0 x_t + \theta_1 y_{t-1} = \delta + \delta_0 x_t + \theta_1(\delta + \delta_0 x_{t-1} + \theta_1 y_{t-2})$$
$$= \delta + \theta_1 \delta + \delta_0 x_t + \theta_1 \delta_0 x_{t-1} + \theta_1^2 y_{t-2}$$

---

[2] *Undergraduate Econometrics, 2nd edition* by Hill, Griffiths and Judge, Wiley (2001), Table 5. Alternatively, go to the Web page http://www.bus.lsu.edu/hill/poe.

Substituting $y_{t-2} = \delta + \delta_0 x_{t-2} + \theta_1 y_{t-3}$ into this expression yields

$$y_t = \delta + \theta_1 \delta + \delta_0 x_t + \theta_1 \delta_0 x_{t-1} + \theta_1^2(\delta + \delta_0 x_{t-2} + \theta_1 y_{t-3})$$
$$= \delta + \theta_1 \delta + \theta_1^2 \delta + \delta_0 x_t + \theta_1 \delta_0 x_{t-1} + \theta_1^2 \delta_0 x_{t-2} + \theta_1^3 y_{t-3}$$

Continuing for a total of j substitutions yields

$$y_t = \delta + \theta_1 \delta + \theta_1^2 \delta + \cdots + \theta_1^j \delta + \delta_0 x_t + \theta_1 \delta_0 x_{t-1} + \theta_1^2 \delta_0 x_{t-2} + \cdots$$
$$+ \theta_1^j \delta_0 x_{t-j} + \theta_1^{j+1} y_{t-(j+1)} \tag{9C.3}$$
$$= \delta(1 + \theta_1 + \theta_1^2 + \cdots + \theta_1^j) + \sum_{s=0}^{j} \delta_0 \theta_1^s x_{t-s} + \theta_1^{j+1} y_{t-(j+1)}$$

Now, let $j \to \infty$, and assume that $-1 < \theta_1 < 1$, an assumption necessary to ensure the lag weights do not get bigger in the more distant past. Then, (9C.3) becomes

$$y_t = \alpha + \sum_{s=0}^{\infty} \delta_0 \theta_1^s x_{t-s} \tag{9C.4}$$

where, using a result on the sum of an infinite geometric progression

$$\alpha = \delta(1 + \theta_1 + \theta_1^2 + \cdots) = \frac{\delta}{1 - \theta_1}$$

Comparing (9C.4) with the general infinite distributed lag representation

$$y_t = \alpha + \sum_{s=0}^{\infty} \beta_s x_{t-s} + e_t$$

reveals that, for the ARDL(1,0) model,

$$\beta_s = \delta_0 \theta_1^s$$

This model is also called a geometric lag model because the lag weights begin at the point δ_0 and then decline geometrically through time according to the relationship $\beta_s = \theta_1 \beta_{s-1}$. The total multiplier showing the long-run effect of a sustained increase in x is

$$\sum_{s=0}^{\infty} \beta_s = \delta_0(1 + \theta_1 + \theta_1^2 + \cdots) = \frac{\delta_0}{1 - \theta_1}$$

The geometric lag model has the advantage of being relatively simple and has been used widely for supply response in agriculture and inventory demand models. There are many instances, however, where it is unreasonable to assume the largest lag weight is the initial one. For example, when modeling monetary or fiscal policy, the peak effect may not occur for several periods. This effect can be captured by including more lagged x's, while more lagged y's will yield weights that decline according to a structure more flexible than the geometrically declining weights.

9C.2 LAG WEIGHTS FOR MORE GENERAL ARDL MODELS

In principle the lag weights for more general ARDL models can be derived following the same steps as those we used for the geometric lag or ARDL(1,0) model, although the algebra is more complicated. In this section we give the weights for the ARDL(2,3) model used in Section 9.7 to capture the relationship between wage rate changes and the inflation rate:

$$y_t = \delta + \delta_0 x_t + \delta_1 x_{t-1} + \delta_2 x_{t-2} + \delta_3 x_{t-3} + \theta_1 y_{t-1} + \theta_2 y_{t-2} + v_t \tag{9C.5}$$

The weights for models with fewer terms (p less than 2 or q less than 3 or both) can be found by setting the relevant coefficients equal to zero. Using recursive substitution, it can be shown that the lag weights for (9C.5) are

$$
\begin{aligned}
\beta_0 &= \delta_0 \\
\beta_1 &= \theta_1 \beta_0 + \delta_1 \\
\beta_2 &= \theta_1 \beta_1 + \theta_2 \beta_0 + \delta_2 \\
\beta_3 &= \theta_1 \beta_2 + \theta_2 \beta_1 + \delta_3 \\
\beta_4 &= \theta_1 \beta_3 + \theta_2 \beta_2 \\
&\ \ \vdots \\
\beta_s &= \theta_1 \beta_{s-1} + \theta_2 \beta_{s-2} \quad \text{for } s \geq 4
\end{aligned}
\tag{9C.6}
$$

Appendix 9D Forecasting: Exponential Smoothing

In Section 9.5 we saw how an autoregressive model can be used to forecast the future value of a variable by making use of past observations on that variable. In this appendix we examine another popular model used for predicting the future value of a variable on the basis of its history—the exponential smoothing method.

Given a sample of observations $(y_1, y_2, \ldots, y_{T-1}, y_T)$, the objective is to forecast the next observation y_{T+1}. One possible forecasting method, one that has some intuitive appeal, is to use the average of past information, say, the average of the last k observations. For example, if we adopt this method with $k = 3$, the proposed forecast is

$$\hat{y}_{T+1} = \frac{y_T + y_{T-1} + y_{T-2}}{3}$$

This forecasting rule is an example of a simple (equally weighted) moving average model with $k = 3$. Note that when $k = 1$, all weight is placed on the most recent value and the forecast is $\hat{y}_{T+1} = y_T$.

Now, let us extend the moving average idea by changing the equal weighting system, where the weights are all $(1/k)$, to one where more weight is put on recent information or, put another way, less weight is placed on observations further into the past. The exponential smoothing model is one such forecasting model; in this case the weights decline (exponentially) as the observations get older. It has the form:

$$\hat{y}_{T+1} = \alpha y_T + \alpha(1-\alpha)^1 y_{T-1} + \alpha(1-\alpha)^2 y_{T-2} + \cdots \tag{9D.1}$$

The weight attached to y_{T-s} is given by $\alpha(1-\alpha)^s$. We assume that $0 < \alpha < 1$, which means that the weights get smaller as s gets larger (as we go further into the past). Also, using results on the infinite sum of a geometric progression, it can be shown that the weights sum to one: $\sum_{s=0}^{\infty} \alpha(1-\alpha)^s = 1$.

However, using information from the infinite past is not convenient for forecasting. Recognizing that:

$$(1-\alpha)\hat{y}_T = \alpha(1-\alpha)y_{T-1} + \alpha(1-\alpha)^2 y_{T-2} + \alpha(1-\alpha)^3 y_{T-3} + \cdots \tag{9D.2}$$

allows us to simplify the model. Substituting (9D.2) into (9D.1) means we can replace an infinite sum by a single term, so that the forecast can be more conveniently presented as

$$\hat{y}_{T+1} = \alpha y_T + (1 - \alpha)\hat{y}_T$$

That is, the forecast for next period is a weighted average of the forecast for the current period and the actual realized value in the current period.

The exponential smoothing method is a versatile forecasting tool, but one needs an estimate of the smoothing parameter α and a value for $\hat{y}_T$ to generate the forecast $\hat{y}_{T+1}$. The value of α can reflect one's judgment about the relative weight of current information; alternatively it can be estimated from historical information by minimizing the sum of squares of the one-step forecast errors $v_{t+1} = y_{t+1} - [\alpha y_t + (1 - \alpha)\hat{y}_t]$.

To illustrate how to compute a series of forecasts and hence the forecast errors, we set the forecast at time $t = 1$ equal to the first value in our time series; that is, $\hat{y}_1 = y_1$. Then, letting $\alpha = 0.1$, for example, we can obtain $\hat{y}_2 = 0.1y_1 + 0.9\hat{y}_1$ and $\hat{y}_3 = 0.1y_2 + 0.9\hat{y}_2$ and so on. By successive substitution, we obtain a whole series of forecasts $\hat{y}_t$ for the sample period $t = 1, 2, \ldots, T$. For a given time series y_t, each value of α yields a different series of in-sample forecasts $\hat{y}_t$. Thus, for each possible value of α there is a different series of forecast errors $v_t = y_t - [\alpha y_{t-1} + (1 - \alpha)\hat{y}_{t-1}]$. To estimate α we choose the nonlinear least squares estimate that minimizes $\sum_{t=2}^{T} v_t^2$.

Chapter *10*

Random Regressors and Moment-Based Estimation

Learning Objectives

Based on the material in this chapter you should be able to

1. Explain why we might sometimes consider explanatory variables in a regression model to be random.

2. Explain the difference between finite sample and large sample properties of estimators.

3. Give an intuitive explanation of why correlation between a random x and the error term causes the least squares estimator to be inconsistent.

4. Describe the "errors-in-variables" problem in econometrics and its consequences for the least squares estimator.

5. Describe the properties of a good instrumental variable.

6. Discuss how the method of moments can be used to derive the least squares and instrumental variables estimators, paying particular attention to the assumptions upon which the derivations are based.

7. Explain why it is important for an instrumental variable to be highly correlated with the random explanatory variable for which it is an instrument.

8. Describe how instrumental variables estimation is carried out in the case of surplus instruments.

9. State the large-sample distribution of the instrumental variables estimator for the simple linear regression model, and how it can be used for the construction of interval estimates and hypothesis tests.

10. Describe a test for the existence of correlation between the error term and the explanatory variables in a model, explaining the null and alternative hypotheses, and the consequences of rejecting the null hypothesis.

Keywords

asymptotic properties
conditional expectation
endogenous variables
errors-in-variables
exogenous variables
finite sample properties
Hausman test

instrumental variable
instrumental variable
  estimator
just identified equations
large sample properties
over identified equations
population moments

random sampling
reduced form equation
sample moments
simultaneous equations bias
test of surplus moment conditions
two-stage least squares estimation
weak instruments

In this chapter we reconsider the linear regression model. We will initially discuss the simple linear regression model, but our comments apply to the general model as well. The usual assumptions we make are

SR1. $y_i = \beta_1 + \beta_2 x_i + e_i \quad i = 1, \ldots, N$

SR2. $E(e_i) = 0$

SR3. $\text{var}(e_i) = \sigma^2$

SR4. $\text{cov}(e_i, e_j) = 0$

SR5. The variable x_i is not random, and it must take at least two different values.

SR6. (optional) $e_i \sim N(0, \sigma^2)$

In Chapter 8, we relaxed the assumption $\text{var}(e_i) = \sigma^2$ that the error variance is the same for all observations. In Chapter 9 we considered regressions with time-series data in which the assumption of serially uncorrelated errors, $\text{cov}(e_i, e_j) = 0$, cannot be maintained.

In this chapter we relax the assumption that variable x is not random. You may have wondered about the validity of this assumption. In our original discussion of random variables in Appendix B, we said that a variable is random if its value is unknown until an experiment is performed. In an economist's nonexperimental world, the values of x_i and y_i are usually revealed at the same time, making x and y random in the same way.

We have considered the variable x to be nonrandom for several reasons. First, when regression is based on data from controlled experiments, or if we are conditioning our results upon the sample we have, it is a proper assumption. Secondly, it simplifies the algebra of least squares. Thirdly, even if x is random, the properties of the least squares estimator still hold under slightly modified assumptions.

The purpose of this chapter is to discuss regression models in which x_i is random and correlated with the error term e_i. We will

- Discuss the conditions under which having a random x is not a problem, and how to test whether our data satisfies these conditions.

- Present cases in which the randomness of x causes the least squares estimator to fail. These are cases where x is correlated with the error e.

- Provide estimators that have good properties even when x_i is random and correlated with the error e_i.

10.1 Linear Regression with Random *x*'s

Let us modify the usual simple regression assumptions as follows:

A10.1 $y_i = \beta_1 + \beta_2 x_i + e_i$ correctly describes the relationship between y_i and x_i in the population, where β_1 and β_2 are unknown (fixed) parameters and e_i is an unobservable random error term.

A10.2   The data pairs (x_i, y_i), $i = 1, \ldots, N$, are obtained by **random sampling**. That is, the data pairs are collected from the same population by a process in which each pair is independent of every other pair. Such data are said to be independent and identically distributed.

A10.3 $E(e_i | x_i) = 0$. The expected value of the error term e_i, **conditional** on the value of x_i, is zero.

A10.4   In the sample, x_i must take at least two different values.

A10.5 $\mathrm{var}(e_i | x_i) = \sigma^2$. The variance of the error term, conditional on x_i, is a constant σ^2.

A10.6 $e_i | x_i \sim N(0, \sigma^2)$. The distribution of the error term, conditional on x_i, is normal.

There is only one new assumption in this list. Assumption A10.2 states that both y_i and x_i are obtained by a sampling process and thus are random. Also, by assuming that the pairs are independent, this implies that assumption SR4 holds as well. In the other assumptions, all we have done is bring back the explicit conditioning notation introduced in Chapter 2.

Because it plays a key role in the properties of the least squares estimator, let us clearly state the interpretation of A10.3, $E(e_i | x_i) = 0$. This assumption implies that we have (i) omitted no important variables, (ii) used the correct functional form, and (iii) there exist no factors that cause the error term e_i to be correlated with x_i.

While the first two of these implications are intuitive, the third may not be.

- If $E(e_i | x_i) = 0$, then we can show that it is also true that x_i and e_i are uncorrelated, and that $\mathrm{cov}(x_i, e_i) = 0$.
- Conversely, if x_i and e_i are correlated, then $\mathrm{cov}(x_i, e_i) \neq 0$, and we can show that $E(e_i | x_i) \neq 0$.

Thus in addition to the usual specification errors of omitted variables and incorrect functional form, assumption A10.3 eliminates correlation between a random explanatory variable x_i and the random error term e_i. We discuss the consequences of correlation between x_i and e_i in Section 10.1.4. In Section 10.2 we will explore some cases in which we can anticipate that correlation will exist between x_i and e_i. In each such case the usual least squares estimation procedure is no longer appropriate.

10.1.1   THE SMALL SAMPLE PROPERTIES OF THE LEAST SQUARES ESTIMATOR

In Chapter 2 we proved the Gauss–Markov theorem. The result that under the classical assumptions, and fixed x's, the least squares estimator is the best linear unbiased estimator, is a **finite sample**, or a **small sample**, property of the least squares estimator. What this means is that the result does not depend on the size of the sample. It holds in every sample, whether the sample size is $N = 20$, 50, or 10,000.

The finite sample properties of the least squares estimator when x is random can be summarized as follows:

1. Under assumptions A10.1–A10.4 the least squares estimator is unbiased.

2. Under assumptions A10.1–A10.5 the least squares estimator is the best linear unbiased estimator of the regression parameters, conditional on the x's, and the usual estimator of σ^2 is unbiased.

3. Under assumptions A10.1–A10.6 the distributions of the least squares estimators, conditional upon the x's, are normal, and their variances are estimated in the usual way. Consequently the usual interval estimation and hypothesis testing procedures are valid.

What these results say is that if x is random, as long as the data are obtained by random sampling, and the other usual assumptions hold, no changes in our regression methods are required.

10.1.2   ASYMPTOTIC PROPERTIES OF THE LEAST SQUARES ESTIMATOR: *x* NOT RANDOM

In this section we examine the large sample properties of the least squares estimator under the classical assumptions SR1–SR5. What happens to the probability distribution of the least squares estimator if we have a very large sample, or when the sample size $N \rightarrow \infty$? The answer is found in two properties of the least squares estimator that we have already established. First, the least squares estimator is unbiased. If we focus on the slope estimator b_2, then $E(b_2) = \beta_2$. Second, the variance of the least squares estimator for the simple linear regression model, $\text{var}(b_2) = \sigma^2 / \Sigma(x_i - \bar{x})^2$, *converges to zero as* $N \rightarrow \infty$. As the sample size gets increasingly large, the probability distribution of the least squares estimator *collapses* about the true parameter. In Figure 10.1 this is illustrated for b_2. As $N \rightarrow \infty$, all the probability is concentrated about β_2. This is a very reassuring result. Its consequence is that as $N \rightarrow \infty$, the probability approaches *one* that a least squares estimate b_2 will be *close* to β_2, no matter how narrowly you define the term "close." The same is true for b_1. Estimators with this property are called **consistent** estimators, and consistency is a nice large sample property of the least squares estimator.

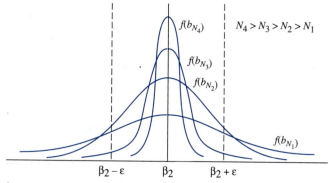

FIGURE **10.1**   An illustration of consistency.

> **REMARK:** Consistency is a "large sample" or "asymptotic" property. We have stated another large sample property of the least squares estimators in Section 2.6. We found that even when the random errors in a regression model are not normally distributed, the least squares estimators still have approximate normal distributions if the sample size N is large enough. How large must the sample size be for these large sample properties to be valid approximations of reality? In a simple regression, 50 observations might be enough. In multiple regression models, the number might be much higher, depending on the quality of the data. What is important for now is that you recognize we are discussing situations in this chapter in which the samples must be large for our conclusions to be valid.

10.1.3 ASYMPTOTIC PROPERTIES OF THE LEAST SQUARES ESTIMATOR: x RANDOM

For the purposes of a "large sample" analysis of the least squares estimator, it is convenient to replace assumption A10.3 by

A10.3* $E(e_i) = 0$ and $\text{cov}(x_i, e_i) = 0$

We can make this replacement because if assumption A10.3 is true it follows that A10.3* is true. That is, $E(e_i \mid x_i) = 0 \Rightarrow \text{cov}(x_i, e_i) = 0$ and $E(e_i \mid x_i) = 0 \Rightarrow E(e_i) = 0$. [See Appendix 10A.] Introducing assumption A10.3* is convenient because we want to investigate how to estimate models in which a random regressor x_i is correlated with the error term e_i, that is, when we violate the assumption that $\text{cov}(x_i, e_i) = 0$. While it does not seem like much of a change, because A10.3* is actually a weaker assumption than A10.3, under A10.3* we cannot show that the least squares estimator is unbiased, or that any of the other finite sample properties hold.

What we can say is the following:

1. Under assumption A10.3*, the least squares estimators are consistent. That is, they converge to the true parameter values as $N \to \infty$.

2. Under assumptions A10.1, A10.2, A10.3*, A10.4, and A10.5, the least squares estimators have approximate normal distributions in large samples, whether the errors are normally distributed or not. Furthermore, our usual interval estimators and test statistics are valid if the sample is large.

> 3. If assumption A10.3* is *not* true, and in particular if $\text{cov}(x_i, e_i) \neq 0$ so that x_i and e_i are correlated, then the least squares estimators are inconsistent. They do not converge to the true parameter values even in very large samples. Furthermore, none of our usual hypothesis testing or interval estimation procedures are valid.

Thus when x is random, the relationship between x_i and e_i is the crucial factor when deciding whether least squares estimation is appropriate or not. If the error term e_i is correlated with x_i (any x_{ki} in the multiple regression model), then the least squares estimator fails. In Section 10.4.1 we provide a way to test whether x_i and e_i are correlated. In the next section we show that if x_i and e_i are correlated, then the least squares estimator fails.

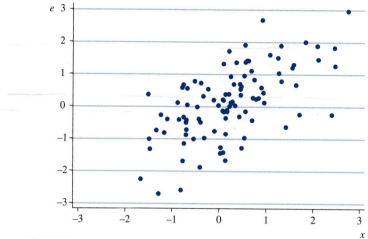

FIGURE **10.2** Plot of correlated x and e.

10.1.4 WHY LEAST SQUARES FAILS

In this section we use a tool of econometrics called the **Monte Carlo simulation** to demonstrate why the least squares estimator fails when $\text{cov}(x_i, e_i) \neq 0$. An algebraic proof is given in Appendix 10B. A Monte Carlo simulation uses artificially created data. By creating data from a known model, we can evaluate how alternative estimation procedures work under a variety of conditions. Specifically, let us specify a simple regression model in which the parameter values are $\beta_1 = 1$ and $\beta_2 = 1$. Thus, the systematic part of the regression model is $E(y) = \beta_1 + \beta_2 x = 1 + 1 \times x$. By adding to $E(y)$ an error term value, which will be a random number we create, we can create a sample value of y.

We want to explore the properties of the least squares estimator when x_i and e_i are correlated. Using random number generators, we create 100 pairs of x_i and e_i values, such that each has a normal distribution with mean zero and variance one and the population correlation between the x_i and e_i values is $\rho_{xe} = 0.6$. These values are plotted in Figure 10.2.

We then create an artificial sample of y values by adding e to the systematic portion of the regression,

$$y = E(y) + e = \beta_1 + \beta_2 x + e = 1 + 1 \times x + e$$

The data values are contained in *ch10.dat*. The least squares estimates are

$$\hat{y} = b_1 + b_2 x = 0.9789 + 1.7034x$$

The values of y, $E(y)$, and $\hat{y}$ are plotted against x in Figure 10.3.

The regression line $E(y) = \beta_1 + \beta_2 x = 1 + x$ is also plotted in this figure. In the "real world" we would never know where this line falls, since we never know the values of the true parameters. Note that the data values *are not* randomly scattered around this regression function, because of the correlation that exists between x_i and e_i. The least squares principle works by fitting a line through the "center" of the data. The fitted line $\hat{y} = 0.9789 + 1.7034x$ is an estimate of the true regression function $E(y) = \beta_1 + \beta_2 x$, but

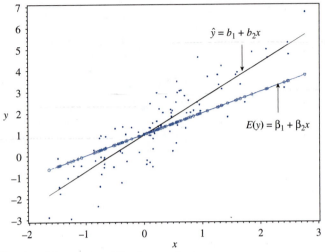

FIGURE *10.3*   Plot of data, true and fitted regressions.

in this case, because x_i and e_i are correlated, the least squares idea is not going to work. When x_i and e_i are positively correlated, the estimated slope tends to be too large relative to the true parameter value (here $b_2 = 1.7034$ compared to the true $\beta_2 = 1$). Furthermore, the systematic overestimation of the slope will not go away in larger samples, and thus the least squares estimators are not correct on average even in large samples. The least squares estimators are inconsistent.

10.2 Cases in Which x and e are Correlated

There are several common situations in which the least squares estimator fails due to the presence of correlation between an explanatory variable and the error term. When an explanatory variable and the error term are correlated, the explanatory variable is said to be **endogenous**. This term comes from simultaneous equations models, which we will consider in Chapter 11, and means "determined within the system." Using this terminology when an explanatory variable is correlated with the regression error, one is said to have an "endogeneity problem."

10.2.1 MEASUREMENT ERROR

The **errors-in-variables** problem occurs when an explanatory variable is measured with error. If we measure an explanatory variable with error, then it is correlated with the error term, and the least squares estimator is inconsistent. As an illustration, consider the following important example. Let us assume that an individual's personal saving, like their consumption, is based on their "permanent" or long-run income. Let $y_i =$ annual savings of the ith worker and let $x_i^* =$ the permanent annual income of the ith worker. A simple regression model representing this relationship is

$$y_i = \beta_1 + \beta_2 x_i^* + v_i \tag{10.1}$$

We have asterisked (*) the permanent income variable because it is difficult, if not impossible, to observe. For the purposes of a regression, suppose that we attempt to measure permanent income using x_i = current income. Current income is a measure of permanent income, but it does not measure permanent income exactly. It is sometimes called a **proxy variable**. To capture this feature let us specify that

$$x_i = x_i^* + u_i \tag{10.2}$$

where u_i is a random disturbance, with mean 0 and variance σ_u^2. With this statement, we are admitting that observed current income only approximates permanent income, and consequently that we have measured permanent income with error. Furthermore, let us assume that u_i is independent of v_i and serially uncorrelated. When we use x_i in the regression in place of x_i^*, we do so by replacement. That is, substitute $x_i^* = x_i - u_i$ into (10.1) to obtain

$$
\begin{aligned}
y_i &= \beta_1 + \beta_2 x_i^* + v_i \\
&= \beta_1 + \beta_2(x_i - u_i) + v_i \\
&= \beta_1 + \beta_2 x_i + (v_i - \beta_2 u_i) \\
&= \beta_1 + \beta_2 x_i + e_i
\end{aligned}
\tag{10.3}
$$

In (10.3) the explanatory variable x_i is random, from the assumption of measurement error in (10.2).

In order to estimate (10.3) by least squares, we must determine whether or not x_i is uncorrelated with the random disturbance e_i. The covariance between these two random variables, using the fact that $E(e_i) = 0$, is

$$
\begin{aligned}
\text{cov}(x_i, e_i) &= E(x_i e_i) = E[(x_i^* + u_i)(v_i - \beta_2 u_i)] \\
&= E(-\beta_2 u_i^2) = -\beta_2 \sigma_u^2 \neq 0
\end{aligned}
\tag{10.4}
$$

The least squares estimator b_2 is an *inconsistent* estimator of β_2 because of the correlation between the explanatory variable and the error term. Consequently, b_2 does not converge to β_2 in large samples. Furthermore, in large or small samples b_2 is *not* approximately normal with mean β_2 and variance $\text{var}(b_2) = \sigma^2 / \Sigma(x_i - \bar{x})^2$. When ordinary least squares fails in this way, is there another estimation approach that works? The answer is yes, as we will see in Section 10.3.

10.2.2 OMITTED VARIABLES

When an omitted variable is correlated with an included explanatory variable, then the regression error will be correlated with the explanatory variable. A classic example is from labor economics. A person's wage is determined in part by their level of education. Let us specify a simple regression model explaining observed hourly wage as

$$WAGE_i = \beta_1 + \beta_2 EDUC_i + e_i \tag{10.5}$$

with $EDUC$ = years of education. What else affects wages? What else is omitted? This introspective experiment should be carried out each time a regression model is formulated. In this case we have omitted many factors, such as experience. We have also omitted ability and motivation. Both of these factors are difficult to measure. Even measures like IQ scores fall short of truly measuring ability, much less a person's motivation. If we omit these factors where do they go? Like all omitted factors, they go into the error term e_i. We can expect that more talented and motivated people have more years of education; therefore, we expect that $\text{cov}(EDUC_i, e_i) \neq 0$. Thus, we can expect that the least squares estimator of the returns to another year of education will be biased and inconsistent.

10.2.3   SIMULTANEOUS EQUATIONS BIAS

Another situation in which an explanatory variable is correlated with the regression error term arises in simultaneous equations models. While this terminology may not sound familiar, students of economics deal with such models from their earliest introduction to supply and demand. Recall that in a competitive market, the prices and quantities of goods are determined jointly by the forces of supply and demand. Thus if P_i = equilibrium price and Q_i = equilibrium quantity, we can say that P_i and Q_i are endogenous, because they are jointly determined within a simultaneous system of two equations, one equation for the supply curve and the other equation for the demand curve. Suppose that we write down the relation

$$Q_i = \beta_1 + \beta_2 P_i + e_i \tag{10.6}$$

We know that changes in price affect the quantities supplied and demanded. But it is also true that changes in quantities supplied and demanded lead to changes in prices. There is a feedback relationship between P_i and Q_i. Because of this feedback, which results because price and quantity are jointly, or simultaneously, determined, we can show that $cov(P_i, e_i) \neq 0$. The least squares estimation procedure will fail if applied to (10.6) because of an endogeneity problem, and the resulting bias (and inconsistency) is called the **simultaneous equations bias**. Supply and demand models permeate economic analysis, and we will treat simultaneous equations models fully in Chapter 11.

10.2.4   LAGGED DEPENDENT VARIABLE MODELS WITH SERIAL CORRELATION

In Chapter 9 we introduced dynamic models. One way to make models dynamic is to introduce a lagged dependent variable into the right-hand side of an equation. That is, $y_t = \beta_1 + \beta_2 y_{t-1} + \beta_3 x_t + e_t$. The lagged variable y_{t-1} is a random regressor, but as long as it is uncorrelated with the error term then the least squares estimator is consistent. However, it is possible when specifying a dynamic model that the errors will be serially correlated. If the errors e_t follow the AR(1) process, $e_t = \rho e_{t-1} + v_t$, then we can see that the lagged dependent variable y_{t-1} must be correlated with the error term e_t, because y_{t-1} depends directly on e_{t-1}, and e_{t-1} directly affects the value of e_t. If $\rho \neq 0$, there will be a correlation between y_{t-1} and e_t. In this case the least squares estimator applied to the lagged dependent variable model will be biased and inconsistent. Thus it is very important to test for the presence of serial correlation in models with lagged dependent variables on the right-hand side. See Section 9.4.2.

10.3 Estimators Based on the Method of Moments

In the simple linear regression model $y_i = \beta_1 + \beta_2 x_i + e_i$, when x_i is random and $cov(x_i, e_i) = E(x_i e_i) \neq 0$, the least squares estimators are biased and inconsistent, with none of their usual nice properties holding. When faced with such a situation we must consider alternative estimation procedures. In this section we discuss the "method of moments" principle of estimation, which is an alternative to the least squares estimation principle. When all the usual assumptions of the linear model hold, the method of moments leads us to the least squares estimator. If x is random and correlated with the error term, the method of moments leads us to an alternative, called instrumental variables estimation or two-stage least squares estimation, that will work in large samples.

10.3.1 METHOD OF MOMENTS ESTIMATION OF A POPULATION MEAN AND VARIANCE

Let us begin with a simple case. The kth moment of a random variable Y is the expected value of the random variable raised to the kth power. That is,

$$E(Y^k) = \mu_k = k\text{th moment of } Y \tag{10.7}$$

Recall that an "expected value" is an average, over an infinite number of experimental outcomes. Consequently, the kth population moment in (10.7) can be estimated consistently using the sample (of size N) analog

$$\widehat{E(Y^k)} = \hat{\mu}_k = k\text{th sample moment of } Y = \Sigma y_i^k / N \tag{10.8}$$

The **method of moments** estimation procedure equates m population moments to m sample moments to estimate m unknown parameters. As an example, let Y be a random variable with mean $E(Y) = \mu$ and the variance expression from equation (B.12) in Appendix B

$$\text{var}(Y) = \sigma^2 = E(Y - \mu)^2 = E(Y^2) - \mu^2 \tag{10.9}$$

In order to estimate the two population parameters μ and σ^2, we must equate two population moments to two sample moments. The first two population and sample moments of Y are

Population moments	Sample moments	
$E(Y) = \mu_1 = \mu$	$\hat{\mu} = \Sigma y_i / N$	(10.10)
$E(Y^2) = \mu_2$	$\hat{\mu}_2 = \Sigma y_i^2 / N$	

Note that for the first population moment μ_1, it is customary to drop the subscript and use μ to denote the mean of Y. With these two moments, we can solve for the unknown mean and variance parameters. Equate the first sample moment to the first population moment to obtain an estimate of the population mean,

$$\hat{\mu} = \Sigma y_i / N = \bar{y} \tag{10.11}$$

Then use (10.9), replacing the second population moment by its sample value, and replacing first moment μ by (10.11)

$$\tilde{\sigma}^2 = \hat{\mu}_2 - \hat{\mu}^2 = \frac{\Sigma y_i^2}{N} - \bar{y}^2 = \frac{\Sigma y_i^2 - N\bar{y}^2}{N} = \frac{\Sigma(y_i - \bar{y})^2}{N} \tag{10.12}$$

The method of moments leads us to the sample mean as an estimator of the population mean. The method of moments estimator of the variance has N in its denominator, rather than the usual $N-1$, so it is not exactly the sample variance we are used to. But in large samples this will not make much difference. In general, method of moments estimators are consistent, and converge to the true parameter values in large samples, but there is no guarantee that they are "best" in any sense.

10.3.2 METHOD OF MOMENTS ESTIMATION IN THE SIMPLE LINEAR REGRESSION MODEL

The definition of a "moment" can be extended to more general situations. In the linear regression model $y_i = \beta_1 + \beta_2 x_i + e_i$, we usually assume that

$$E(e_i) = 0 \Rightarrow E(y_i - \beta_1 - \beta_2 x_i) = 0 \tag{10.13}$$

Furthermore, if x_i is fixed, or random but not correlated with e_i, then

$$E(x_i e_i) = 0 \Rightarrow E[x_i(y_i - \beta_1 - \beta_2 x_i)] = 0 \tag{10.14}$$

Equations (10.13) and (10.14) are moment conditions. If we replace the two population moments by the corresponding sample moments, we have two equations in two unknowns, which define the method of moments estimators for β_1 and β_2,

$$\frac{1}{N}\Sigma(y_i - b_1 - b_2 x_i) = 0$$
$$\frac{1}{N}\Sigma x_i(y_i - b_1 - b_2 x_i) = 0 \tag{10.15}$$

These two equations are equivalent to the least squares "normal" equations [see Chapter 2 Appendix A, equations (2A.3) and (2A.4)] and their solution yields the least squares estimators

$$b_2 = \frac{\Sigma(x_i - \bar{x})(y_i - \bar{y})}{\Sigma(x_i - \bar{x})^2}$$
$$b_1 = \bar{y} - b_2\bar{x}$$

Thus under "nice" assumptions, the method of moments principle of estimation leads us to the same estimators for the simple linear regression model as the least squares principle.

10.3.3 INSTRUMENTAL VARIABLES ESTIMATION IN THE SIMPLE LINEAR REGRESSION MODEL

Problems for least squares arise when x_i is random and correlated with the random disturbance e_i, so that $E(x_i e_i) \neq 0$. This makes the moment condition in (10.14) invalid. Suppose, however, that there is another variable z such that

1. z does not have a direct effect on y, and thus it does not belong on the right-hand side of the model as an explanatory variable.

2. z_i is not correlated with the regression error term e_i. Variables with this property are said to be **exogenous**.

3. z is strongly (or at least not weakly) correlated with x, the endogenous explanatory variable.

A variable z with these properties is called an **instrumental variable**. This terminology arises because while z does not have a direct effect on y, having it will allow us to estimate the relationship between x and y. It is a *tool*, or instrument, that we are using to achieve our objective.

If such a variable z exists, then we can use it to form the moment condition

$$E(z_i e_i) = 0 \Rightarrow E[z_i(y_i - \beta_1 - \beta_2 x_i)] = 0 \tag{10.16}$$

Then we can use the two equations (10.13) and (10.16) to obtain estimates of β_1 and β_2. The sample moment conditions are

$$\frac{1}{N}\Sigma(y_i - \hat{\beta}_1 - \hat{\beta}_2 x_i) = 0$$

$$\frac{1}{N}\Sigma z_i(y_i - \hat{\beta}_1 - \hat{\beta}_2 x_i) = 0 \tag{10.17}$$

Solving these equations leads us to method of moments estimators, which are usually called the **instrumental variable (*IV*) estimators**,

$$\hat{\beta}_2 = \frac{N\Sigma z_i y_i - \Sigma z_i \Sigma y_i}{N\Sigma z_i x_i - \Sigma z_i \Sigma x_i} = \frac{\Sigma(z_i - \bar{z})(y_i - \bar{y})}{\Sigma(z_i - \bar{z})(x_i - \bar{x})}$$

$$\hat{\beta}_1 = \bar{y} - \hat{\beta}_2 \bar{x} \tag{10.18}$$

These new estimators have the following properties:

- They are consistent, if $E(z_i e_i) = 0$ (see Appendix 10C).
- In large samples the instrumental variable estimators have approximate normal distributions. In the simple regression model

$$\hat{\beta}_2 \sim N\left(\beta_2, \frac{\sigma^2}{r_{zx}^2 \Sigma(x_i - \bar{x})^2}\right) \tag{10.19}$$

  where r_{zx}^2 is the squared sample correlation between the instrument z and the random regressor x.
- The error variance is estimated using the estimator

$$\hat{\sigma}_{IV}^2 = \frac{\Sigma(y_i - \hat{\beta}_1 - \hat{\beta}_2 x_i)^2}{N - 2}$$

10.3.3a   The Importance of Using Strong Instruments

Examine the variance expression in (10.19). The denominator includes the squared correlation between the instrument z and the endogenous variable x. We want to obtain an instrument z that is highly correlated with x to improve the efficiency of the instrumental variable estimator. If x and e are uncorrelated, so that least squares is still an option, we can compare the efficiency of the two estimators. Note that we can write the variance of the instrumental variables estimator of β_2 as

$$\text{var}(\hat{\beta}_2) = \frac{\sigma^2}{r_{zx}^2 \Sigma(x_i - \bar{x})^2} = \frac{\text{var}(b_2)}{r_{zx}^2}$$

Because $r_{zx}^2 < 1$ the variance of the instrumental variables estimator will always be larger than the variance of the least squares estimator, and thus it is said to be less efficient. Using the instrumental variables estimation procedure when it is not required leads to wider confidence intervals, and less precise inference, than if least squares estimation is used. If the correlation between z and x is 0.1, then the variance of the instrumental variables estimator is 100 times as large as the variance of the least squares estimator. If the correlation between z and x is 0.5, then the variance of the instrumental variables estimator is four times as large as the variance of the least squares estimator.

In recent years there has been a great deal of research on the behavior of the instrumental variables estimator when the instrument is weakly correlated with the endogenous variable x. When using a weak instrument, the instrumental variables estimator can be badly biased, even in large samples, and its distribution is not approximately normal. Thus point estimates can be substantially off, 95% confidence intervals may not work 95% of the time, and hypothesis tests using the $\alpha = 0.05$ level of significance may not have a probability of Type I error equal to 0.05. The bottom line is that when instruments are weak, instrumental variables estimation is not reliable.

10.3.3b   An Illustration Using Simulated Data

Let us return to the simulation, or Monte Carlo, experiment introduced in Section 10.1.4. Recall that we artificially created a sample of $N = 100$ observations from the true model $y = 1 + x + e$, where x and e are normally distributed variables with true means 0 and variances 1. We set the population correlation between x and e to be $\rho_{xe} = 0.6$. Least squares estimation yields

$$\hat{y}_{OLS} = 0.9789 + 1.7034x$$
$$\text{(se)} \quad (0.088) \quad (0.090)$$

As noted earlier, the estimated slope is far from the true value $\beta_2 = 1$.

In the process of creating the artificial data (*ch10.dat*), we also created two instrumental variables both of which are uncorrelated with the error term. The correlation between the first instrument z_1 and x is $\rho_{xz_1} = 0.5$, and the correlation between the second instrument z_2 and x is $\rho_{xz_2} = 0.3$. The *IV* estimates using z_1 are

$$\hat{y}_{IV\_z_1} = 1.1011 + 1.1924x$$
$$\text{(se)} \quad (0.109) \quad (0.195)$$

and the *IV* estimates using z_2 are

$$\hat{y}_{IV\_z_2} = 1.3451 + 0.1724x$$
$$\text{(se)} \quad (0.256) \quad (0.797)$$

Using z_1, the stronger instrument, yields an estimate of the slope of 1.1924 with a standard error of 0.195, which is about twice the standard error of the least squares estimate. Using the weaker instrument z_2 produces a slope estimate of 0.1724, which is far from the true value, and a standard error of 0.797, which is about eight times as large as the least squares standard error. The results with the weaker instrument are far less satisfactory than the estimates based on the stronger instrument z_1.

Another problem that an instrument can have is that it is not uncorrelated with the error term, as it is supposed to be. The variable z_3 is correlated with x, with correlation $\rho_{xz_3} = 0.5$, but it is correlated with the error term e, with correlation $\rho_{ez_3} = 0.3$. Thus z_3 is not a valid instrument. What happens if we use instrumental variables estimation with the invalid instrument? The results are

$$\hat{y}_{IV\_z_3} = 0.9640 + 1.7657x$$
$$\text{(se)} \quad (0.095) \quad (0.172)$$

As you can see, using the invalid instrument produces a slope estimate even further from the true value than the least squares estimate. Using an invalid instrumental variable means that the instrumental variables estimator will be inconsistent, just like the least squares estimator.

10.3.3c An Illustration Using a Wage Equation

In Section 10.2 we introduced an important example, the estimation of the relationship between wages, specifically log($WAGE$), and years of education ($EDUC$). We will use the data on married women in the file *mroz.dat* to examine this relationship, in light of issues discussed in this chapter. Let us specify a simple model in which ln($WAGE$) depends on years of education, years of work experience, and experience squared.

$$\ln(WAGE) = \beta_1 + \beta_2 EDUC + \beta_3 EXPER + \beta_4 EXPER^2 + e$$

When we specify an equation for estimation, we must always question our specification, asking what we might have omitted. There are several factors we might think of, such as labor market conditions, region of the country, and union membership. However, labor economists are most concerned about the omission of a variable measuring ability. It is logical that a person's ability (and industriousness) may affect the quality of their work and their wage. These variables are components of the error term e, since we usually have no measure for them. The problem is that not only might ability affect wages, but more able individuals may also spend more years in school, causing a correlation between the error term e and the education variable ($EDUC$). If such a correlation exists, then $EDUC$ is endogenous and the least squares estimator of the wage equation is biased and inconsistent. The least squares estimates and their standard errors are

$$\widehat{\ln(WAGE)} = -0.5220 + 0.1075 \times EDUC + 0.0416 \times EXPER - 0.0008 \times EXPER^2$$
$$\text{(se)} \quad (0.1986) \ (0.0141) \qquad\qquad (0.0132) \qquad\qquad (0.0004)$$

We estimate that an additional year of education increases wages by approximately 10.75%, holding everything else constant. If ability has a positive effect on wages, then this estimate will be overstated,[1] as the contribution of ability is attributed to the education variable.

To carry out instrumental variables estimation, we require a variable that does not belong in the wage equation itself, that is correlated with $EDUC$, but is uncorrelated with the person's ability, or intelligence. Such variables are difficult to obtain, but in Thomas Mroz's data, we have the number of years of education for the woman's mother. The mother's education itself does not belong in the daughter's wage equation, and it is reasonable to propose that more educated mothers are more likely to have more educated daughters. Thus two of the conditions for a valid instrumental variable seem satisfied. The remaining question is whether a woman's ability and intelligence are correlated with her mother's education? To be a valid instrument, these variables must be uncorrelated. We will assume so for illustration purposes.

To implement instrumental variables estimation, we first obtain the least squares estimates of what is called the **reduced form equation** for $EDUC$. The reduced form equation

---

[1] See Appendix 10B for a discussion of the large sample bias of the least squares estimator.

has explanatory variables that include all the exogenous variables in the original equation, plus any instrumental variables. The least squares estimates are

$$\widehat{EDUC} = 9.7751 + 0.0489 \times EXPER - 0.0013 \times EXPER^2 + 0.2677 \times MOTHEREDUC$$
$$\text{(se)} \quad (0.4249) \ (0.0417) \qquad\qquad (0.0012) \qquad\qquad (0.0311)$$

Note that coefficient of *MOTHEREDUC* is very significant, with a *t*-value of 8.6. This is important, as it indicates that our instrument is correlated with the variable we suspect to be endogenous, even after accounting for the other exogenous variables in the model.

Estimating the reduced form equation is the first stage in the two-stage least squares approach to instrumental variables estimation. To implement the second stage, we obtain the predicted values of education from the reduced form equation, $\widehat{EDUC}$, and insert them into the wage equation to replace *EDUC*. Then we estimate the resulting equation by least squares. While this two-step process yields proper instrumental variables estimates, the accompanying standard errors are not correct. It is always preferable to use software commands designed for instrumental variables, or two-stage least squares estimation. The instrumental variables estimates of the wage equation are

$$\widehat{\ln(WAGE)} = 0.1982 + 0.0493 \times EDUC + 0.0449 \times EXPER - 0.0009 \times EXPER^2$$
$$\text{(se)} \quad (0.4729) \ (0.0374) \qquad\qquad (0.0136) \qquad\qquad (0.0004)$$

Note two changes as compared to the least squares estimates. First, the estimated return to education is 4.93%, which is lower than the least squares estimate. This is consistent with the fact that the least squares estimator tends to overestimate the effect of education. Also notice, however, that the standard error on the coefficient of education (0.0374) is over 2.5 times larger than the standard error reported with the least squares estimates (0.0141). This reflects the fact that even with good instrumental variables the instrumental variables estimator is not efficient, as discussed in Section 10.3.3a. How can we improve the efficiency of the instrumental variables estimator? We can obtain a larger sample, if possible, or we can obtain more and stronger instrumental variables.

10.3.4 INSTRUMENTAL VARIABLES ESTIMATION WITH SURPLUS INSTRUMENTS

In the simple regression model, we need only one instrumental variable, yielding two moment conditions like (10.17), which we solve for the two unknown model parameters. Usually, however, we have more instrumental variables at our disposal than are necessary. For example, let w be another variable that does not directly affect y, and that is correlated with x but uncorrelated with e, so that we have the additional moment condition

$$E(w_i e_i) = E[w_i(y_i - \beta_1 - \beta_2 x_i)] = 0$$

Now we have three sample moment conditions

$$\frac{1}{N}\Sigma(y_i - \hat{\beta}_1 - \hat{\beta}_2 x_i) = \hat{m}_1 = 0$$

$$\frac{1}{N}\Sigma z_i(y_i - \hat{\beta}_1 - \hat{\beta}_2 x_i) = \hat{m}_2 = 0 \qquad (10.20)$$

$$\frac{1}{N}\Sigma w_i(y_i - \hat{\beta}_1 - \hat{\beta}_2 x_i) = \hat{m}_3 = 0$$

In (10.20) we have three equations with only two unknowns. We could simply throw away one of the conditions and use the remaining two to solve for the unknowns. However, throwing away good information is hardly ever a good idea. An alternative that uses all of the moment conditions is to choose values for $\hat{\beta}_1$ and $\hat{\beta}_2$ satisfying (10.20) as closely as possible. One way to do this is to use the least squares principle, choosing $\hat{\beta}_1$ and $\hat{\beta}_2$ to minimize the sum of squares $\hat{m}_1^2 + \hat{m}_2^2 + \hat{m}_3^2$. It is best, however, to use weighted least squares, putting the greatest weight on the moments with the smaller variances. While the exact details are beyond the scope of this book, the values of $\hat{\beta}_1$ and $\hat{\beta}_2$ that minimize this weighted sum of squares can be obtained using a two-step process.

1. Regress x on a constant term, z and w, and obtain the predicted values $\hat{x}$.
2. Use $\hat{x}$ as an instrumental variable for x.

This leads to the two sample moment conditions

$$\frac{1}{N}\Sigma(y_i - \hat{\beta}_1 - \hat{\beta}_2 x_i) = 0$$
$$\frac{1}{N}\Sigma\hat{x}_i(y_i - \hat{\beta}_1 - \hat{\beta}_2 x_i) = 0 \tag{10.21}$$

Solving these conditions, and using the fact that $\bar{\hat{x}} = \bar{x}$, we have

$$\hat{\beta}_2 = \frac{\Sigma(\hat{x}_i - \bar{\hat{x}})(y_i - \bar{y})}{\Sigma(\hat{x}_i - \bar{\hat{x}})(x_i - \bar{x})} = \frac{\Sigma(\hat{x}_i - \bar{x})(y_i - \bar{y})}{\Sigma(\hat{x}_i - \bar{x})(x_i - \bar{x})}$$
$$\hat{\beta}_1 = \bar{y} - \hat{\beta}_2 \bar{x} \tag{10.22}$$

These instrumental variables estimators, derived using the method of moments, are also called **two-stage least squares (2SLS) estimators**, because they can be obtained using two least squares regressions like we did for the wage equation in the previous section.

- Stage 1 is the regression of x on a constant term, z and w, to obtain the predicted values $\hat{x}$. This first stage is called the **reduced form** model estimation, with the terminology becoming clear in Chapter 11.
- Stage 2 is ordinary least squares estimation of the simple linear regression

$$y_i = \beta_1 + \beta_2 \hat{x}_i + error_i \tag{10.23}$$

Least squares estimation of (10.23) is numerically equivalent to obtaining the instrumental variables estimates using (10.22). Since two-stage least squares estimation and instrumental variables estimation are equivalent, we will simply refer to instrumental variables (*IV*) estimation in all cases.

Another useful result is that the approximate, large sample, variance of $\hat{\beta}_2$ is given by the usual formula for the variance of the least squares estimator of (10.23),

$$\text{var}(\hat{\beta}_2) = \frac{\sigma^2}{\Sigma(\hat{x}_i - \bar{x})^2} \tag{10.24}$$

Unfortunately, least squares software cannot be used to obtain appropriate standard errors and t-values, because the estimator of the error variance must be based on the residuals from the original model, $y_i = \beta_1 + \beta_2 x_i + e_i$, yielding

$$\hat{\sigma}_{IV}^2 = \frac{\Sigma(y_i - \hat{\beta}_1 - \hat{\beta}_2 x_i)^2}{N - 2}$$

Thus the appropriate estimator of the variance of $\hat{\beta}_2$ is

$$\widehat{\text{var}(\hat{\beta}_2)} = \frac{\hat{\sigma}_{IV}^2}{\sum(\hat{x}_i - \bar{x})^2} \tag{10.25}$$

This estimated variance can be used as a basis for t-tests of significance and interval estimation of parameters. Econometric software will automatically use the proper variance estimator if a two-stage least squares or instrumental variables estimation option is chosen.

10.3.4a   An Illustration Using Simulated Data

Returning to our simulated data, discussed in Section 10.3.3b, what is the outcome of two-stage least squares estimation using the two instruments z_1 and z_2? First, we estimate the reduced form model, a regression of x on the two instruments z_1 and z_2,

$$\begin{aligned}
\hat{x} = 0.1947 + 0.5700z_1 + 0.2068z_2 \\
\text{(se)} \ \ (0.079) \quad (0.089) \quad \ (0.077)
\end{aligned} \tag{10.26}$$

Using the predicted value $\hat{x}$ as an instrumental variable as in (10.22), or applying least squares to the modified equation (10.23), we obtain the instrumental variables estimates

$$\begin{aligned}
\hat{y}_{IV\_z_1,z_2} = 1.1376 + 1.0399x \\
\text{(se)} \quad \ \ (0.116) \quad (0.194)
\end{aligned} \tag{10.27}$$

The standard errors are based on the estimated error variance in (10.25).

Using the two valid instruments yields an estimate of the slope of 1.0399, which, in this example, is close to the true value of $\beta_2 = 1$. Two-stage least squares estimation takes the instruments we have, and forms combinations of them in an optimal way, as shown in (10.26). In the simple regression model, we have two parameters to estimate and thus need only two moment conditions, and the two moment conditions produced by 2SLS are given in (10.21).

10.3.4b   An Illustration Using a Wage Equation

In Section 10.3.3c we illustrated instrumental variables estimation of a wage equation for married women using "mother's education" as an instrument. Let us add "father's education" as an additional instrumental variable. The reduced form equation estimates are in Table 10.1.

Note that the two instrumental variables are statistically significant, establishing their correlation with education. The instrumental variables estimates are

$$\begin{aligned}
\ln(WAGE) = 0.0481 + 0.0614EDUC + 0.0442EXPER - 0.0009EXPER^2 \\
\text{(se)} \quad \ \ (0.4003) \ \ (0.0314) \qquad \ \ (0.0134) \qquad \quad (0.0004)
\end{aligned}$$

Table 10.1   **Reduced Form Equation**

Variable	Coefficient	Std. Error	t-Statistic	Prob.
C	9.1026	0.4266	21.3396	0.0000
$EXPER$	0.0452	0.0403	1.1236	0.2618
$EXPER2$	-0.0010	0.0012	-0.8386	0.4022
$MOTHEREDUC$	0.1576	0.0359	4.3906	0.0000
$FATHEREDUC$	0.1895	0.0338	5.6152	0.0000

Compared to the previous results, we see that there is an increase in the estimate of the return to education to 6.14%, and a slight reduction in the standard error. The estimated return to education is statistically significant now, whereas it was not when only the mother's education was used as an instrument.

10.3.5 INSTRUMENTAL VARIABLES ESTIMATION IN A GENERAL MODEL

To extend our analysis to a more general setting, consider the multiple regression model $y = \beta_1 + \beta_2 x_2 + \cdots + \beta_K x_K + e$. Suppose that among the explanatory variables $(x_1 = 1, x_2, \ldots, x_K)$ we know, or suspect, that several may be correlated with the error term e. Divide the variables into two groups, with the first G variables $(x_1 = 1, x_2, \ldots, x_G)$ being exogenous variables that are uncorrelated with the error term e. The second group of $B = K - G$ variables $(x_{G+1}, x_{G+2}, \ldots, x_K)$ is correlated with the regression error, and thus they are endogenous. The multiple regression model including all K variables is then

$$y = \underbrace{\beta_1 + \beta_2 x_2 + \cdots + \beta_G x_G}_{G \text{ exogenous variables}} + \underbrace{\beta_{G+1} x_{G+1} + \cdots + \beta_K x_K}_{B \text{ endogenous variables}} + e \qquad (10.28)$$

In order to carry out *IV* estimation, we must have at least as many instrumental variables as we have endogenous variables. Suppose we have L instrumental variables, $z_1, z_2, \ldots, z_L$. Such notation is invariably confusing and cumbersome. It may help to keep things straight to think of $G = Good$ explanatory variables, $B = Bad$ explanatory variables, and $L = Lucky$ instrumental variables, since we are lucky to have them. Then we have *The Good, The Bad, and The Lucky*.

It is a necessary condition for *IV* estimation that $L \geq B$. If $L = B$, then there are just enough instrumental variables to carry out *IV* estimation. The model parameters are said to be **just identified** or **exactly identified** in this case. The term **identified** is used to indicate that the model parameters can be consistently estimated. If $L > B$, then we have more instruments than are necessary for *IV* estimation, and the model is sometimes said to be **overidentified**.

The first step of two-stage least squares estimation is to estimate B reduced form equations, one for each explanatory variable that is endogenous. On the left-hand side of the reduced form equations, we have an endogenous variable. On the right-hand side, we have *all* the exogenous variables, including the G explanatory variables that are exogenous, and the L instrumental variables, which also must be exogenous. The B reduced form equations are

$$x_{G+j} = \gamma_{1j} + \gamma_{2j} x_2 + \cdots + \gamma_{Gj} x_G + \theta_{1j} z_1 + \cdots + \theta_{Lj} z_L + v_j, \quad j = 1, \ldots, B \quad (10.29)$$

The reduced form parameters (γ's and θ's) take different values in each reduced form equation, which is why they have a "j" subscript. We have omitted the observation subscript for simplicity. Since the right-hand side variables are all exogenous, we can estimate these reduced form equations by least squares, and then obtain the predicted values

$$\hat{x}_{G+j} = \hat{\gamma}_{1j} + \hat{\gamma}_{2j} x_2 + \cdots + \hat{\gamma}_{Gj} x_G + \hat{\theta}_{1j} z_1 + \cdots + \hat{\theta}_{Lj} z_L, \quad j = 1, \ldots, B$$

This comprises the first stage of two-stage least squares estimation.

In the second stage of estimation, we apply least squares to

$$y = \beta_1 + \beta_2 x_2 + \cdots + \beta_G x_G + \beta_{G+1} \hat{x}_{G+1} + \cdots + \beta_K \hat{x}_K + error \qquad (10.30)$$

This two-stage estimation process leads to proper instrumental variables estimates, but it should not be done this way in applied work. Use econometric software designed for two-stage least squares or instrumental variables estimation so that standard errors, t-statistics, and other test statistics will be computed properly.

10.3.5a   Hypothesis Testing with Instrumental Variables Estimates

We may be interested in testing hypotheses about the regression parameters based on the two-stage least squares/instrumental variables estimates. When testing the null hypothesis $H_0 : \beta_k = c$, use of the test statistic $t = (\hat{\beta}_k - c)/\text{se}(\hat{\beta}_k)$ is valid in large samples. We know that as $N \rightarrow \infty$, the $t_{(N-K)}$ distribution converges to the standard normal distribution $N(0,1)$. If the degrees of freedom $N - K$ are large, then critical values from the two distributions will be very close. It is common, but not universal, practice to use critical values, and p-values, based on the $t_{(N-K)}$ distribution rather than the more strictly appropriate $N(0,1)$ distribution. The reason is that tests based on the t-distribution tend to work better in samples of data that are not large.

Another issue is whether to use standard errors that are "robust" to the presence of heteroskedasticity (in cross-section data) or autocorrelation and heteroskedasticity (in time-series data). These options were described in Chapters 8 and 9 for the linear regression model, and they are also available in most software packages for *IV* estimation. Such corrections to standard errors require large samples in order to work properly.

When using software to test a joint hypothesis, such as $H_0 : \beta_2 = c_2, \beta_3 = c_3$, the test may be based on the chi-square distribution with the number of degrees of freedom equal to the number of hypotheses (J) being tested. The test itself may be called a "Wald" test, or a likelihood ratio (*LR*) test, or a Lagrange multiplier (*LM*) test. These testing procedures are all asymptotically equivalent and are discussed in Appendix C.8.4. However, the test statistic reported may be called an F-statistic with J numerator degrees of freedom and $N - K$ denominator degrees of freedom. This F-value is often calculated by dividing one of the chi-square tests statistics, such as the Wald statistic, by J. The motivation for using the F-test is to achieve better performance in small samples. Asymptotically, the tests will all lead to the same conclusion. See Chapter 6, Appendix 6A, for some related discussion. Once again, joint tests can be made "robust" to potential heteroskedasticity or autocorrelation problems, and this is an option with many software packages.

10.3.5b   Goodness-of-Fit with Instrumental Variables Estimates

We discourage the use of measures like R^2 outside the context of least squares estimation. When there are endogenous variables on the right-hand side of a regression equation, the concept of measuring how well the variation in y is explained by the x variables breaks down, because as we discussed in Section 10.2, these models exhibit feedback. This logical problem is paired with a numerical one. If our model is $y = \beta_1 + \beta_2 x + e$, then the *IV* residuals are $\hat{e} = y - \hat{\beta}_1 - \hat{\beta}_2 x$. Many software packages will report the goodness-of-fit measure $R^2 = 1 - \Sigma \hat{e}_i^2 / \Sigma (y_i - \bar{y})^2$. Unfortunately, this quantity can be negative when based on *IV* estimates.

10.4 Specification Tests

We have shown that if an explanatory variable is correlated with the regression error term, the least squares estimator fails. We have shown that if a strong instrumental variable is available, the *IV* estimator is consistent and approximately normally distributed in large samples. But, if we use a weak instrument, or an instrument that is invalid in the sense that it is not uncorrelated with the regression error, then *IV* estimation can be as bad, or worse, than using the least squares estimator. Given this unappetizing menu of choices, several questions come to mind:

1. Can we test for whether x is correlated with the error term? This might give us a guide of when to use least squares and when to use *IV* estimators.

2. Can we test whether our instrument is sufficiently strong to avoid the problems associated with "weak" instruments?

3. Can we test if our instrument is valid, and uncorrelated with the regression error, as required?

These questions will be answered in this section.

10.4.1   THE HAUSMAN TEST FOR ENDOGENEITY

In the previous sections we discussed the fact that the least squares estimator fails if there is correlation between an explanatory variable and the error term. We also provided an estimator, the instrumental variables estimator, that can be used when the least squares estimator fails. The question we address in this section is how to test for the presence of a correlation between an explanatory variable and the error term, so that we can use the appropriate estimation procedure.

The null hypothesis is $H_0 : \text{cov}(x_i, e_i) = 0$ against the alternative that $H_1 : \text{cov}(x_i, e_i) \neq 0$. The idea of the test is to compare the performance of the least squares estimator to an instrumental variables estimator. Under the null and alternative hypotheses we know the following:

- If the null hypothesis is true, both the least squares estimator and the instrumental variables estimator are consistent. Thus, in large samples the difference between them converges to zero. That is, $q = (b_{OLS} - \hat{\beta}_{IV}) \to 0$. Naturally, if the null hypothesis is true, use the more efficient estimator, which is the least squares estimator.

- If the null hypothesis is false, the least squares estimator is not consistent, and the instrumental variables estimator is consistent. Consequently, the difference between them does not converge to zero in large samples. That is, $q = (b_{OLS} - \hat{\beta}_{IV}) \to c \neq 0$. If the null hypothesis is not true, use the instrumental variables estimator, which is consistent.

There are several forms of the test, usually called the **Hausman test**, in recognition of econometrician Jerry Hausman's pioneering work on this problem, for these null and alternative hypotheses. One form of the test directly examines the differences between the least squares and instrumental variables estimates, as we have described above. Some computer software programs implement this test for the user, which can be computationally difficult to carry out.[2]

---

[2] Some software packages compute Hausman tests with K, or $K-1$, degrees of freedom, where K is the total number of regression parameters. This is incorrect. Use the correct degrees of freedom B, equal to the number of potentially endogenous right-hand side variables. See (10.28).

An alternative form of the test is very easy to implement and is the one we recommend. See Appendix 10D for an explanation of the test's logic. In the regression $y_i = \beta_1 + \beta_2 x_i + e_i$, we wish to know whether x_i is correlated with e_i. Let z_1 and z_2 be instrumental variables for x. At a minimum one instrument is required for each variable that might be correlated with the error term. Then carry out the following steps:

1. Estimate the reduced form model $x_i = \gamma_1 + \theta_1 z_{i1} + \theta_2 z_{i2} + v_i$ by least squares, including on the right-hand side all instrumental variables and all exogenous variables not suspected to be endogenous, and obtain the residuals

$$\hat{v}_i = x_i - \hat{\gamma}_1 - \hat{\theta}_1 z_{i1} - \hat{\theta}_2 z_{i2}$$

    If more than one explanatory variables are being tested for endogeneity, repeat this estimation for each one.

2. Include the residuals computed in step 1 as an explanatory variable in the original regression, $y_i = \beta_1 + \beta_2 x_i + \delta \hat{v}_i + e_i$. Estimate this "artificial regression" by least squares, and employ the usual t-test for the hypothesis of significance

$$H_0 : \delta = 0 \quad (\text{no correlation between } x_i \text{ and } e_i)$$
$$H_1 : \delta \neq 0 \quad (\text{correlation between } x_i \text{ and } e_i)$$

3. If more than one variable is being tested for endogeneity, the test will be an F-test of joint significance of the coefficients on the included residuals.

The t- and F-tests in steps 2 and 3 can be made robust if heteroskedasticity and/or autocorrelation are potential problems.

10.4.2 TESTING FOR WEAK INSTRUMENTS

If the instruments we choose are weak, the instrumental variables estimator can suffer large biases and standard errors, and its large sample distribution may not be approximately normal. Consider the model

$$y = \beta_1 + \beta_2 x_2 + \cdots + \beta_G x_G + \beta_{G+1} x_{G+1} + e$$

Suppose that $x_2, \ldots, x_G$ are exogenous and uncorrelated with the error term e, while x_{G+1} is endogenous. Further, suppose that we have one instrumental variable z_1. How can we determine whether it is a "strong" or "weak" instrument? The key is to examine the strength of the relationship between z_1 and the endogenous variable x_{G+1} *after* accounting for the influence of the other exogenous variables already included in the model. The reduced form equation in this case is

$$x_{G+1} = \gamma_1 + \gamma_2 x_2 + \cdots + \gamma_G x_G + \theta_1 z_1 + v$$

In order for z_1 to qualify as an instrument, the coefficient θ_1 in this reduced form equation *must not* be zero. Thus we can test the null hypothesis $H_0 : \theta_1 = 0$ against the alternative hypothesis $H_1 : \theta_1 \neq 0$. Unfortunately, just rejecting the null hypothesis at the $\alpha = 0.05$ level of significance is not enough to insure that we do not have a weak instrument problem. The null hypothesis must be *soundly* rejected. A common rule of thumb is that if the F-test statistic takes a value less than 10, or if the t-statistic is less than 3.3, the instrument is weak.[3]

---

[3] For more on this issue see Stock and Watson, *Introduction to Econometrics*, Addison-Wesley, 2003, pp. 348–352. At an advanced graduate level, see Cameron and Trivedi, *Microeconometrics: Methods and Applications*, Cambridge, 2005, pp. 104–110.

If we have $L > 1$ instruments available then the reduced form equation is

$$x_{G+1} = \gamma_1 + \gamma_2 x_2 + \cdots + \gamma_G x_G + \theta_1 z_1 + \cdots \theta_L z_L + v$$

We require only one instrument to carry out *IV* estimation. We test the null hypothesis $H_0: \theta_1 = 0, \theta_2 = 0, \ldots, \theta_L = 0$ against the alternative that at least one of the θ's is not zero. We can use an F-test for this joint null hypothesis, but again, if the F-value is less than 10 we should be concerned that we are using weak instruments.

For models with $B > 1$ endogenous explanatory variables, there must be $L \geq B$ instruments. To test instrument strength, an F-test should be done in each of the reduced form equations. However, these individual F-tests do not constitute an overall, joint test, and having each $F > 10$ does not guarantee that we have avoided a weak instrument problem. The research on this topic is still developing.

A final diagnostic is to simply compare the standard errors of the *IV* estimates to the standard errors of the least squares estimates. From (10.19) we know that weak instruments lead to large standard errors for the *IV* estimator. If the *IV* standard errors are much larger than the least squares standard errors, this is another indication that instruments are weak.

What should one do if weak instruments are encountered? This is a difficult question that is being researched heavily at this time. One answer is to search among the instruments and discard the weakest of them. This is possible only if surplus instruments are available in the first place.

10.4.3 TESTING INSTRUMENT VALIDITY

A valid instrument z must be uncorrelated with the regression error term, so that $\text{cov}(z_i, e_i) = 0$. If this condition fails then the resulting moment condition, like (10.16), is invalid and the *IV* estimator will not be consistent. Unfortunately, not every instrument can be tested for validity. In order to compute the *IV* estimator for an equation with B possibly endogenous variables, we must have at least B instruments. The validity of this minimum number of required instruments cannot be tested. In the case in which we have $L > B$ instruments available, we can test the validity of the $L - B$ extra, or surplus, moment conditions.[4]

An intuitive approach is the following. From the set of L instruments, form groups of B instruments and compute the *IV* estimates using each different group. If all the instruments are valid, then we would expect all the *IV* estimates to be similar. Rather than do this, there is a test of the validity of the surplus moment conditions that is easier to compute. The steps are

1. Compute the *IV* estimates $\hat{\beta}_k$ using all available instruments, including the G variables $x_1 = 1, x_2, \ldots, x_G$ that are presumed to be exogenous, and the L instruments $z_1, \ldots, z_L$.

2. Obtain the residuals $\hat{e} = y - \hat{\beta}_1 - \hat{\beta}_2 x_2 - \cdots - \hat{\beta}_K x_K$.

3. Regress $\hat{e}$ on all the available instruments described in step 1.

4. Compute NR^2 from this regression, where N is the sample size and R^2 is the usual goodness-of-fit measure.

---

[4] Econometric jargon for surplus moment conditions is "overidentifying restrictions." A surplus of moment conditions means we have more than enough for identification, hence "overidentifying." Moment conditions like (10.16) can be thought of as restrictions on parameters.

5. If all of the surplus moment conditions are valid, then $NR^2 \sim \chi^2_{(L-B)}$.[5] If the value of the test statistic exceeds the $100(1-\alpha)$-percentile (i.e., the critical value) from the $\chi^2_{(L-B)}$ distribution, then we conclude that at least one of the surplus moment conditions is not valid.

If we reject the null hypothesis that all the surplus moment conditions are valid, then we are faced with trying to determine which instrument(s) are invalid and how to weed them out.

10.4.4   NUMERICAL EXAMPLES USING SIMULATED DATA

To illustrate the tests, we will use the simulated data (*ch10.dat*) that we introduced first in Section 10.1.4 and then used again in Section 10.3.3.

10.4.4a   The Hausman Test
To implement the Hausman test, we first estimate the reduced form equation, which is shown in (10.26) using the instruments z_1 and z_2. Compute the residuals

$$\hat{v} = x - \hat{x} = x - 0.1947 - 0.5700z_1 - 0.2068z_2 \tag{10.31}$$

Include the residuals as an extra variable in the regression equation and apply least squares,

$$\hat{y} = 1.1376 + 1.0399x + 0.9957\hat{v}$$
$$(\text{se})\ \ (0.080)\quad (0.133)\quad\ (0.163)$$

The t-statistic for the null hypothesis that the coefficient of $\hat{v}$ is zero is 6.11. The critical value comes from the t-distribution with 97 degrees of freedom and is 1.985, and thus we reject the null hypothesis that x is uncorrelated with the error term and conclude that it is endogenous.

10.4.4b   Test for Weak Instruments
The test for weak instruments again begins with estimation of the reduced form. If we consider using just z_1 as an instrument, the estimated reduced form is

$$\hat{x} = 0.2196 + 0.5711z_1$$
$$(t)\qquad\qquad (6.23)$$

The t-statistic 6.23 corresponds to an F-value of 38.92 that is well above the guideline value of 10. If we use just z_2 as an instrument, the estimated reduced form is

$$\hat{x} = 0.2140 + 0.2090z_2$$
$$(t)\qquad\qquad (2.28)$$

While the t-statistic 2.28 indicates statistical significance at the 0.05 level, the corresponding F-value is $5.21 < 10$, indicating that z_2 is a weak instrument. The reduced form equation using both instruments is shown in (10.26), and the F-test for their joint significance is 24.28, indicating that we have at least one strong instrument.

---

[5] This test is valid if errors are homoskedastic and is sometimes called the Sargan test. If the errors are heteroskedastic, there is a more general test called Hansen's J-test that is provided by some software. A very advanced reference is Hayashi, *Econometrics*, Princeton, 2000, pp. 227–228.

10.4.4c Testing Surplus Moment Conditions

If we use z_1 and z_2 as instruments, there is one surplus moment condition. The IV estimates are shown in (10.27). Calculate the residuals from this equation, and then regress them on an intercept, z_1 and z_2 to obtain $\hat{e} = 0.0189 + 0.0881z_1 - 0.1818z_2$. The R^2 from this regression is 0.03628, and $NR^2 = 3.628$. The 0.05 critical value for the chi-square distribution with one degree of freedom is 3.84, thus we fail to reject the validity of the surplus moment condition.

If we use z_1, z_2, and z_3 as instruments, there are two surplus moment conditions. The IV estimates using these three instruments are $\hat{y}_{IV\_z_1,z_2,z_3} = 1.0626 + 1.3535x$. Obtaining the residuals and regressing them on the instruments yields

$$\hat{e} = 0.0207 - 0.1033z_1 - 0.2355z_2 + 0.1798z_3$$

The R^2 from this regression is 0.1311, and $NR^2 = 13.11$. The 0.05 critical value for the chi-square distribution with two degrees of freedom is 5.99, thus we reject the validity of the two surplus moment conditions. This test does not identify the problem instrument, but since we first tested the validity of z_1 and z_2 and failed to reject their validity, and then found that adding z_3 led us to reject the validity of the surplus moment conditions, the instrument z_3 seems to be the culprit.

10.4.5 SPECIFICATION TESTS FOR THE WAGE EQUATION

In Section 10.3.4b we examined a ln(*WAGE*) equation for married women, using the two instruments "mother's education" and "father's education" for the potentially endogenous explanatory variable education (*EDUC*).

To implement the Hausman test we first obtain the reduced form estimates, which are shown in Table 10.1. Using these estimates we calculate the least squares residuals $\hat{v} = \overline{EDUC} - EDUC$. Insert the residuals in the ln(*WAGE*) equation as an extra variable, and estimate the resulting augmented regression using least squares. The resulting estimates are shown in Table 10.2

The Hausman test of the endogeneity is based on the t-test of significance of the reduced form residuals, $\hat{v}$. If we reject the null hypothesis that the coefficient is zero, we conclude that education is endogenous. Note that the coefficient of the reduced form residuals (*VHAT*) is significant at the 10% level of significance using a two-tail test. While this is not strong evidence of the endogeneity of education, it is sufficient cause for concern to consider using instrumental variables estimation. Second, note that the coefficient estimates of the remaining variables, but not their standard errors, are identical to their instrumental variables estimates. This feature of the regression-based Hausman test is explained in Appendix 10D.

The instrumental variables estimator does not work well with weak instrumental variables. In fact, instrumental variables estimation can be worse than using the least

Table 10.2 **Hausman Test Auxiliary Regression**

Variable	Coefficient	Std. Error	t-Statistic	Prob.
C	0.0481	0.3946	0.1219	0.9030
EDUC	0.0614	0.0310	1.9815	0.0482
EXPER	0.0442	0.0132	3.3363	0.0009
EXPER2	−0.0009	0.0004	−2.2706	0.0237
VHAT	−0.0582	0.0348	−1.6711	0.0954

squares estimator if instruments are weak. To test for weak instruments, we can test the joint significance of the two proposed instruments *MOTHEREDUC* and *FATHEREDUC* using a standard *F*-test. Since we have only one potentially endogenous variable in the wage equation, the minimum number of instrumental variables we need is one. Given that we are using two instruments, we require that at least one of them be significant in the reduced form. The *F*-test null hypothesis is that both coefficients are zero, and if we reject this null hypothesis we conclude that at least one of the coefficients is nonzero. The resulting *F*-statistic value is 55.4, which has a *p*-value less than 0.0001. Thus we can safely conclude that at least one of the two instruments is relevant, and the value is greater than the rule-of-thumb threshold of 10 that was mentioned in Section 10.4.2.

In order to be valid, the instruments *MOTHEREDUC* and *FATHEREDUC* should be uncorrelated with the regression error term. As discussed in Section 10.4.3, we cannot test the validity of both instruments, only the "overidentifying" or surplus instrument. Since we have two instruments, and only one potentially endogenous variable, we have $L - B = 1$ extra instrument. The test is carried out by regressing the residuals from the $\ln(WAGE)$ equation, calculated using the instrumental variables estimates, on all available exogenous and instrumental variables. The test statistic is NR^2 from this artificial regression, and R^2 is the usual goodness-of-fit measure. If the surplus instruments are valid, then the test statistic has an asymptotic $\chi^2_{(1)}$ distribution, where the degrees of freedom are the number of surplus instruments. If the test statistic value is greater than the critical value from this distribution, then we reject the null hypothesis that the surplus instrument is valid. For the artificial regression $R^2 = 0.000883$, and the test statistic value is $NR^2 = 428 \times 0.000883 = 0.3779$. The 0.05 critical value for the chi-square distribution with one degree of freedom is 3.84, thus we fail to reject the surplus instrument as valid. With this result we are reassured that our instrumental variables estimator for the wage equation is consistent.

10.5 Exercises

10.5.1 PROBLEMS

10.1 The geometric lag model (Chapter 9, Appendix C1) reduces with some algebra to $y_t = \beta_1 + \beta_2 y_{t-1} + \beta_3 x_t + v_t$ with random error $v_t = (e_t - \phi e_{t-1})$.
   (a) Is least squares estimation viable in this model? If not, why not?
   (b) Explain why x_{t-1}, x_{t-2} are potentially useful instrumental variables.
   (c) Describe the steps (not a software command) you would take to implement $2SLS/IV$ estimation in this case.

10.2 The labor supply of married women has been a subject of a great deal of economic research. Consider the following supply equation specification

$$HOURS = \beta_1 + \beta_2 WAGE + \beta_3 EDUC + \beta_4 AGE + \beta_5 KIDSL6 + \beta_6 KIDS618$$

$$+ \beta_7 NWIFEINC + e$$

where *HOURS* is the supply of labor, *WAGE* is hourly wage, *EDUC* is years of education, *KIDSL6* is the number of children in the household who are less than 6 years old, *KIDS618* is the number between 6 and 18 years old, and *NWIFEINC* is household income from sources other than the wife's employment.
   (a) Discuss the signs you expect for each of the coefficients.
   (b) Explain why this supply equation cannot be consistently estimated by least squares regression.

(c) Suppose we consider the woman's labor market experience *EXPER* and its square, *EXPER*^{2}, to be instruments for *WAGE*. Explain how these variables satisfy the logic of instrumental variables.

(d) Is the supply equation identified? Explain.

(e) Describe the steps (not a computer command) you would take to obtain *2SLS* estimates.

10.5.2 COMPUTER EXERCISES

10.3 To examine the quantity theory of money, Brumm (2005) ["Money Growth, Output Growth, and Inflation: A Reexamination of the Modern Quantity Theory's Linchpin Prediction," *Southern Economic Journal*, 71(3), 661–667] specifies the equation

$$INFLATION = \beta_1 + \beta_2 MONEY\ GROWTH + \beta_3 OUTPUT\ GROWTH + e$$

where *INFLATION* is the growth rate of the general price level, *MONEY GROWTH* is the growth rate of the money supply, and *OUTPUT GROWTH* is the growth rate of national output. According to theory we should observe that $\beta_1 = 0$, $\beta_2 = 1$, and $\beta_3 = -1$. Dr. Brumm kindly provided us the data he used in his paper, which is contained in the file *brumm.dat*. It consists of 1995 data on 76 countries.

(a) Estimate the model by least squares and test
 (i) the *strong* joint hypothesis that $\beta_1 = 0$, $\beta_2 = 1$, and $\beta_3 = -1$.
 (ii) the *weak* joint hypothesis $\beta_2 = 1$ and $\beta_3 = -1$.

(b) Examine the least squares residuals for the presence of heteroskedasticity related to the variable *MONEY GROWTH*.

(c) Obtain robust standard errors for the model and compare them to the least squares standard errors.

(d) It is argued that *OUTPUT GROWTH* may be endogenous. Four instrumental variables are proposed, *INITIAL* = initial level of real GDP, *SCHOOL* = a measure of the population's educational attainment, *INV* = average investment share of GDP, and *POPRATE* = average population growth rate. Using these instruments obtain instrumental variables (2SLS) estimates of the inflation equation.

(e) Test the strong and weak hypotheses listed in (a) using the *IV* estimates. If your software permits make the tests robust to heteroskedasticity.

(f) Use the Hausman test to check the endogeneity of *OUTPUT GROWTH*. Because the regression errors may be heteroskedastic, use robust standard errors when estimating the auxiliary regression.

(g) Test the validity of the overidentifying restrictions.

(h) Test the relevance of the instruments using a joint F-test as described in Section 10.4.2. If your software permits, use a robust joint test.

10.4 The 25 values of x and e in *ivreg1.dat* were generated artificially. Use your computer software to carry out the following:

(a) Create the value of the dependent variable y from the model $y = \beta_1 + \beta_2 x + e = 1 + 1 \times x + e$ by the method described in Section 10.1.4

(b) In the same graph, plot the value of y against x, and the regression function $E(y) = 1 + 1 \times x$. Do the data fall randomly about the regression function?

(c) Using the data on y created in part (a) and x, obtain the least squares estimates of the parameters β_1 and β_2. Compare the estimated values of the parameters to the true values.

(d) Plot the data and the fitted least squares regression line $\hat{y} = b_1 + b_2 x$. Compare this plot to the one in part (b).

(e) Compute the least squares residuals from the least squares regression in part (d). Find the sample correlation matrix of the variables x, e, and the least squares residuals $\hat{e} = y - b_1 - b_2 x$. Comment on the values of the correlations. Which of these correlations could you *not* compute using a sample of data collected from the real world?

10.5* Using your computer software, and the 50 observations on savings (y), income (x), and averaged income (z) in *savings.dat*

(a) Estimate a least squares regression of savings on income.

(b) Estimate the relation between savings and income (x) using the instrumental variables estimator, with instrument z, using econometric software designed for instrumental variables, or two-stage least squares, estimation.

(c) Using the steps outlined in Section 10.4.1, carry out the Hausman test (via an artificial regression) for the existence of correlation between x and the random disturbance e.

(d) Use two least squares regressions to obtain the *IV* estimates in part (b). Compare the estimates, standard errors, and t-statistics to those in part (b) and comment on the differences.

10.6 The 500 values of x, y, z_1, and z_2 in *ivreg2.dat* were generated artificially. The variable $y = \beta_1 + \beta_2 x + e = 3 + 1 \times x + e$.

(a) The explanatory variable x follows a normal distribution with mean zero and variance $\sigma_x^2 = 2$. The random error e is normally distributed with mean zero and variance $\sigma_e^2 = 1$. The covariance between x and e is 0.9. Using the algebraic definition of correlation, determine the correlation between x and e.

(b) Given the values of y and x, and the values of $\beta_1 = 3$ and $\beta_2 = 1$, solve for the values of the random disturbances e. Find the sample correlation between x and e and compare it to your answer in (a).

(c) In the same graph, plot the value of y against x, and the regression function $E(y) = 3 + 1 \times x$. Note that the data do not fall randomly about the regression function.

(d) Estimate the regression model $y = \beta_1 + \beta_2 x + e$ by least squares using a sample consisting of the first $N = 10$ observations on y and x. Repeat using $N = 20$, $N = 100$, and $N = 500$. What do you observe about the least squares estimates? Are they getting closer to the true values as the sample size increases, or not? If not, why not?

(e) The variables z_1 and z_2 were constructed to have normal distributions with means 0 and variances 1, and to be correlated with x but uncorrelated with e. Using the full set of 500 observations, find the sample correlations between z_1, z_2, x, and e. Will z_1 and z_2 make good instrumental variables? Why? Is one better than the other? Why?

(f) Estimate the model $y = \beta_1 + \beta_2 x + e$ by instrumental variables using a sample consisting of the first $N = 10$ observations and the instrument z_1. Repeat using $N = 20$, $N = 100$, and $N = 500$. What do you observe about the *IV* estimates? Are they getting closer to the true values as the sample size increases, or not? If not, why not?

(g) Estimate the model $y = \beta_1 + \beta_2 x + e$ by instrumental variables using a sample consisting of the first $N = 10$ observations and the instrument z_2. Repeat using

$N=20$, $N=100$, and $N=500$. What do you observe about the *IV* estimates? Are they getting closer to the true values as the sample size increases, or not? If not, why not? Comparing the results using z_1 alone to those using z_2 alone, which instrument leads to more precise estimation? Why is this so?

(h) Estimate the model $y=\beta_1 + \beta_2 x + e$ by instrumental variables using a sample consisting of the first $N=10$ observations and the instruments z_1 and z_2. Repeat using $N=20$, $N=100$, and $N=500$. What do you observe about the *IV* estimates? Are they getting closer to the true values as the sample size increases, or not? If not, why not? Is estimation more precise using two instruments than one, as in parts (f) and (g)?

10.7* A consulting firm run by Mr. John Chardonnay is investigating the relative efficiency of wine production at 75 California wineries. John sets up the production function

$$Q_i = \beta_1 + \beta_2 MGT_i + \beta_3 CAP_i + \beta_4 LAB_i + e_i$$

where Q_i is an index of wine output for the ith winery, taking into account both quantity and quality, MGT_i is a variable that reflects the efficiency of management, CAP_i is an index of capital input, and LAB_i is an index of labor input. Because he cannot get data on management efficiency, John collects observations on the number years of experience ($XPER_i$) of each winery manager and uses that variable in place of MGT_i. The 75 observations are stored in the file *chard.dat*.

(a) Estimate the revised equation using least squares and comment on the results.

(b) Find corresponding interval estimates for wine output at wineries that have the sample average values for labor and capital and have managers with
  (i) 10 years experience
  (ii) 20 years experience
  (iii) 30 years experience.

(c) John is concerned that the proxy variable $XPER_i$ might be correlated with the error term. He decides to do a Hausman test, using the manager's age (AGE_i) as an instrument for $XPER_i$. Regress $XPER_i$ on AGE_i, CAP_i and LAB_i and save the residuals. Include these residuals as an extra variable in the equation you estimated in part (a), and comment on the outcome of the Hausman test.

(d) Use the instrumental variables estimator to estimate the equation

$$Q_i = \beta_1 + \beta_2 XPER_i + \beta_3 CAP_i + \beta_4 LAB_i + e_i$$

with AGE_i, CAP_i, and LAB_i as the instrumental variables. Comment on the results and compare them with those obtained in part (a).

(e) Find corresponding interval estimates for wine output at wineries that have the sample average values for labor and capital and have managers with
  (i) 10 years experience
  (ii) 20 years experience
  (iii) 30 years experience.
Compare these interval estimates with those obtained in part (b).

10.8 The labor supply of married women has been a subject of a great deal of economic research. A classic work[6] is that of Professor Tom Mroz, who kindly provided us his data. The data file is *mroz.dat* and the variable definitions are in the file *mroz.def*. The

---

[6] Mroz, T.A. (1987) "The sensitivity of an empirical model of a married woman's hours of work to economic and statistical assumptions," *Econometrica*, 55, 765–800.

data file contains information on women who have worked in the previous year and those who have not. The variable indicating whether a woman worked is *LFP*, labor force participation, which takes the value 1 if a woman worked and 0 if she did not. Use only the data on women who worked for the following exercises. Consider the following supply equation specification

$$HOURS = \beta_1 + \beta_2 \ln(WAGE) + \beta_3 EDUC + \beta_4 AGE + \beta_5 KIDSL6$$
$$+ \beta_6 KIDS618 + \beta_7 NWIFEINC + e$$

The variable *NWIFEINC* is defined as

$$NWIFEINC = FAMINC - WAGE \times HOURS$$

(a) Considering the woman's labor market experience *EXPER* and its square, $EXPER^2$ to be instruments for $\ln(WAGE)$, test the endogeneity of $\ln(WAGE)$ using the Hausman test.

(b) Estimate the reduced form equation

$$\ln(WAGE) = \pi_1 + \pi_2 EDUC + \pi_3 AGE + \pi_4 KIDSL6 + \pi_5 KIDS618$$
$$+ \pi_6 NWIFEINC + \pi_7 EXPER + \pi_8 EXPER^2 + v$$

using least squares estimation and test the joint significance of *EXPER* and $EXPER^2$. Do these instruments seem adequate?

(c) In this problem we have one surplus instrument. Check the validity of the surplus instrument using the test suggested in Section 10.4.3. What do you conclude about the validity of the overidentifying variable?

(d) It is also possible in the supply equation that the woman's level of education is endogenous, due to the omission of ability from the model. Discuss the suitability of using as instruments the woman's mother's education (*MOTHEREDUC*), her father's education (*FATHEREDUC*), her husband's education (*HEDUC*), and the woman's number of siblings (*SIBLINGS*).

(e) Estimate the reduced form equations for *EDUC* and $\ln(WAGE)$ including all instruments in (b) and the potential instruments listed in (d). In each reduced form equation test the joint significance of *EXPER*, $EXPER^2$, *MOTHEREDUC*, *FATHEREDUC*, *HEDUC*, and *SIBLINGS*.

(f) Use the results of (e) to carry out a Hausman test of the endogeneity of *EDUC* and $\ln(WAGE)$.

(g) Compute the *2SLS* estimates of the supply equation, assuming that *EDUC* and $\ln(WAGE)$ are endogenous. Discuss the estimates' signs and significance. Are there any surprises?

(h) Test the validity of the overidentifying instruments based on part (g).

(i) Write a 200-word summary of what you have discovered in this exercise about the labor supply of married women.

10.9 Consider a supply model for edible chicken, which the U.S. Department of Agriculture calls "broilers." The data for this exercise is in the file *newbroiler.dat*, which is adapted from the data provided by Epple and McCallum (2006).[7] The data

---

[7] "Simultaneous equation econometrics: The missing example," *Economic Inquiry*, 44(2), 374–384. We would like to thank Professor Bennett McCallum for his generous help.

are annual, 1950–2001, but in the estimations use data from 1960–1999. The supply equation is

$$\ln(QPROD_t) = \beta_1 + \beta_2 \ln(P_t) + \beta_3 \ln(PF_t) + \beta_4 TIME_t + \ln(QPROD_{t-1}) + e_t^s$$

where $QPROD$ = aggregate production of young chickens, P = real price index of fresh chicken, PF = real price index of broiler feed, $TIME = 1, \ldots, 52$. This supply equation is dynamic, with lagged production on the right-hand side. This predetermined variable is known at time t and is treated as exogenous. $TIME (= 1, 2, \ldots, 52)$ is included to capture technical progress in production. Some potential *external* instrumental variables are $\ln(Y_t)$ where Y is real per capita income; $\ln(PB_t)$ where PB is the real price of beef; $POPGRO$ = percentage population growth from year $t - 1$ to t; $\ln(P_{t-1})$ = lagged log of real price of chicken; $\ln(EXPTS)$ = log of exports of chicken.

(a) Estimate the supply equation by least squares. Discuss the estimation results. Are the signs and significance what you anticipated?

(b) Estimate the supply equation using an instrumental variables estimator with all available instruments. Compare these results to those in (a).

(c) Test the endogeneity of $\ln(P_t)$ using the regression-based Hausman test described in Section 10.4.1.

(d) Check whether the instruments are adequate, using the test for weak instruments described in Section 10.4.2. What do you conclude?

(e) Do you suspect the validity of any instruments on logical grounds? If so, which ones, and why? Check the instrument validity using the test procedure described in Section 10.4.3.

Appendix 10A Conditional and Iterated Expectations

In this appendix we provide some results related to conditional expectations. See Appendix B.3 for preliminary definitions.

10A.1 CONDITIONAL EXPECTATIONS

In Appendix B.3, we defined the conditional probability distribution. If X and Y are two random variables with joint probability distribution $f(x, y)$, then the conditional probability distribution of Y given X is $f(y|x)$. We can use this conditional *pdf* to compute the **conditional mean** of Y given X. That is, we can obtain the expected value of Y given that $X = x$. The conditional expectation $E(Y|X = x)$ is the average (or mean) value of Y given that X takes the value x. In the discrete case it is defined to be

$$E(Y|X = x) = \sum_y yP(Y = y|X = x) = \sum_y yf(y|x) \tag{10A.1}$$

Similarly we can define the **conditional variance** of Y given X. This is the variance of the conditional distribution of Y given X. In the discrete case it is

$$\text{var}(Y|X = x) = \sum_y \left[y - E(Y|X = x)\right]^2 f(y|x)$$

10A.2   ITERATED EXPECTIONS

The **law of iterated expectations** says that the expected value of Y is equal to the expected value of the conditional expectation of Y given X. That is,

$$E(Y) = E_X[E(Y|X)] \tag{10A.2}$$

What this means becomes clearer with the following demonstration that it is true in the discrete case. We will use two facts about probability distributions discussed in Appendix B.3. First, the marginal *pdf* of Y is $f(y) = \Sigma_x f(x, y)$ and second, the joint *pdf* of X and Y can be expressed as $f(x, y) = f(y|x) f(x)$ [see Appendix B, equation (B.5)]. Then,

$$E(Y) = \sum_y yf(y) = \sum_y y\left[\sum_x f(x, y)\right]$$

$$= \sum_y y\left[\sum_x f(y|x) f(x)\right]$$

$$= \sum_x \left[\sum_y yf(y|x)\right] f(x) \qquad \text{(by changing order of summation)}$$

$$= \sum_x E(Y|X = x) f(x)$$

$$= E_X[E(Y|X)]$$

In the final expression $E_X[\ ]$ means that the expectation of the term in brackets is taken assuming that X is random. So the expected value of Y can be found by finding its conditional expectation given X, and then taking the expected value of the result with respect to X.

Two other results can be shown to be true in the same way:

$$E(XY) = E_X[XE(Y|X)] \tag{10A.3}$$

and

$$\text{cov}(X, Y) = E_X[(X - \mu_X)E(Y|X)] \tag{10A.4}$$

10A.3   REGRESSION MODEL APPLICATIONS

The results above relate to assumption A10.3* made in Section 10.1.3. In the regression model $y_i = \beta_1 + \beta_2 x_i + e_i$, we have assumed that the conditional mean of y_i is $E(y_i|x_i) = \beta_1 + \beta_2 x_i$. Equivalently we have assumed that $E(e_i|x_i) = 0$. Conditional on x, the expected value of the error term is zero. Using the law of iterated expectations (10A.2), it then follows that the *unconditional* expectation of the error is also zero,

$$E(e_i) = E_x[E(e_i|x_i)] = E_x[0] = 0 \tag{10A.5}$$

Next, using (10A.3),

$$E(x_i e_i) = E_x[x_i E(e_i|x_i)] = E_x[x_i 0] = 0 \tag{10A.6}$$

and using (10A.4)

$$\text{cov}(x_i, e_i) = E_x[(x_i - \mu_x)E(e_i|x_i)] = E_x[(x_i - \mu_x)0] = 0 \qquad (10\text{A}.7)$$

Thus, if $E(e_i|x_i) = 0$ it follows that $E(e_i) = 0$, $E(x_i e_i) = 0$, and $\text{cov}(x_i, e_i) = 0$. However, from (10A.7), if $E(e_i|x_i) \neq 0$ then $\text{cov}(x_i, e_i) \neq 0$.

Appendix 10B The Inconsistency of Least Squares

Here we provide an algebraic proof that the least squares estimator is not consistent when $\text{cov}(x_i, e_i) \neq 0$. Our regression model is $y_i = \beta_1 + \beta_2 x_i + e_i$. Under A10.3* $E(e_i) = 0$, so that $E(y_i) = \beta_1 + \beta_2 E(x_i)$. Then,

- subtract this expectation from the original equation,

$$y_i - E(y_i) = \beta_2[x_i - E(x_i)] + e_i$$

- multiply both sides by $x_i - E(x_i)$

$$[x_i - E(x_i)][y_i - E(y_i)] = \beta_2[x_i - E(x_i)]^2 + [x_i - E(x_i)]e_i$$

- take expected values of both sides

$$E[x_i - E(x_i)][y_i - E(y_i)] = \beta_2 E[x_i - E(x_i)]^2 + E\{[x_i - E(x_i)]e_i\},$$

or

$$\text{cov}(x, y) = \beta_2 \text{var}(x) + \text{cov}(x, e)$$

- solve for β_2

$$\beta_2 = \frac{\text{cov}(x, y)}{\text{var}(x)} - \frac{\text{cov}(x, e)}{\text{var}(x)} \qquad (10\text{B}.1)$$

Equation (10B.1) is the basis for showing when the least squares estimator is consistent, and when it is not.

If we can assume that $\text{cov}(x_i, e_i) = 0$, then

$$\beta_2 = \frac{\text{cov}(x, y)}{\text{var}(x)} \qquad (10\text{B}.2)$$

The least squares estimator can be expressed as

$$b_2 = \frac{\Sigma(x_i - \bar{x})(y_i - \bar{y})}{\Sigma(x_i - \bar{x})^2} = \frac{\Sigma(x_i - \bar{x})(y_i - \bar{y})/(N-1)}{\Sigma(x_i - \bar{x})^2/(N-1)} = \frac{\widehat{\text{cov}(x, y)}}{\widehat{\text{var}(x)}} \qquad (10\text{B}.3)$$

This shows that the least squares estimator b_2 is the sample analog of the population relationship in equation (10B.2). The sample variance and covariance converge to the true variance and covariance as the sample size N increases, so that the least squares estimator converges to β_2. That is, if $cov(x_i, e_i) = 0$ then

$$b_2 = \frac{\widehat{cov(x, y)}}{\widehat{var(x)}} \rightarrow \frac{cov(x, y)}{var(x)} = \beta_2$$

showing that the least squares estimator is consistent.

On the other hand, if x and e are correlated, then

$$\beta_2 = \frac{cov(x, y)}{var(x)} - \frac{cov(x, e)}{var(x)}$$

The least squares estimator now converges to

$$b_2 \rightarrow \frac{cov(x, y)}{var(x)} = \beta_2 + \frac{cov(x, e)}{var(x)} \neq \beta_2 \qquad (10B.4)$$

In this case b_2 is an inconsistent estimator of β_2 and the amount of bias that exists even asymptotically, when samples can be assumed to be very large, is $cov(x, e)/var(x)$. The direction of the bias depends on the sign of the covariance between x and e. If factors in the error are positively correlated with the explanatory variable x, then the least squares estimator will overestimate the true parameter.

Appendix 10C The Consistency of the *IV* Estimator

The demonstration that the instrumental variables estimator is consistent follows the logic used in Appendix 10B. The *IV* estimator can be expressed as

$$\hat{\beta}_2 = \frac{\Sigma(z_i - \bar{z})(y_i - \bar{y})/(N-1)}{\Sigma(z_i - \bar{z})(x_i - \bar{x})/(N-1)} = \frac{\widehat{cov(z, y)}}{\widehat{cov(z, x)}} \qquad (10C.1)$$

The sample covariance converges to the true covariance in large samples, so we can say

$$\hat{\beta}_2 \rightarrow \frac{cov(z, y)}{cov(z, x)} \qquad (10C.2)$$

If the instrumental variable z is not correlated with x in both the sample data and in the population, then the instrumental variable estimator fails, since that would mean a zero in the denominator of $\hat{\beta}_2$ in (10C.1) and (10C.2). Thus for an instrumental variable to be valid, it must be uncorrelated with the error term e but correlated with the explanatory variable x.

Now, follow the same steps that led to (10B.1). We obtain

$$\beta_2 = \frac{cov(z, y)}{cov(z, x)} - \frac{cov(z, e)}{cov(z, x)} \qquad (10C.3)$$

If we can assume that $cov(z, e) = 0$, a condition we imposed on the choice of the instrumental variable z, then the instrumental variables estimator in equation (10C.2) converges in large samples to β_2,

$$\hat{\beta}_2 \rightarrow \frac{cov(z, y)}{cov(z, x)} = \beta_2 \qquad (10C.4)$$

Thus if $\text{cov}(z, e) = 0$ and $\text{cov}(z, x) \neq 0$, then the instrumental variable estimator of β_2 is consistent, in a situation in which the least squares estimator is not consistent due to correlation between x and e.

Appendix 10D The Logic of the Hausman Test

In Section 10.4.1 we present a test for whether or not an explanatory variable is endogenous using an artificial regression. Let us explore how and why this test might work. The simple regression model is

$$y = \beta_1 + \beta_2 x + e \tag{10D.1}$$

If x is correlated with the error term e, then x is endogenous and the least squares estimator is biased and inconsistent.

An instrumental variable z must be correlated with x but uncorrelated with e in order to be valid. A correlation between z and x implies that there is a linear association between them (see Appendix B.4.3). This means that we can describe their relationship as a regression

$$x = \pi_0 + \pi_1 z + v \tag{10D.2}$$

There is a correlation between x and z if, and only if, $\pi_1 \neq 0$. This regression is called a "reduced form" equation for reasons that you will discover in Chapter 11. The standard regression assumptions apply to (10D.2), in particular the error term v has mean zero, $E(v) = 0$. We can divide x into two parts, a systematic part and a random part, as

$$x = E(x) + v \tag{10D.3}$$

where $E(x) = \pi_0 + \pi_1 z$. If we knew π_0 and π_1, we could substitute (10D.3) into the simple regression model (10D.1) to obtain

$$\begin{aligned} y = \beta_1 + \beta_2 x + e &= \beta_1 + \beta_2 [E(x) + v] + e \\ &= \beta_1 + \beta_2 E(x) + \beta_2 v + e \end{aligned} \tag{10D.4}$$

Now, suppose for a moment that $E(x)$ and v can be observed and are viewed as explanatory variables in the regression $y = \beta_1 + \beta_2 E(x) + \beta_2 v + e$. Will least squares work when applied to this equation? The explanatory variable $E(x)$ is not correlated with the error term e (or v). The problem, if there is one, comes from a correlation between v (the random part of x) and e. In fact, in the regression (10D.1), any correlation between x and e implies correlation between v and e because $v = x - E(x)$.

We cannot exactly create the partition in (10D.3) because we do not know π_0 and π_1. However, we can consistently estimate the reduced form equation (10D.2) by least squares to obtain the fitted reduced form model $\hat{x} = \hat{\pi}_0 + \hat{\pi}_1 z$ and the residuals $\hat{v} = x - \hat{x}$, which we can rearrange to obtain an estimated analog of (10D.3),

$$x = \hat{x} + \hat{v} \tag{10D.5}$$

Substitute (10D.5) into the original equation (10D.1) to obtain

$$\begin{aligned} y = \beta_1 + \beta_2 x + e &= \beta_1 + \beta_2 [\hat{x} + \hat{v}] + e \\ &= \beta_1 + \beta_2 \hat{x} + \beta_2 \hat{v} + e \end{aligned} \tag{10D.6}$$

To reduce confusion, let the coefficient of $\hat{v}$ be denoted as γ, so that (10D.6) becomes

$$y = \beta_1 + \beta_2 \hat{x} + \gamma \hat{v} + e \tag{10D.7}$$

If we omit $\hat{v}$ from (10D.7) the regression becomes

$$y = \beta_1 + \beta_2 \hat{x} + e \tag{10D.8}$$

The least squares estimates of β_1 and β_2 in (10D.8) *are* the *IV* estimates, as defined in (10.22). Then, recall from Section 6.6.1, equation (6.23), that if we omit a variable from a regression that is uncorrelated with the included variable(s), there is no omitted variables bias, and in fact the least squares estimates are unchanged! This holds true in (10D.7) because the least squares residuals $\hat{v}$ are uncorrelated with $\hat{x}$ and the intercept variable. Thus the least squares estimates of β_1 and β_2 in (10D.7) and (10D.8) are identical, and are equal to the *IV* estimates. Consequently, the least squares estimators of β_1 and β_2 in (10D.7) are consistent whether or not x is exogenous, because they are the *IV* estimators.

What about γ? If x is exogenous, and hence v and e are uncorrelated, then the least squares estimator of γ in (10D.7) will also converge in large samples to β_2. However, if x is endogenous then the least squares estimator of γ in (10D.7) will *not* converge to β_2 in large samples because $\hat{v}$, like v, is correlated with the error term e. This observation makes it possible to test for whether x is exogenous by testing the equality of the estimates of β_2 and γ in (10D.7). If we reject the null hypothesis $H_0 : \beta_2 = \gamma$, then we reject the exogeneity of x, and conclude that it is endogenous.

Carrying out the test is made simpler by playing a trick on (10D.7). Add and subtract $\beta_2 \hat{v}$ to the right-hand side to obtain

$$
\begin{aligned}
y &= \beta_1 + \beta_2 \hat{x} + \gamma \hat{v} + e + \beta_2 \hat{v} - \beta_2 \hat{v} \\
&= \beta_1 + \beta_2 (\hat{x} + \hat{v}) + (\gamma - \beta_2) \hat{v} + e \\
&= \beta_1 + \beta_2 x + \delta \hat{v} + e
\end{aligned}
\tag{10D.9}
$$

Thus instead of testing $H_0 : \beta_2 = \gamma$, we can simply use an ordinary t-test of the null hypothesis $H_0 : \delta = 0$ in (10D.9), which is exactly the test we described in Section 10.4.1. This is much easier because ordinary software automatically prints out the t-statistic for this hypothesis test.

Chapter 11

Simultaneous Equations Models

Learning Objectives

Based on the material in this chapter you should be able to

1. Explain why estimation of a supply and demand model requires an alternative to ordinary least squares.
2. Explain the difference between exogenous and endogenous variables.
3. Define the "identification" problem in simultaneous equations models.
4. Define the reduced form of a simultaneous equations model and explain its usefulness.
5. Explain why it is acceptable to estimate reduced form equations by least squares.
6. Describe the two-stage least squares estimation procedure for estimating an equation in a simultaneous equations model, and how it resolves the estimation problem for least squares.

Keywords

endogenous variables	reduced form equation	simultaneous equations
exogenous variables	reduced form errors	structural parameters
identification	reduced form parameters	two-stage least squares

For most of us, our first encounter with economic models comes through studying supply and demand models, in which the market price and quantity of goods sold are *jointly determined* by the equilibrium of supply and demand. In this chapter we consider econometric models for data that are jointly determined by two or more economic relations. These **simultaneous equations** models differ from those we have considered in previous chapters because in each model there are *two* or more dependent variables rather than just one.

Simultaneous equations models also differ from most of the econometric models we have considered so far because they consist of a *set of equations*. For example, price and quantity are determined by the interaction of two equations, one for supply and the other for demand. Simultaneous equations models, which contain more than one dependent variable and more than one equation, require special statistical treatment. The least squares estimation procedure *is not* appropriate in these models and we must develop new ways to obtain reliable estimates of economic parameters.

Some of the concepts in this chapter were introduced in Chapter 10. However, reading Chapter 10 is *not* a prerequisite for reading Chapter 11, which is self-contained. If you *have* read Chapter 10, you will observe that much of what you learned there will carry over to this chapter, and how simultaneous equations models fit into the big picture. If you *have not* read Chapter 10, the references back to portions of it provide a deeper understanding of material presented in this chapter. This chapter on simultaneous equations is presented separately because its treatment was the first major contribution of econometrics to the wider field of statistics, and because of its importance in economic analysis.

11.1 A Supply and Demand Model

Supply and demand *jointly* determine the market price of a good and the quantity that is sold. Graphically, you recall that market equilibrium occurs at the intersection of the supply and demand curves, as shown in Figure 11.1. An econometric model that explains market price and quantity should consist of two equations, one for supply and the other for demand. It will be a simultaneous equations model since both equations working together determine price and quantity. A very simple model might look like the following:

$$\text{Demand:} \quad Q = \alpha_1 P + \alpha_2 X + e_d \tag{11.1}$$

$$\text{Supply:} \quad Q = \beta_1 P + e_s \tag{11.2}$$

Based on economic theory we expect the supply curve to be positively sloped, $\beta_1 > 0$, and the demand curve to be negatively sloped, $\alpha_1 < 0$. In this model we assume that the quantity demanded (Q) is a function of price (P) and income (X). Quantity supplied is taken to be a function of only price. We have omitted the intercepts to make the algebra easier. In practice we would include intercept terms in these models.

The point we wish to make very clear is that it takes *two* equations to describe the supply and demand equilibrium. The *two* equilibrium values, for price and quantity, P^* and Q^*, respectively, are determined at the same time. In this model the variables P and Q are called **endogenous** variables because their values are determined within the system we have created. The endogenous variables P and Q are *dependent* variables and both are random

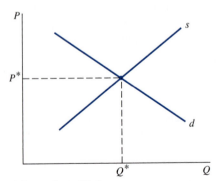

FIGURE **11.1**   Supply and demand equilibrium.

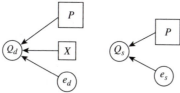

FIGURE **11.2** Influence diagrams for two regression models.

variables. The income variable X has a value that is determined outside this system. Such variables are said to be **exogenous**, and these variables are treated like usual "x" explanatory variables.

Random errors are added to the supply and demand equations for the usual reasons, and we assume that they have the usual properties

$$E(e_d) = 0, \quad \text{var}(e_d) = \sigma_d^2$$
$$E(e_s) = 0, \quad \text{var}(e_s) = \sigma_s^2 \qquad (11.3)$$
$$\text{cov}(e_d, e_s) = 0$$

Let us emphasize the difference between simultaneous equations models and regression models using influence diagrams. An "influence diagram" is a graphical representation of relationships between model components. In the previous chapters we would have modeled the supply and demand relationships as separate regressions, implying the influence diagrams in Figure 11.2. In this diagram the circles represent endogenous dependent variables and error terms. The squares represent exogenous explanatory variables. In regression analysis the direction of the influence is one-way: from the explanatory variable and the error term to the dependent variable. In this case there is no equilibrating mechanism that will lead quantity demanded to equal quantity supplied at a market-clearing price. For price to adjust to the market clearing equilibrium, there must be an influence running from P to Q and from Q to P.

Recognizing that price P and quantity Q are *jointly determined*, and that there is feedback between them, suggests the influence diagram in Figure 11.3. In the simultaneous equations model we see the two-way influence, or feedback, between P and Q because they are jointly determined. The random error terms e_d and e_s affect both P and Q, suggesting a correlation between each of the endogenous variables and each of the random error terms. As we will see this leads to failure of the least squares estimator in simultaneous equations models. Income X is an exogenous variable that affects the endogenous variables, but there is no feedback from P and Q to X.

The fact that P is an endogenous variable on the right-hand side of the supply and demand equations means that we have an explanatory variable that is random. This is contrary to the usual assumption of "fixed explanatory variables," but as we explained in Chapter 10, this by itself does not mean that standard regression analysis is inappropriate. The real problem

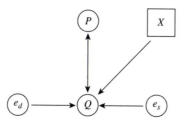

FIGURE **11.3** Influence diagram for a simultaneous equations model.

is that the endogenous regressor P is correlated with the random errors, e_d and e_s, which has a devastating impact on our usual least squares estimation procedure, making the least squares estimator biased and inconsistent.

11.2 The Reduced Form Equations

The two structural equations (11.1) and (11.2) can be solved to express the endogenous variables P and Q as functions of the exogenous variable X. This reformulation of the model is called the **reduced form** of the structural equation system. The reduced form is very important in its own right, and it also helps us understand the structural equation system. To find the reduced form we solve (11.1) and (11.2) simultaneously for P and Q.

To solve for P, set Q in the demand and supply equations to be equal,

$$\beta_1 P + e_s = \alpha_1 P + \alpha_2 X + e_d$$

Then solve for P,

$$P = \frac{\alpha_2}{(\beta_1 - \alpha_1)} X + \frac{e_d - e_s}{(\beta_1 - \alpha_1)} \tag{11.4}$$

$$= \pi_1 X + v_1$$

To solve for Q, substitute the value of P in (11.4) into either the demand or supply equation. The supply equation is simpler, so we will substitute P into (11.2) and simplify.

$$Q = \beta_1 P + e_s$$

$$= \beta_1 \left[\frac{\alpha_2}{(\beta_1 - \alpha_1)} X + \frac{e_d - e_s}{(\beta_1 - \alpha_1)} \right] + e_s \tag{11.5}$$

$$= \frac{\beta_1 \alpha_2}{(\beta_1 - \alpha_1)} X + \frac{\beta_1 e_d - \alpha_1 e_s}{(\beta_1 - \alpha_1)}$$

$$= \pi_2 X + v_2$$

The parameters π_1 and π_2 in (11.4) and (11.5) are called **reduced form parameters**. The error terms v_1 and v_2 are called **reduced form errors**.

The reduced form equations can be estimated consistently by least squares. The explanatory variable X is determined outside this system. It is not correlated with the disturbances v_1 and v_2, which themselves have the usual properties of zero mean, constant variances, and zero covariance. Thus the least squares estimator is BLUE for the purposes of estimating π_1 and π_2.

The reduced form equations are important for economic analysis. These equations relate the *equilibrium* values of the endogenous variables to the exogenous variables. Thus, if there is an increase in income X, π_1 is the expected increase in price, after market adjustments lead to a new equilibrium for P and Q. Similarly, π_2 is the expected increase in the equilibrium value of Q. (*Question*: how did we determine the directions of these changes?) Secondly, and using the same logic, the estimated reduced form equations can be used to *predict* values of equilibrium price and quantity for different levels of income. Clearly CEOs and other market analysts are interested in the ability to forecast both prices and quantities sold of their products. It is the estimated reduced form equations that make such predictions possible.

11.3 The Failure of Least Squares

In this section we explain why the least squares estimator should not be used to estimate an equation in a simultaneous equations model. For reasons that will become clear in the next section, we focus on the supply equation. In the supply equation (11.2), the endogenous variable P on the right-hand side of the equation is *correlated* with the error term e_s. We will give an intuitive explanation for the existence of this correlation here. An algebraic explanation is in Appendix 11A.

Suppose there is a small change, or blip, in the error term e_s, say Δe_s. Trace the effect of this change through the system. The blip Δe_s in the error term of (11.2) is directly transmitted to the equilibrium value of P. This follows from the reduced form (11.4) that has P on the left and e_s on the right. Every change in the supply equation error term e_s has a direct linear effect upon P. Since $\beta_1 > 0$ and $\alpha_1 < 0$, if $\Delta e_s > 0$, then $\Delta P < 0$. Thus, every time there is a change in e_s, there is an associated change in P in the opposite direction. Consequently, P and e_s are negatively correlated.

The failure of least squares estimation for the supply equation can be explained as follows: least squares estimation of the relation between Q and P gives "credit" to price (P) for the effect of changes in the error term (e_s). This occurs because we do not observe the change in the error term, but only the change in P resulting from its correlation with the error e_s. The least squares estimator of β_1 will *understate* the true parameter value in this model, because of the negative correlation between the endogenous variable P and the error term e_s. In large samples, the least squares estimator will tend to be negatively biased in this model. This bias persists even if the sample size goes to infinity, and thus the least squares estimator is inconsistent. This means that the probability distribution of the least squares estimator will ultimately "collapse" about a point that is not the true parameter value as the sample size $N \to \infty$. See Section 10.1.2 for a general discussion of "large sample" properties of estimators, and see Appendix 11A for an algebraic derivation. Here, we summarize by saying:

> The least squares estimator of parameters in a structural simultaneous equation is biased and inconsistent because of the correlation between the random error and the endogenous variables on the right-hand side of the equation.

11.4 The Identification Problem

In the supply and demand model given by (11.1) and (11.2)

- the parameters of the demand equation, α_1 and α_2, *cannot* be consistently estimated by *any* estimation method, but
- the slope of the supply equation, β_1, can be consistently estimated.

How are we able to make such statements? The answer is quite intuitive and it can be illustrated graphically. What happens when income X changes? The demand curve shifts and a new equilibrium price and quantity are created. In Figure 11.4 we show the demand curves d_1, d_2, and d_3 and equilibria, at points a, b, and c, for three levels of income. As income changes, data on price and quantity will be observed around the

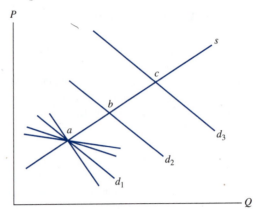

FIGURE 11.4   The effect of changing income.

intersections of supply and demand. The random errors e_d and e_s cause small shifts in the supply and demand curves, creating equilibrium observations on price and quantity that are scattered about the intersections at points a, b, and c.

The data values will trace out the *supply curve*, suggesting that we can fit a line through them to estimate the slope β_1. The data values fall along the supply curve because income is *present* in the demand curve and *absent* from the supply curve. As income changes, the demand curve shifts but the supply curve remains fixed, resulting in observations along the supply curve.

There are *no* data values falling along any of the demand curves, and there is no way to estimate their slope. Any one of an infinite number of demand curves passing through the equilibrium points could be correct. Given the data, there is no way to distinguish the true demand curve from all the rest. Through the equilibrium point a we have drawn a few demand curves, each of which could have generated the data we observe.

The problem lies with the model that we are using. There is no variable in the supply equation that will shift it relative to the demand curve. If we were to add a variable to the supply curve, say W, then each time W changed the supply curve would shift and the demand curve would stay fixed. The shifting of supply relative to a fixed demand curve (since W is *absent* from the demand equation) would create equilibrium observations along the demand curve, making it possible to estimate the slope of the demand curve and the effect of income on demand.

It is the *absence* of variables in one equation, that are *present* in another equation, that makes parameter estimation possible. A general rule, which is called a condition for *identification* of an equation, is this:

> **A NECESSARY CONDITION FOR IDENTIFICATION:** In a system of M simultaneous equations, which jointly determine the values of M endogenous variables, at least $M - 1$ variables must be absent from an equation for estimation of its parameters to be possible. When estimation of an equation's parameters is possible, then the equation is said to be *identified*, and its parameters can be estimated consistently. If less than $M - 1$ variables are omitted from an equation, then it is said to be *unidentified* and its parameters cannot be consistently estimated.

In our supply and demand model there are $M = 2$ equations, so we require at least $M - 1 = 1$ variable to be omitted from an equation to identify it. There are a total of three variables: P, Q, and X. In the demand equation none of the variables are omitted; thus it is unidentified and its parameters cannot be estimated consistently. In the supply equation, one variable, income (X), is omitted; the supply curve is identified and its parameter can be estimated.

The identification condition must be checked *before* trying to estimate an equation. If an equation is not identified, then changing the model must be considered, before it is estimated. However, changing the model should not be done in a haphazard way; no important variable should be omitted from an equation just to identify it. The structure of a simultaneous equations model should reflect your understanding of how equilibrium is achieved and should be consistent with economic theory. Creating a false model is not a good solution to the identification problem.

This paragraph is for those who have read Chapter 10. The necessary condition for identification can be expressed in an alternative but equivalent fashion. The two-stage least squares estimation procedure was developed in Chapter 10 and shown to be an instrumental variables estimator. This procedure is developed further in the next section. The number of instrumental variables required for estimation of an equation within a simultaneous equations model is equal to the number of right-hand side endogenous variables. In a typical equation within a simultaneous equations model, several exogenous variables appear on the right-hand-side. Thus instruments must come from those exogenous variables omitted from the equation in question. Consequently, identification requires that the number of excluded exogenous variables in an equation be at least as large as the number of included right-hand-side endogenous variables. This ensures an adequate number of instrumental variables.

11.5 Two-Stage Least Squares Estimation

The most widely used method for estimating the parameters of an identified structural equation is called **two-stage least squares**, which is often abbreviated as 2*SLS*. The name comes from the fact that it can be calculated using two least squares regressions. We will explain how it works by considering the supply equation in (11.2). Recall that we cannot apply the usual least squares procedure to estimate β_1 in this equation because the endogenous variable P on the right-hand side of the equation is correlated with the error term e_s.

The variable P is composed of a systematic part, which is its expected value $E(P)$, and a random part, which is the reduced form random error v_1. That is,

$$P = E(P) + v_1 = \pi_1 X + v_1 \tag{11.6}$$

In the supply equation (11.2) the portion of P that causes problems for the least squares estimator is v_1, the random part. It is v_1 that causes P to be correlated with the error term e_s. Suppose we *knew* the value of π_1. Then we could replace P in (11.2) by (11.6) to obtain

$$
\begin{aligned}
Q &= \beta_1[E(P) + v_1] + e_s \\
&= \beta_1 E(P) + (\beta_1 v_1 + e_s) \\
&= \beta_1 E(P) + e_*
\end{aligned}
\tag{11.7}
$$

In (11.7) the explanatory variable on the right-hand side is $E(P)$. It is not a random variable and it is not correlated with the error term e_*. We could apply least squares to (11.7) to consistently estimate β_1.

Of course, we cannot use the variable $E(P) = \pi_1 X$ in place of P, since we do not know the value of π_1. However, we can *estimate* π_1 using $\hat{\pi}_1$ from the reduced form equation for P. Then, a consistent estimator for $E(P)$ is

$$\hat{P} = \hat{\pi}_1 X$$

Using $\hat{P}$ as a replacement for $E(P)$ in (11.7) we obtain

$$Q = \beta_1 P + \hat{e}_* \tag{11.8}$$

In large samples, $\hat{P}$ and the random error $\hat{e}_*$ are uncorrelated, and consequently the parameter β_1 can be consistently estimated by applying least squares to (11.8).

Estimating (11.8) by least squares generates the so-called **two-stage least squares** estimator of β_1, which is consistent and normally distributed in large samples. To summarize, the *two stages* of the estimation procedure are

1. Least squares estimation of the reduced form equation for P and the calculation of its predicted value, $\hat{P}$.

2. Least squares estimation of the structural equation in which the right-hand-side endogenous variable P is replaced by its predicted value $\hat{P}$.[1]

11.5.1   THE GENERAL TWO-STAGE LEAST SQUARES ESTIMATION PROCEDURE

The two-stage least squares estimation procedure can be used to estimate the parameters of any identified equation within a simultaneous equations system. In a system of M simultaneous equations let the endogenous variables be $y_1, y_2, \ldots, y_M$. Let there be K exogenous variables, $x_1, x_2, \ldots, x_K$. Suppose the first structural equation within this system is

$$y_1 = \alpha_2 y_2 + \alpha_3 y_3 + \beta_1 x_1 + \beta_2 x_2 + e_1 \tag{11.9}$$

If this equation is identified, then its parameters can be estimated in the two steps:

1. Estimate the parameters of the reduced form equations

$$y_2 = \pi_{12} x_1 + \pi_{22} x_2 + \cdots + \pi_{K2} x_K + v_2$$
$$y_3 = \pi_{13} x_1 + \pi_{23} x_2 + \cdots + \pi_{K3} x_K + v_3$$

by least squares and obtain the predicted values

$$\hat{y}_2 = \hat{\pi}_{12} x_1 + \hat{\pi}_{22} x_2 + \cdots + \hat{\pi}_{K2} x_K$$
$$\hat{y}_3 = \hat{\pi}_{13} x_1 + \hat{\pi}_{23} x_2 + \cdots + \hat{\pi}_{K3} x_K \tag{11.10}$$

---

[1] The discussion above is an intuitive explanation of the two-stage least squares estimator. For a general explanation of this estimation method, see Section 10.3. There we derive the two-stage least squares estimator and discuss its properties.

2. Replace the endogenous variables, y_2 and y_3, on the right-hand side of the structural equation (11.9) by their predicted values from (11.10)

$$y_1 = \alpha_2 \hat{y}_2 + \alpha_3 \hat{y}_3 + \beta_1 x_1 + \beta_2 x_2 + e_1^*$$

Estimate the parameters of this equation by least squares.

11.5.2   THE PROPERTIES OF THE TWO-STAGE LEAST SQUARES ESTIMATOR

We have described how to obtain estimates for structural equation parameters in identified equations. The properties of the two-stage least squares estimator are

- The 2SLS estimator is a biased estimator, but it is consistent.
- In large samples the 2SLS estimator is approximately normally distributed.
- The variances and covariances of the 2SLS estimator are unknown in small samples, but for large samples we have expressions for them, which we can use as approximations. These formulas are built into econometric software packages, which report standard errors, and t-values, just like an ordinary least squares regression program.
- If you obtain 2SLS estimates by applying two least squares regressions using ordinary least squares regression software, the standard errors and t-values reported in the *second* regression are *not* correct for the 2SLS estimator. Always use specialized 2SLS or instrumental variables software when obtaining estimates of structural equations.

11.6 An Example of Two-Stage Least Squares Estimation

Truffles are a gourmet delight. They are edible fungi that grow below the ground. In France they are often located by collectors who use pigs to sniff out the truffles and "point" to them. Actually the pigs dig frantically for the truffles because pigs have an insatiable taste for them, as do the French, and they must be restrained from "pigging out" on them. Consider a supply and demand model for truffles:

$$\text{Demand:} \quad Q_i = \alpha_1 + \alpha_2 P_i + \alpha_3 PS_i + \alpha_4 DI_i + e_i^d \qquad (11.11)$$

$$\text{Supply:} \quad Q_i = \beta_1 + \beta_2 P_i + \beta_3 PF_i + e_i^s \qquad (11.12)$$

In the demand equation Q is the quantity of truffles traded in a particular French market-place, indexed by i, P is the market price of truffles, PS is the market price of a substitute for real truffles (another fungus much less highly prized), and DI is per capita monthly disposable income of local residents. The supply equation contains the market price and quantity supplied. Also it includes PF, the price of a factor of production, which in this case is the hourly rental price of truffle-pigs used in the search process. In this model we assume that P and Q are endogenous variables. The exogenous variables are PS, DI, PF, and the intercept variable.

11.6.1 IDENTIFICATION

Before thinking about estimation, check the identification of each equation. The rule for identifying an equation is that in a system of M equations at least $M - 1$ variables must be omitted from each equation in order for it to be identified. In the demand equation the variable PF is not included and thus the necessary $M - 1 = 1$ variable is omitted. In the supply equation both PS and DI are absent; more than enough to satisfy the identification condition. Note too that the variables that are omitted are different for each equation, ensuring that each contains at least one *shift* variable not present in the other. We conclude that each equation in this system is identified and can thus be estimated by two-stage least squares.

Why are the variables omitted from their respective equations? Because economic theory says that the price of a factor of production should affect supply but not demand, and the price of substitute goods and income should affect demand and not supply. The specifications we used are based on the microeconomic theory of supply and demand.

11.6.2 THE REDUCED FORM EQUATIONS

The reduced form equations express each endogenous variable, P and Q, in terms of the exogenous variables PS, DI, PF, and the intercept variable, plus an error term. They are

$$Q_i = \pi_{11} + \pi_{21}PS_i + \pi_{31}DI_i + \pi_{41}PF_i + v_{i1}$$
$$P_i = \pi_{12} + \pi_{22}PS_i + \pi_{32}DI_i + \pi_{42}PF_i + v_{i2}$$

We can estimate these equations by least squares since the right-hand-side variables are exogenous and uncorrelated with the random errors v_{i1} and v_{i2}. The data file *truffles.dat* contains 30 observations on each of the endogenous and exogenous variables. The price P is measured in $ per ounce, Q is measured in ounces, PS is measured in $ per ounce, DI is in $1000, and PF is the hourly rental rate ($) for a truffle-finding pig. A few of the observations are shown in Table 11.1. The results of the least squares estimations of the reduced form equations for Q and P are reported in Table 11.2.

In Table 11.2a we see that the estimated coefficients are statistically significant and thus we conclude that the exogenous variables affect the quantity of truffles traded, Q, in this reduced form equation. The $R^2 = 0.697$, and the overall F-statistic is 19.973, which has a p-value of less than 0.0001. In Table 11.2b the estimated coefficients are statistically

Table 11.1 **Representative Truffle Data**

OBS	P	Q	PS	DI	PF
1	29.64	19.89	19.97	2.103	10.52
2	40.23	13.04	18.04	2.043	19.67
3	34.71	19.61	22.36	1.870	13.74
4	41.43	17.13	20.87	1.525	17.95
5	53.37	22.55	19.79	2.709	13.71
		Summary statistics			
Mean	62.72	18.46	22.02	3.53	22.75
Std. Dev.	18.72	4.61	4.08	1.04	5.33

Table 11.2a   **Reduced Form for Quantity of Truffles (Q)**

Variable	Coefficient	Std. Error	t-Statistic	Prob.
C	7.8951	3.2434	2.4342	0.0221
PS	0.6564	0.1425	4.6051	0.0001
DI	2.1672	0.7005	3.0938	0.0047
PF	−0.5070	0.1213	−4.1809	0.0003

Table 11.2b   **Reduced Form for Price of Truffles (P)**

Variable	Coefficient	Std. Error	t-Statistic	Prob.
C	−32.5124	7.9842	−4.0721	0.0004
PS	1.7081	0.3509	4.8682	0.0000
DI	7.6025	1.7243	4.4089	0.0002
PF	1.3539	0.2985	4.5356	0.0001

significant, indicating that the exogenous variables have an effect on market price P. The $R^2 = 0.889$ implies a good fit of the reduced form equation to the data. The overall F-statistic value is 69.189 that has a p-value of less than 0.0001, indicating that the model has statistically significant explanatory power.

11.6.3   THE STRUCTURAL EQUATIONS

The reduced form equations are used to obtain $\hat{P}_i$ that will be used in place of P_i on the right-hand side of the supply and demand equations in the second stage of two-stage least squares. From Table 11.2b we have

$$\hat{P}_i = \hat{\pi}_{12} + \hat{\pi}_{22}PS_i + \hat{\pi}_{32}DI_i + \hat{\pi}_{42}PF_i$$

$$= -32.512 + 1.708PS_i + 7.603DI_i + 1.354PF_i$$

The *2SLS* results are given in Tables 11.3a and 11.3b. The estimated demand curve results are in Table 11.3a. Note that the coefficient of price is negative, indicating that as the market price rises, the quantity demanded of truffles declines, as predicted by the law of demand. The standard errors that are reported are obtained from *2SLS* software. They and the t-values are valid in large samples. The p-value indicates that the estimated slope of the demand curve is significantly different from zero. Increases in the price of the substitute for truffles increase the demand for truffles, which is a characteristic of substitute goods. Finally the effect of income is positive, indicating that truffles are a normal good. All of these variables

Table 11.3a   **2SLS Estimates for Truffle Demand**

Variable	Coefficient	Std. Error	t-Statistic	Prob.
C	−4.2795	5.5439	−0.7719	0.4471
P	−0.3745	0.1648	−2.2729	0.0315
PS	1.2960	0.3552	3.6488	0.0012
DI	5.0140	2.2836	2.1957	0.0372

Table 11.3b   **2SLS Estimates for Truffle Supply**

Variable	Coefficient	Std. Error	t-Statistic	Prob.
C	20.0328	1.2231	16.3785	0.0000
P	0.3380	0.0249	13.5629	0.0000
PF	−1.0009	0.0825	−12.1281	0.0000

have statistically significant coefficients and thus have an effect upon the quantity demanded.

The supply equation results appear in Table 11.3b. As anticipated, increases in the price of truffles increase the quantity supplied, and increases in the rental rate for truffle-seeking pigs, which is an increase in the cost of a factor of production, reduces supply. Both of these variables have statistically significant coefficient estimates.

11.7 Supply and Demand at the Fulton Fish Market

The Fulton Fish Market has operated in New York City for over 150 years. The prices for fish are determined daily by the forces of supply and demand. Kathryn Graddy[2] collected daily data on the price of whiting (a common type of fish), quantities sold, and weather conditions during the period December 2, 1991 to May 8, 1992. These data are in the file *fultonfish.dat*. Fresh fish arrive at the market about midnight. The wholesalers, or dealers, sell to buyers for retail shops and restaurants. The first interesting feature of this example is to consider whether prices and quantities are *simultaneously* determined by supply and demand at all.[3] We might consider this a market with a fixed, perfectly inelastic supply. At the start of the day, when the market is opened, the supply of fish available for the day is fixed. If supply is fixed, with a vertical supply curve, then price is demand determined, with higher demand leading to higher prices, but no increase in the quantity supplied. If this is true then the feedback between prices and quantities is eliminated. Such models are said to be **recursive** and the demand equation can be estimated by ordinary least squares rather than the more complicated two-stage least squares procedure.

However whiting fish can be kept for several days before going bad, and dealers can decide to sell less, and add to their inventory, or buffer stock, if the price is judged too low, in hope for better prices the next day. Or, if the price is unusually high on a given day, then sellers can increase the day's catch with additional fish from their buffer stock. Thus despite the perishable nature of the product, and the daily resupply of fresh fish, daily price is simultaneously determined by supply and demand forces. The key point here is that "simultaneity" does not require that events occur at a simultaneous moment in time.

Let us specify the demand equation for this market as

$$\ln(QUAN_t) = \alpha_1 + \alpha_2\ln(PRICE_t) + \alpha_3 MON_t + \alpha_4 TUE_t + \alpha_5 WED_t$$
$$+ \alpha_6 THU_t + e_t^d \tag{11.13}$$

---

[2] See Kathryn Graddy (2006) "The Fulton Fish Market," *Journal of Economic Perspectives*, 20(2), 207–220. The authors would like to thank Professor Graddy for permission to use the data from her study.

[3] The authors thank Peter Kennedy for this observation. See Kathryn Graddy and Peter E. Kennedy (2006) "When are supply and demand determined recursively rather than simultaneously? Another look at the Fulton Fish Market data," working paper. See http://www.economics.ox.ac.uk/members/kathryn.graddy/research.htm.

where $QUAN_t$ is the quantity sold, in pounds, and $PRICE_t$ the average daily price per pound. Note that we are using the subscript "t" to index observations for this relationship because of the time series nature of the data. The remaining variables are dummy variables for the days of the week, with Friday being omitted. The coefficient α_2 is the price elasticity of demand, which we expect to be negative. The daily dummy variables capture day-to-day shifts in demand. The supply equation is

$$\ln(QUAN_t) = \beta_1 + \beta_2\ln(PRICE_t) + \beta_3 STORMY_t + e_t^s \qquad (11.14)$$

The coefficient β_2 is the price elasticity of supply. The variable $STORMY$ is a dummy variable indicating stormy weather during the previous 3 days. This variable is important in the supply equation because stormy weather makes fishing more difficult, reducing the supply of fish brought to market.

11.7.1 IDENTIFICATION

Prior to estimation, we must determine if the supply and demand equation parameters are identified. The necessary condition for an equation to be identified is that in this system of $M = 2$ equations, it must be true that at least $M - 1 = 1$ variable must be omitted from each equation. In the demand equation the weather variable $STORMY$ is omitted, but it does appear in the supply equation. In the supply equation, the four daily dummy variables that are included in the demand equation are omitted. Thus the demand equation shifts daily, while the supply remains fixed (since the supply equation does not contain the daily dummy variables), thus tracing out the supply curve, making it identified, as shown in Figure 11.4. Similarly, stormy conditions shift the supply curve relative to a fixed demand, tracing out the demand curve, and making it identified.

11.7.2 THE REDUCED FORM EQUATIONS

The reduced form equations specify each endogenous variable as a function of all exogenous variables

$$\ln(QUAN_t) = \pi_{11} + \pi_{21}MON_t + \pi_{31}TUE_t + \pi_{41}WED_t + \pi_{51}THU_t$$
$$+ \pi_{61}STORMY_t + v_{t1} \qquad (11.15)$$

$$\ln(PRICE_t) = \pi_{12} + \pi_{22}MON_t + \pi_{32}TUE_t + \pi_{42}WED_t + \pi_{52}THU_t$$
$$+ \pi_{62}STORMY_t + v_{t2} \qquad (11.16)$$

These reduced form equations can be estimated by least squares because the right-hand-side variables are all exogenous and uncorrelated with the reduced form errors v_{t1} and v_{t2}. Using the Graddy's data (*fultonfish.dat*) we estimate these reduced form equations and report them in Table 11.4. Estimation of the reduced form equations is the first step of two-stage least squares estimation of the supply and demand equations. It is a requirement for successful two-stage least squares estimation that the estimated coefficients in the reduced form for the right-hand-side endogenous variable be statistically significant. We have specified the

Table 11.4a   **Reduced Form for ln(Quantity) Fish**

Variable	Coefficient	Std. Error	t-Statistic	Prob.
C	8.8101	0.1470	59.9225	0.0000
STORMY	−0.3878	0.1437	−2.6979	0.0081
MON	0.1010	0.2065	0.4891	0.6258
TUE	−0.4847	0.2011	−2.4097	0.0177
WED	−0.5531	0.2058	−2.6876	0.0084
THU	0.0537	0.2010	0.2671	0.7899

Table 11.4b   **Reduced Form for ln(Price) Fish**

Variable	Coefficient	Std. Error	t-Statistic	Prob.
C	−0.2717	0.0764	−3.5569	0.0006
STORMY	0.3464	0.0747	4.6387	0.0000
MON	−0.1129	0.1073	−1.0525	0.2950
TUE	−0.0411	0.1045	−0.3937	0.6946
WED	−0.0118	0.1069	−0.1106	0.9122
THU	0.0496	0.1045	0.4753	0.6356

structural equations (11.13) and (11.14) with ln($QUAN$) as the left-hand-side variable and ln($PRICE$) as the right-hand-side endogenous variable. Thus the key reduced form equation is (11.16) for ln($PRICE$). In this equation

- To identify the supply curve, the daily dummy variables must be jointly significant. This implies that at least one of their coefficients is statistically different from zero, meaning that there is at least one significant shift variable in the demand equation, which permits us to reliably estimate the supply equation.

- To identify the demand curve, the variable $STORMY$ must be statistically significant, meaning that supply has a significant shift variable, so that we can reliably estimate the demand equation.

Why is this so? The identification discussion in Section 11.4 requires only the presence of shift variables, not their significance. The answer comes from a great deal of econometric research in the past decade, which shows that the two-stage least squares estimator performs very poorly if the shift variables are not strongly significant.[4] Recall that to implement two-stage least squares we take the predicted value from the reduced form regression and include it in the structural equations in place of the right-hand-side endogenous variable. That is, we calculate

$$\widehat{\ln(PRICE_t)} = \hat{\pi}_{12} + \hat{\pi}_{22}MON_t + \hat{\pi}_{32}TUE_t + \hat{\pi}_{42}WED_t + \hat{\pi}_{52}THU_t + \hat{\pi}_{62}STORMY_t$$

where $\hat{\pi}_{k2}$ are the least squares estimates of the reduced form coefficients, and then replace ln($PRICE$) with $\widehat{\ln(PRICE_t)}$. To illustrate our point let us focus on the problem of

---

[4] See James H. Stock and Mark W. Watson (2007) *Introduction to Econometrics, 2nd edition*, Pearson Education, Appendix 12.5 for a more technical, but still intuitive discussion.

Table 11.5   *2SLS* **Estimates for Fish Demand**

Variable	Coefficient	Std. Error	t-Statistic	Prob.
C	8.5059	0.1662	51.1890	0.0000
ln(PRICE)	−1.1194	0.4286	−2.6115	0.0103
MON	−0.0254	0.2148	−0.1183	0.9061
TUE	−0.5308	0.2080	−2.5518	0.0122
WED	−0.5664	0.2128	−2.6620	0.0090
THU	0.1093	0.2088	0.5233	0.6018

estimating the supply equation (11.14) and take the extreme case that $\hat{\pi}_{22} = \hat{\pi}_{32} = \hat{\pi}_{42} = \hat{\pi}_{52} = 0$, meaning that the coefficients on the daily dummy variables are all identically zero. Then

$$\overline{\ln(PRICE_t)} = \hat{\pi}_{12} + \hat{\pi}_{62}STORMY_t$$

If we replace ln(PRICE) in the supply equation (11.14) with this predicted value, there will be *exact* collinearity between $\overline{\ln(PRICE_t)}$ and the variable *STORMY*, which is already in the supply equation, and two-stage least squares will fail. If the coefficient estimates on the daily dummy variables are not exactly zero, but are jointly insignificant, it means there will be severe collinearity in the second stage, and while the two-stage least squares estimates of the supply equation can be computed, they will be unreliable. In Table 11.4b, showing the reduced form estimates for (11.16), none of the daily dummy variables are statistically significant. Also, the joint *F*-test of significance of the daily dummy variables has *p*-value 0.65, so that we cannot reject the null hypothesis that all these coefficients are zero.[5] In this case the supply equation is not identified in practice, and we will not report estimates for it.

However, *STORMY* is statistically significant, meaning that the demand equation may be reliably estimated by two-stage least squares. An advantage of two-stage least squares estimation is that each equation can be treated and estimated separately, so the fact that the supply equation is not reliably estimable does not mean that we cannot proceed with estimation of the demand equation. The check of statistical significance of the sets of shift variables for the structural equations should be carried out each time a simultaneous equations model is formulated.

11.7.3   TWO-STAGE LEAST SQUARES ESTIMATION OF FISH DEMAND

Applying two-stage least squares estimation to the demand equation we obtain the results as given in Table 11.5. The price elasticity of demand is estimated to be −1.12, meaning that a 1% increase in fish price leads to about a 1.12% decrease in the quantity demanded, and this estimate is statistically significant at the 5% level. The dummy variable coefficients are negative and statistically significant for Tuesday and Wednesday, indicating that demand is lower on these days relative to Friday.

---

[5] Even if the variables are jointly significant there may be a problem. The significance must be "strong." An *F*-value <10 is cause for concern. This problem is the same as that of weak instruments in instrumental variables estimation. See Section 10.4.2.

11.8 Exercises

11.8.1 PROBLEMS

11.1 Can you suggest a method for using the reduced form equations (11.4) and (11.5) to obtain an estimate of the slope of the supply function $Q = \beta_1 P + e_s$? In particular, suppose that the estimated reduced form equations are $\hat{P} = 18X$ and $\hat{Q} = 5X$. What is an estimated value of β_1? (*Hint:* look at the expressions for π_1 and π_2).

11.2 Supply and demand curves as traditionally drawn in economics principles classes have price (P) on the vertical axis and quantity (Q) on the horizontal axis.
   (a) Take the estimates in Table 11.3 and on graph paper accurately sketch the supply and demand equations. For these sketches set the values of the exogenous variables DI, PS, and PF to be $DI^* = 3.5$, $PF^* = 23$, and $PS^* = 22$.
   (b) What are the equilibrium values of P and Q from (a)?
   (c) Calculate the predicted equilibrium values of P and Q using the estimated reduced form equations from Table 11.2, using the same values of the exogenous variables as those in (a). Compare these predicted equilibrium values to those in (b). Do they seem to agree, or not?
   (d) On the graph from part (a), show the consequences of increasing income from $DI^* = 3.5$ to $DI^{**} = 4.5$, holding the values of PF and PS at the values given in (a).
   (e) Calculate the change in equilibrium price P and quantity Q in (d) based on your sketch.
   (f) Using the results in part (e), calculate the income elasticity of demand implied by the shift in part (d). Calculate an estimate of the income elasticity of demand from the estimated reduced form equation in Table 11.2a and compare to your graphical solution.

11.3 Suppose you want to estimate a wage equation for married women of the form

$$\ln(WAGE) = \beta_1 + \beta_2 HOURS + \beta_3 EDUC + \beta_4 EXPER + e$$

where $WAGE$ is hourly wage, $HOURS$ is the number of hours worked per week, $EDUC$ is years of education, and $EXPER$ is years of experience. Your classmate observes that higher wages can bring forth increased work effort, and that married women with young children may reduce their hours of work to take care of them, so that there may be an auxiliary relationship such as

$$HOURS = \alpha_1 + \alpha_2 \ln(WAGE) + \alpha_3 KIDS + u$$

where $KIDS$ is the number of children under the age of six in the woman's household.
   (a) Can the wage equation be estimated satisfactorily using the least squares estimator? If not, why not?
   (b) Is the wage equation "identified"? What does the term identification mean in this context?
   (c) If you seek an alternative to least squares estimation for the wage equation, suggest an estimation procedure and how (step by step and NOT a computer command) it is carried out.

11.4   Consider the following simultaneous equations model. Assume that x is exogenous.

$$y_1 = \beta x + e$$

$$y_2 = \alpha y_1 + u$$

(a) How would you estimate the parameter β? Is it identified?
(b) How would you estimate the parameter α? Is it identified?

11.8.2   COMPUTER EXERCISES

11.5   (a) Use your computer software for two-stage least squares or instrumental variables estimation, and the 30 observations in the file *truffles.dat* to obtain *2SLS* estimates of the system in equations (11.11) and (11.12). Compare your results to those in Table 11.3.

(b) Using the *2SLS* estimated equations, compute the price elasticity of supply and demand "at the means." The summary statistics for the data are given in Table 11.1. [*Hint*: See Appendix A, equation (A.7).] Comment on the signs and magnitudes of these elasticities.

11.6   Estimate equations (11.11) and (11.12) by least squares regression, ignoring the fact that they form a simultaneous system. Use the data in *truffles.dat*. Compare your results to those in Table 11.3. Do the signs of the least squares estimates agree with economic reasoning?

11.7*   Supply and demand curves as traditionally drawn in economics principles classes have price (P) on the vertical axis and quantity (Q) on the horizontal axis.

(a) Rewrite the truffle demand and supply equations in (11.11) and (11.12) with price P on the left-hand side. What are the anticipated signs of the parameters in this rewritten system of equations?

(b) Using the data in the file *truffles.dat*, estimate the supply and demand equations that you have formulated in (a) using two-stage least squares. Are the signs correct? Are the estimated coefficients significantly different from zero?

(c) Estimate the price elasticity of demand "at the means" using the results from (b).

(d) On graph paper accurately sketch the supply and demand equations using the estimates from part (b). For these sketches set the values of the exogenous variables DI, PS, and PF to be $DI^* = 3.5$, $PF^* = 23$, and $PS^* = 22$.

(e) What are the equilibrium values of P and Q obtained in part (d)? Calculate the predicted equilibrium values of P and Q using the estimated reduced form equations from Table 11.2, using the same values of the exogenous variables. How well do they agree?

(f) Estimate the supply and demand equations that you have formulated in (a) using ordinary least squares. Are the signs correct? Are the estimated coefficients significantly different from zero? Compare the results to those in part (b).

11.8*   The labor supply of married women has been a subject of a great deal of economic research. A classic work[6] is that of Professor Tom Mroz, who kindly provided us his data. The data file is *mroz.dat* and the variable definitions are in the file *mroz.def*. The data file contains information on women who have worked in the previous year

---

[6] Mroz, T.A. (1987) "The sensitivity of an empirical model of a married woman's hours of work to economic and statistical assumptions," *Econometrica*, 55, 765–800.

and those who have not. The variable indicating whether a woman worked is *LFP*, labor force participation, which takes the value 1 if a woman worked and 0 if she did not.

(a) Calculate the summary statistics for the variables: wife's age, number of children less than 6 years old in the household, and the family income for the women who worked ($LFP = 1$) and those who did not ($LFP = 0$). Comment on any differences you observe.

(b) Consider the following supply equation specification

$$HOURS = \beta_1 + \beta_2 \ln(WAGE) + \beta_3 EDUC + \beta_4 AGE + \beta_5 KIDSL6$$
$$+ \beta_6 KIDS618 + \beta_7 NWIFEINC + e$$

The variable *NWIFEINC* is defined as

$$NWIFEINC = FAMINC - WAGE \times HOURS$$

What signs do you expect each of the coefficients to have, and why? What does *NWIFEINC* measure?

(c) Estimate the supply equation in (b) using least squares regression on *only the women who worked* ($LFP = 1$). You must create *NWIFEINC* and $\ln(WAGE)$. Did things come out as expected? If not, why not?

(d) Estimate the reduced form equation by least squares for the women who worked

$$\ln(WAGE) = \pi_1 + \pi_2 EDUC + \pi_3 AGE + \pi_4 KIDSL6 + \pi_5 KIDS618$$
$$+ \pi_6 NWIFEINC + \pi_7 EXPER + \pi_8 EXPER^2 + v$$

Based on the estimated reduced form, what is the effect upon wage of an additional year of education?

(e) Check the identification of the supply equation, considering the availability of the extra instruments *EXPER* and its square.

(f) Estimate the supply equation by two-stage least squares, using software designed for this purpose. Discuss the signs and significance of the estimated coefficients.

11.9 This exercise examines a supply and demand model for edible chicken, which the U.S. Department of Agriculture calls "broilers." The data for this exercise is in the file *newbroiler.dat*, which is adapted from the data provided by Epple and McCallum (2006).[7]

(a) Consider the demand equation

$$\ln(Q_t) = \alpha_1 + \alpha_2 \ln(Y_t) + \alpha_3 \ln(P_t) + \alpha_4 \ln(PB_t) + e_t^d$$

where $Q =$ per capita consumption of chicken, in pounds; $Y =$ real per capita income; $P =$ real price of chicken; $PB =$ real price of beef. What are the endogenous variables? What are the exogenous variables?

---

[7] "Simultaneous equation econometrics: The missing example," *Economic Inquiry*, 44(2), 374–384. We would like to thank Professor Bennett McCallum for his generous help.

(b) The demand equation in (a) suffers from severe serial correlation. In the AR(1) model $e_t^d = \rho e_{t-1}^d + v_t^d$ the value of ρ is near 1. Epple and McCallum estimate the model in "first difference" form,

$$\ln(Q_t) = \alpha_1 + \alpha_2\ln(Y_t) + \alpha_3\ln(P_t) + \alpha_4\ln(PB_t) + e_t^d$$
$$-[\ln(Q_{t-1}) = \alpha_1 + \alpha_2\ln(Y_{t-1}) + \alpha_3\ln(P_{t-1}) + \alpha_4\ln(PB_{t-1}) + e_{t-1}^d]$$
$$\overline{\Delta\ln(Q_t) = \alpha_2\Delta\ln(Y_t) + \alpha_3\Delta\ln(P_t) + \alpha_4\Delta\ln(PB_t) + v_t^d}$$

(i) What changes do you notice after this transformation? (ii) Are the parameters of interest affected? (iii) If $\rho = 1$ have we solved the serial correlation problem? (iv) What is the interpretation of the "Δ" variables like $\Delta\ln(Q_t)$? (*Hint:* see Appendix A.4.6) (v) What is the interpretation of the parameter α_2? (vi) What signs do you expect for each of the coefficients? Explain.

(c) The supply equation is

$$\ln(QPROD_t) = \beta_1 + \beta_2\ln(P_t) + \beta_3\ln(PF_t) + \beta_4 TIME_t$$
$$+ \beta_5\ln(QPROD_{t-1}) + e_t^s$$

where $QPROD$ = aggregate production of young chickens, PF = nominal price index of broiler feed, $TIME$ = time index with $1950 = 1$ to $2001 = 52$. This supply equation is dynamic, with lagged production on the right-hand side. This predetermined variable is known at time t and is treated as exogenous. $TIME$ is included to capture technical progress in production. (i) What are the endogenous variables? (ii) What are the exogenous variables? (iii) What is the interpretation of the parameter β_2? (iv) What signs do you expect for each of the parameters?

(d) Is the order condition for identification satisfied for the demand equation in (b) (in differenced form) and the supply equation in (c)?

(e) Use the data from 1960 to 1999 to estimate the reduced form equation for $\Delta\ln(P_t)$. (i) Discuss the estimated model, including the signs and significance of the estimated coefficients. (ii) Use the estimated reduced form equation to predict the approximate percentage change in prices for the year 2000 and its 95% prediction (confidence) interval. Is the actual value within the interval?

(f) Use the data from 1960 to 1999 to estimate the reduced form equation for $\ln(P_t)$. (i) Discuss the estimated model, including the signs and significance of the estimated coefficients. (ii) Use the estimated reduced form equation to predict the real price for the year 2000 and its 95% prediction (confidence) interval. Is the actual value within the interval?

(g) Use the data from 1960 to 1999 to estimate the two equations by two-stage least squares, using the exogenous variables in the system as instruments. (i) Discuss your results, paying particular attention to the signs, magnitudes, and significance of the estimated coefficients? (ii) Interpret the numerical magnitudes of the estimates for α_2 and β_2.

(h) Reestimate the supply equation using the log of exports, $\ln(EXPTS)$, as an additional instrumental variable. Discuss the logic of using this variable as an instrument? (*Hint:* What characteristics do good instruments have?)

11.10 Reconsider the example used in Section 11.7 on the supply and demand for fish at the Fulton Fish Market. The data are in the file *fultonfish.dat*.

(a) Carry out two-stage least squares estimation of the supply equation in equation (11.14). Comment on the signs and significance of the estimated coefficients. What is your estimate of the elasticity of supply?

(b) It is possible that bad weather on shore reduces attendance at restaurants, which in turn may reduce the demand for fish at the market. Add the variables *RAINY* and *COLD* to the demand equation in (11.13). Derive the algebraic reduced form for $\ln(PRICE)$ for this new specification.

(c) Estimate the reduced form you derived in (b) by least squares. Test the joint significance of the variables *MON, TUE, WED, THU, RAINY,* and *COLD.* Are these variables jointly significant at the $\alpha = 0.05$ level? Is the addition of *RAINY* and *COLD* to the demand sufficient to allow reliable two-stage least squares estimation of the supply equation? Explain.

(d) Obtain two-stage least squares estimates and ordinary least squares estimates of the augmented demand equation in part (b) and the supply equation (11.14). Discuss the estimates, their signs, and significance. Are the estimates consistent with economic theory?

(e) Augment the supply equation with the variable *MIXED,* which indicates poor but not *STORMY* weather conditons. For the demand equation, use the augmented model in part (b). Derive the algebraic reduced form for $\ln(PRICE)$ for this new specification. Estimate this reduced form by least squares. Test the joint significance of the variables *MON, TUE, WED, THU, RAINY,* and *COLD.* Has this improved the chances of estimating the supply equation by two-stage least squares? Explain your answer.

(f) Estimate the supply and demand equations in (e) by two-stage least squares and ordinary least squares and discuss the results.

11.11 Reconsider the example used in Section 11.7 on the supply and demand for fish at the Fulton Fish Market. The data are in the file *fultonfish.dat.* In this exercise we explore the behavior of the market on days in which changes in fish inventories are large relative to those days on which inventory changes are small. Graddy and Kennedy (2006) anticipate that prices and quantities will demonstrate simultaneity on days with large changes in inventories, as these are days when sellers are demonstrating their responsiveness to prices. On days when inventory changes are small, the anticipation is that feedback between prices and quantities is broken, and simultaneity is no longer an issue.

(a) Use the subset of data for days in which inventory change is large, as indicated by the variable $CHANGE = 1$. Estimate the reduced form equation (11.16) and test the significance of *STORMY.* Discuss the importance of this test for the purpose of estimating the demand equation by two-stage least squares.

(b) Obtain the least squares residuals $\hat{v}_{t2}$ from the reduced form equation estimated in (a). Carry out a Hausman test[8] for the endogeneity of $\ln(PRICE)$ by adding $\hat{v}_{t2}$ as an extra variable to the demand equation in (11.13), estimating the resulting model by least squares, and testing the significance of $\hat{v}_{t2}$ using a standard t-test. If $\hat{v}_{t2}$ is a significant variable in this augmented regression then we may conclude that $\ln(PRICE)$ is endogenous. Based on this test, what do you conclude?

(c) Estimate the demand equation using two-stage least squares and ordinary least squares using the data when $CHANGE = 1$, and discuss these estimates. Compare them to the estimates in Table 11.5.

---

[8] This test is introduced in Section 10.4.1 and further discussed in Appendix 10D.

(d) Estimate the reduced form equation (11.16) for the data when $CHANGE = 0$. Compare these reduced form estimates to those in (a) and those in Table 11.4b.

(e) Obtain the least squares residuals $\hat{v}_{t2}$ from the reduced form equation estimated in (d). Carry out a Hausman test for the endogeneity of $\ln(PRICE)$, as described in part (b). Based on this test, what do you conclude?

(f) Obtain the two-stage least squares and the ordinary least squares estimates for the demand equation for the data when $CHANGE = 0$. Compare these estimates to each other and to the estimates in (c). Discuss the relationships between them.

Appendix 11A An Algebraic Explanation of the Failure of Least Squares

First, let us obtain the covariance between P and e_s.

$$
\begin{aligned}
\text{cov}(P, e_s) &= E[P - E(P)][e_s - E(e_s)] \\
&= E(Pe_s) && (\text{since } E(e_s) = 0) \\
&= E[\pi_1 X + v_1]e_s && (\text{substitute for } P) \\
&= E\left[\frac{e_d - e_s}{\beta_1 - \alpha_1}\right]e_s && (\text{since } \pi_1 X \text{ is exogenous}) && (11A.1) \\
&= \frac{-E(e_s^2)}{\beta_1 - \alpha_1} && (\text{since } e_d, e_s \text{ assumed uncorrelated}) \\
&= \frac{-\sigma_s^2}{\beta_1 - \alpha_1} < 0
\end{aligned}
$$

What impact does the negative covariance in (11A.1) have on the least squares estimator? The least squares estimator of the supply equation (11.2) (which does not have an intercept term) is

$$b_1 = \frac{\sum P_i Q_i}{\sum P_i^2} \tag{11A.2}$$

Substitute for Q from the supply equation (11.2) and simplify,

$$b_1 = \frac{\sum P_i(\beta_1 P_i + e_{si})}{\sum P_i^2} = \beta_1 + \sum\left(\frac{P_i}{\sum P_i^2}\right)e_{si} = \beta_1 + \sum h_i e_{si} \tag{11A.3}$$

where $h_i = P_i / \sum P_i^2$. The expected value of the least squares estimator is

$$E(b_1) = \beta_1 + \sum E(h_i e_{si}) \neq \beta_1$$

The least squares estimator is biased because e_s and P are correlated implying $E(h_i e_{si}) \neq 0$.

In large samples there is a similar failure. Multiply through the supply equation by price P, take expectations, and solve.

$$PQ = \beta_1 P^2 + Pe_s$$

$$E(PQ) = \beta_1 E(P^2) + E(Pe_s)$$

$$\beta_1 = \frac{E(PQ)}{E(P^2)} - \frac{E(Pe_s)}{E(P^2)}$$

In large samples, as $N \to \infty$, sample analogs of expectations, which are averages, converge to the expectations. That is, $\sum Q_i P_i / N \to E(PQ)$, $\sum P_i^2 / N \to E(P^2)$. Consequently, because the covariance between P and e_s is negative, from (11A.1),

$$b_1 = \frac{\sum Q_i P_i / N}{\sum P_i^2 / N} \to \frac{E(PQ)}{E(P^2)} = \beta_1 + \frac{E(Pe_s)}{E(P^2)} = \beta_1 - \frac{\sigma_s^2 / (\beta_1 - \alpha_1)}{E(P^2)} < \beta_1$$

The least squares estimator of the slope of the supply equation (11.2), in large samples, converges to a value less than β_1.

Chapter *12*

Nonstationary Time–Series Data and Cointegration

Learning Objectives

Based on the material in this chapter, you should be able to

1. Explain the differences between stationary and nonstationary time-series processes.
2. Describe the general behavior of an autoregressive process and a random walk process.
3. Explain why we need "unit root" tests, and state implications of the null and alternative hypotheses.
4. Explain what is meant by the statement that a series is "integrated of order 1" or I(1).
5. Perform Dickey–Fuller and augmented Dickey–Fuller tests for stationarity.
6. Explain the meaning of a "spurious regression."
7. Explain the concept of cointegration and test whether two series are cointegrated.
8. Explain how to choose an appropriate model for regression analysis with time-series data.

Keywords

autoregressive process	order of integration	stochastic process
cointegration	random walk process	stochastic trend
Dickey–Fuller tests	random walk with drift	tau statistic
difference stationary	spurious regressions	trend stationary
mean reversion	stationary	unit root tests
nonstationary		

In 2003 the Nobel[1] Prize in Economics was awarded jointly to two distinguished econometricians: Professor Robert F. Engle "for methods of analyzing economic time series with time-varying volatility (ARCH)" and Professor Clive W.J. Granger "for methods of analyzing economic time series with common trends (cointegration)." The aim of this and the following two chapters is to discuss the background that prompted these

---

[1] For more details, see http://nobelprize.org/economics/laureates/.

contributions, and to show how the proposed methods have revolutionized the way we conduct econometrics with time-series data.

The analysis of time-series data is of vital interest to many groups, such as macroeconomists studying the behavior of national and international economies, finance economists analyzing the stock market, and agricultural economists predicting supplies and demands for agricultural products. For example, if we are interested in forecasting the growth of gross domestic product or inflation, we look at various indicators of economic performance and consider their behavior over recent years. Alternatively, if we are interested in a particular business, we analyze the history of the industry in an attempt to predict potential sales. In each of these cases, we are analyzing time-series data.

We have already worked with time-series data in Chapter 9 and discovered how regression models for these data often have special characteristics designed to capture their dynamic nature. We saw how including lagged values of the dependent variable or explanatory variables as regressors, or considering lags in the errors, can be used to model dynamic relationships. We also showed how autoregressive models can be used in forecasting. However, an important assumption maintained throughout Chapter 9 was that the variables have a property called stationarity. It is time now to learn the difference between stationary and nonstationary variables. Many economic variables are nonstationary and, as you will learn, the consequences of nonstationary variables for regression modeling are profound.

The aim of this chapter is to discuss the time-series concepts of **stationarity** (and **nonstationarity**) and **cointegration**. The seminal contributions of the Nobel laureates are to show that the econometric consequences of nonstationarity can be quite severe and to offer methods to overcome them.

12.1 Stationary and Nonstationary Variables

Plots of the time series of some important economic variables for the US economy are displayed in Figure 12.1. The data for these figures can be found in the file *usa.dat*. The figures on the left-hand side are the real gross domestic product (a measure of aggregate economic production), the annual inflation rate (a measure of changes in the aggregate price level), the Federal Funds rate (the interest rate on overnight loans between banks), and the 3-year Bond rate (interest rate on a financial asset to be held for 3 years). Observe how the GDP variable displays upward trending behavior, while the inflation rate appears to "wander up and down" with no discernable pattern or trend. Similarly, both the Federal Funds rate and the Bond rate show "wandering up and down" behavior. The figures on the right-hand side of Figure 12.1 are the changes of the corresponding variables on the left-hand side.

The change in a variable is an important concept that is used repeatedly in this chapter; it is worth dwelling on its definition. The change in a variable y_t, also known as its first difference, is given by $\Delta y_t = y_t - y_{t-1}$. Thus Δy_t is the change in the value of the variable y from period $t - 1$ to period t.

The time series of the changes on the right-hand side of Figure 12.1 display behavior that can be described as irregular ups and downs, or more like fluctuations. Note that while changes in the inflation rate and the two interest rates appear to fluctuate around a constant value, the changes in the GDP variable appear to fluctuate around an upward trend. The first question we address in this chapter is: which data series represent stationary variables and which are observations on nonstationary variables?

Formally, a time series y_t is stationary if its mean and variance are constant over time, and if the covariance between two values from the series depends only on the length of time

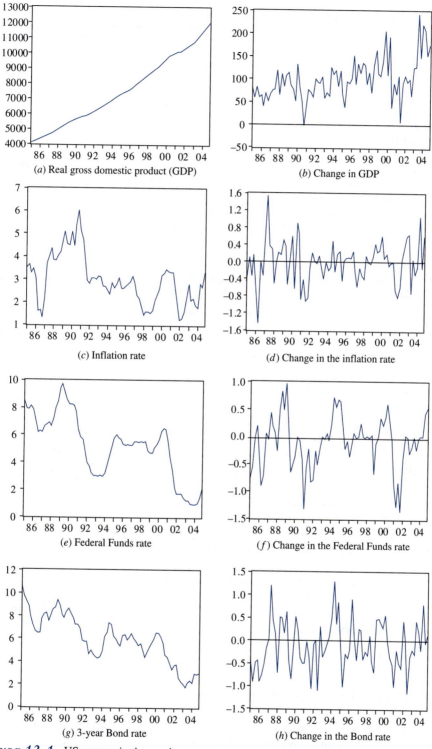

(a) Real gross domestic product (GDP)

(b) Change in GDP

(c) Inflation rate

(d) Change in the inflation rate

(e) Federal Funds rate

(f) Change in the Federal Funds rate

(g) 3-year Bond rate

(h) Change in the Bond rate

FIGURE *12.1* US economic time series.

Table 12.1   **Sample Means of Time Series Shown in Figure 12.1**

Variable	Sample periods	
	1985:1 to 1994:4	1995:1 to 2004:4
Real GDP (a)	5587.7	9465.4
Inflation rate (c)	3.5	2.4
Federal Funds rate (e)	6.3	4.1
Bond rate (g)	7.2	4.7
Change in GDP (b)	79.9	119.1
Change in the inflation rate (d)	−0.03	0.02
Change in the Federal Fund rate (f)	−0.1	−0.1
Change in the Bond rate (h)	−0.1	−0.1

separating the two values, and not on the actual times at which the variables are observed. That is, the time series y_t is stationary if for all values, and every time period, it is true that:

$$E(y_t) = \mu \quad \text{(constant mean)} \tag{12.1a}$$

$$\text{var}(y_t) = \sigma^2 \quad \text{(constant variance)} \tag{12.1b}$$

$$\text{cov}(y_t, y_{t+s}) = \text{cov}(y_t, y_{t-s}) = \gamma_s \quad \text{(covariance depends on } s, \text{not } t) \tag{12.1c}$$

The first condition, that of a constant mean, is the feature that has received the most attention. To appreciate this condition for stationarity look at the plots shown in Figure 12.1 and their sample means shown in Table 12.1. With the exception of the change in GDP, the sample means for the change variables shown on the right-hand side of Figure 12.1 are similar across different sample periods, whereas the sample means for the variables in the original levels, shown on the left-hand side, as well as the change in GDP, differ across sample periods. Thus, while the inflation rate, the Federal Funds rate, and the Bond rate display characteristics of nonstationarity, their changes display characteristics of stationarity. For GDP, both its level and its change display characteristics of nonstationarity. Nonstationary series with nonconstant means are often described as **not** having the property of **mean reversion**. That is, stationary series have the property of mean reversion.

Looking at the sample means of time-series variables is a convenient indicator as to whether a series is stationary or nonstationary, but this does not constitute a hypothesis test. A formal test is described in Section 12.3. However, before we introduce the test, it is useful to revisit the first-order autoregressive model that was introduced in Chapter 9.

12.1.1 THE FIRST-ORDER AUTOREGRESSIVE MODEL

Let y_t be an economic variable that we observe over time. In line with most economic variables, we assume that y_t is random, since we cannot perfectly predict it. We never know the values of random variables until they are observed. The econometric model generating a time-series variable y_t is called a **stochastic** or **random process**. A sample of observed y_t values is called a particular **realization** of the stochastic process. It is one of many possible paths that the stochastic process could have taken. Univariate time-series models are examples of stochastic processes where a single variable y is related to past values of itself and current and past error terms. In contrast to regression modeling, univariate time-series models do not contain any explanatory variables (no x's).

The autoregressive model of order 1, the AR(1) model, is a useful univariate time-series model for explaining the difference between stationary and nonstationary series. It is given by

$$y_t = \rho y_{t-1} + v_t, \quad |\rho| < 1 \tag{12.2a}$$

where the errors v_t are independent, with zero mean and constant variance σ_v^2, and may be normally distributed. In the context of time-series models, the errors are sometimes known as "shocks" or "innovations." As we will see, the assumption $|\rho| < 1$ implies y_t is stationary. The AR(1) process shows that each realization of the random variable y_t contains a proportion ρ of last period's value y_{t-1} plus an error v_t drawn from a distribution with mean 0 and variance σ_v^2. Since we are concerned with only one lag, the model is described as an autoregressive model of order 1. In general an AR(p) model includes lags of the variable y_t up to y_{t-p}. An example of an AR(1) time series with $\rho = 0.7$, and independent $N(0,1)$ random errors is shown in Figure 12.2a. Note that the data have been artificially generated. Observe how the time series fluctuates around zero and has no trend-like behavior, a characteristic of stationary series.

The value "zero" is the constant mean of the series, and it can be determined by doing some algebra known as recursive substitution. Consider the value of y at time $t = 1$, then its value at time $t = 2$ and so on. These values are

$$y_1 = \rho y_0 + v_1$$
$$y_2 = \rho y_1 + v_2 = \rho(\rho y_0 + v_1) + v_2 = \rho^2 y_0 + \rho v_1 + v_2$$
$$\vdots$$
$$y_t = v_t + \rho v_{t-1} + \rho^2 v_{t-2} + \cdots + \rho^t y_0$$

The mean of y_t is

$$E(y_t) = E(v_t + \rho v_{t-1} + \rho^2 v_{t-2} + \cdots) = 0$$

since the error v_t has zero mean and the value of $\rho^t y_0$ is negligible for a large t. The variance can be shown to be a constant $\sigma_v^2/(1 - \rho^2)$ while the covariance between two errors s periods apart γ_s can be shown to be $\sigma_v^2 \rho^s/(1 - \rho^2)$. Thus, the AR(1) model in (12.2a) is a classic example of a stationary process with a zero mean.

Real world data rarely have a zero mean. We can introduce a nonzero mean μ by replacing y_t in (12.2a) with $(y_t - \mu)$ as follows:

$$(y_t - \mu) = \rho(y_{t-1} - \mu) + v_t$$

which can then be rearranged as

$$y_t = \alpha + \rho y_{t-1} + v_t, \quad |\rho| < 1 \tag{12.2b}$$

where $\alpha = \mu(1 - \rho)$. That is, we can accommodate a nonzero mean in y_t by either working with the "de-meaned" variable $(y_t - \mu)$ or introducing the intercept term α in the

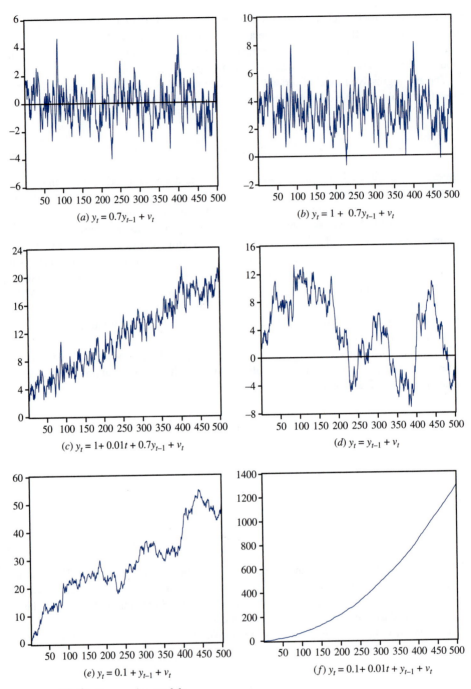

FIGURE 12.2   Time-series models.

autoregressive process of y_t as in (12.2b). Corresponding to these two ways, we describe the "de-meaned" variable $(y_t - \mu)$ as being stationary around zero, or the variable y_t as stationary around its mean value $\mu = \alpha/(1 - \rho)$.

An example of a time series that follows this model, with $\alpha = 1$, $\rho = 0.7$ is shown in Figure 12.2b. We have used the same values of the error v_t as in Figure 12.2a, so the figure shows the added influence of the constant term. Note that the series now fluctuates around a nonzero value. This nonzero value is the constant mean of the series

$$E(y_t) = \mu = \alpha/(1 - \rho) = 1/(1 - 0.7) = 3.33$$

Another extension to (12.2a) is to consider an AR(1) model fluctuating around a linear trend $(\mu + \delta t)$. As we have seen in Figure 12.1, some real world data appear to exhibit a trend. In this case, we let the "de-trended" series $(y_t - \mu - \delta t)$ behave like an autoregressive model

$$(y_t - \mu - \delta t) = \rho(y_{t-1} - \mu - \delta(t-1)) + v_t, \quad |\rho| < 1$$

which can be rearranged as

$$y_t = \alpha + \rho y_{t-1} + \lambda t + v_t \tag{12.2c}$$

where $\alpha = (\mu(1 - \rho) + \rho\delta)$ and $\lambda = \delta(1 - \rho)$. An example of a time series that can be described by this model with $\rho = 0.7, \alpha = 1$, and $\delta = 0.01$ is shown in Figure 12.2c. The de-trended series $(y_t - \mu - \delta t)$ also has a constant variance and covariances that depend only on the time separating observations, not the time at which they are observed. In other words, the "de-trended" series is stationary. An astute reader may have noted that the mean of y_t, $E(y_t) = \mu + \delta t$ depends on t, which implies that y_t is nonstationary. While this observation is correct, when $|\rho| < 1$, y_t is more usually described as stationary around the deterministic trend line $\mu + \delta t$. This is discussed further in Section 12.5.2.

12.1.2 RANDOM WALK MODELS

Consider the special case of $\rho = 1$ in equation (12.2a)

$$y_t = y_{t-1} + v_t \tag{12.3a}$$

This model is known as the random walk model. Equation (12.3a) shows that each realization of the random variable y_t contains last period's value y_{t-1} plus an error v_t. An example of a time series that can be described by this model is shown in Figure 12.2d. These time series are called **random walks** because they appear to wander slowly upward or downward, with no real pattern; the values of sample means calculated from subsamples of observations will be dependent on the sample period. This is a characteristic of nonstationary series.

We can understand the "wandering" behavior of random walk models by doing some recursive substitution.

$$y_1 = y_0 + v_1$$
$$y_2 = y_1 + v_2 = (y_0 + v_1) + v_2 = y_0 + \sum_{s=1}^{2} v_s$$
$$\vdots$$
$$y_t = y_{t-1} + v_t = y_0 + \sum_{s=1}^{t} v_s$$

The random walk model contains an initial value y_0 (often set to zero because it is so far in the past that its contribution to y_t is negligible) plus a component that is the sum of the past stochastic terms $\sum_{s=1}^{t} v_s$. This latter component is often called the **stochastic trend**. This term arises because a stochastic component v_t is added for each time t and because it causes the time series to trend in unpredictable directions. If the variable y_t is subjected to a sequence of positive shocks, $v_t > 0$, followed by a sequence of negative shocks, $v_t < 0$, it will have the appearance of wandering upward then downward.

We have used the fact that y_t is a sum of errors to explain graphically the nonstationary nature of the random walk. We can also use it to show algebraically that the conditions for stationarity do not hold. Recognizing that the v_t are independent, taking the expectation and the variance of y_t yields, for a fixed initial value y_0,

$$E(y_t) = y_0 + E(v_1 + v_2 + \cdots + v_t) = y_0$$

$$\text{var}(y_t) = \text{var}(v_1 + v_2 + \cdots + v_t) = t\sigma_v^2$$

The random walk has a mean equal to its initial value and a variance that increases over time, eventually becoming infinite. Although the mean is constant, the increasing variance implies that the series may not return to its mean, and so sample means taken for different periods are not the same.

Another nonstationary model is obtained by adding a constant term to (12.3a)

$$y_t = \alpha + y_{t-1} + v_t \tag{12.3b}$$

This model is known as the **random walk with drift**. Equation (12.3b) shows that each realization of the random variable y_t contains an intercept (the drift component α) plus last period's value y_{t-1} plus the error v_t. An example of a time series that can be described by this model (with $\alpha = 0.1$) is shown in Figure 12.2e. Notice how the time-series data appear to be "wandering" as well as "trending" upward. In general, random walk with drift models show definite trends either upward (when the drift α is positive) or downward (when the drift α is negative).

Again, we can get a better understanding of this behavior by applying recursive substitution:

$$y_1 = \alpha + y_0 + v_1$$
$$y_2 = \alpha + y_1 + v_2 = \alpha + (\alpha + y_0 + v_1) + v_2 = 2\alpha + y_0 + \sum_{s=1}^{2} v_s$$
$$\vdots$$
$$y_t = \alpha + y_{t-1} + v_t = t\alpha + y_0 + \sum_{s=1}^{t} v_s$$

The value of y at time t is made up of an initial value y_0, the stochastic trend component $(\sum_{s=1}^{t} v_s)$ and now a **deterministic trend** component $t\alpha$. It is called a deterministic trend because a fixed value α is added for each time t. The variable y wanders up and down as well as increases by a fixed amount at each time t. The mean and variance of y_t are

$$E(y_t) = t\alpha + y_0 + E(v_1 + v_2 + v_3 + \cdots + v_t) = t\alpha + y_0$$
$$\text{var}(y_t) = \text{var}(v_1 + v_2 + v_3 + \cdots + v_t) = t\sigma_v^2$$

In this case both the constant mean and constant variance conditions for stationarity are violated.

We can extend the random walk model even further by adding a time trend:

$$y_t = \alpha + \delta t + y_{t-1} + v_t \tag{12.3c}$$

An example of a time series that can be described by this model (with $\alpha = 0.1$; $\delta = 0.01$) is shown in Figure 12.2f. Note how the addition of a time-trend variable t strengthens the trend behavior. We can see the amplification using the same algebraic manipulation as before:

$$y_1 = \alpha + \delta + y_0 + v_1$$

$$y_2 = \alpha + \delta 2 + y_1 + v_2 = \alpha + 2\delta + (\alpha + \delta + y_0 + v_1) + v_2 = 2\alpha + 3\delta + y_0 + \sum_{s=1}^{2} v_s$$

$$\vdots$$

$$y_t = \alpha + \delta t + y_{t-1} + v_t = t\alpha + \left(\frac{t(t+1)}{2}\right)\delta + y_0 + \sum_{s=1}^{t} v_s$$

where we have used the formula for a sum of an arithmetic progression,

$$1 + 2 + 3 + \cdots + t = t(t+1)/2$$

The additional term has the effect of strengthening the trend behavior.

To recap, we have considered the autoregressive class of models and have shown that they display properties of stationarity when $|\rho| < 1$. We have also discussed the random walk class of models when $\rho = 1$. We showed that random walk models display properties of nonstationarity. Now, go back and compare the real world data in Figure 12.1 with those in Figure 12.2. Ask yourself what models might have generated the different data series in Figure 12.1. In the next few sections we shall consider how to test which series in Figure 12.1 exhibit properties associated with stationarity, and which series exhibit properties associated with nonstationarity.

12.2 Spurious Regressions

The main reason why it is important to know whether a time series is stationary or nonstationary before one embarks on a regression analysis is that there is a danger of obtaining apparently significant regression results from unrelated data when nonstationary series are used in regression analysis. Such regressions are said to be **spurious**.

To illustrate the problem, let us take two independent random walks:

$$rw_1: \quad y_t = y_{t-1} + v_{1t}$$

$$rw_2: \quad x_t = x_{t-1} + v_{2t}$$

where v_{1t} and v_{2t} are independent $N(0,1)$ random errors. Two such series are shown in Figure 12.3a—the data are in the file *spurious.dat*. These series were generated independently and, in truth, have no relation to one another, yet when we plot them, as we have done in Figure 12.3b, we see a positive relationship between them. If we estimate a simple regression of series one (rw_1) on series two (rw_2), we obtain the following results:

$$\widehat{rw_{1t}} = 17.818 + 0.842\, rw_{2t}, \quad R^2 = 0.70$$

$$(t) \qquad\qquad (40.837)$$

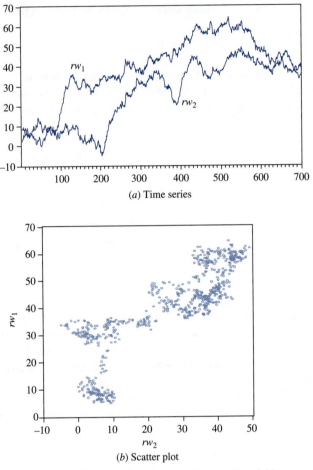

(a) Time series

(b) Scatter plot

FIGURE **12.3** Time series and scatter plot of two random walk variables.

This result suggests that the simple regression model fits the data well $(R^2 = 0.70)$,[2] and that the estimated slope is significantly different from zero. In fact, the t-statistic is huge! These results are, however, completely meaningless, or spurious. The apparent significance of the relationship is false. It results from the fact that we have related one series with a stochastic trend to another series with another stochastic trend. In fact, these series have nothing in common nor are they causally related in any way. Similar and more dramatic results are obtained when random walk with drift series are used in regressions.

In other words, when nonstationary time series are used in a regression model, the results may spuriously indicate a significant relationship when there is none. In these cases the least squares estimator and least squares predictor do not have their usual properties, and t-statistics are not reliable. Since many macroeconomic time series are nonstationary, it is particularly important to take care when estimating regressions with macroeconomic variables.

How then can we test whether a series is stationary or nonstationary and how do we conduct regression analysis with nonstationary data? The former is discussed in Section 12.3, while the latter is considered in Section 12.4.

---

[2] Typically, such regressions will also have low Durbin–Watson statistics, see Appendix 9B.

12.3 Unit Root Tests for Stationarity

There are many tests for determining whether a series is stationary or nonstationary. The most popular one, and the one that we discuss, is the Dickey–Fuller test. As noted in our discussion of the autoregressive and random walk models, stochastic processes can include or exclude a constant term and can include or exclude a time trend. There are three variations of the Dickey–Fuller test designed to take account of the role of the constant term and the trend. We begin by describing the test equations and hypotheses for these three cases and then outline the testing procedure.

12.3.1 DICKEY–FULLER TEST 1 (NO CONSTANT AND NO TREND)

This test is based on the discussion in Section 12.1 where we note that the AR(1) process $y_t = \rho y_{t-1} + v_t$ is stationary when $|\rho| < 1$, but, when $\rho = 1$, it becomes the nonstationary random walk process $y_t = y_{t-1} + v_t$. Hence, one way to test for stationarity is to examine the value of ρ. In other words, we test whether ρ is equal to one or significantly less than one. Tests for this purpose are known as **unit root tests for stationarity**.

To formalize this procedure a little more, consider again the AR(1) model:

$$y_t = \rho y_{t-1} + v_t \tag{12.4}$$

where the v_t are independent random errors with zero mean and constant variance σ_v^2. We can test for nonstationarity by testing the null hypothesis that $\rho = 1$ against the alternative that $|\rho| < 1$, or simply $\rho < 1$. This one-sided (lower tail) test is put into a more convenient form by subtracting y_{t-1} from both sides of (12.4) to obtain:

$$y_t - y_{t-1} = \rho y_{t-1} - y_{t-1} + v_t$$
$$\Delta y_t = (\rho - 1)y_{t-1} + v_t$$
$$= \gamma y_{t-1} + v_t \tag{12.5a}$$

where $\gamma = \rho - 1$ and $\Delta y_t = y_t - y_{t-1}$. Then, the hypotheses can be written in terms of either ρ or γ as follows:

$$H_0 : \rho = 1 \Leftrightarrow H_0 : \gamma = 0$$
$$H_1 : \rho < 1 \Leftrightarrow H_1 : \gamma < 0$$

Note that the null hypothesis is that the series is nonstationary. In other words, if we do not reject the null, we conclude that it is a nonstationary process; if we reject the null hypothesis that $\gamma = 0$, then we conclude that the series is stationary.

12.3.2 DICKEY–FULLER TEST 2 (WITH CONSTANT BUT NO TREND)

The second Dickey–Fuller test includes a constant term in the test equation:

$$\Delta y_t = \alpha + \gamma y_{t-1} + v_t \tag{12.5b}$$

The null and alternative hypotheses are the same as before. In this case, if we do not reject the null hypothesis that $\gamma = 0$ (or $\rho = 1$), we conclude that the series is nonstationary. If we reject the null hypothesis that $\gamma = 0$, we conclude that the series is stationary.

12.3.3 Dickey–Fuller Test 3 (With Constant and With Trend)

The third Dickey–Fuller test includes a constant and a trend in the test equation:

$$\Delta y_t = \alpha + \gamma y_{t-1} + \lambda t + v_t \qquad (12.5c)$$

As before the null and alternative hypotheses are $H_0 : \gamma = 0$ and $H_1 : \gamma < 0$. If we do not reject the null hypothesis that $\gamma = 0$ ($\rho = 1$), we conclude that the series is nonstationary. If we reject the null hypothesis that $\gamma = 0$, we conclude that the series is stationary.

12.3.4 The Dickey–Fuller Testing Procedure

When carrying out a Dickey–Fuller test, a useful first step is to plot the time series of the original observations on the variable. A suitable equation for the test is then chosen on the basis of a visual inspection of the plot.

- If the series appears to be wandering or fluctuating around a sample average of zero, use test equation (12.5a).
- If the series appears to be wandering or fluctuating around a sample average that is nonzero, use test equation (12.5b).
- If the series appears to be wandering or fluctuating around a linear trend, use test equation (12.5c).

To test the hypothesis in all three cases, we simply estimate the test equation by least squares and examine the t-statistic for the hypothesis that $\gamma = 0$. Unfortunately this t-statistic no longer has the t-distribution that we have used previously to test zero null hypotheses for regression coefficients. A problem arises because, when the null hypothesis is true, y_t is nonstationary and has a variance that increases as the sample size increases. This increasing variance alters the distribution of the usual t-statistic when H_0 is true. To recognize this fact the statistic is often called a τ **(tau) statistic**, and its value must be compared to specially generated critical values. Note that critical values are generated for the three different tests because, as we have seen in Section 12.1, the addition of the constant term and the time-trend term changes the behavior of the time series.

Originally these critical values were tabulated by the statisticians Professor David Dickey and Professor Wayne Fuller. The values have since been refined, but in deference to the seminal work, unit root tests using these critical values have become known as **Dickey–Fuller tests**. Table 12.2 contains the critical values for the *tau* (τ) statistic for the three cases; they are valid in large samples for a one-tail test.

Note that the Dickey–Fuller critical values are more negative than the standard critical values (shown in the last row). This implies that the τ-statistic must take larger (negative) values than usual for the null hypothesis of nonstationarity $\gamma = 0$ to be rejected in favor of the alternative of stationarity $\gamma < 0$. Specifically, to carry out this one-tail test of significance, if τ_c is the critical value obtained from Table 12.2, we reject the null hypothesis of nonstationarity if $\tau \leq \tau_c$. If $\tau > \tau_c$ then we do not reject the null hypothesis that the series y_t is nonstationary. Expressed in a casual way, but one that avoids the proliferation of "double negatives," $\tau \leq \tau_c$ suggests the series is stationary while $\tau > \tau_c$ suggests nonstationarity.

An important extension of the Dickey–Fuller test allows for the possibility that the error term is autocorrelated. Such autocorrelation is likely to occur if our earlier models did not

Table 12.2 **Critical Values for the Dickey–Fuller Test**

Model	1%	5%	10%
$\Delta y_t = \gamma y_{t-1} + v_t$	−2.56	−1.94	−1.62
$\Delta y_t = \alpha + \gamma y_{t-1} + v_t$	−3.43	−2.86	−2.57
$\Delta y_t = \alpha + \lambda t + \gamma y_{t-1} + v_t$	−3.96	−3.41	−3.13
Standard critical values	−2.33	−1.65	−1.28

Note: These critical values are taken from R. Davidson and J.G. MacKinnon (1993), *Estimation and Inference in Econometrics*, New York: Oxford University Press, p. 708.

have sufficient lag terms to capture the full dynamic nature of the process. Using the model with an intercept as an example, the extended test equation is

$$\Delta y_t = \alpha + \gamma y_{t-1} + \sum_{s=1}^{m} a_s \Delta y_{t-s} + v_t \qquad (12.6)$$

where $\Delta y_{t-1} = (y_{t-1} - y_{t-2})$, $\Delta y_{t-2} = (y_{t-2} - y_{t-3}), \ldots$. We add as many lagged first difference terms as we need to ensure that the residuals are not autocorrelated. As we discovered in Sections 9.3.2 and 9.3.3, including lags of the dependent variable can be used to eliminate autocorrelation in the errors. The number of lagged terms can be determined by examining the autocorrelation function (ACF) of the residuals v_t, or the significance of the estimated lag coefficients a_s. The unit root tests based on (12.6) and its variants (intercept excluded or trend included) are referred to as **augmented Dickey–Fuller tests**. The hypotheses for stationarity and nonstationarity are expressed in terms of γ in the same way and the test critical values are the same as those for the Dickey–Fuller test shown in Table 12.2. When $\gamma = 0$, in addition to saying the series is nonstationary, we also say the series has a **unit root**. In practice, we always use the augmented Dickey–Fuller test (rather than the nonaugmented version) to ensure the errors are uncorrelated.

12.3.5 THE DICKEY–FULLER TESTS: AN EXAMPLE

As an example, consider the two interest rate series—the Federal Funds rate (F_t) and the 3-year Bond rate (B_t)—plotted in Figure 12.1e and 12.1g, respectively. Both series exhibit wandering behavior, so we suspect that they may be nonstationary variables. When performing Dickey–Fuller tests, we need to decide whether to use (12.5a) with no constant, or (12.5b) that includes a constant term, or (12.5c) that includes a constant and a deterministic time trend t. As suggested earlier, (12.5b) is the appropriate test equation because the series fluctuate around a nonzero mean. We also have to decide on how many lagged difference terms to include on the right-hand side of the equation. Following procedures described in Section 9.4, we find that the inclusion of one lagged difference term is sufficient to eliminate autocorrelation in the residuals in both cases. The results from estimating the resulting equations are

$$\widehat{\Delta F_t} = 0.178 - 0.037 F_{t-1} + 0.672 \Delta F_{t-1}$$
$$(tau) \qquad (-2.090)$$

$$\widehat{\Delta B_t} = 0.285 - 0.056 B_{t-1} + 0.315 \Delta B_{t-1}$$
$$(tau) \qquad (-1.976)$$

The *tau* value (τ) for the Federal Funds rate is -2.090, and the 5% critical value for $tau(\tau_c)$ is -2.86. Again, recall that to carry out this one-tail test of significance, we reject the null hypothesis of nonstationarity if $\tau \leq \tau_c$. If $\tau > \tau_c$ then we do not reject the null hypothesis that the series is nonstationary. In this case, since $-2.090 > -2.86$, we do not reject the null hypothesis that the series is nonstationary. Similarly, the *tau* value for the Bond rate is greater than the 5% critical value of -2.86 and again we do not reject the null hypothesis that the series is nonstationary. Expressed another way, there is insufficient evidence to suggest F_t and B_t are stationary.

12.3.6   ORDER OF INTEGRATION

Up to this stage, we have discussed only whether a series is stationary or nonstationary. We can take the analysis another step forward and consider a concept called the "order of integration." Recall that, if y_t follows a random walk, then $\gamma = 0$ and the first difference of y_t becomes

$$\Delta y_t = y_t - y_{t-1} = v_t$$

An interesting feature of the series $\Delta y_t = y_t - y_{t-1}$ is that it is stationary since v_t, being an independent $(0, \sigma_v^2)$ random variable, is stationary. Series like y_t, which can be made stationary by taking the first difference, are said to be **integrated of order 1**, and denoted as **I(1)**. Stationary series are said to be integrated of order zero, **I(0)**. In general, the order of integration of a series is the minimum number of times it must be differenced to make it stationary.

For example, to determine the order of integration of F and B, we then ask the next question: is the first difference of the Federal Funds rate $(\Delta F_t = F_t - F_{t-1})$ stationary? Is the first difference of the Bond rate $(\Delta B_t = B_t - B_{t-1})$ stationary? Their plots, in Figure 12.1f and 12.1h, seem to suggest that they are stationary.

The results of the Dickey–Fuller test for a random walk applied to the first differences are given below:

$$\widehat{\Delta(\Delta F)}_t = -0.340(\Delta F)_{t-1}$$
$$(tau) \quad (-4.007)$$

$$\widehat{\Delta(\Delta B)}_t = -0.679(\Delta B)_{t-1}$$
$$(tau) \quad (-6.415)$$

where $\Delta(\Delta F)_t = \Delta F_t - \Delta F_{t-1}$ and $\Delta(\Delta B)_t = \Delta B_t - \Delta B_{t-1}$. Note that the null hypotheses are that the variables ΔF and ΔB are not stationary. Also, because the series ΔF and ΔB appear to fluctuate around zero, we use the test equation without the intercept term. Based on the large negative value of the *tau* statistic $(-4.007 < -1.94)$, we reject the null hypothesis that ΔF_t is nonstationary and accept the alternative that it is stationary. We similarly conclude that ΔB_t is stationary $(-6.415 < -1.94)$

This result implies that while the level of the Federal Funds rate (F_t) is nonstationary, its first difference (ΔF_t) is stationary. We say that the series F_t is I(1) because it had to be differenced once to make it stationary $[\Delta F_t$ is I(0)$]$. Similarly we have also shown that the Bond rate (B_t) is integrated of order 1. In the next section we investigate the implications of these results for regression modeling.

12.4 Cointegration

As a general rule, nonstationary time-series variables should not be used in regression models, to avoid the problem of spurious regression. However, there is an exception to this rule. If y_t and x_t are nonstationary I(1) variables, then we expect their difference, or any linear combination of them, such as $e_t = y_t - \beta_1 - \beta_2 x_t,$[3] to be I(1) as well. However, there is an important case when $e_t = y_t - \beta_1 - \beta_2 x_t$ is a stationary I(0) process. In this case y_t and x_t are said to be **cointegrated**. Cointegration implies that y_t and x_t share similar stochastic trends, and, since the difference e_t is stationary, they never diverge too far from each other.

A natural way to test whether y_t and x_t are cointegrated is to test whether the errors $e_t = y_t - \beta_1 - \beta_2 x_t$ are stationary. Since we cannot observe e_t, we test the stationarity of the least squares residuals, $\hat{e}_t = y_t - b_1 - b_2 x_t$ using a Dickey–Fuller test. The test for cointegration is effectively a test of the stationarity of the residuals. If the residuals are stationary, then y_t and x_t are said to be cointegrated; if the residuals are nonstationary, then y_t and x_t are not cointegrated, and any apparent regression relationship between them is spurious.

The test for stationarity of the residuals is based on the test equation:

$$\Delta \hat{e}_t = \gamma \hat{e}_{t-1} + v_t \tag{12.7}$$

where $\Delta \hat{e}_t = \hat{e}_t - \hat{e}_{t-1}$. As before, we examine the t (or *tau*) statistic for the estimated slope coefficient. Note that the regression has no constant term because the mean of the regression residuals is zero. Also, since we are basing this test upon **estimated** values of the residuals, the critical values will be different from those in Table 12.2. The proper critical values for a test of cointegration are given in Table 12.3. The test equation can also include extra terms like $\Delta \hat{e}_{t-1}, \Delta \hat{e}_{t-2}, \ldots$ on the right-hand side if they are needed to eliminate autocorrelation in v_t.

There are three sets of critical values. Which set we use depends on whether the residuals $\hat{e}_t$ are derived from a regression equation without a constant term [like (12.8a)] or a regression equation with a constant term [like (12.8b)], or a regression equation with a constant and a time trend [like (12.8c)].

$$\text{Equation 1:} \quad \hat{e}_t = y_t - b\,x_t \tag{12.8a}$$

$$\text{Equation 2:} \quad \hat{e}_t = y_t - b_2 x_t - b_1 \tag{12.8b}$$

$$\text{Equation 3:} \quad \hat{e}_t = y_t - b_2 x_t - b_1 - \hat{\delta}t \tag{12.8c}$$

Ta b l e 12.3   **Critical Values for the Cointegration Test**

Regression model	1%	5%	10%
(1) $y_t = \beta x_t + e_t$	−3.39	−2.76	−2.45
(2) $y_t = \beta_1 + \beta_2 x_t + e_t$	−3.96	−3.37	−3.07
(3) $y_t = \beta_1 + \delta t + \beta_2 x_t + e_t$	−3.98	−3.42	−3.13

Note: These critical values are taken from J. Hamilton (1994), *Time Series Analysis*, Princeton University Press, p. 766.

---

[3] A linear combination of x and y is a new variable $z = a_0 + a_1 x + a_2 y$. Here we set the constants $a_0 = -\beta_1$, $a_1 = -\beta_2$, and $a_2 = 1$, and call z the series e.

12.4.1 AN EXAMPLE OF A COINTEGRATION TEST

To illustrate, let us test whether $y_t = B_t$ and $x_t = F_t$, as plotted in Figure 12.1e and 12.1g, are cointegrated. We have already shown that both series are nonstationary. The estimated least squares regression between these variables is

$$\hat{B}_t = 1.644 + 0.832F_t, \quad R^2 = 0.881$$
$$(t) \quad (8.437)(24.147)$$

(12.9)

and the unit root test for stationarity in the estimated residuals $(\hat{e}_t = B_t - 1.644 - 0.832F_t)$ is

$$\Delta\hat{e}_t = -0.314\hat{e}_{t-1} + 0.315\Delta\hat{e}_{t-1}$$
$$(tau) \quad (-4.543)$$

Note that this is the augmented Dickey–Fuller version of the test with one lagged term Δe_{t-1} to correct for autocorrelation. Since there is a constant term in (12.9), we use the equation 2 critical values in Table 12.3.

The null and alternative hypotheses in the test for cointegration are

H_0: the series are not cointegrated $\Leftrightarrow$ residuals are nonstationary

H_1: the series are cointegrated $\Leftrightarrow$ residuals are stationary

Similar to the one-tail unit root tests, we reject the null hypothesis of no cointegration if $\tau \leq \tau_c$, and we do not reject the null hypothesis that the series are not cointegrated if $\tau > \tau_c$. The *tau* statistic in this case is -4.543 that is less than the critical value -3.37 at the 5% level of significance. Thus, we reject the null hypothesis that the least squares residuals are nonstationary and conclude that they are stationary. This implies that the Bond rate and the Federal Funds rate are cointegrated. In other words, there is a fundamental relationship between these two variables (the estimated regression relationship between them is valid and not spurious) and the estimated values of the intercept and slope are 1.644 and 0.832, respectively.

The result—that the Federal Funds and Bond rates are cointegrated—has major economic implications! It means that when the Federal Reserve implements monetary policy by changing the Federal Funds rate, the Bond rate will also change thereby ensuring that the effects of monetary policy are transmitted to the rest of the economy. In contrast, the effectiveness of monetary policy would be severely hampered if the Bond and Federal Funds rates were spuriously related as this implies that their movements, fundamentally, have little to do with each other.

12.5 Regression When There is No Cointegration

Thus far, we have shown that regression with I(1) variables is acceptable providing those variables are cointegrated, allowing us to avoid the problem of spurious results. We also know that regression with stationary I(0) variables, that we studied in Chapter 9, is acceptable. What happens when there is no cointegration between I(1) variables? In this case, the sensible thing to do is to convert the nonstationary series to stationary series and to use the techniques discussed in Chapter 9 to estimate dynamic relationships between the stationary variables. However, we stress that this step should be taken only when we fail to find cointegration between the I(1) variables. Regression with cointegrated I(1) variables makes the least squares estimator "super-consistent"[4] and, moreover, it is economically useful to establish relationships between the levels of economic variables.

How we convert nonstationary series to stationary series, and the kind of model we estimate, depend on whether the variables are **difference stationary** or **trend stationary**. In the former case, we convert the nonstationary series to its stationary counterpart by taking first differences. In the latter case, we convert the nonstationary series to its stationary counterpart by de-trending. We now explore these issues.

12.5.1   FIRST DIFFERENCE STATIONARY

Consider a variable y_t that behaves like the random walk model:

$$y_t = y_{t-1} + v_t$$

This is a nonstationary series with a "stochastic" trend, but it can be rendered stationary by taking the first difference:

$$\Delta y_t = y_t - y_{t-1} = v_t$$

The variable y_t is said to be a **first difference stationary** series. Recall that this means that y is said to be integrated of order 1. Now suppose that Dickey–Fuller tests reveal that two variables, y and x, that you would like to relate in a regression, are first difference stationary, I(1), and not cointegrated. Then, a suitable regression involving only stationary variables is one that relates changes in y to changes in x, with relevant lags included, and no intercept. For example, using one lagged Δy_t and a current and lagged Δx_t, we have

$$\Delta y_t = \theta \Delta y_{t-1} + \beta_0 \Delta x_t + \beta_1 \Delta x_{t-1} + e_t \tag{12.10a}$$

Now consider a series y_t that behaves like a random walk with drift:

$$y_t = \alpha + y_{t-1} + v_t$$

and note that y can be rendered stationary by taking the first difference:

$$\Delta y_t = \alpha + v_t$$

The variable y_t is also said to be a **first difference stationary** series, even though it is stationary around a constant term. Now suppose again that y and x are I(1) and not cointegrated. Then an example of a suitable regression equation, again involving stationary variables, is obtained by adding a constant to (12.10a). That is,

$$\Delta y_t = \alpha + \theta \Delta y_{t-1} + \beta_0 \Delta x_t + \beta_1 \Delta x_{t-1} + e_t \tag{12.10b}$$

In line with Section 9.7, the models in (12.10a) and (12.10b) are autoregressive distributed lag models with first-differenced variables. In general, since there is often doubt about the role of the constant term, the usual practice is to include an intercept term in the regression.

---

[4] Consistency means that as $T \to \infty$ the least squares estimator converges to the true parameter value. Super-consistency means that it converges to the true value at a faster rate.

12.5.2 TREND STATIONARY

Consider a model with a constant term, a trend term and a stationary error term,

$$y_t = \alpha + \delta t + v_t$$

The variable y_t is said to be **trend stationary** because it can be made stationary by removing the effect of the deterministic (constant and trend) components

$$y_t - \alpha - \delta t = v_t$$

A series like this is, strictly speaking, not an I(1) variable, but is described as stationary around a deterministic trend. Thus, if y and x are two trend-stationary variables, a possible autoregressive distributed lag model is

$$y_t^* = \theta y_{t-1}^* + \beta_0 x_t^* + \beta_1 x_{t-1}^* + e_t \tag{12.11}$$

where $y_t^* = y_t - \alpha_1 - \delta_1 t$ and $x_t^* = x_t - \alpha_2 - \delta_2 t$ are the de-trended data (the coefficients (α_1, δ_1) and (α_2, δ_2) can be estimated by least squares).

As an alternative to using the de-trended data for estimation, a constant term and a trend term can be included directly into the equation. For example, by substituting y_t^* and x_t^* into (12.11), it can be shown that estimating (12.11) is equivalent to estimating

$$y_t = \alpha + \delta t + \theta y_{t-1} + \beta_0 x_t + \beta_1 x_{t-1} + e_t$$

where $\alpha = \alpha_1(1 - \theta_1) - \alpha_2(\beta_0 + \beta_1) + \theta_1 \delta_1 + \beta_1 \delta_2$ and $\delta = \delta_1(1 - \theta_1) - \delta_2(\beta_0 + \beta_1)$. In practice, this is usually the preferred option as it is relatively more straightforward.

To summarize

- If variables are stationary, or I(1) and cointegrated, we can estimate a regression relationship between the levels of those variables without fear of encountering a spurious regression.

- If the variables are I(1) and not cointegrated, we need to estimate a relationship in first differences, with or without the constant term.

- If they are trend stationary, we can either de-trend the series first and then perform regression analysis with the stationary (de-trended) variables or, alternatively, estimate a regression relationship that includes a trend variable. The latter alternative is typically applied.

12.6 Exercises

12.6.1 Problems

12.1   (a) Consider an AR(1) model

$$y_t = \rho y_{t-1} + v_t, \quad |\rho| < 1$$

Rewrite y as a function of lagged errors. (*Hint*: perform recursive substitution.) What is the mean and variance of y? What is the covariance between y_t and y_{t-2}?

(b) Consider a random walk model

$$y_t = y_{t-1} + v_t$$

Rewrite y as a function of lagged errors. What is the mean and variance of y? What is the covariance between y_t and y_{t-2}?

12.2   Figure 12.4 (data file *unit.dat*) shows plots of four time series. Since W and Y appear to be fluctuating around a nonzero mean, a Dickey–Fuller test 2 (with constant but no trend) was performed on these variables. Since X and Z appear to be fluctuating around a trend, a Dickey–Fuller test 3 (with constant and trend) was performed for these two variables. The results are shown below.

$$\widehat{\Delta W_t} = 0.757 - 0.091 W_{t-1}$$
$$(tau) \qquad (-3.178)$$

$$\widehat{\Delta Y_t} = 0.031 - 0.039 Y_{t-1}$$
$$(tau) \qquad (-1.975)$$

$$\widehat{\Delta X_t} = 0.782 - 0.092 X_{t-1} + 0.009t$$
$$(tau) \qquad (-3.099)$$

$$\widehat{\Delta Z_t} = 0.332 - 0.036 Z_{t-1} + 0.005t$$
$$(tau) \qquad (-1.913)$$

Which series are stationary and which are nonstationary?

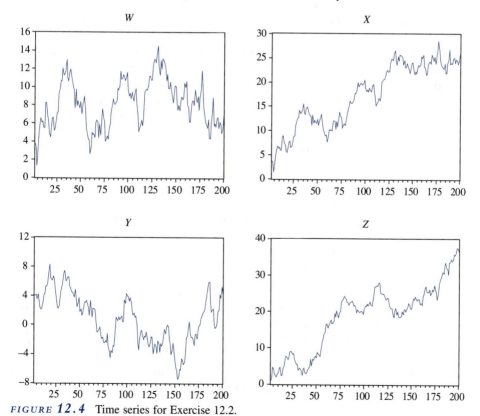

FIGURE 12.4   Time series for Exercise 12.2.

12.6.2 COMPUTER EXERCISES

12.3* The data file *oil.dat* contains 88 annual observations on the price of oil (in 1967 constant dollars) for the period 1883–1970.
(a) Plot the data. Do the data look stationary or nonstationary?
(b) Use a unit root test to demonstrate that the series is stationary.
(c) What do you conclude about the order of integration of this series?

12.4 The data file *bond.dat* contains 102 monthly observations on AA railroad bond yields for the period January 1968 to June 1976.
(a) Plot the data. Do railroad bond yields appear stationary or not?
(b) Use a unit root test to demonstrate that the series is nonstationary.
(c) Find the first difference of the bond yield series and test for stationarity.
(d) What do you conclude about the order of integration of this series?

12.5* The data file *oz.dat* contains quarterly data on disposable income and consumption in Australia from 1985.1 to 2005.2.
(a) Test each of these series for stationarity.
(b) What do you conclude about the "order of integration" of each of these series?
(c) Is consumption cointegrated with or spuriously related to disposable income?

12.6 The data file *texas.dat* contains 57 quarterly observations on the real price of oil (*RPO*), Texas nonagricultural employment (*TXNAG*), and nonagricultural employment in the rest of the US (*USNAG*). The data cover the period 1974:Q1 through 1988:Q1 and were used in a study by Fomby and Hirschberg [T.B. Fomby and J.G. Hirschberg, "Texas in Transition: Dependence on Oil and the National Economy," *Federal Reserve Bank of Dallas Economic Review,* January 1989, 11–28].
(a) Show that the **levels** of the variables *TXNAG* and *USNAG* are nonstationary variables.
(b) At what significance level do you conclude that the **changes** $DTX = TXNAG - TXNAG(-1)$ and $DUS = USNAG - USNAG(-1)$ are stationary variables.
(c) Are the nonstationary variables *TXNAG* and *USNAG* cointegrated or spuriously related?
(d) Are the stationary variables *DTX* and *DUS* related?
(e) What is the difference between (d) and (c)?

12.7 The data file *usa.dat* contains the data shown in Figure 12.1. Consider the two time series, real GDP and the inflation rate.
(a) Are the series stationary or nonstationary? Which Dickey–Fuller test (no constant, no trend; with constant, no trend; or with constant and with trend) did you use?
(b) What do you conclude about the order of integration of these series?
(c) Forecast GDP and inflation for 2005:2.

12.8 The data file *canada.dat* contains monthly Canadian/US exchange rates for the period 1971:01 to 2006:12. Split the observations into two sample periods—a 1971:01-1987:12 sample period and a 1988:01-2006:12 sample period.
(a) Perform a unit root test on the data for each sample period. Which Dickey–Fuller test did you use?
(b) Are the results for the two sample periods consistent?
(c) Perform a unit root test for the full sample 1971:01-2006:12. What is the order of integration of the data?

12.9 The data file *csi.dat* contains the Consumer Sentiment Index (CSI), produced by the University of Michigan for the sample period 1978:01 to 2006:12.
 (a) Perform all three Dickey–Fuller tests. Are the results consistent? If not, why not?
 (b) Based on a graphical inspection of the data, which test should you have used?
 (c) Does the CSI suggest that consumers "remember" and "retain" news information for a short time or for a long time?

12.10 The data file *mexico.dat* contains real GDP for Mexico and the Unites States from the first quarter of 1980 to the fourth quarter of 2006. Both series have been standardized so that the average value in 2000 is 100.
 (a) Perform the test for cointegration between Mexico and the Unites States for all three test equations in (12.8). Are the results consistent?
 (b) The theory of convergence in economic growth suggests the two GDPs should be proportional and cointegrated. That is, there should be a cointegrating relationship that does not contain an intercept or a trend. Do your results support this theory?
 (c) If the variables are not cointegrated, what should you do if you are interested in testing the relationship between Mexico and the United States?

Chapter 13

VEC and VAR Models: An Introduction to Macroeconometrics

Learning Objectives

Based on the material in this chapter, you should be able to do the following:

1. Explain why economic variables are dynamically interdependent.
2. Explain the VEC model.
3. Explain the importance of error correction.
4. Explain the VAR model.
5. Explain the relationship between a VEC model and a VAR model.
6. Explain how to estimate the VEC and VAR models for the bivariate case.
7. Explain how to generate impulse response functions and variance decompositions for the simple case when the variables are not contemporaneously interdependent and when the shocks are not correlated.

Keywords

dynamic relationships
error correction
forecast error variance decomposition
identification problem

impulse response functions
VAR model
VEC model

In Chapter 12, we studied the time-series properties of data and cointegrating relationships between pairs of nonstationary series. In those examples, we assumed that one of the variables was the dependent variable (let us call it y_t) and the other was the independent variable (say x_t), and we treated the relationship between y_t and x_t like a regression model. However, a priori, unless we have good reasons not to, we could just as easily have assumed that y_t is the independent variable and x_t is the dependent variable. Put simply, we are working with two variables $\{y_t, x_t\}$ and the two possible regression models relating them are

$$y_t = \beta_{10} + \beta_{11}x_t + e_t^y, \quad e_t^y \sim N(0, \sigma_y^2) \tag{13.1a}$$

$$x_t = \beta_{20} + \beta_{21}y_t + e_t^x, \quad e_t^x \sim N(0, \sigma_x^2) \tag{13.1b}$$

In this bivariate (two series) system there can be only one unique relationship between x_t and y_t, and so it must be the case that $\beta_{21} = 1/\beta_{11}$ and $\beta_{20} = -\beta_{10}/\beta_{11}$. A bit of terminology: for (13.1a) we say that we have normalized on y (meaning the coefficient in front of y is set to 1) whereas for (13.1b) we say that we have normalized on x (meaning the coefficient in front of x is set to 1).

Is it better to write the relationship as (13.1a) or (13.1b), or is it better to recognize that, in many relationships, variables like y and x are simultaneously determined? The aim of this chapter is to explore the causal relationship between pairs of time-series variables. In doing so, we shall be extending our study of time-series data to take account of their dynamic properties and interactions. In particular, we will discuss the **vector error correction (VEC)** and **vector autoregressive (VAR)** models. We will learn how to estimate a VEC model when there is cointegration between I(1) variables, and how to estimate a VAR model when there is no cointegration.

Some important terminology emerges here. Univariate analysis examines a single data series. Bivariate analysis examines a pair of series. The term **vector** indicates that we are considering a number of series, two, three, or more. The term "vector" is a generalization of the univariate and bivariate cases.

13.1 VEC and VAR Models

Let us begin with two time-series variables y_t and x_t and generalize the discussion about dynamic relationships in Chapter 9 to yield a system of equations:

$$
\begin{aligned}
y_t &= \beta_{10} + \beta_{11}y_{t-1} + \beta_{12}x_{t-1} + v_t^y \\
x_t &= \beta_{20} + \beta_{21}y_{t-1} + \beta_{22}x_{t-1} + v_t^x
\end{aligned}
\tag{13.2}
$$

The equations in (13.2) describe a system in which each variable is a function of its own lag, and the lag of the other variable in the system. In this case, the system contains two variables y and x. In the first equation y_t is a function of its own lag y_{t-1} and the lag of the other variable in the system x_{t-1}. In the second equation x_t is a function of its own lag x_{t-1} and the lag of the other variable in the system y_{t-1}. Together the equations constitute a system known as a vector autoregression (VAR). In this example, since the maximum lag is of order 1, we have a VAR(1).

If y and x are stationary I(0) variables, the above system can be estimated using least squares applied to each equation. If, however, y and x are nonstationary I(1) and not cointegrated, then, as discussed in Chapter 12, we work with the first differences. In this case, the VAR model is

$$
\begin{aligned}
\Delta y_t &= \beta_{11}\Delta y_{t-1} + \beta_{12}\Delta x_{t-1} + v_t^{\Delta y} \\
\Delta x_t &= \beta_{21}\Delta y_{t-1} + \beta_{22}\Delta x_{t-1} + v_t^{\Delta x}
\end{aligned}
\tag{13.3}
$$

All variables are now I(0), and the system can again be estimated by least squares. To recap: the VAR model is a general framework to describe the dynamic interrelationship between stationary variables. Thus, if y and x are stationary I(0) variables, the system in equation (13.2) is used. On the other hand, if y and x are I(1) variables but they are not cointegrated, we examine the interrelation between them using a VAR framework in first differences (13.3).

If y and x are I(1) and cointegrated, then we need to modify the system of equations to allow for the cointegrating relationship between the I(1) variables. We do this for two reasons. First, as economists, we like to retain and use valuable information about the cointegrating relationship and second, as econometricians, we like to ensure that we use the best technique that takes into account the properties of the time-series data. Recall the chapter on simultaneous equations— the cointegrating equation is one way of introducing simultaneous interactions without requiring the data to be stationary. Introducing the cointegrating relationship leads to a model known as the VEC model. We turn now to this model.

Consider two nonstationary variables y_t and x_t that are integrated of order 1; $y_t \sim I(1)$ and $x_t \sim I(1)$ and which we have shown to be cointegrated, so that

$$y_t = \beta_0 + \beta_1 x_t + e_t \qquad (13.4)$$

Note that we could have chosen to normalize on x. Whether we normalize on y or x is often determined from economic theory; the critical point is that there can be at most one fundamental relationship between the two variables.

The VEC model is a special form of the VAR for I(1) variables that are cointegrated. The VEC model is

$$\Delta y_t = \alpha_{10} + \alpha_{11}(y_{t-1} - \beta_0 - \beta_1 x_{t-1}) + v_t^y$$
$$\Delta x_t = \alpha_{20} + \alpha_{21}(y_{t-1} - \beta_0 - \beta_1 x_{t-1}) + v_t^x \qquad (13.5a)$$

which we can expand as

$$y_t = \alpha_{10} + (\alpha_{11} + 1)y_{t-1} - \alpha_{11}\beta_0 - \alpha_{11}\beta_1 x_{t-1} + v_t^y$$
$$x_t = \alpha_{20} + \alpha_{21}y_{t-1} - \alpha_{21}\beta_0 - (\alpha_{21}\beta_1 - 1)x_{t-1} + v_t^x \qquad (13.5b)$$

Comparing (13.5b) with (13.2) shows the VEC as a VAR where the I(1) variable y_t is related to other lagged variables (y_{t-1} and x_{t-1}) and where the I(1) variable x_t is also related to the other lagged variables (y_{t-1} and x_{t-1}). Note, however, that the two equations contain the common cointegrating relationship.

The coefficients α_{11}, α_{21} are known as error correction coefficients, so named because they show how much Δy_t and Δx_t respond to the cointegrating error $y_{t-1} - \beta_0 - \beta_1 x_{t-1} = e_{t-1}$. The idea that the error leads to a correction comes about because of the conditions put on α_{11}, α_{21} to ensure stability, namely $(-1 < \alpha_{11} \leq 0)$ and $(0 \leq \alpha_{21} < 1)$. To appreciate this idea, consider a positive error $e_{t-1} > 0$ that occurred because $y_{t-1} > (\beta_0 + \beta_1 x_{t-1})$. A negative error correction coefficient in the first equation (α_{11}) ensures that Δy falls, while the positive error correction coefficient in the second equation (α_{21}) ensures that Δx rises, thereby correcting the error. Having the error correction coefficients less than 1 in absolute value ensures that the system is not explosive.

The error correction model has become an extremely popular model because its interpretation is intuitively appealing. Think about two nonstationary variables, say consumption (let us call it y_t) and income (let us call it x_t), that we expect to be related (cointegrated). Now think about a change in your income Δx_t, say a pay raise! Consumption will most likely increase, but it may take you a while to change your consumption pattern in response to a change in your pay. The VEC model allows us to examine how much consumption will change in response to a change in the explanatory variable (the cointegration part, $y_t = \beta_0 + \beta_1 x_t + e_t$), as well as the speed of the change (the error correction part, $\Delta y_t = \alpha_{10} + \alpha_{11}(e_{t-1}) + v_t^y$ where e_{t-1} is the cointegrating error).

There is one final point to discuss—the role of the intercept terms. Thus far, we have introduced an intercept term in the cointegrating equation (β_0) as well as in the VEC (α_{10} and α_{20}). However, doing so can create a problem. To see why, we collect all the intercept terms and rewrite (13.5b) as

$$
\begin{aligned}
y_t &= (\alpha_{10} - \alpha_{11}\beta_0) + (\alpha_{11} + 1)y_{t-1} - \alpha_{11}\beta_1 x_{t-1} + v_t^y \\
x_t &= (\alpha_{20} - \alpha_{21}\beta_0) + \alpha_{21}y_{t-1} - (\alpha_{21}\beta_1 - 1)x_{t-1} + v_t^x
\end{aligned}
\tag{13.5c}
$$

If we estimate each equation by least squares, we obtain estimates of composite terms $(\alpha_{10} - \alpha_{11}\beta_0)$ and $(\alpha_{20} - \alpha_{21}\beta_0)$, and we are not able to disentangle the separate effects of β_0, α_{10}, and α_{20}. In the next section, we discuss a simple two-step least squares procedure that gets around this problem. However, the lesson here is to check whether and where an intercept term is needed.

13.2 Estimating a Vector Error Correction Model

There are many econometric methods to estimate the error correction model. The most straightforward is to use a two-step least squares procedure. First, use least squares to estimate the cointegrating relationship $y_t = \beta_0 + \beta_1 x_t + e_t$ and generate the lagged residuals $\hat{e}_{t-1} = y_{t-1} - b_0 - b_1 x_{t-1}$.

Second, use least squares to estimate the equations:

$$
\Delta y_t = \alpha_{10} + \alpha_{11}\hat{e}_{t-1} + v_t^y
\tag{13.6a}
$$

$$
\Delta x_t = \alpha_{20} + \alpha_{21}\hat{e}_{t-1} + v_t^x
\tag{13.6b}
$$

Note that all the variables in equation (13.6) (Δy, Δx and $\hat{e}$) are stationary (recall that for y and x to be cointegrated, the residuals $\hat{e}$ must be stationary). Hence, the standard regression analysis studied in earlier chapters may be used to test the significance of the parameters. The usual residual diagnostic tests may be applied.

We need to be careful here about how we combine stationary and nonstationary variables in a regression model. Cointegration is about the relationship between I(1) variables. The cointegrating equation does not contain I(0) variables. The corresponding VEC model, however, relates the change in an I(1) variable (the I(0) variables Δy and Δx) to other I(0) variables, namely the cointegration residuals $\hat{e}_{t-1}$ and, if required, other stationary variables may be added. In other words, we should not mix stationary and nonstationary variables: an I(0) dependent variable on the left-hand side of a regression equation should be "explained" by other I(0) variables on the right-hand side and an I(1) dependent variable on the left-hand side of a regression equation should be "explained" by other I(1) variables on the right-hand side.

13.2.1 EXAMPLE

In Figure 13.1 the quarterly real GDP of a small economy (Australia) and a large economy (United States) for the sample period 1970.1 to 2000.4 are displayed. Note that the series have been scaled so that both economies show a real GDP value of 100 in 2000. They appear in the file *gdp.dat*. It appears from the figure that both series are nonstationary and possibly cointegrated.

Formal unit root tests of the series confirm that they are indeed nonstationary. To check for cointegration we obtain the fitted equation in (13.7) (the intercept term is omitted

FIGURE **13.1**   Real gross domestic products (GDP).

because it has no economic meaning):

$$\hat{A}_t = 0.985U_t, \quad R^2 = 0.995 \tag{13.7}$$

where A denotes real GDP for Australia and U denotes real GDP for the United States. Note that we have normalized on A because it makes more sense to think of a small economy responding to a large economy. We then performed a test for stationarity of the residuals $\hat{e}_t = A_t - 0.985U_t$. The estimated unit root test equation for the residuals is

$$\widehat{\Delta e_t} = -0.128\hat{e}_{t-1}$$
$$(tau) \quad (-2.889) \tag{13.8}$$

Since the cointegrating relationship does not contain an intercept term [see Chapter 12, equation (12.8a)], the 5% critical value is -2.76. The unit root t-value of -2.889 is less than -2.76. We reject the null of no cointegration and we conclude that the two real GDP series are cointegrated. This result implies that economic activity in the small economy (Australia, A_t) is linked to economic activity in the large economy (United States, U_t). If U_t were to increase by one unit, A_t would increase by 0.985. But the Australian economy may not respond fully by this amount within the quarter. To ascertain how much it will respond within a quarter, we estimate the error correction model by least squares. The estimated VEC model for $\{A_t, U_t\}$ is

$$\widehat{\Delta A_t} = 0.492 - 0.099\hat{e}_{t-1}$$
$$(t) \qquad\qquad (2.077)$$
$$\widehat{\Delta U_t} = 0.510 + 0.030\hat{e}_{t-1}$$
$$(t) \qquad\qquad (0.789) \tag{13.9}$$

The results show that both error correction coefficients are of the appropriate sign. The negative error correction coefficient in the first equation (-0.099) indicates that ΔA falls, while the positive error correction coefficient in the second equation (0.030) indicates that ΔU rises, when there is a positive cointegrating error: ($\hat{e}_{t-1} > 0$ or $A_{t-1} > 0.985U_{t-1}$).

This behavior (negative change in A and positive change in U) "corrects" the cointegrating error. The error correction coefficient (-0.099) is significant at the 5% level; it indicates that the quarterly adjustment of A_t will be about 10% of the deviation of A_{t-1} from its cointegrating value $0.985U_{t-1}$. This is a slow rate of adjustment. However, the error correction coefficient in the second equation (0.030) is insignificant; it suggests that ΔU does not react to the cointegrating error. This outcome is consistent with the view that the small economy is likely to react to economic conditions in the large economy, but not vice versa.

13.3 Estimating a VAR Model

The VEC is a multivariate dynamic model that incorporates a cointegrating equation. It is relevant when, for the two variable case, we have two variables, say y and x, that are both I(1), but are cointegrated. Now we ask: what should we do if we are interested in the interdependencies between y and x, but they are not cointegrated? In this case, we estimate a vector autoregressive (VAR) model as shown in (13.3).

As an example, consider Figure 13.2 that shows the log of GDP (denoted as G) and log of the CPI (denoted as P) for the US economy over the period 1960:1 to 2004:4. The data are in the file *growth.dat*.

The fitted least squares regression of G_t on P_t is

$$\hat{G}_t = 1.632 + 0.624P_t$$
$$(t) \quad (41.49) \quad (61.482)$$

For this fitted model $R^2 = 0.955$ and the t-statistics are very large, a seemingly strong result. Based on the plots the series appear to be nonstationary. To test for cointegration, compute the least squares residual $\hat{e}_t = G_t - 1.632 - 0.624P_t$. The Dickey-Fuller regression is

$$\widehat{\Delta e_t} = -0.009\hat{e}_{t-1}$$
$$(tau) \quad (-0.977) \tag{13.10}$$

The potential cointegrating relationship contains an intercept term to capture the component of GDP that is independent of the CPI. Thus, the 5% critical value of the test for stationarity

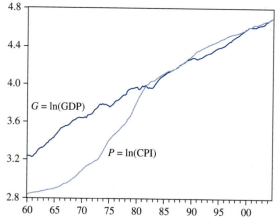

FIGURE 13.2 Real GDP and the consumer price index (CPI) in logarithms.

in the cointegrating residuals is -3.37 [see Chapter 12, equation (12.8b)]. Since the *tau* (unit root *t*-value) of -0.977 is greater than -3.37, it indicates that the errors are nonstationary and hence that the relationship between G (i.e., $\ln(GDP)$) and P (i.e., $\ln(CPI)$) is spurious. That is, we have no cointegration. Thus we would not apply a VEC model to examine the dynamic relationship between aggregate price P and output G. Instead we estimate a VAR model for the set of I(0) variables $\{\Delta P_t, \Delta G_t\}$.

For illustrative purposes, the order of lag in this example has been restricted to 1. In general, one should test for the significance of lag terms greater than 1. The results are

$$\widehat{\Delta P_t} = 0.001 + 0.827\Delta P_{t-1} + 0.046\Delta G_{t-1} \tag{13.11a}$$
$$(t) \quad (2.017)(18.494) \qquad (1.165)$$

$$\widehat{\Delta G_t} = 0.010 - 0.327\Delta P_{t-1} + 0.228\Delta G_{t-1} \tag{13.11b}$$
$$(t) \quad (7.845)(-4.153) \qquad (3.256)$$

The first equation (13.11a) shows that the quarterly growth in price (ΔP_t) is significantly related to its own past value (ΔP_{t-1}) but insignificantly related to the quarterly growth in last period's GDP (ΔG_{t-1}). The second equation (13.11b) shows that ΔG_t is significantly positively related to its own past value and significantly negatively related to last period's change in price (i.e., inflation). The constant terms capture the fixed component in the change in log price (which is a measure of inflation) and the change in $\ln(GDP)$ (which is a measure of the change in economic activity, or growth in the economy).

Having estimated these models can we infer anything else? If the system is subjected to a price (demand) shock, what is the effect of the shock on the dynamic path of inflation and growth? Will inflation rise and by how much? If the system is also subjected to a quantity (supply) shock, what is the contribution of a price versus a quantity shock on the variation of output? We turn now to some analysis suited to addressing these questions.

13.4 Impulse Responses and Variance Decompositions

Impulse response functions and variance decompositions are techniques that are used by macroeconometricians to analyze problems such as the effect of an oil price shock on inflation and GDP growth, and the effect of a change in monetary policy on the economy.

13.4.1 IMPULSE RESPONSE FUNCTIONS

Impulse response functions show the effects of shocks on the adjustment path of the variables. To help us understand this we shall first consider a univariate series.

13.4.1a The Univariate Case

Consider a univariate series $y_t = \rho y_{t-1} + v_t$ and subject it to a shock of size v in period 1. Assume an arbitrary starting value of y at time zero: $y_0 = 0$. Since we are interested in the dynamic path, the starting point is irrelevant. At time $t = 1$, following the shock, the value of y will be: $y_1 = \rho y_0 + v_1 = v$. Assume that there are no subsequent shocks in later time periods $[v_2 = v_3 = \cdots = 0]$, at time $t = 2$, $y_2 = \rho y_1 = \rho v$. At time $t = 3$, $y_3 = \rho y_2 = \rho(\rho y_1) = \rho^2 v$, and so on. Thus the time-path of y following the shock is $\{v, \rho v, \rho^2 v, \ldots\}$. The values of the coefficients $\{1, \rho, \rho^2, \ldots\}$ are known as multipliers, and the time-path of y following the shock is known as the impulse response function.

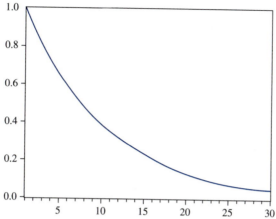

FIGURE **13.3** Impulse responses for an AR(1) model $y_t = 0.9\,y_{t-1} + e_t$ following a unit shock.

To illustrate, assume that $\rho = 0.9$ and let the shock be unity: $v = 1$. According to the analysis, y will be $\{1, 0.9, 0.81, \ldots\}$, approaching zero over time. This impulse response function is plotted in Figure 13.3. It shows us what happens to y after a shock. In this case, y initially rises by the full amount of the shock and then it gradually returns to the value before the shock.

13.4.1b   The Bivariate Case

Now, let us consider an impulse response function analysis with two time series based on a bivariate VAR system of stationary variables:

$$
\begin{aligned}
y_t &= \delta_{10} + \delta_{11} y_{t-1} + \delta_{12} x_{t-1} + v_t^y \\
x_t &= \delta_{20} + \delta_{21} y_{t-1} + \delta_{22} x_{t-1} + v_t^x
\end{aligned}
\tag{13.12}
$$

In this case, there are two possible shocks to the system—one to y and the other to x. Thus we are interested in four impulse response functions—the effect of a shock to y on the time-paths of y and x and the effect of a shock to x on the time-paths of y and x.

The actual mechanics of generating impulse responses in a system is complicated by (i) the fact that one has to allow for interdependent dynamics (the multivariate analog of generating the multipliers) and (ii) one has to identify the correct shock from unobservable data. Taken together, these two complications lead to what is known as the **identification problem**. In this chapter, we consider a special case where there is no identification problem.[1] This special case occurs when the system described in (13.12) is a true representation of the dynamic system—namely, y is related only to lags of y and x, and x is related only to lags of y and x. In other words, y and x are related in a dynamic fashion, but not contemporaneously. The current value x_t does not appear in the equation for y_t and the current value y_t does not appear in the equation for x_t. Also, we need to assume the errors v_t^x and v_t^y are independent of each other (contemporaneously uncorrelated). In addition, we assume $v^y \sim N(0, \sigma_y^2)$ and $v^x \sim N(0, \sigma_x^2)$.

---

[1] Appendix 13A introduces the general problem.

Consider the case when there is a one standard deviation shock (alternatively called an **innovation**) to y so that at time $t = 1$, $v_1^y = \sigma_y$, and v_t^y is zero thereafter. Assume $v_t^x = 0$ for all t. It is traditional to consider a standard deviation shock (innovation) rather than a unit shock to overcome measurement issues. Assume $y_0 = x_0 = 0$. Also, since we are focusing on how a shock *changes* the paths of y and x, we can ignore the intercepts. Then

1.   When $t = 1$, the effect of a shock of size σ_y on y is $y_1 = v_1^y = \sigma_y$, and the effect on x is $x_1 = v_1^x = 0$.

2.   When $t = 2$, the effect of the shock on y is

$$y_2 = \delta_{11}y_1 + \delta_{12}x_1 = \delta_{11}\sigma_y + \delta_{12}0 = \delta_{11}\sigma_y$$

and the effect on x is

$$x_2 = \delta_{21}y_1 + \delta_{22}x_1 = \delta_{21}\sigma_y + \delta_{22}0 = \delta_{21}\sigma_y.$$

3.   When $t = 3$, the effect of the shock on y is

$$y_3 = \delta_{11}y_2 + \delta_{12}x_2 = \delta_{11}\delta_{11}\sigma_y + \delta_{12}\delta_{21}\sigma_y$$

and the effect on x is

$$x_3 = \delta_{21}y_2 + \delta_{22}x_2 = \delta_{21}\delta_{11}\sigma_y + \delta_{22}\delta_{21}\sigma_y.$$

By repeating the substitutions for $t = 4, 5, \ldots$, we obtain the impulse response of the shock (or innovation) to y on y as $\sigma_y\{1, \delta_{11}, (\delta_{11}\delta_{11} + \delta_{12}\delta_{21}), \ldots\}$ and the impulse response of a shock to y on x as $\sigma_y\{0, \delta_{21}, (\delta_{21}\delta_{11} + \delta_{22}\delta_{21}), \ldots\}$.

Now consider what happens when there is a one standard deviation shock to x so that at time $t = 1$, $v_1^x = \sigma_x$, and v_t^x is zero thereafter. Assume $v_t^y = 0$ for all t. In the first period after the shock, the effect of a shock of size σ_x on y is $y_1 = v_1^y = 0$, and the effect of the shock on x is $x_1 = v_1^x = \sigma_x$. Two periods after the shock, when $t = 2$, the effect on y is

$$y_2 = \delta_{11}y_1 + \delta_{12}x_1 = \delta_{11}0 + \delta_{12}\sigma_x = \delta_{12}\sigma_x$$

and the effect on x is

$$x_2 = \delta_{21}y_1 + \delta_{22}x_1 = \delta_{21}0 + \delta_{22}\sigma_x = \delta_{22}\sigma_x$$

Again, by repeated substitutions, we obtain the impulse response of a shock to x on y as $\sigma_x\{0, \delta_{12}, (\delta_{11}\delta_{12} + \delta_{12}\delta_{22}), \ldots\}$, and the impulse response of a shock to x on x as $\sigma_x\{1, \delta_{22}, (\delta_{21}\delta_{12} + \delta_{22}\delta_{22}), \ldots\}$. Figure 13.4 shows the four impulse response functions for numerical values: $\sigma_y = 1, \sigma_x = 2, \delta_{11} = 0.7, \delta_{12} = 0.2, \delta_{21} = 0.3$ and $\delta_{22} = 0.6$.

The advantage of examining impulse response functions (and not just VAR coefficients) is that they show the size of the impact of the shock plus the rate at which the shock dissipates, allowing for interdependencies.

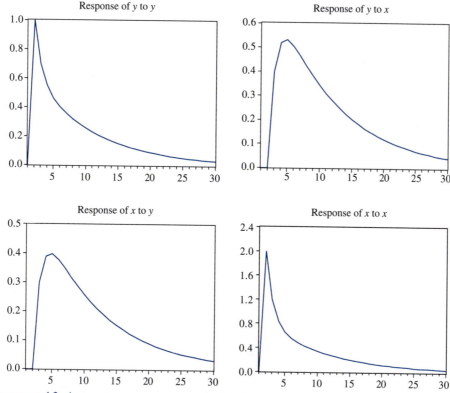

FIGURE **13.4**   Impulse responses to standard deviation shock.

13.4.2   FORECAST ERROR VARIANCE DECOMPOSITIONS

Another way to disentangle the effects of various shocks is to consider the contribution of each type of shock to the forecast error variance.

13.4.2a   Univariate Analysis
Consider again the univariate series, $y_t = \rho y_{t-1} + v_t$. The best one-step ahead forecast (alternatively the forecast one period ahead) is

$$y_{t+1}^F = E_t[\rho y_t + v_{t+1}]$$

where E_t is the expected value conditional on information at time t (i.e., we are interested in the mean value of y_{t+1} using what is known at time t). At time t the conditional expectation $E_t[\rho y_t] = \rho y_t$ is known, but the error v_{t+1} is unknown, and so its conditional expectation is zero. Thus, the best forecast of y_{t+1} is ρy_t and the forecast error is

$$y_{t+1} - E_t[y_{t+1}] = y_{t+1} - \rho y_t = v_{t+1}$$

The variance of the one-step forecast error is $\text{var}(v_{t+1}) = \sigma^2$. Suppose we wish to forecast two steps ahead, then, using the same logic, the two-step forecast becomes

$$y_{t+2}^F = E_t[\rho y_{t+1} + v_{t+2}] = E_t[\rho(\rho y_t + v_{t+1}) + v_{t+2}] = \rho^2 y_t$$

and the two-step forecast error becomes

$$y_{t+2} - E_t[y_{t+2}] = y_{t+2} - \rho^2 y_t = \rho v_{t+1} + v_{t+2}$$

In this case, the variance of the forecast error is $\text{var}(\rho v_{t+1} + v_{t+2}) = \sigma^2(\rho^2 + 1)$ showing that the variance of forecast error increases as we increase the forecast horizon.

In this univariate example, there is only one shock that leads to a forecast error. Hence the forecast error variance is 100% due to its own shock. The exercise of attributing the source of the variation in the forecast error is known as variance decomposition.

13.4.2b Bivariate Analysis

We can perform a variance decomposition for our special bivariate example where there is no identification problem. Ignoring the intercepts (since they are constants), the one–step ahead forecasts are

$$y_{t+1}^F = E_t[\delta_{11}y_t + \delta_{12}x_t + v_{t+1}^y] = \delta_{11}y_t + \delta_{12}x_t$$

$$x_{t+1}^F = E_t[\delta_{21}y_t + \delta_{22}x_t + v_{t+1}^x] = \delta_{21}y_t + \delta_{22}x_t$$

The corresponding one-step ahead forecast errors and variances are

$$FE_1^y = y_{t+1} - E_t[y_{t+1}] = v_{t+1}^y \quad \text{var}(FE_1^y) = \sigma_y^2$$

$$FE_1^x = x_{t+1} - E_t[x_{t+1}] = v_{t+1}^x \quad \text{var}(FE_1^x) = \sigma_x^2$$

Hence in the first period, all variation in the forecast error for y is due to its own shock. Likewise, 100% of the forecast error for x can be explained by its own shock. Using the same technique, the two–step ahead forecast for y is

$$\begin{aligned} y_{t+2}^F &= E_t[\delta_{11}y_{t+1} + \delta_{12}x_{t+1} + v_{t+2}^y] \\ &= E_t[\delta_{11}(\delta_{11}y_t + \delta_{12}x_t + v_{t+1}^y) + \delta_{12}(\delta_{21}y_t + \delta_{22}x_t + v_{t+1}^x) + v_{t+2}^y] \\ &= \delta_{11}(\delta_{11}y_t + \delta_{12}x_t) + \delta_{12}(\delta_{21}y_t + \delta_{22}x_t) \end{aligned}$$

and that for x is

$$\begin{aligned} x_{t+2}^F &= E_t[\delta_{21}y_{t+1} + \delta_{22}x_{t+1} + v_{t+2}^x] \\ &= E_t[\delta_{21}(\delta_{11}y_t + \delta_{12}x_t + v_{t+1}^y) + \delta_{22}(\delta_{21}y_t + \delta_{22}x_t + v_{t+1}^x) + v_{t+2}^x] \\ &= \delta_{21}(\delta_{11}y_t + \delta_{12}x_t) + \delta_{22}(\delta_{21}y_t + \delta_{22}x_t) \end{aligned}$$

The corresponding two-step ahead forecast errors and variances are (recall that we are working with the special case of independent errors)

$$FE_2^y = y_{t+2} - E_t[y_{t+2}] = [\delta_{11}v_{t+1}^y + \delta_{12}v_{t+1}^x + v_{t+2}^y]$$

$$\text{var}(FE_2^y) = \delta_{11}^2\sigma_y^2 + \delta_{12}^2\sigma_x^2 + \sigma_y^2$$

$$FE_2^x = x_{t+2} - E_t[x_{t+2}] = [\delta_{21}v_{t+1}^y + \delta_{22}v_{t+1}^x + v_{t+2}^x]$$

$$\text{var}(FE_2^x) = \delta_{21}^2\sigma_y^2 + \delta_{22}^2\sigma_x^2 + \sigma_x^2$$

We can decompose the total variance of the forecast error for y, $(\delta_{11}^2\sigma_y^2 + \delta_{12}^2\sigma_x^2 + \sigma_y^2)$, into that due to shocks to y, $(\delta_{11}^2\sigma_y^2 + \sigma_y^2)$, and that due to shocks to x, $(\delta_{12}^2\sigma_x^2)$. This decomposition is often expressed in proportional terms. The proportion of the two-step forecast error variance of y explained by its "own" shock is

$$(\delta_{11}^2 \sigma_y^2 + \sigma_y^2)/(\delta_{11}^2 \sigma_y^2 + \delta_{12}^2 \sigma_x^2 + \sigma_y^2)$$

and the proportion of the two-step forecast error variance of y explained by the "other" shock is

$$(\delta_{12}^2 \sigma_x^2)/(\delta_{11}^2 \sigma_y^2 + \delta_{12}^2 \sigma_x^2 + \sigma_y^2)$$

Similarly, the proportion of the two-step forecast error variance of x explained by its "own" shock is

$$(\delta_{22}^2 \sigma_x^2 + \sigma_x^2)/(\delta_{21}^2 \sigma_y^2 + \delta_{22}^2 \sigma_x^2 + \sigma_x^2)$$

and the proportion of the forecast error of x explained by the "other" shock is

$$(\delta_{21}^2 \sigma_y^2)/(\delta_{21}^2 \sigma_y^2 + \delta_{22}^2 \sigma_x^2 + \sigma_x^2)$$

For our numerical example with $\sigma_y = 1$, $\sigma_x = 2$, $\delta_{11} = 0.7$, $\delta_{12} = 0.2$, $\delta_{21} = 0.3$, and $\delta_{22} = 0.6$, we find that 90.303% of the two-step forecast error variance of y is due to y, and only 9.697% is due to x.

To sum up, suppose you were interested in the relationship between economic growth and inflation. A VAR model will tell you whether they are significantly related to each other; an impulse response analysis will show how growth and inflation react dynamically to shocks, and a variance decomposition analysis will be informative about the sources of volatility.

13.4.2c   The General Case

The example above assumes that x and y are not contemporaneously related and that the shocks are uncorrelated. There is no identification problem, and the generation and interpretation of the impulse response functions and decomposition of the forecast error variance are straightforward. In general, this is unlikely to be the case. Contemporaneous interactions and correlated errors complicate the identification of the nature of shocks and hence the interpretation of the impulses and decomposition of the causes of the forecast error variance. This topic is discussed in greater detail in textbooks devoted to time-series analysis.[2] A description of how the identification problem can arise is given in Appendix 13A.

13.5 Exercises

13.5.1   PROBLEMS

13.1   Consider the following first-order VAR model of stationary variables.

$$y_t = \delta_{11} y_{t-1} + \delta_{12} x_{t-1} + v_t^y$$
$$x_t = \delta_{21} y_{t-1} + \delta_{22} x_{t-1} + v_t^x$$

Under the assumption that there is no contemporaneous dependence, determine the impulse responses, four periods after a standard deviation shock for

---

[2] One reference you might consider is Lütkepohl, H. (2005) *Introduction to Multiple Time Series Analysis*, Springer, Chapter 9.

    (a) y following a shock to y
    (b) y following a shock to x
    (c) x following a shock to y
    (d) x following a shock to x

13.2 Consider the first-order VAR model in Exercise 13.1. Under the assumption that there is no contemporaneous dependence determine
    (a) the contribution of a shock to y on the variance of the three-step ahead forecast error for y;
    (b) the contribution of a shock to x on the variance of the three-step ahead forecast error for y;
    (c) the contribution of a shock to y on the variance of the three-step ahead forecast error for x;
    (d) the contribution of a shock to x on the variance of the three-step ahead forecast error for x.

13.3 The VEC model is a special form of the VAR for I(1) variables that are cointegrated. Consider the following VEC model:

$$\Delta y_t = \alpha_{10} + \alpha_{11}(y_{t-1} - \beta_0 - \beta_1 x_{t-1}) + v_t^y$$

$$\Delta x_t = \alpha_{20} + \alpha_{21}(y_{t-1} - \beta_0 - \beta_1 x_{t-1}) + v_t^x$$

The VEC model may also be rewritten as a VAR, but the two equations will contain common parameters:

$$y_t = \alpha_{10} + (\alpha_{11} + 1)y_{t-1} - \alpha_{11}\beta_0 - \alpha_{11}\beta_1 x_{t-1} + v_t^y$$

$$x_t = \alpha_{20} + \alpha_{21}y_{t-1} - \alpha_{21}\beta_0 - (\alpha_{21}\beta_1 - 1)x_{t-1} + v_t^x$$

    (a) Suppose you were given the following results of an estimated VEC model.

$$\widehat{\Delta y_t} = 2 - 0.5(y_{t-1} - 1 - 0.7x_{t-1})$$

$$\widehat{\Delta x_t} = 3 + 0.3(y_{t-1} - 1 - 0.7x_{t-1})$$

    Rewrite the model in the VAR form.
    (b) Now suppose you were given the following results of an estimated VAR model, but you were also told that y and x are cointegrated.

$$\hat{y}_t = 0.7y_{t-1} + 0.3 + 0.24x_{t-1}$$

$$\hat{x}_t = 0.6y_{t-1} - 0.6 + 0.52x_{t-1}$$

    Rewrite the model in the VEC form.

13.5.2 COMPUTER EXERCISES

13.4 The data file *gdp.dat* contains quarterly data on the real GDP of Australia (*AUS*) and real GDP of the United States (*USA*) for the sample period 1970.1 to 2000.4.
    (a) Are the series stationary or nonstationary?
    (b) Test for cointegration allowing for an intercept term. You will find that the intercept is negative. Is this sensible? If not, repeat the test for cointegration excluding the constant term.
    (c) Save the cointegrating residuals and estimate the VEC model.

13.5   The data file *growth.dat* contains the log of GDP (G) and the log of the CPI (P) for the US economy over the period 1960:1 to 2004:4.
(a) Are the series stationary or nonstationary?
(b) Test for cointegration allowing for an intercept term. Are the series cointegrated?
(c) Estimate a VAR model for the set of I(0) variables $\{\Delta P_t, \Delta G_t\}$.

13.6   The data file *vec.dat* contains 100 observations on 2 generated series of data, x and y. The variables are nonstationary and cointegrated without a constant term. Save the cointegrating residuals (*res*) and estimate the VEC model. As a check, the results for the case normalized on y are

$$\widehat{\Delta y_t} = -0.576(res_{t-1})$$
$$(t) \quad (-6.158)$$

$$\widehat{\Delta x_t} = 0.450(res_{t-1})$$
$$(t) \quad (4.448)$$

(a) The residuals from the error correction model should not be autocorrelated. Is this the case?
(b) Note that one of the error correction terms is negative and the other is positive. Explain why this is necessary.

13.7   The data file *var.dat* contains 100 observations on 2 generated series of data, w and z. The variables are nonstationary but not cointegrated. Estimate a VAR model of changes in the variables. As a check, the results are (the intercept terms were not significant):

$$\widehat{\Delta w_t} = 0.743\Delta w_{t-1} + 0.214\Delta z_{t-1}$$
$$(t) \quad (11.403) \qquad (2.893)$$

$$\widehat{\Delta z_t} = -0.155\Delta w_{t-1} + 0.641\Delta z_{t-1}$$
$$(t) \quad (-2.293) \qquad (8.338)$$

(a) The residuals from the VAR model should not be autocorrelated. Is this the case?
(b) Determine the impulse responses for the first two periods. (You may assume the special condition that there is no contemporaneous dependence.)
(c) Determine the variance decompositions for the first two periods.

13.8   The quantity theory of money says that there is a direct relationship between the quantity of money in the economy and the aggregate price level. Put simply, if the quantity of money doubles then the price level should also double. Figure 13.5 shows the percentage change in a measure of the quantity of money (M) and the percentage change in a measure of aggregate prices (P) for the United States between 1961:1 and 2005:4 (data file *qtm.dat*). A VEC model was estimated as follows:

$$\widehat{\Delta P_t} = -0.016(P_{t-1} - 1.004M_{t-1} + 0.039) + 0.514\Delta P_{t-1} - 0.005\Delta M_{t-1}$$
$$(t) \qquad (2.127) \qquad (3.696) \qquad (1.714) \ (7.999) \qquad (0.215)$$

$$\widehat{\Delta M_t} = 0.067(P_{t-1} - 1.004M_{t-1} + 0.039) - 0.336\Delta P_{t-1} - 0.340\Delta M_{t-1}$$
$$(t) \qquad (3.017) \qquad (3.696) \qquad (1.714) \ (1.796) \qquad (4.802)$$

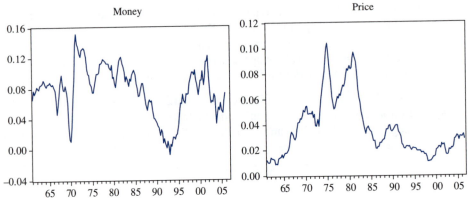

FIGURE **13.5**   Percentage changes in money and price.

(a) Identify the cointegrating relationship between P and M. Is the quantity theory of money supported?

(b) Identify the error-correction coefficients. Is the system stable?

(c) The above results were estimated using a system approach. Derive the cointegrating residuals and confirm that the series is indeed an $I(0)$ variable.

(d) Estimate a VEC model using the cointegrating residuals. (Your results should be the same as above.)

13.9   Research into the Phillips curve is concerned with providing empirical evidence of a tradeoff between inflation and unemployment. Can an economy experience lower unemployment if it is prepared to accept higher inflation? Figure 13.6 plots the changes in a measure of the unemployment rate (DU) and the changes in a measure of inflation (DP) for the United States for the sample period 1970:01 to 2006:12 (data file *phillips.dat*). A VAR model was estimated as follows:

$$\Delta DU_t = 0.145 DU_{t-1} + 0.006 DP_{t-1}$$
$$(t) \quad (3.074) \quad\quad (0.235)$$

$$\Delta DP_t = -0.209 DU_{t-1} + 0.333 DP_{t-1}$$
$$(t) \quad (-2.369) \quad\quad (7.442)$$

(a) Is there evidence of an inverse relationship between the change in the unemployment rate (DU) and the change in the inflation rate (DP)?

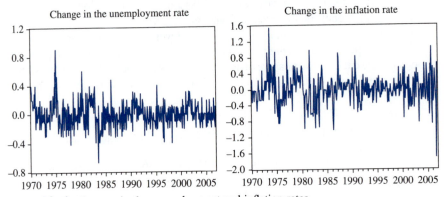

FIGURE **13.6**   Changes in the unemployment and inflation rates.

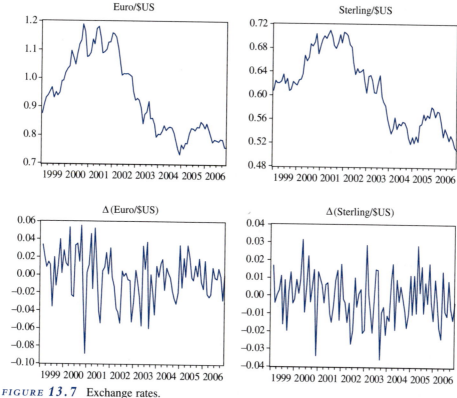

FIGURE *13.7* Exchange rates.

(b) What is the response of DU at time $t+1$ following a unit shock to DU at time t?
(c) What is the response of DP at time $t+1$ following a unit shock to DU at time t?
(d) What is the response of DU at time $t+2$?
(e) What is the response of DP at time $t+2$?

13.10 Figure 13.7 shows the time series for two exchange rates—the EURO per $US and the STERLING per $US (data file *sterling.dat*). Both the levels and the changes in the data are shown.
(a) Which set of data would you consider using to estimate a VEC model and which set to estimate a VAR. Why?
(b) Apply the two-step approach suggested in this chapter to estimate a VEC model.
(c) Estimate a VAR model paying attention to the order of the lag.

Appendix 13A The Identification Problem[3]

A bivariate dynamic system with contemporaneous interactions (also known as a structural model) is written as

$$y_t + \beta_1 x_t = \alpha_1 y_{t-1} + \alpha_2 x_{t-1} + e_t^y$$
$$x_t + \beta_2 y_t = \alpha_3 y_{t-1} + \alpha_4 x_{t-1} + e_t^x \tag{13A.1}$$

---

[3] This appendix requires a basic understanding of matrix notation.

which can be more conveniently expressed in matrix form as

$$\begin{bmatrix} 1 & \beta_1 \\ \beta_2 & 1 \end{bmatrix} \begin{bmatrix} y_t \\ x_t \end{bmatrix} = \begin{bmatrix} \alpha_1 & \alpha_2 \\ \alpha_3 & \alpha_4 \end{bmatrix} \begin{bmatrix} y_{t-1} \\ x_{t-1} \end{bmatrix} + \begin{bmatrix} e_t^y \\ e_t^x \end{bmatrix}$$

or rewritten in symbolic form as $BY_t = AY_{t-1} + E_t$, where

$$B = \begin{bmatrix} 1 & \beta_1 \\ \beta_2 & 1 \end{bmatrix} \quad A = \begin{bmatrix} \alpha_1 & \alpha_2 \\ \alpha_3 & \alpha_4 \end{bmatrix} \quad E = \begin{bmatrix} e_t^y \\ e_t^x \end{bmatrix}$$

A VAR representation (also known as reduced-form model) is written as

$$\begin{align} y_t &= \delta_1 y_{t-1} + \delta_2 x_{t-1} + v_t^y \\ x_t &= \delta_3 y_{t-1} + \delta_4 x_{t-1} + v_t^x \end{align} \tag{13A.2}$$

or in matrix form as: $Y_t = CY_{t-1} + V_t$, where

$$C = \begin{bmatrix} \delta_1 & \delta_2 \\ \delta_3 & \delta_4 \end{bmatrix} \quad V = \begin{bmatrix} v_t^y \\ v_t^x \end{bmatrix}$$

Clearly, there is a relationship between (13.A.1) and (13A.2): $C = B^{-1}A$ and $V = B^{-1}E$. The special case considered in the chapter assumes that there are no contemporaneous interactions ($\beta_1 = \beta_2 = 0$), making B an identity matrix. There is no identification problem in this case because the VAR residuals can be unambiguously "identified" as shocks to y or as shocks to x: $v^y = e^y$, $v^x = e^x$. The generation and interpretation of the impulse responses and variance decompositions are unambiguous.

In general, however, B is not an identity matrix, making v^y and v^x weighted averages of e^y and e^x. In this general case, impulse responses and variance decompositions based on v^y and v^x are not meaningful or useful because we cannot be certain about the source of the shocks. A number of methods exist for "identifying" the structural model from its reduced form.

Chapter *14*

Time-Varying Volatility and ARCH Models: An Introduction to Financial Econometrics

Learning Objectives

Based on the material in this chapter, you should be able to do the following:

1. Explain the difference between a constant and a time-varying variance of the error term.
2. Explain the term "conditionally normal."
3. Perform a test for ARCH effects.
4. Estimate an ARCH model.
5. Forecast volatility.
6. Explain the difference between ARCH and GARCH specifications.
7. Explain the distinctive features of a T-GARCH model and a GARCH-in-mean model.

Keywords

ARCH	GARCH
ARCH-in-mean	GARCH-in-mean
conditional and unconditional forecasts	T-ARCH and T-GARCH
conditionally normal	time-varying variance

In Chapter 12, our focus was on time-varying mean processes and macroeconomic time series. We were concerned with stationary and nonstationary variables and in particular, macroeconomic variables like GDP, inflation, and interest rates. The nonstationary nature of the variables implied that they had **means that change over time**. In this chapter we are concerned with **variances that change over time**, that is, time-varying variance processes. The model we focus on is called the autoregressive conditional heteroskedastic (ARCH) model.

Nobel Prize winner Robert Engle's original work on ARCH was concerned with the volatility of inflation. However, it is the applications of the ARCH model to financial time series that established and consolidated the significance of his contribution. For this reason, the examples used in this chapter will be based on financial time series. As we will see, financial time series have characteristics that are well represented by models with dynamic variances. The particular aims of this chapter are to discuss the modeling of dynamic variances using the ARCH class of models of volatility, the estimation of these models, and their use in forecasting.

14.1 The ARCH Model

To begin consider a simple regression model:

$$y_t = \beta_0 + e_t \tag{14.1a}$$

$$e_t \sim N(0, \sigma_t^2) \tag{14.1b}$$

$$\sigma_t^2 = \alpha_0 \tag{14.1c}$$

The first equation (14.1a) says that variable y_t can be explained by a constant β_0 and an error term e_t. The second equation (14.1b) says that the error term is normally distributed with mean 0 and variance σ_t^2. The third equation (14.1c) says that the variance is a constant α_0. We can think of this model as a simple version of the simple regression model studied in Chapters 2–4. It is a simple version of the simple regression model because it contains only a constant term and no explanatory variable. Explanatory variables can be included in (14.1a), but omitting them in the first instance allows us to focus on the essential features of ARCH.

Now make three changes that we will justify later. First, let the error variance be time varying (so that it is heteroskedastic over time) and, following popular usage, call it h_t; that is, let $\sigma_t^2 = h_t$. Second, let the distribution of the error be **conditionally normal** $e_t|I_{t-1} \sim N(0, h_t)$, where I_{t-1} represents the information available at time $t-1$. Third, let h_t be a function of a constant term and the lagged error squared e_{t-1}^2. Putting all this together yields

$$y_t = \beta_0 + e_t \tag{14.2a}$$

$$e_t|I_{t-1} \sim N(0, h_t) \tag{14.2b}$$

$$h_t = \alpha_0 + \alpha_1 e_{t-1}^2, \quad \alpha_0 > 0, \quad 0 \le \alpha_1 < 1 \tag{14.2c}$$

Equations (14.2b) and (14.2c) describe the ARCH class of models. The name—ARCH—conveys the fact that we are working with time-varying variances (heteroskedasticity) that depend on (are conditional on) lagged effects (autocorrelation). This particular example is an ARCH(1) model since the time-varying variance h_t is a function of a constant term (α_0) plus a term lagged once, the square of the error in the previous period $(\alpha_1 e_{t-1}^2)$. The coefficients α_0 and α_1 have to be positive to ensure a positive variance. The coefficient α_1 must be less than 1, otherwise h_t will continue to increase over time, eventually exploding. Conditional normality means that the distribution is a function of known information at time $t-1$. That is, when $t = 2$, $e_2|I_1 \sim N(0, \alpha_0 + \alpha_1 e_1^2)$ and when $t = 3$, $e_3|I_2 \sim N(0, \alpha_0 + \alpha_1 e_2^2)$, and so on. In this particular case, conditioning on I_{t-1} is equivalent to conditioning on the square of the error in the previous period e_{t-1}^2. So (14.2b) means that conditional on e_{t-1}^2, assuming that its value is known or given, e_t has a normal distribution.

The ARCH model has become a very important econometric model because it is able to capture stylized features of real world volatility. Before we explore these features, it is useful to consider first the distinction between conditional and unconditional forecasts and hence the motivation for the 'C' in ARCH.

14.1.1 CONDITIONAL AND UNCONDITIONAL FORECASTS

Suppose you are working with an AR(1) model $y_t = \rho y_{t-1} + e_t$, $|\rho| < 1$, and, at time t, you would like to use the model to forecast the value of y_{t+1}. The conditional forecast of y_{t+1} is the conditional mean $E(y_{t+1}|I_t) = \rho y_t$. It is conditional on the information set at time t, namely, $I_t = \{y_t\}$. As a general principle, conditional forecasts are better than unconditional, because the latest information is used. The forecast error is $(y_{t+1} - \rho y_t)$, which in this case is e_{t+1}. Hence the variance of the forecast error is $E_t(y_{t+1} - \rho y_t)^2 = E_t(e_{t+1})^2 = \sigma^2$, where E_t is another way to write an expectation conditional on information at time t.

Now imagine the same situation, except that you are interested in an unconditional forecast. An unconditional forecast is not conditional on any past values of y, but uses instead the unconditional mean of y_{t+1} implied by its model, in this case the AR(1) model. To obtain the unconditional mean of y_{t+1}, we use successive substitution to obtain y_{t+1} as the sum of an infinite series of the error terms. To show this algebraically, note that if $y_t = \rho y_{t-1} + e_t$, then $y_{t-1} = \rho y_{t-2} + e_{t-1}$ and $y_{t-2} = \rho y_{t-3} + e_{t-2}$, and so on. Hence $y_{t+1} = e_{t+1} + \rho e_t + \rho^2 e_{t-1} + \cdots + \rho^t y_0$, where the final term $\rho^t y_0$ is assumed to be negligible. The unconditional forecast, in the context of this AR(1) model, is

$$E(y_{t+1}) = E(e_{t+1} + \rho e_t + \rho^2 e_{t-1} + \cdots) = 0$$

because $E(e_{t-j}) = 0$ for all j.

The unconditional forecast error is $(y_{t+1} - 0)$. Its variance is

$$E(y_{t+1} - 0)^2 = \text{var}(y_{t+1}) = E(e_{t+1} + \rho e_t + \rho^2 e_{t-1} + \cdots)^2$$

$$= E(e_{t+1}^2 + \rho^2 e_t^2 + \rho^4 e_{t-1}^2 + \cdots)$$

$$= \sigma^2(1 + \rho^2 + \rho^4 + \cdots) = \frac{\sigma^2}{1 - \rho^2}$$

because $E(e_{t-j}e_{t-i}) = \sigma^2$ when $i = j$; $E(e_{t-j}e_{t-i}) = 0$ when $i \neq j$ and the sum of a geometric series $(1 + \rho^2 + \rho^4 + \cdots)$ is $1/(1 - \rho^2)$.

Since $[1/(1 - \rho^2)] > 1$, it follows that the unconditional variance $[\sigma^2/(1 - \rho^2)]$ is always greater than the conditional variance (σ^2). This result is a general one; conditioning one's forecast on more information improves the precision of that forecast. Thus, there are efficiency advantages from using conditional forecasting. In the context of the ARCH(1) model, knowing the squared error in the previous period e_{t-1}^2 improves our knowledge about the likely magnitude of the variance in period t.

14.2 Time-Varying Volatility

The ARCH model has become a popular one because its variance specification can capture commonly observed features of the time series of financial variables; in particular, it is useful for modeling **volatility** and especially changes in volatility over time. To appreciate

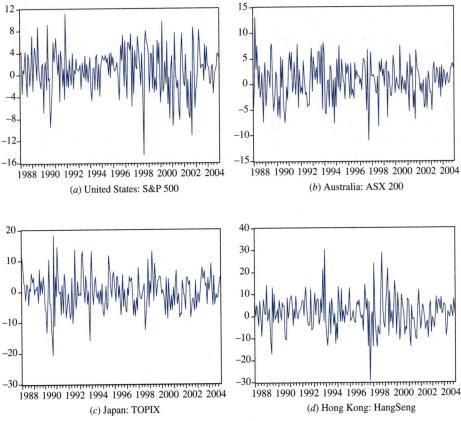

(a) United States: S&P 500

(b) Australia: ASX 200

(c) Japan: TOPIX

(d) Hong Kong: HangSeng

FIGURE 14.1   Time series of returns to stock indices.

what we mean by volatility and time-varying volatility, and how it relates to the ARCH model, let us look at some stylized facts about the behavior of financial variables, for example, the returns to stock price indices (also known as share price indices).

Figure 14.1 shows the time series of the monthly returns to a number of stock prices; namely, the US S&P500, the Australian S&P/ASX 200, the Japanese TOPIX, and the Hong Kong HangSeng over the period 1988:01 to 2004:12 (data file *returns.dat*). The values of these series change rapidly from period to period in an apparently unpredictable manner; we say the series are volatile. Furthermore, there are periods when large changes are followed by further large changes and periods when small changes are followed by further small changes. In this case the series are said to display time-varying volatility as well as "clustering" of changes.

Figure 14.2 shows the histograms of the returns. All returns display non-normal properties. We can see this more clearly if we draw normal distributions (using the respective sample means and sample variances) on top of these histograms. Note that there are more observations around the mean and in the tails. Distributions with these properties—more peaked around the mean and relatively fat tails—are said to be **leptokurtic**.

Note that the assumption that the conditional distribution for $(y_t|I_{t-1})$ is normal, an assumption that we made in equation (14.2b), does not necessarily imply that the unconditional distribution for y_t is normal. When we collect empirical observations on y_t into a histogram, we are constructing an estimate of the unconditional distribution for y_t. What we have observed is that the unconditional distribution for y_t is leptokurtic.

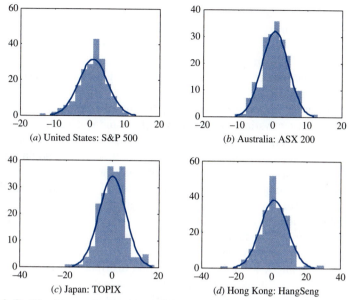

FIGURE **14.2** Histograms of returns to various stock indices.

To illustrate how the ARCH model can be used to capture changing volatility and the leptokurtic nature of the distribution for y_t, we generate some simulated data for two models. In both cases we set $\beta_0 = 0$ so that $y_t = e_t$. The top panel in Figure 14.3 illustrates the case when $\alpha_0 = 1$, $\alpha_1 = 0$. These values imply $\text{var}(y_t|I_{t-1}) = h_t = 1$. This variance is

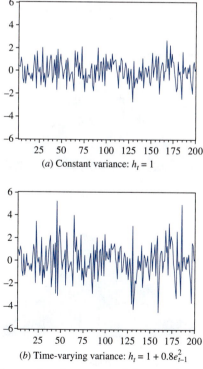

FIGURE **14.3** Simulated examples of constant and time-varying variances.

constant and not time varying because $\alpha_1 = 0$. The bottom panel in Figure 14.3 illustrates the case when $\alpha_0 = 1$, $\alpha_1 = 0.8$, the case of a time-varying variance given by $\text{var}(y_t|I_{t-1}) = h_t = \alpha_0 + \alpha_1 e_{t-1}^2 = 1 + 0.8 e_{t-1}^2$. Note that, relative to the series in the top panel, volatility in the bottom panel is not constant; rather, it changes over time and it clusters—there are periods of small changes (for example, around observation 100) and periods of big changes (around observation 175).

In Figure 14.4 we present histograms of y_t for the two cases. The top panel is the histogram for the constant variance case where $(y_t|I_{t-1})$ and y_t have the same distribution, namely the noise process $y_t \sim N(0, 1)$ because $h_t = 1$. The bottom panel is the histogram for the time-varying variance case. We know that the conditional distribution for $(y_t|I_{t-1})$ is $N(0, h_t)$. But what about the unconditional distribution for y_t? Again, we can check for normality by superimposing a normal distribution on top of the histogram. In this case, to allow for a meaningful comparison with the histogram in the top panel, we plot the standardized observations of y_t. That is for each observation we subtract the sample mean and divide by the sample standard deviation. This transformation ensures that the distribution will have a zero mean and variance 1, but it preserves the shape of the distribution. Comparing the two panels, we note that the second distribution has higher frequencies around the mean (zero) and higher frequencies in the tails (outside ± 3). This feature of time series with ARCH errors—the unconditional distribution of y_t is non-normal—is consistent with what we observed in the stock return series.

Thus, the ARCH model is intuitively appealing because it seems sensible to explain volatility as a function of the errors e_t. These errors are often called "shocks" or "news" by financial analysts. They represent the unexpected! According to the ARCH model, the larger the shock the greater the volatility in the series. In addition, this model captures volatility clustering, as big changes in e_t are fed into further big changes in h_t via the lagged effect e_{t-1}. The simulations show how well the ARCH model mimics the behavior of financial time series shown in Figure 14.1, including their non-normal distributions.

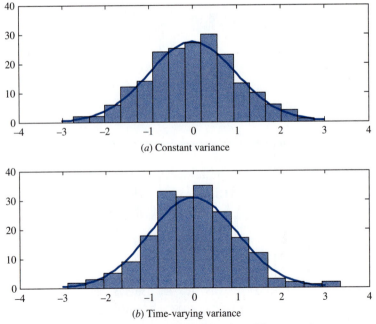

(a) Constant variance

(b) Time-varying variance

FIGURE 14.4 Frequency distributions of the simulated models.

14.3 **Testing, Estimating, and Forecasting**

14.3.1 Testing for ARCH Effects

A Lagrange multiplier (*LM*) test is often used to test for the presence of ARCH effects. To perform this test, first estimate the **mean equation**, which can be a regression of the variable on a constant (like 14.1), or it may include other variables. Then save the estimated residuals $\hat{e}_t$ and obtain their squares $\hat{e}_t^2$. To test for first-order ARCH, regress $\hat{e}_t^2$ on the squared residuals lagged $\hat{e}_{t-1}^2$:

$$\hat{e}_t^2 = \gamma_0 + \gamma_1 \hat{e}_{t-1}^2 + v_t \tag{14.3}$$

where v_t is a random term. The null and alternative hypotheses are

$$H_0 : \gamma_1 = 0 \qquad\qquad H_1 : \gamma_1 \neq 0$$

If there are no ARCH effects, then $\gamma_1 = 0$ and the fit of (14.3) will be poor and the equation R^2 will be low. If there are ARCH effects, we expect the magnitude of $\hat{e}_t^2$ to depend on its lagged values and the R^2 will be relatively high. The *LM* test statistic is $(T - q)R^2$ where T is the sample size, q is the number of $\hat{e}_{t-j}^2$ terms on the right-hand side of (14.3), and R^2 is the coefficient of determination. If the null hypothesis is true, then the test statistic $(T - q)R^2$ is distributed (in large samples) as $\chi_{(q)}^2$, where q is the order of lag, and $T - q$ is the number of complete observations; in this case, $q = 1$. If $(T - q)R^2 \geq \chi_{(1-\alpha,q)}^2$, then we reject the null hypothesis that $\gamma_1 = 0$ and conclude that ARCH effects are present.

To illustrate the test, consider the returns from buying shares in the hypothetical company BrightenYourDay (BYD) Lighting. The time series and histogram of the returns are shown in Figure 14.5 (data file *byd.dat*). The time series shows evidence of time-varying volatility and clustering, and the unconditional distribution is non-normal.

To perform the test for ARCH effects, first estimate a mean equation that in this example is $r_t = \beta_0 + e_t$, where r_t is the monthly return on shares of BYD. Second, retrieve the estimated residuals. Third, estimate equation (14.3). The results for the ARCH test are

$$\hat{e}_t^2 = 0.908 + 0.353\hat{e}_{t-1}^2 \quad R^2 = 0.124$$
$$(t) \qquad\qquad (8.409)$$

The *t*-statistic suggests a significant first-order coefficient. The sample size is 500 giving an *LM* test value of $(T - q)R^2 = 61.876$. Comparing the computed test value to the 5% critical value of a $\chi_{(1)}^2$ distribution $(\chi_{(0.95,1)}^2 = 3.841)$ leads to the rejection of the null hypothesis. In other words, the residuals show the presence of ARCH(1) effects.

14.3.2 Estimating ARCH Models

ARCH models are estimated by the maximum likelihood method. Estimation details are beyond the scope of this book, but the maximum likelihood method (see Appendix C.8) is programmed in most econometric software.

Equation (14.4) shows the results from estimating an ARCH(1) model applied to the monthly returns from buying shares in the company BrightenYourDayLighting. The

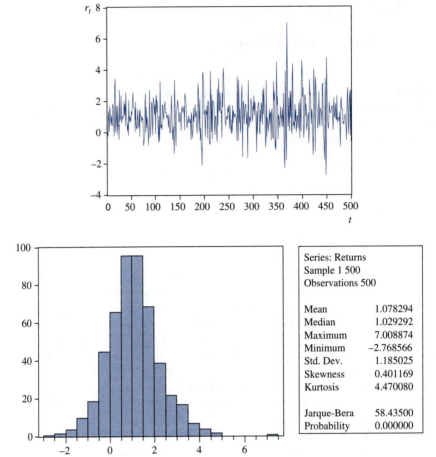

FIGURE **14.5** Time series and histogram of returns for BYD Lighting.

estimated mean of the series is described in (14.4a) while the estimated variance is given in (14.4b).

$$\hat{r}_t = \hat{\beta}_0 = 1.063 \tag{14.4a}$$

$$\hat{h}_t = \hat{\alpha}_0 + \hat{\alpha}_1 \hat{e}_{t-1}^2 = 0.642 + 0.569 \hat{e}_{t-1}^2 \tag{14.4b}$$
$$(t) \qquad\qquad (5.536)$$

The t-statistic of the first-order coefficient (5.536) suggests a significant ARCH(1) coefficient. Recall that one of the requirements of the ARCH model is that $\alpha_0 > 0$ and $\alpha_1 > 0$ so that the implied variances are positive. Note that the estimated coefficients $\hat{\alpha}_0$ and $\hat{\alpha}_1$ satisfy this condition.

14.3.3 FORECASTING VOLATILITY

Once we have estimated the model, we can use it to forecast next period's return r_{t+1} and the conditional volatility h_{t+1}. When one invests in shares, it is important to choose them not just

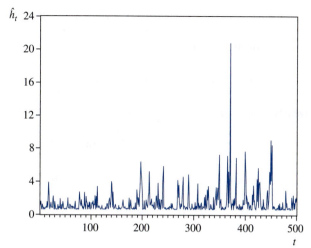

FIGURE **14.6**   Plot of conditional variance.

on the basis of their mean returns, but also on the basis of their risk. Volatility gives us a measure of their risk.

For our case study of investing in BrightenYourDayLighting, the forecast return and volatility are

$$\hat{r}_{t+1} = \hat{\beta}_0 = 1.063 \tag{14.5a}$$

$$\hat{h}_{t+1} = \hat{\alpha}_0 + \hat{\alpha}_1(r_t - \hat{\beta}_0)^2 = 0.642 + 0.569(r_t - 1.063)^2 \tag{14.5b}$$

The first equation (14.5a) gives the estimated return that, because it does not change over time, is both the conditional and unconditional mean return. The estimated error in period t, given by $\hat{e}_t = r_t - \hat{r}_t$, can then be used to obtain the estimated conditional variance (14.5b). The time series of the conditional variance does change over time and is shown in Figure 14.6. Note how the conditional variance around observation 370 coincides with the period of large changes in returns shown in Figure 14.5.

14.4 Extensions

The ARCH(1) model can be extended in a number of ways. One obvious extension is to allow for more lags. In general, an ARCH(q) model that includes lags $e_{t-1}^2, \ldots, e_{t-q}^2$ has a conditional variance function that is given by

$$h_t = \alpha_0 + \alpha_1 e_{t-1}^2 + \alpha_2 e_{t-2}^2 \cdots + \alpha_q e_{t-q}^2 \tag{14.6}$$

In this case the variance or volatility in a given period depends on the magnitudes of the squared errors in the past q periods. Testing, estimating, and forecasting, are natural extensions of the case with one lag.

14.4.1   THE GARCH MODEL—GENERALIZED ARCH

One of the shortcomings of an ARCH(q) model is that there are $q + 1$ parameters to estimate. If q is a large number, we may lose accuracy in the estimation. The generalized

ARCH model, or GARCH, is an alternative way to capture long lagged effects with fewer parameters. It is a special generalization of the ARCH model and it can be derived as follows. First, consider equation (14.6) but write it as

$$h_t = \alpha_0 + \alpha_1 e_{t-1}^2 + \beta_1 \alpha_1 e_{t-2}^2 + \beta_1^2 \alpha_1 e_{t-3}^2 + \cdots$$

In other words, we have imposed a geometric lag structure on the lagged coefficients of the form $\alpha_s = \alpha_1 \beta_1^{s-1}$. This structure is similar to that imposed on the lag structure for a mean function in Appendix 9C. Next, add and subtract $\beta_1 \alpha_0$ and rearrange terms as follows:

$$h_t = (\alpha_0 - \beta_1 \alpha_0) + \alpha_1 e_{t-1}^2 + \beta_1(\alpha_0 + \alpha_1 e_{t-2}^2 + \beta_1 \alpha_1 e_{t-3}^2 + \cdots)$$

Then, since $h_{t-1} = \alpha_0 + \alpha_1 e_{t-2}^2 + \beta_1 \alpha_1 e_{t-3}^2 + \beta_1^2 \alpha_1 e_{t-4}^2 + \cdots$, we may simplify to

$$h_t = \delta + \alpha_1 e_{t-1}^2 + \beta_1 h_{t-1} \tag{14.7}$$

where $\delta = (\alpha_0 - \beta_1 \alpha_0)$. This generalized ARCH model is denoted as GARCH(1,1). It can be viewed as a special case of the more general GARCH (p,q) model, where p is the number of lagged h terms and q is the number of lagged e^2 terms. We also note that we need $\alpha_1 + \beta_1 < 1$ for stationarity; if $\alpha_1 + \beta_1 \geq 1$ we have a so-called "integrated GARCH" process, or IGARCH.

The GARCH(1,1) model is a very popular specification because it fits many data series well. It tells us that the volatility changes with lagged shocks (e_{t-1}^2) but there is also momentum in the system working via h_{t-1}. One reason why this model is so popular is that it can capture long lags in the shocks with only a few parameters. A GARCH(1,1) model with three parameters $(\delta, \alpha_1, \beta_1)$ can capture similar effects to an ARCH(q) model requiring the estimation of $(q+1)$ parameters, where q is large, say $q \geq 6$.

To illustrate the GARCH(1,1) specification, consider again the returns to our shares in BrightenYourDayLighting, which we reestimate (by maximum likelihood) under the new model. The results are

$$\hat{r}_t = 1.049$$

$$\hat{h}_t = 0.401 + 0.492\, \hat{e}_{t-1}^2 + 0.238\, \hat{h}_{t-1}$$

$$(t) \qquad\qquad (4.834) \qquad (2.136)$$

The significance of the coefficient in front of $\hat{h}_{t-1}$ suggests that the GARCH(1,1) model is better than the ARCH(1) results shown in (14.4). A plot of the mean equation and the time-varying variance is shown in Figure 14.7a and 14.7b.

14.4.2 ALLOWING FOR AN ASYMMETRIC EFFECT

A standard ARCH model treats bad "news" (negative $e_{t-1} < 0$) and good "news" (positive $e_{t-1} > 0$) symmetrically, that is, the effect on the volatility h_t is the same $(\alpha_1 e_{t-1}^2)$. However, the effects of good and bad news may have asymmetric effects on volatility. In general, when negative news hits a financial market, asset prices tend to enter a turbulent phase and volatility increases, but with positive news volatility tends to be small and the market enters a period of tranquility.

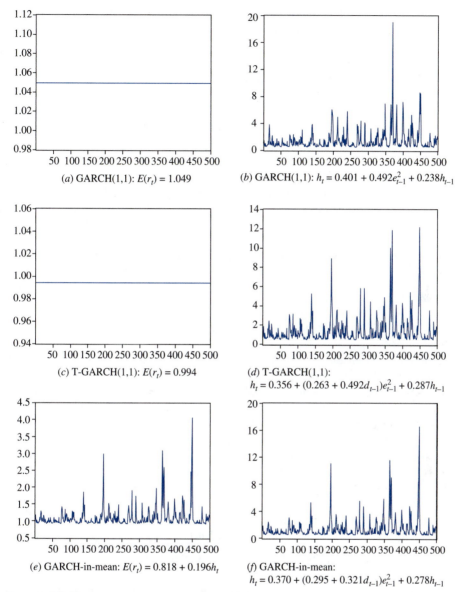

(a) GARCH(1,1): $E(r_t) = 1.049$

(b) GARCH(1,1): $h_t = 0.401 + 0.492e_{t-1}^2 + 0.238h_{t-1}$

(c) T-GARCH(1,1): $E(r_t) = 0.994$

(d) T-GARCH(1,1):
$h_t = 0.356 + (0.263 + 0.492d_{t-1})e_{t-1}^2 + 0.287h_{t-1}$

(e) GARCH-in-mean: $E(r_t) = 0.818 + 0.196h_t$

(f) GARCH-in-mean:
$h_t = 0.370 + (0.295 + 0.321d_{t-1})e_{t-1}^2 + 0.278h_{t-1}$

FIGURE 14.7 Estimated means and variances of ARCH models.

The threshold ARCH model, or T-ARCH, is one example where positive and negative news are treated asymmetrically. In the T-GARCH version of the model, the specification of the conditional variance is

$$h_t = \delta + \alpha_1 e_{t-1}^2 + \gamma d_{t-1} e_{t-1}^2 + \beta_1 h_{t-1}$$

$$d_t = \begin{cases} 1 & e_t < 0 \quad \text{(bad news)} \\ 0 & e_t \geq 0 \quad \text{(good news)} \end{cases} \tag{14.8}$$

where γ is known as the asymmetry or leverage term. When $\gamma = 0$, the model collapses to the standard GARCH form. Otherwise, when the shock is positive (i.e., good news) the effect on volatility is α_1, but when the news is negative (i.e., bad news) the effect on volatility is $\alpha_1 + \gamma$. Hence, if γ is significant and positive, negative shocks have a larger effect on h_t than positive shocks.

The returns to our shares in BrightenYourDayLighting were reestimated with a T-GARCH(1,1) specification. The results are

$$\hat{r}_t = 0.994$$

$$\hat{h}_t = 0.356 + 0.263\hat{e}_{t-1}^2 + 0.492d_{t-1}\hat{e}_{t-1}^2 + 0.287\,\hat{h}_{t-1}$$

$$(t) \qquad\qquad (3.267) \qquad (2.405) \qquad\qquad (2.488)$$

These results show that when the market observes good news (positive e_t), the contribution of e_t^2 to volatility h_{t+1} is by a factor 0.263, whereas when the market observes bad news (negative e_t), the contribution of e_t^2 to volatility h_{t+1} is by a factor $(0.263 + 0.492)$. Overall, negative shocks create greater volatility in financial markets. Figure 14.7b and 14.7d compare the conditional variance of the symmetric GARCH model with that generated by the T-GARCH model. Note how the T-GARCH model highlighted the period around observation 200 as another period of turbulence (see Figure 14.5 for the time series of the returns).

14.4.3   GARCH-IN-MEAN AND TIME-VARYING RISK PREMIUM

Another popular extension of the GARCH model is the "GARCH-in-mean" model. The positive relationship between risk (often measured by volatility) and return is one of the basic tenets of financial economics. As risk increases so does the mean return. Intuitively, the return to risky assets tends to be higher than the return to safe assets (low variation in returns) to compensate an investor for taking on the risk of buying the volatile share. However, while we have estimated the mean equation to model returns, and have estimated a GARCH model to capture time-varying volatility, we have not used the risk to explain returns. This is the aim of the GARCH-in-mean models.

The equations of a GARCH-in-mean model are shown below:

$$y_t = \beta_0 + \theta h_t + e_t \tag{14.9a}$$

$$e_t | I_{t-1} \sim N(0, h_t) \tag{14.9b}$$

$$h_t = \delta + \alpha_1 e_{t-1}^2 + \beta_1 h_{t-1}, \quad \delta > 0,\ 0 \le \alpha_1 < 1,\ 0 \le \beta_1 < 1 \tag{14.9c}$$

The first equation is the mean equation; it now shows the effect of the conditional variance on the dependent variable. In particular, note that the model postulates that the conditional variance h_t affects y_t by a factor θ. The other two equations are as before.

The returns to shares in BrightenYourDayLighting were reestimated as a GARCH-in-mean model. The results are

$$\hat{r}_t = 0.818 + 0.196h_t$$

$$(t) \qquad\qquad (2.915)$$

$$\hat{h}_t = 0.370 + 0.295\hat{e}_{t-1}^2 + 0.321d_{t-1}\hat{e}_{t-1}^2 + 0.278\hat{h}_{t-1}$$

$$(t) \qquad\qquad (3.426) \qquad (1.979) \qquad\qquad (2.678)$$

The results show that as volatility increases, the returns correspondingly increase by a factor of 0.196. In other words, this result supports the usual view in financial markets—high risk, high return. The GARCH-in-mean model is shown in Figure 14.7e and 14.7f. Note that the expected mean return is no longer a constant value, but rather it has high values (e.g., around observation 200) that coincide with higher conditional variances.

One last point before we leave this section. The first equation of the GARCH-in-mean model is sometimes written as a function of the time-varying standard deviation $\sqrt{h_t}$, that is, $y_t = \beta_0 + \theta\sqrt{h_t} + e_t$. This is because both measures—variance and standard deviation—are used by financial analysts to measure risk. There are no hard and fast rules about which measure to use. Exercise 14.8 illustrates the case when we use $\sqrt{h_t}$. A standard t test of significance is often used to decide which is the more suitable measure.

14.5 Exercises

14.5.1 Problems

14.1 The ARCH model is sometimes presented in the following multiplicative form:

$$y_t = \beta_0 + e_t$$
$$e_t = z_t \sqrt{h_t}, \quad z_t \sim N(0,1)$$
$$h_t = \alpha_0 + \alpha_1 e_{t-1}^2, \quad \alpha_0 > 0, \quad 0 \le \alpha_1 < 1.$$

This form describes the distribution of the standardized residuals $e_t/\sqrt{h_t}$ as standard normal z_t. However, the properties of e_t are not altered.
(a) Show that the conditional mean $E(e_t|I_{t-1}) = 0$.
(b) Show that the conditional variance $E(e_t^2|I_{t-1}) = h_t$.
(c) Show that $e_t|I_{t-1} \sim N(0, h_t)$.

14.2 The equations of an ARCH-in-mean model are shown below:

$$y_t = \beta_0 + \theta h_t + e_t$$
$$e_t|I_{t-1} \sim N(0, h_t)$$
$$h_t = \delta + \alpha_1 e_{t-1}^2 \quad \delta > 0, \ 0 \le \alpha_1 < 1$$

Let y_t represent the return from a financial asset and let e_t represent "news" in the financial market. Now use the third equation to substitute out h_t in the first equation, to express the return as

$$y_t = \beta_0 + \theta(\delta + \alpha_1 e_{t-1}^2) + e_t$$

(a) If θ is zero, what is $E_t(y_{t+1})$, the conditional mean of y_{t+1}? In other words, what do you expect next period's return to be, given information today?
(b) If θ is not zero, what is $E_t(y_{t+1})$? What extra information have you used here to forecast the return?

14.3 Consider the following T-ARCH model:

$$h_t = \delta + \alpha_1 e_{t-1}^2 + \gamma d_{t-1} e_{t-1}^2$$

$$d_t = \begin{cases} 1 & e_t < 0 & \text{(bad news)} \\ 0 & e_t \ge 0 & \text{(good news)} \end{cases}$$

(a) If γ is zero, what are the values of h_t when $e_{t-1} = -1$, when $e_{t-1} = 0$ and when $e_{t-1} = 1$?

(b) If γ is not zero, what are the values of h_t when $e_{t-1} = -1$, when $e_{t-1} = 0$ and when $e_{t-1} = 1$? What is the key difference between the case $\gamma = 0$ and $\gamma \neq 0$?

14.5.2 COMPUTER EXERCISES

14.4 The data file *share.dat* contains time-series data on the Straits Times share price index of Singapore.

(a) Compute the time series of returns using the formula $r_t = 100 \times \ln(y_t/y_{t-1})$, where y_t is the share price index. Generate the correlogram of returns up to at least order 12 since the frequency of the data is monthly. Is there evidence of autocorrelation? If yes, it indicates the presence of significant lagged mean effects.

(b) Square the returns and generate the correlogram of squared returns. Is there evidence of significant lagged effects? If yes, it indicates the presence of significant lagged variance effects.

14.5 The data file *euro.dat* contains 204 monthly observations on the returns to the Euro share price index for the period 1988:01 to 2004:12. A plot of the returns data is shown in Figure 14.8a, together with its histogram in Figure 14.8b.

(a) What do you notice about the volatility of returns? Identify the periods of big changes and the periods of small changes.

(b) Is the distribution of returns normal? Is this the unconditional or conditional distribution?

(c) Perform a Lagrange multiplier test for the presence of first-order ARCH and check that you obtain the following results:

$$\hat{e}_t^2 = 20.509 + 0.237\hat{e}_{t-1}^2, \quad (T-1)R^2 = 11.431$$
$$(t) \qquad\qquad (3.463)$$

Is there evidence of ARCH effects?

(d) Estimate an ARCH(1) model and check that you obtain the following results:

$$\hat{r}_t = 0.879, \quad \hat{h}_t = 20.604 + 0.230\hat{e}_{t-1}^2$$
$$(t) \quad (2.383) \qquad (10.968) \ (2.198)$$

Interpret the results.

(e) A plot of the conditional variance is shown in Figure 14.8c. Do the periods of high and low conditional variance coincide with the periods of big and small changes in returns?

14.6 Figure 14.9 shows the time series for monthly changes to the $US/$A exchange rate and its histogram for the period 1985:01 to 2004:12 (data file *exrate.dat*).

(a) Comment on the unconditional distribution of the series. Is it normal?

(b) Estimate a GARCH(1,1) model and check that you obtain the following results:

$$\hat{s}_t = 0.059, \quad \hat{h}_t = 0.288 + 0.066\hat{e}_{t-1}^2 + 0.898\hat{h}_{t-1}$$
$$(t) \quad (0.318) \qquad (1.190) \ (1.873) \qquad (16.458)$$

where s denotes the change in the exchange rate. Interpret the results.

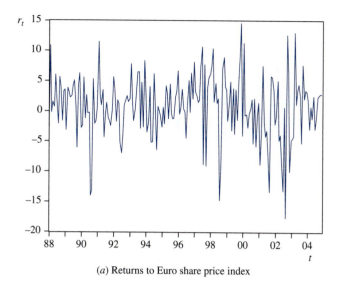

(*a*) Returns to Euro share price index

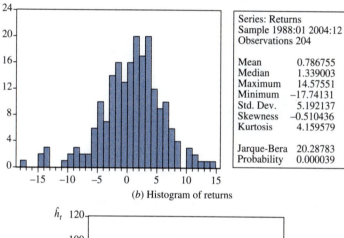

Series: Returns	
Sample 1988:01 2004:12	
Observations 204	
Mean	0.786755
Median	1.339003
Maximum	14.57551
Minimum	−17.74131
Std. Dev.	5.192137
Skewness	−0.510436
Kurtosis	4.159579
Jarque-Bera	20.28783
Probability	0.000039

(*b*) Histogram of returns

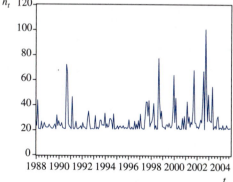

(*c*) Estimated conditional variance $\hat{h}_t$

FIGURE **14.8**   Graphs for Exercise 14.5.

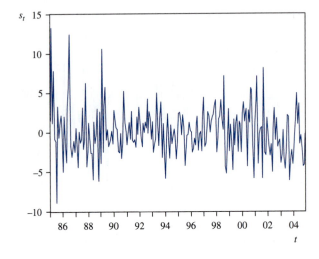

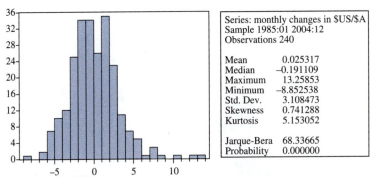

FIGURE **14.9** Graphs for Exercise 14.6: Changes in $US/$A exchange rate.

(c) The table below contains information about actual changes and the estimated conditional variance for the last 6 months of the sample. What is the forecast of the conditional variance for 2005:01?

	Actual change	Expected change	Estimated conditional variance
	s	$\hat{s}$	$\hat{h}_t$
2004:07	−1.40	0.059	9.16
2004:08	−0.36	0.059	8.66
2004:09	−1.92	0.059	9.08
2004:10	−4.30	0.059	7.80
2004:11	−4.12	0.059	8.56
2004:12	−0.19	0.059	9.14
2005:01			

14.7 Figure 14.10 shows the weekly returns to the US S&P500 for the sample period January 1990 to December 2004 (data file *sp.dat*).

(a) Estimate an ARCH(1) model and check that you obtain the following results:

$$\hat{r}_t = 0.197 \quad \hat{h}_t = 3.442 + 0.253\hat{e}_{t-1}^2$$
$$(t) \quad (2.899) \quad\quad (22.436) \ (5.850)$$

What is the value of the conditional variance when the last period's shock was positive, $e_{t-1} = +1$? When the last period's shock was negative, $e_{t-1} = -1$?

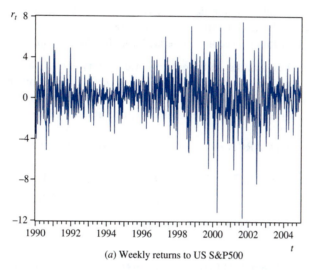

(a) Weekly returns to US S&P500

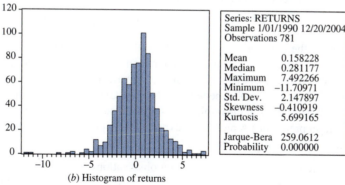

Series: RETURNS	
Sample 1/01/1990 12/20/2004	
Observations 781	
Mean	0.158228
Median	0.281177
Maximum	7.492266
Minimum	−11.70971
Std. Dev.	2.147897
Skewness	−0.410919
Kurtosis	5.699165
Jarque-Bera	259.0612
Probability	0.000000

(b) Histogram of returns

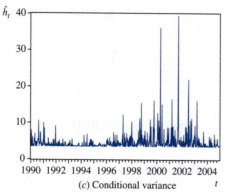

(c) Conditional variance

FIGURE 14.10 Graphs for Exercise 14.7.

(b) Estimate a T-ARCH model and check that you obtain the following results:

$$\hat{r}_t = 0.147, \quad \hat{h}_t = 3.437 + (0.123 + 0.268d_{t-1})\hat{e}_{t-1}^2$$
$$(t) \quad (2.049) \qquad (22.963) \quad (2.330) \quad (2.944)$$

(c) What is the value of the conditional variance when the last period's shock was positive, $e_{t-1} = +1$? When the last period's shock was negative, $e_{t-1} = -1$?

(d) Is the asymmetric T-ARCH model better than the symmetric ARCH model in a financial econometric sense? *Hint*: look at the statistical tests for significance. Is the asymmetric T-ARCH model better than the symmetric ARCH model in a financial economic sense? *Hint*: look at the implications of the results.

14.8 Figure 14.11 shows the daily term premiums between a 180-day bank bill rate and a 90-day bank rate for the period July 1996 to December 1998 (data file *term.dat*). Preliminary unit root tests confirm that the series may be treated as a stationary series, although the value of ρ, the autocorrelation coefficient, is quite high (about 0.9).

(a) Estimate a GARCH model and check that you obtain the following results:

$$\hat{r}_t = -2.272, \quad \hat{h}_t = 1.729 + 0.719\hat{e}_{t-1}^2 + 0.224\,\hat{h}_{t-1}$$
$$(t) \qquad\qquad\qquad (6.271) \quad (6.282) \qquad (3.993)$$

(b) Estimate a GARCH-in-mean model and check that you obtain the following results:

$$\hat{r}_t = -3.376 + 0.211\sqrt{h_t}, \quad \hat{h}_t = 1.631 + 0.730\hat{e}_{t-1}^2 + 0.231\,\hat{h}_{t-1}$$
$$(t) \qquad\qquad (2.807) \qquad\qquad (5.333) \quad (6.327) \qquad (4.171)$$

What is the contribution of volatility to the term premium?

(c) Is the GARCH-in-mean model better than the GARCH model in a financial econometric sense? (*Hint*: look at the statistical tests for significance.) Is the GARCH-in-mean better than the GARCH model in a financial economic sense? (*Hint*: look at the implications of the results, in particular the behavior of the term premium.) A plot of the expected term premium estimated for parts (a) and (b) is shown in Figure 14.11.

14.9 The data file *gold.dat* contains 200 daily observations on the returns to shares in a company specializing in gold bullion for the period December 13, 2005 to September 18, 2006.

(a) Plot the returns data. What do you notice about the volatility of returns? Identify the periods of big changes and the periods of small changes.

(b) Generate the histogram of returns. Is the distribution of returns normal? Is this the unconditional or conditional distribution?

(c) Perform a Lagrange multiplier test for the presence of first-order ARCH.

(d) Estimate a GARCH(1,1) model. Are the coefficients of the correct sign and magnitude?

(e) How would you use the estimated GARCH(1,1) model to improve your forecasts of returns?

14.10 The seminal paper about ARCH by Robert Engle was concerned with the variance of UK inflation. The data file *uk.dat* contains seasonally adjusted data on the UK consumer price index (*ukcpi*) for the sample period 1957:06 to 2006:06.

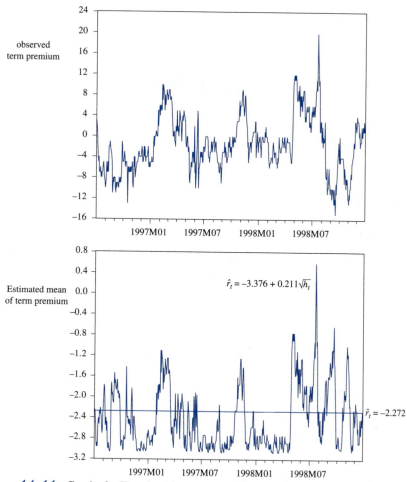

FIGURE **14.11**   Graphs for Exercise 14.8.

(a) Compute the monthly rate of inflation (y) for the sample period 1957:07 to 2006:06 using the formula:

$$y = 100 \times \left[\frac{(ukcpi - ukcpi(-1))}{ukcpi(-1)} \right]$$

(b) Estimate a T-GARCH-in-mean model and check that you obtain the following results:

$$\hat{y}_t = -0.407 + 1.983\sqrt{h_t}$$
$$(t) \quad (-2.862) \quad (5.243)$$

$$\hat{h}_t = 0.022 + (0.211 - 0.221d_{t-1})e_{t-1}^2 + 0.782\,\hat{h}_{t-1}$$
$$(4.697) \quad (8.952)(-8.728) \qquad (27.677)$$

(c) The negative asymmetric effect (-0.221) suggests that negative shocks (such as falls in prices) reduce volatility in inflation. Is this a sensible result for inflation?

(d) What does the positive in-mean effect (1.983) tell you about inflation in the UK and volatility in prices?

Chapter 15

Panel Data Models

Learning Objectives

Based on the material in this chapter you should be able to

1. Explain how a data panel differs from either a cross section or time series of data.

2. Explain how "seemingly unrelated regressions" are related to one another, and how this knowledge leads to improved estimation.

3. Explain how the fixed effects model allows for differences in the parameter values for each individual cross-section in a data panel.

4. Compare and contrast the least squares dummy variable estimator to the fixed effects estimator.

5. Compare and contrast the fixed effects model to the random effects model. Explain what leads us to consider individual differences to be random.

6. Explain the error assumptions in the random effects model, and what characteristic leads us to consider generalized least squares estimation.

7. Describe the steps required to obtain GLS estimates for the random effects estimator.

8. Explain why endogeneity is a potential problem in random effects models and how it affects our choice of estimator.

9. Use your software to estimate seemingly unrelated regressions, fixed effects models, and random effects models for panel data.

10. Test for contemporaneous correlation in a seemingly unrelated regression model.

11. Test for the existence of fixed and/or random effects and use the Hausman test to assess whether the random effects estimator is inconsistent.

Keywords

balanced panel
Breusch–Pagan test
cluster corrected standard errors
contemporaneous correlation
endogeneity
error components model
fixed effects estimator
fixed effects model
Hausman test
heterogeneity

least squares dummy variable model
LM test
panel corrected standard errors
pooled panel data regression
pooled regression
random effects estimator
random effects model
seemingly unrelated regressions
unbalanced panel

A panel of data consists of a group of cross-sectional units (people, households, firms, states, or countries) who are observed over time. We will often refer to such units as individuals, with the term "individual" being used generically, even when the unit of interest is not a person. Let us denote the number of cross-sectional units (individuals) by N, and number of time periods in which we observe them as T. Panel data come in several different "flavors," each of which introduces new challenges and opportunities. Peter Kennedy[1] describes the different types of panel data sets as

- "long and narrow," with "long" describing the time dimension and "narrow" implying a relatively small number of cross-sectional units, or
- "short and wide," indicating that there are many individuals observed over a relatively short period of time, or
- "long and wide," indicating that both N and T are relatively large.

A "long and narrow" panel may consist of data on several firms over a period of time. A classic example is the data analyzed by Grunfeld, which track the investment in plant and equipment by $N = 10$ large firms for $T = 20$ years. This panel is narrow because it consists of only $N = 10$ firms. It is "long" because $T > N$.

Many microeconomic analyses are performed on panel data sets with thousands of individuals who are followed through time. For example, the Panel Study of Income Dynamics (PSID) has followed approximately 8000 families since 1968.[2] The U.S. Department of Labor conducts National Longitudinal Surveys (NLS) such as NLSY79, "a nationally representative sample of 12,686 young men and women who were 14–22 years old when they were first surveyed in 1979.[3] These individuals were interviewed annually through 1994 and are currently interviewed on a biennial basis." Such data sets are "wide" and "short" because N is much, much larger than T. Using panel data we can account for individual differences, or **heterogeneity**. Furthermore, these data panels are becoming long enough so that dynamic factors, such as spells of employment and unemployment, can be studied. While these very large data sets are rich in information, they require the use of considerable computing power.

Macroeconomists who study economic growth across nations employ data that is "long" and "wide." The Penn World Table[4] provides purchasing power parity and national income accounts converted to international prices for 188 countries for some or all of the years 1950–2004, which we may roughly characterize as having both large N and large T.

Finally, it is possible to have cross-sectional and time-series data that do not constitute a panel. We may collect a sample of data on individuals from a population at several points in time, but the individuals are not the same in each time period. Such data can be used to analyze a "natural experiment," for example, when a law affecting some individuals changes, such as a change in unemployment insurance in a particular state. Using data before and after the policy change, and on groups of affected and unaffected people, the effects of the policy change can be measured.

Our interest in this chapter is how to use all available data to estimate econometric models describing the behavior of the individual cross-section units over time. Such data

---

[1] *A Guide to Econometrics*, 5th edition, MIT Press, 2003 Chapter 17.
[2] See http://psidonline.isr.umich.edu/.
[3] See http://www.bls.gov/nls/.
[4] See http://pwt.econ.upenn.edu/.

allow us to control for individual differences and study dynamic adjustment, and to measure the effects of policy changes. For each type of data we must take care not only with error assumptions, but also with our assumptions about whether, how and when, parameters may change across individuals and/or time.

15.1 Grunfeld's Investment Data

There are a number of issues regarding the specification of models for pooling cross-section and time-series data. We introduce these issues with a very famous example. The factors affecting the investment behavior by firms were studied by Grunfeld[5] using a panel of data. His example and data, which are simply referred to in the literature as "the Grunfeld data," have been used many times to illustrate the issues involved in modeling panel data.

Investment demand is the purchase of durable goods by both households and firms. In terms of total spending, investment spending is the volatile component. Therefore, understanding what determines investment is crucial to understanding the sources of fluctuations in aggregate demand. In addition, a firm's net fixed investment, which is the flow of additions to capital stock or replacements for worn out capital, is important because it determines the future value of the capital stock and thus affects future labor productivity and aggregate supply.

There are several interesting and elaborate theories that seek to describe the determinants of the investment process for the firm. Most of these theories evolve to the conclusion that perceived profit opportunities (expected profits or present discounted value of future earnings), and desired capital stock are two important determinants of a firm's fixed business investment. Unfortunately, neither of these variables is directly observable. Therefore, in formulating our economic model, we use observable proxies for these variables instead.

In terms of expected profits, one alternative is to identify the present discounted value of future earnings as the market value of the firm's securities. The price of a firm's stock represents and contains information about these expected profits. Consequently, the stock market value of the firm at the beginning of the year, denoted for firm "i" in time period "t" as V_{it}, may be used as a proxy for expected profits.

In terms of desired capital stock, expectations play a definite role. To catch these expectations effects, one possibility is to use a model that recognizes that actual capital stock in any period is the sum of a large number of past desired capital stocks. Thus, we use the beginning of the year actual capital stock, denoted for the ith firm as K_{it}, as a proxy for permanent desired capital stock.

Focusing on these explanatory variables, an economic model for describing gross firm investment for the ith firm in the tth time period, denoted INV_{it}, may be expressed as

$$INV_{it} = f\left(V_{it}, K_{it}\right) \qquad (15.1)$$

Our concern is how we might take this general economic model and specify an econometric model that adequately represents a panel of real-world data. The data (see *grunfeld.dat*) consist of $T = 20$ years of data (1935–1954) for $N = 10$ large firms.

[5] Grunfeld, Y. (1958) *The Determinants of Corporate Investment*. Unpublished Ph.D. thesis, Department of Economics, University of Chicago. Grunfeld, Y. and Z. Griliches (1960) "Is Aggregation Necessarily Bad?" *Review of Economics and Statistics*, 42, 1–13.

Let $y_{it} = INV_{it}$ denote values for the dependent variable and $x_{2it} = V_{it}$ and $x_{3it} = K_{it}$ denote values for the explanatory variables. A very flexible linear regression model that corresponds to (15.1) is

$$y_{it} = \beta_{1it} + \beta_{2it}x_{2it} + \beta_{3it}x_{3it} + e_{it} \tag{15.2}$$

In this general model the intercepts and slope parameters are permitted to differ for each firm in each time period. The model cannot be estimated in its current form, because there are more unknown parameters than data points. However, there are many types of simplifying assumptions that will make (15.2) operational. Which assumptions are useful to make depends in part on whether the data are long or short, narrow or wide. The assumptions deal with determining which parameters, if any, vary across individuals and/or time, and with alternative error assumptions. Is there heteroskedasticity or serial correlation, or are there other types of error correlations? In the following sections we consider three models that can be characterized according to the assumptions made about the parameters and the errors, and the type of data for which they are suitable. They are the **seemingly unrelated regressions** model, the **fixed effects** model, and the **random effects** model for estimating economic relationships using panel data.

15.2 Sets of Regression Equations

For expository purposes we will consider only two firms at this point, General Electric and Westinghouse. Because we have just two firms we will specify the cross-sectional indicator i to be either GE or WE. These two firms are similar in the range of products they offer, which includes everything from home appliances to light bulbs.

In (15.2) we began by assuming that the investment relationships are linear in the variables, and that the regression parameters are different for every individual in every time period. Before we can estimate the model, a new assumption that leads to fewer parameters is necessary. How can we alter what we assume about the parameter values? If the parameters are fixed for all time periods and are the same for all the firms, which is the extreme opposite of the completely flexible assumption in (15.2), then we can specify the investment equations for the two firms to be

$$INV_{GE,t} = \beta_1 + \beta_2 V_{GE,t} + \beta_3 K_{GE,t} + e_{GE,t} \quad t = 1,\dots,20$$
$$INV_{WE,t} = \beta_1 + \beta_2 V_{WE,t} + \beta_3 K_{WE,t} + e_{WE,t} \quad t = 1,\dots,20 \tag{15.3a}$$

Having the parameter values for the two firms identical, as we have specified in (15.3a), means we may treat the two models as a single, **pooled regression**, and use the 40 data points to estimate the parameters β_1, β_2, and β_3. In a general notation this model is

$$y_{it} = \beta_1 + \beta_2 x_{2it} + \beta_3 x_{3it} + e_{it} \quad i = 1, 2; \quad t = 1,\dots,20 \tag{15.3b}$$

where $i = 1$ corresponds to GE and $i = 2$ corresponds to WE. However, the question that must be asked is "Are we willing to assume that these two firms have identical investment behavior?" Compared to the general model in (15.2), this is a strong assumption, one that we may not want to impose.

For these "long and narrow" data we can estimate separate investment regressions for the two firms. A more flexible specification than (15.3) is to assume that the parameters are different for each of the equations (firms) but are fixed across time, so that the model becomes

$$INV_{GE,t} = \beta_{1,GE} + \beta_{2,GE}V_{GE,t} + \beta_{3,GE}K_{GE,t} + e_{GE,t} \quad t = 1,\ldots,20$$

$$INV_{WE,t} = \beta_{1,WE} + \beta_{2,WE}V_{WE,t} + \beta_{3,WE}K_{WE,t} + e_{WE,t} \quad t = 1,\ldots,20$$

(15.4a)

Expressed generally this is

$$y_{it} = \beta_{1i} + \beta_{2i}x_{2it} + \beta_{3i}x_{3it} + e_{it} \quad i = 1, 2; \quad t = 1,\ldots,20 \qquad (15.4b)$$

It is often said that when working with panel data, the "subscripts tell the story." Comparing (15.3) to (15.4) we can see that this slogan contains a measure of truth. By adding the subscript "i" to the parameter values, we are saying that the parameters vary across the cross-sectional units, but *not* across time. The presence of the "i" subscript represents an assumption about economic behavior that is embodied in (15.4).

For the moment we make the usual least squares assumptions about the errors in (15.4). That is,

$$E(e_{GE,t}) = 0 \quad \text{var}(e_{GE,t}) = \sigma_{GE}^2 \quad \text{cov}(e_{GE,t}, e_{GE,s}) = 0$$

$$E(e_{WE,t}) = 0 \quad \text{var}(e_{WE,t}) = \sigma_{WE}^2 \quad \text{cov}(e_{WE,t}, e_{WE,s}) = 0$$

(15.5)

Assumption (15.5) says that the errors in both investment functions (i) have zero mean, (ii) are homoskedastic with constant variance, and (iii) are not correlated over time; autocorrelation does not exist. Note, however, that the two equations do have different error variances σ_{GE}^2 and σ_{WE}^2. Under these assumptions, and in the absence of contemporaneous correlation that we introduce in the next section, the best we can do is apply least squares estimation to each equation separately. The 40 observations on investment by General Electric and Westinghouse are in the file *grunfeld2.dat*. The least squares estimates of the two investment equations are reported in Table 15.1.

If the variances of the two error terms are equal, so that $\sigma_{GE}^2 = \sigma_{WE}^2 = \sigma^2$, then we can combine the two equations using the dummy variable format of Section 7.3.3. Let D_i be a dummy variable equal to 1 for the Westinghouse observations and 0 for the General Electric observations. Specify a model with slope and intercept dummy variables,

$$INV_{it} = \beta_{1,GE} + \delta_1 D_i + \beta_{2,GE}V_{it} + \delta_2(D_i \times V_{it}) + \beta_{3,GE}K_{it} + \delta_3(D_i \times K_{it}) + e_{it} \quad (15.6)$$

Table 15.1 **Least Squares Estimates of Separate Investment Equations**

Equation	Variable	Coefficient	Std. Error	t-Statistic	Prob.
GE	C	−9.9563	31.3743	−0.3173	0.7548
	V	0.0266	0.0156	1.7057	0.1063
	K	0.1517	0.0257	5.9015	0.0000
	$R^2 = 0.7053$	SSE = 13216.59			
WE	C	−0.5094	8.0153	−0.0636	0.9501
	V	0.0529	0.0157	3.3677	0.0037
	K	0.0924	0.0561	1.6472	0.1179
	$R^2 = 0.7444$	SSE = 1773.23			

Table 15.2 **Least Squares Estimates from the Dummy Variable Model**

Variable	Coefficient	Std. Error	t-Statistic	Prob.
C	−9.9563	23.6264	−0.4214	0.6761
D	9.4469	28.8054	0.3280	0.7450
V	0.0266	0.0117	2.2651	0.0300
$D \times V$	0.0263	0.0344	0.7668	0.4485
K	0.1517	0.0194	7.8369	0.0000
$D \times K$	−0.0593	0.1169	−0.5070	0.6155

Equation (15.6) represents a pooled set of 40 observations, and as we learned in Section 7.3.3, it is just another way of writing (15.4). The least squares estimates from (15.6) will be identical to the least squares estimates obtained by estimating the two equations in (15.4) separately. The only difference will be in the standard errors. In Table 15.2 we report the dummy variable model estimates.

Note that the estimates of $\beta_{k,GE}$, $k = 1, 2, 3$ are identical to those in Table 15.1, and the estimates of $\beta_{k,WE}$, $k = 1, 2, 3$ in Table 15.1 are given by the estimates of $\beta_{k,GE} + \delta_k$, $k = 1, 2, 3$ in Table 15.2. However, as noted, their standard errors are different, which is a consequence of the two separate regressions in Table 15.1 allowing for error variances that differ for the two firms, while the dummy variable regression in Table 15.2 assumes that the variance of the error term is constant across all 40 observations.

We can use the Goldfeld–Quandt test (Section 8.4.2) to test the null hypothesis $H_0: \sigma^2_{GE} = \sigma^2_{WE}$, which we reject at the $\alpha = 0.05$ level of significance, leading us to prefer the results in Table 15.1. So far, since we have nothing to link the two equations together, we have received no gain from combining data from the two firms. In the following section we will provide a meaningful linkage.

15.3 Seemingly Unrelated Regressions

An assumption under which a joint estimation procedure is better than separate least squares estimation is

$$\text{cov}(e_{GE,t}, e_{WE,t}) = \sigma_{GE,WE} \tag{15.7}$$

This assumption says that the error terms in the two equations, at the same point in time, are correlated. This kind of correlation is called a **contemporaneous correlation**. To understand why $e_{GE,t}$ and $e_{WE,t}$ might be correlated, recall that these errors contain the influence on investment of factors that have been omitted from the equations. Such factors might include capacity utilization, current and past interest rates, liquidity, and the general state of the economy. Since the two firms are similar in many respects, it is likely that the effects of the omitted factors on investment by General Electric will be similar to their effect on investment by Westinghouse. If so, then $e_{GE,t}$ and $e_{WE,t}$ will be capturing similar effects and will be correlated. Adding the contemporaneous correlation assumption (15.7) has the effect of introducing additional information that is not included when we carry out separate least squares estimation of the two equations.

The pooled dummy variable model (15.6) represents a way to "stack" the 40 observations for the *GE* and *WE* equations into one regression. We have seen that allowing for the variances of the error terms for the two firms to differ, $\sigma^2_{GE} \neq \sigma^2_{WE}$, means that the error term

Table 15.3 **SUR Estimates of Investment Equations**

Equation	Variable	Coefficient	Std. Error	t-Statistic	Prob.
	C	−27.7193	29.3212	−0.95	0.351
GE	V	0.0383	0.0144	2.66	0.012
	K	0.1390	0.0250	5.56	0.000
	C	−1.2520	7.5452	−0.17	0.869
WE	V	0.0576	0.0145	3.96	0.000
	K	0.0640	0.0530	1.21	0.236

Note: p-values computed from $t_{(34)}$ distribution.

e_{it} in the pooled dummy variable model in (15.6) will be heteroskedastic; it will have variance σ^2_{GE} when $i = GE$ and variance σ^2_{WE} when $i = WE$. What are the implications of (15.7) for the same error term e_{it} in (15.6)? It means that all 40 errors will not be uncorrelated. The 20 General Electric errors are uncorrelated with each other, and the 20 Westinghouse errors are uncorrelated with each other, but the assumption of contemporaneous correlation in (15.7) implies that the first Westinghouse error will be correlated with the first General Electric error, the second Westinghouse error will be correlated with the second General Electric error, and so on. This information cannot be utilized when the equations are estimated separately. However, it can be utilized to produce better estimates when the equations are jointly estimated as they are in the dummy variable model.

To improve the precision of the dummy variable model estimates we use **seemingly unrelated regressions** estimation, which is a generalized least squares estimation procedure. It estimates the two investment equations jointly, accounting for the fact that the variances of the error terms are different for the two equations *and* accounting for the contemporaneous correlation between the errors of the GE and WE equations. In order to implement the SUR estimation procedure we must first estimate each of the unknown variances and the contemporaneous covariance. The exact details of the estimation procedure are complicated and we will not present them here.[6] Econometric software includes commands for SUR (or SURE) that carry out the following steps: (i) Estimate the equations separately using least squares; (ii) Use the least squares residuals from step (i) to estimate σ^2_{GE}, σ^2_{WE}, and $\sigma_{GE,WE}$; (iii) Use the estimates from step (ii) to estimate the two equations jointly within a generalized least squares framework.

Estimates of the coefficients of the two investment functions are presented in Table 15.3. Since the SUR technique utilizes the information on the correlation between the error terms, it is more precise than the least squares estimation procedure. This fact is supported by the standard errors of the SUR estimates in Table 15.3 that are lower than those of the least squares estimates in Table 15.1.[7] You should be cautious, however, when making judgments about precision on the basis of standard errors. Standard errors are themselves estimates; in any one sample it is possible for a standard error for SUR to be greater than a corresponding least squares standard error even when SUR is a better estimator than least squares. From an economic standpoint our estimated coefficients for the capital stock and value variables have the expected positive signs. Also, all are significantly different from zero except for the

---

[6] For details see William E. Griffiths, R. Carter Hill, and George G. Judge (1993) *Learning and Practicing Econometrics* (Wiley), Chapter 17. A more advanced reference is William Greene (2003) *Econometric Analysis*, 5th edition (Prentice-Hall), Chapter 14.

[7] Note that we do not compare the SUR estimates to those in Table 15.2 because it incorporates the assumption that the two error variances are equal, a hypothesis that we have rejected.

coefficient of capital stock in the Westinghouse equation. This coefficient has a low t-value and hence is estimated with limited precision.

Equations that exhibit contemporaneous correlation were called "seemingly unrelated" by University of Chicago econometrician Arnold Zellner when he developed the SUR estimation procedure. The equations seem to be unrelated, but the additional information provided by the correlation between the equation errors means that joint generalized least squares estimation is better than single equation least squares estimation.

15.3.1 SEPARATE OR JOINT ESTIMATION?

Is it always better to estimate two or more equations jointly? Or are there circumstances when it is just as good to estimate each equation separately?

There are two situations where separate least squares estimation is just as good as the SUR technique. The first of these cases is when the equation errors are not contemporaneously correlated. If the errors are not contemporaneously correlated, there is nothing linking the two equations, and separate estimation cannot be improved upon.

The second situation is less obvious. Indeed, some advanced algebra is needed to prove that least squares and SUR give *identical* estimates when the same explanatory variables appear in each equation. By the "same explanatory variables" we mean exactly the same variables with the same observations on those variables. For example, suppose we are interested in estimating demand equations for beef, chicken, and pork. Since these commodities are all substitutes, it is reasonable to specify the quantity demanded for each as a function of the price of beef, the price of chicken, and the price of pork, as well as income. The same variables with the same observations appear in all three equations. Even if the errors of these equations are correlated, as is quite likely, the use of SUR will not yield an improvement over separate estimation.

If the explanatory variables in each equation are different, then a test to see if the correlation between the errors is significantly different from zero is of interest. If a null hypothesis of zero correlation is not rejected, then there is no evidence to suggest that SUR will improve on separate least squares estimation. To carry out such a test we compute the squared correlation

$$r^2_{GE,WE} = \frac{\hat{\sigma}^2_{GE,WE}}{\hat{\sigma}^2_{GE}\,\hat{\sigma}^2_{WE}} = \frac{(207.5871)^2}{(777.4463)(104.3079)} = (0.729)^2 = 0.53139$$

The variance estimates $\hat{\sigma}^2_{GE}$ and $\hat{\sigma}^2_{WE}$ are the usual ones from separate least squares estimation. The estimated covariance is computed from

$$\hat{\sigma}_{GE,WE} = \frac{1}{\sqrt{T-K_{GE}}\sqrt{T-K_{WE}}} \sum_{t=1}^{20} \hat{e}_{GE,t}\hat{e}_{WE,t} = \frac{1}{T-3} \sum_{t=1}^{20} \hat{e}_{GE,t}\hat{e}_{WE,t}$$

where K_{GE} and K_{WE} are the numbers of parameters in the GE and WE equations, respectively. The reason for the odd looking divisor is that in seemingly unrelated regressions the number of variables in each equation might be different, and this is one way to correct for the number of parameters estimated. In this case $K_{GE} = K_{WE} = 3$.

The correlation $r_{GE,WE} = 0.729$ indicates a strong contemporaneous correlation between errors of the General Electric and Westinghouse investment equations. To check the statistical significance of $r^2_{GE,WE}$, we can test the null hypothesis $H_0 : \sigma_{GE,WE} = 0$. If $\sigma_{GE,WE} = 0$, then $LM = Tr^2_{GE,WE}$ is a Lagrange multiplier test statistic that is distributed as a $\chi^2_{(1)}$ random variable in large samples. The 5% critical value of a χ^2 distribution with one degree of freedom is 3.84. The value of the test statistic from our data is $LM = 10.628$. Hence we reject the null hypothesis of no correlation between $e_{GE,t}$ and $e_{WE,t}$, and conclude that there are potential efficiency gains from estimating the two investment equations jointly using SUR.

If we are testing for the existence of correlated errors for more than two equations, the relevant test statistic is equal to T times the sum of squares of all the correlations; the probability distribution under H_0 is a χ^2 distribution with degrees of freedom equal to the number of correlations. For example, with three equations, denoted by subscripts "1," "2," and "3," the null hypothesis is

$$H_0 : \sigma_{12} = \sigma_{13} = \sigma_{23} = 0$$

and the $\chi^2_{(3)}$ test statistic is

$$LM = T\left(r_{12}^2 + r_{13}^2 + r_{23}^2\right)$$

In the general case of an SUR system with M equations, the statistic becomes

$$LM = T \sum_{i=2}^{M} \sum_{j=1}^{i-1} r_{ij}^2$$

Under the null hypothesis that there are no contemporaneous correlations, this LM statistic has a χ^2-distribution with $M(M-1)/2$ degrees of freedom, in large samples.

There are many economic problems where we have cause to consider a system of equations. The investment function example was one; estimation of demand functions, like the meat functions we alluded to in this section, is another. Further examples are given in the exercises.

15.3.2   TESTING CROSS-EQUATION HYPOTHESES

Suppose we are interested in whether the equations for Westinghouse and General Electric have identical coefficients. That is, we are interested in testing

$$H_0 : \beta_{1,GE} = \beta_{1,WE}, \quad \beta_{2,GE} = \beta_{2,WE}, \quad \beta_{3,GE} = \beta_{3,WE} \tag{15.8}$$

against the alternative that at least one pair of coefficients is not equal. In Section 7.3.3 this hypothesis was tested under the assumption of equal error variances and no error correlation. It was called the Chow test. It is also possible to test hypotheses such as (15.8) when the more general error assumptions of the SUR model are relevant. Because of the complicated nature of the model, the test statistic can no longer be calculated simply as an F-test statistic based on residuals from restricted and unrestricted models. Most econometric software will perform an F-test and/or a Wald χ^2-test in a multi-equation framework such as we have here. In the context of SUR equations both tests are large sample approximate tests. The F-statistic has J numerator degrees of freedom and $(MT-K)$ denominator degrees of freedom, where J is the number of hypotheses, M is the number of equations, K is the total number of coefficients in the whole system, and T is the number of time-series observations per equation. The χ^2-statistic has J degrees of freedom. For our particular example, we find that $F = 2.92$ with a p-value of 0.0479, based on the $F_{(3,34)}$ distribution. The chi-square test statistic is $\chi^2 = 8.77$ with a p-value of 0.0326 based on the $\chi^2_{(3)}$ distribution. Thus, from the results of both tests, we reject the null hypothesis of equal coefficients.

The equality of coefficients is not the only cross-equation hypothesis that can be tested. Any restrictions on parameters in different equations can be tested. Such restrictions are particularly relevant when estimating equations derived from demand and production theory.

15.4 The Fixed Effects Model

The SUR model in the previous section can be used when the panel data set is "long and narrow," meaning that we have only a few cross-sectional units. If we have a panel data set that is "short and wide," meaning that there are many cross-sectional units and relatively few time-series observations, then the SUR model is no longer of practical value. Imagine having a panel of data with $N = 1000$ cross-sectional observations on individuals. In the SUR framework we would then have 1000 separate equations, which are too many to evaluate. The fixed effects model that we discuss in this section is useful in a wide variety of situations, and it can be applied to panel data with any number of individual, cross-sectional observations.

To introduce the fixed effects model as a method for pooling time-series and cross-section data, we will continue the Grunfeld investment data example used in the previous sections. Consequently the "individuals" we discuss below are firms. Later in the chapter we will introduce a larger microeconomic panel data example.

Return to equation (15.2), which is

$$y_{it} = \beta_{1it} + \beta_{2it}x_{2it} + \beta_{3it}x_{3it} + e_{it} \tag{15.9}$$

This model is very flexible. It allows each parameter to change for each individual in each time period. However, we cannot consistently estimate the $3 \times N \times T$ parameters in (15.9) with only NT total observations. A simplification of (15.9) that is possible to estimate allows the intercepts for each firm to vary, but restricts the slope parameters to be constant across all firms and time periods. That is,

$$\beta_{1it} = \beta_{1i}, \quad \beta_{2it} = \beta_2, \quad \beta_{3it} = \beta_3 \tag{15.10}$$

This model of parameter variation specifies that *only* the *intercept* parameter varies, not the slope parameters, and the intercept varies only across individuals and not over time. Also, we will make the assumption that the errors e_{it} are independent, with mean zero and constant variance σ_e^2, for all individuals and in all time periods. Given this assumption, and (15.10), it follows that *all behavioral differences between individual firms and over time are captured by the intercept*. Individual intercepts are included to "control" for these firm specific differences. The resulting econometric model is

$$y_{it} = \beta_{1i} + \beta_2 x_{2it} + \beta_3 x_{3it} + e_{it} \tag{15.11}$$

15.4.1 A DUMMY VARIABLE MODEL

The model in (15.11) is conceptually very simple. We simply have to include an intercept dummy variable for each individual. If the number of individuals is small, this can be done by brute force. This is the approach we demonstrate first. The Grunfeld data (*grunfeld.dat*) consists of $T = 20$ annual observations on $N = 10$ firms. To implement the dummy variable version of (15.11), we define the 10 dummy variables

$$D_{1i} = \begin{cases} 1 & i = 1 \\ 0 & \text{otherwise} \end{cases}, D_{2i} = \begin{cases} 1 & i = 2 \\ 0 & \text{otherwise} \end{cases}, D_{3i} = \begin{cases} 1 & i = 3 \\ 0 & \text{otherwise} \end{cases}, \text{ and so on.}$$

Then (15.11) can be written

$$INV_{it} = \beta_{11}D_{1i} + \beta_{12}D_{2i} + \cdots + \beta_{1,10}D_{10i} + \beta_2 V_{2it} + \beta_3 K_{3it} + e_{it} \qquad (15.12)$$

This specification is sometimes called the **least squares dummy variable** model or the **fixed effects** model. Compared to the model setups in Section 7.3.2, and in the SUR specification, the dummy variables in (15.12) are introduced in a slightly different way, using 10 dummy variables, one for each firm, and no constant term. The dummy variable coefficients β_{1i} are equal to the firm intercepts and are called by various names, including "firm specific constants" and "firm fixed effects."

To make (15.12) consistent with our earlier treatments, we would specify a constant and nine dummy variables. Each dummy variable coefficient would be equal to the difference between the intercept for its firm and the intercept for the base firm for which we did not specify a dummy variable. The specification in (15.12) is more convenient for our current discussion. However, you should recognize that the two alternatives are just different ways of looking at the same model.

If the error terms e_{it} are independent with mean zero and constant variance σ_e^2 for all observations, the best linear unbiased estimator of equation (15.12) is the least squares estimator. The results from this estimation appear in Table 15.4. The estimated coefficients for $V =$ firm value and $K =$ capital stock have small standard errors, implying that their influence on investment has been accurately estimated.

Table 15.4   **Dummy Variable Estimation of Fixed Effects Model**

Variable	Coefficient	Std. Error	t-Statistic	Prob.
D1	−69.1435	49.6855	−1.3916	0.1657
D2	100.8624	24.9137	4.0485	0.0001
D3	−235.1187	24.4183	−9.6288	0.0000
D4	−27.6350	14.0698	−1.9641	0.0510
D5	−115.3169	14.1620	−8.1427	0.0000
D6	−23.0736	12.6612	−1.8224	0.0700
D7	−66.6829	12.8376	−5.1943	0.0000
D8	−57.3586	13.9856	−4.1013	0.0001
D9	−87.2770	12.8851	−6.7735	0.0000
D10	−6.5463	11.8199	−0.5538	0.5803
V	0.1098	0.0119	9.2596	0.0000
K	0.3106	0.0174	17.8835	0.0000

$SSE = 522855$

Table 15.5   **Least Squares Estimates of the Pooled Model**

Variable	Coefficient	Std. Error	t-Statistic	Prob.
C	−43.0245	9.4979	−4.5299	0.0000
V	0.1154	0.0058	19.7892	0.0000
K	0.2319	0.0255	9.1079	0.0000

$SSE = 1749128$

The firm intercepts vary considerably, and some of them have large t-values, suggesting that the assumption of differing intercepts for different firms is appropriate. To confirm this fact we can test the following hypothesis.

$$H_0 : \beta_{11} = \beta_{12} = \cdots = \beta_{1N}$$

$$H_1 : \text{the } \beta_{1i} \text{ are not all equal} \qquad (15.13)$$

These $N - 1 = 9$ joint null hypotheses are tested using the usual F-test statistic. In the restricted model all the intercept parameters are equal. If we call their common value β_1, then the restricted model is $INV_{it} = \beta_1 + \beta_2 V_{it} + \beta_3 K_{it} + e_{it}$. The least squares estimates of this restricted model, in which all the data are pooled together, are shown in Table 15.5.

The sum of squared residuals from the restricted model, SSE_R, comes from this pooled model. The unrestricted sum of squared residuals, SSE_U, comes from the dummy variable model. With these two values we can construct the F-statistic as

$$F = \frac{(SSE_R - SSE_U)/J}{SSE_U/(NT - K)}$$

$$= \frac{(1749128 - 522855)/9}{522855/(200 - 12)}$$

$$= 48.99$$

If the null hypothesis is true, then $F \sim F_{(9,188)}$. The value of the test statistic $F = 48.99$ yields a p-value of less than 0.0001; we reject the null hypothesis that the intercept parameters for all firms are equal. We conclude that there are differences in firm intercepts, and that the data should not be pooled into a single model with a common intercept parameter.

15.4.2   THE FIXED EFFECTS ESTIMATOR

The technique of including a dummy variable for each individual is feasible when the number of individuals is small. However, if we have a very large number of individuals, this approach will not work. Today's typical computer simply cannot handle that computing task quickly and accurately. Luckily there is a fantastic trick that makes estimating the fixed effects model with a large number of individuals relatively easy.

Take the data on individual i

$$y_{it} = \beta_{1i} + \beta_2 x_{2it} + \beta_3 x_{3it} + e_{it} \quad t = 1, \ldots, T \qquad (15.14)$$

Average the data across time, by summing both sides of the equation and dividing by T

$$\frac{1}{T} \sum_{t=1}^{T} (y_{it} = \beta_{1i} + \beta_2 x_{2it} + \beta_3 x_{3it} + e_{it})$$

Using the fact that the parameters do not change over time, we can simplify this as

$$\bar{y}_i = \frac{1}{T}\sum_{t=1}^{T} y_{it} = \beta_{1i} + \beta_2 \frac{1}{T}\sum_{t=1}^{T} x_{2it} + \beta_3 \frac{1}{T}\sum_{t=1}^{T} x_{3it} + \frac{1}{T}\sum_{t=1}^{T} e_{it}$$

$$= \beta_{1i} + \beta_2 \bar{x}_{2i} + \beta_3 \bar{x}_{3i} + \bar{e}_i$$

(15.15)

The "bar" notation $\bar{y}_i$ indicates that we have averaged the values of y_{it} over time. Then, subtract (15.15) from (15.14), term by term, to obtain

$$y_{it} = \beta_{1i} + \beta_2 x_{2it} + \beta_3 x_{3it} + e_{it}$$

$$- \quad (\bar{y}_i = \beta_{1i} + \beta_2 \bar{x}_{2i} + \beta_3 \bar{x}_{3i} + \bar{e}_i)$$

(15.16)

$$y_{it} - \bar{y}_i = \beta_2(x_{2it} - \bar{x}_{2i}) + \beta_3(x_{3it} - \bar{x}_{3i}) + (e_{it} - \bar{e}_i)$$

In the last line of (15.16) note that the intercept parameter β_{1i} has fallen out. These data are said to be in "deviation from the individual's mean" form, and if we repeat this process for each individual, then we have a transformed model

$$\tilde{y}_{it} = \beta_2 \tilde{x}_{2it} + \beta_3 \tilde{x}_{3it} + \tilde{e}_{it}$$

(15.17)

The "tilde" notation $\tilde{y}_{it} = y_{it} - \bar{y}_i$ indicates that the variables are in deviation from the mean form. In Table 15.6 we show a few observations for firms 1 and 2, General Motors and US Steel. The variable y is investment, INV, and x_2 is the value of the firm V. The average of the $T = 20$ years of data on each firm is computed. For example, the average value of INV for General Motors over this 20-year period was \$608.02 million (1947 dollars). This value is subtracted from each value of INV for General Motors. This process is repeated for each variable for each firm.

The gain from the transformation in (15.17) is that the least squares estimates of the parameters β_2 and β_3 from (15.17) are identical to the least squares estimates from the full

Table 15.6 Data in Deviation from the Mean Form

i	t	y_{it}	$\sum y_{it}/T$	$y_{it} - \sum y_{it}/T$	x_{2it}	$\sum x_{2it}/T$	$x_{2it} - \sum x_{2it}/T$
1	1	317.6	608.02	−290.42	3078.5	4333.845	−1255.345
1	2	391.8	608.02	−216.22	4661.7	4333.845	327.855
				.			.
1	19	1304.4	608.02	696.38	6241.7	4333.845	1907.855
1	20	1486.7	608.02	878.68	5593.6	4333.845	1259.755
2	1	209.9	410.46	−200.56	1362.4	1971.825	−609.425
2	2	355.3	410.46	−55.16	1807.1	1971.825	−164.725
				.			.
2	19	641	410.46	230.54	2031.3	1971.825	59.475
2	20	459.3	410.46	48.84	2115.5	1971.825	143.675

$y_{it} = INV_{it}, \; x_{2it} = V_{it}$

Table 15.7 **Fixed Effects Estimation of Investment Equation**

Variable	Coefficient	Std. Error	t-Statistic	Prob.
C	-58.7290	12.4463	-4.7186	0.0000
V	0.1098	0.0119	9.2596	0.0000
K	0.3106	0.0174	17.8835	0.0000

dummy variable model shown in (15.12). Furthermore, the least squares residuals from (15.17) are the same as the least squares residuals from (15.12). The proof of this result is difficult,[8] so we will simply demonstrate that it is true by example. In the data file *grunfeld3.dat* we provide the investment data, with the group means for each variable and the variables in deviation from the mean form. The least squares fitted model is

$$\widetilde{INV}_{it} = 0.1098\,\widetilde{V}_{it} + 0.3106\,\widetilde{K}_{it}$$
$$(\text{se}^*)\quad (0.0116)\quad (0.0169) \tag{15.18}$$

The estimates and the sum of squared least squares residuals ($SSE = 522855$) from (15.18) are identical to those in Table 15.4. The standard errors from this least squares regression on the transformed data are slightly different from those in Table 15.4. This is because the estimate of the error variance used by the least squares software when estimating (15.18) is $\hat{\sigma}_{e*}^2 = SSE/(NT - 2)$ when what is required is $\hat{\sigma}_e^2 = SSE/(NT - N - 2)$. The SSE from (15.18) is identical to the SSE from the dummy variable model, so the difference between $\hat{\sigma}_{e*}^2$ and $\hat{\sigma}_e^2$ lies in the divisor. The calculation of $\hat{\sigma}_{e*}^2$ ignores the loss of $N = 10$ degrees of freedom from correcting the variables by their sample means. The correct divisor is $NT - N - 2 = 188$, which is the degrees of freedom in the dummy variable model, taking into account both the dummy variables and explanatory variables. If we multiply the standard errors in (15.18) by the correction factor

$$\sqrt{(NT - 2)/(NT - N - 2)} = \sqrt{198/188} = 1.02625$$

the resulting standard errors are identical to those in Table 15.4.

When using software designed to carry out fixed effects estimation automatically, these corrections will have already been done. In Table 15.7 we report the results in the format used by two econometric software packages (EViews and Stata). Note that value V and capital K have coefficient estimates and standard errors that are identical to the dummy variable model in Table 15.4. The reported constant term C is the average of the estimated coefficients on the cross-section dummy variables. That is, $C = N^{-1}\sum_{i=1}^{N} b_{1i}$, where the b_{1i} are the least squares estimates of the parameters β_{1i} in (15.12), and are the coefficients of the dummy variables in Table 15.4. Other software may report the results in a different format.

It is usually the case that when estimating panel data models, we are most interested in the coefficients of the explanatory variables and not the individual intercept parameters. Recall that the intercept parameters are the coefficients of the dummy variables and are also called the fixed effects. Although they are typically of lower priority, these coefficients can be

---

[8] See George G. Judge, R. Carter Hill, William E. Griffiths, Helmut Lütkepohl, and Tsoung-Chao Lee (1988) *Introduction to the Theory and Practice of Econometrics*, 2nd edition, Wiley, Section 11.4. The proof involves matrix algebra.

"recovered" by using the fact that the least squares fitted regression passes through the point of the means, just as it did in the simple regression model. That is,

$$\bar{y}_i = b_{1i} + b_2\bar{x}_{2i} + b_3\bar{x}_{3i}$$

where b_2 and b_3 are the estimates obtained from (15.17), and b_{1i} denotes the estimates of individual specific constants, or fixed effects. Given b_2 and b_3, we can compute the fixed effects as

$$b_{1i} = \bar{y}_i - b_2\bar{x}_{2i} - b_3\bar{x}_{3i} \quad i = 1, \ldots, N \tag{15.19}$$

Econometric software packages usually make it possible to recover these estimates.

15.4.3   FIXED EFFECTS ESTIMATION USING A MICROECONOMIC PANEL

In the Grunfeld investment example there are only 10 cross sections, and it is easy to simply include intercept dummy variables for each. However, microeconometric analyses make use of large data sets with many individuals. For example, the National Longitudinal Surveys (NLS) conducted by the US Department of Labor have a database on women who were between 14 and 24 years old in 1968. To illustrate we use a subsample of $N = 716$ women who were interviewed in 1982, 1983, 1985, 1987, and 1988. The sample consists of women who were employed, and whose schooling was completed, when interviewed. The data file is named *nls_panel.dat*[9] and it contains 3580 lines of data. Panel data observations are usually stacked, with all the time-series observations for one individual on top of the next. The observations on a few variables for the first three women in the NLS panel are shown in Table 15.8. The first column *ID* identifies the individual and *YEAR* represents the year in which the information was collected. These identifying variables must be present so that your software will properly identify the cross-section and time-series units. Then there are observations on each of the variables. In a typical panel there are some observations with missing values, usually denoted as "." or "NA." We have removed all the missing values in the data file *nls_panel.dat*. In microeconomic panels the individuals are not always interviewed the same number of times, leading to an **unbalanced panel** in which the number of time-series observations is different across individuals. The data file *nls_panel.dat* is, however, a **balanced panel**; for each individual we observe five time-series observations. A larger, unbalanced panel is in the file *nls.dat*. Most modern software packages can handle both balanced and unbalanced panels with ease.

To employ the dummy variable approach to control for individual effects, we would have to include $N = 716$ dummy variables. Using such a brute force approach in this case is infeasible, and, as we have seen, unnecessary since we can use the fixed effects estimation approach, which basically involves some data management and then a least squares regression.

To illustrate the fixed effects estimator, consider a wage equation with dependent variable ln(*WAGE*) and explanatory variables years of education (*EDUC*), total labor force experience (*EXPER*) and its square (*EXPER2*), tenure in current job (*TENURE*) and its square (*TENURE2*), and dummy variables *BLACK*, *SOUTH*, and *UNION*. If you try to estimate this

---

[9] The data in *nls_panel.dat* and *nls.dat* are subsets of the *nlswork.dta* data used by the software Stata as an illustration. See *Stata Longitudinal/Panel Data, Reference Manual, Release 9*, StataCorp, 2005. We thank Stata for permission to use the data for illustration purposes.

Table 15.8 **Representative Observations from NLS Panel Data**

ID	YEAR	ln(WAGE)	EDUC	COLLGRAD	BLACK	UNION	EXPER	TENURE
1	82	1.8083	12	0	1	1	7.6667	7.6667
1	83	1.8634	12	0	1	1	8.5833	8.5833
1	85	1.7894	12	0	1	1	10.1795	1.8333
1	87	1.8465	12	0	1	1	12.1795	3.7500
1	88	1.8564	12	0	1	1	13.6218	5.2500
2	82	1.2809	17	1	0	0	7.5769	2.4167
2	83	1.5159	17	1	0	0	8.3846	3.4167
2	85	1.9302	17	1	0	0	10.3846	5.4167
2	87	1.9190	17	1	0	1	12.0385	0.3333
2	88	2.2010	17	1	0	1	13.2115	1.7500
3	82	1.8148	12	0	0	0	11.4167	11.4167
3	83	1.9199	12	0	0	1	12.4167	12.4167
3	85	1.9584	12	0	0	0	14.4167	14.4167
3	87	2.0071	12	0	0	0	16.4167	16.4167
3	88	2.0899	12	0	0	0	17.8205	17.7500

specification you will discover that your computer software will either send you an error message, or it will drop the variables *EDUC* and *BLACK*. Why does this happen? The fixed effects estimator is equivalent to including a dummy variable for each cross section. The dummy variable is 1 for all time periods for that cross section, and 0 otherwise. Any variable that does not change over time will be exactly collinear with this dummy variable, and estimation will fail. To look at this feature another way, when deviations from individual means are created, as in (15.17), the variables corresponding to *EDUC* and *BLACK* will consist completely of zeros, because in this sample none of the women increased their education over the years, so *EDUC* is constant for each woman. Similarly, *BLACK* is constant across time, either 1 for all periods for black women, or 0 for all women who were another race. The fixed effects model cannot include variables that are constant for each individual across time. Dropping these variables, the estimation results are contained in Table 15.9. The estimates suggest that overall market experience and job tenure have positive but diminishing effects on ln(*WAGE*). Being in the south is associated with wages that are 1.6% less than in other regions, and union members enjoy wages that are about 6.4% higher, holding other factors constant. These results are interpreted just like those in a linear regression model. An advantage of using panel data is that we are able to hold constant

Table 15.9 **Fixed Effects Estimates of a Wage Equation**

Variable	Coefficient	Std. Error	*t*-Statistic	Prob.
C	1.4500	0.0401	36.1244	0.0000
EXPER	0.0411	0.0066	6.2059	0.0000
EXPER2	−0.0004	0.0003	−1.4965	0.1346
TENURE	0.0139	0.0033	4.2433	0.0000
TENURE2	−0.0009	0.0002	−4.3536	0.0000
SOUTH	−0.0163	0.0361	−0.4515	0.6516
UNION	0.0637	0.0143	4.4688	0.0000

individual differences, which allows us to focus on the marginal effects of the included explanatory variables.

To test for the presence of individual differences, we carry out the F-test of the null hypothesis in equation (15.13). In this case we have $J = N - 1 = 715$ joint hypotheses. The F-statistic value is 19.66. The degrees of freedom for the test are $J = 715$ and $NT - N - (K - 1) = (716)(5) - 716 - 6 = 2858$, and the $\alpha = 0.01$ critical value is $F_c = 1.0$. Thus we reject the null hypothesis of no fixed effect differences between these women; it is proper to include individual fixed effects in the model.

15.5 The Random Effects Model

The individuals included in a microeconomic data panel may be selected at random from a larger population. The young women selected for inclusion in the NLS data set were randomly selected from the population of all women who were between 14 and 24 years old in 1968. This is the population of interest. When using such data it is important to take into account the "data generation process," which in this case is random sampling.

In the fixed effects model (15.14) we assumed that all individual differences were captured by differences in the intercept parameter. The intercepts β_{1i} were considered to be "fixed" parameters that we could estimate directly using the least squares estimator. In the **random effects model** we again assume that all individual differences are captured by the intercept parameters, but we also recognize that the individuals in our sample were randomly selected, and thus we treat the individual differences as *random* rather than fixed, as we did in the fixed effects dummy variable model. Random individual differences can be included in our model by specifying the intercept parameters β_{1i} to consist of a fixed part that represents the population average, $\overline{\beta}_1$, and random individual differences from the population average, u_i. In equation form this breakdown is

$$\beta_{1i} = \overline{\beta}_1 + u_i \tag{15.20}$$

The random individual differences u_i, which are called **random effects**, are analogous to random error terms, and we make the same standard assumptions about them, namely that they have zero mean, are uncorrelated across individuals, and have a constant variance σ_u^2, so that

$$E(u_i) = 0, \quad \text{cov}(u_i, u_j) = 0, \quad \text{var}(u_i) = \sigma_u^2 \tag{15.21}$$

If we substitute (15.20) into (15.14) we obtain

$$\begin{aligned} y_{it} &= \beta_{1i} + \beta_2 x_{2it} + \beta_3 x_{3it} + e_{it} \\ &= (\overline{\beta}_1 + u_i) + \beta_2 x_{2it} + \beta_3 x_{3it} + e_{it} \end{aligned} \tag{15.22}$$

In this expression $\overline{\beta}_1$ is a fixed population parameter, and u_i is a random effect. We can rearrange (15.22) to make it resemble a familiar regression equation,

$$\begin{aligned} y_{it} &= \overline{\beta}_1 + \beta_2 x_{2it} + \beta_3 x_{3it} + (e_{it} + u_i) \\ &= \overline{\beta}_1 + \beta_2 x_{2it} + \beta_3 x_{3it} + v_{it} \end{aligned} \tag{15.23}$$

where now $\bar{\beta}_1$ is the intercept parameter and the error term v_{it} is composed of a component u_i that represents a random individual effect and the component e_{it} that is the usual regression random error. The combined error is

$$v_{it} = u_i + e_{it} \tag{15.24}$$

Because the random effects regression error in (15.24) has two components, one for the individual and the other for the regression, the random effects model is often called an **error components model**.

15.5.1 ERROR TERM ASSUMPTIONS

We make the usual assumptions about the regression error e_{it}, that it has zero mean, constant variance σ_e^2, and is uncorrelated over time, so that $\text{cov}(e_{it}, e_{is}) = 0$. One further error assumption is that the individual effects u_i are not correlated with the regression error e_{it}, so that $\text{cov}(u_i, e_{it}) = 0$. Using these assumptions about u_i and e_{it}, we can show that the error term v_{it} in (15.24) has zero mean

$$E(v_{it}) = E(u_i + e_{it}) = E(u_i) + E(e_{it}) = 0 + 0 = 0$$

and a constant, homoskedastic, variance:

$$
\begin{aligned}
\sigma_v^2 = \text{var}(v_{it}) &= \text{var}(u_i + e_{it}) \\
&= \text{var}(u_i) + \text{var}(e_{it}) + 2\text{cov}(u_i, e_{it}) \\
&= \sigma_u^2 + \sigma_e^2
\end{aligned}
\tag{15.25}
$$

So far these error properties are the usual ones. Differences appear when we consider correlations between the error terms v_{it}. There are several correlations that can be considered.

1. The correlation between two individuals, i and j, at the same point in time, t. The covariance for this case is given by

$$
\begin{aligned}
\text{cov}(v_{it}, v_{jt}) = E(v_{it} v_{jt}) &= E\big[(u_i + e_{it})(u_j + e_{jt})\big] \\
&= E(u_i u_j) + E(u_i e_{jt}) + E(e_{it} u_j) + E(e_{it} e_{jt}) \\
&= 0 + 0 + 0 + 0 = 0
\end{aligned}
$$

2. The correlation between errors on the same individual (i) at different points in time, t and s. The covariance for this case is given by

$$
\begin{aligned}
\text{cov}(v_{it}, v_{is}) = E(v_{it} v_{is}) &= E\big[(u_i + e_{it})(u_i + e_{is})\big] \\
&= E(u_i^2) + E(u_i e_{is}) + E(e_{it} u_i) + E(e_{it} e_{is}) \\
&= \sigma_u^2 + 0 + 0 + 0 \\
&= \sigma_u^2
\end{aligned}
\tag{15.26}
$$

3. The correlation between errors for different individuals in different time periods. The covariance for this case is

$$\text{cov}(v_{it}, v_{js}) = E(v_{it}v_{js}) = E\big[(u_i + e_{it})(u_j + e_{js})\big]$$

$$= E(u_iu_j) + E(u_ie_{js}) + E(e_{it}u_j) + E(e_{it}e_{js})$$

$$= 0 + 0 + 0 + 0 = 0$$

What we have shown is that the errors $v_{it} = u_i + e_{it}$ are correlated over time for a given individual, but are otherwise uncorrelated. The correlation is caused by the component u_i that is common to all time periods. It is constant over time, and in contrast to the AR(1) error model [Section 9.2.2], it does not decline as the observations get further apart in time. It is given by

$$\rho = \text{corr}(v_{it}, v_{is}) = \frac{\text{cov}(v_{it}, v_{is})}{\sqrt{\text{var}(v_{it})\text{var}(v_{is})}} = \frac{\sigma_u^2}{\sigma_u^2 + \sigma_e^2} \tag{15.27}$$

The correlation equals the proportion of the variance in the total error term v_{it} that is attributable to the variance of the individual component u_i.

15.5.2 TESTING FOR RANDOM EFFECTS

The magnitude of the correlation ρ in (15.27) is an important feature of the random effects model. If $u_i = 0$ for every individual, then there are no individual differences and no heterogeneity to account for. In such a case the pooled linear regression model (15.3) is appropriate, and there is no need for either a fixed or a random effects model. We are assuming that the error component u_i has expectation zero, $E(u_i) = 0$. If in addition u_i has a variance of *zero*, then it is said to be a degenerate random variable; it is a constant with value equal to zero. In this case, if $\sigma_u^2 = 0$, then the correlation $\rho = 0$, and there is no random individual heterogeneity present in the data. We can test for the presence of heterogeneity by testing the null hypothesis $H_0 : \sigma_u^2 = 0$ against the alternative hypothesis $H_1 : \sigma_u^2 > 0$. If the null hypothesis is rejected, then we conclude that there are random individual differences among sample members, and that the random effects model is appropriate. On the other hand, if we fail to reject the null hypothesis, then we have no evidence to conclude that random effects are present.

The Lagrange multiplier (*LM*) principle for test construction is very convenient in this case, because *LM* tests require estimation of only the restricted model that assumes that the null hypothesis is true. If the null hypothesis is true, then $u_i = 0$, and the random effects model in (15.23) reduces to

$$y_{it} = \bar{\beta}_1 + \beta_2 x_{2it} + \beta_3 x_{3it} + e_{it}$$

The best estimator for this model is the least squares estimator. The test statistic is based on the least squares residuals

$$\hat{e}_{it} = y_{it} - \bar{b}_1 - b_2 x_{2it} - b_3 x_{3it}$$

The test statistic is due to Breusch and Pagan, and for balanced panels[10] it is

$$LM = \frac{NT}{2(T-1)} \left\{ \frac{\sum\limits_{i=1}^{N} \left(\sum\limits_{t=1}^{T} \hat{e}_{it} \right)^2}{\sum\limits_{i=1}^{N} \sum\limits_{t=1}^{T} \hat{e}_{it}^2} - 1 \right\} \tag{15.28}$$

The test works because the numerator will contain terms like $2e_{i1}e_{i2} + 2e_{i2}e_{i3} + \cdots$ whose sum will not be significantly different from zero if there is no correlation over time for each individual, and will reflect a positive correlation if there is one. If the sum of the cross product terms is not significant, the first term in the curly brackets is not significantly different from one.

If the null hypothesis $H_0 : \sigma_u^2 = 0$ is true, i.e., there are no random effects, then the LM statistic in (15.28) has a distribution (in large samples) that is chi-square with one degree of freedom, reflecting the fact that we are testing a single hypothesis. That is, $LM \sim \chi_{(1)}^2$ if the null hypothesis is true. We reject the null hypothesis and accept the alternative $H_1 : \sigma_u^2 > 0$ if $LM \geq \chi_{(1-\alpha,1)}^2$, where $\chi_{(1-\alpha,1)}^2$ is the $100(1 - \alpha)$ percentile of the $\chi_{(1)}^2$ distribution. This critical value is 3.8415 if $\alpha = 0.05$ and is 6.6349 if $\alpha = 0.01$. Rejecting the null hypothesis leads us to conclude that random effects are present.

15.5.3 ESTIMATION OF THE RANDOM EFFECTS MODEL

The random effects model (15.23) has errors with zero expectation, and a constant variance $\sigma_v^2 = \sigma_u^2 + \sigma_e^2$. The complicating factor is due to a special type of serial correlation—the errors for each cross-sectional unit are intercorrelated with correlation $\rho = \sigma_u^2 / (\sigma_u^2 + \sigma_e^2)$. Under these assumptions the least squares estimator is unbiased and consistent, but not minimum variance. Also, the usual least squares standard errors are incorrect. A generalization of White's heteroskedasticity correction can be applied for "clusters" of observations, which here are the groups of T observations on each individual. Cluster corrected standard errors allow for any type of heteroskedasticity across individuals and general intercorrelation among the observations on the individual.[11]

The generalized least squares (GLS) estimator is the minimum variance estimator for the random effects model. As was the case when we had heteroskedasticity or autocorrelation, we can obtain the GLS estimator in the random effects model by applying least squares to a transformed model. The transformed model is

$$y_{it}^* = \bar{\beta}_1 x_{1it}^* + \beta_2 x_{2it}^* + \beta_3 x_{3it}^* + v_{it}^* \tag{15.29}$$

where the transformed variables are

$$y_{it}^* = y_{it} - \alpha \bar{y}_i, \quad x_{1it}^* = 1 - \alpha, \quad x_{2it}^* = x_{2it} - \alpha \bar{x}_{2i}, \quad x_{3it}^* = x_{3it} - \alpha \bar{x}_{3i} \tag{15.30}$$

---

[10] The statistic can be generalized to cases with unbalanced panels. Check your software for the form used in this case. Nevertheless, it will be a chi-square test statistic with one degree of freedom.

[11] Cluster corrected standard errors are an option in Stata 9.2. A very advanced reference is Jeffery Wooldridge (2002) *Econometric Analysis of Cross Section and Panel Data*, MIT Press, page 152.

Table 15.10   **Random Effects Estimates of a Wage Equation**

Variable	Coefficient	Std. Error	t-Statistic	Prob.
C	0.5339	0.0797	6.6974	0.0000
EDUC	0.0733	0.0053	13.7694	0.0000
EXPER	0.0436	0.0063	6.8745	0.0000
EXPER2	−0.0006	0.0003	−2.1404	0.0324
TENURE	0.0142	0.0032	4.4789	0.0000
TENURE2	−0.0008	0.0002	−3.8868	0.0001
BLACK	−0.1167	0.0301	−3.8721	0.0001
SOUTH	−0.0818	0.0224	−3.6579	0.0003
UNION	0.0802	0.0132	6.0846	0.0000

The variables $\bar{y}_i, \bar{x}_{2i}$, and $\bar{x}_{3i}$ are the individual means defined in (15.15). The transformed error term is $v_{it}^* = v_{it} - \alpha \bar{v}_i$. The key transformation parameter α is defined as

$$\alpha = 1 - \frac{\sigma_e}{\sqrt{T\sigma_u^2 + \sigma_e^2}}$$

It can be shown that the v_{it}^* have constant variance σ_e^2 and are uncorrelated. The proof is long and tedious, so we will not inflict it on you.[12]

Because the transformation parameter α depends on the unknown variances σ_e^2 and σ_u^2, these variances need to be estimated before least squares can be applied to (15.29). Some details of how the estimates $\hat{\sigma}_e^2$ and $\hat{\sigma}_u^2$ are obtained can be found in Appendix 15.A. Then, least squares is applied to (15.29) with σ_e^2 and σ_u^2 replaced by $\hat{\sigma}_e^2$ and $\hat{\sigma}_u^2$ in the parameter α.

15.5.4   AN EXAMPLE USING THE NLS DATA

In Section 15.4.3 we introduced the use of a microeconomic data panel. Because the women in the survey were randomly selected from a larger population, it makes sense to treat individual differences between the 716 women as random effects. Recall that the wage equation has dependent variable ln(*WAGE*) and explanatory variables years of education (*EDUC*), total labor force experience (*EXPER*) and its square, tenure in current job (*TENURE*) and its square, and dummy variables *BLACK*, *SOUTH*, and *UNION*. Before carrying out random effects estimation, we test for the presence of random effects using the *LM* test statistic in (15.28). The value of the test statistic is $LM = 3859.28$, which of course far exceeds the critical value from the $\chi_{(1)}^2$ distribution. We conclude that there is strong evidence of individual heterogeneity.

The random effects estimates are given in Table 15.10. Note that with the random effects estimation procedure, we are able to estimate the effects of years of education and race on ln(*WAGE*). We estimate that the return to education is about 7.3%, and that blacks have wages about 12% lower than whites, everything else held constant. These effects are not estimable using the fixed effects approach. Living in the south leads to wages about 8% lower, and union membership leads to wages about 8% higher, everything else held constant.

---

[12] The details can be found in *Econometric Analysis of Cross Section and Panel Data*, by Jeffrey Wooldridge (MIT Press, 2002), page 286. This text is very advanced and presumes skill with matrix algebra.

For these data the estimates of the error components (the standard deviations) are $\hat{\sigma}_u = 0.3291$ and $\hat{\sigma}_e = 0.1951$. The estimated correlation in (15.27) is $\hat{\rho} = 0.74$. Thus a large fraction of the total error variance is attributable to individual heterogeneity. The estimate of the transformation parameter α is

$$\hat{\alpha} = 1 - \frac{\hat{\sigma}_e}{\sqrt{T\hat{\sigma}_u^2 + \hat{\sigma}_e^2}} = 1 - \frac{0.1951}{\sqrt{5(0.1083) + 0.0381}} = 0.7437$$

Using this value to transform the data as in (15.30), then applying least squares to the transformed regression model in (15.29), yields the random effects estimates. Recall that the fixed effects estimator implicitly uses a transformation parameter value of 1. The random effects estimates of the parameters common to both models are similar because the value $\hat{\alpha} = 0.7437$ is not too far from 1.

15.5.5 COMPARING FIXED AND RANDOM EFFECTS ESTIMATORS

We have two sets of estimates for the wage equation based on the NLS data. Naturally, we would like to know which one to use and report in our research report. If random effects are present, so that $\sigma_u^2 > 0$, then the random effects estimator is preferred for several reasons. First, the random effects estimator takes into account the random sampling process by which the data were obtained. Second, the random effects estimator permits us to estimate the effects of variables that are individually time-invariant, such as race or gender, and in the NLS data, the years of education. Thirdly, the random effects estimator is a generalized least squares estimation procedure, and the fixed effects estimator is a least squares estimator. In large samples, the GLS estimator has a smaller variance than the least squares estimator.

The greater precision of the random effects estimator and its ability to estimate the effects of time-invariant variables are related. To estimate the effects of the explanatory variables on y, the fixed effects estimator only uses information from variation in the x's and y over time, for each individual. It does not use information on how changes in y across different individuals could be attributable to the different x-values for those individuals. These differences are picked up by the fixed effects. In contrast, the random effects estimator uses both sources of information.

15.5.5a Endogeneity in the Random Effects Model

However, there is a potential problem when using random effects estimation. If the random error $v_{it} = u_i + e_{it}$ is correlated with any of the right-hand side explanatory variables in a random effects model, such as (15.23), then the least squares and GLS estimators of the parameters are biased and inconsistent. The problem of **endogenous regressors** was first considered in a general context in Chapter 10 where we considered the general problem of using regression analysis when explanatory variables are random (see Section 10.2). The problem arose again in Chapter 11 when we considered simultaneous equations models. The problem is common in random effects models, because the individual specific error component u_i may well be correlated with some of the explanatory variables. In the NLS wage equation example we considered in the previous section, think about the individual characteristics that are captured by the error component u_i. A person's ability, industriousness, and perseverance are variables not explicitly included in the wage equation, and thus these factors are included in u_i. These characteristics may well be correlated with a woman's years of education completed, her previous job market experience, and job tenure. If this is the case, then the random effects estimator is inconsistent. It will attribute the effects of the error component to the included explanatory factors.

Another example may help reinforce the idea. Let us consider the problem of estimating a cost function for producing a particular output. Suppose we have a panel of data consisting of time-series observations on outputs, costs, and inputs from various production facilities scattered across the country. Each plant has a manager, or management team, whose quality is not always directly measurable. If we estimate a cost function, with cost per unit as the dependent variable, and inputs (labor, materials, energy, etc.) as explanatory variables, then it is very possible that unmeasured managerial qualities, contained in u_i, will be correlated with the explanatory variables. More efficient, better managers may use fewer inputs to produce the same level of output. Such a correlation will cause the random effects estimator to be inconsistent.

15.5.5b The Fixed Effects Estimator in a Random Effects Model
In the panel data context, a simple alternative to random effects exists that is consistent in the presence of a correlation between the random error component u_i and any of the explanatory variables x_{kit}. The fixed effects estimator is consistent even in the presence of such correlation. To see why, let us return to the derivation of the fixed effects estimator in Section 15.4.2. The panel data regression (15.23), including the error component u_i, is

$$y_{it} = \overline{\beta}_1 + \beta_2 x_{2it} + \beta_3 x_{3it} + (u_i + e_{it}) \tag{15.31}$$

The first step in fixed effects estimation is to average the panel observations for each individual over time,

$$\overline{y}_i = \frac{1}{T}\sum_{t=1}^{T} y_{it} = \overline{\beta}_1 + \beta_2 \frac{1}{T}\sum_{t=1}^{T} x_{2it} + \beta_3 \frac{1}{T}\sum_{t=1}^{T} x_{3it} + \frac{1}{T}\sum_{t=1}^{T} u_i + \frac{1}{T}\sum_{t=1}^{T} e_{it} \tag{15.32}$$

$$= \overline{\beta}_1 + \beta_2 \overline{x}_{2i} + \beta_3 \overline{x}_{3i} + u_i + \overline{e}_i$$

Subtracting (15.32) from (15.31), term by term, we have

$$y_{it} = \overline{\beta}_1 + \beta_2 x_{2it} + \beta_3 x_{3it} + u_i + e_{it}$$
$$\underline{- \quad (\overline{y}_i = \overline{\beta}_1 + \beta_2 \overline{x}_{2i} + \beta_3 \overline{x}_{3i} + u_i + \overline{e}_i)} \tag{15.33}$$
$$y_{it} - \overline{y}_i = \beta_2(x_{2it} - \overline{x}_{2i}) + \beta_3(x_{3it} - \overline{x}_{3i}) + (e_{it} - \overline{e}_i)$$

which is exactly the same result as in (15.16). The fixed effects transformation, putting the data in deviation from the mean form, *eliminates* the random effect u_i as well as any other time-invariant factors. The least squares estimator of (15.17) is consistent, converging to the true values as $N \to \infty$, whether the random effect u_i is correlated with the regressors or not. In this sense, it is always safe to use the fixed effects estimator to estimate panel data models.

15.5.5c A Hausman Test
To check for any correlation between the error component u_i and the regressors in a random effects model, we can use a **Hausman test**. The test compares the coefficient estimates from the random effects model to those from the fixed effects model. The idea underlying Hausman's test is that both the random effects and fixed effects estimators are consistent if there is no correlation between u_i and the explanatory variables x_{kit}. If both estimators are consistent, then they should converge to the true parameter values β_k in large samples. That is, in large samples the random effects and fixed effects estimates should be similar. On the

other hand, if u_i is correlated with any x_{kit} the random effects estimator is inconsistent, while the fixed effects estimator remains consistent. Thus in large samples the fixed effects estimator converges to the true parameter values, but the random effects estimator converges to some other value that is not the value of the true parameters. In this case, we expect to see differences between the fixed and random effects estimates.

Examine the fixed effects and random effects estimates in Tables 15.9 and 15.10. Recall that the fixed effects estimator is unable to estimate coefficients on time-invariant variables like *BLACK* and, in the NLS data, *EDUC*. Except for the coefficients on *SOUTH* the estimates do not seem that different, but as we have learned many times, casual inspection of the values is not a statistical test. The Hausman test in this context can be carried out for specific coefficients, using a t-test or, jointly, using an F-test or a chi-square test. Let us consider the t-test first. Let the parameter of interest be β_k; denote the fixed effects estimate as $b_{FE,k}$ and the random effects estimate as $b_{RE,k}$. Then the t-statistic for testing that there is no difference between the estimators is

$$t = \frac{b_{FE,k} - b_{RE,k}}{\left[\widehat{\operatorname{var}(b_{FE,k})} - \widehat{\operatorname{var}\left(b_{RE,k}\right)} \right]^{1/2}} = \frac{b_{FE,k} - b_{RE,k}}{\left[\operatorname{se}\left(b_{FE,k}\right)^2 - \operatorname{se}\left(b_{RE,k}\right)^2 \right]^{1/2}} \quad (15.34)$$

In this t-statistic it is important that the denominator is the estimated variance of the fixed effects estimator minus the estimated variance of the random effects estimator. The reason is that under the null hypothesis that u_i is uncorrelated with any of the explanatory variables, the random effects estimator will have a smaller variance than the fixed effects estimator, at least in large samples. Consequently, we expect to find $\widehat{\operatorname{var}(b_{FE,k})} - \widehat{\operatorname{var}(b_{RE,k})} > 0$, which is necessary for a valid test. A second interesting feature of this test statistic is that

$$\operatorname{var}\left(b_{FE,k} - b_{RE,k}\right) = \operatorname{var}(b_{FE,k}) + \operatorname{var}(b_{RE,k}) - 2\operatorname{cov}(b_{FE,k}, b_{RE,k})$$

$$= \operatorname{var}(b_{FE,k}) - \operatorname{var}(b_{RE,k})$$

The unexpected result in the last line occurs because Hausman proved that, in this particular case, $\operatorname{cov}(b_{FE,k}, b_{RE,k}) = \operatorname{var}(b_{RE,k})$.

Let us apply the t-test to the coefficients of *SOUTH* in Tables 15.9 and 15.10. The test statistic value is

$$t = \frac{b_{FE,k} - b_{RE,k}}{\left[\operatorname{se}\left(b_{FE,k}\right)^2 - \operatorname{se}\left(b_{RE,k}\right)^2 \right]^{1/2}} = \frac{-0.0163 - (-0.0818)}{\left[(0.0361)^2 - (0.0224)^2 \right]^{1/2}} = 2.3137$$

Using the standard 5% large sample critical value of 1.96, we reject the hypothesis that the estimators yield identical results. Our conclusion is that the random effects estimator is inconsistent, and we should use the fixed effects estimator, or we should attempt to improve the model specification. The null hypothesis will be rejected for any reason that makes the two sets of estimates different, including a misspecified model. There may be nonlinearities in the relationship we have not captured with our model, and other explanatory variables may be relevant. The p-value of the test is 0.02069. Thus, if we had chosen the 1% level of significance, we would have not rejected the null hypothesis.

More commonly the Hausman test is automated by software packages to contrast the complete set of common estimates. That is, we carry out a test of a joint hypothesis comparing all the coefficients in Table 15.9, except the intercept, to the corresponding estimates in Table 15.10. If there is no correlation between the error component u_i and the values of x_{kit}, then the six variables common to the two tables (*EXPER, EXPER2, TENURE, TENURE2, SOUTH*, and *UNION*) will have coefficient estimates with similar magnitudes. The Hausman contrast[13] test jointly checks how close the differences between the pairs of coefficients are to zero. The calculated value of this chi-square statistic is 20.73. We are comparing the values of six coefficients, and the test statistic has an asymptotic chi-square distribution with six degrees of freedom. The 5% critical value for this distribution is 12.5916 and the 1% critical value is 16.8119. On the basis of the joint test we reject the null hypothesis that the difference between the estimators is zero even at the 1% level of significance. Again this implies that we should use the fixed effects estimator in this case, or revisit the specification of our model.

15.6 **Exercises**

15.6.1 PROBLEMS

15.1   This exercise uses data from the paper Zhenjuan Liu and Thanasis Stengos, "Non-linearities in Cross Country Growth Regressions: A Semiparametric Approach," *Journal of Applied Econometrics*, 14(5), 1999, 527–538. There are observations on 86 countries, in three time periods, 1960, 1970, and 1980. The authors attempt to explain each country's growth rate (*G*) in terms of the explanatory variables: *POP* = population growth, *INV* = the share of output allocated to investment, *IGDP* = initial level of GDP in 1960 in real terms, *SEC* = human capital measured as the enrollment rate in secondary schools. We are considering three cross-sectional regressions, one for each of the years 1960, 1970, and 1980.

$$G_{60} = \alpha_1 + \alpha_2 POP_{60} + \alpha_3 INV_{60} + \alpha_4 IGDP_{60} + \alpha_5 SEC_{60} + e_{60}$$

$$G_{70} = \beta_1 + \beta_2 POP_{70} + \beta_3 INV_{70} + \beta_4 IGDP_{70} + \beta_5 SEC_{70} + e_{70}$$

$$G_{80} = \gamma_1 + \gamma_2 POP_{80} + \gamma_3 INV_{80} + \gamma_4 IGDP_{80} + \gamma_5 SEC_{80} + e_{80}$$

Estimating a three equation seemingly unrelated regression system, we obtain the estimated equations

$G_{60} = 0.0231 - 0.2435 POP_{60} + 0.1280 INV_{60} - 0.0000021 IGDP_{60} + 0.0410 SEC_{60}$ $R^2 = 0.289$
(se)   (0.0195) (0.2384)   (0.0333)   (0.0000020)   (0.0172)

$G_{70} = 0.0185 - 0.4336 POP_{70} + 0.1870 INV_{70} - 0.0000026 IGDP_{70} + 0.0127 SEC_{70}$ $R^2 = 0.302$
(se)   (0.0313) (0.4029)   (0.0397)   (0.0000018)   (0.0184)

$G_{80} = 0.0423 - 0.8156 POP_{80} + 0.1155 INV_{80} - 0.0000007 IGDP_{80} + 0.0028 SEC_{80}$ $R^2 = 0.387$
(se)   (0.0265) (0.2997)   (0.0297)   (0.0000013)   (0.0141)

(a)   Comment on the signs of the coefficients. Can you explain these signs in terms of the expected impact of the explanatory variables on growth rate?

---

[13] Details of the joint test are beyond the scope of this book. A very advanced reference that contains a careful exposition of the *t*-test, the chi-square test, and a regression based alternative that may be preferable, see *Econometric Analysis of Cross Section and Panel Data* by Jeffrey Wooldridge (MIT, 2002), pp. 288–291.

(b) Does human capital appear to influence growth rate?
(c) The estimated correlations between the errors for the three equations are

$$r_{12} = 0.1084 \quad r_{13} = 0.1287 \quad r_{23} = 0.3987$$

Carry out a hypothesis test to see if SUR estimation is preferred over separate least squares estimation.
(d) Consider the following null hypothesis

$$H_0: \alpha_2 = \beta_2, \ \beta_2 = \gamma_2, \ \alpha_3 = \beta_3, \ \beta_3 = \gamma_3, \ \alpha_4 = \beta_4, \ \beta_4 = \gamma_4,$$
$$\alpha_5 = \beta_5, \ \beta_5 = \gamma_5$$

with the alternative hypothesis being that at least one of the equalities being tested is false. What is the economic interpretation of these hypotheses?
(e) The appropriate chi-squared test statistic value (*Hint:* see Section 15.3.2) is 12.309. Using Table 3 at the end of the book, do you reject the null hypothesis at the 5% level of significance? Using your statistical software, compute the p-value for this test.
(f) Using the information in (e), carry out an F-test of the null hypothesis in (d). What do you conclude? What is the p-value of this test?

15.2 The system of equations in Exercise 15.1 is estimated with some restrictions imposed on the parameters. The restricted estimations are as follows:

$$G_{60} = 0.0352 - 0.4286POP_{60} + 0.1361INV_{60} - 0.0000011IGDP_{60} + 0.0150SEC_{60}$$
(se) (0.0153) (0.1889)   (0.0206)   (0.0000010)   (0.0100)

$$G_{70} = 0.0251 - 0.4286POP_{70} + 0.1361INV_{70} - 0.0000011IGDP_{70} + 0.0150SEC_{70}$$
(se) (0.0159) (0.1889)   (0.0206)   (0.0000010)   (0.0100)

$$G_{80} = 0.0068 - 0.4286POP_{80} + 0.1361INV_{80} - 0.0000011IGDP_{80} + 0.0150SEC_{80}$$
(se) (0.0164) (0.1889)   (0.0206)   (0.0000010)   (0.0100)

What restrictions have been imposed?
(a) Comment on any substantial differences between these results and those in Exercise 15.1.
(b) The null hypothesis $H_0: \alpha_1 = \beta_1, \ \beta_1 = \gamma_1$ is tested against the alternative that at least one of the equalities is not true. The resulting chi-square test statistic value is 93.098. Using Table 3 at the end of the book, test the null hypothesis at the 1% level of significance. (*Hint:* see Section 15.3.2). Compute the p-value for the test.

15.3 Another way to estimate the model in Exercise 15.2 is to pool all the observations and use dummy variables for each of the years 1960, 1970, and 1980.
(a) If you estimate the model this way, what different assumptions are you making about the error terms, relative to the assumptions made for Exercise 15.2.
(b) The results for the estimated dummy variable model appear in Table 15.11. Report the estimated equation. Comment on any differences or similarities with the estimates obtained in Exercise 15.2.
(c) Does the RESET test suggest the equation is misspecified?

Table 15.11 **Dummy Variable Regression Model for Exercise 15.3**

Dependent Variable: G
Included observations: 258

Variable	Coefficient	Std. Error	t-Statistic	Prob.
D60	0.031527	0.014673	2.148656	0.0326
D70	0.020514	0.015297	1.341000	0.1811
D80	0.002896	0.015794	0.183381	0.8546
POP	−0.436464	0.182325	−2.393881	0.0174
INV	0.162829	0.020750	7.847380	0.0000
IGDP	−1.43E-06	9.42E-07	−1.516792	0.1306
SEC	0.014886	0.009759	1.525366	0.1284

$R^2 = 0.406$ $SSE = 0.094778$

Ramsey RESET Test:
F-statistic $= 1.207756$ ⠀⠀⠀⠀⠀⠀⠀⠀p-value $= 0.300612$

15.6.2 COMPUTER EXERCISES

15.4* Consider the following three demand equations

$$\ln(Q_{1t}) = \beta_{11} + \beta_{12} \ln(P_{1t}) + \beta_{13} \ln(Y_t) + e_{1t}$$

$$\ln(Q_{2t}) = \beta_{21} + \beta_{22} \ln(P_{2t}) + \beta_{23} \ln(Y_t) + e_{2t}$$

$$\ln(Q_{3t}) = \beta_{31} + \beta_{32} \ln(P_{3t}) + \beta_{33} \ln(Y_t) + e_{3t}$$

where Q_{it} is the quantity consumed of the ith commodity, $i = 1, 2, 3$ in the tth time period, $t = 1, 2, \ldots, 30$, P_{it} is the price of the ith commodity in time t, and Y_t is disposable income in period t. The commodities are meat $(i = 1)$, fruits and vegetables $(i = 2)$, and cereals and bakery products $(i = 3)$. Prices and income are in real terms, and all data are in index form. They can be found in the file *demand.dat*.

(a) Estimate each equation by least squares and test whether the equation errors for each household are correlated. Report the estimates and their standard errors. Do the elasticities have the expected signs?

(b) Estimate the system jointly using the SUR estimator. Report the estimates and their standard errors. Do they differ much from your results in part (a)?

(c) Test the joint null hypothesis that all income elasticities are equal to unity. (Consult your software to see how such a test is implemented.)

15.5 In the model

$$\ln\left(\frac{GAS}{CAR}\right) = \beta_1 + \beta_2 \ln\left(\frac{Y}{POP}\right) + \beta_3 \ln\left(\frac{P_{MG}}{P_{GDP}}\right) + \beta_4 \ln\left(\frac{CAR}{POP}\right) + e$$

GAS/CAR is motor gasoline consumption per car, Y/POP is per capita real income, P_{MG}/P_{GDP} is real motor gasoline price, and CAR/POP is the stock of cars per capita. The data file *gascar.dat* contains 19 time-series observations on the above variables for the countries Austria, Belgium, Canada, Denmark, France, and Germany. The data are a subset of those used by Baltagi, B.H. and J.M. Griffin (1983), "Gasoline Demand in the OECD: An Application of Pooling and Testing Procedures," *European Economic Review*, 22, 117–137. Consider a set of six equations, one for each country.

(a) Compare least squares and SUR estimates of the coefficients of each equation. Comment on the signs.
(b) Test for contemporaneous correlation.
(c) Using the SUR-estimated equations
   (i) Test the hypothesis that corresponding slope coefficients in different equations are equal.
   (ii) Test the hypothesis that $\ln(CAR/POP)$ should be omitted from all six equations.

15.6 The U.S. Secretary of Agriculture asks a staff economist to provide a basis for determining cattle inventories in the Midwest, Southwest, and West regions. Let $i = 1, 2, 3$ denote the three regions. The economist hypothesizes that in each region, cattle numbers at the end of the year (C_{it}) depend on average price during the year (P_{it}), rainfall during the year (R_{it}), and cattle numbers at the end of the previous year $(C_{i,t-1})$. Because growing conditions are quite different in the three regions, three separate equations are specified, one for each region. They are as follows:

$$C_{1t} = \beta_{11} + \beta_{12}P_{1t} + \beta_{13}R_{1t} + \beta_{14}C_{1,t-1} + e_{1t}$$

$$C_{2t} = \beta_{21} + \beta_{22}P_{2t} + \beta_{23}R_{2t} + \beta_{24}C_{2,t-1} + e_{2t}$$

$$C_{3t} = \beta_{31} + \beta_{32}P_{3t} + \beta_{33}R_{3t} + \beta_{34}C_{3,t-1} + e_{3t}$$

(a) What signs would you expect on the various coefficients? Why?
(b) Under what assumptions about the e_{it} should the three equations be estimated jointly as a set rather than individually?
(c) Use the data that appear in the file *cattle.dat* to find separate least squares estimates for each equation, and the corresponding standard errors.
(d) Test for the existence of contemporaneous correlation between the e_{it}.
(e) Estimate the three equations jointly using the seemingly unrelated regression technique. Compare these results with those obtained in (c) in terms of reliability and economic feasibility.

15.7◆Consider the production function

$$Q_i = f(K_i, L_i)$$

where Q_i is output, K_i is capital, and L_i is labor, all for the ith firm. Suppose the function $f(\cdot)$ is a CES or constant elasticity of substitution production function. The elasticity of substitution that we denote by ω measures the degree to which capital and labor are substituted when the factor price ratio changes. Let P_i be the price of output, R_i be the price of capital, and W_i the price of labor. If the function $f(\cdot)$ is a CES production function, then the conditions for profit maximization, with errors attached, are

$$\ln\left(\frac{Q_i}{L_i}\right) = \gamma_1 + \omega \ln\left(\frac{W_i}{P_i}\right) + e_{1i}, \quad \text{where } e_{1i} \sim N(0, \sigma_1^2)$$

$$\ln\left(\frac{Q_i}{K_i}\right) = \gamma_2 + \omega \ln\left(\frac{R_i}{P_i}\right) + e_{2i}, \quad \text{where } e_{2i} \sim N(0, \sigma_2^2)$$

Since these equations are linear in γ_1, γ_2, and ω, some version(s) of least squares can be used to estimate these parameters. Data on 20 firms appear in the file *cespro.dat*.

(a) Find separate least squares estimates of each of the first-order conditions. Compare the two estimates of the elasticity of substitution.

(b) Test for contemporaneous correlation between e_{1i} and e_{2i}.

(c) Estimate the two equations using generalized least squares, allowing for the existence of contemporaneous correlation.

(d) Repeat part (c), but impose a restriction so that only one estimate of the elasticity of substitution is obtained. (Consult your software to see how to impose such a restriction.) Comment on the results.

(e) Compare the standard errors obtained in parts (a), (c), and (d). Do they reflect the efficiency gains that you would expect?

(f) If $\omega = 1$, the CES production function becomes a Cobb–Douglas production function. Use the results in (d) to test whether a Cobb–Douglas production function is adequate.

15.8 This exercise illustrates the transformation that is necessary to produce generalized least squares estimates for the random effects model. It utilizes the data on the investment example in the file *grunfeld.dat*.

(a) Compute the sample means for *INV*, *V*, and *K* for each of the 10 firms. (We can denote these means as $(\bar{y}_i, \bar{x}_{2i}, \bar{x}_{3i})$, $i = 1, 2, \ldots, 10$.)

(b) Show that the error variance estimate from regressing $\bar{y}_i$ on $\bar{x}_{2i}$ and $\bar{x}_{3i}$ is

$$\hat{\sigma}_*^2 = \overline{\sigma_u^2 + \sigma_e^2/T} = 7218.2329$$

(c) Show that the error variance estimate from the dummy variable model is $\hat{\sigma}_e^2 = 2781.1445$

(d) Show that

$$\alpha = 1 - \sqrt{\frac{\hat{\sigma}_e^2}{T\hat{\sigma}_*^2}} = 0.8612$$

(e) Apply least squares to the regression model

$$y_{it}^* = \bar{\beta}_1 x_{1it}^* + \beta_2 x_{2it}^* + \beta_3 x_{3it}^* + v_{it}^*$$

where the transformed variables are given by

$$y_{it}^* = y_{it} - \alpha\bar{y}_i, \quad x_{1it}^* = 1 - \alpha$$

$$x_{2it}^* = x_{2it} - \alpha\bar{x}_{2i}, \quad x_{3it}^* = x_{3it} - \alpha\bar{x}_{3i}$$

How do these estimates compare with those obtained by applying the automatic random effects command in your software?

15.9* The file *liquor.dat* contains observations on annual expenditure on liquor (L) and annual income (X) (both in thousands of dollars) for 40 randomly selected households for three consecutive years. Consider the model

$$L_{it} = \beta_{1i} + \beta_2 X_{it} + e_{it}$$

where $i = 1, 2, \ldots, 40$ refers to household and $t = 1, 2, 3$ refers to year; the e_{it} are assumed to be uncorrelated with $e_{it} \sim N(0, \sigma_e^2)$.
(a) Compare the alternative estimates for β_2, and their corresponding standard errors, that are obtained under the following circumstances:
   (i) The different household intercepts are modeled using dummy variables.
   (ii) Only average data are available, averaged over the 3 years.
   (iii) The β_{1i} are random drawings with mean $\bar{\beta}_1$ and variance σ_u^2.
   Comment on the estimates and their relative precision.
(b) Test the hypothesis that all household intercepts are equal.

15.10 Consider the NLS panel data on young women discussed in Section 15.4.3. However, let us consider only years 1987 and 1988. These data are contained in the file *nls_panel2.dat*. We are interested in the wage equation that relates the logarithm of WAGE to EXPER, its square EXPER2, SOUTH, and UNION.
(a) Estimate the $\ln(WAGE)$ model by least squares separately for each of the years 1987 and 1988. How do the results compare? For these individual year estimations, what are you assuming about the regression parameter values across individuals (heterogeneity)?
(b) Estimate the $\ln(WAGE)$ equation using both years of data, pooling them into a single regression. For this estimation, what are you assuming about the regression parameter values across individuals (heterogeneity) and the variance of the error term?
(c) The $\ln(WAGE)$ equation specified as a fixed effects model that allows for heterogeneity across individuals is

$$\ln(WAGE_{it}) = \beta_{1i} + \beta_2 EXPER_{it} + \beta_3 EXPER_{it}^2 + \beta_4 SOUTH_{it} + \beta_5 UNION_{it} + e_{it}$$

Explain any differences in assumptions between this model and the models in parts (a) and (b).
(d) Estimate the fixed effects model in part (c) and test the null hypothesis that the intercept parameter is identical for all women in the sample. What does this imply about the estimation results in (b)?
(e) Suppose you wish to obtain the results in (d) but do not have access to specialized software for fixed effects estimation. The model in part (c) holds for all time periods t. Write down the model for time period $t - 1$. Subtract this model from the one in part (c). What happens to the heterogeneity term? Using your computer software, create the necessary first differences of the variables, for example, $DLWAGE_{it} = \ln(WAGE_{it}) - \ln(WAGE_{i,t-1})$. Estimate the wage equation using the differenced data, omitting an intercept term. Compare your results to the fixed effects estimates in part (d).

(f) Create a dummy variable that is equal to 1 for 1988 and 0 otherwise. Add it to the specification in part (c) and estimate the resulting model by fixed effects. What is the interpretation of the coefficient of this variable? Is it statistically significant?

(g) Using the differenced data in part (e), estimate the wage equation in part (f), but including an intercept term. What is the interpretation of the intercept?

15.11 Consider the NLS panel data on young women discussed in Section 15.4.3. However, let us consider only years 1987 and 1988. These data are contained in the file *nls_panel2.dat*. We are interested in the wage equation that relates the logarithm of *WAGE* to *EDUC*, *EXPER*, its square *EXPER2*, *BLACK*, *SOUTH*, and *UNION*.

(a) Estimate the ln(*WAGE*) model by least squares separately for each of the years 1987 and 1988. How do the results compare? For these individual year estimations, what are you assuming about the regression parameter values across individuals (heterogeneity)?

(b) Estimate the ln(*WAGE*) equation using both years of data, pooling them into a single regression. For this estimation, what are you assuming about the regression parameter values across individuals (heterogeneity) and the variance of the error term?

(c) Allowing heterogeneity across individuals, the wage equation is

$$\ln(WAGE_{it}) = \beta_{1i} + \beta_2 EDUC_i + \beta_3 EXPER_{it} + \beta_4 EXPER_{it}^2$$
$$+ \beta_5 BLACK_i + \beta_6 SOUTH_{it} + \beta_7 UNION_{it} + e_{it}$$

Explain any differences in assumptions between this model and the models in parts (a) and (b). Explain why the variables *EDUC* and *BLACK* have the subscripts i rather than i and t, like the other variables.

(d) Estimate the model shown in part (c) using the fixed effects estimator. Test the null hypothesis that the intercept parameter is identical for all women in the sample. What do you conclude?

(e) Estimate the model shown in part (c) using the random effects estimator. Test the null hypothesis that there are no random effects. What do you conclude?

(f) What is the estimated return on an additional year of education in the random effects model? Is it statistically significant? Construct a 95% interval estimate for this parameter.

(g) Explain why it is possible to estimate a return to education in part (e) but not in part (d).

(h) Using the *t*-test statistic in equation (15.34), test at the $\alpha = 0.05$ level the difference between the fixed effects and random effects estimates of the coefficients on *EXPER*, its square *EXPER2*, *SOUTH*, and *UNION*. Do we reject, or fail to reject, the hypotheses that the difference between the estimates is zero? If there are significant differences between any of the coefficients, should we rely on the fixed effects estimates or the random effects estimates? Explain your choice.

15.12 What is the relationship between crime and punishment? This important question has been examined by Cornwell and Trumbull[14] using a panel of data from North Carolina. The cross sections are 90 counties, and the data are annual for the years

---

[14] "Estimating the Economic Model of Crime with Panel Data," *Review of Economics and Statistics*, 76, 1994, 360–366. The data was kindly provided by the authors.

1981–1987. The data are in the file *crime.dat*. In these models the crime rate is explained by variables describing the deterrence effect of the legal system, wages in the private sector (which represents returns to legal activities), socioeconomic conditions such as population density and the percentage of young males in the population, and annual dummy variables to control for time effects. The authors argue that there may be heterogeneity across counties (unobservable county specific characteristics).

(a) What signs do you anticipate for the coefficients? What should happen to the crime rate if (i) deterrence increases, (ii) wages in the private sector increase, or (iii) population density or the percentage of young males increases?

(b) Consider a model in which the crime rate (*LCRMRTE*) is a function of the probability of arrest (*LPRBARR*), the probability of conviction (*LPRBCONV*), the probability of a prison sentence (*LPRBPRIS*), the average prison sentence (*LAVGSEN*), and the average weekly wage in the manufacturing sector (*LWMFG*). Note that the logarithms of the variables are used in each case. Estimate this model by least squares. (i) Discuss the signs of the estimated coefficients and their significance. Are they as you expected? (ii) Interpret the coefficient on *LPRBARR*.

(c) Estimate the model in (b) using a fixed effects estimator. (i) Discuss the signs of the estimated coefficients and their significance. Are they as you expected? (ii) Interpret the coefficient on *LPRBARR* and compare it to the estimate in (b). What do you conclude about the deterrent effect of the probability of arrest? (iii) Interpret the coefficient on *LAVGSEN*. What do you conclude about the severity of punishment as a deterrent?

(d) In the fixed effects estimation from part (c), test whether the county level effects are jointly zero, or not.

(e) To the specification in part (b) add the population density (*LDENSITY*) and the percentage of young males (*LPCTYMLE*), as well as dummy variables for the years 1982–1987 (*D82–D87*). (i) Compare the results obtained by using least squares (with no county effects) and the fixed effects estimator. (ii) Test the joint significance of the year dummy variables. Does there appear to be a trend effect? (iii) Interpret the coefficient of *LWMFG* in both estimations.

(f) Based on these results, what public policies would you advocate to deal with crime in the community?

15.13 Macroeconomists are interested in factors that explain economic growth. An aggregate production function specification was studied by Duffy and Papageorgiou.[15] The data are in the file *ces.dat*. They consist of cross-sectional data on 82 countries for 28 years, 1960–1987.

(a) Estimate a Cobb–Douglas production function $LY_{it} = \beta_1 + \beta_2 LK_{it} + \beta_3 LL_{it} + e_{it}$ where *LY* is the log of GDP, *LK* is the log of capital, and *LL* is the log of labor. Interpret the coefficients on *LK* and *LL*. Test the hypothesis that there are constant returns to scale, $\beta_2 + \beta_3 = 1$.

(b) Add a time trend variable $t = 1, 2, \ldots, 28$, to the specification in (a). Interpret the coefficient of this variable. Test its significance. What effect does this addition have on the estimates of β_2 and β_3?

[15] "A Cross-Country Empirical Investigation of the Aggregate Production Function Specification," *Journal of Economic Growth*, 5, 83–116, 2000. The authors thank Chris Papageorgiou for providing the data.

(c) Assume $\beta_2 + \beta_3 = 1$. Solve for β_3 and substitute this expression into the model in (b). Show that the resulting model is $LYL_{it} = \beta_1 + \beta_2 LKL_{it} + \lambda t + e_{it}$ where LYL is the log of the output–labor ratio, and LKL is the log of the capital–labor ratio. Estimate this restricted, constant returns to scale, version of the Cobb–Douglas production function. Compare the estimate of β_2 from this specification to that in part (b).

(d) Estimate the model in (b) using a fixed effects estimator. Test the hypothesis that there are no cross-country differences. Compare the estimates to those in part (b).

(e) Using the results in (d), test the hypothesis that $\beta_2 + \beta_3 = 1$. What do you conclude about constant returns to scale?

(f) Estimate the restricted version of the Cobb–Douglas model in (c) using the fixed effects estimator. Compare the results to those in part (c). Which specification do you prefer? Explain your choice.

(g) Using the specification in (b), replace the time trend variable t with dummy variables $D2$–$D28$. What is the effect of using this dummy variable specification rather than the single time trend variable?

15.14 Because of worries about increasing costs of running the Australian national health scheme, Prime Minister John Howard asks for information on medical expenditures by individuals. The government's health economists take a random sample of 200 individuals and collect annual data over a 5-year period. They specify the following model:

$$MEDEXP_{it} = \beta_{1i} + \beta_2 \ln(INC_{it}) + \beta_3 AGE_{it} + \beta_4 AGE_{it}^2 + \beta_5 INSUR_{it} + e_{it}$$

where $i = 1, 2, \ldots, 200$, $t = 1, 2, \ldots, 5$, $MEDEXP_{it}$ = annual medical expenditure in hundreds of dollars (includes expenditure before government or insurance refunds and the full cost of prescription drugs), INC_{it} = annual income in thousands of dollars, AGE_{it} = age in years, and $INSUR_{it} = 1$ if individual i has private health insurance in year t and 0 otherwise. Data appear in the file *medical.dat*.

(a) Can you suggest a reason why income was included in the equation as the log of income?

(b) Can you suggest why age was included as AGE and AGE^2?

(c) Estimate the model using
  (i) Least squares under the assumption that $\beta_{11} = \beta_{12} = \cdots = \beta_{1,200}$.
  (ii) A fixed effects estimator.
  (iii) A random effects estimator.

(d) Using the results from the least squares and fixed effects estimators in part (c) test the null hypothesis that the individual intercepts are all equal.

(e) What can you say about the effect of income on medical expenditure?

(f) Compare the results from the fixed and random effects models.

(g) Using the results from the random effects model
  (i) What is the effect of age on medical expenditure?
  (ii) Does having private health insurance influence medical expenditure? By how much?

(h) For individuals who did not change their insurance status over the 5-year period, $INSUR_{it}$ is either 1 or 0 in all the time periods. Those who did change their insurance status will have 1s in some year(s) and 0s in others. Suppose that nobody in the sample changed their insurance status. The fixed effects estimator would fail. Why?

15.15 The file *rice.dat* contains 352 observations on 44 rice farmers in the Tarlac region of the Phillipines for the 8 years 1990–1997. Variables in the data set are tonnes of freshly threshed rice (*PROD*), hectares planted (*AREA*), person-days of hired and family labor (*LABOR*), and kilograms of fertilizer (*FERT*).
   (a) Estimate the production function

$$\ln(PROD_{it}) = \beta_{1it} + \beta_2 \ln(AREA_{it}) + \beta_3 \ln(LABOR_{it}) + \beta_4 \ln(FERT_{it}) + e_{it}$$

under the following assumptions (where relevant use a fixed rather than a random effects estimator):
   (i) $\beta_{1it} = \beta_1$ (see Exercise 5.13)
   (ii) $\beta_{1it} = \beta_{1i}$
   (iii) $\beta_{1it} = \beta_{1t}$
   (iv) β_{1it} can be different over time and farms
   (b) Comment on the sensitivity of the estimates of the input elasticities to the assumption made about the intercept.
   (c) Which of the estimated models do you prefer? Perform a series of hypothesis tests to help you make your decision.

15.16 Using the data set from Exercise 15.15, consider the model

$$\ln(PROD_{it}) = \beta_{1t} + \beta_{2t} \ln(AREA_{it}) + \beta_{3t} \ln(LABOR_{it}) + \beta_{4t} \ln(FERT_{it}) + e_{it}$$

   (a) Estimate three seemingly unrelated regressions for the years 1995, 1996, and 1997 and report the results.
   (b) What assumptions are you making when you estimate the equations in (a)? How would you interpret what was called contemporaneous correlation in Section 15.3? Is this correlation significant?
   (c) Test the hypothesis that the input elasticities are the same in all 3 years.

Appendix 15A Estimation of Error Components

The random effects model is

$$y_{it} = \bar{\beta}_1 + \beta_2 x_{2it} + \beta_3 x_{3it} + (u_i + e_{it}) \tag{15A.1}$$

where u_i is the individual specific error and e_{it} is the usual regression error. We will discuss the case for a balanced panel, with T time-series observations for each of N individuals. To implement generalized least squares estimation, we need to consistently estimate σ_u^2, the variance of the individual specific error component, and σ_e^2, the variance of the regression error.

The regression error variance σ_e^2 comes from the fixed effects estimator. In (15.33) we transform the panel data regression into "deviation about the individual mean" form

$$y_{it} - \bar{y}_i = \beta_2(x_{2it} - \bar{x}_{2i}) + \beta_3(x_{3it} - \bar{x}_{3i}) + (e_{it} - \bar{e}_i) \tag{15A.2}$$

The least squares estimator of this equation yields the same estimates and sum of squared residuals (denoted here by SSE_{DV}) as least squares applied to a model that includes a dummy variable for each individual in the sample. A consistent estimator of σ_e^2 is obtained by dividing SSE_{DV} by the appropriate degrees of freedom, which is $NT - N - K_{slopes}$, where K_{slopes} is the number of parameters that are present in the transformed model (15A.2)

$$\hat{\sigma}_e^2 = \frac{SSE_{DV}}{NT - N - K_{slopes}} \tag{15A.3}$$

The estimator of σ_u^2 requires a bit more work. We begin with the time-averaged observations in (15.32)

$$\bar{y}_i = \bar{\beta}_1 + \beta_2 \bar{x}_{2i} + \beta_3 \bar{x}_{3i} + u_i + \bar{e}_i \quad i = 1, \ldots, N \tag{15A.4}$$

The least squares estimator of (15A.4) is called the **between estimator**, as it uses variation between individuals as a basis for estimating the regression parameters. This estimator is unbiased and consistent, but not minimum variance under the error assumptions of the random effects model. The error term in this model is $u_i + \bar{e}_i$; it is uncorrelated across individuals, and has homoskedastic variance

$$
\begin{aligned}
\text{var}(u_i + \bar{e}_i) &= \text{var}(u_i) + \text{var}(\bar{e}_i) = \text{var}(u_i) + \text{var}\left(\frac{1}{T} \sum_{t=1}^{T} e_{it}\right) \\
&= \sigma_u^2 + \frac{1}{T^2} \text{var}\left(\sum_{t=1}^{T} e_{it}\right) = \sigma_u^2 + \frac{T\sigma_e^2}{T^2} \\
&= \sigma_u^2 + \frac{\sigma_e^2}{T}
\end{aligned} \tag{15A.5}
$$

We can estimate the variance in (15A.5) by estimating the between regression in (15A.4), and dividing the sum of squared residuals, SSE_{BE}, by the degrees of freedom $N - K_{BE}$, where K_{BE} is the total number of parameters in the between regression, including the intercept parameter. Then

$$\widehat{\sigma_u^2 + \frac{\sigma_e^2}{T}} = \frac{SSE_{BE}}{N - K_{BE}} \tag{15A.6}$$

With this estimate in hand we can estimate σ_u^2 as

$$\hat{\sigma}_u^2 = \widehat{\sigma_u^2 + \frac{\sigma_e^2}{T}} - \frac{\hat{\sigma}_e^2}{T} = \frac{SSE_{BE}}{N - K_{BE}} - \frac{SSE_{DV}}{T(NT - N - K_{slopes})} \tag{15A.7}$$

We have obtained the estimates of σ_u^2 and σ_e^2 using what is called the Swamy–Arora method. This method is implemented in software packages and is well established. We note, however, that it is possible in finite samples to obtain an estimate $\hat{\sigma}_u^2$ in (15A.7) that is negative, which is obviously infeasible. If this should happen, one option is simply to set $\hat{\sigma}_u^2 = 0$, which implies that there are no random effects. Alternatively, your software may offer other options for estimating the variance components, which you might try.

Chapter 16

Qualitative and Limited Dependent Variable Models

Learning Objectives

Based on the material in this chapter, you should be able to

1. Give some examples of economic decisions in which the observed outcome is a binary variable.

2. Explain why probit, or logit, is usually preferred to least squares when estimating a model in which the dependent variable is binary.

3. Give some examples of economic decisions in which the observed outcome is a choice among several alternatives, both ordered and unordered.

4. Compare and contrast the multinomial logit model to the conditional logit model.

5. Give some examples of models in which the dependent variable is a count variable.

6. Discuss the implications of censored data for least squares estimation.

7. Describe what is meant by the phrase "sample selection."

Keywords

binary choice models
censored data
conditional logit
count data models
feasible generalized least squares
Heckit
identification problem
independence of irrelevant alternatives (IIA)
index models
individual and alternative specific variables
individual specific variables
latent variables
likelihood function
limited dependent variables
linear probability model
logistic random variable

logit
log-likelihood function
marginal effect
maximum likelihood estimation
multinomial choice models
multinomial logit
odds ratio
ordered choice models
ordered probit
ordinal variables
Poisson random variable
Poisson regression model
probit
selection bias
Tobit model
truncated data

In this book we focus primarily on econometric models in which the dependent variable is continuous and fully observable; quantities, prices, and outputs are examples of such variables. However, microeconomics is a general theory of choice, and many of the choices that individuals and firms make cannot be measured by a continuous outcome variable. In this chapter we examine some fascinating models that are used to describe choice behavior, and which do not have the usual continuous dependent variable. Our descriptions will be brief, since we will not go into all the theory, but we will reveal to you a rich area of economic applications.

We also introduce a class of models with dependent variables that are *limited*. By that, we mean that they are continuous, but their range of values is constrained in some way and their values are not completely observable. Alternatives to least squares estimation must be considered for such cases, since the least squares estimator is both biased and inconsistent.

16.1 Models with Binary Dependent Variables

Many of the choices that individuals and firms make are "either–or" in nature. For example, a high school graduate decides to attend college or not. A worker decides to drive to work or to get there another way. A household decides to purchase a house or to rent. A firm decides to advertise its product on the Internet or it decides against such advertising. As economists we are interested in explaining why particular choices are made, and what factors enter into the decision process. We also want to know *how much* each factor affects the outcome. Such questions lead us to the problem of constructing a statistical model of binary, either–or, choices. Such choices can be represented by a binary (dummy) variable that takes the value 1 if one outcome is chosen, and takes the value 0 otherwise. The binary variable describing a choice is the dependent variable rather than an independent variable. This fact affects our choice of a statistical model.

The list of economic applications in which choice models may be useful is a long one. These models are useful in any economic setting in which an agent must choose one of two alternatives. Examples include the following:

- An economic model explaining why some states in the United States have ratified the Equal Rights Amendment and others have not.
- An economic model explaining why some individuals take a second, or third, job and engage in "moonlighting."
- An economic model of why some legislators in the U.S. House of Representatives vote for a particular bill and others do not.
- An economic model of why the federal government awards development grants to some large cities and not to others.
- An economic model explaining why some loan applications are accepted and others are not at a large metropolitan bank.
- An economic model explaining why some individuals vote "yes" for increased spending in a school board election and others vote "no."
- An economic model explaining why some female college students decide to study engineering and others do not.

This list illustrates the great variety of circumstances in which a model of binary choice may be used. In each case an economic decision maker chooses between two mutually exclusive outcomes.

We will illustrate **binary choice models** using an important problem from transportation economics. How can we explain an individual's choice between driving (private transportation) and taking the bus (public transportation) when commuting to work, assuming, for simplicity, that these are the only two alternatives? We represent an individual's choice by the dummy variable

$$y = \begin{cases} 1 & \text{individual drives to work} \\ 0 & \text{individual takes bus to work} \end{cases} \tag{16.1}$$

If we collect a random sample of workers who commute to work, then the outcome y will be unknown to us until the sample is drawn. Thus, y is a random variable. If the probability that an individual drives to work is p, then $P[y = 1] = p$. It follows that the probability that a person uses public transportation is $P[y = 0] = 1 - p$. The probability function for such a binary random variable is

$$f(y) = p^y(1 - p)^{1-y}, \quad y = 0, 1 \tag{16.2}$$

where p is the probability that y takes the value 1. This discrete random variable has expected value $E(y) = p$ and variance $\text{var}(y) = p(1 - p)$.

What factors might affect the probability that an individual chooses one transportation mode over the other? One factor will certainly be how long it takes to get to work one way or the other. Define the explanatory variable

$$x = (\text{commuting time by bus} - \text{commuting time by car})$$

There are other factors that affect the decision, but let us focus on this single explanatory variable. *A priori* we expect that as x increases, and commuting time by bus increases relative to commuting time by car, an individual would be more inclined to drive. That is, we expect a positive relationship between x and p, the probability that an individual will drive to work.

16.1.1 THE LINEAR PROBABILITY MODEL

For these models usual least squares estimation methods are not the best choices. Instead, **maximum likelihood estimation** (see Appendix C.8) is the usual method chosen. However, we begin by illustrating the least squares method and its difficulties in this context.

In regression analysis we break the dependent variable into fixed and random parts. If we do this for the random variable y, we have

$$y = E(y) + e = p + e \tag{16.3}$$

We then relate the fixed, systematic portion of y to explanatory variables that we believe help explain its expected value. We are assuming that the probability of driving is related to the difference in driving times, x, in the transportation example. Assuming that the relationship is linear,

$$E(y) = p = \beta_1 + \beta_2 x \tag{16.4}$$

The linear regression model for explaining the choice variable y is called the **linear probability model**. It is given by

$$y = E(y) + e = \beta_1 + \beta_2 x + e \tag{16.5}$$

One problem with the linear probability model is that the error term is heteroskedastic; the variance of the error term e varies from one observation to another. The probability density functions for y and e are:

y-Value	e-Value	Probability
1	$1 - (\beta_1 + \beta_2 x)$	$p = \beta_1 + \beta_2 x$
0	$-(\beta_1 + \beta_2 x)$	$1 - p = 1 - (\beta_1 + \beta_2 x)$

Using these values it can be shown that the variance of the error term e is

$$\text{var}(e) = (\beta_1 + \beta_2 x)(1 - \beta_1 - \beta_2 x)$$

If we adopt the linear probability model (16.5), we should use generalized least squares estimation. This is generally done by first estimating the model (16.5) by least squares, then the estimated variance of the error term is

$$\hat{\sigma}_i^2 = \widehat{\text{var}(e_i)} = (b_1 + b_2 x_i)(1 - b_1 - b_2 x_i) \tag{16.6}$$

Using this estimated variance the data can be transformed as $y_i^* = y_i / \hat{\sigma}_i$ and $x_i^* = x_i / \hat{\sigma}_i$, then the model $y_i^* = \beta_1 \hat{\sigma}_i^{-1} + \beta_2 x_i^* + e_i^*$ is estimated by least squares to produce the **feasible generalized least squares** estimates. Both least squares and feasible generalized least squares are consistent estimators of the regression parameters.

In practice certain difficulties may arise with the implementation of this procedure. They are related to another problem with the linear probability model—that of obtaining probability values that are less than 0 or greater than 1. If we estimate the parameters of (16.5) by least squares, we obtain the fitted model explaining the systematic portion of y. This systematic portion is p, the probability that an individual chooses to drive to work. That is,

$$\hat{p} = b_1 + b_2 x \tag{16.7}$$

When using this model to predict behavior, by substituting alternative values of x, we can easily obtain values of $\hat{p}$ that are less than 0 or greater than 1. Values like these do not make sense as probabilities, and we are left in a difficult situation. It also means that some of the estimated variances in (16.6) may be negative. The standard fix-up is to set negative $\hat{p}$ values to a small value like 0.01, and values of $\hat{p}$ greater than 1 to 0.99. Making these changes will not hurt in large samples.

The underlying feature that causes these problems is that the linear probability model (16.4) implicitly assumes that increases in x have a constant effect on the probability of choosing to drive,

$$\frac{dp}{dx} = \beta_2 \tag{16.8}$$

That is, as x increases the probability of driving continues to increase at a constant rate. However, since $0 \leq p \leq 1$, a constant rate of increase is impossible. To overcome this problem we consider the nonlinear **probit** model.

16.1.2   THE PROBIT MODEL

To keep the choice probability p within the interval $[0,1]$, a nonlinear S-shaped relationship between x and p can be used. In Figure 16.1a such a curve is illustrated. As x increases, the probability curve rises rapidly at first, and then begins to increase at a decreasing rate. The *slope* of this curve gives the change in probability given a unit change in x. The slope is not constant as in the linear probability model.

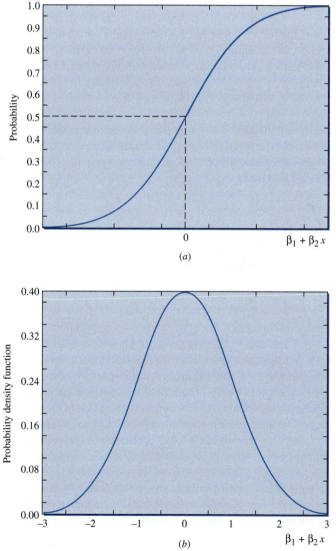

FIGURE *16.1*   (*a*) Standard normal cumulative distribution function. (*b*) Standard normal probability density function.

A functional relationship that is used to represent such a curve is the probit function. The probit function is related to the standard normal probability distribution. If Z is a standard normal random variable, then its probability density function is

$$\phi(z) = \frac{1}{\sqrt{2\pi}} e^{-0.5z^2}$$

The probit function is

$$\Phi(z) = P[Z \le z] = \int_{-\infty}^{z} \frac{1}{\sqrt{2\pi}} e^{-0.5u^2} \, du \tag{16.9}$$

If you are not familiar with integral calculus, ignore the last expression in (16.9). This mathematical expression is the probability that a standard normal random variable falls to the left of point z. In geometric terms it is the area under the standard normal probability density function to the left of z. The function $\Phi(z)$ is the cumulative distribution function (*cdf*) that we have worked with to compute normal probabilities.

The probit statistical model expresses the probability p that y takes the value 1 to be

$$p = P[Z \le \beta_1 + \beta_2 x] = \Phi(\beta_1 + \beta_2 x) \tag{16.10}$$

where $\Phi(z)$ is the probit function. The probit model is said to be *nonlinear* because (16.10) is a nonlinear function of β_1 and β_2. If β_1 and β_2 were known, we could use (16.10) to find the probability that an individual will drive to work. However, since these parameters are not known, we will estimate them.

16.1.3 INTERPRETATION OF THE PROBIT MODEL

The probit model is represented by (16.10). In this model we can examine the effect of a 1-unit change in x on the probability that $y = 1$ by considering the derivative,

$$\frac{dp}{dx} = \frac{d\Phi(t)}{dt} \cdot \frac{dt}{dx} = \phi(\beta_1 + \beta_2 x)\beta_2 \tag{16.11}$$

where $t = \beta_1 + \beta_2 x$ and $\phi(\beta_1 + \beta_2 x)$ is the standard normal probability density function evaluated at $\beta_1 + \beta_2 x$. To obtain this result we have used the chain rule of differentiation. We estimate this effect by replacing the unknown parameters by their estimates $\tilde{\beta}_1$ and $\tilde{\beta}_2$.

In Figure 16.1 we show the probit function $\Phi(z)$ and the standard normal probability density function $\phi(z)$ just below it. The expression in (16.11) shows the effect of an increase in x on p. The effect depends on the slope of the probit function, which is given by $\phi(\beta_1 + \beta_2 x)$ and the magnitude of the parameter β_2. Equation (16.11) has the following implications:

1. Since $\phi(\beta_1 + \beta_2 x)$ is a probability density function, its value is always *positive*. Consequently the sign of dp/dx is determined by the sign of β_2. In the transportation problem we expect β_2 to be positive so that $dp/dx > 0$; as x increases we expect p to increase.

2. As x changes, the value of the function $\phi(\beta_1 + \beta_2 x)$ changes. The standard normal probability density function reaches its maximum when $z = 0$, or when $\beta_1 + \beta_2 x = 0$.

In this case $p = \Phi(0) = 0.5$ and an individual is equally likely to choose car or bus transportation. It makes sense that in this case the effect of a change in x has its greatest effect, since the individual is "on the borderline" between car and bus transportation. The slope of the probit function $p = \Phi(z)$ is at its maximum when $z = 0$, the borderline case.

3. On the other hand, if $\beta_1 + \beta_2 x$ is large, say near 3, then the probability that the individual chooses to drive is very large and close to 1. In this case a change in x will have relatively little effect since $\phi(\beta_1 + \beta_2 x)$ will be nearly 0. The same is true if $\beta_1 + \beta_2 x$ is a large negative value, say near -3. These results are consistent with the notion that if an individual is "set" in their ways, with p near 0 or 1, the effect of a small change in commuting time will be negligible.

The results of a probit model can also be used to predict an individual's choice. The ability to predict discrete outcomes is very important in many applications. For example, banks prior to approving loans predict the probability that an applicant will default. If the probability of default is high, then the loan is either not approved or additional conditions, such as extra collateral or a higher interest rate, are imposed.

In order to predict the probability that an individual chooses the alternative $y = 1$, we can use the probability model $p = \Phi(\beta_1 + \beta_2 x)$. In the following section we describe how to obtain estimates $\tilde{\beta}_1$ and $\tilde{\beta}_2$ of the unknown parameters. Using these we estimate the probability p to be

$$\hat{p} = \Phi(\tilde{\beta}_1 + \tilde{\beta}_2 x) \tag{16.12}$$

By comparing to a threshold value, like 0.5, we can predict choice using the rule

$$\hat{y} = \begin{cases} 1 & \hat{p} \geq 0.5 \\ 0 & \hat{p} < 0.5 \end{cases}$$

16.1.4 MAXIMUM LIKELIHOOD ESTIMATION OF THE PROBIT MODEL

Suppose we randomly select three individuals and observe that the first two drive to work and the third takes the bus; $y_1 = 1$, $y_2 = 1$, and $y_3 = 0$. Furthermore suppose that the values of x, in minutes, for these individuals are $x_1 = 15$, $x_2 = 20$, and $x_3 = 5$. What is the joint probability of observing $y_1 = 1$, $y_2 = 1$, and $y_3 = 0$? The probability function for y is given by (16.2), which we now combine with the probit model (16.10) to obtain

$$f(y_i) = [\Phi(\beta_1 + \beta_2 x_i)]^{y_i}[1 - \Phi(\beta_1 + \beta_2 x_i)]^{1-y_i}, \quad y_i = 0, 1 \tag{16.13}$$

If the three individuals are independently drawn, then the joint probability density function for y_1, y_2, and y_3 is the product of the marginal probability functions:

$$f(y_1, y_2, y_3) = f(y_1) f(y_2) f(y_3)$$

Consequently, the probability of observing $y_1 = 1$, $y_2 = 1$, and $y_3 = 0$ is

$$P[y_1 = 1, y_2 = 1, y_3 = 0] = f(1, 1, 0) = f(1) f(1) f(0)$$

Substituting in (16.13), and the values of x_i, we have

$$P[y_1 = 1, y_2 = 1, y_3 = 0]$$
$$= \Phi[\beta_1 + \beta_2(15)] \times \Phi[\beta_1 + \beta_2(20)] \times \{1 - \Phi[\beta_1 + \beta_2(5)]\} \qquad (16.14)$$

In statistics, the function (16.14), which gives us the probability of observing the sample data, is called the **likelihood function**. Intuitively it makes sense to choose as estimates for β_1 and β_2 the values $\tilde{\beta}_1$ and $\tilde{\beta}_2$ that maximize the probability, or likelihood, of observing the sample. Unfortunately there are no formulas that give us the values for $\tilde{\beta}_1$ and $\tilde{\beta}_2$ as there are in least squares estimation of the linear regression model. Consequently, we must use the computer and techniques from numerical analysis to obtain $\tilde{\beta}_1$ and $\tilde{\beta}_2$. On the surface, this appears to be a difficult task, because $\Phi(z)$ from (16.9) is such a complicated function. As it turns out, however, using a computer to maximize (16.14) is a relatively easy process.

An interesting feature of the maximum likelihood estimation procedure is that while its properties in small samples are not known, we can show that in large samples the maximum likelihood estimator is normally distributed, consistent, and *best*, in the sense that no competing estimator has smaller variance.

Econometric software packages contain the maximum likelihood estimation procedure for the probit model, and thus it is not difficult to estimate the parameters β_1 and β_2 in practice. However, in order for the maximum likelihood estimation procedure to be reliable, large samples are required. Our expression in (16.14) was limited to three observations for illustration only, and maximum likelihood estimation should not be carried out with such a small amount of data. In Section 16.1.5 we give an empirical example based on a larger sample.

16.1.5 AN EXAMPLE

Ben-Akiva and Lerman[1] have sample data on automobile and public transportation travel times and the alternative chosen for $N = 21$ individuals. A few of these observations are given in Table 16.1; the complete set of data is in the file *transport.dat*. In this table the variable $DTIME_i$ = (bus time − auto time) and the dependent variable $AUTO_i = 1$ if automobile transportation is chosen.

Using the complete sample of data, and a numerical optimization program for the probit model (such programs are available in most econometric packages), we can obtain the maximum likelihood estimates of the parameters,

$$\tilde{\beta}_1 + \tilde{\beta}_2 DTIME_i = -0.0644 + 0.0299 DTIME_i$$
$$(\text{se}) \qquad\qquad (0.3992)\ (0.0103) \qquad (16.15)$$

Table 16.1 **Sample Observations on Travel Choice**

Auto time	Bus time	*DTIME*	*AUTO*
52.9	4.4	−48.5	0
4.1	28.5	24.4	0
4.1	86.9	82.8	1
56.2	31.6	−24.6	0

---

[1] *Discrete Choice Analysis*, MIT Press, 1985.

The values in parentheses below the parameter estimates are estimated standard errors that are valid in large samples. These standard errors can be used to carry out hypothesis tests and construct interval estimates in the usual way, with the qualification that they are valid in large samples. The negative sign of $\tilde{\beta}_1$ implies that when commuting times via bus and auto are equal so $DTIME = 0$, individuals have a bias against driving to work, relative to public transportation, though the estimated coefficient is not statistically significant. The positive sign of $\tilde{\beta}_2$ indicates that an increase in public transportation travel time relative to auto travel time increases the probability that an individual will choose to drive to work, and this coefficient is statistically significant.

Suppose that we wish to estimate the marginal effect of increasing public transportation time, given that travel via public transportation currently takes 20 minutes longer than auto travel. Using (16.11)

$$\widehat{\frac{dp}{dDTIME}} = \phi(\tilde{\beta}_1 + \tilde{\beta}_2 DTIME)\tilde{\beta}_2 = \phi(-0.0644 + 0.0299 \times 20)(0.0299)$$

$$= \phi(0.5355)(0.0299) = 0.3456 \times 0.0299 = 0.0104$$

For the probit probability model, an incremental (1-minute) increase in the travel time via public transportation increases the probability of travel via auto by approximately 0.01, given that taking the bus already requires 20 minutes more travel time than driving.

The estimated parameters of the probit model can also be used to "predict" the behavior of an individual who must choose between auto and public transportation to travel to work. If an individual is faced with the situation that it takes 30 minutes longer to take public transportation than to drive to work, then the estimated probability that auto transportation will be selected is calculated using (16.12)

$$\hat{p} = \Phi(\tilde{\beta}_1 + \tilde{\beta}_2 DTIME) = \Phi(-0.0644 + 0.0299 \times 30) = 0.798$$

Since the estimated probability that the individual will choose to drive to work is 0.798, which is greater than 0.5, we "predict" that when public transportation takes 30 minutes longer than driving to work, the individual will choose to drive.

16.2 The Logit Model for Binary Choice

Probit model estimation is numerically complicated because it is based on the normal distribution. A frequently used alternative to the probit model for binary choice situations is the logit model. These models differ only in the particular S-shaped curve used to constrain probabilities to the [0,1] interval. If L is a **logistic random variable**, then its probability density function is

$$\lambda(l) = \frac{e^{-l}}{(1 + e^{-l})^2}, \quad -\infty < l < \infty \tag{16.16}$$

The corresponding cumulative distribution function, unlike the normal distribution, has a closed form expression, which makes analysis somewhat easier. The cumulative distribution function for a logistic random variable is

$$\Lambda(l) = p[L \leq l] = \frac{1}{1 + e^{-l}} \tag{16.17}$$

In the logit model, the probability p that the observed value y takes the value 1 is

$$p = P[L \le \beta_1 + \beta_2 x] = \Lambda(\beta_1 + \beta_2 x) = \frac{1}{1 + e^{-(\beta_1 + \beta_2 x)}} \qquad (16.18)$$

This can be expressed in a more generally useful form. The probability that $y = 1$ can be written as

$$p = \frac{1}{1 + e^{-(\beta_1 + \beta_2 x)}} = \frac{\exp(\beta_1 + \beta_2 x)}{1 + \exp(\beta_1 + \beta_2 x)}$$

The probability that $y = 0$ is

$$1 - p = \frac{1}{1 + \exp(\beta_1 + \beta_2 x)}$$

Represented in this way, the logit model can be extended to cases in which the choice is between more than two alternatives, as we will see in Section 16.3.

In maximum likelihood estimation of the logit model, the probability given in (16.18) is used to form the likelihood function (16.14) by inserting "Λ" for "Φ". To interpret the logit estimates, the derivative in (16.11) is still valid, using (16.16) instead of the normal probability density function.

The shapes of the logistic and normal probability density functions are somewhat different, and maximum likelihood estimates of β_1 and β_2 will be different. However, the marginal probabilities and the predicted probabilities differ very little in most cases.

16.3 Multinomial Logit

In probit and logit models the decision maker chooses between two alternatives. Clearly we are often faced with choices involving more than two alternatives. These are called **multinomial choice** situations. Examples include the following:

- If you are shopping for a laundry detergent, which one do you choose? Tide, Cheer, Arm & Hammer, Wisk, and so on. The consumer is faced with a wide array of alternatives. Marketing researchers relate these choices to prices of the alternatives, advertising, and product characteristics.
- If you enroll in the business school, will you major in economics, marketing, management, finance, or accounting?
- If you are going to a mall on a shopping spree, which mall will you go to, and why?
- When you graduated from high school, you had to choose between not going to college and going to a private 4-year college, a public 4-year college, or a 2-year college. What factors led to your decision among these alternatives?

It would not take you long to come up with other illustrations. In each of these cases, researchers wish to relate the observed choice to a set of explanatory variables. More specifically, as in probit and logit models, they wish to explain and predict the probability that an individual with a certain set of characteristics chooses one of the alternatives. The estimation and interpretation of such models is, in principle, similar to that in logit and probit models. The models themselves go under the names **multinomial logit, conditional logit**, and **multinomial probit**. We will discuss the most commonly used logit models.

16.3.1   MULTINOMIAL LOGIT CHOICE PROBABILITIES

Suppose that a decision maker must choose between several distinct alternatives. Let us focus on a problem with $J = 3$ alternatives. An example might be the choice facing a high school graduate. Shall I attend a 2-year college, a 4-year college, or not go to college? The factors affecting this choice might include household income, the student's high school grades, family size, race, the student's gender, and the parent's education. As in the logit and probit models, we will try to explain the probability that the ith person will choose alternative j,

$$p_{ij} = P[\text{individual } i \text{ chooses alternative } j]$$

In our example there are $J = 3$ alternatives, denoted by $j = 1, 2,$ or 3. These numerical values have no meaning because the alternatives in general have no particular ordering and are assigned arbitrarily. You can think of them as categories A, B, and C.

If we assume a single explanatory factor, x_i, then, in the multinomial logit specification, the probabilities of individual i choosing alternatives $j = 1, 2, 3$ are

$$p_{i1} = \frac{1}{1 + \exp(\beta_{12} + \beta_{22}x_i) + \exp(\beta_{13} + \beta_{23}x_i)}, \quad j = 1 \tag{16.19a}$$

$$p_{i2} = \frac{\exp(\beta_{12} + \beta_{22}x_i)}{1 + \exp(\beta_{12} + \beta_{22}x_i) + \exp(\beta_{13} + \beta_{23}x_i)}, \quad j = 2 \tag{16.19b}$$

$$p_{i3} = \frac{\exp(\beta_{13} + \beta_{23}x_i)}{1 + \exp(\beta_{12} + \beta_{22}x_i) + \exp(\beta_{13} + \beta_{23}x_i)}, \quad j = 3 \tag{16.19c}$$

The parameters β_{12} and β_{22} are specific to the second alternative, and β_{13} and β_{23} are specific to the third alternative. The parameters specific to the first alternative are set to zero to solve an **identification problem** and to make the probabilities sum to 1.[2] Setting $\beta_{11} = \beta_{21} = 0$ leads to the "1" in the numerator of p_{i1} and the "1" in the denominator of each part of (16.19). Specifically, the term that would be there is $\exp(\beta_{11} + \beta_{21}x_i) = \exp(0 + 0x_i) = 1$.

A distinguishing feature of the multinomial logit model in (16.19) is that there is a single explanatory variable that describes the individual, *not* the alternatives facing the individual. To distinguish the alternatives we give them different parameter values. This situation is common in the social sciences, where surveys record many characteristics of the individuals, and choices they made.

16.3.2   MAXIMUM LIKELIHOOD ESTIMATION

Let y_{i1}, y_{i2}, and y_{i3} be dummy variables that indicate the choice made by individual i. If alternative 1 is selected, then $y_{i1} = 1$, $y_{i2} = 0$, and $y_{i3} = 0$. If alternative 2 is selected, then $y_{i1} = 0$, $y_{i2} = 1$, and $y_{i3} = 0$. In this model each individual must choose one, and only one, of the available alternatives.

---

[2] Some software may choose the parameters of the last (Jth) alternative to set to zero, or perhaps the most frequently chosen group. Check your software documentation.

Estimation of this model is by maximum likelihood. Suppose that we observe three individuals, who choose alternatives 1, 2, and 3, respectively. Assuming that their choices are independent, then the probability of observing this outcome is

$$
\begin{aligned}
P(y_{11} = 1, y_{22} = 1, y_{33} = 1) &= p_{11} \times p_{22} \times p_{33} \\
&= \frac{1}{1 + \exp(\beta_{12} + \beta_{22}x_1) + \exp(\beta_{13} + \beta_{23}x_1)} \\
&\times \frac{\exp(\beta_{12} + \beta_{22}x_2)}{1 + \exp(\beta_{12} + \beta_{22}x_2) + \exp(\beta_{13} + \beta_{23}x_2)} \\
&\times \frac{\exp(\beta_{13} + \beta_{23}x_3)}{1 + \exp(\beta_{12} + \beta_{22}x_3) + \exp(\beta_{13} + \beta_{23}x_3)} \\
&= L(\beta_{12}, \beta_{22}, \beta_{13}, \beta_{23})
\end{aligned}
$$

In the last line we recognize that this joint probability depends on the unknown parameters and is in fact the likelihood function. Maximum likelihood estimation seeks those values of the parameters that maximize the likelihood or, more specifically, the **log-likelihood function**, which is easier to work with mathematically. In a real application the number of individuals will be greater than three, and computer software will be used to maximize the log-likelihood function numerically. While the task might look daunting, finding the maximum likelihood estimates in this type of model is fairly simple.

16.3.3 POST-ESTIMATION ANALYSIS

Given that we can obtain maximum likelihood estimates of the parameters, which we denote as $\tilde{\beta}_{12}$, $\tilde{\beta}_{22}$, $\tilde{\beta}_{13}$, and $\tilde{\beta}_{23}$, what can we do then? The first thing we might do is estimate the probability that an individual will choose alternative 1, 2, or 3. For the value of the explanatory variable x_0, we can calculate the predicted probabilities of each outcome being selected using (16.19). For example, the probability that such an individual will choose alternative 1 is

$$
\tilde{p}_{01} = \frac{1}{1 + \exp(\tilde{\beta}_{12} + \tilde{\beta}_{22}x_0) + \exp(\tilde{\beta}_{13} + \tilde{\beta}_{23}x_0)}
$$

The predicted probabilities for alternatives 2 and 3, $\tilde{p}_{02}$ and $\tilde{p}_{03}$, can similarly be obtained. If we wanted to predict which alternative would be chosen, we might choose to predict that alternative j will be chosen if $\tilde{p}_{0j}$ is the maximum of the estimated probabilities.

Because the model is such a complicated nonlinear function of the β's, it will not surprise you to learn that the β's are not "slopes." In these models the **marginal effect** is the effect of a change in x, everything else held constant, on the probability that an individual chooses alternative $m = 1, 2,$ or 3. It can be shown[3] that

$$
\left. \frac{\Delta p_{im}}{\Delta x_i} \right|_{\text{all else constant}} = \frac{\partial p_{im}}{\partial x_i} = p_{im}\left[\beta_{2m} - \sum_{j=1}^{3} \beta_{2j} p_{ij} \right] \tag{16.20}
$$

---

[3] One can quickly become overwhelmed by the mathematics when seeking references on this topic. Two relatively friendly sources, with good examples, are *Regression Models for Categorical and Limited Dependent Variables* by J. Scott Long (Sage Publications, 1997) [see Chapter 6] and *Quantitative Models in Marketing Research* by Philip Hans Franses and Richard Paap (Cambridge University Press, 2001) [see Chapter 5]. At a much more advanced level see *Econometric Analysis*, 5th edition by William Greene (Prentice-Hall, 2003) [see Section 21.7].

Recall that the model we are discussing has a single explanatory variable, x_i, and that $\beta_{21} = 0$.

Alternatively, and somewhat more simply, the difference in probabilities can be calculated for two specific values of x_i. If x_a and x_b are two values of x_i, then the estimated change in probability of choosing alternative 1 $[m = 1]$ when changing from x_a to x_b is

$$\widetilde{\Delta p_1} = \tilde{p}_{b1} - \tilde{p}_{a1}$$

$$= \frac{1}{1 + \exp(\tilde{\beta}_{12} + \tilde{\beta}_{22}x_b) + \exp(\tilde{\beta}_{13} + \tilde{\beta}_{23}x_b)}$$

$$- \frac{1}{1 + \exp(\tilde{\beta}_{12} + \tilde{\beta}_{22}x_a) + \exp(\tilde{\beta}_{13} + \tilde{\beta}_{23}x_a)}$$

This approach is good if there are certain scenarios that you as a researcher have in mind as typical or important cases, or if x is a dummy variable with only two values, $x_a = 0$ and $x_b = 1$.

Another useful interpretive device is the **odds ratio**. It shows how many times more likely category j is to be chosen relative to the first category and is given by

$$\frac{P(y_i = j)}{P(y_i = 1)} = \frac{p_{ij}}{p_{i1}} = \exp(\beta_{1j} + \beta_{2j}x_i), \quad j = 2, 3 \tag{16.21}$$

The effect on the odds ratio of changing the value of x_i is given by the derivative

$$\frac{\partial(p_{ij}/p_{i1})}{\partial x_i} = \beta_{2j}\exp(\beta_{1j} + \beta_{2j}x_i), \quad j = 2, 3 \tag{16.22}$$

The value of the exponential function $\exp(\beta_{1j} + \beta_{2j}x_i)$ is always positive. Thus the sign of β_{2j} tells us whether a change in x_i will make the jth category more or less likely relative to the first category.

An interesting feature of the odds ratio (16.21) is that the odds of choosing alternative j rather than alternative 1 does not depend on how many alternatives there are in total. There is the implicit assumption in logit models that the odds between any pair of alternatives is **independent of irrelevant alternatives (IIA)**. This is a strong assumption, and if it is violated multinomial logit may not be a good modeling choice. It is especially likely to fail if several alternatives are similar. There are tests for the validity of the IIA assumption; however, describing it and alternatives to multinomial logit models is far beyond the scope of this book.[4]

16.3.4 AN EXAMPLE

The National Education Longitudinal Study of 1988 (NELS:88) was the first nationally representative longitudinal study of eighth grade students in public and private schools in the United States. It was sponsored by the National Center for Education Statistics. In 1988, some 25,000 eighth graders, their parents, their teachers, and their principals were surveyed. In 1990, these same students (who were then mostly 10th graders, and some dropouts), their teachers, and principals were surveyed again. In 1992, the second follow-up survey was conducted of students, mostly in the 12th grade, but dropouts, parents, teachers, school

---

[4] An advanced but classic reference for this material is *Limited Dependent and Qualitative Variables in Econometrics* by G. S. Maddala (Cambridge University Press, 1983), especially Chapter 3.

Table 16.2   **Maximum Likelihood Estimates of PSE Choice**

Parameters	Estimates	Standard errors	*t*-Statistics
β_{12}	2.5064	0.4183	5.99
β_{22}	−0.3088	0.0523	−5.91
β_{13}	5.7699	0.4043	14.27
β_{23}	−0.7062	0.0529	−13.34

administrators, and high school transcripts were also surveyed. The third follow-up was in 1994, after most students had graduated.[5]

We have taken a subset of the total data, namely those who stayed in the panel of data through the third follow-up. On this group we have complete data on the individuals and their households, high school grades, and test scores, as well as their post-secondary education choices. In the file *nels_small.dat* we have 1000 observations on students who chose, upon graduating from high school, either no college (*PSECHOICE*=1), a 2-year college (*PSECHOICE*=2), or a 4-year college (*PSECHOICE*=3). For illustration purposes we focus on the explanatory variable *GRADES*, which is an index ranging from 1.0 (highest level, A+ grade) to 13.0 (lowest level, F grade) and represents combined performance in English, Math, and Social Studies.

Of the 1000 students, 22.2% selected not to attend a college upon graduation, 25.1% selected to attend a 2-year college, and 52.7% attended a 4-year college. The average value of *GRADES* is 6.53, with highest grade 1.74 and lowest grade 12.33. The estimated values of the parameters and their standard errors are given in Table 16.2. We selected the group who did not attend a college to be our base group, so that the parameters $\beta_{11} = \beta_{21} = 0$.

Based on these estimates, what can we say? Recall that a larger numerical value of *GRADES* represents a poorer academic performance. The parameter estimates for the coefficients of *GRADES* are negative and statistically significant. Using expression (16.22) on the effect of a change in an explanatory variable on the odds ratio, this means that if the value of *GRADES* increases, the probability that high school graduates will choose a 2-year or a 4-year college goes down, relative to the probability of not attending college. This is the anticipated effect, as we expect that a poorer academic performance will increase the odds of not attending college.

We can also compute the predicted probability of each type of college choice using (16.19) for given values of *GRADES*. In our sample the median value of *GRADES* is 6.64, and the top 5th percentile value is 2.635. What are the choice probabilities of students with these grades? In Table 16.3 we show that the probability of choosing No College is 0.181 for the student with median grades, but this probability is reduced to 0.018 for students with top grades. Similarly, the probability of choosing a 2-year school is 0.286 for the average student but is 0.097 for the better student. Finally, the average student has a 0.533 chance of selecting a 4-year college, but the better student has a 0.886 chance of selecting a 4-year college.

The marginal effect of a change in *GRADES* on the choice probabilities can be calculated using (16.20). The marginal effect again depends on particular values for *GRADES*, and we report these in Table 16.3 for the median and 5th percentile students. An increase in

---

[5] The study and data are summarized in *National Education Longitudinal Study: 1988–1994, Descriptive Summary Report With an Essay on Access and Choice in Post-Secondary Education*, by Allen Sanderson, Bernard Dugoni, Kenneth Rasinski, and John Taylor, C. Dennis Carroll project officer, NCES 96-175, National Center for Education Statistics, March 1996.

Table 16.3 **Effects of Grades on Probability of PSE Choice**

PSE choice	GRADES	$\hat{p}$	Marginal effect
No college	6.64	0.181	0.084
	2.635	0.018	0.012
2-Year college	6.64	0.286	0.045
	2.635	0.097	0.033
4-Year college	6.64	0.533	−0.128
	2.635	0.886	−0.045

GRADES of 1 point (worse performance) increases the probabilities of choosing either no college or a 2-year college and reduces the probability of attending a 4-year college. The probability of attending a 4-year college declines more for the average student than for the top student, given the 1-point increase in *GRADES*. Note that for each value of *GRADES* the sum of the predicted probabilities is 1, and the sum of the marginal effects is zero, except for rounding error. This is a feature of the multinomial logit specification.

As you can see there are many interesting questions we can address with this type of model.

16.4 Conditional Logit

Suppose that a decision maker must choose between several distinct alternatives, just as in the multinomial logit model. In a marketing context, suppose our decision is between three types ($J = 3$) of soft drinks, say Pepsi, 7-Up, and Coke Classic, in 2-liter bottles. Shoppers will visit their supermarkets and make a choice, based on prices of the products and other factors. With the advent of supermarket scanners at checkout, data on purchases (what brand, how many units, and the price paid) are recorded. Of course we also know the prices of the products that the consumer did not buy on a particular shopping occasion. The key point is that if we collect data on soda purchases from a variety of supermarkets, over a period of time, we observe consumer choices from the set of alternatives and we know the prices facing the shopper on each trip to the supermarket.

Let y_{i1}, y_{i2}, and y_{i3} be dummy variables that indicate the choice made by individual i. If alternative 1 (Pepsi) is selected, then $y_{i1} = 1$, $y_{i2} = 0$, and $y_{i3} = 0$. If alternative 2 (7-Up) is selected, then $y_{i1} = 0$, $y_{i2} = 1$, and $y_{i3} = 0$. If alternative 3 (Coke) is selected, then $y_{i1} = 0$, $y_{i2} = 0$, and $y_{i3} = 1$. The price facing individual i for brand j is $PRICE_{ij}$. That is, the price of Pepsi, 7-Up, and Coke is potentially different for each customer who purchases soda. Remember, different customers can shop at different supermarkets and at different times. Variables like price are **individual and alternative specific** because they vary from individual to individual and are different for each choice the consumer might make. This type of information is very different from what we assumed was available in the multinomial logit model, where the explanatory variable x_i was **individual specific**; it did not change across alternatives.

16.4.1 CONDITIONAL LOGIT CHOICE PROBABILITIES

Our objective is to understand the factors that lead a consumer to choose one alternative over another. We construct a model for the probability that individual i chooses alternative j

$$p_{ij} = P[\text{individual } i \text{ chooses alternative } j]$$

The conditional logit model specifies these probabilities as

$$p_{ij} = \frac{\exp(\beta_{1j} + \beta_2 PRICE_{ij})}{\exp(\beta_{11} + \beta_2 PRICE_{i1}) + \exp(\beta_{12} + \beta_2 PRICE_{i2}) + \exp(\beta_{13} + \beta_2 PRICE_{i3})}$$

(16.23)

Note that unlike the probabilities for the multinomial logit model in (16.19), there is only one parameter β_2 relating the effect of each price to the choice probability p_{ij}. We have also included alternative specific constants (intercept terms). These cannot all be estimated, and one must be set to zero. We will set $\beta_{13} = 0$.

Estimation of the unknown parameters is by maximum likelihood. Suppose that we observe three individuals, who choose alternatives 1, 2, and 3, respectively. Assuming that their choices are independent, then the probability of observing this outcome is

$$P(y_{11} = 1, y_{22} = 1, y_{33} = 1) = p_{11} \times p_{22} \times p_{33}$$

$$= \frac{\exp(\beta_{11} + \beta_2 PRICE_{11})}{\exp(\beta_{11} + \beta_2 PRICE_{11}) + \exp(\beta_{12} + \beta_2 PRICE_{12}) + \exp(\beta_2 PRICE_{13})}$$

$$\times \frac{\exp(\beta_{12} + \beta_2 PRICE_{22})}{\exp(\beta_{11} + \beta_2 PRICE_{21}) + \exp(\beta_{12} + \beta_2 PRICE_{22}) + \exp(\beta_2 PRICE_{23})}$$

$$\times \frac{\exp(\beta_2 PRICE_{33})}{\exp(\beta_{11} + \beta_2 PRICE_{31}) + \exp(\beta_{12} + \beta_2 PRICE_{32}) + \exp(\beta_2 PRICE_{33})}$$

$$= L(\beta_{11}, \beta_{12}, \beta_2)$$

16.4.2   POST-ESTIMATION ANALYSIS

How a change in price affects the choice probability is different for "own price" changes and "cross price" changes. Specifically it can be shown that the own price effect is

$$\frac{\partial p_{ij}}{\partial PRICE_{ij}} = p_{ij}(1 - p_{ij})\beta_2$$

(16.24)

The sign of β_2 indicates the direction of the own price effect.

The change in probability of alternative j being selected if the price of alternative k changes $(k \neq j)$ is

$$\frac{\partial p_{ij}}{\partial PRICE_{ik}} = -p_{ij} p_{ik} \beta_2$$

(16.25)

The cross price effect is in the opposite direction of the own price effect.

An important feature of the conditional logit model is that the odds ratio between alternatives j and k is

$$\frac{p_{ij}}{p_{ik}} = \frac{\exp(\beta_{1j} + \beta_2 PRICE_{ij})}{\exp(\beta_{1k} + \beta_2 PRICE_{ik})} = \exp[(\beta_{1j} - \beta_{1k}) + \beta_2(PRICE_{ij} - PRICE_{ik})]$$

The odds ratio depends on the difference in prices, but not on the prices themselves. As in the multinomial logit model this ratio does not depend on the total number of alternatives, and

Table 16.4 **Conditional Logit Parameter Estimates**

Variables	Estimates	Standard errors	t-Statistics	p-Values
PRICE(β_2)	−2.2964	0.1377	−16.68	0.000
PEPSI(β_{11})	0.2832	0.0624	4.54	0.000
7-UP(β_{12})	0.1038	0.0625	1.66	0.096

there is the implicit assumption of the independence of irrelevant alternatives (IIA). See the discussion at the end of Section 16.3.3. Models that do not require the IIA assumption have been developed, but they are difficult. These include the **multinomial probit** model, which is based on the normal distribution, and the **nested logit** and **mixed logit** models.[6]

16.4.3 AN EXAMPLE

We observe 1822 purchases, covering 104 weeks and 5 stores, in which a consumer purchased 2-liter bottles of either Pepsi (34.6%), 7-Up (37.4%), or Coke Classic (28%). These data are in the file *cola.dat*. In the sample the average price of Pepsi was $1.23, of 7-Up $1.12, and of Coke $1.21. We estimate the conditional logit model shown in (16.23), and the estimates are shown in Table 16.4.

　　We see that all the parameter estimates are significantly different from zero at a 10% level of significance, and the sign of the coefficient of *PRICE* is negative. This means that a rise in the price of an individual brand will reduce the probability of its purchase, and the rise in the price of a competitive brand will increase the probability of its purchase. To get a feel for the magnitudes involved, we predict the probability of a Pepsi purchase, given that the price of Pepsi is $1, the price of 7-Up is $1.25, and the price of Coke is $1.10. These values can be chosen to describe a particular scenario of interest when analyzing brand choice. The estimated probability of selecting Pepsi is then

$$\hat{p}_{i1} = \frac{\exp(\tilde{\beta}_{11} + \tilde{\beta}_2 \times 1.00)}{\exp(\tilde{\beta}_{11} + \tilde{\beta}_2 \times 1.00) + \exp(\tilde{\beta}_{12} + \tilde{\beta}_2 \times 1.25) + \exp(\tilde{\beta}_2 \times 1.10)} = 0.4832$$

If we raise the price of Pepsi to $1.10, we estimate that the probability of its purchase falls to 0.4263. If the price of Pepsi stays at $1.00 but we increase the price of Coke by 15 cents, then we estimate that the probability of a consumer selecting Pepsi rises by 0.0445. These numbers indicate to us the responsiveness of brand choice to changes in prices, much like elasticities.

16.5 Ordered Choice Models

The choice options in multinomial and conditional logit models have no natural ordering or arrangement. However, in some cases choices are ordered in a specific way. Examples include the following:

1. Results of opinion surveys in which responses can be strongly disagree, disagree, neutral, agree, or strongly agree.

---

[6] For a brief description of these models at an advanced level see *Econometric Analysis*, 5th edition by William Greene (Prentice-Hall, 2003), pp. 725–729.

2. Assignment of grades or work performance ratings. Students receive grades A, B, C, D, and F, which are ordered on the basis of a teacher's evaluation of their performance. Employees are often given evaluations on scales such as Outstanding, Very Good, Good, Fair, and Poor, which are similar in spirit.

3. Standard and Poor's rates bonds as AAA, AA, A, BBB, and so on, as a judgment about the credit worthiness of the company or country issuing a bond, and how risky the investment might be.

4. Levels of employment are unemployed, part-time, or full-time.

When modeling these types of outcomes, numerical values are assigned to the outcomes, but the numerical values are **ordinal** and reflect only the ranking of the outcomes. In the first example, we might assign a dependent variable y the values

$$y = \begin{cases} 1 & \text{strongly disagree} \\ 2 & \text{disagree} \\ 3 & \text{neutral} \\ 4 & \text{agree} \\ 5 & \text{strongly agree} \end{cases}$$

In Section 16.3 we considered the problem of choosing what type of college to attend after graduating from high school as an illustration of a choice among unordered alternatives. However, in this particular case there may in fact be natural ordering. We might rank the possibilities as

$$y = \begin{cases} 3 & \text{4-year college (the full college experience)} \\ 2 & \text{2-year college (a partial college experience)} \\ 1 & \text{no college} \end{cases} \tag{16.26}$$

The usual linear regression model is not appropriate for such data, because in regression we would treat the y-values as having some numerical meaning when they do not. In the next section we discuss how probabilities of each choice might be modeled.

16.5.1 ORDINAL PROBIT CHOICE PROBABILITIES

When faced with a ranking problem, we develop a "sentiment" about how we feel concerning the alternative choices, and the higher the sentiment the more likely a higher ranked alternative will be chosen. This sentiment is, of course, unobservable to the econometrician. Unobservable variables that enter decisions are called **latent variables**, and we will denote our sentiment toward the ranked alternatives by y_i^*, with the "star" reminding us that this variable is unobserved.

Microeconomics is well described as the "science of choice." Economic theory will suggest that certain factors (observable variables) may affect how we feel about the alternatives facing us. As a concrete example, let us think about what factors might lead a high school graduate to choose among the alternatives "no college," "2-year college," and "4-year college" as described by the ordered choices in (16.26). Some factors that affect this choice are household income, the student's high school grades, how close a 2- or 4-year college is to the home, whether parents had attended a 4-year college, and so on. For simplicity, let us focus on the single explanatory variable *GRADES*. The model is then

$$y_i^* = \beta GRADES_i + e_i$$

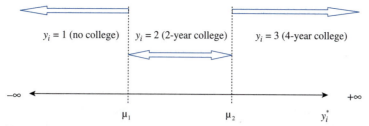

FIGURE 16.2 Ordinal choices relative to thresholds.

This model is not a regression model because the dependent variable is unobservable. Consequently it is sometimes called an **index model**. The error term is present for the usual reasons. The choices we observe are based on a comparison of "sentiment" toward higher education y_i^* relative to certain thresholds, as shown in Figure 16.2.

Because there are $M = 3$ alternatives, there are $M - 1 = 2$ thresholds μ_1 and μ_2, with $\mu_1 < \mu_2$. The index model does not contain an intercept because it would be exactly collinear with the threshold variables. If sentiment toward higher education is in the lowest category, then $y_i^* \leq \mu_1$ and the alternative "no college" is chosen, if $\mu_1 < y_i^* \leq \mu_2$ then the alternative "2-year college" is chosen, and if sentiment toward higher education is in the highest category, then $y_i^* > \mu_2$ and "4-year college" is chosen. That is,

$$y = \begin{cases} 3 \text{ (4-year college)} & \text{if} \quad y_i^* > \mu_2 \\ 2 \text{ (2-year college)} & \text{if} \quad \mu_1 < y_i^* \leq \mu_2 \\ 1 \text{ (no college)} & \text{if} \quad y_i^* \leq \mu_1 \end{cases}$$

We are able to represent the probabilities of these outcomes if we assume a particular probability distribution for y_i^*, or equivalently for the random error e_i. If we assume that the errors have the standard normal distribution, $N(0, 1)$, an assumption that defines the ordered probit model, then we can calculate the following:

$$P(y = 1) = P(y_i^* \leq \mu_1) = P(\beta GRADES_i + e_i \leq \mu_1)$$
$$= P(e_i \leq \mu_1 - \beta GRADES_i)$$
$$= \Phi(\mu_1 - \beta GRADES_i)$$

$$P(y = 2) = P(\mu_1 < y_i^* \leq \mu_2) = P(\mu_1 < \beta GRADES_i + e_i \leq \mu_2)$$
$$= P(\mu_1 - \beta GRADES_i < e_i \leq \mu_2 - \beta GRADES_i)$$
$$= \Phi(\mu_2 - \beta GRADES_i) - \Phi(\mu_1 - \beta GRADES_i)$$

and the probability that $y = 3$ is

$$P(y = 3) = P(y_i^* > \mu_2) = P(\beta GRADES_i + e_i > \mu_2)$$
$$= P(e_i > \mu_2 - \beta GRADES_i)$$
$$= 1 - \Phi(\mu_2 - \beta GRADES_i)$$

16.5.2 ESTIMATION AND INTERPRETATION

Estimation, as with previous choice models, is by maximum likelihood. If we observe a random sample of $N = 3$ individuals, with the first not going to college ($y_1 = 1$), the second attending a 2-year college ($y_2 = 2$), and the third attending a 4-year college ($y_3 = 3$), then the likelihood function is

$$L(\beta, \mu_1, \mu_2) = P(y_1 = 1) \times P(y_2 = 2) \times P(y_3 = 3)$$

Note that the probabilities depend on the unknown parameters μ_1 and μ_2 as well as the index function parameter β. These parameters are obtained by maximizing the log-likelihood function using numerical methods. While this is no easy task, econometric software includes options for both **ordered probit**, which depends on the errors being standard normal, and **ordered logit**, which depends on the assumption that the random errors follow a logistic distribution. Most economists will use the normality assumption, but many other social scientists use the logistic. In the end, there is little difference between the results.

The types of questions we can answer with this model are the following:

1. What is the probability that a high school graduate with $GRADES = 2.5$ (on a 13-point scale, with 1 being the highest) will attend a 2-year college? The answer is obtained by plugging in the specific value of $GRADES$ into the predicted probability based on the maximum likelihood estimates of the parameters,

    $$\hat{P}(y = 2|GRADES = 2.5) = \Phi(\tilde{\mu}_2 - \tilde{\beta} \times 2.5) - \Phi(\tilde{\mu}_1 - \tilde{\beta} \times 2.5)$$

2. What is the difference in probability of attending a 4-year college for two students, one with $GRADES = 2.5$ and another with $GRADES = 4.5$? The difference in the probabilities is calculated directly as

    $$\hat{P}(y = 3|GRADES = 4.5) - \hat{P}(y = 3|GRADES = 2.5)$$

3. If we treat $GRADES$ as a continuous variable, what is the marginal effect on the probability of each outcome, given a 1-unit change in $GRADES$? These derivatives are

    $$\frac{\partial P(y = 1)}{\partial GRADES} = -\phi(\mu_1 - \beta GRADES) \times \beta$$

    $$\frac{\partial P(y = 2)}{\partial GRADES} = [\phi(\mu_1 - \beta GRADES) - \phi(\mu_2 - \beta GRADES)] \times \beta$$

    $$\frac{\partial P(y = 3)}{\partial GRADES} = \phi(\mu_2 - \beta GRADES) \times \beta$$

In these expressions "$\phi(\cdot)$" denotes the probability density function of a standard normal distribution, and its values are always positive. Consequently the sign of the parameter β is opposite the direction of the marginal effect for the lowest category, but it indicates the direction of the marginal effect for the highest category. The direction of the marginal effect for the middle category goes one way or the other, depending on the sign of the difference in brackets.

Table 16.5 **Ordered Probit Parameter Estimates**

Parameters	Estimates	Standard errors
β	-0.3066	0.0191
μ_1	-2.9456	0.1468
μ_2	-2.0900	0.1358

There are a variety of other devices that can be used to analyze the outcomes of ordered choice models, including some useful graphics. For more on these see (from a social science perspective) *Regression Models for Categorical and Limited Dependent Variables* by J. Scott Long (Sage Publications, 1997, Chapter 5) or (from a marketing perspective) *Quantitative Models in Marketing Research* by Philip Hans Franses and Richard Paap (Cambridge University Press, 2001, Chapter 6).

16.5.3 AN EXAMPLE

To illustrate we use the college choice data introduced in Section 16.3 and contained in the file *nels_small.dat*. We treat *PSECHOICE* as an ordered variable with "1" representing the least favored alternative (no college) and "3" denoting the most favored alternative (4-year college). The estimation results are in Table 16.5.

The estimated coefficient of *GRADES* is negative, indicating that the probability of attending a 4-year college goes down when *GRADES* increase (indicating a worse performance), and the probability of the lowest ranked choice, attending no college, increases. Let us examine the marginal effects of an increase in *GRADES* on attending a 4-year college. For a student with median grades (6.64) the marginal effect is -0.1221, and for a student in the 5th percentile (2.635) the marginal effect is -0.0538. These are similar in magnitude to the marginal effects shown in Table 16.3.

Had we simply estimated the relationship between *PSECHOICE* and *GRADES* using a linear regression model we would have obtained

$$\widehat{PSECHOICE} = 3.4703 - 0.1784 GRADES$$

These estimates imply that the "marginal effect" of *GRADES* is -0.1784. This approach incorrectly gives a numerical interpretation to the values of *PSECHOICE* and thus the estimated values have little meaning.

16.6 Models for Count Data

When the dependent variable in a regression model is a count of the number of occurrences of an event, the outcome variable is $y = 0, 1, 2, 3, \ldots$ These numbers are actual counts, and thus different from the ordinal numbers of the previous section. Examples include the following:

- The number of trips to a physician a person makes during a year.
- The number of fishing trips taken by a person during the previous year.
- The number of children in a household.

- The number of automobile accidents at a particular intersection during a month.
- The number of televisions in a household.
- The number of alcoholic drinks a college student takes in a week.

While we are again interested in explaining and predicting probabilities, such as the probability that an individual will take two or more trips to the doctor during a year, the probability distribution we use as a foundation is the Poisson, not the normal or the logistic. If Y is a Poisson random variable, then its probability function is

$$f(y) = P(Y = y) = \frac{e^{-\lambda}\lambda^y}{y!}, \quad y = 0, 1, 2, \ldots \tag{16.27}$$

The factorial (!) term $y! = y \times (y-1) \times (y-2) \times \cdots \times 1$. This probability function has one parameter, λ, which is the mean (and variance) of Y. That is, $E(Y) = \text{var}(Y) = \lambda$. In a regression model we try to explain the behavior of $E(Y)$ as a function of some explanatory variables. We do the same here, keeping the value of $E(Y) \geq 0$ by defining

$$E(Y) = \lambda = \exp(\beta_1 + \beta_2 x) \tag{16.28}$$

This choice defines the **Poisson regression model** for count data.

16.6.1   MAXIMUM LIKELIHOOD ESTIMATION

The parameters β_1 and β_2 can be estimated by maximum likelihood. Suppose we randomly select $N = 3$ individuals from a population and observe that their counts are $y_1 = 0, y_2 = 2$, and $y_3 = 2$, indicating 0, 2, and 2 occurrences of the event for these three individuals. Recall that the likelihood function is the joint probability function of the observed data, interpreted as a function of the unknown parameters. That is,

$$L(\beta_1, \beta_2) = P(Y = 0) \times P(Y = 2) \times P(Y = 2)$$

This product of functions like (16.27) will be very complicated and difficult to maximize. However, in practice, maximum likelihood estimation is carried out by maximizing the logarithm of the likelihood function, or

$$\ln L(\beta_1, \beta_2) = \ln P(Y = 0) + \ln P(Y = 2) + \ln P(Y = 2)$$

Using (16.28) for λ, the log of the probability function is

$$\ln[P(Y = y)] = \ln\left[\frac{e^{-\lambda}\lambda^y}{y!}\right] = -\lambda + y\ln(\lambda) - \ln(y!)$$
$$= -\exp(\beta_1 + \beta_2 x) + y \times (\beta_1 + \beta_2 x) - \ln(y!)$$

Then the log-likelihood function, given a sample of N observations, becomes

$$\ln L(\beta_1, \beta_2) = \sum_{i=1}^{N} \{-\exp(\beta_1 + \beta_2 x_i) + y_i \times (\beta_1 + \beta_2 x_i) - \ln(y_i!)\}$$

This log-likelihood function is a function of only β_1 and β_2 once we substitute in the data values (y_i, x_i). The log-likelihood function itself is still a nonlinear function of the unknown parameters, and the maximum likelihood estimates must be obtained by numerical methods. Econometric software has options that allow for the maximum likelihood estimation of count models with the click of a button.

16.6.2   INTERPRETATION IN THE POISSON REGRESSION MODEL

As in other modeling situations we would like to use the estimated model to predict outcomes, determine the marginal effect of a change in an explanatory variable on the mean of the dependent variable, and test the significance of coefficients.

Prediction of the conditional mean of y is straightforward. Given the maximum likelihood estimates $\tilde{\beta}_1$ and $\tilde{\beta}_2$, and given a value of the explanatory variable x_0, then

$$\widehat{E(y_0)} = \tilde{\lambda}_0 = \exp(\tilde{\beta}_1 + \tilde{\beta}_2 x_0)$$

This value is an estimate of the expected number of occurrences observed, if x takes the value x_0. The probability of a particular number of occurrences can be estimated by inserting the estimated conditional mean into the probability function, as

$$\widehat{P(Y = y)} = \frac{\exp(-\tilde{\lambda}_0)\tilde{\lambda}_0^y}{y!}, \quad y = 0, 1, 2, \ldots$$

The marginal effect of a change in a continuous variable x in the Poisson regression model is not simply given by the parameter, because the conditional mean model is a nonlinear function of the parameters. Using our specification that the conditional mean is given by $E(y_i) = \lambda_i = \exp(\beta_1 + \beta_2 x_i)$, and using rules for derivatives of exponential functions, we obtain the marginal effect

$$\frac{\partial E(y_i)}{\partial x_i} = \lambda_i \beta_2 \tag{16.29}$$

To estimate this marginal effect, replace the parameters by their maximum likelihood estimates and select a value for x. The marginal effect is different depending on the value of x chosen. A useful fact about the Poisson model is that the conditional mean $E(y_i) = \lambda_i = \exp(\beta_1 + \beta_2 x_i)$ is always positive, because the exponential function is always positive. Thus the direction of the marginal effect can be determined from the sign of the coefficient β_2.

Equation (16.29) can be expressed as a percentage, which can be useful:

$$\frac{\%\Delta E(y)}{\Delta x_i} = 100\frac{\partial E(y_i)/E(y_i)}{\partial x_i} = 100\beta_2\%$$

If x is not transformed, then a 1-unit change in x leads to $100\beta_2\%$ change in the conditional mean.

Suppose the conditional mean function contains a dummy variable, how do we calculate its effect? If $E(y_i) = \lambda_i = \exp(\beta_1 + \beta_2 x_i + \delta D_i)$ we can examine the conditional expectation when $D = 0$ and when $D = 1$.

$$E(y_i|D_i = 0) = \exp(\beta_1 + \beta_2 x_i)$$

$$E(y_i|D_i = 1) = \exp(\beta_1 + \beta_2 x_i + \delta)$$

Then, the percentage change in the conditional mean is

$$100\left[\frac{\exp(\beta_1 + \beta_2 x_i + \delta) - \exp(\beta_1 + \beta_2 x_i)}{\exp(\beta_1 + \beta_2 x_i)}\right]\% = 100[e^\delta - 1]\%$$

This is identical to the expression we obtained for the effect of a dummy variable in a log-linear model. See Section 7.5.

Finally, hypothesis testing can be carried out using standard methods. The maximum likelihood estimators are asymptotically normal with a variance of a known form. The actual expression for the variance is complicated and involves matrix expressions, so we will not report the formula here.[7] Econometric software has the variance expressions encoded, and along with parameter estimates, it will provide standard errors, t-statistics, and p-values, which are used as always.

16.6.3 AN EXAMPLE

The Olympic Games are a subject of great interest to the global community. Rightly or wrongly the attention focuses on the number of medals won by each country. Andrew Bernard and Meghan Busse[8] examined the effect of a country's economic resources on the number of medals won. The data are in the file *olympics.dat*. Using the data from 1988, we estimate a Poisson regression explaining the number of medals won (*MEDALTOT*) as a function of the logarithms of population and gross domestic product (1995 dollars). These results are given in Table 16.6.

Both the size of the country and wealth of the country have a positive and significant effect on the number of medals won. Using these estimates, the estimated conditional mean number of medals won for the country with median population (5921270) and median GDP (5.51E + 09) is 0.8634. If we keep GDP at the median value but raise population to the 75th percentile (1.75E + 7), the estimated mean is 1.0495. And if we keep population at the median but raise GDP to the 75th percentile (5.18E + 10), the estimated mean number of medals is 3.1432. Alternatively, we can estimate the mean outcome for a specific county. In 1988 the population in the United Kingdom was 5.72E + 7 and its GDP was 1.01E + 12. The estimated mean number of medals was 26.2131. They in fact won a total of 24 medals.

Table 16.6 **Poisson Regression Estimates**

Variable	Coefficient	Std. Error	t-Statistic	p-Value
INTERCEPT	−15.8875	0.5118	−31.0420	0.0000
ln*(POP)*	0.1800	0.0323	5.5773	0.0000
ln*(GDP)*	0.5766	0.0247	23.3238	0.0000

[7] See *Regression Models for Categorical and Limited Dependent Variables* by J. Scott Long (Sage Publications, 1997, Chapter 8). A much more advanced and specialized reference is *Regression Analysis of Count Data* by A. Colin Cameron and Pravin K. Trivedi (Cambridge University Press, 1998).

[8] "Who Wins the Olympic Games: Economic Resources and Medal Totals," *The Review of Economics and Statistics*, 2004, 86(1), 413–417. The data were kindly provided by Andrew Bernard.

16.7 Limited Dependent Variables

In the previous sections of this chapter we reviewed choice behavior models that have dependent variables that are discrete variables. When a model has a discrete dependent variable, the usual regression methods we have studied must be modified. In this section we present another case in which standard least squares estimation of a regression model fails.

16.7.1 CENSORED DATA

An example that illustrates the situation is based on Thomas Mroz's (1987) study of married women's labor force participation and wages. The data are in the file *mroz.dat* and consist of 753 observations on married women. Of these 325 did not work outside the home, and thus had no hours worked and no reported wages. The histogram of hours worked is shown in Figure 16.3. The histogram shows the large fraction of women who did not enter the labor force. This is an example of **censored data**, meaning that a substantial fraction of the observations on the dependent variable take a limit value, which is zero in the case of market hours worked by married women. Other natural examples include variables like charitable giving or damage caused by a hurricane. In these examples a sample of households will yield a large number of households who give nothing or who have no hurricane damage.

In Section 2.2 we explained the type of data generation process for which least squares regression can be successful. Refer back to Figure 2.3. There we show the probability density functions for the dependent variable y, at different x-values, centered on the regression function

$$E(y|x) = \beta_1 + \beta_2 x \qquad (16.30)$$

This leads to sample data being scattered along the regression function. Least squares regression works by fitting a line through the center of a data scatter, and in this case such a

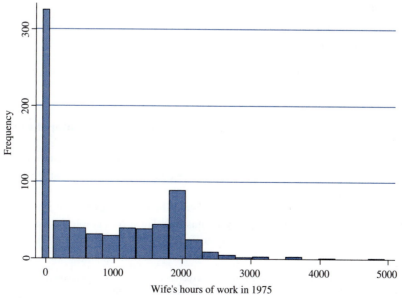

FIGURE *16.3* Histogram of wife's hours of work in 1975.

strategy works fine, because the true regression function also fits through the middle of the data scatter.

Unfortunately, in situations like we have with the supply of labor by married women, when a substantial number of observations have dependent variable values taking the limit value of zero, the regression function $E(y|x)$ is no longer given by (16.30). Instead $E(y|x)$ is a complicated nonlinear function of the regression parameters β_1 and β_2, the error variance σ^2, and x. The least squares estimators of the regression parameters obtained by running a regression of y on x are biased and inconsistent—least squares estimation fails.

If having all the limit observations present is the cause of the problem, then why not drop them out? This does not work either. The regression function becomes the expected value of y, conditional on the y-values being positive, or $E(y|x, y > 0)$. Once again it can be shown that this regression function is nonlinear and not equal to (16.30).

16.7.2   A Monte Carlo Experiment

Let us illustrate these concepts using a simulated sample of data (*tobit.dat*). Using simulation is an excellent way to learn econometrics. It requires us to understand how the data are obtained under a particular set of assumptions.[9] In this example we give the parameters the specific values $\beta_1 = -9$ and $\beta_2 = 1$. The observed sample is obtained within the framework of an **index** or **latent variable model**, similar to the one discussed in Section 16.5 on the ordered probit model. Let the latent variable be

$$y_i^* = \beta_1 + \beta_2 x_i + e_i = -9 + x_i + e_i \tag{16.31}$$

with the error term assumed to have a normal distribution, $e_i \sim N(0, \sigma^2 = 16)$. The observable outcome y_i takes the value zero if $y_i^* \leq 0$, but $y_i = y_i^*$ if $y_i^* > 0$. In the simulation we

- Create $N = 200$ random values of x_i that are spread evenly (or uniformly) over the interval [0, 20]. We will keep these fixed in further simulations.
- Obtain $N = 200$ random values e_i from a normal distribution with mean 0 and variance 16.
- Create $N = 200$ values of the latent variable $y_i^* = -9 + x_i + e_i$.
- Obtain $N = 200$ values of the observed y_i using

$$y_i = \begin{cases} 0 & \text{if } y_i^* \leq 0 \\ y_i^* & \text{if } y_i^* > 0 \end{cases}$$

The 200 observations obtained this way constitute a sample that is **censored** with a lower limit of zero. The latent data are plotted in Figure 16.4. In this figure the line labeled $E(y^*)$ has intercept -9 and slope 1. The values of the latent variable y_i^* are scattered along this regression function. If we observed these data we could estimate the parameters using the least squares principle, by fitting a line through the center of the data.

However, we do not observe all the latent data. When the values of y_i^* are zero or less, we observe $y_i = 0$. We observe y_i^* when they are positive. These observable data, along with the fitted least squares regression, are shown in Figure 16.5.

---

[9] Peter Kennedy is an advocate of using Monte Carlo experiments in teaching econometrics. See "Using Monte Carlo Studies for Teaching Econometrics," in: W. Becker and M. Watts (Eds.), *Teaching Undergraduate Economics: Alternatives to Chalk and Talk*, Cheltenham, UK: Edward Elgar, 1998, pp. 141–159; see also Peter Kennedy (2003) *A Guide to Econometrics*, 5th edition, Cambridge, MA: MIT Press, pp. 24–27.

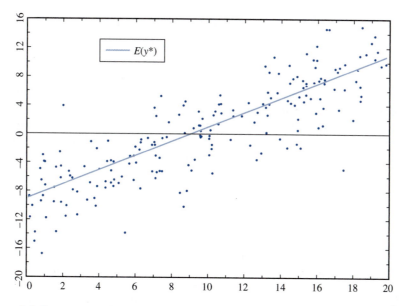

FIGURE **16.4**   Uncensored sample data and regression function.

The least squares principle will fail to estimate $\beta_1 = -9$ and $\beta_2 = 1$ because the observed data do not fall along the underlying regression function $E(y^*|x) = \beta_1 + \beta_2 x = -9 + x$. In Figure 16.5 we show the estimated regression function for the 200 observed y-values, which is given by

$$\hat{y}_i = -2.1477 + 0.5161x_i$$
$$\text{(se)} \quad (0.3706) \ (0.0326)$$

(16.32a)

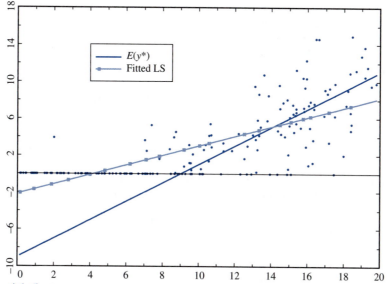

FIGURE **16.5**   Censored sample data, and latent regression function and least squares fitted line.

If we restrict our sample to include only the 100 positive y-values, the fitted regression is

$$\hat{y}_i = -3.1399 + 0.6388x_i$$
$$\text{(se)} \quad (1.2055) \quad (0.0827)$$

(16.32b)

In a Monte Carlo simulation we repeat this process of creating $N = 200$ observations, and applying least squares estimation, many times. This is analogous to "repeated sampling" in the context of experimental statistics. In this case we repeat the process $NSAM = 1000$ times, keeping the x-values fixed and drawing new error values e, recording each time the values of the estimates we obtain. At the end, we can compute the average values of the estimates, recorded in *tobitmc.dat*, which is the Monte Carlo "expected value,"

$$E_{MC}(b_k) = \frac{1}{NSAM} \sum_{m=1}^{NSAM} b_{k(m)}$$

(16.33)

where $b_{k(m)}$ is the estimate of β_k in the mth Monte Carlo sample.

If we apply the least squares estimation procedure to all the observed censored data (i.e., including observations $y = 0$), the average value of the estimated intercept is -2.0465 and the average value of the estimated slope is 0.5434. If we discard the $y = 0$ observations and apply least squares to just the positive y observations, these averages are -1.9194 and 0.5854, respectively. The least squares estimates are biased by a substantial amount, compared to the true values $\beta_1 = -9$ and $\beta_2 = 1$. This bias will not disappear no matter how large the sample size we consider, because the least squares estimators are inconsistent when data are censored.

16.7.3 MAXIMUM LIKELIHOOD ESTIMATION

If the dependent variable is censored, having a lower limit and/or an upper limit, then the least squares estimators of the regression parameters are biased and inconsistent. In this case we can apply an alternative estimation procedure, which is called **Tobit** in honor of James Tobin, winner of the 1981 Nobel Prize in Economics, who first studied this model. Tobit is a maximum likelihood procedure that recognizes that we have data of two sorts, the limit observations ($y = 0$) and the nonlimit observations ($y > 0$). The two types of observations that we observe, the limit observations and those that are positive, are generated by the latent variable y_i^* crossing the zero threshold or not crossing that threshold. The (**probit**) probability that $y_i = 0$ is

$$P(y_i = 0) = P(y_i^* \leq 0) = 1 - \Phi[(\beta_1 + \beta_2 x_i)/\sigma]$$

If we observe a positive value of y_i, then the term that enters the likelihood function is the normal probability density function with mean $\beta_1 + \beta_2 x_i$ and variance σ^2. The full likelihood function is the product of the probabilities that the limit observations occur times the probability density functions for all the positive, nonlimit, observations. Using "large pi" notation to denote multiplication, the likelihood function is

$$L(\beta_1, \beta_2, \sigma) = \prod_{y_i=0} \left\{ 1 - \Phi\left(\frac{\beta_1 + \beta_2 x_i}{\sigma}\right) \right\}$$
$$\times \prod_{y_i>0} \left\{ (2\pi\sigma^2)^{-\frac{1}{2}} \exp\left(-\frac{1}{2\sigma^2}(y_i - \beta_1 - \beta_2 x_i)^2\right) \right\}$$

This complicated looking likelihood is maximized numerically and is routinely available in econometric software.[10] The maximum likelihood estimator is consistent and asymptotically normal, with a known covariance matrix.[11]

Using the artificial data in *tobit.dat*, we obtain the fitted values

$$\tilde{y}_i = -10.2773 + 1.0487x_i$$
$$(\text{se}) \quad (1.0970) \quad (0.0790) \tag{16.34}$$

These estimates are much closer to the true values $\beta_1 = -9$ and $\beta_2 = 1$, especially when compared to the least squares estimates in (16.32). Maximum likelihood estimation also yields an estimate of σ (true value equals 4) of 3.5756 with a standard error of 0.2610.

The Monte Carlo simulation experiment results from Section 16.7.2 are summarized in Table 16.7. The column "MC average" reports the average estimates over the 1000 Monte Carlo samples, as calculated using (16.33). While the least squares estimates based on all the data and the least squares estimates based only on data corresponding to positive y-values are not close to the true values, the Tobit estimates are very close. The standard errors reported in (16.34) are valid in large samples, and we can see that they do reflect the actual variability of the estimates, as measured by their sample standard deviation, labeled "Std. Dev." in Table 16.7.

A word of caution is in order about commercial software packages. There are many algorithms available for obtaining maximum likelihood estimates, and different packages use different ones, which may lead to slight differences (in perhaps the third or fourth decimal) in the parameter estimates and their standard errors. When carrying out important research, it is a good tip to confirm empirical results with a second software package, just to be sure they give essentially the same numbers.

16.7.4 TOBIT MODEL INTERPRETATION

In the Tobit model the parameters β_1 and β_2 are the intercept and slope of the latent variable model (16.31). In practice we are interested in the marginal effect of a change in x

Table 16.7 **Censored Data Monte Carlo Results**

Estimator	Parameter	MC average	Std. Dev.
Least squares	β_1	−2.0465	0.2238
	β_2	0.5434	0.0351
	σ	2.9324	0.1675
Least squares $y > 0$	β_1	−1.9194	0.9419
	β_2	0.5854	0.0739
	σ	3.3282	0.2335
Tobit	β_1	−9.0600	1.0248
	β_2	1.0039	0.0776
	σ	3.9813	0.2799

[10] Tobit requires data on both the limit values of $y = 0$, and also the nonlimit values for which $y > 0$. Sometimes it is possible that we do not observe the limit values; in such a case the sample is said to be truncated. In this case Tobit does not apply; however, there is a similar maximum likelihood procedure, called **truncated regression**, for such a case. An advanced reference is William Greene (2003) *Econometric Analysis*, 5th edition, Prentice-Hall, Section 22.2.3.

[11] The asymptotic covariance matrix can be found in *Introduction to the Theory and Practice of Econometrics*, 2nd edition, by George G. Judge, R. Carter Hill, William E. Griffiths, Helmut Lütkepohl, and Tsoung-Chao Lee (John Wiley and Sons, 1988), Section 19.3.2.

on either the regression function of the observed data $E(y|x)$ or the regression function conditional on $y > 0$, $E(y|x, y > 0)$. As we indicated earlier, these functions are not straight lines. Their graphs are shown in Figure 16.6. The slope of each changes at each value of x. The slope of $E(y|x)$ has a relatively simple form, being a scale factor times the parameter value; it is

$$\frac{\partial E(y|x)}{\partial x} = \beta_2 \Phi\left(\frac{\beta_1 + \beta_2 x}{\sigma}\right) \tag{16.35}$$

where Φ is the cumulative distribution function (*cdf*) of the standard normal random variable that is evaluated at the estimates and a particular x-value. Because the *cdf* values are positive, the sign of the coefficient tells the direction of the marginal effect, but the magnitude of the marginal effect depends on both the coefficient and the *cdf*. If $\beta_2 > 0$, as x increases the *cdf* function approaches 1, and the slope of the regression function approaches that of the latent variable model, as is shown in Figure 16.6. This marginal effect can be shown to consist of two factors, one representing the change from the portion of the population for which $y = 0$ and the other for the portion of the population for which $y > 0$. This breakdown is called the "McDonald–Moffit" decomposition.[12]

16.7.5 AN EXAMPLE

If we wish to estimate a model explaining the market hours worked by a married woman, what explanatory variables would we include? Factors that would tend to pull a woman into the labor force are her education and her prior labor market experience. Factors that may

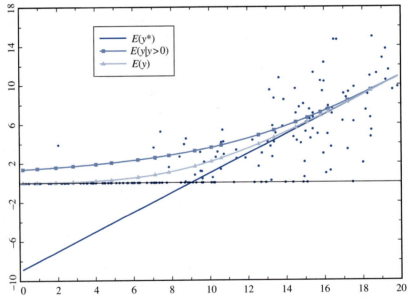

FIGURE 16.6 Censored sample data, and regression functions for observed and positive *y*-values.

[12] J. F. McDonald and R. A. Moffit (1980) "The Uses of Tobit Analysis," *Review of Economics and Statistics*, 62, 318–321. Jeffrey M. Wooldridge (2006) *Introductory Econometrics: A Modern Approach*, 3rd edition, Thompson/South-Western, Section 17.2 has a relatively friendly presentation.

reduce her incentive to work are her age and, the presence of young children in the home.[13] Thus we might propose the regression model

$$HOURS = \beta_1 + \beta_2 EDUC + \beta_3 EXPER + \beta_4 AGE + \beta_4 KIDSL6 + e \qquad (16.36)$$

where *KIDSL6* is the number of children less than 6 years old in the household. Using Mroz's data we obtain the estimates shown in Table 16.8. As previously argued, the least squares estimates are unreliable because the least squares estimator is both biased and inconsistent. The Tobit estimates have the anticipated signs and are all statistically significant at the 0.01 level. To compute the scale factor required for calculation of the marginal effects, we must choose values of the explanatory variables. We choose the sample means for *EDUC* (12.29), *EXPER* (10.63), and *AGE* (42.54) and assume one small child at home (rather than the mean value of 0.24). The calculated scale factor is $\tilde{\Phi} = 0.3638$. Thus the marginal effect on observed hours of work of another year of education is

$$\frac{\partial E(HOURS)}{\partial EDUC} = \tilde{\beta}_2 \tilde{\Phi} = 73.29 \times 0.3638 = 26.34$$

That is, we estimate that another year of education will increase a wife's hours of work by about 26 hours, conditional upon the assumed values of the explanatory variables.

16.7.6 SAMPLE SELECTION

If you consult an econometrician concerning an estimation problem, the first question you will usually hear is, "How were the data obtained?" If the data are obtained by

Table 16.8 **Estimates of Labor Supply Function**

Estimator	Variable	Estimate	Std. Error
Least squares	INTERCEPT	1335.31	235.65
	EDUC	27.09	12.24
	EXPER	48.04	3.64
	AGE	−31.31	3.96
	KIDSL6	−447.85	58.41
Least squares hours > 0	INTERCEPT	1829.75	292.54
	EDUC	−16.46	15.58
	EXPER	33.94	5.01
	AGE	−17.11	5.46
	KIDSL6	−305.31	96.45
Tobit	INTERCEPT	1349.88	386.30
	EDUC	73.29	20.47
	EXPER	80.54	6.29
	AGE	−60.77	6.89
	KIDSL6	−918.92	111.66
	SIGMA	1133.70	42.06

[13] This equation does not include wages, which is jointly determined with hours. The model we propose may be considered a reduced form equation. See Section 11.2.

random sampling, then classic regression methods, such as least squares, work well. However, if the data are obtained by a sampling procedure that is not random, then standard procedures do not work well. Economists regularly face such data problems. A famous illustration comes from labor economics. If we wish to study the determinants of the wages of married women, we face a **sample selection** problem. If we collect data on married women, and ask them what wage rate they earn, many will respond that the question is not relevant since they are homemakers. We only observe data on market wages when the woman chooses to enter the workforce. One strategy is to ignore the women who are homemakers, omit them from the sample, then use least squares to estimate a wage equation for those who work. This strategy fails, the reason for the failure being that our sample is not a random sample. The data we observe are "selected" by a systematic process for which we do not account.

A solution to this problem is a technique called **Heckit**, named after its developer, Nobel Prize winning econometrician James Heckman. This simple procedure uses two estimation steps. In the context of the problem of estimating the wage equation for married women, a probit model is first estimated explaining why a woman is in the labor force or not. In the second stage, a least squares regression is estimated relating the wage of a working woman to education, experience, and so on, and a variable called the "inverse Mills ratio," or IMR. The IMR is created from the first step probit estimation and accounts for the fact that the observed sample of working women is not random.

16.7.6a The Econometric Model

The econometric model describing the situation is composed of two equations. The first is the **selection equation** that determines whether the variable of interest is observed. The sample consists of N observations; however, the variable of interest is observed only for $n < N$ of these. The selection equation is expressed in terms of a latent variable z_i^* that depends on one or more explanatory variables w_i, and is given by

$$z_i^* = \gamma_1 + \gamma_2 w_i + u_i, \quad i = 1, \ldots, N \tag{16.37}$$

For simplicity we will include only one explanatory variable in the selection equation. The latent variable is not observed, but we do observe the binary variable

$$z_i = \begin{cases} 1 & z_i^* > 0 \\ 0 & \text{otherwise} \end{cases} \tag{16.38}$$

The second equation is the linear model of interest. It is

$$y_i = \beta_1 + \beta_2 x_i + e_i, \quad i = 1, \ldots, n, \quad N > n \tag{16.39}$$

A **selectivity problem** arises when y_i is observed only when $z_i = 1$ and if the errors of the two equations are correlated. In such a situation the usual least squares estimators of β_1 and β_2 are biased and inconsistent.

Consistent estimators are based on the conditional regression function[14]

$$E(y_i | z_i^* > 0) = \beta_1 + \beta_2 x_i + \beta_\lambda \lambda_i, \quad i = 1, \ldots, n \tag{16.40}$$

---

[14] Further explanation of this material requires understanding the truncated normal distribution, which is beyond the scope of this book. See William Greene (2003) *Econometric Analysis*, 5th edition, Prentice-Hall, pp.780–783.

where the additional variable λ_i is the "inverse Mills ratio." It is equal to

$$\lambda_i = \frac{\phi(\gamma_1 + \gamma_2 w_i)}{\Phi(\gamma_1 + \gamma_2 w_i)} \tag{16.41}$$

where, as usual, $\phi(\cdot)$ denotes the standard normal probability density function and $\Phi(\cdot)$ denotes the cumulative distribution function for a standard normal random variable. While the value of λ_i is not known, the parameters γ_1 and γ_2 can be estimated using a probit model, based on the observed binary outcome z_i in (16.38). Then the estimated IMR,

$$\tilde{\lambda}_i = \frac{\phi(\tilde{\gamma}_1 + \tilde{\gamma}_2 w_i)}{\Phi(\tilde{\gamma}_1 + \tilde{\gamma}_2 w_i)}$$

is inserted into the regression equation as an extra explanatory variable, yielding the estimating equation

$$y_i = \beta_1 + \beta_2 x_i + \beta_\lambda \tilde{\lambda}_i + v_i, \quad i = 1,\dots,n \tag{16.42}$$

Least squares estimation of this equation yields consistent estimators of β_1 and β_2. A word of caution, however, as the least squares estimator is inefficient relative to the maximum likelihood estimator, and the usual standard errors and t-statistics produced after estimation of (16.42) are incorrect. Proper estimation of standard errors requires the use of specialized software for the "Heckit" model.

16.7.6b Heckit Example: Wages of Married Women

As an example we will reconsider the analysis of wages earned by married women using the Mroz (1987) data, *mroz.dat*. In the sample of 753 married women, 428 have market employment and nonzero earnings. First, let us estimate a simple wage equation, explaining ln(*WAGE*) as a function of the woman's education, *EDUC*, and years of market work experience (*EXPER*), using the 428 women who have positive wages. The result is

$$\ln(WAGE) = -0.4002 + 0.1095EDUC + 0.0157EXPER \qquad R^2 = 0.1484$$
$$(t) \qquad (-2.10) \qquad (7.73) \qquad\qquad (3.90) \tag{16.43}$$

The estimated return to education is about 11%, and the estimated coefficients of both education and experience are statistically significant.

The Heckit procedure starts by estimating a probit model of labor force participation. As explanatory variables we use the woman's age, her years of education, a dummy variable for whether she has children, and the marginal tax rate that she would pay upon earnings if employed. The estimated probit model is

$$\widehat{P(LFP=1)} = \Phi(1.1923 - 0.0206AGE + 0.0838EDUC - 0.3139KIDS - 1.3939MTR)$$
$$(t) \qquad\qquad (-2.93) \qquad (3.61) \qquad (-2.54) \qquad (-2.26)$$

As expected, the effects of age, the presence of children, and the prospects of higher taxes significantly reduce the probability that a woman will join the labor force, while education increases it. Using the estimated coefficients we compute the inverse Mills ratio for the 428 women with market wages

$$\tilde{\lambda} = IMR = \frac{\phi(1.1923 - 0.0206AGE + 0.0838EDUC - 0.3139KIDS - 1.3939MTR)}{\Phi(1.1923 - 0.0206AGE + 0.0838EDUC - 0.3139KIDS - 1.3939MTR)}$$

This is then included in the wage equation, and least squares estimation applied to obtain

$$\ln(WAGE) = 0.8105 + 0.0585EDUC + 0.0163EXPER - 0.8664IMR$$

(t)	(1.64)	(2.45)	(4.08)	(−2.65)	(16.44)
(t-adj)	(1.33)	(1.97)	(3.88)	(−2.17)	

Two results are of note. First, the estimated coefficient of the inverse Mills ratio is statistically significant, implying that there is a selection bias present in the least squares results (16.43). Second, the estimated return to education has fallen from approximately 11% to approximately 6%. The upper row of t-statistics is based on standard errors as usually computed when using least squares regression. The usual standard errors do not account for the fact that the inverse Mills ratio is itself an estimated value. The correct standard errors,[15] which do account for the first stage probit estimation, are used to construct the "adjusted t-statistics" reported in (16.44). As you can see the adjusted t-statistics are slightly smaller, indicating that the adjusted standard errors are somewhat larger than the usual ones.

In most instances it is preferable to estimate the full model, both the selection equation and the equation of interest, jointly by maximum likelihood. While the nature of this procedure is beyond the scope of this book, it is available in some software packages. The maximum likelihood estimated wage equation is

$$\ln(WAGE) = 0.6686 + 0.0658EDUC + 0.0118EXPER$$

(t)	(2.84)	(3.96)	(2.87)

The standard errors based on the full information maximum likelihood procedure are smaller than those yielded by the two-step estimation method.

16.8 Exercises[16]

16.1   In Section 16.1.5 we present an example of transportation choice. Use the sample data on automobile and public transportation times in *transport.dat* for the following exercises.

(a) Estimate the linear probability model $AUTO = \beta_1 + \beta_2 DTIME + e$ using least squares estimation. What is the estimated marginal effect of an increase in *DTIME* on the probability of a person choosing automobile transportation given that $DTIME = 20$?

---

[15] The formulas are very complicated. See William Greene (2003) *Econometric Analysis*, 5th edition, Prentice-Hall, pp.784–785. There are several software packages, such as Stata and LIMDEP, that report correct standard errors.

[16] All exercises in this chapter are computer based.

(b) For each sample observation, calculate the predicted probability of choosing automobile transportation $\widehat{P(AUTO)} = b_1 + b_2 DTIME$. Are all the predicted probabilities plausible?

(c) Using the error variance in equation (16.6) compute the feasible generalized least squares estimates of the linear probability model. If a predicted probability was zero or negative, replace it by 0.01; if a predicted probability was greater than or equal to 1, replace it by 0.99. Compare these estimates to those from part (a).

(d) Using generalized least squares, as we have done in part (c), cures the basic deficiency of the linear probability model. True or false? Explain your answer.

(e) For each of the 21 observations, estimate the probability of choosing automobile transportation using the generalized least squares estimates of the linear probability model. Predict the choice of transportation mode using the rule $\widehat{AUTO} = 1$ if the predicted probability is 0.5 or larger, otherwise $\widehat{AUTO} = 0$. Define a successful prediction to be when we predict that a person will choose the automobile $(\widehat{AUTO} = 1)$ when they actually did $(AUTO = 1)$, OR when we predict that a person will choose public transportation $(\widehat{AUTO} = 0)$ when they did $(AUTO = 0)$. Calculate the percentage of correct predictions in the $N = 21$ cases.

(f) Compare the percentage of correct predictions from the linear probability model to that for the probit model.

16.2* In Section 16.1.5 we present an example of transportation choice. Use the sample data on automobile and public transportation times in *transport.dat* for the following exercises.

(a) Estimate the logit model explaining the choice of automobile transportation as a function of difference in travel time $(DTIME)$. Compare the parameter estimates and their standard errors to the estimates from the probit model in equation (16.15).

(b) Based on the logit model results, estimate the marginal effect of an increase in $DTIME$ given that $DTIME = 20$. Use (16.11) but replace the standard normal density function $\phi(\cdot)$ by the logistic density function $\lambda(\cdot)$ given in (16.16). Compare this result to that for the probit model in Section 16.1.5, where the estimated marginal effect is 0.0104.

(c) Using the logit estimates, calculate the probability of a person choosing automobile transportation given that the time differential $DTIME = 30$. Compare this value to the probit estimate of the probability of choosing automobile transportation, which is 0.798.

(d) For each of the 21 observations, estimate the probability of choosing automobile transportation using the logit model. Predict the choice of transportation mode using the rule $\widehat{AUTO} = 1$ if the predicted probability is 0.5 or larger, otherwise $\widehat{AUTO} = 0$. Define a successful prediction to be when we predict that a person will choose the automobile $(\widehat{AUTO} = 1)$ when they actually did $(AUTO = 1)$, OR when we predict that a person will choose public transportation $(\widehat{AUTO} = 0)$ when they did $(AUTO = 0)$. Calculate the percentage of correct predictions in the $N = 21$ cases.

16.3* Dhillon, Shilling, and Sirmans ("Choosing Between Fixed and Adjustable Rate Mortgages," *Journal of Money, Credit and Banking*, 19(1), 1987, 260–267) estimate a probit model designed to explain the choice by homebuyers of fixed versus adjustable rate mortgages. They use 78 observations from a bank in Baton Rouge, Louisiana, taken over the period January, 1983 to February, 1984. These data are contained in the file *sirmans.dat. ADJUST* = 1 if an adjustable mortgage is chosen. The explanatory variables, and their anticipated signs, are *FIXRATE* $(+)$ = fixed interest rate ; *MARGIN* $(-)$ =the variable rate $-$ the fixed rate; *YIELD* $(-)$ =the 10-year Treasury rate less the 1-year rate; *MATURITY* $(-)$ = ratio of maturities on adjustable to fixed rates; *POINTS* $(-)$ = ratio of points paid on an adjustable mortgage to those paid on a fixed rate mortgage; *NETWORTH* $(+)$ = borrower's net worth.

(a) Obtain the least squares estimates of the linear probability model explaining the choice of an adjustable mortgage, using the explanatory variables listed above. Obtain the predicted values from this estimation. Are the signs consistent with expectations? Are the predicted values between 0 and 1?

(b) Estimate the model of mortgage choice using probit. Are the signs consistent with expectations? Are the estimated coefficients statistically significant?

(c) Using the probit estimates from part (b), estimate the probability $\hat{p}$ of choosing an adjustable rate mortgage for each sample observation. What percentage of the outcomes do we successfully predict, using the rule that if $\hat{p} \geq 0.5$ we predict that an adjustable rate mortgage will be chosen.

(d) Estimate the marginal effect of an increase in the variable *MARGIN*, with all explanatory variables fixed at their sample means. Explain the meaning of this value.

16.4 Use the data on college choice contained in *nels_small.dat*. These data are discussed in Section 16.3.

(a) Define a variable *COLLEGE* that equals 1 if a high school graduate chooses either a 2-year or a 4-year college, and zero otherwise. What percentage of the high school graduates attended college?

(b) Estimate a probit model explaining *COLLEGE*, using as explanatory variables *GRADES*, 13-point scale with 1 indicating highest grade and 13 the lowest; *FAMINC*, gross family income in $1000; *FAMSIZ*, number of family members; *PARCOLL*, = 1 if most educated parent had a college degree; *FEMALE*, = 1 if female; and *BLACK*, = 1 if black. Are the signs of the estimated coefficients consistent with your expectations? Explain. Are the estimated coefficients statistically significant?

(c) Using the estimates in (b), predict the probability of attending college for a black female with *GRADES* = 5, *FAMINC* = sample mean, from a household with five members, with a parent who attended college. Repeat this probability calculation with *GRADES* = 10.

(d) Repeat the calculations in (c) for (i) a white female, and (ii) a white male.

(e) Reestimate the model in (b), but omitting the variables *PARCOLL*, *BLACK*, and *FEMALE*. How are the signs and significance of the remaining coefficients affected?

(f) Test the joint significance of *PARCOLL*, *BLACK*, and *FEMALE* using a likelihood ratio test. [*Hint:* The test statistic is LR = 2(log-likelihood of unrestricted model – log-likelihood of restricted model). The test statistic is chi-square with 3 degrees of freedom if the null hypothesis is true.]

16.5 Use the data on college choice contained in *nels_small.dat*. These data are discussed in Section 16.3. In this exercise you will consider only those students who chose to attend a college, either a 2-year or a 4-year college. Within this subsample, define a variable *FOURYR* = 1 if the student attended a 4-year college, and 0 otherwise.

(a) What percentage of the high school graduates who attended college selected a 4-year college? What percentage of those choosing a 4-year college are female? What percentage of those choosing a 4-year college are black?

(b) Estimate a probit model explaining *FOURYR*, using as explanatory variables *GRADES*, 13-point scale with 1 indicating highest grade and 13 the lowest; *FAMINC*, gross family income in $1000; and *FAMSIZ*, number of family members. Are the signs of the estimated coefficients consistent with your expectations? Explain. Are the estimated coefficients statistically significant?

(c) Reestimate the model in (b) separately for the populations of black students and white students $(BLACK = 0)$. Compare and contrast these results.

16.6   Use the data on college choice contained in *nels_small.dat*. These data are discussed in Section 16.3.

(a) Estimate a multinomial logit model explaining *PSECHOICE*. Use the group who did not attend college as the base group. Use as explanatory variables *GRADES, FAMINC, FEMALE,* and *BLACK*. Are the estimated coefficients statistically significant?

(b) Compute the estimated probability that a white male student with median values of *GRADES* and *FAMINC* will attend a 4-year college.

(c) Compute the odds that a white male student with median values of *GRADES* and *FAMINC* will attend a 4-year college rather than not attend any college.

(d) Compute the change in probability of attending a 4-year college for a white male student with median *FAMINC* whose *GRADES* change from 6.64 (the median value) to 4.905 (top 25th percentile).

(e) From the full data set create a subsample, omitting the group who attended a 2-year college. Estimate a logit model explaining student's choice between attending a 4-year college and not attending college, using the same explanatory variables in (a). Compute the odds that a white male student with median values of *GRADES* and *FAMINC* will attend a 4-year college rather than not attend any college. Compare the result to that in (c).

16.7   In Section 16.4.3 we considered a conditional logit model of choice among three brands of soda: Coke, Pepsi, and 7-Up. The data are in the file *cola.dat*.

(a) In addition to *PRICE*, the data file contains dummy variables indicating whether the product was "featured" at the time (*FEATURE*) or whether there was a store display (*DISPLAY*). Estimate a conditional logit model explaining choice of soda using *PRICE, DISPLAY,* and *FEATURE* as explanatory variables. Discuss the signs of the estimated coefficients and their significance. (*Note:* In this model do not include alternative specific intercept terms.)

(b) Compute the odds of choosing *COKE* relative to *PEPSI* and *7-UP* if the price of each is $1.25 and no display or feature is present.

(c) Compute the odds of choosing *COKE* relative to *PEPSI* and *7-UP* if the price of each is $1.25 and a display is present for *COKE*, but not for the others, and none of the items is featured.

(d) Compute the change in the probability of purchase of each type of soda if the price of *COKE* changes from $1.25 to $1.30, with the prices of the *PEPSI* and *7-UP* remaining at $1.25. Assume that a display is present for *COKE*, but not for the others, and none of the items is featured.

(e) Add the alternative specific "intercept" terms for *PEPSI* and *7-UP* to the model in (a). Estimate the conditional logit model. Compute the odds ratios in (c) based upon these new estimates.

(f) Based on the estimates in (e), calculate the effects of the price change in (d) on the choice probability for each brand.

16.8   In Section 16.5.1 we described an ordinal probit model for post-secondary education choice and estimated a simple model in which the choice depended simply on the student's *GRADES*.

(a) Using the estimates in Table 16.5, calculate the probability that a student will choose no college, a 2-year college, and a 4-year college if the student's grades are the median value, *GRADES* = 6.64. Recompute these probabilities assuming that *GRADES* = 4.905. Discuss the probability changes. Are they what you anticipated? Explain.

(b) Expand the ordered probit model to include family income (*FAMINC*), family size (*FAMSIZ*), and the dummy variables *BLACK* and *PARCOLL*. Discuss the estimates, their signs, and significance. (*Hint:* Recall that the sign indicates the direction of the effect for the highest category, but is opposite for the lowest category).

(c) Test the joint significance of the variables added in (b) using a likelihood ratio test.

(d) Compute the probability that a black student from a household of four members, including a parent who went to college, and household income of $52,000, will attend a 4-year college if (i) *GRADES* = 6.64 and (ii) *GRADES* = 4.905.

(e) Repeat (d) for a "non-black" student and discuss the differences in your findings.

16.9   In Section 16.6.3 we estimated a Poisson regression explaining the number of Olympic Games medals won by various countries as a function of the logarithms of population and gross domestic product (in 1995 dollars). The estimated coefficients are in Table 16.6.

(a) In 1988 Australia had *GDP* = 3.0E + 11 and a population of 16.5 million. Predict the number of medals that Australia would win. They did win 14 medals. Calculate the probability that Australia would win 10 medals or more.

(b) In 1988 Canada had *GDP* = 5.19E + 11 and a population of 26.9 million. Predict the number of medals that Canada would win. They did win 10 medals. Calculate the probability that they would win 15 medals or less.

(c) Use the combined data on years 1992 and 1996 to estimate the model explaining medals won as a function of the logarithms of population and gross domestic product. Compare these estimates to those in Table 16.6.

(d) In addition to population and *GDP*, the file *olympics.dat* contains a dummy variable (*SOVIET*) to indicate that a country was part of the former Soviet Union. The dummy variable *HOST* indicates the country hosting the Olympic Games. Using again the combined data for 1992 and 1996, estimate the Poisson regression model that adds these two variables to the specification. Discuss the results. Are the signs what you expected? Are the added variables statistically significant?

(e) A variable similar to *SOVIET* is *PLANNED*, which includes nonmarket, typi- cally communist countries. Use this variable instead of *SOVIET* and repeat (d). Which model do you prefer, the one with *SOVIET* or the one with *PLANNED*? Why?

(f) In 2000, the *GDP* (in 1995 US $) of Australia was 3.22224E + 11 and that of Canada was 6.41256E + 11. The Australian population in 2000 was 19.071 million, and that of Canada was 30.689 million. Using these figures, predict the number of medals won by Canada and Australia based on the estimates in part (e). Note that the 2000 games were held in Sydney, Australia. In

2000, Australia won 58 medals and Canada won 14. How close were your predictions?

16.10 Bernard and Busse use the Olympic Games data in *olympics.dat* to examine the share of medals won by countries. The total number of medals awarded in 1988 was 738, in 1992 there were 815 medals awarded, and in 1996, 842 medals were awarded. Using these totals, compute the share of medals (*SHARE*) won by each country in each of these years.

(a) Construct a histogram for the variable *SHARE*. What do you observe? What percent of the observations are zero?

(b) Estimate a least squares regression explaining *SHARE* as a function of the logarithms of population and real GDP, and the dummy variables *HOST* and *SOVIET*. (i) Discuss the estimation results. (ii) Plot the residuals against ln(*GDP*). Do they appear random? (iii) Use your computer software to compute the skewness and kurtosis values of the residuals. How do these values compare to those for the normal distribution, which has skewness of zero and kurtosis of 3?

(c) In 2000, the *GDP* (in 1995 US $) of Australia was 3.22224E + 11 and that of Canada was 6.41256E + 11. The Australian population in 2000 was 19.071 million, and that of Canada was 30.689 million. Predict the share of medals won by Canada and Australia based on the estimates in part (b). Note that the 2000 games were held in Sydney, Australia. In 2000, Australia won 58 medals and Canada won 14 out of the 929 medals awarded. How close were your predicted shares?

(d) Estimate the model described in (b) using Tobit. Compare the parameter estimates to those in (b).

(e)◆ In the Tobit model the expected value of the dependent variable, conditional on the fact that it is positive, is given by an expression like equation (16.40). Specifically it is $E(y_i|y_i > 0) = \beta_1 + \beta_2 x_i + \sigma \lambda_i$ where $\lambda_i = \phi(z_i)/\Phi(z_i)$ is the inverse Mills ratio and $z_i = (\beta_1 + \beta_2 x_i)/\sigma$. Use the information in part (c) to predict the share of medals won by Australia and Canada. Are these predicted shares closer to the true shares, or not?

16.11 Is there a formula that can predict the outcome of the Oscar Award for the Best Picture? In *The Wall Street Journal* (February 25, 2005, pages W1 and W4) the research of Professor Andrew Bernard is summarized. The file *oscar.dat* contains information on the nominees for Best Picture since 1984, kindly provided by Dr. Bernard. The variables are *YEAR*, *TITLE*, a dummy variable *WINNER* indicating the Oscar for Best Picture, the total number of Oscar *NOMINATIONS*, the number of Golden Globe awards (*GGLOBES*) won, and a dummy variable indicating whether or not the film was a comedy (*COMEDY*).

(a) Using all observations from 1984–2003, estimate a probit model to predict the Oscar winner using *NOMINATIONS* and *GGLOBES* as explanatory factors. Are the coefficients significant and of anticipated signs?

(b) Calculate the marginal effect of an additional *NOMINATION* on the probability of winning the Oscar.

(c) Calculate the marginal effect of an additional Golden Globe Award on the probability of winning the Oscar.

(d) Predict the probability of winning for each film up through 2003. Using the rule that the highest predicted probability predicts the winner, compute the percentage of correct predictions by this model.

(e) Using the model estimated in (a), predict the winner in 2004. The actual winner was "Million Dollar Baby."

16.12 Predicting U.S. presidential election outcomes is a weekly event in the year prior to an election. In the 2000 election Republican George W. Bush defeated Democrat Al Gore, and in 2004 George Bush defeated Democrat John F. Kerry. The data file *vote2.dat* contains data on these two elections. By state and for the 2 years we report the dummy variable $DEM = 1$ if the popular vote favored the democratic candidate, $INCOME =$ state median income, $HS =$ percentage of the population with at least a high school degree, $BA =$ percentage of the population with at least a bachelor's degree, $DENSITY =$ population per square mile, and $REGION = 3$ for southwest, 2 for south, and 1 otherwise.

(a) Calculate summary statistics for the variables $INCOME$, HS, BA, and $DENSITY$ if (i) $DEM = 1$ and $YEAR = 2000$ and (ii) $DEM = 0$ and $YEAR = 2000$. What major differences, if any, do you observe?

(b) Estimate a probit model explaining the observed binary outcome DEM for the year 2000. Use as explanatory variables $INCOME$, BA, and $DENSITY$. Which factors are statistically significant, and what is the direction of their effect?

(c) Use the results in (b) to predict the outcome of the 2004 election. What percentage of state outcomes did you predict correctly?

(d) Estimate the model in (b) using 2004 data. What differences, if any, do you observe?

Chapter 17

Writing an Empirical Research Report and Sources of Economic Data

In the preceding chapters we emphasized (i) the formulation of an econometric model from an economic model, (ii) estimation of the econometric model by an appropriate procedure, (iii) interpretation of the estimates, and (iv) inferences, in the form of interval estimates, hypothesis tests, and predictions. In this chapter we recognize that specifying the model, selecting an estimation method, and obtaining the data are all part of an econometric research project. In particular, we discuss the selection of a suitable topic for a research project, the essential components of a research report, and sources of economic data.

17.1 Selecting a Topic for an Economics Project

Economic research is an adventure and can be *fun*! A research project is an opportunity to investigate a topic of importance in which you are interested. However, before you begin the actual research and writing of a report, it is a good idea to give some quality thinking time to the selection of your topic. Then, once you have an idea formulated, it is wise to write an abstract of the project, summarizing what you know and what you hope to learn. These two steps are the focus of this section.

17.1.1 CHOOSING A TOPIC

Choosing a good research topic is essential if you are to complete a class project successfully. A starting point is the question, "What are my interests?" Interest in a particular topic will add pleasure to the research effort. Also, if you begin working on an interesting question, other questions will usually occur to you. These new questions may put another light on the original topic, or they may represent new paths to follow, which are even more interesting to you.

By the time you have completed several semesters of economics classes, you will find yourself enjoying some areas more than others. For each of us, specialized areas such as industrial organization, public finance, resource economics, monetary economics, environmental economics, and international trade hold a different appeal. If you are generally interested in one of these areas, but do not have a specific idea of where to start in the selection of a topic, speak with your instructor. He or she will be able to suggest some ideas that will give you a start and may cite some published research for you to read, or may suggest specific professional journals that carry applied research articles on a general area. If you find an area or topic in which you are interested, consult the *Journal of Economic Literature* for a list of related journal articles. The *JEL* has a classification scheme that makes isolating particular areas of study an easy task.

Once you have tentatively identified a problem on which you wish to work, the next issues are pragmatic ones. Over the course of one semester, you will not have sufficient time to collect your own data to use in a project. Thus you must find out whether suitable data are available for the problem you have identified. Once again your instructor may be of help in this regard.

We have so far identified two aspects of a good research topic: the topic should be of interest to you and data that are relevant to the topic should be readily available. The third aspect of a good project is again a pragmatic one: you should be able to finish in the time remaining in your semester. This requires not only the availability of the data, but also implies that you are familiar with the econometric procedures that are appropriate for analyzing the data, and also that you can implement them on the computer, or learn the procedure in a reasonable period of time.

17.1.2 WRITING AN ABSTRACT

After you have selected a specific topic, it is a good idea to write up a brief abstract. Writing the abstract will help you to focus your thoughts about what you really want to do, and you can show it to your instructor for preliminary approval and comments. The abstract should be short, usually not more than 500 words, and should include

1. a concise statement of the problem;
2. comments on the information that is available with one or two key references;
3. a description of the research design that includes
    (a) the economic model,
    (b) the econometric estimation and inference methods,
    (c) data sources,
    (d) estimation, hypothesis testing, and prediction procedures;
4. the potential contribution of the research.

17.2 A Format for Writing a Research Report

Economic research reports have a standard format in which the various steps of the research project are discussed and the results interpreted. The following outline is typical.

1. *Statement of the problem:* The place to start your report is with a summary of the questions you wish to investigate, why they are important and who should be interested in the results. This introductory section should be nontechnical, and it should motivate the reader to continue reading the paper. It is also useful to map out the contents of the following sections of the report.

2. *Review of the literature:* Briefly summarize the relevant literature in the research area you have chosen and clarify how your work extends our knowledge. By all means cite the works of others who have motivated your research, but keep it brief. You do not have to survey everything that has been written on the topic.

3. *The economic model:* Specify the economic model that you used, and define the economic variables. State the model's assumptions and identify hypotheses that

you wish to test. Economic models can get complicated. Your task is to explain the model clearly, but as briefly and simply as possible. Do not use unnecessary technical jargon. Use simple terms instead of complicated ones when possible. Your objective is to display the quality of your thinking, not the extent of your vocabulary.

4. *The econometric model:* Discuss the econometric model that corresponds to the economic model. Make sure you include a discussion of the variables in the model, the functional form, the error assumptions, and any other assumptions that you make. Use notation that is as simple as possible, and do not clutter the body of the paper with long proofs or derivations. These can go into a technical appendix.

5. *The data:* Describe the data you used, the source of the data and any reservations you have about their appropriateness.

6. *The estimation and inference procedures:* Describe the estimation methods you used and why they were chosen. Explain hypothesis testing procedures and their usage.

7. *The empirical results and conclusions:* Report the parameter estimates, their interpretation, and the values of test statistics. Comment on their statistical significance, their relation to previous estimates, and their economic implications.

8. *Possible extensions and limitations of the study:* Your research will raise questions about the economic model, data, and estimation techniques. What future research is suggested by your findings and how might you go about it?

9. *Acknowledgments:* It is appropriate to recognize those who have commented on and contributed to your research. This may include your instructor, a librarian who helped you find data, a fellow student who read and commented on your paper.

10. *References:* An alphabetical list of the literature you cite in your study, as well as references to the data sources you used.

Once you have written the first draft, use your computer's software "spell-checker" to check for errors. Have a friend read the paper, make suggestions for clarifying the prose, and check your logic and conclusions. Before you submit the paper you should eliminate as many errors as possible. Typos, missing references, and incorrect formulas can spell doom for an otherwise excellent paper. Some do's and don'ts are summarized nicely, and with good humor, by Deidre N. McClosky in *Economical Writing, 2ⁿᵈ Edition* (Prospect Heights, IL: Waveland Press, Inc., 1999). While it is not a pleasant topic to discuss, you should be aware of the rules of plagiarism. You must not use someone else's words as if they were your own. If you are unclear about what you can and cannot use, check with the style manuals listed in the next paragraph, or consult your instructor.

The paper should have clearly defined sections and subsections. The equations, tables, and figures should be numbered. References and footnotes should be formatted in an acceptable fashion. A style guide is a good investment. Two classic ones are

- *The Chicago Manual of Style: The Essential Guide for Writers, Editors, and Publishers (15th Edition)* (2003, University of Chicago Press.)

- *A Manual for Writers of Research Papers, Theses, and Dissertations, Seventh Edition: Chicago Guides to Writing, Editing, and Publishing* by Kate L. Turabian, Wayne C. Booth, Gregory G. Colomb, and Joseph M. Williams (April 2007, University of Chicago Press.)

On the Web, *The Economist Style Guide* can be found at http://www.economist.com/research/styleguide/

17.3 Sources of Economic Data

Economic data are much easier to obtain after the World Wide Web was developed. In this section we direct you to some places on the Internet where economic data are accessible and also list some traditional data sources.

17.3.1 LINKS TO ECONOMIC DATA ON THE INTERNET

There are a number of fantastic sites on the World Wide Web for obtaining economic data. The following three sources provide links to many specific data sources.

Resources for Economists (RFE) (http://www.rfe.org) is a primary gateway to resources on the Internet for economists. This excellent site is the work of Bill Goffe. There you will find links to sites for economic data and to sites of general interest to economists. The **Data** link has these broad data categories:

- *U.S. macro and regional data:* Here you will find links to various data sources such as the Bureau of Economic Analysis, Bureau of Labor Statistics, *Economic Reports of the President*, and the Federal Reserve Banks.

- *Other U.S. data:* Here you will find links to the U.S. Census Bureau, as well as links to many panel and survey data sources. The gateway to U.S. Government agencies is FedStats (http://www.fedstats.gov/). Once there, click on *Agencies* to see a complete list of US Government agencies and links to their homepages.

- *World and non-US data:* Here there are links to world data, such as the CIA Factbook, and the Penn World Tables. International organizations such as the Asian Development Bank, the International Monetary Fund, the World Bank, and so on. There are also links to sites with data on specific countries and sectors of the world.

- *Finance and financial markets:* Here there are links to sources of United States and world financial data on variables such as exchange rates, interest rates, and share prices.

- *Journal data and program archives:* Some economic journals post data used in articles. Links to these journals are provided here. Many of the articles in these journals will be beyond the scope of undergraduate economics majors.

Business and Economics Data links (http://www.econ-datalinks.org/) is a site maintained by the Business and Economics Statistics Section of the American Statistical Association. It provides links to economics and financial data sources of interest to economists and business statisticians, along with an assessment of the quality of each site.

Resources for Econometricians: A link that contains a range of resources for econometricians is *Econometrics Journal* online. The specific link to data sources is http://www.feweb.vu.nl/econometriclinks/#data

Some Web sites make extracting data relatively easy. For example, **Economagic** (http://www.Economagic.com) is an excellent and easy-to-use source of macro time series (some 100,000 series available). The data series are easily viewed in a copy and paste format, or graphed.

Data Web sites are constantly being created. Some recent examples include

- Time-Web: http://www.bized.co.uk/timeweb/
- Statistical Resources on the Web: http://www.lib.umich.edu/govdocs/stats.html
- Business, Financial, and Economic Data: http://www.forecasts.org/data/

17.3.2 TRADITIONAL SOURCES OF ECONOMIC DATA

Your library contains a wealth of business and economic data. To locate these data you can take several approaches. First, your school's Web page may contain a link to the library and there you may find links describing available resources. Second, you might search using your library's computerized database. Third, you might ask a librarian. Some well-known data sources are the following.

At the international level, macro data are published by agencies such as the International Monetary Fund (IMF), the Organization for Economic Development (OECD), the United Nations (UN), and the Food and Agriculture Organization (FAO). Some examples of publications of these agencies that include a wide array of data include

International Financial Statistics (IMF, monthly)

Basic Statistics of the Community (OECD, annual)

Consumer Price Indices in the European Community (OECD, annual)

World Statistics (UN, annual)

Yearbook of National Accounts Statistics (UN, annual)

FAO Trade Yearbook (annual).

The major sources of US economic data are the Bureau of Economic Analysis (BEA), the Bureau of the Census (BC), the Bureau of Labor Statistics (BLS), the Federal Reserve (FR), and the Statistical Reporting Service of the Department of Agriculture (USDA). Some examples of publications of these US agencies that include a wide array of macroeconomic data include

Survey of Current Business (BEA, monthly)

Handbook of Basic Economic Statistics (Bureau of Economic Statistics, Inc., monthly)

Monthly Labor Review (BLS, monthly)

Federal Reserve Bulletin (FR, monthly)

Statistical Abstract of the US (BC, annual)

Economic Report of the President (annual)

Agricultural Statistics (USDA, annual)

Agricultural Situation Reports (USDA, monthly)

Economic Indicators (Council of Economic Advisors, monthly).

17.3.3 INTERPRETING ECONOMIC DATA

In many cases it is easier to obtain economic data than it is to understand the meaning of the data. It is essential when using macroeconomic or financial data that you understand the definitions of the variables. Just what is the index of leading economic indicators? What is included in personal consumption expenditures? You may find the answers to some questions like these in your textbooks. Another resource you might find useful is *A Guide to Everyday Economic Statistics*, 6th edition [Gary E. Clayton and Martin Gerhard Giesbrecht (2003) Boston: Irwin/McGraw-Hill]. This slender volume examines how economic statistics are constructed and how they can be used.

17.4 Exercises

17.1 Check out in your library the latest *Economic Report of the President*. Become acquainted with the aggregate income, employment, and production data and their sources that are reported therein. Note how these data are used in the narrative portion of the report.

17.2 Locate the *Survey of Current Business* in your library and describe its contents.

17.3 Visit an Internet site devoted to economic data. Download data on the monthly prime interest rate for the past 10 years and graph it against time.

17.4 Choose two economic articles containing empirical work that use some of the techniques we have discussed in this book. Critique their format and the clarity of their writing.

Review of Math Essentials

Learning Objectives

Based on the material in this appendix, you should be able to

1. Work with single and double summation operations.
2. Explain the relationship between exponential functions and natural logarithms.
3. Explain and apply scientific notation.
4. Define a linear relationship, as opposed to a nonlinear relationship.
5. Compute the elasticity at a point on a linear function or any of the functions in Table A.2.
6. Explain the key features of the log-linear functional form.
7. Explain the key features of the log-log functional form.
8. Explain the key features of the linear-log functional form.

Keywords

absolute value	inequalities	partial derivative
antilogarithm	integers	percentage change
asymptote	intercept	Phillips curve
ceteris paribus	irrational numbers	quadratic function
cubic function	linear relationship	rational numbers
derivative	logarithm	real numbers
double summation	log-linear function	reciprocal function
e	log-log function	relative change
elasticity	marginal effect	scientific notation
exponential function	natural logarithm	slope
exponents	nonlinear relationship	summation sign

We assume that you have studied basic math. Hopefully you understand the calculus concepts of differentiation and integration, though these tools are not *required* for success in this class. In this appendix we review some essential concepts that you may wish to consult from time to time.

A.1 Summation

Throughout this book we will use a **summation sign**, denoted by the Greek symbol Σ, to shorten algebraic expressions. For example, let x represent an economic variable, such as the number of 1-liter bottles of diet soda sold at a grocery store on a particular day. We might like to obtain the total number of bottles sold over the first 15 days of the month. Denote these quantities by $x_1, x_2, \ldots, x_{15}$. The total quantity we seek is the sum of these daily values, or $x_1 + x_2 + \cdots + x_{15}$. Rather than write this sum out each time, we will represent the sum as $\sum_{i=1}^{15} x_i$, so that $\sum_{i=1}^{15} x_i = x_1 + x_2 + \cdots + x_{15}$. If we sum n terms, a general number, then the summation will be $\sum_{i=1}^{n} x_i = x_1 + x_2 + \cdots + x_n$. In this notation

- The symbol Σ is the capital Greek letter sigma and means "the sum of."
- The letter i is called the **index of summation**. This letter is arbitrary and may also appear as t, j, or k.
- The expression $\sum_{i=1}^{n} x_i$ is read "the sum of the terms x_i, from i equal to 1 to n."
- The expression $\sum_{i=1}^{n} x_i$ is also written as $\sum_{i=1}^{n} x_i$. Both forms mean the same thing.
- The numbers 1 and n are the **lower limit** and **upper limit** of summation.

The following rules apply to the summation operation.

1. The sum of n values $x_1, \ldots, x_n$ is
$$\sum_{i=1}^{n} x_i = x_1 + x_2 + \cdots + x_n$$

2. If a is a constant then
$$\sum_{i=1}^{n} a x_i = a \sum_{i=1}^{n} x_i$$

3. If a is a constant then
$$\sum_{i=1}^{n} a = a + a + \cdots + a = na$$

4. If X and Y are two variables, then
$$\sum_{i=1}^{n} (x_i + y_i) = \sum_{i=1}^{n} x_i + \sum_{i=1}^{n} y_i$$

5. If X and Y are two variables, then
$$\sum_{i=1}^{n} (a x_i + b y_i) = a \sum_{i=1}^{n} x_i + b \sum_{i=1}^{n} y_i$$

6. The arithmetic mean (average) of n values of X is
$$\bar{x} = \frac{\sum_{i=1}^{n} x_i}{n} = \frac{x_1 + x_2 + \cdots + x_n}{n}$$

7. A property of the average is that
$$\sum_{i=1}^{n} (x_i - \bar{x}) = \sum_{i=1}^{n} x_i - \sum_{i=1}^{n} \bar{x} = \sum_{i=1}^{n} x_i - n\bar{x} = \sum_{i=1}^{n} x_i - \sum_{i=1}^{n} x_i = 0$$

8. We often use an abbreviated form of the summation notation. For example, if $f(x)$ is a function of the values of X,

$$\sum_{i=1}^{n} f(x_i) = f(x_1) + f(x_2) + \cdots + f(x_n)$$

$$= \sum_{i} f(x_i) \quad (\text{``sum over all values of the index } i\text{''})$$

$$= \sum_{x} f(x) \quad (\text{``sum over all possible values of } X\text{''})$$

9. Several summation signs can be used in one expression. Suppose the variable Y takes n values and X takes m values, and let $f(x, y) = x + y$. Then the **double summation** of this function is

$$\sum_{i=1}^{m} \sum_{j=1}^{n} f(x_i, y_j) = \sum_{i=1}^{m} \sum_{j=1}^{n} (x_i + y_j)$$

To evaluate such expressions, work from the innermost sum outward. First set $i = 1$ and sum over all values of j, and so on. That is,

$$\sum_{i=1}^{m} \sum_{j=1}^{n} f(x_i, y_j) = \sum_{i=1}^{m} [f(x_i, y_1) + f(x_i, y_2) + \cdots + f(x_i, y_n)]$$

The *order* of summation does not matter, so

$$\sum_{i=1}^{m} \sum_{j=1}^{n} f(x_i, y_j) = \sum_{j=1}^{n} \sum_{i=1}^{m} f(x_i, y_j)$$

A.2 Some Basics

A.2.1 NUMBERS

Integers are the whole numbers, $0, \pm1, \pm2, \pm3, \ldots$. The positive integers are the counting numbers. **Rational** numbers can be written as a/b, where a and b are integers, and $b \neq 0$. The **real numbers** can be represented by points on a line. There are an uncountable number of real numbers and they are not all rational. Numbers such as $\pi \cong 3.1415927$ and $\sqrt{2}$ are said to be **irrational** since they cannot be expressed as ratios and have only decimal representations. Numbers like $\sqrt{-2}$ are not real numbers. The **absolute value** of a number is denoted by $|a|$. It is the positive part of the number, so that $|3| = 3$ and $|-3| = 3$.

Inequalities among numbers obey certain rules. The notation $a < b$, a is less than b, means that a is to the left of b on the number line and that $b - a > 0$. If a is less than or equal to b, it is written as $a \leq b$. Three basic rules are as follows:

$$\text{If } a < b, \text{ then } a + c < b + c$$

$$\text{If } a < b, \text{ then } \begin{cases} ac < bc & \text{if } c > 0 \\ ac > bc & \text{if } c < 0 \end{cases}$$

$$\text{If } a < b \text{ and } b < c, \text{ then } a < c$$

A.2.2 EXPONENTS

Exponents are defined as follows:

$$x^n = xx \cdots x \ (n \text{ terms}) \text{ if } n \text{ is a positive integer}$$
$$x^0 = 1 \text{ if } x \neq 0. \quad 0^0 \text{ is not defined}$$

Some common rules for working with exponents, assuming x and y are real, m and n are integers, and a and b are rational, are as follows:

$$x^{-n} = \frac{1}{x^n} \text{ if } x \neq 0. \text{ For example, } x^{-1} = \frac{1}{x}$$

$$x^{1/n} = \sqrt[n]{x}. \text{ For example, } x^{1/2} = \sqrt{x} \text{ and } x^{-1/2} = \frac{1}{\sqrt{x}}$$

$$x^{m/n} = (x^{1/n})^m. \text{ For example, } 8^{4/3} = (8^{1/3})^4 = 2^4 = 16$$

$$x^a x^b = x^{a+b}, \quad \frac{x^a}{x^b} = x^{a-b}$$

$$\left(\frac{x}{y}\right)^a = \frac{x^a}{y^a}, \quad (xy)^a = x^a y^a$$

A.2.3 SCIENTIFIC NOTATION

Scientific notation is useful for very large or very small numbers. A number in scientific notation is written as a number between 1 and 10 multiplied by a power of 10. So, for example, $5.1 \times 10^5 = 510{,}000$, and $0.00000034 = 3.4 \times 10^{-7}$. Scientific notation makes handling large numbers much easier because complex operations can be broken into simpler ones. For example,

$$510{,}000 \times 0.00000034 = (5.1 \times 10^5) \times (3.4 \times 10^{-7})$$
$$= (5.1 \times 3.4) \times (10^5 \times 10^{-7})$$
$$= 17.34 \times 10^{-2}$$
$$= 0.1734$$

and

$$\frac{510{,}000}{0.00000034} = \frac{5.1 \times 10^5}{3.4 \times 10^{-7}} = \frac{5.1}{3.4} \times \frac{10^5}{10^{-7}} = 1.5 \times 10^{12}$$

Computer programs sometimes write $5.1 \times 10^5 = 5.1\text{E}5$ or $5.1\text{D}5$ and $3.4 \times 10^{-7} = 3.4\text{E} - 7$ or $3.4\text{D} - 7$.

A.2.4 LOGARITHMS AND THE NUMBER e

Logarithms are simply exponents. If $x = 10^b$, then b is the logarithm of x to the base 10. The irrational number $e \cong 2.718282$ is used in mathematics and statistics as the base for logarithms. If $x = e^b$, then b is the logarithm of x to the base e. Logarithms using the

Table A.1   **Some Natural Logarithms**

x	$\ln(x)$
1	0
10	2.3025851
100	4.6051702
1000	6.9077553
10,000	9.2103404
100,000	11.512925
1,000,000	13.815511

number e as base are called **natural logarithms**. All logarithms in this book are natural logarithms. We express the natural logarithm of x as $\ln(x)$,

$$\ln(x) = \ln(e^b) = b$$

Note that $\ln(1) = 0$, using the laws of exponents. Table A.1 gives the logarithms of some powers of 10. Note that logarithms have a compressed scale compared to the original numbers. Since logarithms are exponents, they follow similar rules:

$$\ln(xy) = \ln(x) + \ln(y)$$
$$\ln(x/y) = \ln(x) - \ln(y)$$
$$\ln(x^a) = a \ln(x)$$

For example, if $x = 1000$ and $y = 10,000$, then

$$\ln(1000 \times 10,000) = \ln(1000) + \ln(10,000)$$
$$= 6.9077553 + 9.2103404$$
$$= 16.118096$$

What is the advantage of this? The value of xy is a multiplication problem, which by using logarithms we can turn into an addition problem. We need a way to go backwards, from the logarithm of a number to the number itself. By definition,

$$x = e^{\ln(x)} = \exp[\ln(x)]$$

When there is an **exponential function** with a complicated exponent, the notation **exp** is often used, so that $e^{(\bullet)} = \exp(\bullet)$. The exponential function is the **antilogarithm** because we can recover the value of x using it. Then,

$$1000 \times 10,000 = \exp(16.118096) = 10,000,000$$

You will not be doing lots of calculations like these, but the knowledge of logarithms and exponents is quite critical in economics and econometrics. As you will see in the following sections, many of the relationships we study in economics are formulated in terms of logarithms and exponents in real-world applications.

A.3 Linear Relationships

In economics and econometrics, we study linear and nonlinear relationships between variables. In this section we review basic characteristics of straight lines. We will also stress "marginal" analysis and marginal effects.

Let y and x be variables. The standard form for a linear relationship is

$$y = \beta_1 + \beta_2 x \tag{A.1}$$

In econometrics we use Greek letters for the slope and intercept. In Figure A.1 the slope is β_2 and the y-intercept is β_1. The symbol "Δ" represents "a change in," so "Δx" is read as "a change in x." The slope of the line is $\beta_2 = \Delta y / \Delta x$.

The slope parameter β_2 is very meaningful to economists as it is the **marginal effect** of a change in x on y. To see this, solve the **slope** definition $\beta_2 = \Delta y / \Delta x$ for Δy, obtaining

$$\Delta y = \beta_2 \Delta x \tag{A.2}$$

If x changes by one unit, $\Delta x = 1$, then $\Delta y = \beta_2$. The marginal effect, β_2, is always the same for a linear relationship like (A.1) because the slope is constant.

The **intercept** parameter indicates where the linear relationship crosses the vertical axis, that is, it is the value of y when x is zero,

$$y = \beta_1 + \beta_2 x = \beta_1 + \beta_2 0 = \beta_1$$

A simple economic example will give these definitions some context. Let $y =$ total cost of production (TC) and $x =$ quantity of output produced (Q), then $TC = \beta_1 + \beta_2 Q$. The intercept is the total cost incurred when output is zero, which in the short run is "fixed cost." The slope is the change in total cost over the change in output, $\Delta TC / \Delta Q$, which is the marginal cost, so in this simple example $\beta_2 = MC$.

For those of you who know calculus, recall that the **derivative** of a function is its slope, and in this case

$$\frac{dy}{dx} = \beta_2 \tag{A.3}$$

The derivative is the change in y given an infinitesimal change in x, and for a linear function like (A.1) it is constant and equal to $\beta_2 = \Delta y / \Delta x$. The "infinitesimal" does not matter here since the function is linear.

If our linear relationship is extended to include another variable, then

$$y = \beta_1 + \beta_2 x_2 + \beta_3 x_3 \tag{A.4}$$

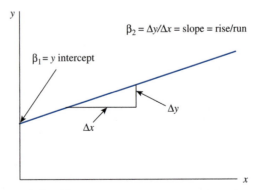

FIGURE A.1   A linear relationship.

This is the equation of a plane, with y-intercept β_1. The slope parameters must now be interpreted more carefully. The value of y is affected by both variables x_2 and x_3, and in order to deduce the marginal effect of either variable on y, we must hold the other constant and not let it change. This is the **ceteris paribus** assumption of economics, which means "holding all other factors constant." Then

$$\beta_2 = \frac{\Delta y}{\Delta x_2} \text{ given that } x_3 \text{ is held constant}$$

$$\beta_3 = \frac{\Delta y}{\Delta x_3} \text{ given that } x_2 \text{ is held constant}$$

(A.5)

Again, to give this some meaning, suppose that y is output Q, and x_2 is labor input, L, and x_3 is capital input, K. While not realistic, let us assume a linear production relationship,

$$Q = \beta_1 + \beta_2 L + \beta_3 K$$

Now,

$$\beta_2 = \frac{\Delta Q}{\Delta L} \text{ given that capital } K \text{ is held constant}$$

$$= MP_L, \text{ the marginal product of labor input}$$

(A.6)

Thus β_2 is interpreted as the marginal effect, once we make clear that all other things are held constant. Furthermore, the marginal effect is constant because of our assumption of a linear relationship in (A.4).

For those of you who have had some calculus, the simple derivative is replaced by a **partial derivative** in this multivariate context

$$\frac{\partial y}{\partial x_2} = \beta_2, \quad \frac{\partial y}{\partial x_3} = \beta_3$$

The partial derivative is the derivative with the additional assumption that all other variables are held constant; it is the slope and the marginal effect in the more general function. The words we have used in (A.5) and (A.6) describe partial derivatives of the linear relationship (A.4).

A.3.1 ELASTICITY

Another favorite tool of the economist is **elasticity**, which is the percentage change in one variable associated with a 1% change in another variable. The elasticity of y with respect to a change in x is

$$\varepsilon_{yx} = \frac{\Delta y/y}{\Delta x/x} = \frac{\Delta y}{\Delta x} \times \frac{x}{y} = slope \times \frac{x}{y}$$

(A.7)

The elasticity is seen to be a product of the slope of the relationship and the ratio of an x value to a y value. In a linear relationship, like Figure A.1, while the slope is constant, $\beta_2 = \Delta y/\Delta x$, the elasticity changes at every point on the line. For the linear function $y = 1 + 1x$, at the point $x = 2$ and $y = 3$, the elasticity is $\varepsilon_{yx} = \beta_2(x/y) = 1 \times (2/3) = 0.67$. That is, at the point $(x = 2, y = 3)$ a 1% change in x is associated with a 0.67% change in y. Specifically, at $x = 2$ a 1% ($1\% = 0.01$ in decimal form) change amounts to $\Delta x = 0.01 \times 2 = 0.02$. If x increases to $x = 2.02$, the value of y increases to 3.02. The **relative change** in y is $\Delta y/y = 0.02/3 = 0.0067$. This, however, is not the percentage change in y; it is the decimal equivalent. To obtain the percentage change in y, which we denote $\%\Delta y$, we multiply the relative change $\Delta y/y$ by 100. The **percentage change** in y is

$$\%\Delta y = 100 \times (\Delta y/y) = 100 \times 0.02/3 = 100 \times 0.0067 = 0.67\%$$

To summarize

$\Delta y/y =$ the relative change in y, which is a decimal	(A.8a)
$\%\Delta y =$ percentage change in y	(A.8b)
$\%\Delta y = 100 \times \dfrac{\Delta y}{y}$	(A.8c)

A.4 Nonlinear Relationships

The world is not linear. While linear relationships are intuitive and easy to work with, many real-world economic relationships are nonlinear, such as the total cost and production relationships we used as illustrations in the previous section. Consider the relationship between labor input x and the total output y, holding all other factors constant. The marginal product of labor declines as more labor is added, the phenomena that economists call diminishing returns, leading to a relationship between total output and labor input that is nonlinear, as shown in Figure A.2.

The slope of this curve is not constant. The slope measures the marginal effect of x on y, and for a nonlinear relationship like that in Figure A.2, the slope is different at every point on the curve. The changing slope tells us that the relationship is not linear. Since the slope is different at every point, we can talk only about the effect of small changes in x on y. In (A.2) we replace "Δ," the symbol for "a change in," by "d" that we will take to mean an "infinitesimal change in." The definition of slope at a single point is

$$dy = \beta_2 dx \qquad\qquad (A.9)$$

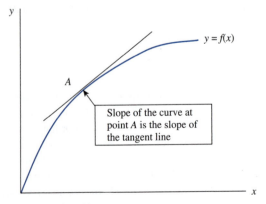

FIGURE *A.2* A nonlinear relationship.

Table A.2   **Some Useful Functions, Their Derivatives and Elasticities**

Name	Function	Slope $= dy/dx$	Elasticity
Linear	$y = \beta_1 + \beta_2 x$	β_2	$\beta_2 \dfrac{x}{y}$
Quadratic	$y = \beta_1 + \beta_2 x + \beta_3 x^2$	$\beta_2 + 2\beta_3 x$	$(\beta_2 + 2\beta_3 x)\dfrac{x}{y}$
Cubic	$y = \beta_1 + \beta_2 x + \beta_3 x^2 + \beta_4 x^3$	$\beta_2 + 2\beta_3 x + 3\beta_4 x^2$	$(\beta_2 + 2\beta_3 x + 3\beta_4 x^2)\dfrac{x}{y}$
Reciprocal	$y = \beta_1 + \beta_2 \dfrac{1}{x}$	$-\beta_2 \dfrac{1}{x^2}$	$-\beta_2 \dfrac{1}{xy}$
Log-log	$\ln(y) = \beta_1 + \beta_2 \ln(x)$	$\beta_2 \dfrac{y}{x}$	β_2
Log-linear	$\ln(y) = \beta_1 + \beta_2 x$	$\beta_2 y$	$\beta_2 x$
Linear-log	$y = \beta_1 + \beta_2 \ln(x)$	$\beta_2 \dfrac{1}{x}$	$\beta_2 \dfrac{1}{y}$

Rearranging this expression gives us (A.3); the derivative is a slope. With a linear equation the slope (derivative) is the constant $dy/dx = \beta_2$. However, with nonlinear equations like that in Figure A.2, the slope (derivative) is not constant but changes as x changes. Here is where knowing a bit of calculus comes in handy, because using the rules of calculus we can find derivatives of a function $y = f(x)$. In Table A.2 we give you formulas for the slopes (derivatives) of functions commonly used in econometrics. Note how they depend on x and/or y. Plots of the functions are given in Figure A.3. Given the slope of the curve, then the elasticity of y with respect to changes in x is given by a slightly modified equation (A.7),

$$\varepsilon_{yx} = \frac{dy/y}{dx/x} = \frac{dy}{dx} \times \frac{x}{y} = slope \times \frac{x}{y} \tag{A.10}$$

A.4.1 QUADRATIC FUNCTION

The quadratic function, $y = \beta_1 + \beta_2 x + \beta_3 x^2$, is the familiar parabola. The y-intercept is β_1. The shape of the curve is dominated by β_3. If $\beta_3 > 0$, then the curve is U-shaped, and representative of average or marginal cost functions, with increasing marginal effects. If $\beta_3 < 0$, then the curve is an inverted-U shape, useful for total product curves, total revenue curves, and curves that exhibit diminishing marginal effects. The slope (derivative) is zero at the point where the function reaches its maximum or minimum. The derivative is zero when $dy/dx = \beta_2 + 2\beta_3 x = 0$, or $x = -\beta_2/(2\beta_3)$.

A.4.2 CUBIC FUNCTION

The cubic function, $y = \beta_1 + \beta_2 x + \beta_3 x^2 + \beta_4 x^3$, can have two **inflection points**, where the function crosses its tangent line and changes from concave to convex, or vice versa. Cubic functions can be used for total cost and total product curves in economics. The derivative of total cost is marginal cost, and the derivative of total product is marginal product. If the "total" curves are cubic, then the "marginal" curves are quadratic functions, a U-shaped curve for marginal cost, and an inverted-U shape for marginal product.

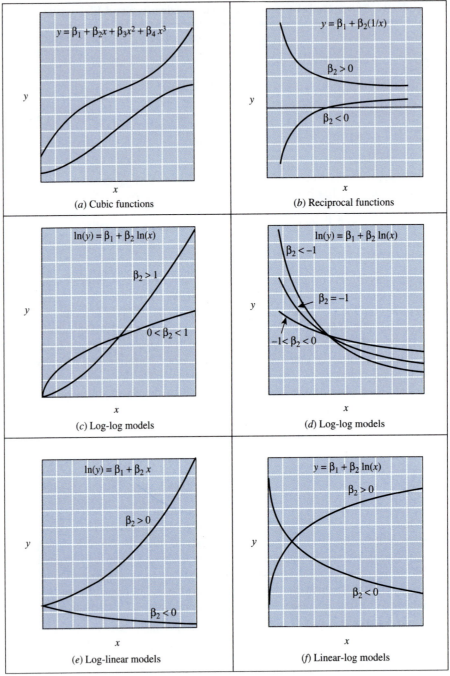

FIGURE A.3   Alternative Functional Forms.

A.4.3   RECIPROCAL FUNCTION

The reciprocal function is $y = \beta_1 + \beta_2(1/x) = \beta_1 + \beta_2 x^{-1}$. As x increases, y approaches the intercept, its **asymptote**, from above or below depending on the sign of β_2. The slope of this curve changes and flattens out as x increases. The elasticity also changes at each point and is opposite in sign to β_2. When $\beta_2 > 0$, the relationship between x and y is an inverse one and the elasticity is negative: a 1% increase in x leads to a reduction in y of $-\beta_2/(xy)\%$.

One possible example is the Phillips Curve, which describes an inverse relationship between growth in wages and the unemployment rate. If we let w_t be the wage rate in year t, then the percentage change in the wage rate from one year to the next is

$$\%\Delta w_t = \frac{w_t - w_{t-1}}{w_{t-1}} \times 100$$

If u_t = unemployment rate in year t, then the Phillips relation can be expressed as

$$\%\Delta w_t = \beta_1 + \beta_2 \frac{1}{u_t}$$

A.4.4 LOG-LOG FUNCTION

The log-log function, $\ln(y) = \beta_1 + \beta_2 \ln(x)$, is widely used to describe demand equations and production functions. The name "log-log" comes from the fact that the logarithm appears on both sides of the equation. In order to use this model, all values of y and x must be positive. The slopes of these curves change at every point, but the elasticity is constant and equal to β_2. The log-log function is a transformation of the equation $y = Ax^{\beta_2}$, with $\beta_1 = \ln(A)$.

Another useful way to think about the log-log function comes from closer inspection of its slope $dy/dx = \beta_2(y/x)$. Rearrange this so that $\beta_2 = (dy/y)/(dx/x)$. Thus the slope of the log-log function exhibits constant *relative* change, whereas the linear function displays constant absolute change.

If $\beta_2 = -1$, then $y = Ax^{-1}$ or $xy = A$. This curve has "unit" elasticity. If we let y = price and x = quantity demanded, then A = total revenue from sales. For every point on the curve $xy = A$, the area under the curve A (total revenue for the demand curve) is constant. Unit elasticity implies that a 1% increase in x is associated with a 1% decrease in y, so that the product xy remains constant.

If $\beta_2 > 0$, then y is an increasing function of x. If $\beta_2 > 1$, then the function increases at an increasing rate. That is, as x increases, the slope increases as well. If $0 < \beta_2 < 1$, then the function is increasing, but at a decreasing rate; as x increases the slope decreases.

A.4.5 LOG-LINEAR FUNCTION

The log-linear model, $\ln(y) = \beta_1 + \beta_2 x$, has a logarithmic term on the left-hand side of the equation and an untransformed (linear) variable on the right-hand side. Both its slope and elasticity change at each point and are the same sign as β_2. Using the antilogarithm we see that $\exp[\ln(y)] = y = \exp(\beta_1 + \beta x)$, so that the log-linear function is an exponential function. The function requires $y > 0$. The slope at any point is $\beta_2 y$, which for $\beta_2 > 0$ means that the marginal effect increases for larger values of y. An economist might say that this function is increasing at an increasing rate.

A.4.6 APPROXIMATING LOGARITHMS

A feature of logarithms that helps greatly in their economic interpretation in this case is that they can be approximated very simply. Let y_1 be a positive value of y, and let y_0 be a value of y that is "close" to y_1. The value of $\ln(y_1)$ can be approximated as

$$\ln(y_1) \cong \ln(y_0) + \frac{1}{y_0}(y_1 - y_0) \tag{A.11}$$

For example, let $y_1 = 1 + x$ and let $y_0 = 1$. Then, as long as x is small,

$$\ln(1 + x) \cong x$$

Also, subtract $\ln(y_0)$ from both sides of (A.11) to obtain

$$\ln(y_1) - \ln(y_0) = \Delta\ln(y) \cong \frac{1}{y_0}(y_1 - y_0) = \frac{\Delta y}{y_0} = \text{relative change in } y$$

The symbol $\Delta\ln(y)$ represents the "difference" between two logarithms. Then, using equation (A.8),

$$100\Delta\ln(y) = 100[\ln(y_1) - \ln(y_0)]$$

$$\cong 100 \times \frac{\Delta y}{y_0} \qquad \qquad (A.12)$$

$$= \%\Delta y = \text{percentage change in } y$$

This approximation works well for values of y_1 and y_0 that are close to each other.

You might well ask how close do y_1 and y_0 have to be before the approximation works well. Suppose that $y_0 = 1$. Then the percentage difference between y_1 and y_0 is

$$\%\Delta y = 100 \times \frac{\Delta y}{y_0} = 100(y_1 - 1)$$

The quantity we are approximating is $100\Delta\ln(y) = 100[\ln(y_1) - \ln(1)] = 100 \times \ln(y_1)$ since $\ln(1) = 0$. The percentage error in the approximation is

$$\%\text{approximation error} = 100\left[\frac{\%\Delta y - 100\Delta\ln(y)}{100\Delta\ln(y)}\right] = 100\left[\frac{(y_1 - 1) - \ln(y_1)}{\ln(y_1)}\right]$$

A few values are reported in Table A.3.

As you can see if y_1 and y_0 differ by 10% then the approximation error is 4.92%. If y_1 and y_0 differ by 20%, then the approximation error is 9.7%. How much approximation error are you willing to tolerate? If you lose 5% on an exam, you still receive an A. If you lose 10%, then you are down to a B.

A.4.7 APPROXIMATING LOGARITHMS IN THE LOG-LINEAR MODEL

With respect to the log-linear model, let us look at an increase in x from x_0 to x_1. The change in the log-linear model is from $\ln(y_0) = \beta_1 + \beta_2 x_0$ to $\ln(y_1) = \beta_1 + \beta_2 x_1$. Then subtracting

Table A.3 **Log Difference Approximation Error**

y_1	$\%\Delta y$	$100\Delta\ln(y)(\%)$	Approximation error (%)
1.01	1.00	0.995	0.50
1.05	5.00	4.88	2.48
1.10	10.00	9.53	4.92
1.15	15.00	13.98	7.33
1.20	20.00	18.23	9.70
1.25	25.00	22.31	12.04

the first equation from the second gives $\ln(y_1) - \ln(y_0) = \beta_2(x_1 - x_0) = \beta_2 \Delta x$. Multiply by 100 to obtain

$$100[\ln(y_1) - \ln(y_0)] \cong \%\Delta y$$
$$= 100\beta_2(x_1 - x_0) \tag{A.13}$$
$$= (100\beta_2) \times \Delta x$$

Thus, for example, a 1-unit increase in x leads to, approximately, a $100 \times \beta_2$ percent change in y. How accurate is this approximation? Let us put things in context. Suppose an electrician's hourly wage rate (in \$US) is determined by a union salary scale that depends only on $x =$ years of experience. Suppose the wage scale is

$$\ln(WAGE) = 3.4011974 + 0.10x$$

Recall that we can recover the wage from this equation by taking the antilogarithm, using the exponential function. The starting wage, at $x = 0$ years experience, is \$30 dollars per hour [using $\exp(3.4011974) = 30$]. After 1 year the hourly wage rate is \$33.155, which is an increase of 10.571%. Our approximate calculation, based only on the wage formula, is $\%\Delta WAGE \cong 100\beta_2\Delta x = 100(0.10)1 = 10.0$, giving a little over a 1/2% approximation error. For smaller values of β_2, or smaller values of Δx, the approximation error is less when using (A.13).

A.4.8 LINEAR-LOG FUNCTION

The linear-log model has a linear term on the left-hand side and a logarithmic term on the right-hand side. Because of the logarithm, this function requires $x > 0$. It is an increasing or decreasing function depending upon the sign of β_2. The slope of the function is β_2/x, so that as x increases the slope decreases in absolute magnitude. If $\beta_2 > 0$, then the function increases at a decreasing rate.

Consider an increase in x from x_0 to x_1. Then $y_0 = \beta_1 + \beta_2 \ln(x_0)$ and $y_1 = \beta_1 + \beta_2 \ln(x_1)$. Subtracting the former from the latter, and using the approximation developed for the log-linear model, gives

$$\Delta y = y_1 - y_0 = \beta_2[\ln(x_1) - \ln(x_0)]$$
$$= \frac{\beta_2}{100} \times 100[\ln(x_1) - \ln(x_0)]$$
$$\cong \frac{\beta_2}{100}(\%\Delta x)$$

The change in y is approximately $(\beta_2/100)$ times the percentage change in x. For example, in a production relationship, suppose output y is a function of only labor input x, and output is given by

$$y = \beta_1 + \beta_2 \ln(x) = 0 + 500\ln(x)$$

The approximate interpretation would be that a 10% change in x would lead to a 50 unit increase in output, based on the calculation

$$\Delta y = \frac{\beta_2}{100}(\%\Delta x) = \frac{500}{100} \times 10 = 50$$

If in fact x increases from 50 to 55, a 10% increase, then output increases by 47.65 units, so the approximation has an error of less than 3%.

> **REMARK:** This appendix was designed to remind you of mathematics concepts you
> have learned, but perhaps forgotten. If you plan to study economics further, or a field
> related to economics, start a collection of mathematics books so that you have ready
> references at your fingertips. At bookstore sales, scour the selections for used mathematics
> books. Also valuable are books with solved problems, such as *Schaum's Outline Series*
> (McGraw-Hill). Also, the Internet is filled with helpful sites on mathematics. For example,
> a Google search of "natural logarithm" yields over 300,000 hits.

A.5 Exercises

A.1* Express each of the following sums in summation notation.
   (a) $x_1 + x_2 + x_3 + x_4$
   (b) $x_3 + x_4$
   (c) $x_1 y_1 + x_2 y_2 + x_3 y_3 + x_4 y_4$
   (d) $x_1 y_2 + x_2 y_3 + x_3 y_4 + x_4 y_5$
   (e) $x_2 y_2^2 + x_3 y_3^2$
   (f) $(x_1 - y_1) + (x_2 - y_2) + (x_3 - y_3)$

A.2* Write out each of the following sums and compute where possible.
   (a) $\sum_{i=1}^4 (a + bx_i)$
   (b) $\sum_{i=1}^3 i^2$
   (c) $\sum_{x=0}^3 (x^2 + 2x + 2)$
   (d) $\sum_{x=2}^4 f(x+2)$
   (e) $\sum_{x=0}^2 f(x, y)$
   (f) $\sum_{x=2}^4 \sum_{y=1}^2 (x + 2y)$

A.3 Let X take four values, $x_1 = 1$, $x_2 = 2$, $x_3 = 3$, $x_4 = 4$.
   (a) Calculate the arithmetic average $\bar{x} = \sum_{i=1}^4 x_i / 4$.
   (b) Calculate $\sum_{i=1}^4 (x_i - \bar{x})$.
   (c) Calculate $\sum_{i=1}^4 (x_i - \bar{x})^2$.
   (d) Calculate $\sum_{i=1}^4 x_i^2 - 4\bar{x}^2$.
   (e) Show algebraically that $\sum_{i=1}^n (x_i - \bar{x})^2 = \sum_{i=1}^n x_i^2 - n\bar{x}^2$.

A.4 Show that $\sum_{i=1}^n (x_i - \bar{x})(y_i - \bar{y}) = \sum_{i=1}^n x_i y_i - n\bar{x}\bar{y}$.

A.5 Let $y = -3 + 0.8x$, where y is the quantity supplied of a good and x is the market
   price.
   (a) State the interpretation of the slope in economic terms.
   (b) Calculate the elasticity at $x = 10$ and $x = 50$, and state their interpretations.

A.6 Suppose the relationship between annual percentage change in wages and the
   unemployment rate, expressed as a percentage, is $\%\Delta w = -2 + 8 \times (1/u)$.

(a) Sketch the curve for values of u between 1 and 10.

(b) Where is the impact of a change in the unemployment rate the largest?

(c) If the unemployment rate is 5%, what is the marginal effect of an increase in the unemployment rate on the annual percentage change in wages?

A.7* Simplify the following expressions:

(a) $x^{1/2}x^{1/3}$

(b) $x^{2/3} \div x^{5/8}$

(c) $(x^4y^4)^{-1/2}$

A.8 (a) The velocity of light is 186,000 miles per second. Write the velocity of light in scientific notation.

(b) Find the number of seconds in a year and write in scientific notation.

(c) Express the distance light travels in 1 year in scientific notation.

A.9 Technology affects agricultural production by increasing yield over time. Let y_t = average wheat production (tonnes per hectare) for the period 1950–2000 ($t = 1, \ldots, 51$) in the Western Australia shire of Chapman Valley.

(a) Suppose production is defined by $y_t = 0.5 + 0.20 \ln(t)$. Plot this curve. Find the slope and elasticity at the point $t = 49$ (1998). State the economic interpretation of these values.

(b) Suppose production is defined by $y_t = 0.80 + 0.0004\,t^2$. Plot this curve. Find the slope and elasticity at the point $t = 49$ (1998). State the economic interpretation of these values.

A.10* Forensic scientists can deduce the amount of arsenic in drinking water from concentrations (in parts per million) in toenails. Let y = toenail concentration and x = drinking water concentration. The following three equations describe the relationship.

$$\ln(y) = 0.8 + 0.4\ln(x)$$
$$y = 1.5 + 0.2\ln(x)$$
$$\ln(y) = -1.75 + 20x$$

(a) Plot each of the functions for $x = 0$ to $x = 0.15$.

(b) Calculate the slope of each function at $x = 0.10$. State the interpretation of the slope.

(c) Calculate the elasticity of each function at $x = 0.10$ and give its interpretation.

A.11* Consider the numbers $x = 4567839$ and $y = 54937.11$.

(a) Write each number in scientific notation.

(b) Use scientific notation to obtain the product xy.

(c) Use scientific notation to obtain the quotient x/y.

(d) Use scientific notation to obtain the sum $x + y$. (*Hint:* Write each number as a numeric part times 10^6.)

Review of Probability Concepts

Learning Objectives

Based on the material in this appendix, you should be able to

1. Explain the difference between a random variable and its values, and give an example.

2. Explain the difference between discrete and continuous random variables, and give examples of each.

3. State the characteristics of a probability density function (*pdf*) for a discrete random variable, and give an example.

4. Compute probabilities of events, given a discrete probability function.

5. Explain the meaning of the following statement: "The probability that the discrete random variable takes the value 2 is 0.3."

6. Explain how the *pdf* of a continuous random variable is different from the *pdf* of a discrete random variable.

7. Show, geometrically, how to compute probabilities given a *pdf* for a continuous random variable.

8. Explain, intuitively, the concept of the mean, or expected value, of a random variable.

9. Use the definition of expected value for a discrete random variable, in equation (B.9), to compute expectations, given a *pdf* $f(x)$ and a function $g(x)$.

10. Define the variance of a discrete random variable, and explain in what sense the values of a random variable are more spread out if the variance is larger.

11. Use a joint *pdf* (table) for two discrete random variables to compute probabilities of joint events and to find the (marginal) *pdf* of each individual random variable.

12. Find the conditional *pdf* for one discrete random variable, given the value of another and their joint *pdf*.

13. Give an intuitive explanation of statistical independence of two random variables and state the conditions that must hold to prove statistical independence. Give examples of two independent random variables and two dependent random variables.

14. Define the covariance and correlation between two random variables, and compute these values given a joint probability function of two discrete random variables.

15. Find the mean and variance of a sum of random variables.

16. Use Table 1 and your computer software to compute probabilities involving normal random variables.

Keywords

binary variable	degrees of freedom	mode
binomial random variable	discrete random variable	normal distribution
cdf	expected value	*pdf*
chi-square distribution	experiment	probability
conditional *pdf*	*F*-distribution	probability density function
conditional probability	joint probability density	random variable
continuous random variable	function	standard deviation
correlation	marginal distribution	standard normal distribution
covariance	mean	statistical independence
cumulative distribution	median	variance
function		

We assume that you have had a basic probability and statistics course. In this appendix we review some essential probability concepts. Section B.1 defines discrete and continuous random variables. Probability distributions are discussed in Section B.2. Section B.3 introduces joint probability distributions, defines conditional probability, and statistical independence. In Section B.4 we review the properties of probability distributions, paying particular attention to expected values and variances. Section B.5 summarizes important facts about probability distributions that we use repeatedly: the normal, *t*, chi-square, and *F* distributions.

B.1 Random Variables

There is a saying: "The only things certain in life are death and taxes." While not the original intent, this bit of wisdom points out that almost everything we encounter in life is uncertain. We do not know how many games our football team will win next season. You do not know what score you will make on the first exam. We do not know what the stock market index will be tomorrow. These events, or outcomes, are uncertain, or random. Probability gives us a way to talk about possible outcomes.

A **random variable** is a variable whose value is unknown until it is observed; in other words it is a variable that is not perfectly predictable. Each random variable has a set of possible values it can take. If W is the number of games our football team wins next year, then W can take the values $0, 1, 2, \ldots, 13$, if there are a maximum of 13 games. This is a **discrete random variable** since it can take only a limited, or countable, number of values. Other examples of discrete random variables are the number of computers owned by a randomly selected household and the number of times you will visit your physician next year. A special case occurs when a random variable can only be one of two possible values—for example, in a phone survey, if you are asked if you are a college graduate or not, your answer can only be "yes" or "no." Outcomes like this can be characterized by a **binary variable** taking the values 1, if yes, or 0, if no. Binary variables are discrete and are used to represent qualitative characteristics such as gender (male or female), or race (white or nonwhite).

The U.S. *GNP* is yet another example of a random variable because its value is unknown until it is observed. In the second quarter of 2007, its value was $13839.4 billion (seasonally adjusted annual rate) dollars. Admittedly, the *GNP* is measured in dollars and it *can* be counted in whole dollars, but the value is so large that counting individual dollars serves no purpose. For practical purposes, *GNP* can take any value in the interval zero to infinity, and it is a **continuous random variable**. Other common macroeconomic variables, like interest rates, investment, and consumption, are also treated as continuous random variables. In Finance, stock market indices, like the Dow–Jones Industrial Index, are also treated as continuous. The key attribute of these variables that makes them continuous is that they can take any value in an interval.

B.2 Probability Distributions

Probability is usually defined in terms of **experiments**. Rolling a die is an experiment and we have six possible outcomes. If the die is fair, then each value will appear $1/6$-th of the time, if the experiment is performed numerous times. The probability of $1/6$-th comes from the fact that we have six equally likely outcomes. However, suppose the die is not fair. If X is the value that appears when the die is rolled, we can say that the probability that $X = 1$ is the proportion of time a "one" appears in a large number of rolls of the die. The die does not have to be "fair" for this definition to work. In general, the probability of an event is its "limiting relative frequency," or the proportion of time it occurs in the long run.

When collecting survey data, a person's educational attainment is often of interest. Let $X = 1$ if a randomly selected person has a college or advanced degree, and $X = 0$ if not. In 2002, 27% of the U.S. population aged 25 and older had at least a college degree[1]. Thus, in this population, the probability that $X = 1$ is 0.27, and this is written as $P(X = 1) = 0.27$. Probabilities must be positive and must sum to 1, so $P(X = 0) = 1 - P(X = 1) = 0.73$. In this example the random variable is discrete, and it makes sense to talk about the probability of specific values occurring.

We can summarize the probabilities of possible outcomes using a **probability density function (*pdf*)**. The *pdf* for a discrete random variable indicates the probability of each possible value occurring. For a discrete random variable X, the value of the probability density function $f(x)$ is the probability that the random variable X takes the value x, $f(x) = P(X = x)$. Because $f(x)$ is a probability, it must be true that $0 \leq f(x) \leq 1$, and if X takes n possible values $x_1, \ldots, x_n$, then the sum of their probabilities must be 1

$$f(x_1) + f(x_2) + \cdots + f(x_n) = 1.$$

For discrete random variables, the *pdf* might be presented as a table, a formula, or a graph. For the binary variable X, indicating whether a person is a college graduate or not, we might report the probabilities in tabular form as in Table B.1.

The probablities can also be reported in equation form as

$$f(x) = (0.27)^x (0.73)^{1-x}$$

which gives $f(1) = (0.27)^1 (0.73)^{1-1} = 0.27$ and $f(0) = (0.27)^0 (0.73)^{1-0} = 0.73$.

---

[1] U.S. Census Bureau, Current Population Survey, 2003 Annual Social and Economic Supplement, Table PINC-03.

Table B.1 **Probabilities of a College Degree**

College Degree	x	$f(x)$
No	0	0.73
Yes	1	0.27

As another example, let X be the number of quarters during a year (3-month periods) in which a college student has a job. The probabilities of the five possible values $x = 0, 1, 2, 3,$ and 4 might be $f(x) = 0.05, 0.50, 0.10, 0.10,$ and $0.25,$ respectively. We can represent the *pdf* for a discrete random variable as a bar graph, so that we can visualize the probabilities of alternative outcomes, as in Figure B.1.

The **cumulative distribution function (*cdf*)** is an alternative way to represent probabilities. The *cdf* of the random variable X, denoted $F(x)$, gives the probability that X is less than or equal to a specific value x. That is,

$$F(x) = P(X \le x)$$

The values of X, the *pdf*, and *cdf* are listed in Table B.2.

Using the *cdf* we can compute the probability that a student works *more* than 2 quarters as

$$P(X > 2) = 1 - P(X \le 2) = 1 - F(2) = 1 - 0.65 = 0.35$$

For standard probability distributions, statistical software programs have *cdf*s preprogrammed as functions, so that it is easy to do probability calculations.

For example, a **binomial random variable** X is the number of successes in n independent trials of identical experiments with probability of success p. Given the number of trials n and the probability of success p, binomial probabilities are given by

$$P(X = x) = f(x) = \binom{n}{x} p^x (1 - p)^{n-x} \tag{B.1}$$

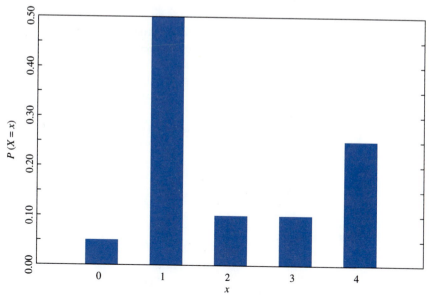

FIGURE *B.1* College employment probabilities.

Table B.2   A pdf and cdf

x	f(x)	F(x)
0	0.05	0.05
1	0.50	0.55
2	0.10	0.65
3	0.10	0.75
4	0.25	1.00

where

$$\binom{n}{x} = \frac{n!}{x!(n-x)!}$$

is the "number of combinations of n items taken x at a time," and $n!$ is "n factorial," which is given by $n! = n(n-1)(n-2)\cdots(2)(1)$. Suppose that the $n = 13$ games the LSU Tigers play are all independent and in each game they have the probability $p = 0.7$ of winning. What is the probability of them winning at least eight games during the season? The answer is

$$P(X \ge 8) = \sum_{x=8}^{13} f(x) = 1 - P(X \le 7) = 1 - F(7)$$

We could compute the probability by brute force using (B.1), but it would be tedious. Using the EViews command @cbinom for the *cdf* of a binomial random variable makes it child's play

$$1 - @cbinom(7, 13, 0.7) = 0.8346$$

Other software has similarly powerful commands.

Continuous random variables can take any value in an interval on the number line and have an uncountable number of values. Consequently the probability of any specific value is zero. For continuous random variables, we talk about outcomes being in a certain range. Figure B.2 illustrates the *pdf* $f(x)$ of a continuous random variable X that takes values from zero to infinity. Areas under the curve represent probabilities that X falls in an interval. For this distribution, $P(X \le 20) = 0.294$ and $P(X \le 40) = 0.649$. Then we can compute $P(20 \le X \le 40) = 0.649 - 0.294 = 0.355$.

How are these areas obtained? The integral from calculus gives the area under a curve, so that

$$P(20 \le X \le 40) = \int_{20}^{40} f(x)dx = 0.355$$

The cumulative distribution function is

$$P(X \le x) = \int_{-\infty}^{x} f(t)dt = F(x)$$

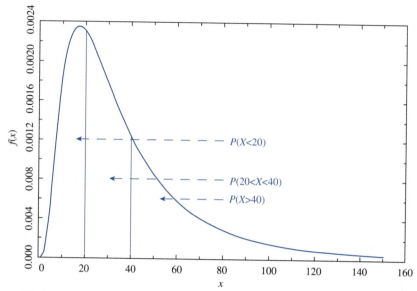

FIGURE **B.2** *pdf* of a continuous random variable.

where $F(x)$ is the *cdf* of X. The probability calculation is

$$P(20 \leq X \leq 40) = F(40) - F(20) = 0.649 - 0.294 = 0.355$$

We will not compute integrals in this book. Instead we will use the computer and compute *cdf* values using simple software commands.

B.3 Joint, Marginal, and Conditional Probability Distributions

Working with more than one random variable requires a **joint probability density function**. A joint *pdf* describes the probabilities of the values that combinations of the variables can take. In the United States during 2002, there were 185,183,000 people at least 25 years old.[2] Suppose we are interested in the probability of randomly selecting from this population someone with a 4-year college degree and who had earnings in 2002. Define two discrete random variables: X, characterizing a person's educational attainment, and Y, whether they had earned income during 2002.

$$X = \begin{cases} 1 & \text{high school diploma or less} \\ 2 & \text{some college} \\ 3 & \text{4-year college degree} \\ 4 & \text{advanced degree} \end{cases}$$

---

[2] U.S. Census Bureau, Current Population Survey, 2003 Annual Social and Economic Supplement, Table PINC-03.

Table B.3 **Joint Probability Function** $f(x, y)$

			x		
y		1	2	3	4
0		0.19	0.06	0.04	0.02
1		0.28	0.19	0.14	0.08

$$Y = \begin{cases} 0 & \text{if had no money earnings in 2002} \\ 1 & \text{if had positive money earnings in 2002} \end{cases}$$

The probabilities of randomly selecting someone with these characteristics is given by the joint *pdf* of X and Y, written as $f(x, y)$, which is given in Table B.3. The probability of randomly selecting someone from this population with a 4-year college degree and who had earnings in 2002 is 0.14, or

$$P(X = 3, Y = 1) = f(3, 1) = 0.14$$

Like the *pdf* of a single random variable, the sum of the joint probabilities is 1, $\sum_x \sum_y f(x, y) = 1$.

B.3.1   MARGINAL DISTRIBUTIONS

Given a joint probability density function, we can obtain the probability distributions of individual random variables, which are also known as **marginal distributions**. If X and Y are two discrete random variables, then

$$f_X(x) = \sum_y f(x, y) \quad \text{for each value } X \text{ can take}$$
$$f_Y(0) = \sum_x f(x, y) \quad \text{for each value } Y \text{ can take}$$
(B.2)

Note that the summations in (B.2) are over the *other* random variable—the one that we are eliminating from the joint probability density function. This operation is sometimes called "summing out" the unwanted variable in the table of joint probabilities. For example, using Table B.3,

$$f_Y(y) = \sum_{x=1}^{4} f(x, y) \quad y = 0, 1$$
$$f_Y(0) = 0.19 + 0.06 + 0.04 + 0.02 = 0.31$$

The joint and marginal distributions are often reported as in Table B.4.

If the random variables are continuous, the idea in (B.2) also works, but with integrals replacing the summation signs.

B.3.2   CONDITIONAL PROBABILITY

What is the probability that a randomly chosen individual will have income *given* that they have a 4-year college degree? This question is about the **conditional probability** of the

Table B.4 **Marginal Distributions for X and Y**

	x				
y	1	2	3	4	$f_Y(y)$
0	0.19	0.06	0.04	0.02	0.31
1	0.28	0.19	0.14	0.08	0.69
$f_X(x)$	0.47	0.25	0.18	0.10	1

outcome $(Y = 1)$ *given* that another has occurred $(X = 3)$. The effect of the conditioning is to reduce the set of possible outcomes. In this case we consider only the 18% of the population with a 4-year college degree. For discrete random variables, the probability that the random variable Y takes the value y *given* that $X = x$ is written $P(Y = y|X = x)$. This conditional probability is given by the **conditional *pdf*** $f(y|x)$:

$$f(y|x) = P(Y = y|X = x) = \frac{P(Y = y, X = x)}{P(X = x)} = \frac{f(x, y)}{f_X(x)} \qquad (B.3)$$

Using the marginal probability $P(X = 3) = 0.18$, the conditional *pdf* of Y given $X = 3$ is

y	$f(y|X = 3)$
0	$0.04/0.18 = 0.22$
1	$0.14/0.18 = 0.78$

The probability of randomly selecting a person with a positive income is 0.78 *if* only college graduates are considered (from the conditional *pdf*), but the probability of randomly selecting a person from the entire population with a positive income is $f_Y(1) = 0.69$ (from the marginal *pdf*). Knowing educational attainment tells us something about the probability of an individual having earned income. Such random variables are dependent in a statistical sense. Two random variables are **statistically independent** if the conditional probability that $Y = y$ given that $X = x$ is the same as the unconditional probability that $Y = y$. Knowing the value of X does not alter the probability distribution of Y. This means, if X and Y are independent random variables, then

$$P(Y = y|X = x) = P(Y = y) \qquad (B.4)$$

Equivalently, if X and Y are independent, then the conditional *pdf* of Y given $X = x$ is the same as the unconditional, or marginal, *pdf* of Y alone,

$$f(y|x) = \frac{f(x, y)}{f_X(x)} = f_Y(y) \qquad (B.5)$$

The converse is also true, so that if (B.4) or (B.5) are true for every possible pair of x and y values, then X and Y are statistically independent.

Solving (B.5) for the joint *pdf*, we can also say that X and Y are statistically independent if their joint *pdf* factors into the product of their marginal *pdf*s

$$f(x, y) = f_X(x) f_Y(y) \qquad (B.6)$$

Table B.5   A Population

1	2	3	4	4
2	3	3	4	4

If (B.6) is true for each and every pair of values x and y, then X and Y are statistically independent. This result extends to more than two random variables. If X, Y, and Z are statistically independent, the joint probability density function can be factored and written as $f(x, y, z) = f_X(x) \cdot f_Y(y) \cdot f_Z(z)$.

B.3.3   A SIMPLE EXPERIMENT

Let us illustrate the use of joint, marginal, and conditional probabilities in the context of a simple experiment. Consider the values in Table B.5 to be a population of interest. If we were to select one cell from the table at random (imagine cutting the table into 10 equally sized pieces of paper, stirring them up, and drawing one piece without looking) that would constitute a **random experiment**. Based on this random experiment we can define several random variables. For example, let X be the numerical value $(x = 1, 2, 3, 4)$ showing on the slip we draw, and let Y be a discrete random variable designating the color of the slip, with $Y = 1$ denoting a shaded slip and $Y = 0$ denoting a slip with no shading (white). The probability distributions for these two random variables are given in Tables B.6 and B.7. We can also specify the joint probability distribution of X and Y, given in Table B.8. Using this joint probability distribution, we can say that the probability of drawing a slip that is white $(Y = 0)$ with the numerical value 2 $(X = 2)$ is $P(X = 2, Y = 0) = 0.1$.

Using this simple experiment we can also illustrate the meaning of conditional probability. What is the probability of drawing a numeric value $X = 2$ given that the slip drawn is shaded, $(Y = 1)$? If we are restricting our attention to only the shaded slips, we are redefining the population of interest. Each numerical value has an equal chance of occurring in this new (shaded) population, so $P(X = x | Y = 1) = 0.25$ for $x = 1, 2, 3, 4$. Or, using the formula (B.3)

$$P(X = 1 | Y = 1) = \frac{P(X = 1, Y = 1)}{P(Y = 1)} = \frac{0.1}{0.4} = 0.25$$

Table B.6   Probability Distribution of Y

Shaded	Y	$f(y)$
No	0	0.6
Yes	1	0.4

Table B.7   Probability Distribution of X

X	$f(x)$
1	0.1
2	0.2
3	0.3
4	0.4

Table B.8 **Joint Probability Function** $f(x, y)$

	x			
y	1	2	3	4
0	0	0.1	0.2	0.3
1	0.1	0.1	0.1	0.1

A key point to remember is that by conditioning we are considering only the subset of a population for which the condition holds. Probability calculations are then based on the "new" population. Because the conditional probability $P(X = 1|Y = 1) = 0.25$ is not equal to the unconditional probability $P(X = 1) = 0.1$, from the full population, we conclude from (B.4) and (B.5) that the numerical value X and the shading Y are not independent random variables

B.4 Properties of Probability Distributions

Figures B.1 and B.2 give us a picture of how frequently values of the random variables will occur. Two key features of a distribution are its center (location) and width (dispersion). Measures of the center are the **mean, median,** and **mode**; measures of dispersion are **variance** and its square root—the **standard deviation.**

B.4.1   MEAN, MEDIAN, AND MODE

The **mean** of a random variable is given by its **mathematical expectation**. If X is a discrete random variable taking the values $x_1, \ldots, x_n$, then the mathematical expectation, or **expected value**, of X is

$$E(X) = x_1 P(X = x_1) + x_2 P(X = x_2) + \cdots + x_n P(X = x_n) \tag{B.7}$$

The expected value, or mean, of X is a weighted average of its values, the weights being the probabilities that the values occur. The mean is often symbolized by μ, or μ_X. It is the average value of the random variable in an infinite number of repetitions of the underlying experiment. For the binary variable in Table B.1

$$E(X) = 0 \times 0.73 + 1 \times 0.27 = 0.27$$

What does this mean? The expected value of X is *not* the value of X we expect to obtain when we draw a person at random from the population, because X only takes the values 0 and 1. The expected value of X, $E(X)$, is the average value of X if we randomly selected *many* individuals from the population. Similarly, if X is the value showing on the roll of a fair die, then the expected value of X is 3.5. If a die is rolled a large number of times, then the average of all values converges to 3.5.

For a discrete random variable, the probability that X takes the value x is given by its *pdf* $f(x)$, $P(X = x) = f(x)$. The expected value in (B.7) can be written equivalently as

$$\mu = E(X) = x_1 f(x_1) + x_2 f(x_2) + \cdots + x_n f(x_n) = \sum_{i=1}^{n} x_i f(x_i) = \sum_x x f(x) \tag{B.8}$$

For continuous random variables, the interpretation of the expected value of X is unchanged—it is the average value of X if many values are obtained by repeatedly performing the underlying random experiment. However, since there are now an uncountable number of values to sum, mathematically we must replace the "summation over all possible values" in (B.8) by the "integral over all possible values," so that for a continuous random variable X, its expected value is

$$\mu = E(X) = \int_{-\infty}^{\infty} x f(x) dx$$

The mean has a flaw as a measure of the center of a probability distribution in that it can be pulled by extreme values. For example, suppose a random variable X can take the values 1, 2, and 1,000,000 with probabilities 0.50, 0.49, and 0.01, respectively. The expected value of X is $E(X) = 10,001.48$. Is that representative of the center of the probability distribution? Perhaps not.

The two other popular measures of the center of a probability distribution are its median and mode. For a continuous distribution, the **median** of X is the value m such that $P(X > m) = P(X < m) = 0.5$. That is, the median value has half the probability on either side. A relevant example is given in Figure B.2, which very closely represents the distribution of earnings in the United States during 2002 for persons aged at least 25 years old (thousands of dollars). In that year the actual median income was \$30,553, and the mean income was \$39,849. While about 65% of incomes are below \$40,000, the fact that some individuals have very high incomes "pulls" the mean to the right. Such a distribution is said to be **skewed**. In symmetric distributions, like the familiar "bell-shaped curve" of the normal distribution, the mean and median are equal. The median for discrete distributions is somewhat more difficult to characterize and may not be unique. For the case in which X takes the values 1, 2, and 1,000,000 with probabilities 0.50, 0.49 and 0.01, respectively, the median is $X = 2$. For the example shown in Table B.2, the median value would be "slightly less than" $X = 1$, which puts us in a quandary because the next lower value is $X = 0$. One could resolve this case by taking $X = 1/2$ as a compromise.

The **mode** is the value of X at which the *pdf* is highest. In the case of Figure B.1, the mode is $X = 1$. For the continuous distribution in Figure B.2 the mode is at $X = 17.09$.

B.4.2   EXPECTED VALUES OF FUNCTIONS OF A RANDOM VARIABLE

Functions of random variables are also random. Expected values are obtained using calculations similar to those in (B.8). If X is a discrete random variable and $g(X)$ is a function of it, then

$$E[g(X)] = \sum_x g(x) f(x) \tag{B.9}$$

The rule also applies when X is continuous, but we replace the sum with an integral. Using (B.9) we can develop some frequently used rules that work for both discrete and continuous random variables. In general $E[g(X)] \neq g[E(X)]$. For example, $E(X^2) \neq [E(X)]^2$. But in certain cases, finding such expectations is easy. If a is a constant, then

$$E(aX) = aE(X) \tag{B.10}$$

To see how this result is obtained, we apply the definition in (B.9)

$$E[g(X)] = \sum g(x) f(x) = \sum axf(x) = a \sum xf(x) = aE(X)$$

In the final step we recognize $E(X)$ from its definition in (B.8). Similarly, if a and b are constants, then we can show that

$$E(aX + b) = aE(X) + b \tag{B.11}$$

If $g_1(X)$ and $g_2(X)$ are functions of X, then

$$E[g_1(X) + g_2(X)] = E[g_1(X)] + E[g_2(X)] \tag{B.12}$$

This rule extends to any number of functions. Remember the "singsong" phrase, the expected value of a sum is always the sum of the expected values.

The **variance** of a discrete or continuous random variable X is the expected value of

$$g(X) = [X - E(X)]^2$$

The variance of a random variable is important in characterizing the scale of measurement and the spread of the probability distribution. We give it the symbol σ^2, which is read "sigma squared." Algebraically, letting $E(X) = \mu$,

$$\text{var}(X) = \sigma^2 = E(X - \mu)^2 = E(X^2) - \mu^2 \tag{B.13}$$

The variance of a random variable is the *average* squared difference between the random variable X and its mean value μ. The larger the variance of a random variable the more "spread out" the values of the random variable are. Figure B.3 shows two distributions, both with mean $\mu = 3$. As we can see, the distribution with the smaller variance (the solid curve) is less spread out about its mean.

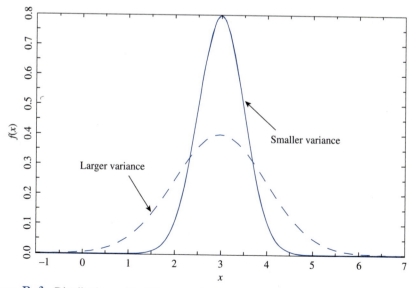

FIGURE **B.3** Distributions with different variances.

The square root of the variance is called the **standard deviation**; it is denoted by σ. It also measures the spread or dispersion of a distribution and has the advantage of being in the same units of measure as the random variable.

A useful property of variances is the following. Let a and b be constants, then

$$\text{var}(aX + b) = a^2 \text{var}(X) \tag{B.14}$$

This result is obtained by using the definition of variance and the rules of expectation, as follows:

$$\text{var}(aX + b) = E[aX + b - E(aX + b)]^2 = E(aX + b - a\mu - b)^2$$

$$= E[a(X - \mu)]^2 = a^2 E(X - \mu)^2 = a^2 \text{var}(X)$$

Two other characteristics of a probability distribution are its **skewness** and **kurtosis**. These are defined as

$$skewness = \frac{E[(X - \mu)^3]}{\sigma^3}$$

and

$$kurtosis = \frac{E[(X - \mu)^4]}{\sigma^4}$$

Skewness measures the lack of symmetry of a distribution. If the distribution is symmetric, then its *skewness* = 0. Distributions with long tails to the left are negatively skewed and *skewness* < 0. Distributions with long tails to the right are positively skewed and *skewness* > 0. Kurtosis measures the "peakedness" of a distribution. A distribution with large kurtosis has more values concentrated near the mean and a relatively high central peak. A distribution that is relatively flat has a lower kurtosis. The benchmark value for kurtosis is "3," which is the kurtosis of the *normal* distribution that we will discuss later in this appendix (Section B.5.1).

B.4.3 EXPECTED VALUES OF SEVERAL RANDOM VARIABLES

A rule similar to (B.9) exists for functions of several random variables. Let X and Y be discrete random variables with joint *pdf* $f(x, y)$. If $g(X, Y)$ is a function of them, then

$$E[g(X, Y)] = \sum_x \sum_y g(x, y) f(x, y) \tag{B.15}$$

Using (B.15) we can show that

$$E(X + Y) = E(X) + E(Y) \tag{B.16}$$

This follows by using the definition (B.15) and using rules of expectation, as follows:

$$E(X + Y) = \sum_x \sum_y (x + y) f(x, y) = \sum_x \sum_y xf(x, y) + \sum_x \sum_y yf(x, y)$$

$$= \sum_x x \sum_y f(x, y) + \sum_y y \sum_x f(x, y) = \sum_x xf(x) + \sum_y yf(y)$$

$$= E(X) + E(Y)$$

In the second line we have used (B.2) to obtain the marginal distributions of X and Y, and the fact that the order of summation does not matter. Using the same logic we can show that

$$E(aX + bY + c) = aE(X) + bE(Y) + c \qquad (B.17)$$

Using (B.15) we can also show that $E(XY) = E(X)E(Y)$ if X and Y are independent. To see this recall that if X and Y are independent then their joint *pdf* factors into the product of the marginal *pdf*'s, $f(x,y) = f(x)f(y)$. Then

$$E(XY) = E[g(X,Y)] = \sum_x \sum_y xy f(x,y) = \sum_x \sum_y xy f(x)f(y)$$
$$= \sum_x x f(x) \sum_y y f(y) = E(X)E(Y)$$

These rules can be extended to more random variables.

One particular application of (B.15) is the derivation of the **covariance** between X and Y. Define a function that is the product of X minus its mean times Y minus its mean,

$$g(X,Y) = (X - \mu_X)(Y - \mu_Y) \qquad (B.18)$$

In Figure B.4 we plot values of X and Y that have been constructed so that $E(X) = E(Y) = 0$. The values fall predominately in quadrants I and III, so that on average the value of $g(x,y) = (x - \mu_X)(y - \mu_Y) > 0$.

We define the covariance between two random variables as the expected (average) value of the product in (B.18),

$$\operatorname{cov}(X,Y) = \sigma_{XY} = E[(X - \mu_X)(Y - \mu_Y)] = E(XY) - \mu_X \mu_Y \qquad (B.19)$$

The covariance σ_{XY} of the variables in Figure B.4 is positive, which tells us that when x values are greater than their mean, then the y values also tend to be greater than their mean; when x values are below their mean, then the y values also tend to be less than their mean. If values tend primarily to fall in quadrants II and IV, then $g(x,y)$ will tend to be negative

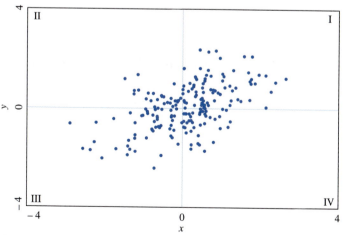

FIGURE **B.4** Correlated data.

and σ_{XY} will be negative. If values are spread evenly across the four quadrants and show neither positive nor negative association, then the covariance is zero. In summary, the sign of σ_{XY} tells us whether the two variables are positively associated or negatively associated.

Interpreting the actual value of σ_{XY} is difficult because X and Y may have different units of measurement. Scaling the covariance by the standard deviations of the variables eliminates the units of measurement and defines the **correlation** between X and Y

$$\rho = \frac{\text{cov}(X, Y)}{\sqrt{\text{var}(X)}\sqrt{\text{var}(Y)}} = \frac{\sigma_{XY}}{\sigma_X \sigma_Y} \tag{B.20}$$

As with the covariance, the correlation ρ between two random variables measures the degree of *linear* association between them. However, unlike the covariance, the correlation must lie between -1 and 1. Thus the correlation between X and Y is 1 or -1 if X is a perfect positive or negative linear function of Y. If there is *no linear* association between X and Y, then $\text{cov}(X, Y) = 0$ and $\rho = 0$. For other values of correlation, the magnitude of the absolute value $|\rho|$ indicates the "strength" of the linear association between the values of the random variables. In Figure B.4 the correlation between X and Y is $\rho = 0.5$.

If X and Y are independent random variables, then the covariance and correlation between them are zero. The converse of this relationship is *not* true. Independent random variables X and Y have zero covariance, indicating that there is no linear association between them. However, just because the covariance or correlation between two random variables is zero *does not* mean that they are necessarily independent. There may be more complicated nonlinear associations such as $X^2 + Y^2 = 1$.

In (B.16) we obtain the expected value of a sum of random variables. We obtain similar rules for variances. If a and b are constants, then

$$\text{var}(aX + bY) = a^2 \text{var}(X) + b^2 \text{var}(Y) + 2ab\,\text{cov}(X, Y) \tag{B.21}$$

$$\text{var}(X + Y) = \text{var}(X) + \text{var}(Y) + 2\,\text{cov}(X, Y) \tag{B.22}$$

$$\text{var}(X - Y) = \text{var}(X) + \text{var}(Y) - 2\,\text{cov}(X, Y) \tag{B.23}$$

If X and Y are independent, or if $\text{cov}(X, Y) = 0$, then

$$\text{var}(aX + bY) = a^2 \text{var}(X) + b^2 \text{var}(Y) \tag{B.24}$$

$$\text{var}(X \pm Y) = \text{var}(X) + \text{var}(Y) \tag{B.25}$$

These rules extend to more random variables. For example, if X, Y, and Z are independent, or uncorrelated, random variables, then the variance of the sum is the sum of the variances,

$$\text{var}(X + Y + Z) = \text{var}(X) + \text{var}(Y) + \text{var}(Z)$$

B.4.4   THE SIMPLE EXPERIMENT AGAIN

In Section B.3.3 we introduced a simple example leading to the probability distributions of the random variables X and Y in Tables B.6 and B.7, and the joint distribution in Table B.8. Let us use this example to review some key concepts introduced in this section.

The expected value of the random variable X, using the probability distribution in Table B.7, is

$$E(X) = \sum_{x=1}^{4} x f(x) = (1 \times 0.1) + (2 \times 0.2) + (3 \times 0.3) + (4 \times 0.4) = 3 = \mu_X$$

What does this mean? Drawing a cell at random from Table B.5 constitutes an experiment. Observe the numerical value X. If we repeat this experiment many times, the values $x = 1, 2, 3,$ and 4 will appear 10%, 20%, 30%, and 40% of the time, respectively. The *average* of all the numerical values will approach $\mu_X = 3$, as the number of draws becomes large. The key point is that the expected value of the random variable is the average value that occurs in many repeated trials of an experiment.

Similarly, the variance of the random variable X is

$$\begin{aligned}
\sigma_X^2 &= E(X - \mu_X)^2 \\
&= [(1-3)^2 \times 0.1] + [(2-3)^2 \times 0.2] + [(3-3)^2 \times 0.3] + [(4-3)^2 \times 0.4] \\
&= (4 \times 0.1) + (1 \times 0.2) + (0 \times 0.3) + (1 \times 0.4) \\
&= 1
\end{aligned}$$

In the many repeated experiments, the average of the numerical values $(X-3)^2$ is 1. The average of the squared difference between the values of the random variable and its mean is the variance of the random variable.

B.5 Some Important Probability Distributions

B.5.1 THE NORMAL DISTRIBUTION

In the previous sections we discussed random variables and their probability density functions in a general way. In real economic contexts some specific probability density functions have been found to be very useful. The most important is the normal distribution. If X is a normally distributed random variable with mean μ and variance σ^2, it can be symbolized as $X \sim N(\mu, \sigma^2)$. The *pdf* of X is

$$f(x) = \frac{1}{\sqrt{2\pi\sigma^2}} \exp\left[\frac{-(x-\mu)^2}{2\sigma^2}\right], \quad -\infty < x < \infty \tag{B.26}$$

where $\exp[a]$ denotes the exponential function e^a. The mean μ and variance σ^2 are the parameters of this distribution and determine its center and dispersion. The range of the continuous normal random variable is from minus infinity to plus infinity. Pictures of the normal probability density functions are given in Figure B.5 for various values of the mean and variance. Note that the normal distribution is symmetric, so that its skewness $= 0$ and its kurtosis $= 3$.

Like all continuous random variables, probabilities involving normal random variables are found as areas under probability density functions. For calculating probabilities both computer software and tabled values make use of the relation between a normal random variable and its "standardized" equivalent. A **standard normal random variable** is one that has a normal probability density function with mean 0 and variance 1. If $X \sim N(\mu, \sigma^2)$, then

$$Z = \frac{X - \mu}{\sigma} \sim N(0, 1) \tag{B.27}$$

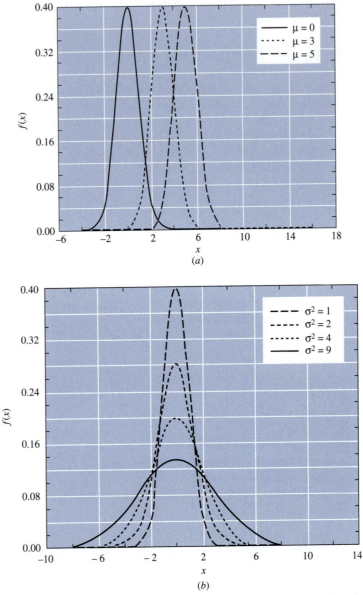

FIGURE **B.5**   (*a*) Normal probability density functions with means μ and variance 1. (*b*) With mean 0 and variance σ^2.

The *cdf* for the standardized normal variable Z is so widely used that it is given its own special symbol, $\Phi(z) = P(Z \le z)$. Computer programs, and Table 1 at the end of this book, give values of $\Phi(z)$. To calculate normal probabilities, remember that the distribution is symmetric, so that $P(Z > a) = P(Z < -a)$, and $P(Z > a) = P(Z \ge a)$, since the probability of any one point is zero for a continuous random variable. If $X \sim N(\mu, \sigma^2)$ and a and b are constants, then

$$P(X \le a) = P\left(\frac{X - \mu}{\sigma} \le \frac{a - \mu}{\sigma}\right) = P\left(Z \le \frac{a - \mu}{\sigma}\right) = \Phi\left(\frac{a - \mu}{\sigma}\right) \qquad \text{(B.28)}$$

$$P(X > a) = P\left(\frac{X - \mu}{\sigma} > \frac{a - \mu}{\sigma}\right) = P\left(Z > \frac{a - \mu}{\sigma}\right) = 1 - \Phi\left(\frac{a - \mu}{\sigma}\right) \tag{B.29}$$

$$P(a \le X \le b) = P\left(\frac{a - \mu}{\sigma} \le Z \le \frac{b - \mu}{\sigma}\right) = \Phi\left(\frac{b - \mu}{\sigma}\right) - \Phi\left(\frac{a - \mu}{\sigma}\right) \tag{B.30}$$

For example, if $X \sim N(3, 9)$, then

$$P(4 \le X \le 6) = P(0.33 \le Z \le 1) = \Phi(1) - \Phi(0.33) = 0.8413 - 0.6293 = 0.2120$$

An interesting and useful fact about the normal distribution is that a weighted sum of normal random variables has a normal distribution. That is, if $X_1 \sim N(\mu_1, \sigma_1^2)$ and $X_2 \sim N(\mu_2, \sigma_2^2)$, then

$$Y = a_1 X_1 + a_2 X_2 \sim N(\mu_Y = a_1 \mu_1 + a_2 \mu_2, \sigma_Y^2 = a_1^2 \sigma_1^2 + a_2^2 \sigma_2^2 + 2a_1 a_2 \sigma_{12}) \tag{B.31}$$

B.5.2   THE CHI-SQUARE DISTRIBUTION

Chi-square random variables arise when standard normal random variables are squared. If $Z_1, Z_2, \ldots, Z_m$ denote m *independent* $N(0, 1)$ random variables, then

$$V = Z_1^2 + Z_2^2 + \cdots + Z_m^2 \sim \chi_{(m)}^2 \tag{B.32}$$

The notation $V \sim \chi_{(m)}^2$ is read as: the random variable V has a chi-square distribution with m **degrees of freedom**. The degrees of freedom parameter m indicates the number of *independent* $N(0, 1)$ random variables that are squared and summed to form V. The value of m determines the entire shape of the chi-square distribution, including its mean and variance

$$E(V) = E\left(\chi_{(m)}^2\right) = m$$
$$\text{var}(V) = \text{var}\left(\chi_{(m)}^2\right) = 2m \tag{B.33}$$

In Figure B.6 graphs of the chi-square distribution for various degrees of freedom are presented. The values of V must be non-negative, $v \ge 0$, because V is formed by squaring and summing m standardized normal $N(0, 1)$ random variables. The distribution has a long tail, or is *skewed*, to the right. As the degrees of freedom m gets larger, however, the distribution becomes more symmetric and "bell-shaped." In fact, as m gets large the chi-square distribution converges to, and essentially becomes, a normal distribution.

The 90th, 95th, and 99th percentile values of the chi-square distribution for selected values of the degrees of freedom are given in Table 3 at the end of the book. These values are often of interest in hypothesis testing.

B.5.3   THE *t*-DISTRIBUTION

A "t" random variable (no upper case) is formed by dividing a standard normal random variable $Z \sim N(0, 1)$ by the square root of an *independent* chi-square random variable, $V \sim \chi_{(m)}^2$, that has been divided by its degrees of freedom m. If $Z \sim N(0, 1)$ and $V \sim \chi_{(m)}^2$, and if Z and V are independent, then

$$t = \frac{Z}{\sqrt{V/m}} \sim t_{(m)} \tag{B.34}$$

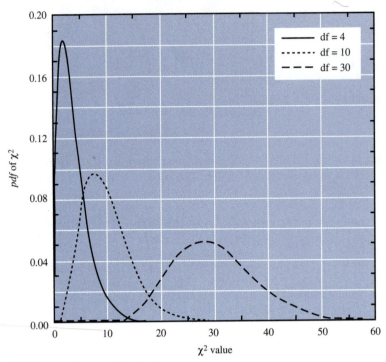

FIGURE **B.6**   The chi-square distribution.

The t-distribution's shape is completely determined by the degrees of freedom parameter, m, and the distribution is symbolized by $t_{(m)}$.

Figure B.7 shows a graph of the t-distribution with $m = 3$ degrees of freedom relative to the $N(0, 1)$. Note that the t-distribution is less "peaked" and more spread out than the $N(0, 1)$. The t-distribution is symmetric, with mean $E(t_{(m)}) = 0$ and variance $\text{var}(t_{(m)}) = m/(m - 2)$. As the degrees of freedom parameter $m \to \infty$, the $t_{(m)}$ distribution approaches the standard normal $N(0, 1)$.

Computer programs have functions for the *cdf* of t-random variables that can be used to calculate probabilities. Since certain probabilities are widely used, Table 2 at the back of this book, and also inside the front cover, contains frequently used percentiles of t-distributions, called **critical values** of the distribution. For example, the 95th percentile of a t-distribution with 20 degrees of freedom is $t_{(0.95,20)} = 1.725$. The t-distribution is symmetric, so Table 2 shows only the right tail of the distribution.

B.5.4   THE F-DISTRIBUTION

An F random variable is formed by the ratio of two independent chi-square random variables that have been divided by their degrees of freedom. If $V_1 \sim \chi^2_{(m_1)}$ and $V_2 \sim \chi^2_{(m_2)}$ and if V_1 and V_2 are independent, then

$$F = \frac{V_1/m_1}{V_2/m_2} \sim F_{(m_1,m_2)} \tag{B.35}$$

The F-distribution is said to have m_1 *numerator degrees of freedom* and m_2 *denominator degrees of freedom*. The values of m_1 and m_2 determine the shape of the distribution, which

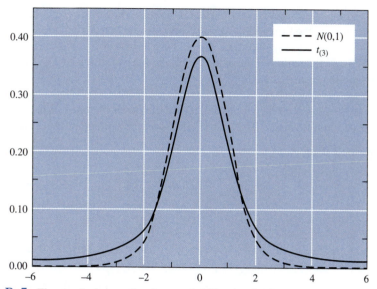

FIGURE *B.7* The standard normal and $t_{(3)}$ probability density functions.

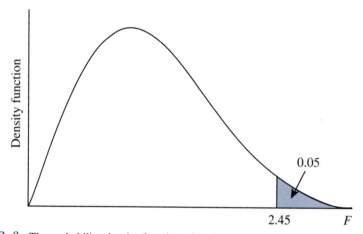

FIGURE *B.8* The probability density function of an $F_{(8,20)}$ random variable.

in general looks like Figure B.8. The range of the random variable is $(0, \infty)$ and it has a long tail to the right. For example, the 95th percentile value for an F-distribution with $m_1 = 8$ numerator degrees of freedom and $m_2 = 20$ denominator degrees of freedom is $F_{(0.95,8,20)} = 2.45$. Critical values for the F-distribution are given in Table 4 (the 95 percentile) and Table 5 (the 99 percentile).

B.6 **Exercises**

B.1* Let X be a discrete random variable with values $x = 0, 1, 2$ and probabilities $P(X = 0) = 0.25$, $P(X = 1) = 0.50$, and $P(X = 2) = 0.25$, respectively.
   (a) Find $E(X)$.
   (b) Find $E(X^2)$.
   (c) Find $\text{var}(X)$.
   (d) Find the expected value and variance of $g(X) = 3X + 2$.

B.2   Let X be a discrete random variable that is the value shown on a single roll of a fair die.
   (a) Represent the probability density function $f(x)$ in tabular form.
   (b) What is the probability that $X = 4$? That $X = 4$ or $X = 5$?
   (c) What is the expected value of X? Explain the meaning of $E(X)$ in this case.
   (d) Find the expected value of X^2.
   (e) Find the variance of X.
   (f) Obtain a die. Roll it 20 times and record the values obtained. What is the average of the first 5 values? The first 10? What is the average of the 20 rolls?

B.3   Let X be a continuous random variable whose probability density function is

$$f(x) = \begin{cases} 2x & 0 \le x \le 1 \\ 0 & otherwise \end{cases}$$

   (a) Sketch the probability density function $f(x)$.
   (b) Geometrically calculate the probability that X falls between 0 and $1/2$.
   (c) Geometrically calculate the probability that X falls between $1/4$ and $3/4$.

B.4   Let the binary random variable X have $pdf\, f(x) = p^x(1-p)^{1-x}$ for $x = 0, 1$.
   (a) Find the mean and variance of X.
   (b) Let $X_1, \ldots, X_n$ be independent discrete $(0,1)$ random variables each with probability density function $f(x)$. The random variable $B = X_1 + X_2 + \cdots + X_n$ has a binomial distribution with parameters n and p. The values of B are $b = 0, \ldots, n$ and represent the number of "successes" (i.e., $X_i = 1$) in n independent trials of an experiment, each with probability p of success. Calculate the mean and variance of B using the rules of expected values and variances. [*Hint:* What is the expected value of a sum? The variance?]
   (c) Let $X_1, \ldots, X_n$ be independent discrete $(0, 1)$ random variables with probability density functions $f(x)$. The random variable $B = X_1 + X_2 + \cdots + X_n$ has a binomial distribution. The random variable $Y = B/n$ is the proportion of successes in n trials of an experiment. Find the mean and variance of Y using the rules of expected values and variances.

B.5   The joint probability density function of two discrete random variables X and Y is given by the following table:

		Y		
		1	3	9
	2	1/8	1/24	1/12
X	4	1/4	1/4	0
	6	1/8	1/24	1/12

   (a) Find the marginal probability density function of Y.
   (b) Find the conditional probability density function of Y given that $X = 2$.
   (c) Find the covariance of X and Y.
   (d) Are X and Y independent?

B.6* Consider the population in Table B.5 and the joint distribution of the random variables X and Y in Table B.8, described in Section B.3.3.
   (a) Find the expected value and variance of the random variable Y, using the probability distribution in Table B.6.

(b) Find the covariance between X and Y.

(c) Find the correlation between X and Y.

B.7 Let $X_1, X_2, \ldots, X_n$ be independent random variables which all have the same probability distribution, with mean μ and variance σ^2. Let

$$\overline{X} = \frac{1}{n} \sum_{i=1}^{n} X_i$$

(a) Use the properties of expected values to show that $E(\overline{X}) = \mu$.

(b) Use the properties of variance to show that $\text{var}(\overline{X}) = \sigma^2/n$. How have you used the assumption of independence?

B.8 Suppose that Y_1, Y_2, Y_3 is a sample of observations from a $N(\mu, \sigma^2)$ population but that Y_1, Y_2, and Y_3 are *not* independent. In fact suppose

$$\text{cov}(Y_1, Y_2) = \text{cov}(Y_2, Y_3) = \text{cov}(Y_1, Y_3) = 0.5\sigma^2$$

Let $\overline{Y} = (Y_1 + Y_2 + Y_3)/3$.

(a) Find $E(\overline{Y})$

(b) Find $\text{var}(\overline{Y})$

B.9*- The length of life (in years) of a personal computer is approximately normally distributed with mean 2.9 years and variance 1.96 years.

(a) What fraction of computers will fail in the first year?

(b) What fraction of computers will last 4 years or more?

(c) What fraction of computers will last at least 2 years?

(d) What fraction of computers will last more than 2.5 years but less than 4 years?

(e) If the manufacturer adopts a warranty policy in which only 5% of the computers have to be replaced, what will be the length of the warranty period?

B.10 Based on long years of experience, an instructor in the principles of economics has determined that in her class the probability distribution of X, the number of students absent on Mondays, is as follows:

x	0	1	2	3	4	5	6	7
$f(x)$	0.005	0.025	0.310	0.340	0.220	0.080	0.019	0.001

(a) Sketch a probability function of X.

(b) Find the probability that on a given Monday either two or three or four students will be absent.

(c) Find the probability that on a given Monday more than three students are absent.

(d) Compute the expected value of the random variable X. Interpret this expected value.

(e) Compute the variance and standard deviation of the random variable X.

(f) Compute the expected value and variance of $Y = 7X + 3$.

B.11* Let X be a continuous random variable with probability density function given by

$$f(x) = -0.5x + 1, \quad 0 \leq x \leq 2$$

(a) Graph the density function $f(x)$.

(b) Find the total area beneath $f(x)$ for $0 \leq x \leq 2$.

(c) Find $P(X \geq 1)$.

(d) Find $P(X \leq 0.5)$.

(e) Find $P(X = 1.5)$.

B.12   Suppose a certain mutual fund has an annual rate of return that is approximately normally distributed with mean (expected value) 10% and standard deviation 4%. Use Table 1 for parts (a)–(c).

(a) Find the probability that your 1-year return will be negative.

(b) Find the probability that your 1-year return will exceed 15%.

(c) If the mutual fund managers modify the composition of its portfolio, they can raise its mean annual return to 12%, but this change will also raise the standard deviation of returns to 5%. Answer parts (a) and (b) in light of these decisions. Would you advise the fund managers to make this portfolio change?

(d) Verify your computations in (a)–(c) using your computer software.

B.13* An investor holds a portfolio consisting of two stocks. She puts 25% of her money in Stock A and 75% into Stock B. Stock A has an expected return of $R_A = 8\%$ and a standard deviation of $\sigma_A = 12\%$. Stock B has an expected return of $R_B = 15\%$ with a standard deviation of $\sigma_B = 22\%$. The portfolio return is $P = 0.25R_A + 0.75R_B$.

(a) Compute the expected return on the portfolio.

(b) Compute the standard deviation of the returns on the portfolio assuming that the two stocks' returns are perfectly positively correlated.

(c) Compute the standard deviation of the returns on the portfolio assuming that the two stocks' returns have a correlation of 0.5.

(d) Compute the standard deviation of the returns on the portfolio assuming that the two stocks' returns are uncorrelated.

Appendix C

Review of Statistical Inference

Learning Objectives

Based on the material in this appendix you should be able to

1. Discuss the difference between a population and a sample, and why we use samples of data as a basis for inference about population parameters.

2. Connect the concepts of a population and a random variable, indicating how the probability density function of a random variable, and the expected value and variance of the random variable, inform us about the population.

3. Explain the difference between the population mean and the sample mean.

4. Explain the difference between an estimate and an estimator, and why the latter is a random variable.

5. Explain the terms sampling variation and sampling distribution.

6. Explain the concept of unbiasedness, and use the rules of expected values to show that the sample mean is unbiased.

7. Explain why we prefer unbiased estimators with smaller variances to those with larger variances.

8. Describe the central limit theorem, and its implications for statistical inference.

9. Explain the relation between the population "standard deviation" and the standard error of the sample mean.

10. Explain the difference between point and interval estimation, and construct and interpret interval estimates of a population mean given a sample of data.

11. Give, in simple terms, a clarification of what the phrase "95% level of confidence" does and does not mean in relation to interval estimation.

12. Explain the purpose of hypothesis testing, and list the elements that must be present when carrying out a test.

13. Discuss the implications of the possible alternative hypotheses when testing the null hypothesis $H_0 : \mu = 7$. Give an economic example in which this hypothesis might be tested against one of the alternatives.

14. Describe the level of significance of a test, and the difference between the level of significance and the p-value of a test.

15. Define Type I error, and its relationship to the level of significance of a test.

16. Explain the difference between one-tail tests and two-tail tests and when one is preferred to the other.

17. Explain the difference and implications between the statements "I accept the null hypothesis" and "I do not reject the null hypothesis."

18. Give an intuitive explanation of maximum likelihood estimation, and describe the properties of the maximum likelihood estimator.

19. List the three types of tests associated with maximum likelihood estimation and comment on their similarities and differences.

Keywords

alternative hypothesis	likelihood function	sample variance
asymptotic distribution	likelihood ratio test	sampling distribution
BLUE	linear estimator	sampling variation
central limit theorem	log-likelihood function	standard error
central moments	maximum likelihood	standard error of the mean
estimate	estimation	standard error of the estimate
estimator	null hypothesis	statistical inference
experimental design	point estimate	test statistic
information measure	population parameter	two-tail tests
interval estimate	p-value	Type I error
Lagrange multiplier test	random sample	Type II error
law of large numbers	rejection region	unbiased estimators
level of significance	sample mean	Wald test

Economists are interested in relationships between economic variables. For example, how much can we expect the sales of Frozen Delight ice cream to rise if we reduce the price by 5%? How much will household food expenditure rise if household income rises by $100 per month? Questions such as these are the main focus of this book.

However, sometimes questions of interest focus on a single economic variable. For example, an airplane seat designer must consider the average hip size of passengers in order to allow adequate room for each person, while still designing the plane to carry the profit maximizing number of passengers. What is the average hip size, or more precisely hip width, of U.S. flight passengers? If a seat 18 inches wide is planned, what percent of customers will not be able to fit? Questions like this must be faced by manufacturers of everything from golf carts to women's jeans. How can we answer these questions? We certainly cannot take the measurements of every man, woman, and child in the U.S. population. This is a situation when statistical inference is used. Infer means "to conclude by reasoning from something known or assumed." **Statistical inference** means that we will draw conclusions about a population based on a sample of data.

C.1 A Sample of Data

To carry out statistical inference we need data. The data should be obtained from the population in which we are interested. For the airplane seat designer this is essentially the entire U.S. population above the age of two, since small children can fly "free" on the laps of

Table C.1 **Sample Hip Size Data**

14.96	14.76	15.97	15.71	17.77
17.34	17.89	17.19	13.53	17.81
16.40	18.36	16.87	17.89	16.90
19.33	17.59	15.26	17.31	19.26
17.69	16.64	13.90	13.71	16.03
17.50	20.23	16.40	17.92	15.86
15.84	16.98	20.40	14.91	16.56
18.69	16.23	15.94	20.00	16.71
18.63	14.21	19.08	19.22	20.23
18.55	20.33	19.40	16.48	15.54

their suffering parents. A separate branch of statistics, called **experimental design**, is concerned with the question of how to actually collect a representative sample. How would you proceed if you were asked to obtain 50 measurements of hip size that is representative of the entire population? This is not such an easy task. Ideally the 50 individuals will be randomly chosen from the population, in such a way that there is no pattern of choices. Suppose we focus on only the population of adult flyers, since usually there are few children on planes. Our experimental design specialist draws a sample that is shown in Table C.1 and stored in the file *hip.dat*.

A first step when analyzing a sample of data is to examine it visually. Figure C.1 is a histogram of the 50 data points. Based on this figure the "average" hip size in this sample seems to be between 16 and 18 inches. For our profit maximizing designer this casual estimate is not sufficiently precise. In the next section we set up an econometric model that will be used as a basis for inference in this problem.

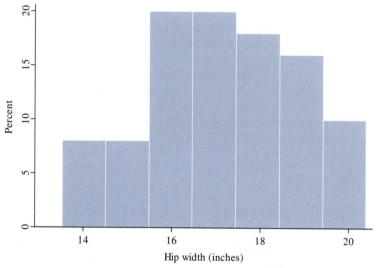

FIGURE *C.1* Histogram of hip sizes.

C.2 An Econometric Model

The data in Table C.1 were obtained by sampling. Sampling from a population is an experiment. The variable of interest in this experiment is an individual's hip size. Before the experiment is performed we do not know what the values will be, thus the hip size of a randomly chosen person is a random variable. Let us denote this random variable as Y. We choose a sample of $N = 50$ individuals, $Y_1, Y_2, \ldots, Y_N$, where each Y_i represents the hip size of a different person. The data values in Table C.1 are specific values of the variables, which we denote as $y_1, y_2, \ldots, y_N$. We assume that the population has a center, which we describe by the expected value of the random variable Y,

$$E(Y) = \mu \tag{C.1}$$

We use the Greek letter μ ("mu") to denote the mean of the random variable Y, and also the mean of the population we are studying. Thus if we knew μ we would have the answer to the question "What is the average hip size of adults in the United States?" To indicate its importance to us in describing the population we call μ a **population parameter**, or, more briefly, a parameter. Our objective is to use the sample of data in Table C.1 to make inferences, or judgments, about the unknown population parameter μ.

The other random variable characteristic of interest is its variability, which we measure by its variance,

$$\operatorname{var}(Y) = E[Y - E(Y)]^2 = E[Y - \mu]^2 = \sigma^2 \tag{C.2}$$

The variance σ^2 is also an unknown population parameter. As described in Appendix B, the variance of a random variable measures the "spread" of a probability distribution about the population mean, with a larger variance meaning a wider spread, as shown in Figure B.3. In the context of the hip data, the variance tells us how much hip sizes can vary from one randomly chosen person to the next. To economize on space we will denote the mean and variance of a random variable as $Y \sim (\mu, \sigma^2)$ where "$\sim$" means "is distributed as." The first element in parentheses is the population mean and the second is the population variance. So far we have not said what kind of probability distribution we think Y has.

The econometric model is not complete. If our sample is drawn randomly, we can assume that $Y_1, Y_2, \ldots, Y_N$ are statistically independent. The hip size of any one individual is independent of the hip size of another randomly drawn individual. Furthermore, we assume that each of the observations we collect is from the population of interest, so each random variable Y_i has the same mean and variance, or $Y_i \sim (\mu, \sigma^2)$. The Y_i constitute a **random sample**, in the statistical sense, because $Y_1, Y_2, \ldots, Y_N$ are statistically independent with identical probability distributions. It is sometimes reasonable to assume that population values are *normally* distributed, which we represent by $Y \sim N(\mu, \sigma^2)$.

C.3 Estimating the Mean of a Population

How shall we estimate the population mean μ given our sample of data values in Table C.1? The population mean is given by the expected value $E(Y) = \mu$. The expected value of a random variable is its average value in the population. It seems reasonable, by analogy, to use the average value in the sample, or **sample mean**, to estimate the population mean. Denote by $y_1, y_2, \ldots, y_N$ the sample of N observations. Then the sample mean is

$$\bar{y} = \Sigma y_i / N \tag{C.3}$$

The notation $\bar{y}$ (pronounced "y-bar") is widely used for the sample mean, and you probably encountered it in your statistics courses. For the hip data in Table C.1 we obtain $\bar{y} = 17.1582$, thus we estimate that the average hip size in the population is 17.1582 inches.

Given the estimate $\bar{y} = 17.1582$ we are inclined to ask, "How good an estimate is 17.1582?" By that we mean how close is 17.1582 to the true population mean, μ? Unfortunately this is an ill-posed question in the sense that it can never be answered. In order to answer it, we would have to know μ, in which case we would not have tried to estimate it in the first place!

Instead of asking about the quality of the *estimate* we will ask about the quality of the *estimation procedure*, or **estimator**. How good is the sample mean as an estimator of the mean of a population? This is a question we can answer. To distinguish between the estimate and the estimator of the population mean μ we will write the estimator as

$$\bar{Y} = \sum_{i=1}^{N} Y_i / N \tag{C.4}$$

In (C.4) we have used Y_i instead of y_i to indicate that this general formula is used whatever the sample values turn out to be. In this context Y_i are random variables, and thus the estimator $\bar{Y}$ is random too.

We do not know the value of the estimator $\bar{Y}$ until a data sample is obtained, and different samples will lead to different values. To illustrate, we collect 10 more samples of size $N = 50$ and calculate the average hip size, as shown in Table C.2. The estimates differ from sample to sample because $\bar{Y}$ is a random variable. This variation, due to collection of different random samples, is called **sampling variation**. It is an inescapable fact of statistical analysis that the estimator $\bar{Y}$ and indeed all statistical estimation procedures are subject to sampling variability. Because of this terminology, an estimator's probability density function is called its **sampling distribution**.

We can determine how good the estimator $\bar{Y}$ is by examining its expected value, variance, and sampling distribution.

Table C.2 **Sample Means from 10 Samples**

Sample	$\bar{y}$
1	17.3544
2	16.8220
3	17.4114
4	17.1654
5	16.9004
6	16.9956
7	16.8368
8	16.7534
9	17.0974
10	16.8770

C.3.1   THE EXPECTED VALUE OF $\bar{Y}$

Write out formula (C.4) fully as

$$\bar{Y} = \sum_{i=1}^{N} \frac{1}{N} Y_i = \frac{1}{N} Y_1 + \frac{1}{N} Y_2 + \cdots + \frac{1}{N} Y_N \qquad \text{(C.5)}$$

From (B.17) the expected value of this sum is the sum of expected values

$$
\begin{aligned}
E(\bar{Y}) &= E\left[\frac{1}{N} Y_1\right] + E\left[\frac{1}{N} Y_2\right] + \cdots + E\left[\frac{1}{N} Y_N\right] \\
&= \frac{1}{N} E[Y_1] + \frac{1}{N} E[Y_2] + \cdots + \frac{1}{N} E[Y_N] \\
&= \frac{1}{N} \mu + \frac{1}{N} \mu + \cdots + \frac{1}{N} \mu \\
&= \mu
\end{aligned}
$$

The expected value of the estimator $\bar{Y}$ *is* the population mean μ that we are trying to estimate. What does this mean? The expectation of a random variable is its average value in many repeated trials of an experiment, which amounts to collecting a large number of random samples from the population. If we did obtain many samples of size N, and obtained their average values, like those in Table C.2, then the average of all *those* values would equal the true population mean μ. This property is a good one for estimators to have. Estimators with this property are called **unbiased estimators**. The sample mean $\bar{Y}$ is an unbiased estimator of the population mean μ.

Unfortunately, while unbiasedness is a good property for an estimator to have, it does not tell us anything about whether our estimate $\bar{y} = 17.1582$, based on a single sample of data, is close to the true population mean value μ or not. To assess how far the estimate might be from μ we will determine the variance of the estimator.

C.3.2   THE VARIANCE OF $\bar{Y}$

The variance of $\bar{Y}$ is obtained using the procedure for finding the variance of a sum of uncorrelated (zero covariance) random variables in (B.24). We can apply this rule if our data are obtained by random sampling, because with random sampling the observations are statistically independent, and thus uncorrelated. Furthermore, we have assumed that $\text{var}(Y_i) = \sigma^2$ for all observations. Carefully note how these assumptions are used in the derivation of the variance of $\bar{Y}$, which we write as $\text{var}(\bar{Y})$:

$$
\begin{aligned}
\text{var}(\bar{Y}) &= \text{var}\left(\frac{1}{N} Y_1 + \frac{1}{N} Y_2 + \cdots + \frac{1}{N} Y_N\right) \\
&= \frac{1}{N^2} \text{var}(Y_1) + \frac{1}{N^2} \text{var}(Y_2) + \cdots + \frac{1}{N^2} \text{var}(Y_N) \\
&= \frac{1}{N^2} \sigma^2 + \frac{1}{N^2} \sigma^2 + \cdots + \frac{1}{N^2} \sigma^2 \\
&= \frac{\sigma^2}{N}
\end{aligned}
\qquad \text{(C.6)}
$$

This result tells us that (i) the variance of $\bar{Y}$ is *smaller* than the population variance, because the sample size $N \geq 2$; and (ii) the larger the sample size the smaller the sampling variation of $\bar{Y}$ as measured by its variance.

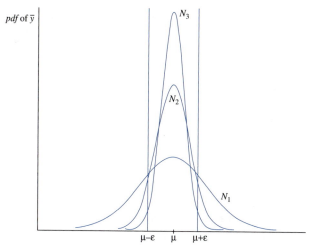

FIGURE C.2   Increasing sample size and sampling distributions of $\overline{Y}$.

C.3.3   THE SAMPLING DISTRIBUTION OF $\overline{Y}$

If the population data are normally distributed, then we say that the random variable Y_i follows a normal distribution. In this case the estimator $\overline{Y}$ also follows a normal distribution. In (B.31) it is noted that weighted averages of normal random variables are normal themselves. From (C.5) we know that $\overline{Y}$ is a weighted average of Y_i. If $Y_i \sim N(\mu, \sigma^2)$, then $\overline{Y}$ is also normally distributed, or $\overline{Y} \sim N(\mu, \sigma^2/N)$.

We can gain some intuition about the meaning and usefulness of the finding that $\overline{Y} \sim N(\mu, \sigma^2/N)$ if we examine Figure C.2.

Each of the normal distributions in this figure is a sampling distribution of $\overline{Y}$. The differences among them are the samples sizes used in estimation. The sample size $N_3 > N_2 > N_1$. Increasing the sample size decreases the variance of the estimator $\overline{Y}$, $\text{var}(\overline{Y}) = \sigma^2/N$, and this increases the probability that the sample mean will be "close" to the true population parameter μ. When examining Figure C.2 recall that an area under a probability density function (*pdf*) measures the probability of an event. If ε represents a positive number, the probability that $\overline{Y}$ falls in the interval between $\mu - \varepsilon$ and $\mu + \varepsilon$ is greater for larger samples. The lesson here is that having more data is better than having less data, because having a larger sample increases the probability of obtaining an estimate "close" or "within ε" of the true population parameter μ.

In our numerical example, suppose we want our estimate of μ to be within 1 inch of the true value. Let us compute the probability of getting an estimate within $\varepsilon = 1$ inch of μ, that is, within the interval $[\mu - 1, \mu + 1]$. For the purpose of illustration assume that the population is normal, $\sigma^2 = 10$ and $N = 40$. Then $\overline{Y} \sim N(\mu, \sigma^2/N = 10/40 = 0.25)$. We can compute the probability that $\overline{Y}$ is within 1 inch of μ by calculating $P[\mu - 1 \leq \overline{Y} \leq \mu + 1]$. To do so we standardize $\overline{Y}$ by subtracting its mean μ and dividing by its standard deviation $\sigma/\sqrt{N}$, and then use the standard normal distribution and Table 1 at the end of the book:

$$P[\mu - 1 \leq \overline{Y} \leq \mu + 1] = P\left[\frac{-1}{\sigma/\sqrt{N}} \leq \frac{\overline{Y} - \mu}{\sigma/\sqrt{N}} \leq \frac{1}{\sigma/\sqrt{N}}\right]$$

$$= P\left[\frac{-1}{\sqrt{0.25}} \leq Z \leq \frac{1}{\sqrt{0.25}}\right]$$

$$= P[-2 \leq Z \leq 2] = 0.9544$$

Thus, if we draw a random sample of size $N = 40$ from a normal population with variance 10, using the sample mean as an estimator will provide an estimate within 1 inch of the true value about 95% of the time. If $N = 80$, the probability that $\overline{Y}$ is within 1 inch of μ increases to 0.995.

C.3.4   THE CENTRAL LIMIT THEOREM

We were able to carry out the above analysis because we assumed that the population we are considering, hip width of U.S. adults, has a normal distribution. This implies that $Y_i \sim N(\mu, \sigma^2)$, and $\overline{Y} \sim N(\mu, \sigma^2/N)$. A question we need to ask is "If the population is not normal, then what is the sampling distribution of the sample mean?" The **central limit theorem** provides an answer to this question.

> **CENTRAL LIMIT THEOREM:** If $Y_1, \ldots, Y_N$ are independent and identically distributed random variables with mean μ and variance σ^2, and $\overline{Y} = \Sigma Y_i/N$, then
>
> $$Z_N = \frac{\overline{Y} - \mu}{\sigma/\sqrt{N}}$$
>
> has a probability distribution that converges to the standard normal $N(0, 1)$ as $N \to \infty$.

This theorem says that the sample average of N independent random variables from *any* probability distribution will have an approximate standard normal distribution after standardizing (i.e., subtracting the mean and dividing by the standard deviation), if the sample is sufficiently large. A shorthand notation is $\overline{Y} \stackrel{a}{\sim} N(\mu, \sigma^2/N)$, where the symbol "$\stackrel{a}{\sim}$" means *asymptotically distributed*. The word **asymptotic** implies that the approximate normality of $\overline{Y}$ depends on having a large sample. Thus even if the population is not normal, if we have a sufficiently large sample, we can carry out calculations like those in the previous section. How large does the sample have to be? In general, it depends on the complexity of the problem, but in the simple case of estimating a population mean, if $N \geq 30$ then you can feel pretty comfortable in assuming that the sample mean is approximately normally distributed, $\overline{Y} \stackrel{a}{\sim} N(\mu, \sigma^2/N)$, as indicated by the central limit theorem.

To illustrate how well the central limit theorem actually works, we carry out a simulation experiment. Let the continuous random variable Y have a triangular distribution, with probability density function

$$f(y) = \begin{cases} 2y & 0 < y < 1 \\ 0 & \text{otherwise} \end{cases}$$

Draw a sketch of the triangular *pdf* to understand its name. The expected value of Y is $\mu = E(Y) = 2/3$ and its variance is $\sigma^2 = \text{var}(Y) = 1/18$. The central limit theorem says that if $Y_1, \ldots, Y_N$ are independent and identically distributed with density $f(y)$ then

$$Z_N = \frac{\overline{Y} - 2/3}{\sqrt{\dfrac{1/18}{N}}}$$

has a probability distribution that approaches the standard normal distribution as N approaches infinity.

We use a random number generator to create random values from the triangular *pdf*. Plotting 10,000 values gives the histogram in Figure C.3a. We generate 10,000 samples of sizes $N = 3, 10$, and 30, compute the sample means of each sample, and create Z_N. Their histograms are shown in Figure C.3 b–d. You see the amazing convergence of the

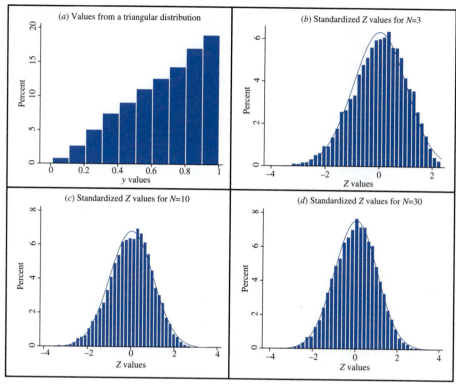

FIGURE *C.3* Central limit theorem.

standardized sample mean's distribution to a distribution that is bell shaped, centered at zero, symmetric, with almost all values between -3 and 3, just like a standard normal distribution, with a sample size as small as $N = 10$.

C.3.5 BEST LINEAR UNBIASED ESTIMATION

Another powerful finding about the estimator $\overline{Y}$ of the population mean is that it is the best of all possible estimators that are both *linear* and *unbiased*. A **linear estimator** is simply one that is a weighted average of Y_i's, such as $\tilde{Y} = \sum a_i Y_i$, where a_i are constants. The sample mean $\overline{Y}$, given in (C.4), is a linear estimator with $a_i = 1/N$. The fact that $\overline{Y}$ is the "best" linear unbiased estimator (BLUE) accounts for its wide use. "Best" means that it is the linear unbiased estimator with the smallest possible variance. In the previous section we demonstrated that it is better to have an estimator with a smaller variance rather than a larger one—because it increases the chances of getting an estimate close to the true population mean μ. This important result about the estimator $\overline{Y}$ is true *if* the sample values $Y_i \sim (\mu, \sigma^2)$ are uncorrelated and identically distributed. It does not depend on the population being normally distributed. A proof of this result is in Section C.9.2.

C.4 Estimating the Population Variance and Other Moments

The sample mean $\overline{Y}$ is an estimate of the population mean μ. The population mean is often called the first moment since it is the expected value of Y to the first power. Higher moments are obtained by taking expected values of higher powers of the random variable, so the second moment of Y is $E(Y^2)$, the third moment is $E(Y^3)$, and so on. When the random variable has its population mean subtracted it is said to be *centered*. Expected values of powers of centered random variables are called **central moments**, and they are often denoted as μ_r, so that the rth central moment of Y is

$$\mu_r = E\left[(Y - \mu)^r\right]$$

The value of the first central moment is zero since $\mu_1 = E\left[(Y - \mu)^1\right] = E(Y) - \mu = 0$. It is the higher central moments of Y that are interesting:

$$\mu_2 = E\left[(Y - \mu)^2\right] = \sigma^2$$
$$\mu_3 = E\left[(Y - \mu)^3\right]$$
$$\mu_4 = E\left[(Y - \mu)^4\right]$$

You recognize that the second central moment of Y is its variance, and the third and fourth moments appear in the definitions of skewness and kurtosis introduced in Section B.4.2. The question we address in this section is, now that we have an excellent estimator of the mean of a population, how do we estimate these higher moments? We will first consider estimation of the population variance, and then address the problem of estimating the third and fourth moments.

C.4.1 ESTIMATING THE POPULATION VARIANCE

The population variance is $\text{var}(Y) = \sigma^2 = E[Y - \mu]^2$. An expected value is an "average" of sorts, so if we knew μ we could estimate the variance by using the sample analog $\tilde{\sigma}^2 = \Sigma(Y_i - \mu)^2/N$. We do not know μ, so replace it by its estimator $\overline{Y}$, giving

$$\tilde{\sigma}^2 = \frac{\Sigma(Y_i - \overline{Y})^2}{N}$$

This estimator is not a bad one. It has a logical appeal, and it can be shown to converge to the true value of σ^2 as the sample size $N \to \infty$, but it is biased. To make it unbiased we divide by $N - 1$ instead of N. This correction is needed since the population mean μ has to be estimated before the variance can be estimated. This change does not matter much in samples of at least 30 observations, but it does make a difference in smaller samples. The unbiased estimator of the population variance σ^2 is

$$\hat{\sigma}^2 = \frac{\Sigma(Y_i - \overline{Y})^2}{N - 1} \tag{C.7}$$

You may remember this estimator from a prior statistics course as the "sample variance." Using the sample variance we can estimate the variance of the estimator $\overline{Y}$ as

$$\widehat{\text{var}(\overline{Y})} = \hat{\sigma}^2/N \tag{C.8}$$

In (C.8) note that we have put a "hat" ($\hat{\ }$) over this variance to indicate that is an estimated variance. The square root of the estimated variance is called the **standard error** of $\bar{Y}$ and is also known as the **standard error of the mean** and the **standard error of the estimate**,

$$se(\bar{Y}) = \sqrt{\widehat{\text{var}(\bar{Y})}} = \hat{\sigma}/\sqrt{N} \tag{C.9}$$

C.4.2 ESTIMATING HIGHER MOMENTS

Recall that central moments are expected values, $\mu_r = E[(Y - \mu)^r]$, and thus they are averages in the population. In statistics the **law of large numbers** says that sample means converge to population averages (expected values) as the sample size $N \to \infty$. We can estimate the higher moments by finding the sample analog and replacing the population mean μ by its estimate $\bar{Y}$, so that

$$\tilde{\mu}_2 = \Sigma(Y_i - \bar{Y})^2/N = \tilde{\sigma}^2$$
$$\tilde{\mu}_3 = \Sigma(Y_i - \bar{Y})^3/N$$
$$\tilde{\mu}_4 = \Sigma(Y_i - \bar{Y})^4/N$$

Note that in these calculations we divide by N and not $N - 1$, since we are using the law of large numbers (i.e., large samples) as justification, and in large samples the correction has little effect. Using these sample estimates of the central moments we can obtain estimates of the skewness coefficient (S) and kurtosis coefficient (K) as

$$\widehat{skewness} = S = \frac{\tilde{\mu}_3}{\tilde{\sigma}^3}$$

$$\widehat{kurtosis} = K = \frac{\tilde{\mu}_4}{\tilde{\sigma}^4}$$

C.4.3 THE HIP DATA

The sample variance for the hip data is

$$\hat{\sigma}^2 = \frac{\Sigma(y_i - \bar{y})^2}{N - 1} = \frac{\Sigma(y_i - 17.1582)^2}{49} = \frac{159.9995}{49} = 3.2653$$

This means that the estimated variance of the sample mean is

$$\widehat{\text{var}(\bar{Y})} = \frac{\hat{\sigma}^2}{N} = \frac{3.2653}{50} = 0.0653$$

and the standard error of the mean is

$$se(\bar{Y}) = \hat{\sigma}/\sqrt{N} = 0.2556$$

The estimated skewness is $S = -0.0138$ and the estimated kurtosis is $K = 2.3315$ using

$$\tilde{\sigma} = \sqrt{\Sigma(Y_i - \overline{Y})^2/N} = \sqrt{159.9995/50} = 1.7889$$

$$\tilde{\mu}_3 = \Sigma(Y_i - \overline{Y})^3/N = -0.0791$$

$$\tilde{\mu}_4 = \Sigma(Y_i - \overline{Y})^4/N = 23.8748$$

Thus the hip data is slightly negatively skewed and is slightly less peaked than would be expected for a normal distribution. Nevertheless, as we will see in Section C.7.4, we cannot conclude that the hip data follow a non-normal distribution.

C.4.4 USING THE ESTIMATES

How can we summarize what we have learned? Our estimates suggest that the hip size of U.S. adults is normally distributed with mean 17.158 inches with a variance of 3.265, $Y \sim N(17.158, 3.265)$. Based on this information, if an airplane seat is 18 inches wide, what percentage of customers will not be able to fit? We can recast this question as asking, what is the probability that a randomly drawn person will have hips larger than 18 inches,

$$P(Y > 18) = P\left(\frac{Y - \mu}{\sigma} > \frac{18 - \mu}{\sigma}\right)$$

We can give an approximate answer to this question by replacing the unknown parameters by their estimates,

$$\widehat{P(Y > 18)} \cong P\left(\frac{Y - \overline{y}}{\hat{\sigma}} > \frac{18 - 17.158}{1.8070}\right) = P(Z > 0.4659) = 0.3207$$

Based on our estimates, 32% of the population would not be able to fit into a seat 18 inches wide.

How large would a seat have to be to fit 95% of the population? If we let y^* denote the required seat size, then

$$\widehat{P(Y \le y^*)} \cong P\left(\frac{Y - \overline{y}}{\hat{\sigma}} \le \frac{y^* - 17.1582}{1.8070}\right) = P\left(Z \le \frac{y^* - 17.1582}{1.8070}\right) = 0.95$$

Using your computer software, or the table of normal probabilities, the value of Z such that $P(Z \le z^*) = 0.95$ is $z^* = 1.645$. Then

$$\frac{y^* - 17.1582}{1.8070} = 1.645 \Rightarrow y^* = 20.1305$$

Thus to accommodate 95% of U.S. adult passengers, we estimate that the seats should be slightly greater than 20 inches wide.

C.5 Interval Estimation

In contrast to a point estimate of the population mean μ, like $\overline{y} = 17.158$, a confidence interval, or an interval estimate, is a range of values that may contain the true population mean. A confidence interval contains information not only about the location of the population mean, but about the precision with which we estimate it.

C.5.1   INTERVAL ESTIMATION: σ^2 KNOWN

Let Y be a normally distributed random variable, $Y \sim N(\mu, \sigma^2)$. Assume that we have a random sample of size N from this population, $Y_1, Y_2, \ldots, Y_N$. The estimator of the population mean is $\overline{Y} = \sum_{i=1}^{N} Y_i / N$. Because we have assumed that Y is normally distributed it is also true that $\overline{Y} \sim N(\mu, \sigma^2/N)$.

For the present, let us assume that the population variance σ^2 is known. This assumption is not likely to be true, but making it allows us to introduce the notion of confidence intervals with few complications. In the next section we introduce methods for the case when σ^2 is unknown. Create a standard normal random variable

$$Z = \frac{\overline{Y} - \mu}{\sqrt{\sigma^2/N}} = \frac{\overline{Y} - \mu}{\sigma/\sqrt{N}} \sim N(0, 1) \tag{C.10}$$

Cumulative probabilities for the standard normal are given by its cumulative distribution function (see Section B.5.1)

$$P[Z \leq z] = \Phi(z)$$

These values are given in Table 1 at the end of this book. Let z_c be a "critical value" for the standard normal distribution, such that $\alpha = 0.05$ of the probability is in the tails of the distribution, with $\alpha/2 = 0.025$ of the probability in the tail to the right of z_c and $\alpha/2 = 0.025$ of the probability in the tail to the left of $-z_c$. The critical value is the 97.5 percentile of the standard normal distribution, $z_c = 1.96$, with $\Phi(1.96) = 0.975$. It is shown in Figure C.4. Thus $P[Z \geq 1.96] = P[Z \leq -1.96] = 0.025$ and

$$P[-1.96 \leq Z \leq 1.96] = 1 - 0.05 = 0.95 \tag{C.11}$$

Substitute (C.10) into (C.11) and rearrange to obtain

$$P[\overline{Y} - 1.96\,\sigma/\sqrt{N} \leq \mu \leq \overline{Y} + 1.96\,\sigma/\sqrt{N}] = 0.95$$

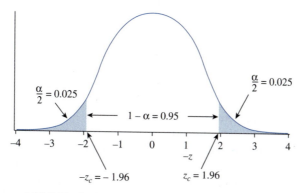

FIGURE **C.4** $\alpha = 0.05$ Critical values for the $N(0, 1)$ distribution.

Table C.3   **30 Values from $N(10, 10)$**

11.939	11.407	13.809
10.706	12.157	7.443
6.644	10.829	8.855
13.187	12.368	9.461
8.433	10.052	2.439
9.210	5.036	5.527
7.961	14.799	9.921
14.921	10.478	11.814
6.223	13.859	13.403
10.123	12.355	10.819

In general,

$$P\left[\overline{Y} - z_c \frac{\sigma}{\sqrt{N}} \leq \mu \leq \overline{Y} + z_c \frac{\sigma}{\sqrt{N}}\right] = 1 - \alpha \tag{C.12}$$

where z_c is the appropriate critical value for a given value of tail probability α such that $\Phi(z_c) = 1 - \alpha/2$. In (C.12) we have defined the interval estimator

$$\overline{Y} \pm z_c \frac{\sigma}{\sqrt{N}} \tag{C.13}$$

Our choice of the phrase interval *estimator* is a careful one. Intervals constructed using (C.13), in repeated sampling from the population, have a $100(1 - \alpha)\%$ chance of containing the population mean μ.

C.5.2   A SIMULATION

In order to use the interval estimator in (C.13) we must have data from a normal population with a known variance. To illustrate the computation, and the meaning of interval estimation, we will create a sample of data using a computer simulation. Statistical software programs contain random number generators. These are routines that create values from a given probability distribution. Table C.3 (*table-c3.dat*) contains 30 random values from a normal population with mean $\mu = 10$ and variance $\sigma^2 = 10$.

The sample mean of these values is $\overline{y} = 10.206$ and the corresponding interval estimate for μ, obtained by applying the interval estimator in (C.13) with a 0.95 probability content, is $10.206 \pm 1.96 \times \sqrt{10/30} = (9.074, 11.338)$. To appreciate how the sampling variability of an interval estimator arises, consider Table C.4 that contains the interval estimate for the sample in Table C.3 as well as the sample means and interval estimates from another 9 samples of size 30, like that in Table C.3. The whole 10 samples are stored in the file *table-c4.dat*.

Table C.4 illustrates the sampling variation of the estimator $\overline{Y}$. The sample mean varies from sample to sample. In this simulation, or Monte Carlo experiment, we know the true population mean, $\mu = 10$, and the estimates $\overline{y}$ are centered at that value. The half-width of the interval estimates is $1.96\sigma/\sqrt{N}$. Note that while the point estimates $\overline{y}$ in Table C.4 fall near the true value $\mu = 10$, not all of the interval estimates contain the true value. Intervals from samples 3, 4, and 6 do not contain the true value $\mu = 10$. However, in 10,000 simulated

Table C.4 **Confidence Interval Estimates from 10 Samples of Data**

Sample	$\bar{y}$	Lower bound	Upper bound
1	10.206	9.074	11.338
2	9.828	8.696	10.959
3	11.194	10.063	12.326
4	8.822	7.690	9.953
5	10.434	9.303	11.566
6	8.855	7.723	9.986
7	10.511	9.380	11.643
8	9.212	8.080	10.343
9	10.464	9.333	11.596
10	10.142	9.010	11.273

samples the average value of $\bar{y} = 10.004$ and 94.86% of intervals constructed using (C.13) contain the true parameter value $\mu = 10$.

These numbers reveal what is, and what is not, true about interval estimates.

- Any one interval estimate may or may not contain the true population parameter value.

- If *many* samples of size N are obtained, and intervals are constructed using (C.13) with $(1 - \alpha) = 0.95$, then 95% of them will contain the true parameter value.

- A 95% level of "confidence" is the probability that the interval estimator will provide an interval containing the true parameter value. Our confidence is in the procedure, not in any one interval estimate.

Since 95% of intervals constructed using (C.13) will contain the true parameter $\mu = 10$, we will be surprised if an interval estimate based on one sample does not contain the true parameter. Indeed, the fact that 3 of the 10 intervals in Table C.4 do not contain $\mu = 10$ is surprising, since out of 10 we would assume that only one 95% interval estimate might not contain the true parameter. This just goes to show that what happens in any one sample, or just a few samples, is not what sampling properties tell us. Sampling properties tell us what happens in many repeated experimental trials.

C.5.3 Interval Estimation: σ^2 Unknown

The standardization in (C.10) assumes that the population variance σ^2 is known. When σ^2 is unknown it is natural to replace it with its estimator $\hat{\sigma}^2$ given in (C.7)

$$\hat{\sigma}^2 = \frac{\sum\limits_{i=1}^{N}(Y_i - \bar{Y})^2}{N - 1}$$

When we do so the resulting standardized random variable has a t-distribution (See Section B.5.3) with $(N - 1)$ degrees of freedom,

$$t = \frac{\bar{Y} - \mu}{\hat{\sigma}/\sqrt{N}} \sim t_{(N-1)} \tag{C.14}$$

The notation $t_{(N-1)}$ denotes a t-distribution with $N - 1$ "degrees of freedom." Let the critical value t_c be the $100(1 - \alpha/2)$-percentile value $t_{(1-\alpha/2,N-1)}$. This critical value has the property that $P[t_{(N-1)} \leq t_{(1-\alpha/2,N-1)}] = 1 - \alpha/2$. Critical values for the t-distribution are contained in Table 2 at the end of the book, and also inside the front cover. If t_c is a critical value from the t-distribution, then

$$P\left[-t_c \leq \frac{\overline{Y} - \mu}{\hat{\sigma}/\sqrt{N}} \leq t_c\right] = 1 - \alpha$$

Rearranging we obtain

$$P\left[\overline{Y} - t_c \frac{\hat{\sigma}}{\sqrt{N}} \leq \mu \leq \overline{Y} + t_c \frac{\hat{\sigma}}{\sqrt{N}}\right] = 1 - \alpha$$

The $100(1 - \alpha)\%$ interval estimator for μ is

$$\overline{Y} \pm t_c \frac{\hat{\sigma}}{\sqrt{N}} \quad \text{or} \quad \overline{Y} \pm t_c \text{se}(\overline{Y}) \qquad \text{(C.15)}$$

Unlike the interval estimator for the known σ^2 case in (C.13), the interval in (C.15) has center *and* width that vary from sample to sample.

> **REMARK:** The confidence interval (C.15) is based upon the assumption that the population is normally distributed, so that $\overline{Y}$ is normally distributed. If the population is not normal, then we invoke the central limit theorem, and say that $\overline{Y}$ is approximately normal in "large" samples, which from Figure C.3 you can see might be as few as 30 observations. In this case we can use (C.15), recognizing that there is an approximation error introduced in smaller samples.

C.5.4   A SIMULATION (CONTINUED)

Table C.5 contains estimated values of σ^2 and interval estimates using (C.15) for the same 10 samples used for Table C.4. For the sample size $N = 30$ and the 95% confidence level the t-distribution critical value $t_c = t_{(0.975,29)} = 2.045$. The estimates $\overline{y}$ are the same as in Table C.4. The estimates $\hat{\sigma}^2$ vary about the true value $\sigma^2 = 10$. Of these

Table C.5   **Interval Estimates Using (C.15) from 10 Samples**

Sample	$\overline{y}$	$\hat{\sigma}^2$	Lower bound	Upper bound
1	10.206	9.199	9.073	11.338
2	9.828	6.876	8.849	10.807
3	11.194	10.330	9.994	12.394
4	8.822	9.867	7.649	9.995
5	10.434	7.985	9.379	11.489
6	8.855	6.230	7.923	9.787
7	10.511	7.333	9.500	11.523
8	9.212	14.687	7.781	10.643
9	10.464	10.414	9.259	11.669
10	10.142	17.689	8.571	11.712

10 intervals, those for samples 4 and 6 do not contain the true parameter $\mu = 10$ Nevertheless, in 10,000 simulated samples 94.82% of them contain the true population mean $\mu = 10$.

C.5.5 INTERVAL ESTIMATION USING THE HIP DATA

We have introduced the empirical problem faced by an airplane seat design engineer. Given a random sample of size $N = 50$ we estimated the mean U.S. hip width to be $\bar{y} = 17.158$ inches. Furthermore we estimated the population variance to be $\hat{\sigma}^2 = 3.265$; thus the estimated standard deviation is $\hat{\sigma} = 1.807$. The standard error of the mean is $\hat{\sigma}/\sqrt{N} = 1.807/\sqrt{50} = 0.2556$. The critical value for interval estimation comes from a t-distribution with $N - 1 = 49$ degrees of freedom. While this value is not in Table 2, the correct value using our software is $t_c = t_{(0.975,49)} = 2.0095752$, which we round to $t_c = 2.01$. To construct a 95% interval estimate we use (C.15), replacing estimates for the estimators, to give

$$\bar{y} \pm t_c \frac{\hat{\sigma}}{\sqrt{N}} = 17.1582 \pm 2.01 \frac{1.807}{\sqrt{50}}$$
$$= [16.6447,\ 17.6717]$$

We estimate that the population mean hip size falls between 16.645 and 17.672 inches. While we do not know if this interval contains the true population mean hip size for sure, we know that the procedure used to create the interval "works" 95% of the time; thus we would be surprised if the interval did not contain the true population value μ.

C.6 Hypothesis Tests About a Population Mean

Hypothesis testing procedures compare a conjecture, or a hypothesis, we have about a population to the information contained in a sample of data. The conjectures we test here concern the mean of a normal population. In the context of the problem faced by the airplane seat designer, suppose that airplanes since 1970 have been designed assuming the mean population hip width is 16.5 inches. Is that figure still valid today?

C.6.1 COMPONENTS OF HYPOTHESIS TESTS

Hypothesis tests use sample information about a parameter, namely its point estimate and its standard error, to draw a conclusion about the hypothesis. In each and every hypothesis test, five ingredients must be present:

COMPONENTS OF HYPOTHESIS TESTS

A *null* hypothesis, H_0
An *alternative* hypothesis, H_1
A test *statistic*
A *rejection* region
A conclusion

C.6.1a   The Null Hypothesis

The "null" hypothesis, which is denoted H_0 (*H-naught*), specifies a value c for a parameter. We write the null hypothesis as $H_0 : \mu = c$. A null hypothesis is the belief we will maintain until we are convinced by the sample evidence that it is not true, in which case we *reject* the null hypothesis.

C.6.1b   The Alternative Hypothesis

Paired with every null hypothesis is a logical alternative hypothesis, H_1, that we will accept if the null hypothesis is rejected. The alternative hypothesis is flexible and depends to some extent on the problem at hand. For the null hypothesis $H_0 : \mu = c$ three possible alternative hypotheses are

- $H_1 : \mu > c$. If we reject the null hypothesis that $\mu = c$, we accept the alternative that μ is greater than c.
- $H_1 : \mu < c$. If we reject the null hypothesis that $\mu = c$, we accept the alternative that μ is less than c.
- $H_1 : \mu \neq c$. If we reject the null hypothesis that $\mu = c$, we accept the alternative that μ takes a value other than (not equal to) c.

C.6.1c   The Test Statistic

The sample information about the null hypothesis is embodied in the sample value of a **test statistic**. Based on the value of a test statistic we decide either to reject the null hypothesis or not to reject it. A test statistic has a very special characteristic: its probability distribution is completely known when the null hypothesis is true, and it has some other distribution if the null hypothesis is not true.

Consider the null hypothesis $H_0 : \mu = c$. If the sample data come from a normal population with mean μ and variance σ^2, then

$$t = \frac{\overline{Y} - \mu}{\hat{\sigma}/\sqrt{N}} \sim t_{(N-1)}$$

If the null hypothesis $H_0 : \mu = c$ is true, then

$$t = \frac{\overline{Y} - c}{\hat{\sigma}/\sqrt{N}} \sim t_{(N-1)} \tag{C.16}$$

If the null hypothesis is not true, then the t-statistic in (C.16) does not have the usual t-distribution.

> **REMARK:** The test statistic distribution in (C.16) is based on an assumption that the population is normally distributed. If the population is not normal, then we invoke the central limit theorem, and say that $\overline{Y}$ is approximately normal in "large" samples. We can use (C.16), recognizing that there is an approximation error introduced if our sample is small.

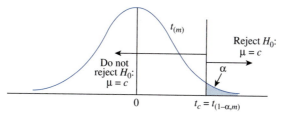

FIGURE **C.5** The rejection region for the one-tail test of $H_0 : \mu = c$ against $H_1 : \mu > c$.

C.6.1d The Rejection Region

The rejection region depends on the form of the alternative. It is the range of values of the test statistic that leads to rejection of the null hypothesis. They are values that are *unlikely* and have low probability of occurring when the null hypothesis is true. The chain of logic is "If a value of the test statistic is obtained that falls in a region of low probability, then it is unlikely that the test statistic has the assumed distribution, and thus it is unlikely that the null hypothesis is true." If the alternative hypothesis is true, then values of the test statistic will tend to be unusually "large" or unusually "small." The terms "large" and "small" are determined by choosing a probability α, called the **level of significance** of the test, which provides a meaning for "an *unlikely* event." The level of significance of the test α is usually chosen to be 0.01, 0.05, or 0.10.

C.6.1e A Conclusion

When you have completed a hypothesis test you should state your conclusion, whether you reject, or do not reject, the null hypothesis. However, we urge you to make it standard practice to say what the conclusion means in the economic context of the problem you are working on, that is, interpret the results in a meaningful way. This should be a point of emphasis in all statistical work that you do.

We will now discuss the mechanics of carrying out alternative versions of hypothesis tests.

C.6.2 ONE-TAIL TESTS WITH ALTERNATIVE "GREATER THAN" ($>$)

If the alternative hypothesis $H_1 : \mu > c$ is true, then the value of the t-statistic (C.16) tends to become larger than usual for the t-distribution. Let the critical value t_c be the $100(1 - \alpha)$-percentile $t_{(1-\alpha, N-1)}$ from a t-distribution with $N - 1$ degrees of freedom. Then $P(t \leq t_c) = 1 - \alpha$, where α is the level of significance of the test. If the t-statistic is greater than or equal to t_c, then we reject $H_0 : \mu = c$ and accept the alternative $H_1 : \mu > c$, as shown in Figure C.5.

If the null hypothesis $H_0 : \mu = c$ is *true*, then the test statistic (C.16) has a t-distribution, and its values would tend to fall in the center of the distribution, where most of the probability is contained. If $t < t_c$, then there is no evidence against the null hypothesis, and we do not reject it.

C.6.3 ONE-TAIL TESTS WITH ALTERNATIVE "LESS THAN" ($<$)

If the alternative hypothesis $H_1 : \mu < c$ is true, then the value of the t-statistic (C.16) tends to become smaller than usual for the t-distribution. The critical value $-t_c$ is the 100α-percentile $t_{(\alpha, N-1)}$ from a t-distribution with $N - 1$ degrees of freedom. Then $P(t \leq -t_c) = \alpha$, where α is the level of significance of the test as shown in Figure C.6.

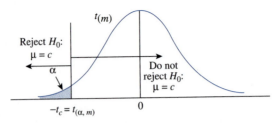

FIGURE **C.6** Critical value for one-tail test $H_0 : \mu = c$ versus $H_1 : \mu < c$.

If $t \leq -t_c$, then we reject $H_0 : \mu = c$ and accept the alternative $H_1 : \mu < c$. If $t > -t_c$, then we do not reject $H_0 : \mu = c$.

> **MEMORY TRICK:** The rejection region for a one-tail test is in the direction of the arrow in the alternative. If alternative is ">", then reject in right tail. If alternative is "<", reject in left tail.

C.6.4   TWO-TAIL TESTS WITH ALTERNATIVE "NOT EQUAL TO" ($\neq$)

If the alternative hypothesis $H_1 : \mu \neq c$ is true, then values of the test statistic may be unusually "large" or unusually "small." The rejection region consists of the two "tails" of the t-distribution, and this is called a two-tail test. In Figure C.7, the critical values for testing $H_0 : \mu = c$ against $H_1 : \mu \neq c$ are depicted. The critical value is the $100(1 - \alpha/2)$-percentile from a t-distribution with $N - 1$ degrees of freedom, $t_c = t_{(1-\alpha/2, N-1)}$, so that $P(t \geq t_c) = P(t \leq -t_c) = \alpha/2$.

If the value of the test statistic t falls in the rejection region, either tail of the $t_{(N-1)}$-distribution, then we reject the null hypothesis $H_0 : \mu = c$ and accept the alternative $H_1 : \mu \neq c$. If the value of the test statistic t falls in the nonrejection region, between the critical values $-t_c$ and t_c, then we do not reject the null hypothesis $H_0 : \mu = c$.

C.6.5   EXAMPLE OF A ONE-TAIL TEST USING THE HIP DATA

Let us illustrate by testing the null hypothesis that the population hip size is 16.5 inches, against the alternative that it is *greater* than 16.5 inches. The following five-step format is recommended.

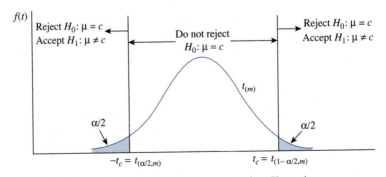

FIGURE **C.7** Rejection region for a test of $H_0 : \mu = c$ against $H_1 : \mu \neq c$

1. The null hypothesis is $H_0 : \mu = 16.5$. The alternative hypothesis is $H_1 : \mu > 16.5$.
2. The test statistic $t = (\bar{Y} - 16.5)/(\hat{\sigma}/\sqrt{N}) \sim t_{(N-1)}$ *if the null hypothesis is true.*
3. Let us select the level of significance $\alpha = 0.05$. The critical value $t_c = t_{(0.95,49)} = 1.6766$ for a t-distribution with $N - 1 = 49$ degrees of freedom. Thus we will reject the null hypothesis in favor of the alternative if $t \geq 1.68$.
4. Using the hip data, the estimate of μ is $\bar{y} = 17.1582$, with estimated variance $\hat{\sigma}^2 = 3.2653$, so $\hat{\sigma} = 1.807$. The value of the test statistic is

$$t = \frac{17.1582 - 16.5}{1.807/\sqrt{50}} = 2.5756.$$

5. *Conclusion:* Since $t = 2.5756 > 1.68$ we *reject* the null hypothesis. The sample information we have is *incompatible* with the hypothesis that $\mu = 16.5$. We accept the alternative that the population mean hip size is greater than 16.5 inches, at the $\alpha = 0.05$ level of significance.

C.6.6 Example of a Two-Tail Test Using the Hip Data

Let us test the null hypothesis that the population hip size is 17 inches, against the alternative that it is *not equal to* 17 inches. The steps of the test are

1. The null hypothesis is $H_0 : \mu = 17$. The alternative hypothesis is $H_1 : \mu \neq 17$.
2. The test statistic $t = (\bar{Y} - 17)/(\hat{\sigma}/\sqrt{N}) \sim t_{(N-1)}$ *if the null hypothesis is true.*
3. Let us select the level of significance $\alpha = 0.05$. In a two-tail test $\alpha/2 = 0.025$ of probability is allocated to each tail of the distribution. The critical value is the 97.5 percentile of the t-distribution, which leaves 2.5% of the probability in the upper tail, $t_c = t_{(0.975,49)} = 2.01$ for a t-distribution with $N - 1 = 49$ degrees of freedom. Thus we will reject the null hypothesis in favor of the alternative if $t \geq 2.01$ or if $t \leq -2.01$.
4. Using the hip data, the estimate of μ is $\bar{y} = 17.1582$, with estimated variance $\hat{\sigma}^2 = 3.2653$, so $\hat{\sigma} = 1.807$. The value of the test statistic is $t = (17.1582 - 17)/(1.807/\sqrt{50}) = 0.6191$.
5. *Conclusion:* Since $-2.01 < t = 0.6191 < 2.01$ we *do not reject* the null hypothesis. The sample information we have is *compatible* with the hypothesis that the population mean hip size $\mu = 17$.

> **WARNING:** Care must be taken here in interpreting the outcome of a statistical test. One of the basic precepts of hypothesis testing is that finding a sample value of the test statistic in the nonrejection region does not make the null hypothesis true! Suppose another null hypothesis is $H_0 : \mu = c^*$, where c^* is "close" to c. If we fail to reject the hypothesis $\mu = c$, then we will likely fail to reject the hypothesis that $\mu = c^*$. In the example above, at the $\alpha = 0.05$ level, we fail to reject the hypothesis that μ is 17, 16.8, 17.2, or 17.3. In fact, in any problem there are many hypotheses that we would fail to reject, but that does not make any of them true. The weaker statements "we do not reject the null hypothesis" or "we fail to reject the null hypothesis" do not send a misleading message.

C.6.7   THE p-VALUE

When reporting the outcome of statistical hypothesis tests it has become common practice to report the **p-value** of the test. If we have the p-value of a test, p, we can determine the outcome of the test by comparing the p-value to the chosen level of significance, α, *without* looking up or calculating the critical values ourselves. The rule is

> **p-VALUE RULE:** Reject the null hypothesis when the p-value is less than, or equal to, the level of significance α. That is, if $p \leq \alpha$ then reject H_0. If $p > \alpha$, then do not reject H_0.

If you have chosen the level of significance to be $\alpha = 0.01, 0.05, 0.10$, or any other value, you can compare it to the p-value of a test and then reject, or not reject, without checking the critical value t_c.

How the p-value is computed depends on the alternative. If t is the calculated value (not the critical value t_c) of the t-statistic with $N - 1$ degrees of freedom, then

- if $H_1 : \mu > c$, $p = $ probability to the right of t
- if $H_1 : \mu < c$, $p = $ probability to the left of t
- if $H_1 : \mu \neq c$, $p = $ *sum* of probabilities to the right of $|t|$ *and* to the left of $-|t|$

The direction of the alternative indicates the tail(s) of the distribution in which the p-value falls.

In Section C.6.5 we used the hip data to test $H_0 : \mu = 16.5$ against $H_1 : \mu > 16.5$. The calculated t-statistic value was $t = 2.5756$. In this case, since the alternative is "greater than" ($>$), the p-value of this test is the probability that a t-random variable with $N - 1 = 49$ degrees of freedom is greater than 2.5756. This probability value cannot be found in the usual t-table of critical values, but it is easily found using the computer. Statistical software packages, and spreadsheets such as Excel, have simple commands to evaluate the *cumulative distribution function* (*cdf*) (see Section B.2) for a variety of probability distributions. If $F_X(x)$ is the *cdf* for a random variable X, then for any value $x = c$, $P[X \leq c] = F_X(c)$. Given such a function for the t-distribution, we compute the desired p-value

$$p = P[t_{(N-1)} \geq 2.576] = 1 - P[t_{(N-1)} \leq 2.576] = 0.0065$$

Given the p-value we can immediately conclude that at $\alpha = 0.01$ or 0.05 we reject the null hypothesis in favor of the alternative, but if $\alpha = 0.001$ we would not reject the null hypothesis.

The logic of the p-value rule is shown in Figure C.8. If 0.0065 of the probability lies to the right of $t = 2.5756$, then the critical value t_c that leaves a probability of $\alpha = 0.01$ $(t_{(0.99,49)})$ or $\alpha = 0.05$ $(t_{(0.95,49)})$ in the tail must be to the left of 2.5756. In this case, when the p-value $\leq \alpha$, it must be true that $t \geq t_c$, and we should reject the null hypothesis for either of these levels of significance. On the other hand, it must be true that the critical value for $\alpha = 0.001$ must fall to the right of 2.5756, meaning that we should not reject the null hypothesis at this level of significance.

For a two-tail test, the rejection region is in the two tails of the t-distribution, and the p-value must similarly be calculated in the two tails of the distribution. For the hip data,

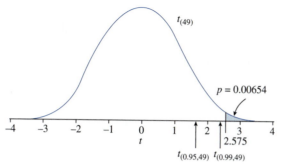

FIGURE *C.8*   *p*-value for a right-tail test.

we tested the null hypothesis $H_0 : \mu = 17$ against $H_1 : \mu \neq 17$, yielding the test statistic value $t = 0.6191$. The *p*-value is

$$p = P[t_{(N-1)} \geq 0.6191] + P[t_{(N-1)} \leq -0.6191] = 2 \times 0.2694 = 0.5387$$

Since the *p*-value $= 0.5387 > \alpha = 0.05$ we do not reject the null hypothesis $H_0 : \mu = 17$ at $\alpha = 0.05$ or any other common level of significance. The two-tail *p*-value is shown in Figure C.9.

C.6.8   A COMMENT ON STATING NULL AND ALTERNATIVE HYPOTHESES

A statistical test procedure cannot prove the truth of a null hypothesis. When we fail to reject a null hypothesis, all the hypothesis test can establish is that the information in a sample of data is *compatible* with the null hypothesis. On the other hand, a statistical test can lead us to *reject* the null hypothesis, with only a small probability, α, of rejecting the null hypothesis when it is actually true. Thus rejecting a null hypothesis is a stronger conclusion than failing to reject it.

The null hypothesis is usually stated in such a way that if our theory is correct, then we will reject the null hypothesis. For example, our airplane seat designer has been operating under the assumption (the maintained or null hypothesis) that the population mean hip width is 16.5 inches. Casual observation suggests that people are getting larger all the time. If we are larger, and if the airline wants to continue to accommodate the same percentage of the population, then the seat widths must be increased. This costly change should be undertaken only if there is statistical evidence that the population hip size is indeed larger. When using a hypothesis test we would like to find out that there is statistical evidence against our current "theory," or

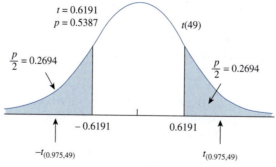

FIGURE *C.9*   The *p*-value for a two-tailed test.

if the data are compatible with it. With this goal, we set up the null hypothesis that the population mean is 16.5 inches, $H_0 : \mu = 16.5$, against the alternative that it is greater than 16.5 inches, $H_1 : \mu > 16.5$. In this case if we reject the null hypothesis we have shown that there has been a "statistically significant" increase in hip width.

You may view the null hypothesis to be too limited in this case, since it is feasible that the population mean hip width is now smaller than 16.5 inches. The hypothesis test of the null hypothesis $H_0 : \mu \leq 16.5$ against the alternative hypothesis $H_1 : \mu > 16.5$ is exactly the same as the test for $H_0 : \mu = 16.5$ against the alternative hypothesis $H_1 : \mu > 16.5$. The test statistic and rejection region are exactly the same. For a one-tail test you can form the null hypothesis in either of these ways.

Finally, it is important to set up the null and alternative hypotheses before you analyze or even collect the sample of data. Failing to do so can lead to errors in formulating the alternative hypothesis. Suppose that we wish to test whether $\mu > 16.5$ and the sample mean is $\bar{y} = 15.5$. Does that mean we should set up the alternative $\mu < 16.5$, to be consistent with the estimate? The answer is no. The alternative is formed to state the conjecture that we wish to establish, $\mu > 16.5$.

C.6.9   TYPE I AND TYPE II ERRORS

Whenever we reject, or do not reject, a null hypothesis there is a chance that we may be making a mistake. This is unavoidable. In any hypothesis testing situation there are two ways that we can make a correct decision and two ways that we can make an incorrect decision.

CORRECT DECISIONS

The null hypothesis is *false* and we decide to *reject* it.
The null hypothesis is *true* and we decide *not* to reject it.

INCORRECT DECISIONS

The null hypothesis is *true* and we decide to *reject* it (a Type I error).
The null hypothesis is *false* and we decide *not* to reject it (a Type II error).

When we reject the null hypothesis we risk what is called a Type I error. The probability of a Type I error is α, the level of significance of the test. When the null hypothesis is true, the t-statistic falls in the rejection region with probability α. Thus hypothesis tests will *reject* a true hypothesis $100\alpha\%$ of the time. The good news here is that we can control the probability of a Type I error by choosing the level of significance of the test, α.

We risk a Type II error when we do not reject the null hypothesis. Hypothesis tests will lead us to fail to reject null hypotheses that are false with a certain probability. The magnitude of the probability of a Type II error is not under our control and cannot be computed because it depends on the true value of μ, which is unknown. However, we do know that

- The probability of a Type II error varies inversely with the level of significance of the test, α, which is the probability of a Type I error. If you choose to make α smaller, the probability of a Type II error increases.
- If the null hypothesis is $\mu = c$, and if the true (unknown) value of μ is *close* to c, then the probability of a Type II error is high.

- The larger the sample size N, the lower the probability of a Type II error, given a level of Type I error α.

An easy to remember example of the difference between Type I and Type II errors is from the U.S. legal system. In a trial, a person is presumed innocent. This is the "null" hypothesis, the alternative hypothesis being that the person is guilty. If we convict an innocent person, then we have rejected a null hypothesis that is true, committing a Type I error. If we fail to convict a guilty person, failing to reject the false null hypothesis, then we commit a Type II error. Which is the more costly error in this context? Is it better to send an innocent person to jail, or to let a guilty person go free? It is better in this case to make the probability of a Type I error very small.

C.6.10 A RELATIONSHIP BETWEEN HYPOTHESIS TESTING AND CONFIDENCE INTERVALS

There is an algebraic relationship between two-tail hypothesis tests and confidence interval estimates that is sometimes useful. Suppose that we are testing the null hypothesis H_0: $\mu = c$ against the alternative $H_1 : \mu \neq c$. If we fail to reject the null hypothesis at the α level of significance, then the value c will fall within a $100(1 - \alpha)\%$ confidence interval estimate of μ. Conversely, if we reject the null hypothesis, then c will fall outside the $100(1 - \alpha)\%$ confidence interval estimate of μ. This algebraic relationship is true because we fail to reject the null hypothesis when $-t_c \leq t \leq t_c$, or when

$$-t_c \leq \frac{\overline{Y} - c}{\hat{\sigma}/\sqrt{N}} \leq t_c$$

which when rearranged becomes

$$\overline{Y} - t_c \frac{\hat{\sigma}}{\sqrt{N}} \leq c \leq \overline{Y} + t_c \frac{\hat{\sigma}}{\sqrt{N}}$$

The endpoints of this interval are the same as the endpoints of a $100(1 - \alpha)\%$ confidence interval estimate of μ. Thus for any value of c within the confidence interval we do not reject $H_0 : \mu = c$ against the alternative $H_1 : \mu \neq c$. For any value of c outside the confidence interval we reject $H_0 : \mu = c$ and accept the alternative $H_1 : \mu \neq c$.

This relationship can be handy if you are given only a confidence interval and want to determine what the outcome of a two-tail test would be.

C.7 Some Other Useful Tests

In this section we very briefly summarize some additional tests. These tests are not only useful in and of themselves, but also illustrate the use of test statistics with chi-square and F-distributions. These distributions were introduced in Section B.5.

C.7.1 TESTING THE POPULATION VARIANCE

Let Y be a normally distributed random variable, $Y \sim N(\mu, \sigma^2)$. Assume that we have a random sample of size N from this population, $Y_1, Y_2, \ldots, Y_N$. The estimator of the population mean is $\overline{Y} = \Sigma Y_i / N$ and the unbiased estimator of the population variance is $\hat{\sigma}^2 = \Sigma(Y_i - \overline{Y})^2 / (N-1)$. To test the null hypothesis $H_0 : \sigma^2 = \sigma_0^2$ we use the test statistic

$$V = \frac{(N-1)\hat{\sigma}^2}{\sigma_0^2} \sim \chi^2_{(N-1)}$$

If the null hypothesis is true, then the test statistic has the indicated chi-square distribution with $N-1$ degrees of freedom. If the alternative hypothesis is $H_1 : \sigma^2 > \sigma_0^2$, then we carry out a one-tail test. If we choose the level of significance $\alpha = 0.05$, then the null hypothesis is rejected if $V \geq \chi^2_{(0.95,N-1)}$, where $\chi^2_{(0.95,N-1)}$ is the 95th percentile of the chi-square distribution with $N-1$ degrees of freedom. These values can be found in Table 3 at the end of this book, or computed using statistical software. If the alternative hypothesis is $H_1 : \sigma^2 \neq \sigma_0^2$, then we carry out a two-tail test, and the null hypothesis is rejected if $V \geq \chi^2_{(0.975,N-1)}$ or if $V \leq \chi^2_{(0.025,N-1)}$. The chi-square distribution is skewed, with a long tail to the right, so we cannot use the properties of symmetry when determining the left and right tail critical values.

C.7.2   TESTING THE EQUALITY OF TWO POPULATION MEANS

Let two normal populations be denoted by $N(\mu_1, \sigma_1^2)$ and $N(\mu_2, \sigma_2^2)$. In order to estimate and test the difference between means, $\mu_1 - \mu_2$, we must have random samples of data from each of the two populations. We draw a sample of size N_1 from the first population, and a sample of size N_2 from the second population. Using the first sample we obtain the sample mean $\overline{Y}_1$ and sample variance $\hat{\sigma}_1^2$; from the second sample we obtain $\overline{Y}_2$ and $\hat{\sigma}_2^2$. How the null hypothesis $H_0 : \mu_1 - \mu_2 = c$ is tested depends on whether the two population variances are equal or not.

Case 1: Population variances are equal   If the population variances are equal, so that $\sigma_1^2 = \sigma_2^2 = \sigma_p^2$, then we use information in both samples to estimate the common value σ_p^2. This "pooled variance estimator" is

$$\hat{\sigma}_p^2 = \frac{(N_1 - 1)\hat{\sigma}_1^2 + (N_2 - 1)\hat{\sigma}_2^2}{N_1 + N_2 - 2}$$

If the null hypothesis $H_0 : \mu_1 - \mu_2 = c$ is true, then

$$t = \frac{(\overline{Y}_1 - \overline{Y}_2) - c}{\sqrt{\hat{\sigma}_p^2 \left(\dfrac{1}{N_1} + \dfrac{1}{N_2}\right)}} \sim t_{(N_1 + N_2 - 2)}$$

As usual we can construct a one-sided alternative, such as $H_1 : \mu_1 - \mu_2 > c$, or the two-sided alternative $H_1 : \mu_1 - \mu_2 \neq c$.

Case 2: Population variances are unequal   If the population variances are not equal, then we cannot use the pooled variance estimate. Instead we use

$$t^* = \frac{(\overline{Y}_1 - \overline{Y}_2) - c}{\sqrt{\dfrac{\hat{\sigma}_1^2}{N_1} + \dfrac{\hat{\sigma}_2^2}{N_2}}}$$

The exact distribution of this test statistic is neither normal nor the usual t-distribution. The distribution of t^* can be approximated by a t-distribution with degrees of freedom

$$df = \frac{(\hat{\sigma}_1^2/N_1 + \hat{\sigma}_2^2/N_2)^2}{\left(\dfrac{(\hat{\sigma}_1^2/N_1)^2}{N_1 - 1} + \dfrac{(\hat{\sigma}_2^2/N_2)^2}{N_2 - 1}\right)}$$

This is one of several approximations that appear in the statistics literature, and your software may well use a different one.

C.7.3   TESTING THE RATIO OF TWO POPULATION VARIANCES

Given two normal populations, denoted by $N(\mu_1, \sigma_1^2)$ and $N(\mu_2, \sigma_2^2)$, we can test the null hypothesis $H_0 : \sigma_1^2/\sigma_2^2 = 1$. If the null hypothesis is true, then the population variances are equal. The test statistic is derived from the results that $(N_1 - 1)\hat{\sigma}_1^2/\sigma_1^2 \sim \chi^2_{(N_1-1)}$ and $(N_2 - 1)\hat{\sigma}_2^2/\sigma_2^2 \sim \chi^2_{(N_2-1)}$. In Section B.5.4 we define an F random variable, which is formed by taking the ratio of two independent chi-square random variables that have been divided by their degrees of freedom. In this case the relevant ratio is

$$F = \frac{\dfrac{(N_1 - 1)\hat{\sigma}_1^2/\sigma_1^2}{(N_1 - 1)}}{\dfrac{(N_2 - 1)\hat{\sigma}_2^2/\sigma_2^2}{(N_2 - 1)}} = \frac{\hat{\sigma}_1^2/\sigma_1^2}{\hat{\sigma}_2^2/\sigma_2^2} \sim F_{(N_1-1,N_2-1)}$$

If the null hypothesis $H_0 : \sigma_1^2/\sigma_2^2 = 1$ is true then the test statistic is $F = \hat{\sigma}_1^2/\hat{\sigma}_2^2$, which has an F-distribution with $N_1 - 1$ numerator and $N_2 - 1$ denominator degrees of freedom. If the alternative hypothesis is $H_1 : \sigma_1^2/\sigma_2^2 \neq 1$, then we carry out a two-tail test. If we choose level of significance $\alpha = 0.05$, then we reject the null hypothesis if $F \geq F_{(0.975,N_1-1,N_2-1)}$ or if $F \leq F_{(0.025,N_1-1,N_2-1)}$, where $F_{(\alpha,N_1-1,N_2-1)}$ denotes the 100α-percentile of the F-distribution with the specified degrees of freedom. If the alternative is one sided, $H_1 : \sigma_1^2/\sigma_2^2 > 1$, then we reject the null hypothesis if $F \geq F_{(0.95,N_1-1,N_2-1)}$.

C.7.4   TESTING THE NORMALITY OF A POPULATION

The tests for means and variances we have developed began with the assumption that the populations were normally distributed. Two questions immediately arise. How well do the tests work when the population is not normal? Can we test for the normality of a population? The answer to the first question is that the tests work pretty well even if the population is not normal if samples are sufficiently large. How large must the samples be? There is no easy answer, since it depends on how "non-normal" the populations are. The answer to the second question is yes, we can test for normality. Statisticians have been vitally interested in this question for a long time, and a variety of tests have been developed, but the tests and underlying theory are very complicated and far outside the scope of this book.

However, we can present a test that is slightly less ambitious. The normal distribution is symmetric and has a bell shape with a peakedness and tail thickness leading to a kurtosis of 3. Thus we can test for departures from normality by checking the skewness and kurtosis from a sample of data. If skewness is not close to zero, and if kurtosis is not close to 3, then we reject the normality of the population. In Section C.4.2 we developed sample measures of skewness and kurtosis

$$\widetilde{skewness} = S = \frac{\tilde{\mu}_3}{\tilde{\sigma}^3}$$

$$\widetilde{kurtosis} = K = \frac{\tilde{\mu}_4}{\tilde{\sigma}^4}$$

The **Jarque–Bera** test statistic allows a joint test of these two characteristics,

$$JB = \frac{N}{6}\left(S^2 + \frac{(K-3)^2}{4}\right)$$

If the true distribution is symmetric and has kurtosis 3, which includes the normal distribution, then the JB test statistic has a chi-square distribution with two degrees of freedom if the sample size is sufficiently large. If $\alpha = 0.05$ then the critical value of the $\chi^2_{(2)}$ distribution is 5.99. We reject the null hypothesis and conclude that the data are non-normal if $JB \geq 5.99$. If we reject the null hypothesis, then we know the data have non-normal characteristics, but we do not know what distribution the population might have.

For the hip data, skewness and kurtosis measures were estimated in Section C.4.3. Plugging these values into the JB test statistic formula we obtain

$$JB = \frac{N}{6}\left(S^2 + \frac{(K-3)^2}{4}\right) = \frac{50}{6}\left((-0.0138)^2 + \frac{(2.3315-3)^2}{4}\right) = 0.9325$$

Since $JB = 0.9325$ is less than the critical value 5.99, we conclude that we cannot reject the normality of the hip data. The p-value for this test is the tail area of a $\chi^2_{(2)}$-distribution to the right of 0.9325,

$$p = P\left[\chi^2_{(2)} \geq 0.9325\right] = 0.6273$$

C.8 Introduction to Maximum Likelihood Estimation[1]

Maximum likelihood estimation is a powerful procedure that can be used when the population distribution is known. In this section we introduce the concept with a very simple but revealing example. Consider the following "Wheel of Fortune" game. You are a contestant faced with two wheels, each of which is partly shaded and partly nonshaded (see Figure C.10). Suppose that, after spinning a wheel, you win if a pointer is in the shaded area and you lose if the pointer is in the nonshaded area. On wheel A 25% of the area is shaded so that the probability of winning is 1/4. On wheel B 75% of the area is shaded so that the probability of winning is 3/4. The game that you must play is this. One of the wheels is chosen and spun three times, with outcomes WIN, WIN, LOSS. You *do not* know which wheel was chosen, and must pick which wheel was spun. Which would you select?

---

[1] This section contains some advanced material.

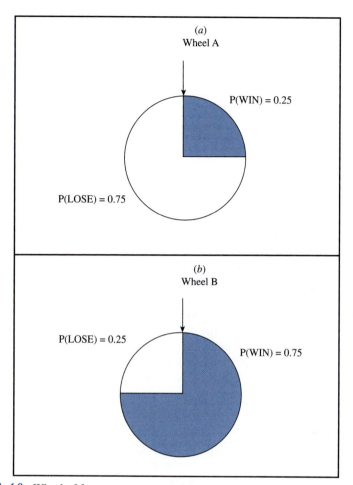

FIGURE C.10   Wheel of fortune game.

One intuitive approach is the following: let p denote the probability of winning on one spin of a wheel. Choosing between wheels A and B means choosing between $p = 1/4$ and $p = 3/4$. You are estimating p, but there are only two possible estimates, and you must choose based on the observed data. Let us compute the probability of each sequence of outcomes for each of the wheels.

For wheel A, with $p = 1/4$, the probability of observing WIN, WIN, LOSS is

$$\frac{1}{4} \times \frac{1}{4} \times \frac{3}{4} = \frac{3}{64} = 0.0469$$

That is, the probability, or **likelihood**, of observing the sequence WIN, WIN, LOSS when $p = 1/4$ is 0.0469.

For wheel B, with $p = 3/4$, the probability of observing WIN, WIN, LOSS is

$$\frac{3}{4} \times \frac{3}{4} \times \frac{1}{4} = \frac{9}{64} = 0.1406$$

The probability, or likelihood, of observing the sequence WIN, WIN, LOSS when $p = 3/4$ is 0.1406.

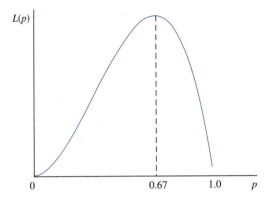

$L(p)$

0   0.67 1.0 p

FIGURE **C.11** A likelihood function.

If we had to choose wheel *A* or *B* based on the available data, we would choose wheel *B* because it has a higher probability of having produced the observed data. It is more *likely* that wheel *B* was spun than wheel *A*, and $\hat{p} = 3/4$ is called the **maximum likelihood estimate** of *p*. The **maximum likelihood principle** seeks the parameter values that maximize the probability, or likelihood, of observing the outcomes actually obtained.

Now suppose *p* can be any probability between 0 and 1, not just $1/4$ or $3/4$. We have one wheel with a proportion of it shaded, which is the probability of WIN, but we do not know the proportion. In three spins we observe WIN, WIN, LOSS. What is the most likely value of *p*? The probability of observing WIN, WIN, LOSS is the likelihood *L* and is

$$L(p) = p \times p \times (1 - p) = p^2 - p^3 \qquad \text{(C.17)}$$

The likelihood *L* depends on the unknown probability *p* of a WIN, which is why we have given it the notation $L(p)$, indicating a functional relationship. We would like to find the value of *p* that maximizes the likelihood of observing the outcomes actually obtained. The graph of the likelihood function (C.17) and the choice of *p* that maximizes this function is shown in Figure C.11. The maximizing value is denoted as $\hat{p}$ and is called the maximum likelihood estimate of *p*. To find this value of *p* we can use calculus. Differentiate $L(p)$ with respect to *p*,

$$\frac{dL(p)}{dp} = 2p - 3p^2$$

Set this derivative to zero,

$$2p - 3p^2 = 0 \Rightarrow p(2 - 3p) = 0$$

There are two solutions to this equation, $p = 0$ or $p = 2/3$. The value that maximizes $L(p)$ is $\hat{p} = 2/3$, which is the maximum likelihood estimate. That is, of all possible values of *p*, between 0 and 1, the value that maximizes the probability of observing two wins and one loss (the order does not matter) is $\hat{p} = 2/3$.

Can we derive a more general formula that can be used for any observed data? In Section B.2 we introduced the concept of probability distributions for discrete random variables. Let us define the random variable *X* that takes the values $x = 1$ (WIN) and $x = 0$ (LOSS) with probabilities p and $1 - p$. The probability function for this random variable can be written in mathematical form as

$$P(X = x) = f(x|p) = p^x(1 - p)^{1-x}, \quad x = 0, 1$$

If we spin the "wheel" N times we observe N sample values $x_1, x_2, \ldots, x_N$. Assuming that the spins are independent, we can form the joint probability function

$$
\begin{aligned}
f(x_1, \ldots, x_N|p) &= f(x_1|p) \times \cdots \times f(x_N|p) \\
&= p^{\Sigma x_i}(1 - p)^{N - \Sigma x_i} \\
&= L(p|x_1, \ldots, x_N)
\end{aligned}
\tag{C.18}
$$

The joint probability function gives the probability of observing a specific set of outcomes, and it is a generalization of (C.17). In the last line we have indicated that the joint probability function is algebraically equivalent to the **likelihood function** $L(p|x_1, \ldots, x_N)$. The notation emphasizes that the likelihood function depends upon the unknown probability p *given* the sample outcomes, which we observe. For notational simplicity we will continue to denote the likelihood function as $L(p)$.

In the "Wheel of Fortune" game the maximum likelihood estimate is that value of p that maximizes $L(p)$. To find this estimate using calculus we use a trick to simplify the algebra. The value of p that maximizes $L(p) = p^2(1 - p)$ is the same value of p that maximizes the **log-likelihood function** $\ln L(p) = 2\ln(p) + \ln(1 - p)$, where "ln" is the natural logarithm. The plot of the log-likelihood function is shown in Figure C.12. Compare Figures C.11 and C.12. The maximum of the likelihood function is $L(\hat{p}) = 0.1481$. The maximum of the log-likelihood function is $\ln L(\hat{p}) = -1.9095$. Both of these maximum values occur at $\hat{p} = 2/3 = 0.6667$.

This trick works for all likelihood and log-likelihood functions and their parameters, so when you see maximum likelihood estimation being discussed it will always be in terms of maximizing the log-likelihood function. For the general problem we are considering the log-likelihood function is the logarithm of (C.18)

$$
\begin{aligned}
\ln L(p) &= \sum_{i=1}^{N} \ln f(x_i|p) \\
&= \left(\sum_{i=1}^{N} x_i\right)\ln(p) + \left(N - \sum_{i=1}^{N} x_i\right)\ln(1 - p)
\end{aligned}
\tag{C.19}
$$

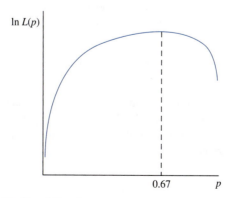

FIGURE **C.12** A log-likelihood function.

The first derivative is

$$\frac{d\ln L(p)}{dp} = \frac{\sum x_i}{p} - \frac{N - \sum x_i}{1 - p}$$

Setting this to zero, and replacing p by $\hat{p}$ to denote the value that maximizes $\ln L(p)$, yields

$$\frac{\sum x_i}{\hat{p}} - \frac{N - \sum x_i}{1 - \hat{p}} = 0$$

To solve this equation multiply both sides by $\hat{p}(1 - \hat{p})$. This gives

$$(1 - \hat{p})\sum x_i - \hat{p}(N - \sum x_i) = 0$$

Finally, solving for $\hat{p}$ yields

$$\hat{p} = \frac{\sum x_i}{N} = \bar{x} \tag{C.20}$$

The estimator $\hat{p}$ is the **sample proportion**; $\sum x_i$ is the total number of 1s (wins) out of N spins. As you can see $\hat{p}$ is also the sample mean of x_i. This result is completely general. Any time we have two outcomes that can occur with probabilities p and $1 - p$, then the maximum likelihood estimate based on a sample of N observations is the sample proportion (C.20). This estimation strategy can be used if you are a pollster trying to estimate the proportion of the population intending to vote for candidate A rather than candidate B, a medical researcher who wishes to estimate the proportion of the population having a particular defective gene, or a marketing researcher trying to discover if the population of customers prefers a blue box or a green box for their morning cereal. Suppose in this latter case, you select 200 cereal consumers at random and ask whether they prefer blue or green boxes. If 75 prefer a blue box, then we would estimate that the population proportion preferring blue is $\hat{p} = \sum x_i/N$ $= 75/200 = 0.375$. Thus we estimate that 37.5% of the population prefers a blue box.

C.8.1   INFERENCE WITH MAXIMUM LIKELIHOOD ESTIMATORS

If we use maximum likelihood estimation, how do we perform hypothesis tests and construct confidence intervals? The answers to these questions are found in some remarkable properties of estimators obtained using maximum likelihood methods. Let us consider a general problem. Let X be a random variable (either discrete or continuous) with a probability density function $f(x|\theta)$, where θ is an unknown parameter. The log-likelihood function, based on a random sample $x_1, \ldots, x_N$ of size N, is

$$\ln L(\theta) = \sum_{i=1}^{N} \ln f(x_i|\theta)$$

If the probability density function of the random variable involved is relatively smooth, and if certain other technical conditions hold, then in large samples the maximum likelihood estimator $\hat{\theta}$ of a parameter θ has a probability distribution that is approximately normal, with expected value θ and a variance $V = \mathrm{var}(\hat{\theta})$ that we will discuss in a moment. That is, we can say

$$\hat{\theta} \stackrel{a}{\sim} N(\theta, V) \tag{C.21}$$

where the symbol $\overset{a}{\sim}$ denotes "asymptotically distributed." The word "asymptotic" refers to estimator properties when the sample size N becomes large, or as $N \to \infty$. To say that an estimator is asymptotically normal means that its probability distribution, which may be unknown when samples are small, becomes approximately normal in large samples. This is analogous to the central limit theorem we discussed in Section C.3.4.

Based on the normality result in (C.21) it will not surprise you that we can immediately construct a t-statistic and obtain both a confidence interval and a test statistic from it. Specifically, if we wish to test the null hypothesis $H_0 : \theta = c$ against a one-tail or two-tail alternative hypothesis then we can use the test statistic

$$t = \frac{\hat{\theta} - c}{\text{se}(\hat{\theta})} \overset{a}{\sim} t_{(N-1)} \tag{C.22}$$

If the null hypothesis is true, then this t-statistic has a distribution that can be approximated by a t-distribution with $N - 1$ degrees of freedom in large samples. The mechanics of carrying out the hypothesis test are exactly those in Section C.6.

If t_c denotes the $100(1 - \alpha/2)$-percentile $t_{(1-\alpha/2, N-1)}$, then a $100(1 - \alpha)\%$ confidence interval for θ is

$$\hat{\theta} \pm t_c \text{se}(\hat{\theta})$$

This confidence interval is interpreted just like those in Section C.5.

> **REMARK:** These asymptotic results in (C.21) and (C.22) hold only in large samples. We have indicated that the distribution of the test statistic can be approximated by a t-distribution with $N - 1$ degrees of freedom. If N is truly large, then the $t_{(N-1)}$-distribution converges to the standard normal distribution $N(0, 1)$ and the $100(1 - \alpha/2)$-percentile value $t_{(1-\alpha/2, N-1)}$ converges to the corresponding percentile from the standard normal distribution. Asymptotic results are used, rightly or wrongly, when the sample size N may not be large. We prefer using the t-distribution critical values, which are adjusted for small samples by the degrees of freedom correction, when obtaining interval estimates and carrying out hypothesis tests.

C.8.2 THE VARIANCE OF THE MAXIMUM LIKELIHOOD ESTIMATOR

A key ingredient in both the test statistic and confidence interval expressions is the standard error $\text{se}(\hat{\theta})$. Where does this come from? Standard errors are square roots of estimated variances. The part we have delayed discussing until now is how we find the variance of the maximum likelihood estimator, $V = \text{var}(\hat{\theta})$. The variance V is given by the inverse of the negative expectation of the second derivative of the log-likelihood function,

$$V = \text{var}(\hat{\theta}) = \left[-E\left(\frac{d^2 \ln L(\theta)}{d\theta^2} \right) \right]^{-1} \tag{C.23}$$

This looks quite intimidating, and you can see why we put it off. What does this mean? First of all, the second derivative measures the curvature of the log-likelihood function. A second

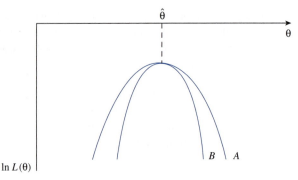

FIGURE **C.13**   Two log-likelihood functions.

derivative is literally the derivative of the derivative. A single derivative, the first, measures the slope of a function or the rate of change of the function. The second derivative measures the rate of change of the slope. To obtain a maximum of the log-likelihood function it must be an "inverted bowl" shape, like those shown in Figure C.13.

At any point to the left of the maximum point the slope of the log-likelihood function is positive. At any point to the right of the maximum the slope is negative. As we progress from left to right the slope is *decreasing* (becoming more negative), so that the second derivative must be negative. A larger absolute magnitude of the second derivative implies a more rapidly changing slope, indicating a more sharply curved log-likelihood. This is important. In Figure C.13 the two log-likelihood functions A and B have the same maximizing value $\hat{\theta}$. Imagine yourself a climber who is trekking up one of these mountains. For which mountain is the summit most clearly defined? For log-likelihood B the summit is a sharp peak, and its maximum is more easily located than that for log-likelihood A. The sharper peak has less "wiggle room" at the summit. The smaller amount of wiggle room means that there is less uncertainty as to the location of the maximizing value $\hat{\theta}$; in estimation terminology, less uncertainty means greater precision, and a smaller variance. The more sharply curved log-likelihood function, the one whose second derivative is larger in absolute magnitude, leads to more precise maximum likelihood estimation, and a maximum likelihood estimator with smaller variance. Thus the variance V of the maximum likelihood estimator is inversely related to the (negative) second derivative. The expected value "E" must be present because this quantity depends on the data and is thus random, so we average over all possible data outcomes.

C.8.3   THE DISTRIBUTION OF THE SAMPLE PROPORTION

It is time for an example. At the beginning of Section C.8 we introduced a random variable X that takes the values $x = 1$ and $x = 0$ with probabilities p and $1 - p$. It has log-likelihood given in (C.19). In this problem the parameter θ that we are estimating is the population proportion p, the proportion of $x = 1$ values in the population. We already know that the maximum likelihood estimator of p is the sample proportion $\hat{p} = \sum x_i / N$. The second derivative of the log-likelihood function (C.19) is

$$\frac{d^2 \ln L(p)}{dp^2} = -\frac{\sum x_i}{p^2} - \frac{N - \sum x_i}{(1 - p)^2} \tag{C.24}$$

To calculate the variance of the maximum likelihood estimator we need the "expected value" of expression (C.24). In the expectation we treat the x_i values as random because these values vary from sample to sample. The expected value of this discrete random variable is obtained using (B.7)

$$E(x_i) = 1 \times P(x_i = 1) + 0 \times P(x_i = 0) = 1 \times p + 0 \times (1 - p) = p$$

Then, using a generalization of (B.17) (the expected value of a sum is the sum of the expected values and constants can be factored out of expectations) we find the expected value of the second derivative as

$$E\left(\frac{d^2 \ln L(p)}{dp^2}\right) = -\frac{\sum E(x_i)}{p^2} - \frac{N - \sum E(x_i)}{(1 - p)^2}$$

$$= -\frac{Np}{p^2} - \frac{N - Np}{(1 - p)^2}$$

$$= -\frac{N}{p(1 - p)}$$

The variance of the sample proportion, which is the maximum likelihood estimator of p, is then

$$V = \text{var}(\hat{p}) = \left[-E\left(\frac{d^2 \ln L(p)}{dp^2}\right)\right]^{-1} = \frac{p(1 - p)}{N}$$

The asymptotic distribution of the sample proportion, which is valid in large samples, is

$$\hat{p} \overset{a}{\sim} N\left(p, \frac{p(1 - p)}{N}\right)$$

To estimate the variance V we must replace the true population proportion by its estimate,

$$\hat{V} = \frac{\hat{p}(1 - \hat{p})}{N}$$

The standard error that we need for hypothesis testing and confidence interval estimation is the square root of this estimated variance

$$\text{se}(\hat{p}) = \sqrt{\hat{V}} = \sqrt{\frac{\hat{p}(1 - \hat{p})}{N}}$$

As a numerical example, suppose a cereal company CEO conjectures that 40% of the population prefers a blue box. To test this hypothesis we construct the null hypothesis $H_0 : p = 0.4$ and use the two-tail alternative $H_1 : p \neq 0.4$. If the null hypothesis is true, then the test statistic $t = (\hat{p} - 0.4)/\text{se}(\hat{p}) \overset{a}{\sim} t_{(N-1)}$. For a sample of size $N = 200$ the critical value from the t-distribution is $t_c = t_{(0.975,199)} = 1.96$. Therefore we reject the null hypothesis if the calculated value of $t \geq 1.96$ or $t \leq -1.96$. If 75 of the respondents prefer a blue box, then the sample proportion is $\hat{p} = 75/200 = 0.375$. The standard error of this estimate is

$$\text{se}(\hat{p}) = \sqrt{\frac{\hat{p}(1 - \hat{p})}{N}} = \sqrt{\frac{0.375 \times 0.625}{200}} = 0.0342$$

The value of the test statistic is

$$t = \frac{\hat{p} - 0.4}{\text{se}(\hat{p})} = \frac{0.375 - 0.4}{0.0342} = -0.7303$$

This value is in the nonrejection region, $-1.96 < t = -0.7303 < 1.96$, so we do not reject the null hypothesis that $p = 0.4$. The sample data are compatible with the conjecture that 40% of the population prefer a blue box.

The 95% interval estimate of the population proportion p who prefer a blue box is

$$\hat{p} \pm 1.96\,\text{se}(\hat{p}) = 0.375 \pm 1.96(0.0342) = [0.3075, 0.4425]$$

We estimate that between 30.8% and 44.3% of the population prefer a blue box.

C.8.4   ASYMPTOTIC TEST PROCEDURES

When using maximum likelihood estimation there are three test procedures that can be used, with the choice depending on which one is most convenient in a given case. The tests are *asymptotically equivalent* and will give the same result in large samples. Suppose that we are testing the null hypothesis $H_0 : \theta = c$ against the alternative hypothesis $H_1 : \theta \neq c$. In (C.22) we have given the t-statistic for carrying out the test. How does this test really work? Basically it is measuring the distance $\hat{\theta} - c$ between the estimate of θ and the hypothesized value c. This distance is normalized by the standard error of $\hat{\theta}$ to adjust for how precisely we have estimated θ. If the distance between the estimate $\hat{\theta}$ and the hypothesized value c is large, then that is taken as evidence against the null hypothesis, and if the distance is large enough we conclude that the null hypothesis is not true.

There are other ways to measure the distance between $\hat{\theta}$ and c that can be used to construct test statistics. Each of the three testing principles takes a different approach to measuring the distance between $\hat{\theta}$ and the hypothesized value.

C.8.4a   The Likelihood Ratio (*LR*) Test

Consider Figure C.14. A log-likelihood function is shown, along with the maximum likelihood estimate $\hat{\theta}$ and the hypothesized value c. Note that the distance between $\hat{\theta}$ and c is also reflected by the distance between the log-likelihood function value evaluated at the maximum likelihood estimate $\ln L(\hat{\theta})$ and the log-likelihood function value evaluated

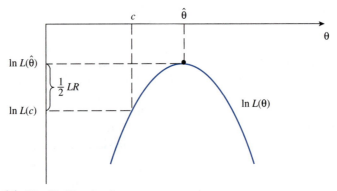

FIGURE C.14   The likelihood ratio test.

at the hypothesized value $\ln L(c)$. We have labeled the difference between these two log-likelihood values $(1/2)\,LR$ for a reason that will become clear. If the estimate $\hat{\theta}$ is close to c, then the difference between the log-likelihood values will be small. If $\hat{\theta}$ is far from c, then the difference between the log-likelihood values will be large. This observation leads us to the **likelihood ratio statistic**, which is twice the difference between $\ln L(\hat{\theta})$ and $\ln L(c)$,

$$LR = 2[\ln L(\hat{\theta}) - \ln L(c)] \tag{C.25}$$

Based on some advanced statistical theory, it can be shown that if the null hypothesis is true then the LR test statistic has a *chi-square* distribution (see Section B.5.2) with $J = 1$ degree of freedom. In more general contexts J is the number of hypotheses being tested and it can be greater than 1. If the null hypothesis is not true, then the LR test statistic becomes large. We reject the null hypothesis at the α level of significance if $LR \geq \chi^2_{(1-\alpha,J)}$, where $\chi^2_{(1-\alpha,J)}$ is the $100(1-\alpha)$ percentile of a chi-square distribution with J degrees of freedom, as shown in Figure C.15. The 90th, 95th, and 99th percentile values of the chi-square distribution for various degrees of freedom are given in Table 3 at the end of the book.

When estimating a population proportion p the log-likelihood function is given by (C.19). The value of p that maximizes this function is $\hat{p} = \sum x_i/N$. Thus, the maximum value of the log-likelihood function is

$$\ln L(\hat{p}) = \left(\sum_{i=1}^{N} x_i\right)\ln \hat{p} + \left(N - \sum_{i=1}^{N} x_i\right)\ln(1-\hat{p})$$
$$= N\hat{p}\ln \hat{p} + (N - N\hat{p})\ln(1-\hat{p})$$
$$= N[\hat{p}\ln \hat{p} + (1-\hat{p})\ln(1-\hat{p})]$$

where we have used the fact that $\sum x_i = N\hat{p}$. For our cereal box problem $\hat{p} = 0.375$ and $N = 200$, so we have

$$\ln L(\hat{p}) = 200[0.375 \times \ln(0.375) + (1 - 0.375)\ln(1 - 0.375)]$$
$$= -132.3126$$

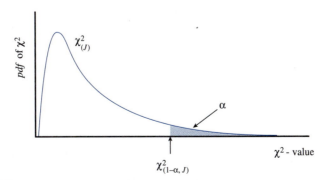

FIGURE **C.15**   Critical value from a chi-square distribution.

The value of the log-likelihood function assuming $H_0: p = 0.4$ is true is

$$\ln L(0.4) = \left(\sum_{i=1}^{N} x_i\right)\ln(0.4) + \left(N - \sum_{i=1}^{N} x_i\right)\ln(1 - 0.4)$$

$$= 75 \times \ln(0.4) + (200 - 75) \times \ln(0.6)$$

$$= -132.5750$$

The problem is to assess whether -132.3126 is significantly different from -132.5750. The *LR* test statistic (C.25) is

$$LR = 2[\ln L(\hat{p}) - \ln L(0.4)] = 2 \times (-132.3126 - (-132.575)) = 0.5247$$

If the null hypothesis $p = 0.4$ is true, then the *LR* test statistic has a $\chi^2_{(1)}$-distribution. If we choose $\alpha = 0.05$, then the test critical value is $\chi^2_{(0.95,1)} = 3.84$, the 95th percentile from the $\chi^2_{(1)}$ distribution. Since $0.5247 < 3.84$ we do not reject the null hypothesis.

C.8.4b The Wald Test

In Figure C.14 it is clear that the distance $(1/2)\,LR$ will depend on the curvature of the log-likelihood function. In Figure C.16 we show two log-likelihood functions with the hypothesized value c and the distances $(1/2)\,LR$ for each of the log-likelihoods. The log-likelihoods have the same maximum value $\ln L(\hat{\theta})$ but the values of the log-likelihood evaluated at the hypothesized value c are different.

The distance $\hat{\theta} - c$ translates into a larger value of $(1/2)\,LR$ for the more highly curved log-likelihood, B. Thus it seems reasonable to construct a test measure by weighting the distance $\hat{\theta} - c$ by the magnitude of the log-likelihood's curvature, which we measure by the negative of its second derivative. This is exactly what the Wald statistic does,

$$W = (\hat{\theta} - c)^2 \left[-\frac{d^2 \ln L(\theta)}{d\theta^2}\right] \tag{C.26}$$

The value of the Wald statistic is larger for log-likelihood function B (more curved) than log-likelihood function A (less curved).

If the null hypothesis is true, then the Wald statistic (C.26) has a $\chi^2_{(1)}$-distribution, and we reject the null hypothesis if $W \geq \chi^2_{(1-\alpha,1)}$. In more general situations we may test $J > 1$ hypotheses jointly, in which case we work with a chi-square distribution with J degrees of freedom, as shown in Figure C.15.

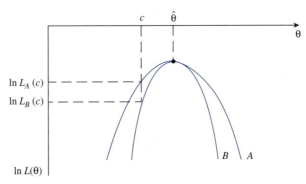

FIGURE C.16 The Wald statistic.

There is a linkage between the curvature of the log-likelihood function and the precision of maximum likelihood estimation. The greater the curvature of the log-likelihood function the smaller the variance V in (C.23) and the more precise maximum likelihood estimation becomes, meaning that we have more **information** about the unknown parameter θ. Conversely, the more information we have about θ the smaller the variance of the maximum likelihood estimator. Using this idea we define an information measure to be the reciprocal of the variance V,

$$I(\theta) = -E\left[\frac{d^2 \ln L(\theta)}{d\theta^2}\right] = V^{-1} \tag{C.27}$$

As the notation indicates the information measure $I(\theta)$ is a function of the parameter θ. Substitute the information measure for the second derivative in the Wald statistic in (C.26) to obtain

$$W = (\hat{\theta} - c)^2 I(\theta) \tag{C.28}$$

In large samples the two versions of the Wald statistic are the same. An interesting connection here is obtained by rewriting (C.28) as

$$W = (\hat{\theta} - c)^2 V^{-1} = (\hat{\theta} - c)^2 / V \tag{C.29}$$

To implement the Wald test we use the estimated variance

$$\hat{V} = [I(\hat{\theta})]^{-1} \tag{C.30}$$

Then, taking the square root, we obtain the t-statistic in (C.22),

$$\sqrt{W} = \frac{\hat{\theta} - c}{\sqrt{\hat{V}}} = \frac{\hat{\theta} - c}{\text{se}(\hat{\theta})} = t$$

That is, the t-test is also a Wald test.

In our blue box–green box example, we know that the maximum likelihood estimate $\hat{p} = 0.375$. To implement the Wald test we calculate

$$I(\hat{p}) = \hat{V}^{-1} = \frac{N}{\hat{p}(1 - \hat{p})} = \frac{200}{0.375(1 - 0.375)} = 853.3333$$

where $V = p(1 - p)/N$ and $\hat{V}$ were obtained in Section C.7.3. Then the calculated value of the Wald statistic is

$$W = (\hat{p} - c)^2 I(\hat{p}) = (0.375 - 0.4)^2 \times 853.3333 = 0.5333$$

In this case the value of the Wald statistic is close in magnitude to the LR statistic and the test conclusion is the same. Also, when testing one hypothesis, the Wald statistic is the square of the t-statistic, $W = t^2 = (-0.7303)^2 = 0.5333$

C.8.4c The Lagrange Multiplier (*LM*) Test

The third testing procedure that comes from maximum likelihood theory is the Lagrange multiplier (*LM*) test. Figure C.17 illustrates another way to measure the distance

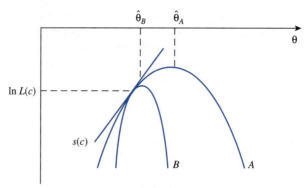

FIGURE C.17 Motivating the Lagrange multiplier test.

between $\hat\theta$ and c. The slope of the log-likelihood function, which is sometimes called the *score*, is

$$s(\theta) = \frac{d \ln L(\theta)}{d\theta} \tag{C.31}$$

The slope of the log-likelihood function depends on the value of θ, as our function notation $s(\theta)$ indicates. The slope of the log-likelihood function at the maximizing value is zero, $s(\hat\theta) = 0$. The *LM* test examines the slope of the log-likelihood function at the point c. The logic of the test is that if $\hat\theta$ is close to c then the slope $s(c)$ of the log-likelihood function evaluated at c should be close to zero. In fact testing the null hypothesis $\theta = c$ is equivalent to testing $s(c) = 0$.

The difference between c and the maximum likelihood estimate $\hat\theta_B$ (maximizing $\ln L_B$) is smaller than the difference between c and $\hat\theta_A$. In contrast to the Wald test, more curvature in the log-likelihood function implies a smaller difference between the maximum likelihood estimate and c. If we use the information measure $I(\theta)$ as our measure of curvature (more curvature means more information), the Lagrange multiplier test statistic can be written as

$$LM = \frac{[s(c)]^2}{I(\theta)} = [s(c)]^2[I(\theta)]^{-1} \tag{C.32}$$

The *LM* statistic for log-likelihood function *A* (less curved) is greater than the *LM* statistic for log-likelihood function *B* (more curved). If the null hypothesis is true, *LM* test statistic (C.32) has a $\chi^2_{(1)}$-distribution, and the rejection region is the same as for the *LR* and Wald tests. The *LM*, *LR*, and Wald tests are asymptotically equivalent and will lead to the same conclusion in sufficiently large samples.

In order to implement the *LM* test we can evaluate the information measure at the point $\theta = c$, so that it becomes

$$LM = [s(c)]^2[I(c)]^{-1}$$

In cases in which the maximum likelihood estimate is difficult to obtain (which it can be in more complex problems) the *LM* test has an advantage because $\hat\theta$ is not required. On the other hand, the Wald test in (C.28) uses the information measure evaluated at the maximum likelihood estimate $\hat\theta$,

$$W = (\hat\theta - c)^2 I(\hat\theta)$$

It is preferred when the maximum likelihood estimate and its variance are easily obtained. The likelihood ratio test statistic (C.25) requires calculation of the log-likelihood function at both the maximum likelihood estimate and the hypothesized value c. As noted the three tests are asymptotically equivalent and the choice of which to use is often made on the basis of convenience. In complex situations the rule of convenience may not be a good one. The likelihood ratio test is relatively reliable in most circumstances, so that if you are in doubt it is a safe one to use.

In the blue box–green box example the value of the score, based on the first derivative shown just below equation (C.19), evaluated at the hypothesized value $c = 0.4$ is

$$s(0.4) = \frac{\sum x_i}{c} - \frac{N - \sum x_i}{1 - c} = \frac{75}{0.4} - \frac{200 - 75}{1 - 0.4} = -20.8333$$

The calculated information measure is

$$I(0.4) = \frac{N}{c(1 - c)} = \frac{200}{0.4(1 - 0.4)} = 833.3333$$

The value of the *LM* test statistic is

$$LM = [s(0.4)]^2 [I(0.4)]^{-1} = [-20.8333]^2 [833.3333]^{-1} = 0.5208$$

Thus in our example the values of the *LR*, Wald, and *LM* test statistics are very similar and give the same conclusion. This was to be expected since the sample size $N = 200$ is large, and the problem is a simple one.

C.9 Algebraic Supplements (Optional)

C.9.1 Derivation of Least Squares Estimator

In this section we illustrate how to use the least squares principle to obtain the sample mean as an estimator of the population mean. Represent a sample of data as $y_1, y_2, \ldots, y_N$. The population mean is $E(Y) = \mu$. The least squares principle says find the value of μ that minimizes

$$S = \sum_{i=1}^{N} (y_i - \mu)^2$$

where S is the sum of squared deviations of the data values from μ.

The motivation for this approach can be deduced from the following example. Suppose you are going shopping at a number of shops along a certain street. Your plan is to shop at one store and return to your car to deposit your purchases. Then you visit a second store and return again to your car, and so on. After visiting each shop you return to your car. Where would you park to minimize the total amount of walking between your car and the shops you visit? You want to minimize the *distance* traveled. Think of the street along which you shop as a number line. The Euclidean distance between a shop located at y_i and your car at point μ is

$$d_i = \sqrt{(y_i - \mu)^2}$$

The squared distance, which is mathematically more convenient to work with, is

$$d_i^2 = (y_i - \mu)^2$$

To minimize the total squared distance between your parking spot μ and all the shops located at $y_1, y_2, \ldots, y_N$ you would minimize

$$S(\mu) = \sum_{i=1}^{N} d_i^2 = \sum_{i=1}^{N} (y_i - \mu)^2$$

which is the sum of squares function. Thus the least squares principle is really the least *squared distance* principle.

Since the values of y_i are known given the sample, the sum of squares function $S(\mu)$ is a function of the unknown parameter μ. Multiplying out the sum of squares we have

$$S(\mu) = \sum_{i=1}^{N} y_i^2 - 2\mu \sum_{i=1}^{N} y_i + N\mu^2 = a_0 - 2a_1\mu + a_2\mu^2$$

For the data in Table C.1 we have

$$a_0 = \Sigma y_i^2 = 14880.1909, \quad a_1 = \Sigma y_i = 857.9100, \quad a_2 = N = 50$$

The plot of the sum of squares parabola is shown in Figure C.18. The minimizing value appears to be a bit larger than 17 in the figure. Now we will determine the minimizing value exactly.

The value of μ that minimizes $S(\mu)$ is the "least squares estimate." From calculus, we know that the minimum of the function occurs where its slope is zero. The function's

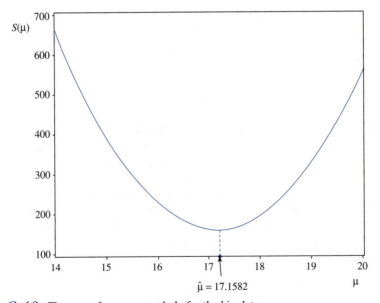

FIGURE C.18   The sum of squares parabola for the hip data.

derivative gives its slope, so by equating the first derivative of $S(\mu)$ to zero and solving, we can obtain the minimizing value exactly. The derivative of $S(\mu)$ is

$$\frac{dS(\mu)}{d\mu} = -2a_1 + 2a_2\mu$$

Setting the derivative to zero determines the least squares estimate of μ, which we denote as $\hat{\mu}$. Setting the derivative to zero,

$$-2a_1 + 2a_2\hat{\mu} = 0$$

Solving for $\hat{\mu}$ yields the formula for the least squares estimate,

$$\hat{\mu} = \frac{a_1}{a_2} = \frac{\sum_{i=1}^{N} y_i}{N} = \bar{y}$$

Thus the least squares estimate of the population mean is the sample mean, $\bar{y}$. This formula can be used in general, for any sample values that might be obtained, meaning that the least squares estimator is

$$\hat{\mu} = \frac{\sum_{i=1}^{N} Y_i}{N} = \bar{Y}$$

For the hip data in Table C.1

$$\hat{\mu} = \frac{\sum_{i=1}^{N} y_i}{N} = \frac{857.9100}{50} = 17.1582$$

Thus we estimate that the average hip size in the population is 17.1582 inches.

C.9.2   BEST LINEAR UNBIASED ESTIMATION

One of the powerful findings about the sample mean (which is also the least squares estimator) is that it is the best of all possible estimators that are both *linear* and *unbiased*. The fact that $\bar{Y}$ is the "best" linear unbiased estimator (BLUE) accounts for its wide use. In this context we mean by "best" that it is the estimator with the smallest variance of all linear and unbiased estimators. It is better to have an estimator with a smaller variance rather than a larger one; it increases the chances of getting an estimate close to the true population mean μ. This important result about the least squares estimator is true *if* the sample values $Y_i \sim (\mu, \sigma^2)$ are uncorrelated and identically distributed. It does not depend on the population being normally distributed. The fact that $\bar{Y}$ is BLUE is so important that we will prove it.

The sample mean is a weighted average of the sample values,

$$\begin{aligned}
\bar{Y} &= \sum_{i=1}^{N} Y_i / N = \frac{1}{N}Y_1 + \frac{1}{N}Y_2 + \cdots + \frac{1}{N}Y_N \\
&= a_1 Y_1 + a_2 Y_2 + \cdots + a_N Y_N \\
&= \sum_{i=1}^{N} a_i Y_i
\end{aligned}$$

where the weights $a_i = 1/N$. Weighted averages are also called linear combinations, thus we call the sample mean a **linear estimator**. In fact any estimator that can be written like $\sum_{i=1}^{N} a_i Y_i$ is a linear estimator. For example, suppose the weights a_i^* are constants different from $a_i = 1/N$. Then we can define another linear estimator of μ as

$$\tilde{Y} = \sum_{i=1}^{N} a_i^* Y_i$$

To ensure that $\tilde{Y}$ is different from $\overline{Y}$ let us define

$$a_i^* = a_i + c_i = \frac{1}{N} + c_i$$

where c_i are constants that are not all zero. Thus

$$\begin{aligned}
\tilde{Y} &= \sum_{i=1}^{N} a_i^* Y_i = \sum_{i=1}^{N} \left(\frac{1}{N} + c_i \right) Y_i \\
&= \sum_{i=1}^{N} \frac{1}{N} Y_i + \sum_{i=1}^{N} c_i Y_i \\
&= \overline{Y} + \sum_{i=1}^{N} c_i Y_i
\end{aligned}$$

The expected value of the new estimator $\tilde{Y}$ is

$$\begin{aligned}
E[\tilde{Y}] &= E\left[\overline{Y} + \sum_{i=1}^{N} c_i Y_i \right] = \mu + \sum_{i=1}^{N} c_i E[Y_i] \\
&= \mu + \mu \sum_{i=1}^{N} c_i
\end{aligned}$$

The estimator $\tilde{Y}$ is not unbiased unless $\sum c_i = 0$. We want to compare the sample mean to other linear and unbiased estimators, so we will assume $\sum c_i = 0$ holds. Now we find the variance of $\tilde{Y}$. The linear unbiased estimator with the smaller variance will be best.

$$\begin{aligned}
\mathrm{var}(\tilde{Y}) &= \mathrm{var}\left(\sum_{i=1}^{N} a_i^* Y_i \right) = \mathrm{var}\left(\sum_{i=1}^{N} \left(\frac{1}{N} + c_i \right) Y_i \right) = \sum_{i=1}^{N} \left(\frac{1}{N} + c_i \right)^2 \mathrm{var}(Y_i) \\
&= \sigma^2 \sum_{i=1}^{N} \left(\frac{1}{N} + c_i \right)^2 = \sigma^2 \sum_{i=1}^{N} \left(\frac{1}{N^2} + \frac{2}{N} c_i + c_i^2 \right) = \sigma^2 \left(\frac{1}{N} + \frac{2}{N} \sum_{i=1}^{N} c_i + \sum_{i=1}^{N} c_i^2 \right) \\
&= \sigma^2/N + \sigma^2 \sum_{i=1}^{N} c_i^2 \qquad \left(\text{since } \sum_{i=1}^{N} c_i = 0 \right) \\
&= \mathrm{var}(\overline{Y}) + \sigma^2 \sum_{i=1}^{N} c_i^2
\end{aligned}$$

It follows that the variance of $\tilde{Y}$ must be greater than the variance of $\overline{Y}$, unless all the c_i values are zero, in which case $\tilde{Y} = \overline{Y}$.

C.10 Exercises

C.1   Suppose $Y_1, Y_2, \ldots, Y_N$ is a random sample from a population with mean μ and variance σ^2. Rather than using all N observations consider an easy estimator of μ that uses only the first two observations

$$Y^* = \frac{Y_1 + Y_2}{2}$$

(a) Show that Y^* is a linear estimator.

(b) Show that Y^* is an unbiased estimator.

(c) Find the variance of Y^*.

(d) Explain why the sample mean of all N observations is a better estimator than Y^*.

C.2   Suppose that Y_1, Y_2, Y_3 is a random sample from a $N(\mu, \sigma^2)$ population. To estimate μ consider the weighted estimator

$$\tilde{Y} = \frac{1}{2} Y_1 + \frac{1}{3} Y_2 + \frac{1}{6} Y_3$$

(a) Show that $\tilde{Y}$ is a linear estimator.

(b) Show that $\tilde{Y}$ is an unbiased estimator.

(c) Find the variance of $\tilde{Y}$ and compare it to the variance of the sample mean $\overline{Y}$.

(d) Is $\tilde{Y}$ as good an estimator as $\overline{Y}$?

(e) If $\sigma^2 = 9$, calculate the probability that each estimator is within 1 unit on either side of μ.

C.3* The hourly sales of fried chicken at Louisiana Fried Chicken are normally distributed with mean 2000 pieces and standard deviation 500 pieces. What is the probability that in a 9-hour day more than 20,000 pieces will be sold?

C.4   Starting salaries for Economics majors have a mean of $47,000 and a standard deviation of $8,000. What is the probability that a random sample of 40 Economics majors will have an average salary of more than $50,000?

C.5* A store manager designs a new accounting system that will be cost effective if the mean monthly charge account balance is more than $170. A sample of 400 accounts is randomly selected. The sample mean balance is $178 and the sample standard deviation is $65. Can the manager conclude that the new system will be cost effective?

(a) Carry out a hypothesis test to answer this question. Use the $\alpha = 0.05$ level of significance.

(b) Compute the p-value of the test.

C.6   An econometric professor's rule of thumb is that students should expect to spend 2 hours outside of class on coursework for each hour in class. For a 3 hour per week class, this means that students are expected to do 6 hours of work outside class. The professor randomly selects eight students from a class, and asks how many hours they studied econometrics during the past week. The sample values are 1, 3, 4, 4, 6, 6, 8, 12.

(a) Assuming that the population is normally distributed, can the professor conclude at the 0.05 level of significance that the students are studying on average at least 6 hours per week?

(b) Construct a 90% confidence interval for the population mean number of hours studied per week.

C.7   Modern labor practices attempt to keep labor costs low by hiring and laying off workers to meet demand. Newly hired workers are not as productive as experienced ones. Assume assembly line workers with experience handle 500 pieces per day. A manager concludes it is cost effective to maintain the current practice if new hires, with a week of training, can process at least 450 pieces per day. A random sample of $N = 50$ trainees is observed. Let Y_i denote the number of pieces each handles on a randomly selected day. The sample mean is $\bar{y} = 460$ and the estimated sample standard deviation is $\hat{\sigma} = 38$.

(a) Carry out a test of whether or not there is evidence to support the conjecture that current hiring procedures are effective, at the 5% level of significance. Pay careful attention when formulating the null and alternative hypotheses.

(b) What exactly would a Type I error be in this example? Would it be a costly one to make?

(c) Compute the p-value for this test.

C.8* To evaluate alternative retirement benefit packages for its employees, a large corporation must determine the mean age of its workforce. Assume that the age of its employees is normally distributed. Since the corporation has thousands of workers a sample is to be taken. If the standard deviation of ages is known to be $\sigma = 21$ years, how large should the sample be to ensure that a 95% interval estimate of mean age is no more than 4 years wide?

C.9 Consider the discrete random variable Y that takes the values $y = 1, 2, 3$, and 4 with probabilities 0.1, 0.2, 0.3, and 0.4, respectively.

(a) Sketch this *pdf*.

(b) Find the expected value of Y.

(c) Find the variance of Y.

(d) If we take a random sample of size $N = 3$ from this distribution, what are the mean and variance of the sample mean, $\bar{Y} = (Y_1 + Y_2 + Y_3)/3$?

C.10 This exercise is a low-tech simulation experiment related to Exercise C.9. It can be a group or class exercise if desired. Have each group member create a set of 10 numbered, identical, slips of paper like the following table.

1	2	2	3	3
3	4	4	4	4

(a) Draw a slip of paper at random and record its value, preferably entering each number into a data file for use with your computer software. Draw a total of 10 times, each time replacing the slip into the pile and stirring them well. Compare the average of these values to the expected value in Exercise C.9(b). Draw 10 more values with replacement. What is the average of all 20 values?

(b) Calculate the sample variance of the 20 values obtained in part (a). Compare this value to the true variance in Exercise C.9(c).

(c) Draw three slips of paper at random, with replacement. Calculate the average of the numbers on these $N = 3$ slips of paper, $\bar{Y} = (Y_1 + Y_2 + Y_3)/3$. Repeat this process at least $NSAM = 20$ times, obtaining $NSAM$ average values, $\bar{Y}_1, \bar{Y}_2, \ldots, \bar{Y}_{NSAM}$. Calculate the sample average and sample variance of these $NSAM$ values. Compare these to the expected value and variance of the sample mean obtained in Exercise C.9(d).

(d) Enter the $NSAM$ values $\bar{Y}_1, \bar{Y}_2, \ldots, \bar{Y}_{NSAM}$ into a data file. Standardize these values by subtracting the true mean and dividing by the true standard deviation of the mean, from Exercise C9(d). Use your computer software to create a histogram. Discuss the central limit theorem and how it relates to the figure you have created.

(e) Repeat parts (c) and (d) using *NSAM* samples of more than $N = 3$ slips of paper, perhaps 5 or 7. How do the histograms compare to the one in part (d)?

(f) Discuss the terms "sampling variation" and "sampling distribution" in the context of the experiments you have performed.

C.11 At the famous Fulton Fish Market in New York city sales of Whiting (a type of fish) vary from day to day. Over a period of several months daily quantities sold (in pounds) were observed. These data are in the file *fultonfish.dat*.

(a) Using the data for Monday sales, test the null hypothesis that the mean quantity sold is greater than or equal to 10,000 pounds a day, against the alternative that the mean quantity sold is less than 10,000 pounds. Use the $\alpha = 0.05$ level of significance. Be sure to (i) state the null and alternative hypotheses, (ii) give the test statistic and its distribution, (iii) indicate the rejection region, including a sketch, (iv) state your conclusion, and (v) calculate the *p*-value for the test. Include a sketch showing the *p*-value.

(b) Assume that daily sales on Tuesday (X_2) and Wednesday (X_3) are normally distributed with means μ_2 and μ_3, and variances σ_2^2 and σ_3^2, respectively. Assume that sales on Tuesday and Wednesday are independent of each other. Test the hypothesis that the variances σ_2^2 and σ_3^2 are equal, against the alternative that the variance on Tuesday is larger. Use the $\alpha = 0.05$ level of significance. Be sure to (i) state the null and alternative hypotheses, (ii) give the test statistic and its distribution, (iii) indicate the rejection region, including a sketch, (iv) state your conclusion, and (v) calculate the *p*-value for the test. Include a sketch showing the *p*-value.

(c) We wish to test the hypothesis that mean daily sales on Tuesday and Wednesday are equal, against the alternative that they are not equal. Using the result in part (b) as a guide to the appropriate version of the test (Section C.7), carry out this hypothesis test using the 5% level of significance.

(d) Let the daily sales for Monday, Tuesday, Wednesday, Thursday, and Friday be denoted as X_1, X_2, X_3, X_4, and X_5, respectively. Assume that $X_i \sim N(\mu_i, \sigma_i^2)$ and that sales from day to day are independent. Define total weekly sales as $W = X_1 + X_2 + X_3 + X_4 + X_5$. Derive the expected value and variance of W. Be sure to show your work and justify your answer.

(e)◆ Referring to part (d), let $E(W) = \mu$. Assume that we estimate μ using

$$\hat{\mu} = \overline{X}_1 + \overline{X}_2 + \overline{X}_3 + \overline{X}_4 + \overline{X}_5$$

where $\overline{X}_i$ is the sample mean for the *i*th day. Derive the probability distribution of $\hat{\mu}$ and construct an approximate (valid in large samples) 95% interval estimate for μ. Justify the validity of your interval estimator.

Appendix *D*

Answers to Selected Exercises

Chapter 2

2.3 (b) $\Sum x_i = 21$ $\Sum y_i = 44$ $\Sum(x_i - \bar{x})(y_i - \bar{y}) = 22$ $\Sum(x_i - \bar{x})^2 = 17.5$
$b_2 = 1.257$ $b_1 = 2.9333$

(c) $\bar{y} = 7.3333$ $\bar{x} = 3.5$ The predicted value for y at $x = \bar{x}$ is $\bar{y}$.

(d) $\hat{e}_1 = -0.19048$ $\hat{e}_2 = 0.55238$ $\hat{e}_3 = 0.29524$
$\hat{e}_4 = -0.96190$ $\hat{e}_5 = -0.21905$ $\hat{e}_6 = 0.52381$
$\Sum \hat{e}_i = 0$

(e) $\Sum x_i \hat{e}_i = 0$

2.6 (a) The intercept estimate $b_1 = -240$ is an estimate of the number of sodas sold when the temperature is 0°F. It is impossible to sell -240 sodas and so this estimate should not be accepted as a sensible one. The slope estimate $b_2 = 6$ is an estimate of the increase in sodas sold when temperature increases by 1°F. This estimate does make sense. One would expect the number of sodas sold to increase as temperature increases.

(b) The predicted number of sodas sold is $\hat{y} = -240 + 6 \times 80 = 240$.

(c) If no sodas are sold, $y = 0$, and $0 = -240 + 6 \times x$ or $x = 40$. Thus, she predicts no sodas will be sold below 40°F.

2.9 (b) $b_1 = 6.0191$ and $b_2 = -0.3857$. The cost of producing the first unit is
$\widehat{UNITCOST}_1 = \exp(b_1) = \exp(6.0191) = 411.208$. The estimate $b_2 = -0.3857$ suggests that a 1% increase in cumulative production will decrease costs by 0.386%. The numbers are sensible.

(c) $\widehat{\mathrm{var}(b_1)} = 0.075553$ $\widehat{\mathrm{var}(b_2)} = 0.001297$ $\widehat{\mathrm{cov}(b_1, b_2)} = -0.009888$

(d) $\hat{\sigma}^2 = 0.049930^2 = 0.002493$.

(e) $\ln(\widehat{UNITCOST}_0) = 6.0191 - 0.0385\ln(2000) = 3.0874526$

$\widehat{UNITCOST}_0 = \exp(3.0874526) = 21.921$

2.12 (b) $\widehat{PRICE} = -18,386 + 81.389SQFT$. The coefficient $b_2 = 81.389$ suggests house price increases by approximately \$81 for each additional square foot in size. If taken literally, the intercept $b_1 = -\$18,386$ suggests a house with zero square feet would cost $-\$18,386$. The model should not be accepted as a serious one in the region of zero square feet.

    (c) Vacant houses: $\widehat{PRICE} = -4793 + 69.908SQFT$
        Occupied houses: $\widehat{PRICE} = -27,169 + 89.259SQFT$
        The marginal cost (change in price) for an additional square foot is higher for occupied houses than for vacant houses. The average price per square foot is higher for vacant houses than for occupied houses when the house size is less than 1156 square feet. For houses larger than 1156 square feet, the price per square foot is higher for occupied houses.

    (d) The magnitude of the residuals tends to be larger for larger sized houses suggesting that SR3 $var(e|x_i) = \sigma^2$ (the homoskedasticity assumption) could be violated.

    (e) $\widehat{PRICE} = -18,386 + 81.389 \times 2000 = \$144,392$

2.14 (b) $\widehat{VOTE} = 51.939 + 0.660GROWTH$

    (c) $\widehat{VOTE} = 53.496 - 0.445INFLATION$

Chapter 3

3.3 (a) Hypotheses are $H_0 : \beta_2 = 0$ against $H_1 : \beta_2 \neq 0$. Rejection region is $t \geq 2.819$ or $t \leq -2.819$. Calculated value of test statistic is $t = 0.310/0.082 = 3.78$. Reject H_0 because $t = 3.78 > 2.819$.

    (b) Hypotheses are $H_0 : \beta_2 = 0$ against $H_1 : \beta_2 > 0$. Rejection region is $t \geq 2.508$. Calculated value of test statistic is $t = 3.78$. Reject H_0 because $t = 3.78 > 2.508$.

    (c) Hypotheses are $H_0 : \beta_2 = 0$ against $H_1 : \beta_2 < 0$. Rejection region is $t \leq -1.717$. Calculated value of test statistic is $t = 3.78$. Do not reject H_0 because $t = 3.78 > -1.717$.

    (d) Hypotheses are $H_0 : \beta_2 = 0.5$ against $H_1 : \beta_2 \neq 0.5$. Rejection region is $t \geq 2.074$ or $t \leq -2.074$. Calculated value of test statistic is $t = (0.31 - 0.5)/0.082 = -2.32$. Reject H_0 because $t = -2.32 < -2.074$.

    (e) $b_2 \pm t_c se(b_2) = 0.310 \pm 2.819 \times 0.082 = (0.079, 0.541)$

3.6 (a) $b_2 \pm 2.145 \times se(b_2) = -0.3857 \pm 2.145 \times 0.03601 = (-0.4629, -0.3085)$. We estimate β_2 to lie between -0.4629 and -0.3085 using a procedure that works 95% of the time in repeated samples.

    (b) Hypotheses are $H_0 : \beta_2 = 0$ against $H_1 : \beta_2 < 0$. Rejection region is $t \leq -1.761$. Calculated value of test statistic is $t = -0.3857/0.03601 = -10.71$. Reject H_0 because $t = -10.71 < -1.761$. Learning does exist.

3.9 (a) Hypotheses are $H_0 : \beta_2 = 0$ against $H_1 : \beta_2 > 0$. Alternative $H_1 : \beta_2 > 0$ is chosen under the assumption that growth, if it does influence the vote, will do so in a positive way. Rejection region is $t \geq 1.699$. Calculated value of test statistic is $t = 0.6599/0.1631 = 4.046$. Reject H_0 because $t = 4.046 > 1.699$. Growth has a positive effect on the vote.

(b) $b_2 \pm 2.045 \times se(b_2) = 0.6599 \pm 2.045 \times 0.1631 = (0.3264, 0.9934)$. Using a procedure that works 95% of the time in repeated samples, we estimate that a 1% increase in the growth rate will increase the percentage vote by an amount between 0.3264% to 0.9934%.

(c) Hypotheses are $H_0 : \beta_2 = 0$ against $H_1 : \beta_2 < 0$. Alternative $H_1 : \beta_2 < 0$ is chosen under the assumption that inflation, if it does influence the vote, will do so in a negative way. Choosing a 5% significance level, the rejection region is $t \leq -1.699$. The value of the test statistic is $t = -0.4450/0.5197 = -0.856$. Do not reject H_0 because $t = -0.856 > -1.699$. Not enough evidence to suggest inflation has a negative effect on the vote.

(d) $b_2 \pm 2.045 \times se(b_2) = -0.4450 \pm 2.045 \times 0.5197 = (-1.508, 0.618)$. This interval estimate suggests a 1% increase in the inflation rate could increase or decrease the percentage vote.

3.11 (a) Hypotheses are $H_0 : \beta_2 = 80$ against $H_1 : \beta_2 \neq 80$. Rejection region is $t \geq 1.963$ or $t \leq -1.963$. Value of test statistic is $t = (81.389 - 80)/1.918 = 0.724$. Do not reject H_0 because $-1.963 < 0.724 < 1.963$.

(b) Hypotheses are $H_0 : \beta_2 = 80$ against $H_1 : \beta_2 \neq 80$. Rejection region is $t \geq 1.965$ or $t \leq -1.965$. Value of test statistic is $t = (69.908 - 80)/2.267 = -4.45$. Reject H_0 because $-4.45 < -1.965$.

(c) Hypotheses are $H_0 : \beta_2 = 80$ against $H_1 : \beta_2 \neq 80$. Rejection region is $t \geq 1.966$ or $t \leq -1.966$. Value of test statistic is $t = (89.259 - 80)/3.039 = 3.05$. Reject H_0 because $3.05 > 1.966$.

(d) Hypotheses are $H_0 : \beta_2 \leq 80$ against $H_1 : \beta_2 > 80$. Using a 5% significance level, rejection region is $t \geq 1.649$. Value of test statistic is $t = 3.05$. Reject H_0 because $3.05 > 1.649$.

(e) Hypotheses are $H_0 : \beta_2 \geq 80$ against $H_1 : \beta_2 < 80$. Using a 5% significance level, rejection region is $t \leq -1.648$. Value of test statistic is $t = -4.45$. Reject H_0 because $-4.45 < -1.648$.

(f) (i) $b_2 \pm 1.963 \times se(b_2) = 81.389 \pm 1.963 \times 1.918 = (77.62, 85.15)$

   (ii) $b_2 \pm 1.965 \times se(b_2) = 69.908 \pm 1.965 \times 2.267 = (65.45, 74.36)$

   (iii) $b_2 \pm 1.966 \times se(b_2) = 89.259 \pm 1.966 \times 3.039 = (83.28, 95.23)$

Chapter 4

4.1 (a) $R^2 = 0.7105$ (b) $R^2 = 0.8455$ (c) $\hat{\sigma}^2 = 6.4104$

4.2 (a) $\hat{y}_t = 5.83 + 8.69x_t^*$ $R^2 = 0.756$ $x_t^* = x_t/10$
      $(1.23)\ (1.17)$

(b) $\hat{y}_t^* = 0.583 + 0.0869x_t$ $R^2 = 0.756$ $\hat{y}_t^* = \hat{y}_t/10$
      $(0.123)\ (0.0117)$

(c) $\hat{y}_t^* = 0.583 + 0.869x_t^*$ $R^2 = 0.756$ $\hat{y}_t^* = \hat{y}_t/10$ $x_t^* = x_t/10$
      $(0.123)\ (0.117)$

4.9 (a) Equation $1: \hat{y}_0 = 1.467$ Equation $2: \hat{y}_0 = 1.251$
      Equation $3: \hat{y}_0 = 1.643$

(b) Equation $1: dy_t/dt = 0.0161$ Equation $2: dy_t/dt = 0.0038$
      Equation $3: dy_t/dt = 0.0348$

(c) Equation $1: (dy_t/dt)(t/y_t) = 0.538$ Equation $2: (dy_t/dt)(t/y_t) = 0.148$
      Equation $3: (dy_t/dt)(t/y_t) = 1.037$

4.11 (a) $\widehat{VOTE_{2000}} = 51.9387 + 0.6599 \times 1.603 = 52.9965$

$\hat{e}_{2000} = VOTE_{2000} - \widehat{VOTE_{2000}} = 50.265 - 52.9965 = -2.7315$

(b) $\widehat{VOTE_{2000}} = 52.0281 + 0.6631 \times 1.603 = 53.091$

$f = VOTE_{2000} - \widehat{VOTE_{2000}} = 50.2650 - 53.091 = -2.826$

(c) $\widehat{VOTE_{2000}} \pm 2.048 \times se(f) = 53.091 \pm 2.048 \times 5.1648 = (42.513, 63.669)$

(d) $GROWTH = -3.209$

4.13 (a) $\ln(PRICE) = 10.5938 + 0.000596 SQFT$

(se)   (0.0219) (0.000013)

Each extra square foot of house size increases price by 0.06%.

$\dfrac{dPRICE}{dSQFT} = \beta_2 \times \overline{PRICE} = 67.23, \quad \dfrac{dPRICE/PRICE}{dSQFT/SQFT} = \beta_2 \times \overline{SQFT} = 0.9607$

(b) $\ln(PRICE) = 4.1707 + 1.0066\ln(SQFT)$

(se)   (0.1655) (0.0225)

An extra 1% of floor space leads to a price that is approximately 1% higher.

$\dfrac{dPRICE}{dSQFT} = \beta_2 \times \dfrac{\overline{PRICE}}{\overline{SQFT}} = 70.444, \quad \dfrac{dPRICE/PRICE}{dSQFT/SQFT} = \beta_2 = 1.0066$

(c) Linear $R^2 = 0.672$ Log-linear $R_g^2 = 0.715$ Log-log $R_g^2 = 0.673$

(d) Log-linear: Jarque-Bera = 78.9 p-value = 0.0000

Log-log: Jarque-Bera = 52.7 p-value = 0.0000

Simple linear: Jarque-Bera = 2456 p-value = 0.0000

None of the models have residuals compatible with the normality assumption, particularly the simple linear one.

(e) Plots of the residuals against $SQFT$ reveal (i) the absolute magnitude of the residuals increases as $SQFT$ increases suggesting that the assumption of homoskedasticity is violated and (ii) for the simple linear model there is a predominance of positive residuals for very small and very large houses, suggesting the functional form is not suitable.

(f) Log-linear model: $\widehat{PRICE} = \exp(b_1 + b_2 \times 2700 + \hat{\sigma}^2/2) = 203,516$

Log-log model: $\widehat{PRICE} = \exp(b_1 + b_2\ln(2700) + \hat{\sigma}^2/2) = 188,221$

Simple linear model: $\widehat{PRICE} = b_1 + b_2 \times 2700 = 201,365$

(g) Log-linear model

$$se(f) = 0.203034\sqrt{1 + \frac{1}{880} + \frac{(2700 - 1611.968)^2}{248768933.1}} = 0.2036$$

95% confidence interval $\exp\left(\widehat{\ln(y_0)} \pm t_c se(f)\right) = [133,683;\ 297,316]$

Log-log model:

$$se(f) = 0.208251\sqrt{1 + \frac{1}{880} + \frac{(7.90101 - 7.3355)^2}{85.34453}} = 0.2088$$

95% confidence interval, $\exp\left(\widehat{\ln(y_0)} \pm t_c \mathrm{se}(f)\right) = [122, 267;\ 277, 454]$

Simple linear model:

$$\mathrm{se}(f) = 30259.2\sqrt{1 + \frac{1}{880} + \frac{(2700 - 1611.968)^2}{248768933.1}} = 30348$$

95% confidence interval $\quad \widehat{y_0} \pm t_c \mathrm{se}(f) = (141, 801;\ 260, 928)$

(h) The log-linear functional form is the best choice. It has the highest R_g^2 value that suggests that this model best fits the data. The simple linear model is not a good choice because the residuals are heavily skewed to the right and hence far from being normally distributed.

Chapter 5

5.1 (a) $\bar{y} = 1$, $\bar{x}_2 = 0$, $\bar{x}_3 = 0$. Thus, $x_{i2}^* = x_{i2}$ and $x_{i3}^* = x_{i3}$. Values for y_i^* are
$y_i^* = [0, 1, 2, -2, -1, -2, 1, 0, 1]$

(b) $\sum y_i^* x_{i2}^* = 13$, $\quad \sum x_{i2}^{*2} = 16$, $\quad \sum y_i^* x_{i3}^* = 4$, $\quad \sum x_{i2}^* x_{i3}^* = 0$, $\quad \sum x_{i3}^{*2} = 10$

(c) $b_2 = \dfrac{13 \times 10 - 4 \times 0}{16 \times 10 - 0^2} = 0.8125 \qquad b_3 = \dfrac{4 \times 16 - 13 \times 0}{16 \times 10 - 0^2} = 0.4$

$b_1 = \bar{y} - b_2 \bar{x}_2 - b_3 \bar{x}_3 = 1$

(d) $\hat{e}_i = [-0.4, 0.9875, -0.025, -0.375, -1.4125, 0.025, 0.6, 0.4125, 0.1875]$

(e) $\hat{\sigma}^2 = \dfrac{\sum \hat{e}_i^2}{N - K} = \dfrac{3.8375}{9 - 3} = 0.6396$

(f) $r_{23} = \dfrac{\sum (x_{i2} - \bar{x}_2)(x_{i3} - \bar{x}_3)}{\sqrt{\sum (x_{i2} - \bar{x}_2)^2 \sum (x_{i3} - \bar{x}_3)^2}} = \dfrac{\sum x_{i2}^* x_{i3}^*}{\sqrt{\sum x_{i2}^{*2} \sum x_{i3}^{*2}}} = 0$

(g) $\mathrm{se}(b_2) = \sqrt{\widehat{\mathrm{var}(b_2)}} = \sqrt{\dfrac{\hat{\sigma}^2}{\sum (x_{i2} - \bar{x}_2)^2 (1 - r_{23}^2)}} = \sqrt{\dfrac{0.6396}{16}} = 0.1999$

(h) $SSE = 3.8375 \quad SST = 16 \quad SSR = 12.1625 \quad R^2 = 0.7602$

5.2 (a) $b_2 \pm t_c \mathrm{se}(b_2) = 0.8125 \pm 2.447 \times 0.1999 = (0.3233, 1.3017)$

(b) Rejection region for a 5% significance level is $t \geq 2.447$ or $t \leq -2.447$. Value of test statistic is $t = (0.8125 - 1)/0.1999 = -0.938$. Do not reject H_0 because $-2.447 < -0.938 < 2.447$.

5.4 (a) $\widehat{WTRANS} = -0.0315 + 0.0414 \ln(TOTEXP) - 0.0001 AGE - 0.0130 NK$

(se) $\qquad\qquad (0.0322)\ (0.0071) \qquad\qquad\qquad (0.0004) \qquad (0.0055)$

$$R^2 = 0.0247$$

(b) $b_2 = 0.0414$. A 10% increase in total expenditure will increase the budget proportion for transportation by 0.004 (see Section A.4.8). Time is likely to be more valuable for households with higher expenditure in which case one would expect a greater proportion of expenditure on quicker more expensive forms of transportation. The increase is not large, however.

$b_3 = -0.0001$. When the age of the head of the household increases by 1 year, the budget share for transport decreases by 0.0001. The expected sign for b_3 could be positive or negative. In any event, the estimated change is small.

$b_4 = -0.0130$. For each additional child the budget share for transport decreases by 0.013. The negative sign means that adding children to a household increases expenditure on other items (such as food and clothing) more than it does on transportation. Alternatively, having more children may lead a household to turn to cheaper forms of transport.

(c) The p-value for testing $H_0 : \beta_3 = 0$ against the alternative $H_1 : \beta_3 \neq 0$ where β_3 is the coefficient of *AGE* is 0.869, suggesting that *AGE* could be excluded from the equation. Similar tests for the coefficients of the other two variables yield p-values less than 0.05.

(d) 0.0247

(e) One-child household:

$$\overline{WTRANS_0} = -0.0315 + 0.0414 \times \ln(98.7) - 0.0001 \times 36 - 0.013 \times 1 = 0.142$$

Two-children household:

$$\overline{WTRANS_0} = -0.0315 + 0.0414 \times \ln(98.7) - 0.0001 \times 36 - 0.013 \times 2 = 0.129$$

5.9 (a) $\beta_2 < 0$ (higher price leads to lower quantity demanded); $\beta_3 > 0, \beta_4 > 0$ (lamb and pork are substitutes); $\beta_5 > 0$ (higher income leads to greater beef consumption).

(b)

Dependent Variable: $\ln(QB)$

	Coeff	Std. Error	t-Stat	p-value
C	4.673	1.660	2.816	0.016
$\ln(PB)$	−0.827	0.183	−4.526	0.001
$\ln(PL)$	0.200	0.213	0.939	0.366
$\ln(PP)$	0.437	0.384	1.139	0.277
$\ln(IN)$	0.102	0.294	0.346	0.735

All estimates have elasticity interpretations. For example, a 1% increase in the price of lamb will lead to a 0.2% increase in the quantity of beef demanded. The signs and magnitudes of the elasticities are reasonable, although, with the exception of the coefficient of the price of beef, their standard errors are relatively large.

(c) The estimated covariance matrix is

	C	$\ln(PB)$	$\ln(PL)$	$\ln(PP)$	$\ln(IN)$
C	2.7542	0.1087	−0.0736	−0.2353	−0.3314
$\ln(PB)$	0.1087	0.0334	0.0040	−0.0107	−0.0326
$\ln(PL)$	−0.0736	0.0040	0.0453	−0.0439	0.0166
$\ln(PP)$	−0.2353	−0.0107	−0.0439	0.1472	−0.0303
$\ln(IN)$	−0.3314	−0.0326	0.0166	−0.0303	0.0864

The standard errors reported in part (b) are the square roots of the diagonal elements in this matrix. The variances and covariances are measures of how the least squares estimates $b_1, b_2, b_3, b_4,$ and b_5 will vary and "covary" in repeated samples.

(d) Using $t_c = 2.179$ for 12 degrees of freedom, 95% confidence intervals are

	β_1	β_2	β_3	β_4	β_5
Lower limit	1.0563	−1.2246	−0.2638	−0.3989	−0.5389
Upper limit	8.2888	−0.4286	0.6632	1.2732	0.7423

5.11 (a) $\widehat{VOTE} = 52.44 + 0.6488\,GROWTH - 0.1862\,INFLATION$

(se)   (1.49) (0.1675)   (0.4320)

$H_0 : \beta_2 = 0$ $H_1 : \beta_2 > 0$ $p\text{-value} = 0.0003$ significant at 10% level
$H_0 : \beta_3 = 0$ $H_1 : \beta_3 < 0$ $p\text{-value} = 0.335$ not significant at 10% level

One-tail tests used because more growth is favorable (and more inflation is not favorable) for reelection of the incumbent party.

(b) $\widehat{VOTE_0} = 52.44 + 0.6488 \times (-4) - 0.1862 \times 4 = 49.104$

(c) $52.44 - 4\beta_2 - 0.1862 \times 4 \geq 50$ when $\beta_2 \leq 0.42467$. For testing $H_0 : \beta_2 \leq 0.42467$ against the alternative $H_1 : \beta_2 > 0.42467$, the t-value is $t = (0.64876 - 0.42467)/0.16746 = 1.338$. For a 5% significance level $t_c = t_{(0.95,28)} = 1.701$. Thus, H_0 is not rejected. The incumbent party might still get elected when $GROWTH = -4\%$.

5.13 (a)

Dependent Variable: ln(*PROD*)				
	Coeff	Std. Error	t-Stat	p-value
C	−1.5468	0.2557	−6.0503	0.0000
ln(*AREA*)	0.3617	0.0640	5.6550	0.0000
ln(*LABOR*)	0.4328	0.0669	6.4718	0.0000
ln(*FERT*)	0.2095	0.0383	5.4750	0.0000

All estimates have elasticity interpretations. For example, a 1% increase in labor will lead to a 0.4328% increase in rice output. All p-values are less than 0.0001 implying all estimates are significantly different from zero at conventional significance levels.

(b) Hypotheses are $H_0 : \beta_2 = 0.5$ against $H_1 : \beta_2 \neq 0.5$. Rejection region is $t \geq 2.59$ or $t \leq -2.59$. Calculated value of test statistic is $t = (0.3617 - 0.5)/0.064 = -2.16$. Do not reject H_0 because $-2.59 < -2.16 < 2.59$.

(c) $b_4 \pm t_c \times se(b_4) = 0.2095 \pm 1.967 \times 0.03826 = (0.134, 0.285)$. This narrow interval implies the fertilizer elasticity has been precisely measured.

(d) Hypotheses are $H_0 : \beta_3 \leq 0.3$ against $H_1 : \beta_3 > 0.3$. Rejection region is $t \geq 1.649$. Calculated value of test statistic is $t = (0.433 - 0.3)/0.067 = 1.99$. Reject H_0 because $1.99 > 1.649$. Reversing the hypotheses and testing $H_0 : \beta_3 \geq 0.3$

against $H_1:\beta_3 < 0.3$, the rejection region is $t \leq -1.649$. The calculated t-value is $t = 1.99$. The null hypothesis is not rejected because $1.99 > -1.649$.

Chapter 6

6.3 (a) Unexplained variation $= SSE = (N-K) \times \hat{\sigma}^2 = 17 \times 2.5193 = 42.828$
Total variation $= SST = SSE/(1-R^2) = 42.8281/0.0534 = 802.02$
Explained variation $= SSR = SST - SSE = 802.0243 - 42.8281 = 759.196$

(b) $b_2 \pm t_c \times se(b_2) = 0.6991 \pm 2.11 \times 0.2203 = (0.234, 1.164)$
$b_3 \pm t_c \times se(b_3) = 1.7769 \pm 2.11 \times 0.19267 = (1.370, 2.183)$

(c) Hypotheses are $H_0:\beta_2 \geq 1$ against $H_1:\beta_2 < 1$. Rejection region for a 5% significance level is $t \leq -1.74$. Calculated value of test statistic is $t = (0.6991 - 1)/0.2203 = -1.37$. Do not reject H_0 because $-1.37 > -1.74$.

(d) Hypotheses are $H_0:\beta_2 = \beta_3 = 0$ against $H_1:\beta_2 \neq 0$ and/or $\beta_3 \neq 0$. Rejection region for a 5% significance level is $F \geq 3.59$. Calculated value of test statistic is

$$F = \frac{SSR/(K-1)}{SSE/(N-K)} = \frac{759.1962/2}{42.8281/17} = 151$$

Reject H_0 because $151 > 3.59$.

(e) $se(2b_2 - b_3) = \sqrt{4 \times 0.048526 + 0.03712 - 2 \times 2 \times (-0.031223)}$
$= 0.59675$

$2b_2 - b_3 = -0.37862$ $t = -0.37862/0.59675 = -0.634$
Do not reject $H_0:2\beta_2 = \beta_3$ because $-2.11 < -0.634 < 2.11$ where $t_c = \pm 2.11$ are the critical values for a 5% significance level.

6.7 (a) The coefficients of $\ln(Y)$, $\ln(K)$, and $\ln(PF)$ are 0.6792, 0.3503, and 0.3219, respectively. Since the model is in log-log form the coefficients are elasticities. The interpretations of these coefficients are that the percentage changes in VC, caused by 1% changes in Y, K, and PF, are 0.6792, 0.3503, and 0.3219, respectively.

(b) An increase in any one of the explanatory variables should lead to an increase in variable cost, with the exception of $\ln(STAGE)$. For a given level of output (passenger-miles) and a given level of capital stock, longer flights should be cheaper than shorter ones. Thus, positive signs are expected for all variables except $\ln(STAGE)$, whose coefficient should be negative. All coefficients have the expected signs with the exception of $\ln(PM)$.

(c) The coefficient of $\ln(PM)$ has a p-value of 0.4966 that is higher than 0.05, indicating that this coefficient is not significantly different from zero.

(d) Augmenting the equation with the squares of the predictions, and squares and cubes of the predictions, yields the RESET test F-values of 3.3803 and 1.8601 with corresponding p-values of 0.0671 and 0.1577, respectively. These two p-values are higher than the conventional 0.05 level of significance indicating that the model is adequate.

(e) The F-value for testing $H_0 : \beta_2 + \beta_3 = 1$ is 6.1048 with a p-value of 0.014. Since $0.014 < 0.05$, reject H_0 and conclude that constant returns to scale do not exist.

(f) The F-value for testing $H_0 : \beta_4 + \beta_5 + \beta_6 = 1$ is 75.4 with a p-value less than 0.0001. We reject H_0 and conclude that a proportional increase in input prices will not lead variable cost to increase by the same proportion.

(g) To test $H_0 : \beta_2 + \beta_3 = 1$ the value of the t statistic is

$$t = \frac{b_2 + b_3 - 1}{se(b_2 + b_3)} = \frac{0.6792 + 0.3503 - 1}{0.01187} = 2.48$$

where $se(b_2 + b_3) = \sqrt{0.002851 + 0.002796 + 2(-0.002753)} = 0.01187$. Reject H_0 because $2.48 > t_{(0.975,261)} = 1.969$. Note $t^2 = (2.48)^2 = 6.15 \approx F = 6.10$. The difference between t^2 and F is due to rounding error. To test $H_0 : \beta_4 + \beta_5 + \beta_6 = 1$ the value of the t-statistic is

$$t = \frac{b_4 + b_5 + b_6 - 1}{se(b_4 + b_5 + b_6)} = \frac{0.2754 + 0.3219 - 0.0683 - 1}{0.0542} = -8.69$$

where $se(b_4 + b_5 + b_6)$ can be calculated as

$$\sqrt{0.001919 + 0.001303 + 0.010068 - 2 \times 0.000088 - 2 \times 0.002159 - 2 \times 0.002929}$$
$$= 0.0542$$

Reject H_0 because $-8.69 < t_{(0.025,261)} = -1.969$. Note $t^2 = (-8.69)^2 = 75.52$ that is approximately equal to $F = 75.43$.

6.10 (a) The restricted and unrestricted least squares estimates and their standard errors appear in the following table. The two sets of estimates are similar except for the noticeable difference in sign for $\ln(PL)$. The positive restricted estimate 0.187 is more in line with our *a priori* views about the cross-price elasticity with respect to liquor than the negative estimate -0.583. Most standard errors for the restricted estimates are less than their counterparts for the unrestricted estimates, supporting the theoretical result that restricted least squares estimates have lower variances.

	CONST	$\ln(PB)$	$\ln(PL)$	$\ln(PR)$	$\ln(I)$
Unrestricted	-3.243	-1.020	-0.583	0.210	0.923
	(3.743)	(0.239)	(0.560)	(0.080)	(0.416)
Restricted	-4.798	-1.299	0.187	0.167	0.946
	(3.714)	(0.166)	(0.284)	(0.077)	(0.427)

(b) The high auxiliary R^2s and sample correlations between the explanatory variables that appear in the following table suggest that collinearity could be a problem. The relatively large standard error and the wrong sign for $\ln(PL)$ are a likely consequence of this correlation.

Variable	Auxiliary R^2	$\ln(PL)$	$\ln(PR)$	$\ln(I)$
		Sample correlation with		
$\ln(PB)$	0.955	0.967	0.774	0.971
$\ln(PL)$	0.955		0.809	0.971
$\ln(PR)$	0.694			0.821
$\ln(I)$	0.964			

(c) The F-value for testing $H_0 : \beta_2 + \beta_3 + \beta_4 + \beta_5 = 0$ is 2.50 with a p-value of 0.127. Also, $F_{(0.95,1,25)} = 4.24$. The restriction is not rejected at the 5% significance level.

(d) $\widehat{\ln(Q_0)} \pm t_c \text{se}(f) = 4.5541 \pm 2.056 \times 0.14446 = [4.257, 4.851]$
$[\exp(4.257), \exp(4.851)] = [70.6, 127.9]$

(e) $\widehat{\ln(Q_0)} \pm t_c \text{se}(f) = 4.4239 \pm 2.060 \times 0.16285 = [4.088, 4.759]$
$[\exp(4.088), \exp(4.759)] = (59.6, 116.7)$

6.12 Log-log model: RESET F-value (one term) $= 0.0075$ with p-value $= 0.932$
RESET F-value (two terms) $= 0.358$ with p-value $= 0.703$

Linear model: RESET F-value (one term) $= 8.838$ with p-value $= 0.0066$
RESET F-value (two terms) $= 4.762$ with p-value $= 0.0186$

The log-log model better reflects the demand for beer.

6.16 (a) Hypotheses are $H_0 : \beta_2 + \beta_3 = 0$ against $H_1 : \beta_2 + \beta_3 > 0$. Rejection region for a 5% significance level is $t \geq 1.701$. Calculated value of test statistic is $t = (0.64876 - 0.18622)/0.48685 = 0.95$. Do not reject H_0 because $0.95 < 1.701$. Standard error is computed from

$$\text{se}(b_2 + b_3) = \sqrt{0.028043 + 0.186606 + 2 \times 0.011186} = 0.48685$$

(b) Hypotheses are $H_0 : \beta_1 + 4\beta_2 + 5\beta_3 \leq 50$ against $H_1 : \beta_1 + 4\beta_2 + 5\beta_3 > 50$. Rejection region is $t \geq 1.701$. Calculated value of test statistic is $t = 4.1075/1.534 = 2.68$. We reject H_0 and conclude Willie will get reelected.

6.18 (a) The F-value for testing $H_0 : \beta_2 = \beta_3$ is 0.342, with a p-value of 0.559. Also, $F_{(0.95,1,348)} = 3.868$. The hypothesis that the land and labor elasticities are equal cannot be rejected at a 5% significance level.

(b) The F-value for testing $H_0 : \beta_2 + \beta_3 + \beta_4 = 1$ is 0.029, with a p-value of 0.864. Also, $F_{(0.90,1,348)} = 2.72$. The hypothesis of constant returns to scale cannot be rejected at a 5% significance level.

(c) The F-value for testing the joint null hypothesis $H_0 : \beta_2 + \beta_3 + \beta_4 = 1$ and $\beta_2 = \beta_3$ is 0.183, with a p-value of 0.833. Also, $F_{(0.95,2,348)} = 3.02$. The joint null hypothesis of constant returns to scale and equality of land and labor elasticities cannot be rejected at a 10% significance level.

(d) After taking logs of the specified input values, the null and alternative hypotheses are $H_0 : \beta_1 + 0.69315\beta_2 + 4.60517\beta_3 + 5.16479\beta_4 = 1.5$ and $H_1 : \beta_1 + 0.69315\beta_2 + 4.60517\beta_3 + 5.16479\beta_4 \neq 1.5$. The F-value is 208, with *p*-value less than 0.0001. The hypothesis that the mean of log output is equal to 1.5 when the inputs are set at the specified levels is rejected.

6.19 (i)   With *FERT* omitted the elasticity for *AREA* changes from 0.3617 to 0.4567, and the elasticity for *LABOR* changes from 0.4328 to 0.5689. The RESET *F*-values (*p*-values) for one and two extra terms are 0.024 (0.877) and 0.779 (0.460), respectively. Omitting *FERT* appears to bias the other elasticities upwards, but the omitted variable is not picked up by the RESET test.

   (ii)   With *LABOR* omitted the elasticity for *AREA* changes from 0.3617 to 0.6633, and the elasticity for *FERT* changes from 0.2095 to 0.3015. The RESET *F*-values (*p*-values) for one and two extra terms are 0.629 (0.428) and 0.559 (0.572), respectively. Omitting *LABOR* also appears to bias the other elasticities upwards, but again the omitted variable is not picked up by the RESET test.

  (iii)   With *AREA* omitted the elasticity for *FERT* changes from 0.2095 to 0.2682, and the elasticity for *LABOR* changes from 0.4328 to 0.7084. The RESET *F*-values (*p*-values) for one and two extra terms are 2.511 (0.114) and 4.863 (0.008), respectively. Omitting *AREA* appears to bias the other elasticities upwards, particularly that for *LABOR*. In this case the omitted variable misspecification has been picked up by the RESET test with two extra terms.

Chapter 7

7.2 (a) The coefficients have the following interpretations:

INTERCEPT: At the beginning of the time period over which observations were taken, on a day that is not Friday, Saturday, or a holiday, and a day that has neither a full moon nor a half moon, the average number of emergency room cases was 94.

T: The average number of emergency room cases has been increasing by 0.0338 per day.

HOLIDAY: The average number of emergency room cases goes up by 13.9 on holidays.

FRIDAY and *SATURDAY*: The average number of emergency room cases goes up by 6.9 and 10.6 on Fridays and Saturdays, respectively.

FULLMOON: The average number of emergency room cases goes up by 2.45 on days when there is a full moon. However, a null hypothesis stating that a full moon has no influence on the number of emergency room cases would not be rejected.

NEWMOON: The average number of emergency room cases goes up by 6.4 on days when there is a new moon. However, a null hypothesis stating that a new moon has no influence on the number of emergency room cases would not be rejected.

Emergency rooms should expect more calls on holidays, Fridays and Saturdays, and also over time, but not necessarily when there is a new moon or a full moon.

  (b) Omitting *FULLMOON* and *NEWMOON* has led to very little change in the remaining coefficients.

  (c) The null and alternative hypotheses are $H_0 : \beta_6 = \beta_7 = 0$ and $H_1 : \beta_6 \neq 0$ and/or $\beta_7 \neq 0$. The value of the test statistic is

$$F = \frac{(SSE_R - SSE_U)/J}{SSE_U/(N-K)} = \frac{(27424.19 - 27108.82)/2}{27108.82/(229-7)} = 1.29$$

Since $1.29 < F_{(0.95,2,222)} = 3.037$, the null hypothesis is not rejected. There is no evidence to support the myths about moons.

7.5 (a) The estimated marginal response of yield to nitrogen is

$$\frac{\partial E(YIELD)}{\partial(NITRO)} = 8.011 - 2 \times 1.944 \times NITRO - 0.567 \times PHOS$$

$$= 7.444 - 3.888 NITRO \qquad \text{when} \quad PHOS = 1$$
$$= 6.877 - 3.888 NITRO \qquad \text{when} \quad PHOS = 2$$
$$= 6.310 - 3.888 NITRO \qquad \text{when} \quad PHOS = 3$$

The effect of additional nitrogen on yield depends on the level of phosphorus. Marginal yield is positive for small values of *NITRO* but becomes negative if too much nitrogen is applied. The level of *NITRO* that achieves maximum yield for a given level of *PHOS* is obtained by setting the first derivative equal to zero. For example, when $PHOS = 1$ the maximum yield occurs when $NITRO = 7.444/3.888 = 1.915$. The larger the amount of phosphorus used, the smaller the amount of nitrogen required to attain the maximum yield.

(b) The estimated marginal response of yield to phosphorous is

$$\frac{\partial E(YIELD)}{\partial(PHOS)} = 4.800 - 2 \times 0.778 \times PHOS - 0.567 \times NITRO$$

$$= 4.233 - 1.556 PHOS \qquad \text{when} \quad NITRO = 1$$
$$= 3.666 - 1.556 PHOS \qquad \text{when} \quad NITRO = 2$$
$$= 3.099 - 1.556 PHOS \qquad \text{when} \quad NITRO = 3$$

Comments similar to those made for part (a) are also relevant here.

(c) (i) The null hypothesis is $H_0: \beta_2 + 2\beta_4 + \beta_6 = 0$. The test statistic value is $t = (8.011 - 2 \times 1.944 - 0.567)/\sqrt{0.233} = 7.367$. The critical *t*-value is ± 2.080. Reject H_0. Marginal yield with respect to nitrogen is not zero when $NITRO = 1$ and $PHOS = 1$.

(ii) The null hypothesis is $H_0: \beta_2 + 4\beta_4 + \beta_6 = 0$. The test statistic value is $t = (8.011 - 4 \times 1.944 - 0.567)/\sqrt{0.040} = -1.660$. The critical *t*-value is ± 2.080. Do not reject H_0. A zero marginal yield with respect to nitrogen is compatible with the data when $NITRO = 1$ and $PHOS = 2$.

(iii) The null hypothesis is $H_0: \beta_2 + 6\beta_4 + \beta_6 = 0$. The test statistic value is $t = (8.011 - 6 \times 1.944 - 0.567)/\sqrt{0.233} = -8.742$. The critical *t*-value is ± 2.080. Reject H_0. Marginal yield with respect to nitrogen is not zero when $NITRO = 1$ and $PHOS = 3$.

(d) The maximizing levels $NITRO^*$ and $PHOS^*$ are those values for *NITRO* and *PHOS* such that the first-order partial derivatives are equal to zero.

$$\frac{\partial E(YIELD)}{\partial(PHOS)} = \beta_3 + 2\beta_5 PHOS^* + \beta_6 NITRO^* = 0$$

$$\frac{\partial E(YIELD)}{\partial(NITRO)} = \beta_2 + 2\beta_4 NITRO^* + \beta_6 PHOS^* = 0$$

The solutions and their estimates are

$$NITRO^* = \frac{2\beta_2\beta_5 - \beta_3\beta_6}{\beta_6^2 - 4\beta_4\beta_5} = \frac{2 \times 8.011 \times (-0.778) - 4.800 \times (-0.567)}{(-0.567)^2 - 4 \times (-1.944)(-0.778)} = 1.701$$

$$PHOS^* = \frac{2\beta_3\beta_4 - \beta_2\beta_6}{\beta_6^2 - 4\beta_4\beta_5} = \frac{2 \times 4.800 \times (-1.944) - 8.011 \times (-0.567)}{(-0.567)^2 - 4 \times (-1.944)(-0.778)} = 2.465$$

The yield maximizing levels of fertilizer are not necessarily the optimal levels. The optimal levels are those for which

$$\frac{\partial E(YIELD)}{\partial(PHOS)} = \frac{PRICE_{PHOS}}{PRICE_{PEANUTS}} \quad \text{and} \quad \frac{\partial E(YIELD)}{\partial(NITRO)} = \frac{PRICE_{NITRO}}{PRICE_{PEANUTS}}$$

7.9 (a) $\widehat{PIZZA} = 129.0 + 1.458INC$
   (t) (2.440)

(b) $\widehat{PIZZA} = 342.9 - 7.576AGE + 2.382INC$
   (t) (-3.270) (3.947)

Pizza consumption responds positively to income and negatively to age, as expected. Both estimated coefficients are significantly different from zero at a 5% significance level. Scaling the income variable (dividing by 1000) has increased the coefficient 1000 times, but has not changed its t-value.

(c) $\widehat{PIZZA} = 161.5 - 2.977AGE + 9.074INC - 0.1602(AGE \times INC)$
   (t) (-0.888) (2.473) (-1.847)

$$\frac{\partial E(\widehat{PIZZA})}{\partial(AGE)} = -2.977 - 0.1602INC, \quad \frac{\partial E(\widehat{PIZZA})}{\partial(INC)} = 9.074 - 0.1602AGE$$

Pizza consumption declines with age and the decline is greater the higher the level of income. Pizza consumption increases with income, but the increase is smaller for older people. Using two-tail tests, the coefficient of income is significant at a 5% level, but the other two coefficients are not. The coefficient of the interaction term is significant at the 5% level if a one-tail test is employed. The coefficients of INC and $AGE \times INC$ have increased 1000 times due to the effects of scaling, but the t-values are unchanged.

(d) The F-value for testing $H_0: \beta_2 = 0, \beta_4 = 0$ is 7.40 with a p-value of 0.002. Reject H_0. Conclude that AGE does affect pizza consumption. The joint test for AGE has established its significance although separate t-tests could not.

(e) The marginal propensity to spend on pizza is

$$\frac{\partial E(PIZZA)}{\partial(INC)} = \beta_3 + \beta_4 AGE$$

Point estimates, standard errors, and 95% interval estimates for this quantity (using $t_c = 2.028$) are given in the following table for the 4 different ages.

The point estimates for the marginal propensity to spend on pizza decline as age increases. However, the confidence intervals are relatively wide, indicating that our information on the marginal propensities is not very reliable. Indeed, all the confidence intervals overlap.

Age	Point estimate	Standard error	Confidence interval	
			Lower	Upper
20	5.870	1.977	1.861	9.878
30	4.268	1.176	1.882	6.653
40	2.665	0.605	1.439	3.892
50	1.063	0.923	−0.809	2.935

(f) $\widehat{PIZZA} = 109.7 - 2.038AGE + 18.325INC - 0.6115(AGE \times INC)$
(t) (-0.575) (1.595) (-1.136)
$+ 0.005466(AGE^2 \times INC)$
(0.850)

$$\frac{\partial E(\widehat{PIZZA})}{\partial(INC)} = 18.325 - 0.6115AGE + 0.005466AGE^2$$

A negative coefficient on $AGE^2 \times INC$ is required for the marginal effect of income to increase with age up to a point and then decline. The estimate is positive, however. This positive estimate and the estimate for β_4 imply the marginal effect of income will decrease with age up to $AGE = 56$ and then increase. It is difficult to reach this conclusion with any confidence, however. The estimates for both β_4 and β_5 are not significantly different from zero.

(g) $\widehat{PIZZA} = 98.5 - 1.720AGE + 22.104INC - 0.9087(AGE \times INC)$
(t) (-0.355) (0.549) (-0.295)
$+ 0.01312(AGE^2 \times INC) - 0.000065(AGE^3 \times INC)$
(0.167) (-0.098)

In both models (f) and (g) none of the coefficients are significant, suggesting that collinearity could be a problem. The high auxiliary R^2s in the table below confirm that there are near exact linear relationships between the explanatory variables.

	R^2 values from auxiliary regressions	
LHS variable	R^2 in part (f)	R^2 in part (g)
INC	0.99796	0.99983
AGE	0.68400	0.82598
$AGE \times INC$	0.99956	0.99999
$AGE^2 \times INC$	0.99859	0.99999
$AGE^3 \times INC$		0.99994

7.12 $\widehat{SCORE} = -39.59 + 47.024AGE - 20.222AGE^2 + 2.749AGE^3$
  (t) (1.691) (-2.272) (2.972)

(a) The t-value of 2.972 on the coefficient of AGE^3 suggests the quadratic would not be adequate. The cubic equation allows for the golfer to improve at an increasing rate, then at a decreasing rate and to then decline in ability.

(b) (i) At the age of 30, where the predicted score is lowest (-6.29).
  (ii) Between the ages of 20 and 25, where the differences between the predictions are increasing.
  (iii) Between the ages of 25 and 30, where the differences between the predictions are declining.
  (iv) At the age of 36.
  (v) At the age of 40.

(c) At the age of 70, the predicted score (relative to par) is 241.71. To break 100 it would need to be less than 28. Thus, he will not be able to break 100 when he is 70.

7.15 (a) *PERSON*: Positive because reputation and knowledge of incumbent is likely to favor his/her reelection, but could be negative if incumbents were, on average, unpopular.
  WAR: Positive, reflecting national feeling during, and immediately after, first and second world wars.

(b) Intercept when there is a Democrat incumbent $= \beta_1 + \beta_7$. Intercept when there is a Republican incumbent $= \beta_1 - \beta_7$. The effect of *PARTY* on the vote is $2\beta_7$ with the sign of β_7 indicating whether incumbency favors Democrats $(\beta_7 > 0)$ or Republicans $(\beta_7 < 0)$.

(c) $\widehat{VOTE} = 49.6 + 0.691GROWTH - 0.775INFLATION + 0.837GOODNEWS$
  (se) (0.103) (0.287) (0.268)

  $+ 3.251PERSON - 3.628DURATION - 2.713PARTY + 3.855WAR$
  (1.301) (1.191) (0.584) (2.634)

All the estimates are statistically significant with the exception of *WAR*. An R^2 of 0.923 suggests the model fits the data well.

(d) $\widehat{VOTE}_{2004} = 56.47$

(e) $\widehat{VOTE}_{2004} \pm t_{(0.975,14)} \times se(f) = 56.47 \pm 2.145 \times 3.0707 = [49.89, 63.06]$

7.17 (a) The distribution for *PRICE* is positively skewed; that for $\ln(PRICE)$ is more symmetric.

(b) $\widehat{\ln(PRICE/1000)} = 3.995 - 0.00245AGE + 0.00891BATHS - 0.0849BEDS$
  (se) (0.00037) (0.0181) (0.0134)
    $+ 0.0637SQFT^* - 0.0183STORIES - 0.0803VACANT$
    (0.0020) (0.0219) (0.0132)

All coefficients are significant with the exception of those for *BATHS* and *STORIES*. All signs are reasonable, although those for *BEDS* and *STORIES* deserve closer scrutiny. They suggest that, for a given floor area, houses with more bedrooms and/or more stories are cheaper.

(c) Since $100(\exp(-0.0803) - 1) = -7.72$, vacancy at the time of sale reduces price by 7.72%.

(d) For $VACANT = 0$

$$\ln\left(\widehat{PRICE}/1000\right) = 3.980 - 0.0020AGE + 0.0193BATHS - 0.0978BEDS$$
$$(\text{se}) \qquad\qquad\qquad (0.0005) \qquad (0.0252) \qquad\qquad (0.0200)$$

$$+ 0.0685SQFT^* - 0.0655STORIES$$
$$(0.0030) \qquad\qquad (0.0337)$$

For $VACANT = 1$

$$\ln\left(\widehat{PRICE}/1000\right) = 3.925 - 0.0029AGE - 0.0103BATHS - 0.0678BEDS$$
$$(\text{se}) \qquad\qquad\qquad (0.0005) \qquad (0.0265) \qquad\qquad (0.0178)$$

$$+ 0.0593SQFT^* + 0.0265STORIES$$
$$(0.0028) \qquad\qquad (0.0285)$$

(e) $F = \dfrac{(33.38128 - 17.5203 - 14.08308)/6}{(17.5203 + 14.08308)/(880 - 12)} = 8.14, \quad F_{(0.95,6,868)} = 2.109$

Reject H_0. The equations for houses vacant at the time of sale and occupied at the time of sale are not the same.

Chapter 8

8.7 (a) $\Sigma x_i = 0 \quad \Sigma y_i = 31.1 \quad \Sigma x_i y_i = 89.35 \quad \Sigma x_i^2 = 52.34$
$\bar{x} = 0 \qquad \bar{y} = 3.8875 \qquad b_1 = 3.8875 \qquad b_2 = 1.7071$

(b) $\hat{e} = (-1.9339, 0.7338, 9.5498, -1.7147, -3.2917, 3.8874, -3.4846, -3.7461)$

(c) $\sum_{i=1}^{8}\left(z_i\ln(\hat{e}_i^2)\right) = 86.4674 \quad \sum_{i=1}^{8} z_i^2 = 178.17 \quad \hat{\alpha} = \dfrac{86.4674}{178.17} = 0.4853$

(d) $\hat{\sigma}_i^2 = (4.9606, 1.1567, 29.879, 9.7860, 2.5145, 27.115, 3.0533, 22.331)$

(e) $\Sigma\hat{\sigma}_i^{-2} = 2.00862 \quad \Sigma\hat{\sigma}_i^{-2}y_i x_i = 15.33594 \quad \Sigma\hat{\sigma}_i^{-2}x_i^2 = 15.44214$

$\dfrac{\Sigma\hat{\sigma}_i^{-2}x_i}{\Sigma\hat{\sigma}_i^{-2}} = -0.38385 \quad \dfrac{\Sigma\hat{\sigma}_i^{-2}y_i}{\Sigma\hat{\sigma}_i^{-2}} = 2.19381 \quad \hat{\beta}_1 = 2.6253 \quad \hat{\beta}_2 = 1.1242$

8.10 (a) $\hat{e}^2 = -123.79 + 23.35x \quad \chi^2 = N \times R^2 = 40 \times 0.13977 = 5.59$
$\chi^2_{(0.95,1)} = 3.84$. Reject H_0 of no heteroskedasticity. Transformation was not adequate.

(b) $\hat{e}^2 = 1.117 + 0.05896x \quad \chi^2 = N \times R^2 = 40 \times 0.02724 = 1.09$
$\chi^2_{(0.95,1)} = 3.84$. Fail to reject H_0 of no heteroskedasticity. Transformation was adequate.

8.13 (a) $\hat{C}_1 = 93.595 + 68.592Q_1 - 10.744Q_1^2 + 1.0086Q_1^3$
$(\text{se}) \qquad\qquad (17.484) \qquad (3.774) \qquad (0.2425)$
(b) $H_0: \beta_1 = 0, \beta_4 = 0 \quad F = 108.4 > F_{(0.95,2,24)} = 3.40 \quad$ Reject H_0
(c) Average cost is a linear function of output when $\beta_1 = 0, \beta_4 = 0$.
(d) $\text{var}(e_t) = \sigma^2 Q_{1t}^2$

8.14 (a) $\hat{C}_1 = 72.774 + 83.659Q_1 - 13.796Q_1^2 + 1.1911Q_1^3$ $\hat{\sigma}_1^2 = 324.85$
  (se)   (23.655)   (4.597)   (0.2721)

$\hat{C}_2 = 51.185 + 108.29Q_2 - 20.015Q_2^2 + 1.6131Q_2^3$ $\hat{\sigma}_2^2 = 847.66$
(se)   (28.933)   (6.156)   (0.3802)

For the marginal cost (MC) curves to be positive for $Q = 0$, and be U-shaped with decreasing MC for small Q and increasing MC for large Q, we require $\beta_2 > 0$, $\beta_3 < 0$, and $\beta_4 > 0$. All estimated coefficients have the expected signs and are estimated relatively precisely. The coefficients from the two equations have similar magnitudes but the estimated error variances are different.

(b) For testing $H_0 : \sigma_1^2 = \sigma_2^2$ against $H_1 : \sigma_1^2 \neq \sigma_2^2$, $F = 847.66/324.85 = 2.61$. Critical values are $F_{(0.05,24,24)} = 0.0504$ and $F_{(0.95,24,24)} = 1.984$. Reject H_0.

(c) Using generalized least squares to accommodate the different variances,

$$\hat{C} = 67.270 + 89.920Q - 15.408Q^2 + 1.3026Q^3$$
(se)   (16.973)   (3.415)   (0.2065)

Some automatic software commands will produce slightly different results if the transformed error variance is restricted to be unity or if the variables are transformed using variance estimates from a pooled regression instead of those from part (a).

(d) We do not reject the null hypothesis that the coefficients are equal because $\chi^2 = 1.24 < \chi^2_{(0.95,4)} = 9.488$, or $F = 0.31 < F_{(0.95,4,48)} = 2.565$.

8.15 (a) Using the squared residuals from (8.28), $\ln(\hat{e}_i^2) = 1.50845 + 0.33804 \, METRO$, giving $\hat{\sigma}_M^2 = 6.3375$ and $\hat{\sigma}_R^2 = 4.5197$. These estimates are much smaller than those obtained from separate subsamples ($\hat{\sigma}_M^2 = 31.824$ and $\hat{\sigma}_R^2 = 15.243$). However, multiplying them by the bias factor $\exp(1.2704)$ yields $\hat{\sigma}_M^2 = 22.576$ and $\hat{\sigma}_R^2 = 16.100$.

(b) $\widehat{WAGE} = -9.705 + 1.218EDUC + 0.133EXPER + 1.530METRO$
  (se)   (1.048) (0.069)   (0.015)   (0.386)

(c) $se(b_1) = 1.212$ $se(b_2) = 0.084$ $se(b_3) = 0.016$ $se(b_4) = 0.345$
White least squares standard errors are larger with the exception of that for b_4.

Chapter 9

9.2 (a) $r_1 = 0.1946$ $r_2 = 0.2007$
  (b) (i) $Z = \sqrt{10} \times 0.1946 = 0.615 < 1.96$. Do not reject $H_0 : \rho_1 = 0$.
    (ii) $Z = \sqrt{10} \times 0.2007 = 0.635 < 1.96$. Do not reject $H_0 : \rho_2 = 0$.

9.5 (a) (i) $\hat{e}_{T+1} = \rho e_T$ (ii) $\hat{e}_{T+2} = \rho^2 e_T$
  (b) $\bar{e}_T = 0.1911$
  (c) $\hat{e}_{T+1} = 0.0807$ $\hat{e}_{T+2} = 0.03406$
  (d) $\widehat{\ln(A_{T+1})} = 3.979$ $\widehat{\ln(A_{T+2})} = 4.095$
  (e) $\hat{A}_{T+1}^{natural} = \exp(3.979) = 53.49$ $\hat{A}_{T+2}^{natural} = \exp(4.095) = 60.03$

  $\hat{A}_{T+1}^{corrected} = \hat{A}_{T+1}^{natural} \exp(0.2584^2/2) = 55.71$

  $\hat{A}_{T+2}^{corrected} = \hat{A}_{T+2}^{natural} \exp(0.2584^2/2) = 62.52$

9.8 (a) $\hat{\beta}_0 = 0.7766$ $\hat{\beta}_1 = -0.2969$ $\hat{\beta}_2 = -0.1200$ $\hat{\beta}_3 = -0.0485$
     $\hat{\beta}_4 = -0.0196$ $\hat{\beta}_5 = -0.0079$ $\hat{\beta}_6 = -0.0032$

9.9 (a) $\widehat{\ln(JV_t)} = 3.503 - 1.612\ln(U_t)$ $b_2 \pm 2.074 \times se(b_2) = (-1.934, -1.289)$
        (se)   (0.283) (0.156)
     (b) $F = 5.047$ with p-value 0.036 or $\chi^2 = 4.650$ with p-value 0.031. It is not
         reasonable to assume the e_t are independent. The confidence interval in (a)
         could be misleading.
     (c) $\widehat{\ln(JV_t)} = 3.503 - 1.600\ln(U_t)$ $\hat{\rho} = 0.4486$
        (se)   (0.249) (0.132)   (0.2029)

     $\hat{\beta}_2 \pm 2.074 \times se(\hat{\beta}_2) = (-1.873, -1.327)$. This confidence interval is nar-
     rower than that in (a). One expects a narrower more precise interval, but a
     direct comparison is difficult because the least squares standard errors are
     incorrect in the presence of AR(1) errors. An examination of the correlogram of
     the residuals from this equation does not reveal any autocorrelation.

9.17 (a) $ROB_t = -5.6204 + 1.5614t + 0.5639ROB_{t-1}$
        (se)   (0.2873) (0.0769)
     Checking the correlogram of the residuals shows a few small but significant
     correlations at long lags.

     (b) $\widehat{ROB_{T+1}} \pm t_c \times \hat{\sigma}_1 = 423.2 \pm 1.981 \times 36.713 = (350, 496)$

     $\widehat{ROB_{T+2}} \pm t_c \times \hat{\sigma}_2 = 420.4 \pm 1.981 \times 42.148 = (337, 504)$

Chapter 10

10.5 (a) $\widehat{SAVINGS} = 4.343 - 0.00512\,INCOME$
        (se)   (0.01116)

     (b) $\widehat{SAVINGS} = 0.988 + 0.0392\,INCOME$
        (se)   (0.0200)

     (c) $\widehat{SAVINGS} = 0.988 + 0.0392\,INCOME - 0.0755\hat{v}$ $t = \dfrac{-0.0755}{0.0201} = -3.76$
        (se)   (0.0154)   (0.0201)

     Reject H_0 and conclude x and e are correlated.

10.7 (a) $\hat{Q} = 1.7623 + 0.1468XPER + 0.4380CAP + 0.2392LAB$
        (se)   (0.0634)   (0.1176)   (0.0998)

     The signs of the coefficients are positive as expected and significantly different
     from zero.
     (b) (i) $\hat{Q}_{(10)} \pm t_c \times se(f)_{(10)} = 9.0647 \pm 1.994 \times 2.785 = (3.511, 14.619)$
         (ii) $\hat{Q}_{(20)} \pm t_c \times se(f)_{(20)} = 10.5331 \pm 1.994 \times 2.802 = (4.947, 16.119)$
         (iii) $\hat{Q}_{(30)} \pm t_c \times se(f)_{(30)} = 12.0015 \pm 1.994 \times 2.957 = (6.106, 17.897)$

     (c) $\hat{Q} = -2.487 + 0.5121\,XPER + 0.3321\,CAP + 0.2400\,LAB - 0.4158\hat{v}$
        (se)   (0.1773)   (0.1242)   (0.0972)   (0.1892)

Conclude that *XPER* and *e* are correlated because $t = -0.416/0.189 = -2.20$ is less than $t_{(0.025,70)} = -1.994$

(d) $\hat{Q} = -2.487 + 0.5121\,XPER + 0.3321\,CAP + 0.2400\,LAB$
     (se) $\qquad\qquad$ (0.2205) $\qquad$ (0.1545) $\qquad$ (0.1209)
     The magnitude of the coefficient of *XPER* is much larger than that obtained in part (a).

(e) (i) $\hat{Q}_{(10)} \pm t_c \times se(f)_{(10)} = 7.6475 \pm 1.994 \times 3.468 = (0.733, 14.562)$
     (ii) $\hat{Q}_{(20)} \pm t_c \times se(f)_{(20)} = 12.7685 \pm 1.994 \times 3.621 = (5.548, 19.989)$
     (iii) $\hat{Q}_{(30)} \pm t_c \times se(f)_{(30)} = 17.890 \pm 1.994 \times 4.891 = (8.137, 27.642)$

These intervals predict a smaller output for managers with 10 years of experience and a higher output for managers with 20 and 30 years of experience, relative to those in part (b).

Chapter 11

11.7 (a) Demand: $\quad P = \delta_1 + \delta_2 Q + \delta_3 PS + \delta_4 DI + u^d, \quad \delta_2 < 0, \delta_3 > 0, \delta_4 > 0$
$\qquad$ Supply: $\quad P = \phi_1 + \phi_2 Q + \phi_3 PF + u^s, \quad \phi_2 > 0, \phi_3 > 0$

(b) Demand: $\quad \hat{P} = -11.43 - 2.671\,Q + 3.461\,PS + 13.39\,DI$
$\qquad$ (se) $\qquad\qquad$ (1.175) $\quad$ (1.116) $\qquad$ (2.75)

$\quad$ Supply: $\quad \hat{P} = -58.80 + 2.937\,Q + 2.958\,PF$
$\qquad$ (se) $\qquad\qquad$ (0.216) $\quad$ (0.156)

All estimated coefficients have the expected signs and are significantly different from zero.

(c) *Elasticity* $= (1/-2.6705) \times (62.724/18.4583) = -1.27$

(d) $P_{EQM} = 62.84 \quad P_{EQM\_RF} = 62.81 \quad Q_{EQM} = 18.25 \quad Q_{EQM\_RF} = 18.26$
The alternative ways of computing equilibrium values yield answers that are almost identical.

(e) Demand: $\quad \hat{P} = -13.62 + 0.1512\,Q + 1.3607\,PS + 12.36\,DI$
$\qquad$ (se) $\qquad\qquad$ (0.4988) $\quad$ (0.594) $\qquad$ (1.83)

$\quad$ Supply: $\quad \hat{P} = -52.88 + 2.661\,Q + 2.922\,PF$
$\qquad$ (se) $\qquad\qquad$ (0.171) $\quad$ (0.148)

The coefficient of *Q* in the demand equation has the wrong sign. The supply estimates are similar to those in part (b); the coefficients of *Q* and *PS* in the demand equation are quite different.

11.8 (a)

Variable	Mean		Standard deviation	
	$LFP = 1$	$LFP = 0$	$LFP = 1$	$LFP = 0$
AGE	41.97	43.28	7.72	8.47
KIDSL6	0.1402	0.3662	0.3919	0.6369
FAMINC	24130	21698	11671	12728

On average, working wives are younger, have fewer children, and a higher family income.

(b) $\beta_2 > 0$: A higher wage leads to an increased labor supply.

$\beta_3 > 0$: A higher level of education is likely to lead to a greater desire to work.

β_4: For working wives AGE varies between 30 and 60. It is not clear whether hours worked will increase or decrease within this age range.

$\beta_5 < 0, \beta_6 < 0$: The presence of children in the household reduces hours worked.

$\beta_7 < 0$: The greater the level of income from the husband and other sources, the less the need to work.

(c) $\widehat{HOURS} = 2114 - 17.41\ln(WAGE) - 14.44EDUC - 7.73AGE$
$$-343KIDSL6 - 115KIDS618 - 0.00425NWIFEINC$$

The signs of $\ln(WAGE)$ and $EDUC$ did not come out as expected.

(d) $\widehat{\ln(WAGE)} = -0.358 + 0.0999EDUC - 0.00352AGE - 0.0559KIDSL6$
$$-0.0176KIDS618 + (5.69 \times 10^{-6})NWIFEINC + 0.407EXPER$$
$$-0.000747EXPER^2$$

An additional year of education increases wage by approximately 10%.

(e) The presence of $EXPER$ and $EXPER^2$ in the reduced form equation and their absence in the supply equation serves to identify the supply equation. The F-value for testing the joint significance of $EXPER$ and $EXPER^2$ in the reduced form equation is 8.25 with corresponding p-value 0.0003, confirming the relevance of these variables.

(f) $\widehat{HOURS} = 2432 + 1545\ln(WAGE) - 177.4EDUC - 10.78AGE - 211KIDSL6$
(se)   (481)   (58.1)   (9.58)   (177)
$$- 47.6KIDS618 - 0.00925NWIFEINC$$
$$(56.9) \qquad (0.00648)$$

The coefficient of $\ln(WAGE)$ has the expected positive sign and is significant; that for education is also significant but has retained the unexpected negative sign. The remaining coefficients have the expected signs but are not significant.

Chapter 12

12.3 (a) A plot of the data shows the series to be fluctuating around a constant value.

(b) A unit root test with a constant and no trend is applied. A Dickey–Fuller test with no augmentation terms yields $t = -3.625$, which is less than the 5% critical value of -2.86, and so we reject the null hypothesis that OIL has a unit root.

(c) The series OIL is integrated of order 0 because it is stationary.

12.5 (a) Since both series appear to be trending, a unit root test with a constant and a trend is applied. For the consumption series, the Dickey–Fuller test with no augmentation terms yields $t = 1.550$, which is greater than the 5% critical value of -3.41, and so we do not reject the null hypothesis that $CONSUMPTION$ has a unit root. For the income series, the Dickey–Fuller test with no augmentation terms yields $t = -0.894$, which is greater than the 5% critical value of -3.41, and so we do not reject the null hypothesis that *INCOME* has a unit root.

(b) To determine the order of integration, we have to conduct a unit root test on the first difference of the series. Since the first differences in both series appear to be fluctuating around a constant value, a unit root test with a constant term is applied. For the first difference in *CONSUMPTION*, the Dickey–Fuller test with no augmentation terms yields $t = -6.579$, which is less than the 5% critical value of -2.86, and so we reject the null hypothesis that the first difference in *CONSUMPTION* has a unit root. Since the first difference in *CONSUMPTION* is stationary, it follows that *CONSUMPTION* is integrated of order 1. For the first difference in *INCOME*, the Dickey–Fuller test with no augmentation terms yields $t = -10.676$, which is less than the 5% critical value of -2.86, and so we reject the null hypothesis that the first difference in *INCOME* has a unit root. Since the first difference of *INCOME* is stationary, it follows that *INCOME* is integrated of order 1. A different result is obtained for *CONSUMPTION* if augmentation terms are included in the test equation.

(c) The residuals from a regression of *CONSUMPTION* on a constant term and *INCOME* are saved and tested for stationarity. A Dickey–Fuller test without a constant and a time trend and with no augmentation terms yields $t = -3.909$, which is less than the 5% critical value of -3.37, and so we reject the null hypothesis that the residuals are not stationary. Since the residuals are stationary, this implies that the variables *CONSUMPTION* and *INCOME* are cointegrated.

Chapter 15

15.4 (a) and (b) Least squares and SUR estimates and standard errors for the demand system appear in the following table

Coefficient	Estimates		Standard deviation	
	LS	SUR	LS	SUR
β_{11}	1.017	2.501	1.354	1.092
β_{12}	-0.567	-0.911	0.215	0.130
β_{13}	1.434	1.453	0.229	0.217
β_{21}	2.463	3.530	1.453	1.232
β_{22}	-0.648	-0.867	0.188	0.125
β_{23}	1.144	1.136	0.261	0.248
β_{31}	4.870	5.021	0.546	0.468
β_{32}	-0.964	-0.999	0.065	0.034
β_{33}	0.871	0.870	0.108	0.103

Both sets of estimates have the expected signs and are significantly different from zero. Comparing the magnitudes of the LS and SUR estimates, we see that the most noticeable difference is in the price elasticities β_{12} and β_{22}. The standard errors of the SUR estimates are lower, reflecting their greater precision. Testing whether the equation errors are correlated, we find $LM = 18.77$, which is greater than the critical value $\chi^2_{(0.95,3)} = 7.81$, suggesting that the errors are correlated.

(c) $H_0 : \beta_{13} = 1$, $\beta_{23} = 1$, $\beta_{33} = 1$. Test values are $F = 1.895$ with a p-value of 0.14 or $\chi^2 = 5.686$ with a p-value of 0.13. Do not reject the hypothesis that all income elasticities are equal to 1.

15.9 (a) (i) $b_2 = 0.0207$ $se(b_2) = 0.0209$

(ii) $\hat{\beta}_2^A = 0.0273$ $se\left(\hat{\beta}_2^A\right) = 0.0075$

(iii) $\hat{\beta}_2 = 0.0266$ $se\left(\hat{\beta}_2\right) = 0.0070$

The estimates for β_2 are similar, but the standard error from the dummy variable estimator is much larger than those from the other two estimators.

(b) $H_0 : \beta_{11} = \beta_{12} = \cdots = \beta_{1,40}$. Test value is $F = 3.175$, which is greater than the critical value $F_{(0.95,39,79)} = 1.551$. Reject the hypothesis that the intercepts are equal.

Chapter 16

16.2 (a) Logit estimates

$\tilde{\beta}_1 = -0.2376$ $se(\tilde{\beta}_1) = 0.7505$ $\tilde{\beta}_2 = 0.05311$ $se(\tilde{\beta}_2) = 0.02064$

These values are quite different from the probit estimates in (16.15).

(b) Marginal effect is 0.0112, a value similar to that from the probit model.

(c) Probability is 0.795, a value similar to that from the probit model.

(d) There are two incorrect predictions, implying a correct prediction rate of 90%.

16.3 (a) $\hat{p} = -0.0708 + 0.160FIXRATE - 0.132MARGIN - 0.793YIELD$
$-0.0341MATURITY - 0.0887POINTS + 0.0289NETWORTH$

The signs are consistent with expectations. There are two negative predictions (observations 29 and 48), but no predictions greater than 1.

(b) $\hat{p} = \Phi(-1.877 + 0.499FIXRATE - 0.431MARGIN - 2.384YIELD$
(se)   (4.121) (0.262)   (0.174)   (1.083)

$-0.0592MATURITY - 0.300POINTS + 0.0838NETWORTH)$
(0.6226)   (0.242)   (0.0379)

Ignoring the intercept and using a 5% significance level and one-tail tests, we find that all coefficients are statistically significant with the exception of those for *MATURITY* and *POINTS*.

(c) The percentage of correct predictions is 75.64%.

(d) Marginal effect $= -0.164$. When the variables are at their mean levels, increasing the difference between the variable rate and the fixed rate decreases the probability of choosing the variable-rate mortgage by an amount of 0.164 per 1% change in the *MARGIN*.

Appendix A

A.1 (a) $\sum_{i=1}^{4} x_i$ (b) $\sum_{i=3}^{4} x_i$ (c) $\sum_{i=1}^{4} x_i y_i$ (d) $\sum_{i=1}^{4} x_i y_{i+1}$ (e) $\sum_{i=2}^{3} x_i y_i^2$

(f) $\sum_{i=1}^{3} (x_i - y_i)$

A.2 (a) $4a + b(x_1 + x_2 + x_3 + x_4)$ (b) $1^2 + 2^2 + 3^2 = 14$

(c) $(0^2 + 2 \times 0 + 2) + (1^2 + 2 \times 1 + 2) + (2^2 + 2 \times 2 + 2)$
$$+ (3^2 + 2 \times 3 + 2) = 34$$

(d) $f(4) + f(5) + f(6)$ (e) $f(0, y) + f(1, y) + f(2, y)$

(f) $\sum_{x=2}^{4} \{(x + 2 \times 1) + (x + 2 \times 2)\} = \sum_{x=2}^{4} (2x + 6) = 36$

A.7 (a) $x^{5/6}$ (b) $x^{1/24}$ (c) $x^{-2}y^{-2}$

A.10 (b) Equation 1: $\dfrac{dy}{dx} = 0.4e^{0.8}x^{-0.6} = 3.544$ when $x = 0.10$.

Equation 2: $\dfrac{dy}{dx} = \dfrac{0.2}{x} = 2$ when $x = 0.10$.

Equation 3: $\dfrac{dy}{dx} = 20e^{-1.75+20x} = 25.68$ when $x = 0.10$.

The slope is the change in y, arsenic concentration in toenails, with respect to a change in x, the concentration of arsenic in drinking water.

(c) Equation 1: $\dfrac{dy}{dx}\dfrac{x}{y} = 0.4$

Equation 2: $\dfrac{dy}{dx}\dfrac{x}{y} = \dfrac{0.2}{1.03948} = 0.192$

Equation 3: $\dfrac{dy}{dx}\dfrac{x}{y} = 20 \times 0.1 = 2$

The elasticity is the percentage change in y, arsenic concentration in toenails, associated with a 1% change in x, the concentration of arsenic in drinking water.

A.11(a) $x = 4.567839 \times 10^6$ $y = 5.493711 \times 10^4$
(b) $xy = 25.094387360529 \times 10^{10} = 2.5094387360529 \times 10^{11}$
(c) $x/y = 0.831467 \times 10^2 = 83.1467$
(d) $x + y = (4.567839 + 0.05493711) \times 10^6 = 4.622776 \times 10^6$

Appendix B

B.1 (a) $E(X) = 1$ (b) $E(X^2) = 1.5$ (c) $\text{var}(X) = 0.5$
(d) $E(3X + 2) = 5$ $\text{var}(3X + 2) = 4.5$

B.6 (a) $E(Y) = 0.4$ $\text{var}(Y) = 0.24$ $E(X) = 3$ $\text{var}(X) = 1$
(b) $E(XY) = 1$ $\text{cov}(X, Y) = 1 - 3 \times 0.4 = -0.2$
(c) $\rho = -0.2/\sqrt{1 \times 0.24} = -0.408$

B.9 (a) 0.087   (b) 0.216   (c) 0.740   (d) 0.396
(e) Warranty period $= 0.597$ years $= 7$ months approximately.

B.11 (b) 1   (c) 0.25   (d) 0.4375   (e) 0

B.13(a) $E(P) = 0.25 \times 8 + 0.75 \times 15 = 13.25\%$
(b) $\text{cov}(R_A, R_B) = 12 \times 22 = 264$ $\sigma_P = 19.5\%$

(c) $\text{cov}(R_A, R_B) = 132$ $\sigma_P = 18.19\%$
(d) $\text{cov}(R_A, R_B) = 0$ $\sigma_P = 16.77\%$

Appendix C

C.3 $P(\overline{X} > 2222) = P(Z > 1.3333) = 0.091$

C.5 Hypotheses are $H_0 : \mu \leq 170$ against $H_1 : \mu > 170$. Rejection region is $t \geq 1.649$. Calculated value of test statistic is $t = \sqrt{400}(178 - 170)/65 = 2.462$. Reject H_0 because $t = 2.462 > 1.649$ and conclude the new system is cost effective. The p-value of the test is 0.007.

C.8 $N \geq \left(\dfrac{1.96 \times 21}{2} \right)^2 = 423.5$. A sample of 424 is needed.

Appendix *E*

Standard Normal Distribution

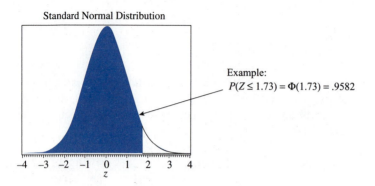

Example:
$P(Z \leq 1.73) = \Phi(1.73) = .9582$

Table 1 **Cumulative Probabilities for the Standard Normal Distribution**
$\Phi(z) = P(Z \leq z)$

z	0.00	0.01	0.02	0.03	0.04	0.05	0.06	0.07	0.08	0.09
0.0	0.5000	0.5040	0.5080	0.5120	0.5160	0.5199	0.5239	0.5279	0.5319	0.5359
0.1	0.5398	0.5438	0.5478	0.5517	0.5557	0.5596	0.5636	0.5675	0.5714	0.5753
0.2	0.5793	0.5832	0.5871	0.5910	0.5948	0.5987	0.6026	0.6064	0.6103	0.6141
0.3	0.6179	0.6217	0.6255	0.6293	0.6331	0.6368	0.6406	0.6443	0.6480	0.6517
0.4	0.6554	0.6591	0.6628	0.6664	0.6700	0.6736	0.6772	0.6808	0.6844	0.6879
0.5	0.6915	0.6950	0.6985	0.7019	0.7054	0.7088	0.7123	0.7157	0.7190	0.7224
0.6	0.7257	0.7291	0.7324	0.7357	0.7389	0.7422	0.7454	0.7486	0.7517	0.7549
0.7	0.7580	0.7611	0.7642	0.7673	0.7704	0.7734	0.7764	0.7794	0.7823	0.7852
0.8	0.7881	0.7910	0.7939	0.7967	0.7995	0.8023	0.8051	0.8078	0.8106	0.8133
0.9	0.8159	0.8186	0.8212	0.8238	0.8264	0.8289	0.8315	0.8340	0.8365	0.8389
1.0	0.8413	0.8438	0.8461	0.8485	0.8508	0.8531	0.8554	0.8577	0.8599	0.8621
1.1	0.8643	0.8665	0.8686	0.8708	0.8729	0.8749	0.8770	0.8790	0.8810	0.8830
1.2	0.8849	0.8869	0.8888	0.8907	0.8925	0.8944	0.8962	0.8980	0.8997	0.9015
1.3	0.9032	0.9049	0.9066	0.9082	0.9099	0.9115	0.9131	0.9147	0.9162	0.9177
1.4	0.9192	0.9207	0.9222	0.9236	0.9251	0.9265	0.9279	0.9292	0.9306	0.9319
1.5	0.9332	0.9345	0.9357	0.9370	0.9382	0.9394	0.9406	0.9418	0.9429	0.9441
1.6	0.9452	0.9463	0.9474	0.9484	0.9495	0.9505	0.9515	0.9525	0.9535	0.9545
1.7	0.9554	0.9564	0.9573	0.9582	0.9591	0.9599	0.9608	0.9616	0.9625	0.9633
1.8	0.9641	0.9649	0.9656	0.9664	0.9671	0.9678	0.9686	0.9693	0.9699	0.9706
1.9	0.9713	0.9719	0.9726	0.9732	0.9738	0.9744	0.9750	0.9756	0.9761	0.9767
2.0	0.9772	0.9778	0.9783	0.9788	0.9793	0.9798	0.9803	0.9808	0.9812	0.9817
2.1	0.9821	0.9826	0.9830	0.9834	0.9838	0.9842	0.9846	0.9850	0.9854	0.9857
2.2	0.9861	0.9864	0.9868	0.9871	0.9875	0.9878	0.9881	0.9884	0.9887	0.9890
2.3	0.9893	0.9896	0.9898	0.9901	0.9904	0.9906	0.9909	0.9911	0.9913	0.9916
2.4	0.9918	0.9920	0.9922	0.9925	0.9927	0.9929	0.9931	0.9932	0.9934	0.9936
2.5	0.9938	0.9940	0.9941	0.9943	0.9945	0.9946	0.9948	0.9949	0.9951	0.9952
2.6	0.9953	0.9955	0.9956	0.9957	0.9959	0.9960	0.9961	0.9962	0.9963	0.9964
2.7	0.9965	0.9966	0.9967	0.9968	0.9969	0.9970	0.9971	0.9972	0.9973	0.9974
2.8	0.9974	0.9975	0.9976	0.9977	0.9977	0.9978	0.9979	0.9979	0.9980	0.9981
2.9	0.9981	0.9982	0.9982	0.9983	0.9984	0.9984	0.9985	0.9985	0.9986	0.9986
3.0	0.9987	0.9987	0.9987	0.9988	0.9988	0.9989	0.9989	0.9989	0.9990	0.9990

Source: This table was generated using the SAS® function PROBNORM

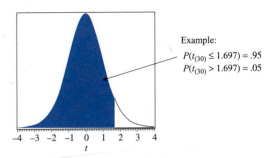

Example:
$P(t_{(30)} \leq 1.697) = .95$
$P(t_{(30)} > 1.697) = .05$

Ta b l e 2   Percentiles of the *t*-distribution

df	$t_{(.90,df)}$	$t_{(.95,df)}$	$t_{(.975,df)}$	$t_{(.99,df)}$	$t_{(.995,df)}$
1	3.078	6.314	12.706	31.821	63.657
2	1.886	2.920	4.303	6.965	9.925
3	1.638	2.353	3.182	4.541	5.841
4	1.533	2.132	2.776	3.747	4.604
5	1.476	2.015	2.571	3.365	4.032
6	1.440	1.943	2.447	3.143	3.707
7	1.415	1.895	2.365	2.998	3.499
8	1.397	1.860	2.306	2.896	3.355
9	1.383	1.833	2.262	2.821	3.250
10	1.372	1.812	2.228	2.764	3.169
11	1.363	1.796	2.201	2.718	3.106
12	1.356	1.782	2.179	2.681	3.055
13	1.350	1.771	2.160	2.650	3.012
14	1.345	1.761	2.145	2.624	2.977
15	1.341	1.753	2.131	2.602	2.947
16	1.337	1.746	2.120	2.583	2.921
17	1.333	1.740	2.110	2.567	2.898
18	1.330	1.734	2.101	2.552	2.878
19	1.328	1.729	2.093	2.539	2.861
20	1.325	1.725	2.086	2.528	2.845
21	1.323	1.721	2.080	2.518	2.831
22	1.321	1.717	2.074	2.508	2.819
23	1.319	1.714	2.069	2.500	2.807
24	1.318	1.711	2.064	2.492	2.797
25	1.316	1.708	2.060	2.485	2.787
26	1.315	1.706	2.056	2.479	2.779
27	1.314	1.703	2.052	2.473	2.771
28	1.313	1.701	2.048	2.467	2.763
29	1.311	1.699	2.045	2.462	2.756
30	1.310	1.697	2.042	2.457	2.750
31	1.309	1.696	2.040	2.453	2.744
32	1.309	1.694	2.037	2.449	2.738
33	1.308	1.692	2.035	2.445	2.733
34	1.307	1.691	2.032	2.441	2.728
35	1.306	1.690	2.030	2.438	2.724
36	1.306	1.688	2.028	2.434	2.719
37	1.305	1.687	2.026	2.431	2.715
38	1.304	1.686	2.024	2.429	2.712
39	1.304	1.685	2.023	2.426	2.708
40	1.303	1.684	2.021	2.423	2.704
50	1.299	1.676	2.009	2.403	2.678
∞	1.282	1.645	1.960	2.326	2.576

Source: This table was generated using the SAS® function TINV

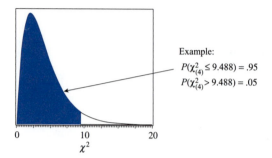

Example:

$P(\chi^2_{(4)} \leq 9.488) = .95$

$P(\chi^2_{(4)} > 9.488) = .05$

Table 3   **Percentiles of the Chi-square distribution**

df	$\chi^2_{(.90,df)}$	$\chi^2_{(.95,df)}$	$\chi^2_{(.975,df)}$	$\chi^2_{(.99,df)}$	$\chi^2_{(.995,df)}$
1	2.706	3.841	5.024	6.635	7.879
2	4.605	5.991	7.378	9.210	10.597
3	6.251	7.815	9.348	11.345	12.838
4	7.779	9.488	11.143	13.277	14.860
5	9.236	11.070	12.833	15.086	16.750
6	10.645	12.592	14.449	16.812	18.548
7	12.017	14.067	16.013	18.475	20.278
8	13.362	15.507	17.535	20.090	21.955
9	14.684	16.919	19.023	21.666	23.589
10	15.987	18.307	20.483	23.209	25.188
11	17.275	19.675	21.920	24.725	26.757
12	18.549	21.026	23.337	26.217	28.300
13	19.812	22.362	24.736	27.688	29.819
14	21.064	23.685	26.119	29.141	31.319
15	22.307	24.996	27.488	30.578	32.801
16	23.542	26.296	28.845	32.000	34.267
17	24.769	27.587	30.191	33.409	35.718
18	25.989	28.869	31.526	34.805	37.156
19	27.204	30.144	32.852	36.191	38.582
20	28.412	31.410	34.170	37.566	39.997
21	29.615	32.671	35.479	38.932	41.401
22	30.813	33.924	36.781	40.289	42.796
23	32.007	35.172	38.076	41.638	44.181
24	33.196	36.415	39.364	42.980	45.559
25	34.382	37.652	40.646	44.314	46.928
26	35.563	38.885	41.923	45.642	48.290
27	36.741	40.113	43.195	46.963	49.645
28	37.916	41.337	44.461	48.278	50.993
29	39.087	42.557	45.722	49.588	52.336
30	40.256	43.773	46.979	50.892	53.672
35	46.059	49.802	53.203	57.342	60.275
40	51.805	55.758	59.342	63.691	66.766
50	63.167	67.505	71.420	76.154	79.490
60	74.397	79.082	83.298	88.379	91.952
70	85.527	90.531	95.023	100.425	104.215
80	96.578	101.879	106.629	112.329	116.321
90	107.565	113.145	118.136	124.116	128.299
100	118.498	124.342	129.561	135.807	140.169
110	129.385	135.480	140.917	147.414	151.948
120	140.233	146.567	152.211	158.950	163.648

Source: This table was generated using the SAS® function CINV

Example:

$P(F_{(4,30)} \le 2.69) = .95$
$P(F_{(4,30)} > 2.69) = .05$

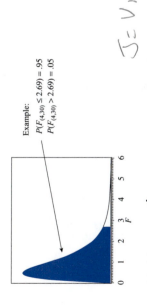

Table 4 95th Percentile for the F-distribution

ν_2/ν_1	1	2	3	4	5	6	7	8	9	10	12	15	20	30	60	∞
1	161.45	199.50	215.71	224.58	230.16	233.99	236.77	238.88	240.54	241.88	243.91	245.95	248.01	250.10	252.20	254.31
2	18.51	19.00	19.16	19.25	19.30	19.33	19.35	19.37	19.38	19.40	19.41	19.43	19.45	19.46	19.48	19.50
3	10.13	9.55	9.28	9.12	9.01	8.94	8.89	8.85	8.81	8.79	8.74	8.70	8.66	8.62	8.57	8.53
4	7.71	6.94	6.59	6.39	6.26	6.16	6.09	6.04	6.00	5.96	5.91	5.86	5.80	5.75	5.69	5.63
5	6.61	5.79	5.41	5.19	5.05	4.95	4.88	4.82	4.77	4.74	4.68	4.62	4.56	4.50	4.43	4.36
6	5.99	5.14	4.76	4.53	4.39	4.28	4.21	4.15	4.10	4.06	4.00	3.94	3.87	3.81	3.74	3.67
7	5.59	4.74	4.35	4.12	3.97	3.87	3.79	3.73	3.68	3.64	3.57	3.51	3.44	3.38	3.30	3.23
8	5.32	4.46	4.07	3.84	3.69	3.58	3.50	3.44	3.39	3.35	3.28	3.22	3.15	3.08	3.01	2.93
9	5.12	4.26	3.86	3.63	3.48	3.37	3.29	3.23	3.18	3.14	3.07	3.01	2.94	2.86	2.79	2.71
10	4.96	4.10	3.71	3.48	3.33	3.22	3.14	3.07	3.02	2.98	2.91	2.85	2.77	2.70	2.62	2.54
15	4.54	3.68	3.29	3.06	2.90	2.79	2.71	2.64	2.59	2.54	2.48	2.40	2.33	2.25	2.16	2.07
20	4.35	3.49	3.10	2.87	2.71	2.60	2.51	2.45	2.39	2.35	2.28	2.20	2.12	2.04	1.95	1.84
25	4.24	3.39	2.99	2.76	2.60	2.49	2.40	2.34	2.28	2.24	2.16	2.09	2.01	1.92	1.82	1.71
30	4.17	3.32	2.92	2.69	2.53	2.42	2.33	2.27	2.21	2.16	2.09	2.01	1.93	1.84	1.74	1.62
35	4.12	3.27	2.87	2.64	2.49	2.37	2.29	2.22	2.16	2.11	2.04	1.96	1.88	1.79	1.68	1.56
40	4.08	3.23	2.84	2.61	2.45	2.34	2.25	2.18	2.12	2.08	2.00	1.92	1.84	1.74	1.64	1.51
45	4.06	3.20	2.81	2.58	2.42	2.31	2.22	2.15	2.10	2.05	1.97	1.89	1.81	1.71	1.60	1.47
50	4.03	3.18	2.79	2.56	2.40	2.29	2.20	2.13	2.07	2.03	1.95	1.87	1.78	1.69	1.58	1.44
60	4.00	3.15	2.76	2.53	2.37	2.25	2.17	2.10	2.04	1.99	1.92	1.84	1.75	1.65	1.53	1.39
120	3.92	3.07	2.68	2.45	2.29	2.18	2.09	2.02	1.96	1.91	1.83	1.75	1.66	1.55	1.43	1.25
∞	3.84	3.00	2.60	2.37	2.21	2.10	2.01	1.94	1.88	1.83	1.75	1.67	1.57	1.46	1.32	1.00

Source: This table was generated using the SAS® function FINV

$J = V_1$

$N - k = V_2$

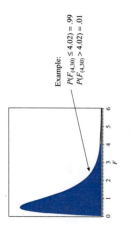

Example:
$P(F_{(4,30)} \le 4.02) = .99$
$P(F_{(4,30)} > 4.02) = .01$

Table 5 **99th Percentile for the F-distribution**

v_2/v_1	1	2	3	4	5	6	7	8	9	10	12	15	20	30	60	∞
1	4052.18	4999.50	5403.35	5624.58	5763.65	5858.99	5928.36	5981.07	6022.47	6055.85	6106.32	6157.28	6208.73	6260.65	6313.03	6365.87
2	98.50	99.00	99.17	99.25	99.30	99.33	99.36	99.37	99.39	99.40	99.42	99.43	99.45	99.47	99.48	99.50
3	34.12	30.82	29.46	28.71	28.24	27.91	27.67	27.49	27.35	27.23	27.05	z26.87	26.69	26.50	26.32	26.13
4	21.20	18.00	16.69	15.98	15.52	15.21	14.98	14.80	14.66	14.55	14.37	14.20	14.02	13.84	13.65	13.46
5	16.26	13.27	12.06	11.39	10.97	10.67	10.46	10.29	10.16	10.05	9.89	9.72	9.55	9.38	9.20	9.02
6	13.75	10.92	9.78	9.15	8.75	8.47	8.26	8.10	7.98	7.87	7.72	7.56	7.40	7.23	7.06	6.88
7	12.25	9.55	8.45	7.85	7.46	7.19	6.99	6.84	6.72	6.62	6.47	6.31	6.16	5.99	5.82	5.65
8	11.26	8.65	7.59	7.01	6.63	6.37	6.18	6.03	5.91	5.81	5.67	5.52	5.36	5.20	5.03	4.86
9	10.56	8.02	6.99	6.42	6.06	5.80	5.61	5.47	5.35	5.26	5.11	4.96	4.81	4.65	4.48	4.31
10	10.04	7.56	6.55	5.99	5.64	5.39	5.20	5.06	4.94	4.85	4.71	4.56	4.41	4.25	4.08	3.91
15	8.68	6.36	5.42	4.89	4.56	4.32	4.14	4.00	3.89	3.80	3.67	3.52	3.37	3.21	3.05	2.87
20	8.10	5.85	4.94	4.43	4.10	3.87	3.70	3.56	3.46	3.37	3.23	3.09	2.94	2.78	2.61	2.42
25	7.77	5.57	4.68	4.18	3.85	3.63	3.46	3.32	3.22	3.13	2.99	2.85	2.70	2.54	2.36	2.17
30	7.56	5.39	4.51	4.02	3.70	3.47	3.30	3.17	3.07	2.98	2.84	2.70	2.55	2.39	2.21	2.01
35	7.42	5.27	4.40	3.91	3.59	3.37	3.20	3.07	2.96	2.88	2.74	2.60	2.44	2.28	2.10	1.89
40	7.31	5.18	4.31	3.83	3.51	3.29	3.12	2.99	2.89	2.80	2.66	2.52	2.37	2.20	2.02	1.80
45	7.23	5.11	4.25	3.77	3.45	3.23	3.07	2.94	2.83	2.74	2.61	2.46	2.31	2.14	1.96	1.74
50	7.17	5.06	4.20	3.72	3.41	3.19	3.02	2.89	2.78	2.70	2.56	2.42	2.27	2.10	1.91	1.68
60	7.08	4.98	4.13	3.65	3.34	3.12	2.95	2.82	2.72	2.63	2.50	2.35	2.20	2.03	1.84	1.60
120	6.85	4.79	3.95	3.48	3.17	2.96	2.79	2.66	2.56	2.47	2.34	2.19	2.03	1.86	1.66	1.38
∞	6.63	4.61	3.78	3.32	3.02	2.80	2.64	2.51	2.41	2.32	2.18	2.04	1.88	1.70	1.47	1.00

Source: This table was generated using the SAS® function FINV

Index

Elasticity

$$\eta = \frac{\text{percentage change in } y}{\text{percentage change in } x} = \frac{\Delta y / y}{\Delta x / x} = \frac{\Delta y}{\Delta x} \cdot \frac{x}{y}$$

$$\eta = \frac{\Delta E(y)/E(y)}{\Delta x / x} = \frac{\Delta E(y)}{\Delta x} \cdot \frac{x}{E(y)} = \beta_2 \cdot \frac{x}{E(y)}$$

Least Squares Expressions Useful for Theory

$$b_2 = \beta_2 + \Sigma w_i e_i$$

$$w_i = \frac{x_i - \bar{x}}{\Sigma(x_i - \bar{x})^2},$$

$$\Sigma w_i = 0, \quad \Sigma w_i x_i = 1, \quad \Sigma w_i^2 = 1/\Sigma(x_i - \bar{x})^2,$$

Properties of the Least Squares Estimators

$$\text{var}(b_1) = \sigma^2 \left[\frac{\Sigma x_i^2}{N\Sigma(x_i - \bar{x})^2} \right] \quad \text{var}(b_2) = \frac{\sigma^2}{\Sigma(x_i - \bar{x})^2}$$

$$\text{cov}(b_1, b_2) = \sigma^2 \left[\frac{-\bar{x}}{\Sigma(x_i - \bar{x})^2} \right]$$

Gauss-Markov Theorem: Under the assumptions SR1-SR5 of the linear regression model the estimators b_1 and b_2 have the *smallest variance of all linear and unbiased estimators* of β_1 and β_2 They are the **B**est **L**inear **U**nbiased **E**stimators (BLUE) of β_1 and β_2

If we make the normality assumption, assumption SR6 about the error term, then the least squares estimators are normally distributed.

$$b_1 \sim N\left(\beta_1, \frac{\sigma^2 \Sigma x_i^2}{N\Sigma(x_i - \bar{x})^2}\right), b_2 \sim N\left(\beta_2, \frac{\sigma^2}{\Sigma(x_i - \bar{x})^2}\right)$$

Estimated Error Variance

$$\hat{\sigma}^2 = \frac{\Sigma \hat{e}_i^2}{N - 2}$$

Estimator Standard Errors

$$\text{se}(b_1) = \sqrt{\widehat{\text{var}(b_1)}}, \ \text{se}(b_2) = \sqrt{\widehat{\text{var}(b_2)}}$$

t-distribution

If assumptions SR1-SR6 of the simple linear regression model hold, then

$$t = \frac{b_k - \beta_k}{\text{se}(b_k)} \sim t_{(N-2)}, \quad k = 1, 2$$

Interval Estimates

$$P[b_2 - t_c \text{se}(b_2) \leq \beta_2 \leq b_2 + t_c \text{se}(b_2)] = 1 - \alpha$$

Hypothesis Testing

Components of Hypothesis Tests
1. A *null* hypothesis, H_0
2. An *alternative* hypothesis, H_1
3. A test *statistic*
4. A *rejection* region
5. A conclusion

If the null hypothesis $H_0 : \beta_2 = c$ is ***true***, then

$$t = \frac{b_2 - c}{\text{se}(b_2)} \sim t_{(N-2)}$$

Rejection rule for a two-tail test: If the value of the test statistic falls in the rejection region, either tail of the *t*-distribution, then we reject the null hypothesis and accept the alternative.

Type I error-The null hypothesis is *true* and we decide to *reject* it

Type II error-The null hypothesis is *false* and we decide *not* to reject it

***p*-value rejection rule:** When the *p*-value of a hypothesis test is *smaller* than the chosen value of α, then the test procedure leads to *rejection* of the null hypothesis.

Prediction

$$y_0 = \beta_1 + \beta_2 x_0 + e_0, \ \hat{y}_0 = b_1 + b_2 x_0, \ f = \hat{y}_0 - y_0$$

$$\widehat{\text{var}(f)} = \hat{\sigma}^2 \left[1 + \frac{1}{N} + \frac{(x_0 - \bar{x})^2}{\Sigma(x_i - \bar{x})^2} \right], \text{se}(f) = \sqrt{\widehat{\text{var}(f)}}$$

A $(1 - \alpha) \times 100\%$ confidence interval, or prediction interval, for y_0

$$\hat{y}_0 \pm t_c \text{se}(f)$$

Goodness of Fit

$$\Sigma(y_t - \bar{y})^2 = \Sigma(\hat{y}_t - \bar{y})^2 + \Sigma \hat{e}_t^2$$

$$SST = SSR + SSE$$

$$R^2 = \frac{SSR}{SST} = 1 - \frac{SSE}{SST} = (\text{corr}(y, \hat{y}))^2$$

Log-Linear Model

$$\ln(y) = \beta_1 + \beta_2 x + e, \ \widehat{\ln(y)} = b_1 + b_2 x$$

$100 \times \beta_2 \approx \%$ change in y given one-unit change in x.

$$\hat{y}_n = \exp(b_1 + b_2 x)$$

$$\hat{y}_c = \exp(b_1 + b_2 x)\exp(\hat{\sigma}^2/2)$$

Prediction interval:

$$\exp[\widehat{\ln(y)} - t_c \text{se}(f)], \ \exp[\widehat{\ln(y)} + t_c \text{se}(f)]$$

Generalized goodness-of-fit measure $R_g^2 = (\text{corr}(y, \hat{y}_n))^2$

Assumptions of the Multiple Regression Model

MR1 $y_i = \beta_1 + \beta_2 x_{i2} + \cdots + \beta_K x_{iK} + e_i$

MR2 $E(y_i) = \beta_1 + \beta_2 x_{i2} + \cdots + \beta_K x_{iK} \Leftrightarrow E(e_i) = 0.$

MR3 $\text{var}(y_i) = \text{var}(e_i) = \sigma^2$

MR4 $\text{cov}(y_i, y_j) = \text{cov}(e_i, e_j) = 0$

MR5   The values of x_{ik} are not random and are not exact linear functions of the other explanatory variables.

MR6 $y_i \sim N[(\beta_1 + \beta_2 x_{i2} + \cdots + \beta_K x_{iK}), \sigma^2]$
      $\Leftrightarrow e_i \sim N(0, \sigma^2)$

Least Squares Estimates in MR Model

Least squares estimates $b_1, b_2, \ldots, b_K$ minimize

$$S(\beta_1, \beta_2, \cdots, \beta_K) = \Sigma(y_i - \beta_1 - \beta_2 x_{i2} - \cdots - \beta_K x_{iK})^2$$

Estimated Error Variance and Estimator Standard Errors

$$\hat{\sigma}^2 = \frac{\Sigma \hat{e}_i^2}{N - K} \qquad \text{se}(b_k) = \sqrt{\widehat{\text{var}(b_k)}}$$